Schooling in Renaissance Italy

T0385522

The Johns Hopkins University
Studies in Historical and Political Science
107th Series (1989)

1. *Schooling in Renaissance Italy: Literacy and Learning, 1300–1600*
by Paul F. Grendler

SCHOOLING IN RENAISSANCE ITALY

Literacy and Learning,
1300–1600

PAUL F. GRENDLER

The Johns Hopkins University Press

BALTIMORE AND LONDON

This book has been brought to publication with the
generous assistance of the National Endowment for
the Humanities.

Originally published in hardcover, 1989
Softshell Books edition, 1991

The Johns Hopkins University Press
701 West 40th Street
Baltimore, Maryland 21211
The Johns Hopkins Press Ltd., London

Frontispiece: Woodcut from *Libro del maestro e del discepulo*
(Venice, 1502)

Part title illustration: Woodcut from *Donato al senno*
(Bologna, 1654)

The paper used in this publication meets the
minimum requirements of American National Standard
for Information Sciences—Permanence of Paper for
Printed Library Materials, ANSI Z39.48-1984.

Library of Congress Cataloging-in-Publication Data

Grendler, Paul F.
    Schooling in Renaissance Italy.

    The Johns Hopkins University studies in historical and
political science ; 107th ser., 1)
    Bibliography: p.
    Includes index.
    1. Education, Medieval—Italy. 2. Education—Italy—
History—16th century. 3. Education—Italy—Curricula—
History. I. Title. II. Series.
LA791.3.G74   1989   370'.945   88-73568
ISBN 0-8018-3725-1 (alk. paper)
ISBN 0-8018-4229-8 (pbk.)

To the memory of
JOHN F. D'AMICO
1947–1987

CONTENTS

Contents

ILLUSTRATIONS

TABLES

PREFACE

An unlikely source planted the seed for this book long before I became aware of it. In the academic year 1971–72, my son, then six, attended an Italian elementary school on the outskirts of Florence. My wife and I found his *quaderni* (notebooks) and description of the pedagogy fascinating. His schooling introduced me to an education somewhat different from that in North America, one that echoed a distant past. I thought no further of the matter until completion of another project led me to look for a new one. My interest in intellectual history within its institutional and social context led me to the elementary and secondary schools of the Italian Renaissance. They were obviously of great importance to their own age and to future centuries. But we did not know much about them beyond the idealized picture presented by humanist pedagogical theorists. What kinds of schools existed? What percentage of potential students attended them? Above all, what did students learn, and how did they learn?

Aware of the papal bull *In sacrosancta beati Petri* of 13 November 1564 requiring all teachers to make professions of faith, I went looking for records of the professions hoping that they might reveal more. In May 1976 I found in the Archivio della Curia Patriarcale of Venice a bundle of professions sworn by Venetian schoolmasters between April 1587 and May 1588. This was the starting point of a broad investigation that has occupied most of my time since 1978.

Numerous friends and librarians helped make this book possible. I am very grateful to Erika Rummel for reading most of the manuscript. Not only did she rescue me from shipwreck on the rocks of Latinity more than once, but her keen eye detected other infelicities. Alexander Dalzell carefully read chapter 9 and guided me through the maze of Latin metrics. Warren Van Egmond clarified the importance of abbaco before his important study appeared in print. David Herlihy, Eleanor Jordan, Nelson Minnich, and W. Keith Percival offered good advice on specific points.

Robert Black and Thomas Deutscher generously allowed me to read their research before publication. Henry Y. K. Tom has been a patient editor. Linda Distad put a long manuscript on the word processor, and Jackie Wehmueller edited the manuscript carefully. Gail Solberg graciously procured two of the illustrations. Charles Trinkaus has offered excellent advice, support, and a brilliant scholarly example over many years. Barbara and Vince Bowen made my many visits to the University of Illinois more than pleasant through their friendship and hospitality. Numerous librarians and archivists have aided my research over the years, especially Fathers Gino Bortolan and Fulvio Parisotto of the Archivio della Curia Patriarcale of Venice. N. Frederick Nash, Mary Ceibert, and Louise Fitton of the Rare Book Room of the Library of the University of Illinois at Urbana-Champaign helped me to use that library's superb collection of fifteenth- and sixteenth-century imprints of the classics.

Financial support came from Canada Council research grants in the summers of 1976 and 1977, a Guggenheim Memorial Fellowship during 1978–79, Social Sciences and Humanities Research Council of Canada Leave Fellowships in 1979–80 and 1985–86, and a fellowship from the Woodrow Wilson International Center for Scholars in Washington, D.C., from September 1982 through February 1983. I was also a Visiting Associate at the Center for Advanced Study of the University of Illinois in 1979–80. I am grateful to these organizations and their staffs.

The expression of my final and most important debt is etched in sadness. John D'Amico was a constant friend and fellow scholar through the research and writing of this book. From our first meeting in Rome in the summer of 1976, our paths frequently and happily ran together: at San Martino a Mensola, Florence, in 1978–79, at the University of Illinois in 1979–80, and in northern Virginia from 1981 through 1986. At every stop, we resumed our ongoing discussion of Italian Renaissance humanism from which I learned so much. He also read the entire manuscript and made many suggestions. His premature death on 9 December 1987 has deprived the field of a brilliant scholar and a warm friend. This book is dedicated to his memory.

NOTE ON QUOTATIONS
AND TRANSLATIONS

Quotations in the text and notes are presented in the original orthography and usually without modernizing the punctuation. This sometimes produces inconsistencies. For example, documents may still employ medieval Latin orthography when describing the appointment of a humanist teacher expected to teach Latin according to classical norms. Italian in these centuries is even more irregular. Finally, all translations are mine unless otherwise indicated.

ABBREVIATIONS

ARCHIVAL

ACPV	Archivio della Curia Patriarcale, Venice
ARSI	Archivum Romanum Societatis Iesu
ASCR	Archivio Storico Capitolino, Rome
ASR	Archivio di Stato, Rome
ASV	Archivio di Stato, Venice
ASVa	Archivio Segreto Vaticano

LIBRARY

BA	Bologna, Archiginnasio
Berg Mai	Bergamo, Mai
BQ	Brescia, Queriniana
BU	Bologna, Universitaria
CU	University of California, Berkeley
DFo	Washington, Folger Shakespeare
FLaur	Florence, Laurenziana
FM	Florence, Marucelliana
FN	Florence, Nazionale Centrale
FPed	Florence, Nazionale Pedagogica
FR	Florence, Riccardiana
ICN	Chicago, Newberry
ICU	Chicago, University of Chicago
IU	University of Illinois, Urbana-Champaign
MA	Milan, Ambrosiana

MB	Milan, Braidense
MH	Cambridge, MA, Harvard University
MT	Milan, Trivulziana
NNC	New York, Columbia University
NNPM	New York, Pierpont Morgan
NYPL	New York, Public Library
PN	Paris, Nationale
PU	Padua, Universitaria
RAles	Rome, Alessandrina Universitaria
RAng	Rome, Angelica
RCas	Rome, Casanatense
RV	Rome, Vallicelliana
RVE	Rome, Vittorio Emanuele II
V	Vatican City, Biblioteca Apostolica
VC	Venice, Museo Civico Correr
VCini	Venice, Fondazione Giorgio Cini
VM	Venice, Marciana

PRINTED SOURCES

Copinger W. Copinger, *Supplement to Hain's Repertorium Bibliographicum*. 3 vols. London, 1895–98; rpt. Milan, 1950.

DBI *Dizionario biografico degli italiani*. Rome, 1960– .

DIP *Dizionario degli istituti di perfezione*. Rome, 1974– .

Goff,
Third
Census Frederick R. Goff, *Incunabula in American Libraries: A Third Census*. New York, 1964.

GW *Gesamtkatalog der Wiegendrucke*. Leipzig, 1925– .

Hain Ludwig Hain, *Repertorium bibliographicum*. 4 vols. Stuttgart, 1826–36; rpt. Milan, 1966.

IGI *Indice generale degli incunaboli delle biblioteche d'Italia*. Edited by T. M. Guarnaschelli and D. Valenziani. 6 vols. Rome, 1943–81.

MP *Monumenta paedagogica Societatis Iesu*. Edited by Ladislaus Lukács. Vol. 1: *1540–1556;* vols. 2 and 3: *1557–1572;* vol. 4: *1573–1580*. Rome, 1965–81.

Reichling Dietrich Reichling, *Appendices ad Hainii-Copingeri Repertorium bibliographicum*. 7 vols. in 1. Munich, 1905–11.

Revised	*A Short-Title Catalogue of Books Printed in England, Scotland,*
STC	*and Ireland and of English Books Printed Abroad.* Edited by
	A. W. Pollard and G. R. Redgrave. London, 1926. 2d ed.
	revised by W. A. Jackson et al. London, 1976– .
STC	*Short-Title Catalogue of Books Printed in Italy and of Italian*
Italian	*Books Printed in Other Countries from 1465 to 1600 Now in the*
	British Museum. London, 1958.

TEACHERS AND PUPILS

Parents and communes erected a large educational establishment by the middle of the fourteenth century. Governments and parents stepped in because the church did not educate secular boys. The merchants and nobles of communal Italy organized education so well that practically every large city and small town across Italy had schools. Detailed examination of the schools of Venice, Florence, and Rome in the High Renaissance reveals both Latin and vernacular schools and how many pupils attended each. Boys from the middle and upper classes constituted the overwhelming majority of pupils, but some working-class boys and a few girls also studied. Clerics, laymen, and a small number of women formed a corps of professional teachers who earned their living in the classroom. Despite great political diversity the schools of Italy manifested many similarities across the peninsula during the Renaissance. The educational structure erected in the late Middle Ages underwent little change until 1600.

CHAPTER ONE

The Organization of Schooling

et those men teach boys who can do nothing greater, whose qualities are a plodding diligence, a rather dull mind, a muddled intellect, ordinary talent, cold-bloodedness, a body tolerant of labor, and a mind contemptuous of glory, desirous of petty gains, and indifferent to boredom. . . . Let them watch boys' fidgety hands, their roving eyes and confused whispering. . . . Neither grammar nor any of the seven liberal arts deserves the entire lifetime of a noble talent. . . . I . . . pity those who waste nearly all their lives in public school.[1]

So Petrarch wrote to a Florentine Latin teacher in 1352. The latter did not "waste" his whole life teaching, but left teaching to become a court secretary in Naples and a papal official in Rome. Fortunately for the children of Italy, a large number of masters stayed in the classroom. And even Petrarch conceded that they performed a useful service: "You teach children; you perform a task for the state."[2]

Pupils attended several different kinds of schools in an educational structure that assumed definite form by 1300 and did not change until the late sixteenth century. A limited number of earlier documents point the way; an abundance of fourteenth-century sources confirm that parents and civil governments created the schools of Renaissance Italy.

THE MEDIEVAL BACKGROUND

A sampling of the earliest concrete references to teachers, usually found in notarial acts because few early Italian civic records have survived, illustrates what little is known about pre-university education in the centuries before 1300. A certain Dominicus grammaticus appeared in

[1]*Rerum familiarium,* bk. 12, no. 3, of 1 April (1352), addressed to Zanobi Mazzuoli da Strada (1315–62). I follow the translation in Petrarca, 1982, pp. 143–44.
[2]Petrarca, 1982, p. 144.

Novara, a town about thirty miles west of Milan, between 941 and 958.[3] A teacher may have signed a document of 862 in Chioggia, at the south-western end of the Venetian lagoon. The names of additional *magistri* who may have been schoolteachers appeared in documents of 1064, 1067, and later at Chioggia.[4] A Giovanni grammatico, a layman, appeared in Forlì in 1102,[5] as did the name of the adult son of Albertus grammaticus in Noàntola (near Bologna) in a document of 1130.[6] Treviso had a grammarian in 1198, who was followed by others in the next century.[7]

Thirteenth-century documents are more abundant and informative. In 1221, a Genoese father hired a notary, who also taught school, to board and instruct his son for five years. After three years, the boy was expected to have learned enough to assist the master in teaching younger or less skilled pupils *Donatum et psalterium*, that is, the elements of Latin grammar and beginning reading. In 1248 a Genoese banker hired a teacher to instruct his two sons in *Donatus* and the psalter to enable them to read Latin correctly.[8]

The first grammarian in Verona for whom documentation can be found appeared in a tax document dated 1226; in the 1270s the Commune of Verona hired a Latin teacher for twenty-five Veronese pounds and the use of a house.[9] A grammarian taught in Bassano (in the Veneto) in 1233, a second in 1292, and a third in 1297.[10] The names of eighty *maestri di grammatica* appeared in Bolognese documents between 1265 and 1328; some, perhaps most, of these Latin teachers must have been pre-university instructors.[11] A *doctor puerorum*, a lay teacher of boys, surfaced in a Floren-tine document of 1275, followed by others in subsequent years.[12] San Gimignano had a Latin teacher in 1270.[13] In Venice, "Master Alexander *scriptor*, who teaches boys" ("magister Alexander scriptor, qui docet pu-

[3]Lizier, 1908, pp. 6–7. Italian local historians studied schooling intensively and well in the late nineteenth and early twentieth centuries in the enthusiastic aftermath of national unity. For comprehensive bibliographies of the older studies, see Barsanti, 1905, pp. 7–31; and Manacorda, 1914, vol. 2:379–99. I do not know of any subsequent comprehensive bibliographies.

[4]Bellemo, 1888, pp. 278–79. *Magister* also meant master of a craft at this time.

[5]Pasini, 1925, p. 5. *Grammatica* meant both Latin grammar and Latin, depending on the context. Similarly, a grammarian taught Latin grammar or elementary Latin (including reading and composition). Hence, I use "grammarian" and "Latin teacher" interchangeably.

[6]Quoted in Manacorda, 1914, vol. 1:138.

[7]Serena, 1912, pp. 58–59.

[8]Massa, 1906, pp. 172–73, quotes from the 1221 contract, and Petti Balbi, 1979, pp. 143–44, quotes it in full. Manacorda, 1914, vol. 1:140–41, analyzes it well. Also see Reynolds, 1937, pp. 255–56.

[9]C. Garibotto, 1921, pp. 5–6; Bolognini, 1896, pp. 1–11.

[10]Chiuppani, 1915, pp. 82–83.

[11]Zaccagnini, 1924, pp. 22–27.

[12]Davidsohn, 1965, p. 214; also see Debenedetti, 1906–7.

[13]Davidsohn, 1965, p. 222.

eros"), witnessed a document in 1287.[14] Milan in 1288 boasted eight "professors of grammar" ("professores artis grammaticae"), who may have been university-level teachers, plus seventy or more grammarians teaching at lower levels.[15]

Commercial mathematics teachers, or *maestri d'abbaco*, also appeared in the thirteenth century, the first in Bologna in 1265.[16] The Commune of Verona in 1277 decided to appoint *unum magistrum rationis abachi*, the first known communal *maestro d'abbaco*, if the commune acted immediately.[17] By 1284 the Commune of Verona had acted; it paid a commercial mathematics teacher an annual stipend of forty *lire veronesi* and the free use of a house.[18]

The early documentation reveals three kinds of schools which can be classified according to their sponsors and financial supporters. The town or city government, called the commune, sponsored and directed communal schools.[19] The commune appointed the teacher, paid his salary, and exercised limited supervision of the curriculum. A free-lance master and the parents of his pupils created an independent school.[20] He opened a school in his home or rented premises and taught all those willing to pay him for his services. Other independent masters taught as household tutors, either living in the home or coming daily to teach; again, parents paid. Ecclesiastical authorities, such as a bishop acting through the cathedral chapter or a religious order in a monastery, sponsored ecclesiastical schools in which clergymen taught other clerics and lay students.

Communal and independent masters dominated; indeed, all the teach-

[14]Bertanza and Dalla Santa, 1907, p. 1.
[15]Manacorda, 1914, vol. 1:142–43.
[16]Zaccagnini, 1924, pp. 32–33.
[17]Bolognini, 1896, p. 11.
[18]E. Garibotto, 1923, p. 315.
[19]A word about terminology. Teachers in Renaissance Italy used the terms *public* and *public school* differently than we use them today. When a teacher said "tengo scuola publica à S. Maria Mater Domini," or "tengo scuola publicamente," he meant that he ran a school in the district of S. Maria Mater Domini that was open to all who were willing to pay him. *Public* meant *open*. ACPV, "Professioni di fede richiesta agli insegnanti, 1587," fols. 205ᵛ, 203ᵛ, et passim; Baldo, 1977, p. 71. To avoid confusion with the modern English meaning of *public school,* and because the local commune, rather than a distant and impersonal "state," directed the school, I use "communal school."
[20]I prefer the term *independent* to the term *private* as a description of schools and teachers, because the English word *private* connotes social exclusivity, which the independent schools lacked. Most accepted anyone who would pay, including boys of modest social status. Manacorda used the terms *free schools (scuole libere),* meaning free of external legal authority (such as that of the bishop), and *lay schools* to differentiate these schools from ecclesiastical schools. I avoid both terms in order to prevent confusion with a modern meaning of *free* ("without charge"), and because many clergymen taught in "lay" schools. I believe that the word *independent* best describes these schools.

ers mentioned so far were communal or independent masters. Italy had very few church schools after 1300.

THE DECLINE OF CHURCH SCHOOLS

Many historians conclude that the church monopolized education in early medieval Italy.[21] Italian historians, on the other hand, point out that some of the few surviving documents mention state and independent schools as well as ecclesiastical schools.[22] They argue for limited continuity: just as early medieval Italian towns rose from the ruins of Roman cities, so state and independent schools may have survived the wreckage of imperial institutions. In truth, not enough is known about Italian pre-university education, or any other kind, in the centuries between the disintegration of the Roman Empire and 1100 to support a definitive statement. A few civil, episcopal, and papal decrees survive, as do scattered references to teachers and schools. But information on their functioning is lacking.

The picture of church schools becomes clearer after 1100; twelfth- and thirteenth-century Italy had a reasonable number of episcopal or cathedral chapter schools and some monastic schools.[23] But much of the information is vague. Episcopal/cathedral schools taught *clericos,* a general term that could mean boys intending to become priests, youths in minor orders, or adult clergymen. It is usually impossible to determine the level and content of the instruction in these church schools; they could have instructed boys in Latin grammar or university-age clerics in theology. That church schools taught significant numbers of lay boys, that is, those not destined for clerical careers, is doubtful. The same uncertainty surrounds the references to clerical teachers. It often is not clear whether they taught under ecclesiastical auspices, as in a cathedral school, or independently. Despite the uncertainty, however, it is likely that the church, through episcopal/cathedral chapter schools and some monastic schools, played a significant role in Italian education between 1100 and 1300. Church schools were probably numerous enough to educate most of those intended for the clerical life, and they may have educated a few lay boys, as well.

But most of these ecclesiastical schools disappeared by 1300. In post-1300 documents, which are abundant, references to church schools are very difficult to find. By contrast, it is clear that communal and indepen-

[21]Delhaye, 1947, p. 211; Richè, 1976, pp. 399–421; Richè, 1979, pp. 174–79, 189–94. General histories of the Middle Ages frequently echo their views.

[22]Salvioli, 1912, pp. 33–42 and 50–123, for notices of schools across Italy before the year 1000; Manacorda, 1914, vol. 1, chs. 1–3; Delhaye, 1947, p. 213; Petti Balbi, 1979, pp. 13–16.

[23]For local examples, see Manacorda, 1914, vol. 1, ch. 4, and vol. 2:283, 286, 288, 295, 297, 299, 302, 305, 308, 311–13, 316, 335.

dent schools appeared in large cities and small towns throughout Italy. The difference is too great to be explained by the chance survival of some records and the loss of others. Church schools suffered drastic decline between 1100 and 1300.

In 1100, two kinds of schools operating under the auspices of a church body and staffed by clergymen existed: (1) monastic schools, meaning schools located in a monastery or convent where members of a religious order taught novices of the order and possibly lay children who either lived in the monastery or came daily to learn; and (2) chapter schools, which were schools run by a chapter of canons attached to a specific church, especially the cathedral. Indeed, *chapter school, episcopal school,* and *cathedral school* were nearly synonymous terms in Italy; almost all the known chapter schools operated under the bishop's direction and were located at the cathedral. Chapter schools had as their principal goal the training of boys intended for the secular priesthood.

Monastic schools underwent profound change when religious orders withdrew from elementary and secondary education. Monastic reformers following the lead of St. Peter Damiani (1007–72) opposed open schools; they insisted that convents train only novices and professed members of the religious order. They believed that the monastic vocation was basically incompatible with such lay activities as teaching Latin to boys.[24]

Monastic reformers thoroughly disapproved of the practice of child oblation, which had given monasteries a corps of children to educate.[25] Oblation was the donation or "offering" (*oblatio*) of a young child to a monastery where he or she would be brought up without further parental control. Parents practiced oblation for a variety of noble and ignoble motives. They might present the child to a monastery in the hope that both givers and child would reap rich spiritual rewards. Poor parents might give up their child so that he might enjoy material benefits the parents could not provide. On the other hand, oblation permitted parents to rid themselves of the offspring of an illegitimate or incestuous union, a child whose presence caused embarrassment. Or parents might practice oblation in order to keep intact the family patrimony for the eldest child; giving siblings to a monastery effectively disinherited them. Social custom and canon law considered oblation to be perpetual: the child would become a monk or nun and could not leave as an adult. Usually the parents made a substantial financial contribution to induce the monastery to accept the child. Still, this probably cost less than rearing a child and then providing a dowry. Monastic reformers objected to various aspects of oblation, but especially to the payment that accompanied it. While canon-

[24]Arnaldi, 1978, p. 13.
[25]Lynch, 1976, pp. 36–60; Boswell, 1984; Klapisch-Zuber, 1985, pp. 108–9.

ists devised penalties to discourage it, reformers fought child oblation by raising the minimum age for novices to 15, 16, 18, or 20, and insisting that they be able to read, write, and chant before admission. Although oblation never completely disappeared, it declined in the thirteenth century. Hence, monasteries did not need to provide much pre-university education.

Although religious orders withdrew from elementary and secondary education, they supported a remarkable revival of theological training. In the thirteenth and fourteenth centuries, the mendicant orders, especially the Dominicans and Franciscans, founded numerous *studia theologiae,* that is, university-level theology schools, in their monasteries across Italy and Europe. These *studia* offered instruction in theology to members of their orders and to outsiders. Some *studia* were located in Italian university towns alongside the faculties of arts and law. Monastic *studia* might give arts instruction as well as theological training, and enroll a few laymen. But they were institutions of higher learning, not elementary and secondary schools.[26] Dante, aged 26 and married, studied theology in the *studium* at Santa Croce in Florence in 1291.[27]

Chapter or cathedral schools also suffered crisis and decline after 1100; the history of Genoese chapter schools illustrates what happened.[28] The earliest documented teacher at Genoa's cathedral chapter appeared in 1111. Others regularly taught there through the twelfth century, training aspirants to the clerical life and some lay children, who seem to have paid for their instruction. But then the common life of the chapter began to decay in the second half of the twelfth century. The cathedral's patrimony was divided into prebends, that is, an individual canon's share of the cathedral's revenue. With it and dispensation from the obligation of residence, a canon might move away. With the rise of universities, a canon with a prebend might leave to attend a university in another city, because Genoa lacked one. Indeed, the papacy encouraged university study in order to raise the educational level of the clergy. In 1219, Pope Honorius III authorized bishops to send clerics away to study at a university; while studying, the clerics might continue to enjoy the revenues of their benefices.[29] Although the papacy tried to arrest the decline of cathedral schools, the decline continued in Genoa. By the second half of the thirteenth century, the number of canons in the Genoese cathedral chapter had fallen to four. The school suffered from the decline of collegiality; by 1313 it appears to have ceased functioning.

[26]G. Barone, 1978, pp. 207–8; Maierù, 1978, pp. 314–15; plus other studies in *Le scuole degli ordini mendicanti,* 1978.

[27]Davidsohn, 1965, pp. 229–30.

[28]The following is based on Petti Balbi, 1979, pp. 16–32. Other scholars noting the decline of chapter life and cathedral schools include Bullough, 1964, pp. 139–40, 142–43; Fonseca, 1984, pp. 267–68, 277; and Rigon, 1984, p. 716, on Padua.

[29]Boyle, 1962, pp. 263–66.

The same happened in Florence. A Florentine cathedral school educated aspirants to the priesthood from the late thirteenth through the first third of the fourteenth century, then disappeared.[30] Ser Lapo Nuti, chaplain to the cathedral chapter and *doctor puerorum*, was active from 1315 through 1339. It is not clear whether he taught independently or was the last of the cathedral school masters.[31]

A series of conciliar and papal decrees tried to strengthen cathedral schools in particular and church schools in general. Canon 18 of the Third Lateran Council of 1179 ordered every cathedral to appoint a teacher to instruct clerics and poor scholars gratis. Canon 11 of the Fourth Lateran Council of 1215 repeated the admonition, ordering cathedrals and other churches to teach grammar and theology if sufficient revenues existed, an important qualification.[32] Additional papal actions of the thirteenth century encouraged young clerics, including parish priests, to attend universities.[33] These actions increased the number of university-trained clergymen but did not prevent the withering of cathedral schools. In retrospect, these famous and frequently cited canons and papal actions signalled a desperate, unsuccessful effort to stem the decay of medieval church schools, at least in Italy.[34]

Pope Eugenius IV (1431–47) attempted to revive cathedral schools. Following his lead, bishops in Bologna, Catania, Florence, Olona, Padua, Pistoia, Tortona, Treviso, Turin, Venice, and Verona founded free cathedral schools for a small number of boys intended for the diocesan priesthood.[35] The schools followed a pattern. The pontiff assigned benefice income sufficient to support eight to a dozen boys and a teacher or two. The Verona *Scola acolytorum* (School for Acolytes) did considerably better under the leadership of energetic bishops. It enrolled twenty-four (later, forty to forty-five) poor boys, who studied a Latin humanistic curriculum and singing under two masters in the fifteenth and sixteenth centuries. When they completed their studies and reached canonical age, the boys became diocesan priests.[36]

The Pistoia cathedral school survived at least to 1502; those of Verona, Venice, and Treviso to the middle of the sixteenth century and beyond.[37]

[30]Davidsohn, 1965, pp. 227–29.

[31]Debenedetti, 1906–7, p. 338.

[32]*Conciliorum*, 1973, pp. 220, 240.

[33]Boyle, 1962.

[34]Manacorda, 1914, vol. 1:163; Verger, 1978, pp. 186–87; Arnaldi, 1976, p. 351; Maccarrone, 1984, pp. 131–32.

[35]Pesce, 1969, vol. 1:120–31; vol. 2:13–17, provides a good survey of the founding of these schools, and detailed information on the founding of Treviso.

[36]Spagnolo, 1904.

[37]For the Pistola school, see Zanelli, 1900, pp. 77–78n. For the Verona school, see the sources in n. 35 above. For the continuing history of the Venetian acolyte school, see ch. 2 herein.

The Vicenza cathedral school, founded in 1460 to instruct a handful of poor priesthood students, also lasted more than a hundred years.[38] The fate of the others is unknown. But they did not always fulfill the hopes of their founders. For example, the religious tone of the Treviso school left something to be desired in the 1560s. Despite the requirement of poverty, noble youths sometimes enrolled in order to avoid criminal prosecution or tax judgments, not to fulfill clerical vocations.[39] In the end, these small cathedral or acolyte schools had but a minimum impact on Renaissance education, because they enrolled only a few clerical students. Tridentine seminary legislation would go much further toward educating diocesan clergy.

Parish schools, in which the parish priest taught the children of the parish, were not common in Renaissance Italy. A few surfaced in several villages in the countryside around Treviso on the Venetian *Terraferma* in the middle and late sixteenth century.[40] Possibly a few more have escaped notice. But the church did not establish or maintain a network of parish schools in Italy.[41] By contrast, the English hierarchy sporadically exhorted and ordered parish priests to teach their parishioners prayers, basic religious doctrine, simple reading, singing, and Latin in decrees from 994 through the 1540s, with the result that England had a limited number of parish schools.[42] The absence of such exhortations in Italy strongly argues that parish schools existed only in rare cases. Had they been numerous, Italian bishops and their vicars-general would have badgered parish priests with instructions for their parish schools in this age of regulatory minutiae. And tight-fisted town councils would not have had to spend money hiring communal masters.

Although the church withdrew from the education of lay children, individual clergymen did not. They moved outside the institutional framework of the church to teach as independent masters in the later Middle Ages. Genoese priests appeared as independent masters outside the walls of chapter, monastery, or parish in the late thirteenth century. They

[38]Mantese, 1964, pp. 711–25.

[39]Liberali, 1971, pp. 37–43.

[40]Liberali, 1971, p. 33, notes evidence—which is not always conclusive—of eight parish schools between 1530 and 1587.

[41]Zafarana, 1984, pp. 510–11, 536–39, notes the absence of references to parish schools in fourteenth-century visitation reports. I have examined a number of detailed diocesan visitation reports after Trent in ASVa, Congregazione del Concilio, Visitationes Apostolicae, plus published reports, without finding any parish schools. Parish schools, or at least parochial schoolmasters, appeared in rural areas in the seventeenth and eighteenth centuries, partly as a consequence of growth in the number of clergy. Priests without benefices taught in order to earn some income from the commune or parents. Hence, their schools were not usually free parish schools sponsored by the church. Deutscher, "Growth." Also see Pesciatini, 1982, pp. 132–35.

[42]Moran, 1985, pp. 77–79, 94, 142–44.

filled the same professional roles as lay masters. Indeed, Genoese lay teachers rightly saw these clergymen as competitors and called on the teachers' guild to protect their interests by restricting clerical masters to ten pupils each.[43] Such tensions did not surface elsewhere, perhaps because no other city had a teachers' guild. In other towns, and eventually in Genoa as well, independent lay and clerical masters shared the teaching profession. A large number of clergymen appeared across Italy as household tutors and neighborhood schoolmasters, and a handful became communal masters between 1300 and 1550.

These clerical masters neither lived nor taught under ecclesiastical roofs, but lived and taught anywhere in the town. Indeed, after Trent, bishops sometimes obliged seminarians to take employment as household tutors after several years of study but before ordination, if they had not secured postings through their own efforts.[44] One suspects that some of these clerics simply continued to teach after ordination. Residence requirements were not always enforced on the Renaissance clergy. Hence, some clerics became independent masters and, like laymen, moved from quarter to quarter and town to town searching for more pupils and better positions.

After 1300 the church educated only the limited number of youths destined for the religious life—and far from all of these—plus a small number of girls in convents. The close association between church and school typical of fourteenth- and fifteenth-century England,[45] and possibly elsewhere, did not prevail in the Italian peninsula.

SCHOOLS IN THE TRECENTO

Italy's urban civilization met its own educational needs, as communal governments and parents founded schools. Even if the decline of church schools left a large pedagogical gap—a supposition, not a proven fact—the church never could have met the demands of the leading commercial society of Europe. Thirteenth- and fourteenth-century Italy needed many notaries, secretaries, and public officials to carry on civic and private business. When merchants recognized the great usefulness of abbaco (commercial mathematics), they wanted schools to teach this skill to their sons and future employees. The merchants who dominated the now wealthy cities and towns believed strongly in the utility of learning and suited action to belief by hiring teachers. The documents reveal few

[43]Petti Balbi, 1979, pp. 96–101.

[44]The example comes from Treviso in 1592; see Liberali, 1971, pp. 81, 162. The seminarians had to be at least 19 and to have completed six years of study before teaching. One suspects that financial reasons dictated this arrangement.

[45]This is the theme of Moran, 1985.

schools before 1300 but an abundance of communal and independent schools in the fourteenth century.

However, the educational surge cannot be precisely dated. The lack of surviving documentation may hide a thirteenth-century initiative; it is also possible that a pedagogical explosion occurred in the Trecento. The most likely explanation embraces both: schooling began to grow in the Duecento and exploded across Italy in the Trecento. The appearance of a literacy requirement for certain professions supports the notion of an expansion of schooling. For example, judges, lawyers, administrators, civil servants, and priests in twelfth- and thirteenth-century Chioggia frequently could not read or write, or could do one but not the other. But in 1333 the Commune of Chioggia decreed that judges and other civic officials must read and write to hold their jobs.[46] Such a law, and its absence earlier, presupposed greater availability of schooling.

By the middle of the Trecento, parents and communes had created a large educational establishment across northern and north-central Italy. A listing of some cities, towns, and hamlets supporting communal or independent schools or both suggests the size of this establishment. Turin had a communal Latin teacher in 1337, and thirty-four other Piedmontese towns and villages had teachers in the fourteenth and fifteenth centuries.[47] Genoa and the nearby towns in Liguria had numerous teachers and schools.[48] The Veneto in northeastern Italy exhibited the same pattern. A communal grammarian taught in Treviso as early as 1316, and numerous other communal and independent masters followed.[49] Bassano had a communal grammarian in 1349, the date of the first extant records.[50] Chioggia had several teachers in the middle of the Trecento; by the 1380s, the commune's relatively high salaries lured grammarians from other towns.[51] Modena had teachers, possibly including communal masters, early in the Trecento.[52] Tuscan towns boasted an abundance of communal and independent schools. An independent Latin teacher was mentioned in a Pistoian document of 1304; the city hired its first communal master in 1322 to teach grammar, logic, and *ars dictandi,* and added a communal *maestro d'abbaco* in 1353.[53] In or about 1360, the Commune of Pistoia, seeking a new communal grammarian, commissioned a visit to other towns to evaluate their teachers: Lucca, Pisa, Siena, San Gimignano, San Miniato, Colle di Val d'Elsa, and Volterra in Tuscany, plus Todi in Umbria and Rieti in Lazio.

[46]Bellemo, 1888, pp. 279–80. Massa, 1906, p. 173, makes a similar point for Genoa.
[47]Gabotto, 1895, pp. 288–350; Sassi, 1880, pp. 14–15; Manacorda, 1914, vol. 2:328–29.
[48]Massa, 1906; Gorrini, 1931–32; Petti Balbi, 1975.
[49]Serena, 1912, pp. 48–49; and Pesce, 1983, pp. 51–63, 164–91, 397–98.
[50]Chiuppani, 1915, p. 85.
[51]Bellemo, 1888, pp. 283, 49.
[52]Bertoni and Vicini, 1904–5, pp. 168–69; Vicini, 1935, pp. 59–60.
[53]Zanelli, 1900, pp. 9–10, 38–39, et passim.

All these towns, even the tiny hamlet of Colle di Val d'Elsa, supported communal Latin teachers at this time.[54] No doubt many other towns, whose records have not been examined or have disappeared, also offered schooling for the young.

COMMUNAL LATIN SCHOOLS

Communes supported education because they judged that educating the young yielded civic and personal benefits. A town might begin by responding to an emergency. In the plague year of 1348, an elementary teacher (*doctor puerorum*) approached the city council of Lucca with a petition. Because of the poverty in the city and the lack of pupils, he could not continue teaching without a stipend from the commune. He meant that the plague had so decimated the youthful population that he did not have enough fee-paying pupils to continue teaching in Lucca. Probably the plague had killed or driven off many teachers, as well, leaving him in a favorable bargaining position. If the parents of Lucca wanted to retain his services, the city would have to put him on the public payroll. The city council responded by noting that boys wandered about the city idly and ignorant of letters for the lack of teachers. "Under the rod of a master," they would achieve "the splendor of learning."[55] The city government granted this teacher a stipend of three *lire di danaro piccolo* per month free of taxes.

The common good, seen in civic and moral terms, quickly became the justification for spending communal funds on a teacher. In 1353 the Luccan Commune spoke of the benefit to the republic (*reipublice utilitas*) of hiring a Latin teacher.[56] In 1371 the city council elaborated: providing grammar instruction to boys would benefit the commune (*pro communi utilitate*). Knowledge of Latin grammar was useful to the young and indispensable to the health of the city. An often-cited *topos* rooted in late antiquity and the early Middle Ages was that Latin grammar was the beginning and foundation of all skill and virtue.[57] In 1436 the tiny village of Chieri (in Piedmont,

---

[54]Bacci, 1895, pp. 88–95.

[55]"ne ipsi pueri hinc inde vacabunde ambulent, et ne ex diutina magistrorum vacatione ignari literarum efficiantur, sed sub magistrali ferula ad decus doctrine valeant pervenire." Barsanti, 1905, pp. 50, 195 (quote, 14 August 1348).

[56]Ibid., p. 210, 21 January 1353.

[57]"Significatur pro communi utilitate quod esset bonum providere de uno alio magistro in scientia gramaticali docto. . . . Verum quod gramaticalis scientia est origo et fundamentum omnium virtutum et scientiarum et propterea summe nedum utile, sed necesse est procurare unum sufficientem virum in tali facultate qui iuvenes erudiat doceat ac moribus disciplinet." Ibid., p. 212, 27 September 1371. Both Flavius Cassiodorus Senator (480–575), in his *Institutiones divinarum et saecularium litterarum,* and Isidore of Seville (c. 570–636), in his *Etymologiarum sive originum libri XX,* praised grammar as the "origo et fundamentum liberalium litterarum." J. Murphy, 1981, pp. 66, 74 n. 110. Appointing a teacher of Latin for the

about twenty miles from Turin) decided to hire a "worthy" teacher for "the benefit of the republic."[58] The phrase had both practical and lofty meaning: schools had to train boys in the language skills needed by prospective civil servants as well as inculcate the wisdom required of future leaders of the commune.

As the ideology of humanism became stronger, town councils stated that learning promoted civic values and personal fulfillment. The Commune of Treviso explained in 1475 that it had to provide capable and grave teachers for the honor and good of the city. Our sons should be instructed and made learned so that later, when heavily engaged in the duties of business, they will not be deficient in letters. They should have the opportunity now to pursue and acquire virtue, knowledge, and good habits, instead of daily squandering their time in the city and its streets where, in the absence of venerable teachers, they acquire bad habits and strong vices.[59] In 1524 the Commune of Treviso directly linked education to civic welfare. Nothing so ennobles and exalts a city as the study of good letters, which make men learned and wise, honorable to their city, useful to the republic, and capable of every civic enterprise.[60] In 1542, the Treviso Commune again coupled civic commitment with the moral and intellectual development of its youth as reasons for hiring a teacher. The study of letters is necessary in order to live civilly and honestly (*viver civil et honesto*). Good teachers are needed to draw youths out of their idleness and indifference to letters.[61]

Italian communes supported education from the late thirteenth through the seventeenth century and beyond. Most of the towns lacking schools in the Trecento added them in the Quattrocento. The commune might embark on state-supported education in response to an emergency, but communal support of education soon became entrenched. The schoolmaster took his place alongside the communal physician and surgeon as a public servant providing services for the common good.[62] Communal schools manifested the self-confidence and pride of the towns and the

good of the community strikingly anticipated civic humanism, as Baron, 1977, p. 611, points out in his discussion of the same move, expressed in nearly identical words by the Commune of Arezzo in 1388.

[58]Quoted in Gabotto, 1895, p. 312.

[59]Liberali, 1971, p. 175.

[60]"Non vi è cosa alcuna che mazor autorità e più sufficientemente possano nobilitar et esaltar una città che lo studio delle buone lettere, facendosi qui uomini dotti e sapienti, onorevoli alla sua città e utili alla sua repubblica, e idonei ad ogni civil impresa." Quoted in Liberali, 1971, pp. 175–76.

[61]Ibid., p. 176. For similar statements in Arezzo, see Black, 1987, pp. 212–13.

[62]As Park, 1985, p. 90, writes, "By the mid-fourteenth century the communal doctor (*medico condotto*) had become a standard institution in many Italian cities and towns as well as in some areas of the countryside." Other cities and towns can be added to those that Park mentions.

merchants who led them. Such towns had either thrown off princely rule entirely or enjoyed the right to manage local affairs. Urban merchants bought and sold, shipped and traded, across Europe and the Levant; their ambition and pride easily embraced the founding of communal schools. Of course, the decision to pay a Latin teacher's salary had personal benefits for the city's leaders: their sons were more likely to attend school than the sons of the laboring classes.

Small towns hired communal masters more often than did large cities. The village of Palazzolo sull'Oglio (midway between Brescia and Bergamo) of 1,200 to 1,300 souls had a communal master in the 1460s.[63] So did many Piedmontese villages in the fourteenth and fifteenth centuries, and tiny villages of a few hundred people or fewer in the Tuscan countryside in the sixteenth and seventeenth centuries.[64] Communal schools appeared in small towns and villages throughout northern and north-central Italy. By contrast, large and powerful cities such as Venice, Milan, and Florence had few communal teachers.

Necessity, rather than a greater commitment to education, drove smaller towns to support communal schools. The leading citizens of small communes lacked the personal wealth to hire household tutors or as a group to support an independent master. They might be the leaders of their own towns and villages, but their overall wealth did not compare with that of their counterparts in the large cities. Hence, the council of a small town used communal revenues to hire a master, who supplemented his salary with student fees. By contrast, the much wealthier merchants, nobles, and professionals of major urban centers who ruled subject lands and commercial empires had ample incomes to hire individual household tutors and to support other independent masters.

Both communal council and individual parent viewed education personally. Each took a direct interest in the hiring of an individual teacher of academic excellence and good character who would, they hoped, implant these qualities in their sons. Erasmus and many others articulated the strong Renaissance belief that the teacher determined the quality of education; hence, hiring a master became a weighty matter. A commune normally hired only one, two, or three communal masters. Renaissance men did not think in terms of establishing an educational "system" in the modern sense, nor did they believe in universal education, which would have required a broader, more impersonal approach.

Communal councils followed a standard procedure in the appointment of masters. They announced their need for a "good, suitable, and compe-

[63]Chiappa, 1964, p. 41, who gives no source for the population figure.
[64]Gabotto, 1895, pp. 288–350; Imberciadori, 1959, pp. 432–37; Pesciatini, 1982. Pescia (between Pistoia and Lucca), with 4,000 to 6,000 inhabitants in the second half of the sixteenth century, had four communal teachers: a Latin teacher, an abbaco master, and two assistants. J. Brown, 1982, pp. 130–31.

tent" teacher to instruct the youth of the city. Teachers from other towns plus independent masters already in the city applied. A commune might initiate its own search. As noted previously, the Commune of Pistoia circa 1360 authorized an official to ascertain the competency, age, current salaries, and willingness to move to Pistoia of the communal grammarians of nine central Italian towns.[65] The Commune of Arezzo wrote letters to neighboring towns inquiring after Latin teachers; it also asked native sons living elsewhere to suggest names and, when necessary, approached masters directly.[66] Communes preferred to appoint masters from out of town. For example, Volterra appointed foreigners, usually men from other Tuscan towns, almost exclusively through the fourteenth and fifteenth centuries.[67] Communes believed that a foreign teacher free of local friendships and enmities plus the claims of relatives brought independence to his post, a principle also followed in the appointment of men to higher civic posts such as *podestà* (chief police and judicial officer) and chancellor.

The commune reviewed the qualifications of the applicants and made the decision. It awarded the successful applicant a *condotta,* a contract specifying the terms and conditions of a renewable appointment for one, two, three, or five years. For example, the Commune of Rovigo normally awarded its masters *condotte* of three years. Between 1483 and 1615, it hired twenty-eight masters whose tenure averaged four and three-quarters years. Two stayed considerably longer, one from 1510 to 1538, another from 1593 to 1615.[68] On rare occasions the commune honored an esteemed master who had already served a number of years with a lifetime appointment. The *condotta* fixed the teacher's salary and authorized him to collect supplementary fees from his students at rates established by the commune. He might also receive one or all of the following: a rent-free house in which to hold classes, live, or both; permission to accept fee-paying boarding students; and a tax exemption.

Communes authorized masters to collect supplementary fees for practical reasons. The government judged public education to be beneficial to the community, but saw no reason to offer it gratis. Occasionally a commune waived pupil fees; more frequently it decreed that, for charitable reasons, a handful of deserving but indigent pupils might attend without payment (see below). But in the vast majority of cases, the commune permitted communal masters to collect additional fees from all students. While the communal council guaranteed that the town would have the services of a good master, the tight-fisted merchants who dominated communal councils did not wish to spend more for education than

[65]Bacci, 1895.
[66]Black, 1987, pp. 180–81.
[67]Battistini, 1919, p. 49.
[68]Cessi, 1896, pp. 13, 17–18.

the minimum, an attitude typical of public authorities of all centuries. So they provided the greater part of the teacher's income, and left it to parents to pay the rest. For example, the Commune of Credenza d'Ivrea (midway between Turin and Aosta in Piedmont) hired a master in 1421, gave him the right to charge additional fees at rates set by the commune, and promised that it would not hire another communal master (but pointedly added that anyone else might open an independent school).[69] If part of the master's income depended on student fees, he would have to teach well in order to attract the number of pupils needed to augment his income significantly. Communal governments approached education with a mixture of commitment to the public good, self-interest, shrewd calculation of the lowest possible expense, and great attention to detail—qualities exhibited in all other areas, as well.

In 1386 the Commune of Chioggia hired a new master to replace the deceased incumbent. It hired Cristoforo Dente, who had previously taught independently in Venice,[70] for two years at an annual salary of sixty gold ducats plus a house (*domo sufitiente*). He might also charge his students fees according to the following schedule: students just beginning to learn to read (*pro pueris a tabula usque ad Donatum*) paid forty soldi per annum, those studying beginning Latin grammar (*pro illis de Donato usque donec erunt de latino*) paid one ducat per annum, those reading Latin at a slightly more advanced level (*qui erunt de latino*) paid six lire per annum, and the most advanced pupils, who read Vergil, Lucan, Terence, Aesop, Prospero, Ovid, and Boethius, paid two ducats annually. Both salary and student fees were to be paid quarterly.[71]

A typical communal master normally taught about thirty students, more of them elementary than advanced.[72] If the Chioggia communal master in the academic year 1386–87 had ten students learning to read, ten more beginning the study of Latin, and five each in the two advanced classes, he earned slightly more than thirty-one ducats in student fees.[73]

---

[69]Gabotto, 1895, p. 328.

[70]Dente taught independently in Venice in 1382 and 1383. After his appointment as communal master at Chioggia, he maintained his house in Venice, served as a witness in Venetian notarial acts through 1416, and may have been a notary himself in Venice from 1412 to 1421. Bertanza and Dalla Santa, 1907, pp. 163n, 173, 177.

[71]See Bellemo, 1888, p. 49, for the full text of the contract. This fee schedule is typical of those that appear in the contracts.

[72]Thirty students was the approximate maximum enrollment of a Latin school taught by a single teacher in sixteenth-century Venice. Schools invariably had more elementary than advanced pupils.

[73]Calculating the income from student fees is a little complicated, because two monetary systems were employed. Salaries and large amounts were often stated in the famous monies of account based on gold, the Venetian ducat and the Florentine florin, which were used elsewhere as well. But people often made payment in a silver system based on 1 lira (lb.) equals 20 soldi (shillings) equals 240 denari (pence), called *lira di piccoli* for the basic coins

With his communal salary of sixty ducats, his annual income from teaching amounted to ninety-one ducats, plus the rent-free use of a house, perhaps worth another few ducats. If he had a larger school and earned additional income from student fees, he probably would have to pay an assistant (*ripetitore*) to drill the elementary pupils. If he had fewer pupils, his income dropped.

Chioggia communal masters of the 1380s and 1390s earned salaries of 50 to 70 ducats plus student fees of 25 to 30 ducats.[74] Their total annual income amounted to between 75 and 100 ducats—good but not extraordinary. In the 1420s a Venetian oarsman in a war galley earned 28 ducats annually in peacetime. A skilled craftsman such as a master shipwright earned 48 ducats annually, a shipwright foreman with supervisory responsibilities earned 100 ducats, and an expert galley builder 200 ducats plus extras.[75] In short, the Chioggia communal master earned three to four times as much as an unskilled laborer, one and one-half to two times as much as a skilled craftsman, about the same or a little less than a foreman-craftsman, and half as much as the galley builder. The communal master probably earned considerably less than a lawyer, less than most university professors, and little compared to professors of law and medicine. Nobles and wealthy merchants enjoyed annual incomes of hundreds and thousands of ducats, far beyond the dreams of a teacher.

Communal masters elsewhere earned similar incomes. In the 1420s the Commune of Volterra hired a teacher at the salary of 80 gold florins annually. He might also charge fees. Beginners just learning the letters of the alphabet paid nothing; students reading the primer paid 1 lira 10 soldi each; students reading *Donatus,* that is, studying the rudiments of Latin grammar, paid 2 lire; students in the first- and second-level Latin classes paid 3 lire each; and students of the most advanced class paid 4 lire each.[76] A class of thirty students divided between the four fee-paying groups in the same proportions as the Chioggia master's class yielded the Volterra master 17 florins 2 lire.[77] He also had the rent-free use of a house in which

---

(*denari piccoli* or silver pennies). One ducat equaled about 90 soldi (or 4 lire 10 soldi) in Venice in the 1380s and 1390s (Cessi, 1968, vol. 2:25). Hence, ten students learning to read paid 40 soldi each, for a total of 400 soldi (4 ducats 2 lire), ten pupils beginning Latin paid 10 ducats, five advanced pupils charged 6 lire each paid 600 soldi (30 lire or 6 ducats 3 lire), and the five most advanced pupils studying at a rate of 2 ducats each paid 10 ducats. Thus, thirty students paid 31 ducats 1 lira in toto. *Condotte* never indicated the value of a rent-free house and seldom mentioned its intended use (teaching, residence, or both).

[74]Chioggia hired another master in 1397 at exactly the same salary and fee schedule that applied in 1386. Bellemo, 1888, pp. 49–50.

[75]The salaries come from Lane, 1944, p. 33.

[76]Battistini, 1919, pp. 15, 34–35.

[77]The florin was worth 79 to 83 soldi, i.e., about 4 lire, in Florence in the 1420s. Goldthwaite, 1980, p. 430.

to live and teach, worth at least another 5 florins.[78] Hence, his annual income reached about 102 florins.

Like his comrade in Chioggia, the Volterra communal master earned more than skilled and unskilled artisans but less than other professionals. In the first half of the fifteenth century, an unskilled laborer in the Florentine building trades might earn 30 florins annually, a skilled artisan such as a mason or a smith up to 50 florins, and a foreman 75 florins.[79] Beginning employees of Florentine merchant-banking houses earned as little as 20 florins annually, others earned 50 to 60 florins, and managers of branch offices 100 florins or more.[80] Florentine lawyers earned 300 florins and more annually.[81]

Other factors also influenced the selection of a master. The Pistoian official of the 1360s searching for a communal master knew these well. He noted that the communal masters of San Miniato and San Gimignano earned 60 florins each, the latter with a ten-year *condotta*. The Pistoian judged the Sienese master to be the best in Tuscany; a poet, he also held degrees in grammar, philosophy, and rhetoric, and could teach any text. He wanted 100 florins to come to Pistoia, although he might be bargained down to 80 or 90. However, he was 60 years old and not in the best of health. The Pistoian observer preferred the communal teacher of Colle di Val d'Elsa, Maestro Nofrio di Siena, who taught Vergil, Lucan, and all other authors, even Dante, plus rhetoric, to those who cared to listen. The official judged him to be the most competent of all those observed, certainly more accomplished than anyone currently teaching in Pistoia. He enjoyed excellent health at age 35. Best of all, he would come to Pistoia for 60 florins.[82] Competence, salary within a certain range, age, length of *condotta,* location, and willingness to move—all influenced a reasonably competitive market for communal teachers.

Whereas most communes across Italy hired schoolmasters for 50, 60, or 70 ducats or florins, plus fees, in the fourteenth, fifteenth, and sixteenth centuries, a few hired masters for as little as 10 or 12 and as much as 200 florins.[83] Proximate circumstances probably mattered more than typical salaries in these cases. Some teachers might be learned, experienced, esteemed, and have friends on the communal council. Others may have been inexperienced and desperate for a position. A small town might have to pay more in order to make the purgatory of living in an isolated village

---

[78]Rent and clothing were not nearly as expensive as food. Ibid., pp. 347–48.

[79]Ibid., pp. 347–50.

[80]Roover, 1966, pp. 43–45.

[81]Martines, 1968, pp. 103–6.

[82]Bacci, 1895. However, Zanelli, 1900, pp. 23–24, believes that this search and the document date from 1382 rather than from the 1360s.

[83]Gabotto, 1895, pp. 279–80.

bearable. Communal masters' salaries fluctuated somewhat, but they did not rise overall in the three centuries.[84] Finally, the condition of the communal treasury also mattered; for example, Volterra in 1532 paid part of its communal masters' stipends in sacks of grain, and the Commune of Rovigo did not hire a master in 1504, preferring to use the education fund to pay the city's debts.[85]

The majority of communes supported one or two masters; a handful went beyond that. Sixteenth-century Volterra had a public reader in law, a music teacher, a grammarian and his assistant (*ripetitore*), and an abbaco teacher—all supported by the public fisc and educational bequests.[86] Lucca in the 1350s funded an elementary reading and writing teacher, an arithmetic and geometry instructor, a grammarian, a teacher of notarial skills, and a master of logic and philosophy.[87] Lucca also helped some of its sons study at universities. Beginning in the 1340s, the commune gave annual subsidies of three, five, or ten florins and sometimes larger sums for periods of up to six years; this program continued through the fifteenth and sixteenth centuries. In 1559 Lucca helped twenty-nine university students, although the figure was usually much lower.[88]

A number of communes dreamed of expanding their handful of masters into a *studium generale,* a university. It was a logical if ambitious step, because Italian municipalities, much more than their northern European counterparts, created and guided universities.[89] By the second quarter of the thirteenth century, Italian communes began to make professorial appointments and pay the bills, practices that lasted into modern times. Moreover, the distinction between lower and higher studies in such fields as grammar and rhetoric was not clearly drawn; a gifted teacher might lead able students into university-level studies. Hence, more than one commune dreamt university dreams. They obtained papal and imperial bulls conveying degree-granting authority and privileges, and set about in a small way to appoint professors.

Several communes appointed a single public reader in a university subject, such as law or medicine, in an effort to initiate higher studies. For example, Volterra appointed a lecturer in law in the 1480s but did not

[84]This is my impression; it is not possible to reach a definite conclusion. And since prices tended to rise, teachers' salaries were worth less by the late sixteenth century.

[85]Battistini, 1919, pp. 42–43 n. 121; Cessi, 1896, p. 14. A number of communes closed the communal school for one or several years for lack of funds, especially in the sixteenth century.

[86]Battistini, 1919, pp. 61–65.

[87]Barsanti, 1905, pp. 239–40.

[88]Ibid., pp. 68–83.

[89]Rashdall, 1936, ch.6.

proceed further.[90] Lucca did. It obtained an imperial charter from Emperor Charles IV in 1369 and a papal bull from Urban VI in 1387 authorizing the establishment of a university and the right to confer degrees. Privileges and bulls could be purchased without difficulty. More important, Lucca tried to appoint a professor of medicine in 1388. But the city failed to establish a *studium generale* at that time. In 1455 the Luccans appropriated four thousand florins to fund a university, more than enough to begin and support a small university. Again they drew back: they conferred a handful of degrees in the fifteenth and sixteenth centuries but failed to establish a university.[91]

That the Luccans drew back at the crucial moment was possibly due to the fear that their prospective *studium* would not compete well with the nearby universities of Florence, Siena, and, later, Pisa. Or perhaps the lackluster career of the university of the larger city of Florence gave them pause. And not all citizens regarded the presence of young, wealthy, and unruly foreign males as a blessing. Residents often viewed university students as threats to public order and female virtue, faults that outweighed their liberal spending habits. In the end, the cautious Luccans, who maintained their independence until 1799 by avoiding external political alliances, abandoned the quest.

Self-confident Italian cities and towns established publicly supported schools across Italy in the Trecento because they viewed education as useful and necessary to lay society. Communal schools never educated the majority of students; indeed, in larger towns they probably enrolled only a small fraction of the student population, leaving a larger fraction to independent schools, and the majority to ignorance. Nevertheless, communal schools probably enrolled a large percentage of the sons of the prominent, the boys who would govern and administer the city in the future. Most important, communal schools manifested a strong and visible public commitment to learning.

The communes took small steps toward universal public education by recognizing that education benefited the community, appointing communal teachers, and requiring them to instruct a few poor students gratis. But the communes went no further, because the leaders of the communes did not see a large part of the population as part of the commune at all. Deep social divisions split late medieval and Renaissance towns and cities; the merchant and noble leaders of the city did not grant the bulk of the population any substantive role in the governance of the commune. Indeed, they viewed the working class of artisans, laborers, and even small merchants as threats to the social order and political health of the com-

[90]Battistini, 1919, p. 73.
[91]Barsanti, 1905, pp. 83–99.

mune. Why should the sons of these people be educated at communal expense? Italian towns and cities also denied universal suffrage and did not impose military conscription. The communes lacked the social unity and ideological consensus necessary for universal education.

COMMUNAL ABBACO SCHOOLS

Communes also hired abbaco masters. As mentioned before, Verona possibly hired one in 1277 and certainly did in 1284. Whether or not Verona supported communal abbaco masters through the fourteenth century is unclear for the lack of sources. Documents do confirm the continuous presence of communal abbaco masters from 1424 through the sixteenth century. After several foreigners, Verona in 1437 hired a Veronese, Baldassare di Battista (c. 1403–c. 1471), the son of a *pezarolo* (that is, a *pezzaio* who cut and sold pieces of shoe leather), at eight *lire veronesi* per month. The appointment confirmed the close bond between abbaco teaching and the commercial world of artisans and merchants. Baldassare's three sons succeeded him; then, in the early sixteenth century, Verona reverted to the common practice of hiring teachers who were not native sons.[92]

City councils supported abbaco teachers for a pragmatic reason: the training of future merchants and their clerks and accountants, and artisans of the building trades. Communes recognized the link between the abbaco schools and the future prosperity of the town. The Commune of Pistoia hired an abbaco teacher (its first known) in 1353 in the expectation that the master would also teach geometry, an extremely useful skill because it would help the citizens to measure and sell land, in the words of the commune.[93] On another occasion, Pistoia justified the expense of a *maestro d'abbaco* on the grounds that merchants and artisans could not work profitably or well without the knowledge of abbaco.[94]

Lucca hired its first communal *abbachista* (abbaco teacher) in 1345 and continued to support one through the early sixteenth century. In 1353 the commune appointed the abbaco teacher to teach children (*fanciulli*) and others who wished to learn. If he did not enroll enough pupils to make it worth his while, he might leave. This indicated that the Great Plague of 1348 to 1351 had reduced the number of children in the city, and that the abbaco teacher might collect supplementary fees, although the contract failed to mention them. Luccan *maestri d'abbaco* also received the rent-free use of a house or a housing allowance. As elsewhere, the abbaco teacher also taught geometry and bookkeeping, and served as accountant to the

---

[92]E. Garibotto, 1923, pp. 315–22.

[93]"quod tam dicta arte discenda quam pro mensurando terram civibus pistoriensibus ementibus et vendentibus utilissimum esset tote civitati," as quoted in Zanelli, 1900, p. 39.

[94]"sine scientia abaci mercatores et artifices utiliter et bene se exercere non possunt," ibid.

commune. In the sixteenth century, Lucca amalgamated the abbaco school with the communal elementary reading and writing school in order to create a vernacular combination school, as in Venice.[95]

Communes took as great pains to appoint good *maestri d'abbaco* as they did to appoint good grammarians. Volterra, which began appointing communal abbaco teachers in 1409, sought to fill a vacant post in 1511 by offering it unsuccessfully to two independent *maestri d'abbaco* from Florence and a third from Pistoia.[96] As with grammarians, communes preferred foreigners, with Tuscans, especially Florentines, winning many posts. Although offering only short-term contracts, communes reappointed and honored the abbaco teachers they liked. Volterra appointed Giovan Battista di Baldassare della Colomba di Pisa in 1520, honored him with citizenship in 1542, and mourned his death in 1552.[97] But communes paid *abbachisti* less than grammarians. Volterra paid its first communal abbaco teacher thirty florins in 1409, when the grammarians received forty to sixty-five. Later in the fifteenth century, Volterra paid the *maestro d'abbaco* sixty florins, the highest salary earned by an *abbachista* there, while paying its communal grammarians eighty or ninety florins.[98] But other towns paid less; salaries of twenty to thirty florins or ducats, plus supplementary fees and housing, were common.

ELEMENTARY AND SECONDARY TEACHERS
ON UNIVERSITY ROLLS

A small number of university towns supported communal masters through the university. Some teachers listed on university rolls taught children in different quarters of the city instead of youths aged 17 to 25 at the *studium,* thus blurring the line between communal school and university. Since the commune financed both, it saw no need to separate them administratively. In addition, Renaissance men to some extent saw Latin learning as a seamless whole.

The wording of an appointment, either in the university roll (*rotulus,* the list of professors and subjects) or in communal documents, usually differentiated the grammar master from the university professor. Sometimes the document stated that the teacher taught boys (*pueros*), which usually meant boys up to and including age 14. Or the appointment of the grammar master was to a school (*master in scholis*) rather than to the university (*studium*). The commune often appointed the grammar master

[95]Barsanti, 1905, pp. 54–57, 196–97, 239–40. For the full curriculum of abbaco schools, see chs. 10 and 11 herein.
[96]Battistini, 1919, p. 45 n. 152.
[97]Ibid., p. 29.
[98]Ibid., pp. 14, 18, 28–29.

to teach in a specific administrative unit of the city (*porta, quarterio, sestiere,* or *rione,* followed by a proper name) which was not the site of the university. The grammar master usually taught (*docere, docendum*), while the professor read or lectured (*legere, legendum*), sometimes in a faculty (*in facultate*). The grammar master received a lower salary than did the university professor, or the same as that received by humanities professors, the lowest paid in Italian Renaissance universities. Finally, the grammar master on the university roll did not have to fulfill the requirement of holding a doctorate or a *licentia docendi,* the degree authorizing one to teach, as the professor did.

For example, in 1439 the Commune of Florence hired a priest, Gregorio of Spoleto, who had a school in the district or parish of Orsanmichele, to teach grammar for one year at a salary of twenty florins (*Presbiter Gregorius de Spoleto, qui tenet scholas in Orto Sancti Michaelis, elettus ad docendum Grammaticam, pro uno anno inchoando ut supra, cum salario florenorum 20*).[99] By contrast, a Florentine communal document of 1458 described Cristoforo Landino as "reading publicly in the University of Florence in the faculty of oratory and poetry" ("legendum publice in Studio florentino in facultate Oratoria et Poesis").[100]

When a commune first listed a pre-university teacher on a university roll is not known, because very few early university rolls and documents survive. University of Perugia rolls of 1365 and 1366 named five grammarians who taught in each of the five *porte* of the city at a pre-university level, the earliest surviving such notice. In 1389 the University of Perugia altered the arrangement slightly by hiring four grammarians at thirty gold florins per annum and one rhetorician at seventy gold florins. The salary of thirty florins confirms the elementary nature of the grammarians' teaching, while the salary of seventy florins leaves the rhetorician's status unclear. In that year the University of Perugia also added a *magister geometricus,* probably a pre-university abbaco teacher.[101]

Grammarians teaching boys became a permanent feature of the University of Florence in the fifteenth century. From 1413 through the first half of the fifteenth century, the university roll included one to three grammarians who taught boys. For example, the roll for the academic year 1422–23 included Antonio Andreucci, teacher of grammar, paid fifty florins for teaching boys.[102] In 1434–35 Maestro Sozzo di Giovanni Gualfredi da

[99]Gherardi, 1881, p. 445. The use of *scholas* (schools) in Renaissance academic documents, including Jesuit papers of the late sixteenth century, is a little disconcerting. One might translate *tenet scholas* more literally as "holds classes" or "teaches classes." But "teaches school" is the meaning.

[100]Ibid., p. 467.

[101]Ermini, 1947, pp. 160–62. Abbaco was never a university subject; see ch. 11 herein.

[102]"magistrum Antonium Andreucci, magistram Grammatice, ad docendum pueris, cum salario florenorum 50." Gherardi, 1881, p. 402. Also noted in Park, 1980, p. 281.

Volterra taught grammar *in scolis* for a salary of twenty florins. Ser Niccolò di Antonio da Pratovecchio earned the same salary for teaching grammar *in scolis* in the academic year 1439–40.[103] An occasional specific reference to *pueri* or *in scolis* and the consistently low salaries (fifteen to fifty florins) confirm the status of these grammarians.[104]

When in the middle of the fifteenth century the University of Florence became financially more secure, the grammarians on the university roll received higher salaries and longer contracts. Because doing so was useful and honorable to the city, the government in 1452 determined to elect two excellent men to teach grammar, "the beginning and foundation of all other sciences," to the boys and youths (*pueri et iuvenes*) of the city. These grammarians received two-year appointments at 100 florins per annum.[105] Such appointments continued; in 1457 the government renewed contracts for two grammarians for five years at 100 florins per annum.[106] In 1469 the city elected four grammarians to teach learning and good habits to the "sons" of the city.[107] In 1471 it appropriated 375 florins to pay the salaries of four teachers for the communal grammar schools.[108] And when in December 1472 the commune authorized the translation of most of the Florentine *studium* to Pisa the following year, it insisted that three or four grammarians and a university-level humanist remain in Florence.[109]

From 1473 through the academic year 1502–3, the university always included on its rolls at least two, and most of the time four, grammarians who taught at a pre-university level in Florence. The rolls listed them as *maestri di squola, magistri grammaticae, magistri scolarum,* and *magistri grammaticae et eloquentiae,* or described their duties as *ad docendum grammaticam* or *grammaticam et rhetoricam.* The title *magister* usually prefaced their names, while university professors were called *dominus.* The grammarians earned 40 to 100 florins per annum, but most often 50 to 65 florins. For example, four pre-university grammarians earned 50 florins each from 1487–88

[103]Park, 1980, pp. 292, 297.

[104]Ibid., pp. 274–309 passim.

[105]"advertentes quod utile esset et honor civitatis, pro eruditione puerorum et iuvenum, ut habeantur duo prestantes magistri Grammatice in civitate nostra, qui instruant diligenter pueros et iuvenes in dicta facultate, que est principium et fundamentum omnium aliarum scientiarum, et qua mediante intellectus habetur omnis scripture latine. . . ." Gherardi, 1881, p. 263, 27 April 1452. Also see Gherardi, p. 465, 17 June 1452.

[106]Ibid., pp. 265–66, 4 August 1457.

[107]"pro erudiendis filiis vestrorum civium in bonis moribus ac doctrina." Ibid., pp. 269, 270, 18 April and 9 November 1469.

[108]Ibid., pp. 493–94, 19 August 1471.

[109]"Et perchè gli è necessario havere nella città di Firenze almeno tre o quattro maestri che insegnino Grammatica, et qualche uno che dia lume degli oratori et poeti et degli ornamenti della lingua latina a quegli cittadini che più oltre non vogliono seguitare gli studii. . . ." Ibid., p. 274, 18 December 1472.

through 1494–95, and 60 or 65 florins from 1495–96 through 1502–3.[110] Unlike a university professor, who frequently changed positions, a grammarian held his post for years; in one case, the position was passed on to a son. Magister Lucas Antonii Bernardi de Colle, who first appeared as a teacher on the university roll of Pisa in 1473, began teaching as a grammarian in Florence in 1481–82, and taught continuously in this capacity from 1481 through the academic year 1498–99. Beginning in the academic year 1497–98, he shared the position with his son Hieronimus, who replaced him in 1499–1500 and taught at least through 1502–3.[111]

Bologna provided more elementary and secondary schools under the auspices of its university than did any other Italian city. Both communal and independent grammarians existed in Bologna by the end of the thirteenth century; since the commune began to appropriate money for the university in 1282, it may have planned to support pre-university teachers for the *quarteri* at that early date.[112] In any case, the first extant roll of the University of Bologna, that of 1384–85, listed three grammarians who taught in the quarter of Porta Nova, where the faculty of arts was located, plus two others who taught in the quarters of Porta Stiera and Porta Ravennate.[113] All received fifty *lire bolognesi,* the same salaries given the majority of university professors in the faculty of arts. Scholars agree that these masters for the quarters taught at pre-university levels.[114]

The Bolognese government continued to fund grammarians for the quarters in the next two and a half centuries. The roll of 1438–39 listed four of them (*ad lecturam grammatice per quarterio*); from that date on, grammarians for the quarters constantly appeared on university rolls.[115] The number fluctuated between four and seven from 1439 to 1456, grew to eight in the 1480s, twelve in 1487–88, and thirteen to fifteen in the last decade of the fifteenth century.[116] Their salaries were the lowest on university rolls. For example, grammarians for the quarters received 25 lire, while professors earned 50, 100, 200, 700, 1,000, and 2,100 lire in the academic year 1506–7.[117] Grammarians also received supplementary fees

[110]Verde, 1973–77, vol. 1:296–383 passim. For some individual grammarians, see vol. 2:120–21, 164–65, 264–65, 286–87, 304–5, 366–67, 390–91, 488–89, 492–93, 534–35, 546–47, 588–89.

[111]Ibid., vol. 1:298–383 passim; vol. 2:456–59.

[112]Zaccagnini, 1924, p. 271; Zaccagnini, 1926, p. 118.

[113]Dallari, 1888–1924, vol. 1:5.

[114]Corradi, 1887, p. 356 n. 1; Cavazza, 1896, pp. 130–32; Zaccagnini, 1926, pp. 88–89, 91–94; Simeoni, 1940, p. 117.

[115]The two surviving rolls (1388–89 and 1407–8) between 1384–85 and 1438–39 fail to mention the grammarians for the quarters. For the 1438–39 mention, see Dallari, 1888–1924, vol. 1:12. The description in the roll of 1467–68 is typical and frequently repeated: "Quatuor gramatici (Quilibet habeat scholas in suo quarterio)." Ibid., p. 76.

[116]Ibid., passim.

[117]Simeoni, 1940, p. 31.

from their students. But beginning in the academic year of 1499–1500, the commune obliged each of the grammarians for the quarters to teach four paupers without charge.[118] Later, the commune specifically described the paupers as boys and added *pro amore Dei* to justify the free instruction.[119] The city of Rome also required its grammarians listed on university rolls to teach a limited number of poor students without charge.

Bologna also provided funds for pre-university teachers. The university rolls of the second half of the fifteenth century listed four or five teachers for arithmetic and geometry, probably abbaco masters who taught at the primary or secondary school level, or both.[120] That the commune extended the obligation of teaching four paupers to the abbaco masters in 1507–8 supports the supposition.[121]

The Commune of Bologna supported through the university administrative structure humanists who taught at a secondary-school level. These schools evolved slowly, or else the rolls only gradually described their instruction accurately. Two to four humanists (*ad lecturam rhetoricae et poesis*), some of them well-known scholars, appeared on the university rolls as university lecturers in the second half of the fifteenth century. In the early sixteenth century the commune added additional humanists to the roll and divided them into groups. In 1503–4 two of the seven humanists taught rhetoric and poetry in "public schools" (not *in studio,* which meant the university), plus grammar, which was a pre-university subject.[122] The roll of 1518–19 drew new distinctions: four of the ten might teach grammar to boys in "private schools" (meaning in the teacher's home or rented quarters rather than at the university) so long as they taught four paupers gratis.[123] The commune did not define the roles and obligations of other humanists, who were simply listed as lecturers in rhetoric and poetry (meaning that they taught at the university).

In 1539–40 the rolls very accurately described the grammarians of the quarters and the lower-level humanists as "schoolmasters" ("ludi magistri").[124] And in 1542–43 the grammarians for the quarters became

---

[118]"Cum hoc quod quilibet eorum gratis instruat et doceat quattuor pauperes verecundos, pro voluntate eorum procuratorum." Dallari, 1888–1924, vol. 2:174.

[119]"Grammatici pro quarterijs (Quilibet eorum doceat quattuor pauperes pueros, amore Dei)." Ibid., vol. 2:162 (1564–65).

[120]Dallari, 1888–1924, vol. 1:46 (1456–57) et passim.

[121]Ibid., p. 199, and frequently repeated in subsequent years.

[122]"(Cum hoc quod legant in scholis publicis et domi grammaticam doceant.)" Ibid., p. 185.

[123]"Legere possint in scholis suis privatis, in quibus etiam pueros grammaticam doceant, cum conditione et obligatione de qua infra." The obligation was the usual one of instructing four paupers without charge. Ibid., p. 22.

[124]"Ad Rethoricam et Poeticam. (Ludi magistri legant quilibet duas lectiones, unam in oratoria alteram in poetica arte. Ad primam horam legere possint in scholis suis privatis, in quibus etiam pueros grammaticam doceant, cum conditione grammaticis apposita ut infra.)"

grammatici secundae classis and the humanists *ludi magistri primae classis*.[125]
The roll of the following year simply listed *grammatici primae classis* (the
humanists) and *grammatici secundae classis* (grammarians for the quarters).[126] In other words, the commune clearly labeled grammarians for the
quarters as elementary school teachers and the humanists as secondary
school teachers, probably what they had been since the beginning of the
century. Finally, in 1528–29, the commune added to the university roll
three writing masters (*ad scribendi artem*), who also had to have been
elementary-level teachers.[127]

The titles of the teaching positions changed but the personnel did not.
Two of the three writing masters of 1528–29 had been grammarians for the
quarters for more than twenty years; they taught writing for another ten to
fifteen years.[128] Most secondary school humanists, grammarians for the
quarters, and writing masters, plus some arithmetic and geometry teachers, held their posts for years and decades, a sure sign that they taught at a
pre-university level. They very seldom advanced to the rank of university
lecturer.[129]

Bolognese communal education under the aegis of the university
reached its apex between 1528–29 and 1555–56, during which time the
commune supported twenty to twenty-four teachers for elementary and
secondary learning. For example, in 1528–29 the commune paid the
salaries of seven secondary school humanists, seven grammarians for the
quarters, three teachers of writing, and five abbaco teachers.[130] In 1537–38
the commune supported six humanists, ten grammarians for the quarters,
three writing masters, and five arithmetic and geometry teachers.[131] But
the number of pre-university instructors dropped to between six and
twelve from the late 1560s through the first decade of the seventeenth

---

And for the grammarians: "Ad Grammaticam. (Ludi magistri quilibet gratis doceat quattuor
pauperes ex verecundis, ut ab eorum procuratoribus mandatum fuerit.)" Ibid., vol. 2:91.

[125]Ibid., p. 100.

[126]Ibid., p. 103.

[127]Ibid., p. 56.

[128]M. Petrus Antonius Salandus served as a grammarian for a quarter from 1503–4
through 1527–28, then as a writing master from 1528–29 through 1544–45. Ibid., vol. 1:185–
213 passim; vol. 2:1–106 passim. M. Hieronymus Pagliarolus taught as a grammarian for a
quarter from 1507–8 through 1527–28, then as a writing master from 1528–29 through 1538–
39. Ibid., vol. 1:199–213 passim; vol. 2:1–88 passim.

[129]The rolls easily verify these two statements. Also see Simeoni, 1940, p. 117. I know of
two exceptions. Iacopo della Croce taught as a grammarian for the quarters in Bologna from
1480–81 until 1495–96, when he became a university humanities lecturer. He taught at the
secondary level in Lucca from 1512 to 1517 and at the university level in Bologna until his
death in 1528. Barsanti, 1905, p. 133 n. 6; Dallari, 1888–1924, vols. 1 and 2 passim. A Roman
maestro del rione found favor with Leo X and advanced to university teaching. See ch. 3 herein.

[130]Dallari, 1888–1924, vol. 2:56.

[131]Ibid., p. 85.

century.[132] The founding and growth of a free Jesuit school in the 1550s and 1560s, and other religious order schools in the ensuing decades, led the commune to reduce its educational support. The number of primary and secondary instructors listed on the rolls of the University of Bologna declined to seven in 1630–31 and four or five in the 1640s.[133]

Bologna in the first half of the sixteenth century came the closest to establishing a comprehensive state school system in the modern meaning of the term. Since each master conducted his own school, the commune at the height of its involvement supported twenty to twenty-four grammar, humanistic, abbaco, and writing schools. The listing of all these pre-university teachers on university rolls hinted at an integrated approach to education which was unusual at the time. Boys mastered Latin at an early age in order to continue studying and using Latin at more advanced levels; they attended grammar, humanistic, and university schools. Writing and abbaco schools, on the other hand, taught the vernacular curriculum.

Only a handful of Italian cities with local universities, notably Perugia, Florence, Bologna, and Rome, followed this path. Most cities and towns had but one or two communal masters enrolling a small number of students.

INDEPENDENT SCHOOLS

The vast majority of students learned in independent schools. No one appointed or directed independent masters; instead, the parents paid a master who educated their sons. Independent schools took a variety of forms. Some independent masters served as household tutors, living and teaching in the home of a noble; others visited daily to teach the children of a wealthy family. Numerous independent masters taught in their own homes or rented rooms fee-paying pupils from the neighborhood. Others led boarding schools that housed, fed, and instructed the children of the wealthy and powerful. The most famous pedagogues of the Renaissance, Guarino Guarini and Vittorino da Feltre, were the independent masters of a boarding school and a court school with boarding facilities, respectively.

Independent teachers played a crucial role in towns lacking a communal master or with only one or two communal masters. Parents and students had to pay to learn. For example, in 1397 a Venetian druggist made a will to ensure that his youngest son would become a doctor. He left half his estate to his oldest and youngest sons together: the eldest would feed, clothe, and send the youngest to learn Latin. Since Venice lacked communal schools at that time, the boy would have to study with an independent master. Having learned Latin, the lad would go on to Padua "to study medicine, or

[132]Ibid., pp. 174–316 passim.
[133]For example, see Dallari, 1888–1924, vol. 2:387, 435, 454, 470.

physic, or surgery, whichever he prefers."[134] Students wanted to learn, "because knowledge is recognizing divine and human things, and man by nature desires to know," began the preamble of a Venetian contract of 1405 between a priest and a teacher. The priest agreed to pay an independent teacher eight gold ducats to teach him Latin.[135]

Teachers and students organized independent schools in several ways to satisfy this educational hunger. In 1373 six fathers signed an agreement with a grammarian to found an independent school in Cles, a village in a mountain valley about thirty miles north of Trent. The six men, who included three notaries, agreed to pay the master a total of 18 marks (180 *lire veronesi*) per annum for four years. For that sum, the teacher would educate eighteen sons and relatives of the men. Should a pupil die, a father was not obligated to pay tuition for the dead child; the other five would make up the difference. Beyond these eighteen pupils, the grammarian might accept as many additional students as he wished who would pay 1 mark (10 *lire veronesi*) each per annum. The master might pocket all the revenue from the first ten additional pupils but only one-third of the income from any pupils beyond twenty-eight; the remaining two-thirds would go to the original six fathers.[136] This contract, so redolent of the Italian commercial world, shared costs while safeguarding the interests of all concerned. It procured the services of a grammarian for a period of years and ensured that he would enjoy an adequate income, but it discouraged an enrollment so large as to threaten the quality of instruction of the original eighteen pupils. Perhaps special circumstances or the remoteness of the locale necessitated such an elaborate agreement. Most parents in larger towns and cities simply hired one of the available independent masters and entered into a simple contract, or paid fees without the formality of a notarized agreement, for their children's education.

Venice had a large complement of independent teachers in the fourteenth and fifteenth centuries. About 850 different teachers appeared in surviving Venetian notarial acts and governmental records between 1300 and 1450, as many as 55 different teachers in a single year in the late fourteenth century.[137] Yet, the total number of active teachers in any year had to have been higher than this. Teachers, like other men, made wills, engaged the services of a notary for other reasons, and witnessed notarial acts only when necessary. Moreover, witnessing a notarial act presupposed a fluency in Latin and the arcane notarial hand probably beyond the

[134]Bertanza and Dalla Santa, 1907, p. 220, 4 September 1397.

[135]"Quia sciencia est divinarum et humanarum rerum cognicio et naturaliter homo scire desiderat. . . ." Ibid., pp. 253–54, 16 July 1405. This is another sign of the lack of church schools; would a priest need to hire an independent master if many ecclesiastical schools existed?

[136]Inama, 1896–97.

[137]Bertanza and Dalla Santa, 1907, pp. 108–21, 160–73, for the years 1371 and 1382.

competence of abbaco masters and elementary Latin instructors. Since notarial acts and governmental records are nets with meshes too large to catch all the pedagogical fish in the Venetian lagoon, one must estimate the total number of active independent teachers to have been two to three times the number recorded in notarial acts. If Venice had as many teachers relative to its population in the late fourteenth century as in 1587–88, then it had 130 to 165 independent masters in the 1370s and 1380s.[138]

The metropolis of Venice had a semi-permanent corps of independent teachers who taught for decades. For example, Iohannes de Cassio, a grammarian in the district of San Moisè, taught from 1310 through 1338.[139] "Zentil de labacho" (Gentile the abachist) taught in Venice from 1305 until his death between 1338 and 1346.[140] Vigilius de Tridento (Trent), a Latin master and notary in the district of San Raffaele, taught from 1356 through 1393.[141]

Some independent teachers occupied very prominent places in the academic lives of the elite of a city. Stefano Plazon from Asola, a village near Mantua, arrived in Venice just before 1520 in order to open an independent Latin school.[142] He enjoyed great pedagogical success in Venice. By 1528 or 1529, Plazon's Venetian academy included an upper school for pupils from about 14 to 18 years of age, a lower school with about 150 students, and 8 boarding students. Students in the lower school paid four, five, or six ducats a year plus tips, for a total of about five hundred ducats annually. The 8 boarding students paid forty ducats and more annually. Even after deducting expenses for assistant teachers, food, and rent, Plazon must have enjoyed an enormous income for a teacher. He also wrote an elementary Latin grammar that had at least five printings and a rhetoric text published at least twice.[143]

Plazon enrolled the sons of the most powerful patricians of the city plus illustrious commoners such as Paolo Manuzio (1512–74), son of Aldo and an important scholar and publisher in his own right. Thirteen noble pupils participated in public academic exercises in April 1524. The first delivered an oration and commentary on Cicero's *Epistulae ad familiares* I.I. Others disputed, responded, recited verses, and translated vernacular prose into Latin. The young scholars thus demonstrated their learning and promise

---

[138]In 1587–88 Venice had 245 active teachers in a population of c. 149,000. Hence, in the late Trecento it may have had 130 to 165 teachers in a population of 80,000 to 100,000. See ch. 2 herein and Beloch, 1961, pp. 3–4.

[139]Bertanza and Dalla Santa, 1907, pp. 2 n. 3, 3–10, 12, 14–15, 17–18, 22, 25, 27.

[140]Ibid., pp. 1, 7, 13, 27, 39, 46.

[141]Ibid., pp. 62–206 passim.

[142]Most of the following is based on Pavanello, 1905, pp. 31, 35–36; and Nardi, 1971, pp. 77–91. Plazon also competed unsuccessfully for a lectureship at the Scuola di San Marco in 1520. See Ross, 1976, p. 548.

[143]See ch. 7 and the Bibliography.

to the influential parents, relatives, and friends in attendance. These public performances, typical of humanistic schools, also served as graduation exercises, as Plazon's 18-year-old nobles then went on to study at higher schools, such as the Scuola di Rialto for philosophy or the Scuola di San Marco for the humanities in Venice, or to the University of Padua. Some noble youths passed directly from Plazon's school into the Great Council to begin their lifelong climb up the ladder of political office.[144] At its height, Plazon's school functioned as a humanist academy for the sons of the highborn and powerful; it must have been the most important of the numerous Latin schools in Venice.

Unfortunately, Plazon and his school fell from grace when he became romantically involved with a woman who bore his illegitimate child. Because Plazon set a bad moral example and allegedly neglected his pupils in his infatuated state, many parents withdrew their children. By Plazon's death circa 1543, the school had precipitously declined.

An independent teacher might also venture out into the countryside to teach. One such teacher set up his school in the *castello* of Cutigliano, a rural area approximately twenty miles north of Pistoia, in 1513. He taught reading, writing, elementary Latin, and abbaco, charging students learning the alphabet (*tavola*) five soldi per month, those learning to read (*salterio*) seven soldi per month, and students of Latin grammar (*il Donato*) and abbaco students ten soldi each, plus "the usual tips." He taught 144 students during the short life of the school. The master earned thirty-two gold ducats and a suit of clothes by teaching from the first of June 1513 through the end of August 1514, less three months lost through illness. If only all my students had paid in full, I would have realized fifty ducats, he lamented. Nevertheless, he earned enough to purchase a farm and retire from teaching. In 1526 he decided to return to the classroom. In preparation, he purchased twenty *tavole di leggere* (hornbooks or ABC sheets), twenty *salterii* (primers), twenty *abbachetti* (abbaco manuals), six *Donati* (elementary Latin grammars), eight *tavole da scrivere* (presumably booklets with writing examples), plus paper and the ingredients to make ink. The teacher then sold these textbooks and supplies to his students.[145]

Independent teachers charged fees for their services which ranged from very high to modest. Not surprisingly, those who taught the sons of nobles earned the highest fees. In 1402 a Venetian noble hired a teacher to instruct one son in the rudiments of reading and writing and a second son in "Donatus and Cato," that is, Latin grammar and elementary Latin

<hr/>

[144]Although the constitutional age for admission to the Great Council was 25, special rules permitted some wealthy and powerful politicians to enter at the ages of 18 and 20.
[145]Zanelli, 1900, pp. 83–84n.

reading. The teacher would receive 20 ducats regardless of how long it took.[146] In 1404 a teacher agreed to board and teach Latin to the son of a noble for six months for 20 ducats.[147] Tutors to nobles sometimes earned even higher fees. In 1497 two noble brothers hired a Latin instructor to teach their sons for 114 ducats.[148] The contract did not indicate the number of children or the duration; nevertheless, few communal teachers earned as much for teaching thirty students for a year.

Commoners normally hired independent masters for two to six, at most ten, ducats per pupil per annum. In 1419 a Venetian teacher agreed to teach one boy Latin for four ducats per annum and a second boy for three ducats per annum.[149] The following year a teacher agreed to teach a boy for five months for four lire, a rate that came to a little more than two ducats per annum.[150] In 1463 a tailor in Murano hired a priestly schoolteacher for two and a half ducats for one year in order to learn Latin grammar and the "office of priests" (the breviary), and to hear lectures on the *Doctrinale* of Alexander de Villedieu.[151] It was a very ambitious syllabus for twelve months.

Another document provides a broader picture of the fees paid by commoner pupils. In 1442 a Venetian teacher drafted a will that listed the sums owed him for instruction: twenty boys owed him one to six ducats each for a total of fifty-six ducats. Three debtors boasted noble names, the rest did not. Among the latter were *Martinus barcharolo* (Martin the boatman), who owed five ducats for the instruction of his *nepos* (nephew or grandson), and *Anthonius murarius* (Anthony the wall builder), who owed ten ducats for the instruction of his two sons. This will and the contracts mentioned above show that commoners often paid two to six ducats per pupil per annum.[152] Hence, an independent teacher with twenty commoner pupils paying an average of four ducats (less from the younger ones, more from the advanced) earned eighty ducats annually—if all fees were collected. Overall, most independent teachers probably earned a little less than communal masters. Those fortunate enough to tutor the sons of nobles earned more.

[146]Bertanza and Dalla Santa, 1907, p. 240, 27 June 1402.
[147]Ibid., p. 246, 9 January 1404. The date has been changed to modern style.
[148]Ibid., p. 338, 22 August 1497.
[149]Ibid., p. 293, 21 May 1419.
[150]Ibid., p. 299, 9 October 1420.
[151]Ibid., p. 329, 30 June 1463. Noble and commoner parents paid similar fees to independent masters in Treviso. See Serena, 1912, pp. 370, 373–74.
[152]Bertanza and Dalla Santa, 1907, pp. 321–24, esp. 322, 26 July 1442, the will of Victor Bonapaxius, son of Iohannes Michael de Ramboldonibus, from Feltre. This is not the famous Vittorino Ramboldoni da Feltre, who was the son of Bruto. The relationship between the two Vittorinos is unknown.

ACADEMIC CALENDAR AND CORPORAL PUNISHMENT

The academic year traditionally began in the fall, often on the Feast of St. Luke (18 October), but school remained in session the year around, Monday through Friday or Saturday.[153] Numerous holidays interrupted the long academic year. *Carnevale,* the seven or eight days before Ash Wednesday, was the longest and tended to lengthen. The Commune of Volterra tried to avoid an increase in its duration by threatening to fine or imprison any student who appeared with mask or drum before the official beginning of *carnevale.* Very long vacations do students more harm than good, the commune huffed.[154] Classes were also dismissed for several days at Easter. Other traditional holidays included liturgical feasts commemorating events in the lives of Jesus and Mary, plus numerous saints' days: all twelve apostles, four doctors of the church, and local and regional patron saints, and often their vigils. Most holidays were full days; some were half-days. The commune typically authorized sixty-five to seventy-five school holidays. This yielded an academic year of about 190 days if classes did not meet on Saturdays, and 240 days if they did.

The school day was long but flexible. The commune organized the school day around universal reference points that fluctuated according to the seasons. Independent teachers probably followed the lead of the communal school. For example, Pistoia in 1511 ordered its communal teachers to present themselves at their schools at sunrise and to teach until the hour of the midday meal. After a lunch break of unspecified length, school resumed until an hour before sunset in winter and until two hours before sunset in summer. However, between 1 March and 1 September the teacher should allow students to stop for the afternoon snack (*merenda*) "as is the custom" at the ringing of the vespers bell sometime in mid-afternoon. After the *merenda* break (probably short), students returned for the rest of the day.[155] Other towns followed this pattern with minor variations.

Such a schedule meant that schools were in session most of the good daylight hours, perhaps six or seven in the winter and about ten in the spring and summer. For example, the school day in Pistoia in 1511 pro-

[153]The Commune of Pistoia scheduled no Saturday classes in 1511 but ordered its teachers to be present Saturday mornings so that students might come for special help. Zanelli, 1900, p. 151. For academic calendars in various towns and cities between 1469 and 1574, see Zanelli, 1900, pp. 56, 108–10, 137–38, 152–53; Barsanti, 1905, pp. 179, 221, 235; Villoslada, 1954, pp. 86–87; and Petti Balbi, 1979, p. 89.

[154]Battistini, 1919, p. 117.

[155]"Debbi tenere la scuola aperta la mactina da che si leva il sole insino a hora desinare. Et da doppo desinare insino a hore XXIII di verno et di state in sino a hore XXII. Ma da dì primo di Maggio insino a dì primo di Settembre ne debbi mandare al tocho di vespro gli scolari a merenda, come è di consuetudine." Zanelli, 1900, p. 152.

ceeded in modern terms as follows. In January lessons began at about 8:00 A.M., halted for lunch at about noon, resumed at 1:00 P.M. or later, and ended at about 4:00 P.M., making a school day of seven hours. In July classes began at about 5:00 A.M., lasted until the midday meal (perhaps 10:00 A.M.), resumed at noon, broke for the *merenda* at mid-afternoon (perhaps 3:00 to 3:30 P.M.) and concluded at about 6:00 P.M. This produced a scholastic day of about ten hours and thirty minutes, but shorter if the midday break lasted longer than two hours. Spring and autumn school days fell between the January and July extremes, as daylight expanded and contracted.[156]

The Commune of Lucca followed a slightly shorter schedule in 1499.[157] It ordered its two elementary teachers to be present at the school at the canonical hour of prime (6:00 A.M. in the summer and sunrise in the winter). In the winter they had to remain until the "Ave Maria" (the ringing of the angelus bell at 6:00 P.M., but perhaps as early as 4:00 P.M. in midwinter), and to nones (about 3:00 P.M.) in the summer. Teachers and students dispersed for a midday meal break of unspecified duration. Hence, the Luccan school day probably lasted six to seven hours in the winter and about eight hours in the summer, assuming that the midday meal took about an hour.

These were somewhat long school days. By contrast, after experimentation, Jesuit schools settled for a five- or six-hour school day evenly divided between morning and afternoon.[158]

Communal school regulations, parent-teacher contracts, and like documents did not mention corporal punishment. Only indirect pieces of evidence brought the subject to light. Textbook illustrations sometimes carried admonitory pictures of switches or short verses threatening the use of the rod. Occasionally a horror story of a student subjected to severe physical abuse appeared; Erasmus, who was obsessed with the matter, related several.[159] On the other hand, taking their cue from Quintilian, Renaissance and Catholic Reformation pedagogical treatises universally condemned all but the lightest physical punishment. They stressed competition and rewards instead.

It is almost impossible to determine how frequently teachers used corporal punishment to punish students for misbehavior or to make them learn. That teachers occasionally beat or otherwise physically punished

[156]Renaissance Italy divided the day into twenty-four one-hour segments beginning at sunset or slightly later. In January, when sunset occurred at about 5:00 P.M. modern time, hour one struck at 6:00 P.M. modern time, hour twelve at 6:00 A.M. modern time, and so on. But in July, when the sun set at about 8:00 P.M., hour one was at 9:00 P.M. modern time, and so on. See MP, 1965–81, vol. 1:76–77 n. 34, 167; and Villoslada, 1954, p. 85, for further explanation.

[157]Barsanti, 1905, p. 215; also see pp. 219–20 (1524), 225 (1546), and 232–33 (1574).

[158]Villoslada, 1954, pp. 85–86.

[159]Erasmus, 1985, pp. xx, xxxv–xxxvi, 41–42, 325–333.

students for disciplinary infractions seems logical. In an era in which injury, illness, fatigue, cold, or hunger inflicted discomfort and pain on many, one can expect that society authorized a good deal of physical force to compel obedience. But the assumption that severe corporal punishment was routine, or that teachers beat students for their inability to learn the past subjunctive tense, seems unwarranted.[160] Moreover, the notion that Italian Renaissance parents felt little love for their children, and remained emotionally detached from their suffering, is contradicted by practically every surviving piece of personal evidence, such as diaries.[161] It is not likely that parents would pay fees to a teacher who routinely beat his pupils. If they were displeased with a teacher, parents could easily find a new independent teacher among the many available. Visitation committees and the knowledge that parents sat on the highest city councils must have deterred communal masters from frequent use of the rod. Until evidence to the contrary appears, it does not seem logical to conclude that teachers frequently inflicted physical punishment on their pupils.

THE LIVES OF TEACHERS

Teachers prepared for their careers in many ways. The lack of guilds allowed individuals to become teachers without earning a degree, a *licentia docendi,* or undergoing examinations.[162] A young man left Vittorino da Feltre's school with knowledge and the master's blessing, which probably counted more toward a successful pedagogical career than a university degree. Only toward the end of the sixteenth century did a few communes examine teachers for competence, which might be acquired in any manner.

A limited number of teachers earned university degrees or at least studied at a university. Some clergymen-turned-pedagogues studied, although not specifically in order to teach grammar and rhetoric, at theological *studia* in a monastery or university town. After Trent some, but not all, clergymen who taught attended seminaries (see ch. 2). Because pre-university teaching resembled a Renaissance craft as much as a profession, teachers, like apprentices, began by assisting established pedagogues. In particular, a youth wishing to become an abbaco master studied under or assisted an experienced abbachist until bold enough to open a new school.

[160]See the sensible remarks of Strauss, 1978, pp. 179–82.

[161]Ariès, 1962, pp. 38–39, misleads the reader on this point as in many other matters.

[162]Genoa was the exception. Founded in 1298, its teachers' guild attempted to examine teacher candidates, require two years' study in a *studium,* and regulate teaching conditions over the next two centuries. However, it enrolled only a small number of Latin teachers (thirteen to twenty-two) and achieved only limited success. Massa, 1906, pp. 180–85; Petti Balbi, 1979, pp. 75–101. Florentine teachers failed to form a guild in the early fourteenth century. Debenedetti, 1906–7, pp. 338–40; Davidsohn, 1965, p. 212.

Son sometimes followed father into teaching. At the bottom of the profession, reading and writing teachers needed only a modicum of skill in order to teach small children basic skills. Knowledge, plus the persuasive powers to win a *condotta* from the commune or to induce parents to send their children, launched a pedagogical career.

Both movement and stability characterized teaching careers. Many taught beyond their native towns. Of the approximately thirty-five teachers recorded in Venetian notarial acts of 1395, fifteen came from northern Italian towns not yet subject to Venice (Brescia and Verona), other cities and regions of Italy (Trent, Cremona, Parma, Reggio, Bologna, and Calabria), and foreign countries (Germany and Portugal).[163] Florentines and other Tuscans often taught abbaco elsewhere in Italy. But once arrived, teachers tended to settle, marry, and die in their adopted homes.

The professional class included lawyers, notaries, governmental secretaries, university professors, physicians, and teachers in no clear order except for teachers at the bottom. The financial and social details of teachers' marriages, children, and homes demonstrated this well. In 1386 a Venetian Latin teacher, Anthonius de Patrianis de Cassia, the son of a Bolognese physician, married Margarite, the daughter of a teacher.[164] She brought him a dowry of 14 lire (about 3 ducats), a sum typical of serving-girl dowries. Anthonius then began to rise in the world. In 1395 the Venetian government, noting that Anthonius had been a citizen for eight years, appointed him to a minor governmental post. In 1402 he bought for 20 lire a house in the district in which he had lived and taught for some time. The following year he gave his daughter a dowry of 310 gold ducats when she married a *physicus,* that is, a university-trained physician licensed to teach.[165] Anthonius bought another house in 1410 for 38 lire. He died in 1412 or 1413 after having solidified his position and that of his family in the professional class.

Another Latin master barely maintained his position in the middle class. In 1473 the Florentine commune appointed Matteo della Rocca to teach Latin for four years at forty florins *di studio,* that is, a florin valued at four lire rather than the standard rate of five and one-half or six.[166] The commune renewed his appointment in 1477 for fifty florins, and again in 1480 for the same salary. In his 1480 tax declaration, Matteo described himself as a "master who teaches Latin and reading to children" ("maestro che insegna grammaticha e legiere a' fanciulli"). He was 46 years old, had a wife aged 32 and six children, and had lived in Florence since at least 1470.

[163]Bertanza and Dalla Santa, 1907, pp. 210–14.

[164]Ibid., pp. 182, 210, 238–39, 242, 273–74, 279, 281, 312.

[165]For the definition of *physicus,* see Park, 1985, pp. 58–59.

[166]The Florentine government usually paid university and communal salaries at the rate of the cheaper florin. Verde, 1973–77, vol. 2:3–4.

The eldest children, sons aged 14 and 13, studied *gramaticha;* three other sons, aged 9, 3, and 2, apparently did not attend school. A daughter, aged 6, had no dowry. Matteo rented the house in which he lived for eight florins per year and the quarters for his school for six florins. He had no net assets and paid no tax.[167]

Teachers sometimes rose from the artisan class below them. Vigilius de Tridento, active as a Latin teacher in Venice between 1356 and 1393, and Magister Nascimbene, who taught in Venice from 1359 until circa 1382, were sons of tailors. Petrus de Mantua, a Venetian Latin teacher from 1363 through 1386, married Lucia, the daughter of a *chalefadius* (either a *calafatore,* a caulker, or a *calefattore,* a worker with heat such as a kilnman).[168]

Latin and abbaco teachers tried to live middle-class lives. They earned more money and had greater social prestige than most artisans, but trailed other professionals. They had modest houses and possessions, including the occasional female domestic slave and property in the countryside to grow food on or rent.[169] They gave their daughters limited dowries, paid nothing or small sums in taxes, and did not win legislative or executive offices in the commune. They married at their own social level, or slightly above (for example, the daughter of a physician) or below (an artisan's daughter).

Teachers could drop into dire poverty. Master Corbaccinus from Florence, a grammarian, began teaching in Venice in 1305 or earlier. Taking note of his long residence in Venice, his good behavior, and especially an unspecified personal injury and the loss of all his possessions as a result of a fire in his small room at San Polo, the Venetian government in 1322 awarded him an annual pension of twenty soldi for teaching (*pro docendo scolares*) for ten years, should he live that long. The tiny annuity was charity rather than payment for teaching. Corbaccinus did survive, but in straitened circumstances. Noting his age, feebleness, and poverty, the government in 1336 gave him twenty soldi without mentioning teaching. Because Corbaccinus had always been a good and learned man, but was now decrepit and poor, the clothes falling from his back, the government in 1339 granted him the larger sum of twenty-five lire (approximately seven ducats). It continued to support Corbaccinus, now living in a monastery, with annual gifts of about twenty soldi from 1340 through 1345.[170] Presumably Corbaccinus then died. One can surmise that the no-

---

[167]Ibid., pp. 488–89; vol. 3:1062. Matteo taught the young Niccolò Machiavelli; see ch. 3 herein.

[168]Bertanza and Dalla Santa, 1907, pp. 97, 105, 147, 148, 157.

[169]For Venetian teachers who owned slaves, see ibid., pp. 134 (6 November 1374), 147 (16 August 1378), 192 (15 May 1389). For the economic and social position of Florentine abbaco masters in the fourteenth and fifteenth centuries, see Van Egmond, 1976, pp. 92–104.

[170]Bertanza and Dalla Santa, 1907, pp. 1–3, 5, 7, 11, 12, 15, 18, 24, 29–31, 33–37, 39.

bles who obtained the state pension for Corbaccinus were former pupils.

The vast majority of teachers loomed large in the lives of their pupils but not elsewhere. There were exceptions. Donato degli Albanzani da Casentino (in the central mountainous region of Italy, near L'Aquila) taught nobles, became a chancellor, and was friends with the leading scholars of his age. Born circa 1325, he lived for some time in Ravenna, where he won Boccaccio's friendship and perhaps taught school. He moved to Venice circa 1356; twelve years later, the government awarded him citizenship in recognition of his dedication and fidelity in teaching "very many" sons of nobles. Petrarch praised him in his letters. Donato's Venetian will of 1371 demonstrated his prosperity and paternal care: he willed his books to his son, aged 18, to use in his studies until he was 25, and he provided a dowry of 400 ducats for his daughter when she reached the age of 14. Donato did not die then, however; he moved back to Ravenna circa 1377, and there received praise for his intelligence from Coluccio Salutati. By 1381 he had moved to Ferrara to serve Duke Alberto Este (ruled 1388–93) in a high office, perhaps as chancellor. He then became tutor to Alberto Este's son Niccolò III (ruled 1393–1441) and a citizen of Ferrara. He made another will in 1411 which left large sums to his daughter and others. Donato died circa 1411 at the age of 85.[171] He achieved the kind of success in his career that most teachers could only dream of: he taught the sons of Venetian patricians and an Este ruler; he attained high office; he basked in the praise of the three greatest intellectual figures of his age; and he became relatively wealthy.

Teachers sometimes manifested their commitment to intellectual values in unusual ways. One Venetian teacher of the 1370s married a woman named Dialetica.[172] After the triumph of the *studia humanitatis,* names reflected Renaissance values. A Venetian teacher of 1429 bore the name Titus Livius de Perlovisiis.[173] Teachers also named their children for classical figures; for example, a sixteenth-century Veronese grammarian christened his children Achille, Valeria, and Pompeo.[174]

Like other men, teachers sometimes committed crimes of violence. In 1346 two Venetian abbaco teachers fought over pupils. One hit the other on the head, causing blood to flow; the authorities fined him 50 lire and imprisoned him for three months.[175] In 1373 a Florentine abbaco teacher

---

[171]Ibid., pp. 95, 97, 119–21, 160–61; Novati, 1890; Martellotti, 1960. Whether Donato became chancellor or referendary is disputed.

[172]Bertanza and Dalla Santa, 1907, pp. 151 (12 October 1379), 167 (28 September 1382), 174 (11 March 1383). Her husband was Benucius de Bonifacio de Pirano, who taught between 1367 and 1382.

[173]Ibid., p. 315 (12 April 1429).

[174]C. Garibotto, 1921, p. 37.

[175]Bertanza and Dalla Santa, 1907, pp. 40–41 (16 August 1346).

then active in Venice assaulted and killed another teacher, also a Florentine, and fled.[176] Venetian courts punished other teachers for stealing from their employers, counterfeiting the city's money, and rape.[177] In the last case, the Venetian government convicted a Latin master in 1378 of raping an 11-year-old girl, sentencing him to six months in prison and levying a fine of 150 ducats, 100 of which went to the girl as her dowry. The teacher continued to teach in Venice through 1395.[178] In 1454 a Venetian abbaco master petitioned the Council of Ten on behalf of his son Francesco, who had fled from prison during a jail break instigated by others. Would the Council of Ten forgive the rest of his sentence so that Francesco might teach abbaco in Brescia? The Council did. Francesco later returned to Venice to teach.[179]

Even though teachers mostly committed ordinary crimes, society held them to be notorious sodomites.[180] Although undeserving of such dubious repute, the pedagogical corps did harbor a few sodomites. In 1360 Nicolao de Eugubio, a *ripetitore* to the sons of a Venetian noble, confessed under torture to sodomizing a 10-year-old pupil, to attempting sodomy with another pupil, and to previous sodomizing in Gubbio. The court sentenced him to be burned.[181]

The *ripetitore* (*repetitor, affirmator,* or *refirmator* in Latin), an assistant teacher or coach, occupied the lowest rung of the pedagogical ladder. *Ripetitori* helped young students to memorize Latin grammar rules, arithmetical functions, and whatever else needed to be learned. They either assisted a master in his school or coached the children of a household.

A management-employee bond, formalized through a contract, joined master and *ripetitore*. In 1299 a Florentine independent Latin teacher hired a *ripetitore;* he was to receive one-third of the school's income except for the Easter and Christmas gifts (a significant omission), which went to the teacher.[182] In 1519 a Florentine abbaco master made a contract with an assistant. The latter agreed to teach in the master's school for three years for a salary of twelve florins a year, or a little more. (Abbaco masters earned between fifty and one hundred florins a year.) Upon leaving the employ of the master, the *ripetitore* might not teach in Florence for three

[176]Ibid., pp. 125–29, 131 (30 March, 22 September 1373).

[177]Ibid., pp. 54–55 (6 March 1350), 334 (24 November 1473–31 August 1474). For Venetian crime and punishment, see Ruggiero, 1980.

[178]Bertanza and Dalla Santa, 1907, Alexander de Parma, on pp. 108, 138, 144–45 (sentence), 157, 172, 176, 181, 190, 199, 206, 213.

[179]Ibid., pp. 326, 332–34 (Troiolus ab abacho and his son Franciscus).

[180]Zaccagnini, 1926, p. 103, who also mentions several sodomy cases involving Bolognese teachers. Sodomy, of course, meant several things in the Renaissance.

[181]Bertanza and Dalla Santa, 1907, pp. 70–71. Other accusations against Venetian teachers for sodomy are found on pp. 292 and 326.

[182]Debenedetti, 1906–7, pp. 340–41n.

months, a clause that prevented him from opening his own school and stealing the master's students.[183]

Communal masters also hired *ripetitori* if they enrolled a large number of pupils. When the Commune of Ivrea (in Piedmont, north of Turin) appointed a communal master in 1427, it specified that if the number of pupils surpassed eighty, the master had to hire a *ripetitore* out of his own pocket.[184] Sometimes a commune chose both master and *ripetitore:* Volterra in 1462 engaged a grammarian *pro scolaribus majoribus* for 70 florins and an assistant *pro scolaribus minoribus* for 120 lire, a little over 22 florins. The master was a foreigner, the *ripetitore* a Volterran.[185]

Even if a father could not afford the services of a household tutor, he might be able to pay a *ripetitore* to coach his children. The *ripetitore,* in turn, supported his own studies in this way. In 1480 a 20-year-old student at the faculty of poetry and rhetoric in Florence served as a *ripetitore* for the four sons, aged 9 through 13, of a Florentine man. Tax returns underline the difference in status of the two. The employer had a net worth of 861 florins and a 3-year-old daughter with a dowry of 1,000 florins. The family of the *ripetitore,* which came from the nearby small town of Empoli, had a net worth of 76 florins and daughters without dowries.[186]

The organization of primary and secondary education was a secular enterprise. Although little is known about the early Middle Ages, it is clear that the church had relinquished most of its educational role by 1300. Communal councils and parents stepped in to found the schools of Renaissance Italy. Fathers paid independent masters to teach their sons Latin or abbaco, and the commune appointed one or more masters to instruct a limited number of the town's pupils. Some cities with a local university added primary and secondary teachers through the administrative apparatus of the faculty of arts. A diverse group of lay and clerical professional teachers taught in the schools. A much larger number of students came to learn.

A close look at the schools of one city during the High Renaissance, roughly between 1450 and 1600, reveals much more about Renaissance schooling.

[183]Goldthwaite, 1972.

[184]Gabotto, 1895, pp. 273, 311.

[185]Battistini, 1919, pp. 18, 49.

[186]Verde, 1973–77, pp. 743 (Nicolaus Michaelis Zeffi, *ripetitore*), 1015 (Ronchagnano di Giovanni di Barduccio, employer).

CHAPTER TWO

Venetian Schools in the High Renaissance

SCHOOLING AND LITERACY IN 1587

remarkable series of documents makes possible a quantitative examination of Venetian education in the High Renaissance. In reaction to the discovery of a few Protestant teachers in Italy, Pope Pius IV, with his bull *In sacrosancta beati Petri* of 13 November 1564, ordered all teachers to profess their Catholic faith before the local bishop or his representative. Venice ordered teachers to obey the bull in 1567–68, and perhaps at other times in the next twenty years, but the records of these professions of faith have not been found.[1] The Republic ordered new professions from its teachers in the spring of 1587, when 237 Venetian teachers professed between 30 April and 30 June, followed by 21 stragglers, some newly arrived in the city and hoping to start schools, in the next eleven months. By the completion of the exercise on 27 May 1588, a total of 256 Venetian masters and 2 *ripetitori*—the Republic obviously did not require *ripetitori* to appear—had professed their Catholicism.[2]

The teachers answered questions about themselves: name, age, town of origin, and civil or ecclesiastical status. All affirmed that they taught Christian doctrine, placed images of Christ, Mary, and the saints on the walls, and neither held nor read prohibited books. Teachers also frequently

---

[1]P. Grendler, 1977, p. 138; Baldo, 1977, pp. 9, 85–88. Some teachers in 1587 mentioned professing their faith on previous occasions. ACPV, "Professioni di fede richiesta agli insegnanti, 1587," fols. 11r, 15v. Teachers in other towns also made professions of faith, but the documentation located to date is brief and general.

[2]ACPV, "Professioni di fede richiesta agli insegnanti, 1587," (hereafter "Professioni di fede"), a bundle of 331 folios. I first read them in May 1976, and reread them in 1979. Now a detailed summary has appeared: Baldo, 1977, who performs a great service in making the documents more accessible. I will cite both the original documents and Baldo when possible; nevertheless, I rely on my own reading and analysis, which sometimes varies slightly from his.

TABLE 2.1
Venetian Teachers and Pupils, 1587–1588

Type of School	Teachers	Pupils
Independent—Latin	160 (65.3%)	c. 1,650 (35.7%)
Communal—Latin.	5 (2.0%)	c. 188 (4.1%)
Church—Latin	8 (3.3%)	c. 322 (7.0%)
Independent—vernacular and abbaco	72 (29.4%)	c. 2,465 (53.3%)
Totals	245	c. 4,625

Source: ACPV, "Professioni di fede."

Note: The table excludes ten independent Latin teachers and three independent vernacular teachers who lacked schools.

told the patriarch's representative about their schools: location, enrollment, sometimes the ages of pupils, and almost always the texts taught. The documents offer a uniquely informative picture of education in the Renaissance.

Sixteenth-century Venice had a typical Renaissance mixture of independent, communal, and church schools (table 2.1). Hence, in 1587–88, about 89 percent of Venetian students (circa 4,115 pupils) studied in independent schools, 7 percent (circa 322) in church schools, and 4 percent (circa 188) in communal schools. This distribution by kind of school probably typified the situation in other large cities such as Milan, Florence, and Rome, because such cities had a large number of wealthy nobles and merchants who could afford to hire independent masters, including household tutors. Few of the very wealthy needed to rely on communal schools to educate their children. On the other hand, one or two communal masters probably taught a larger proportion of the total school population in villages and towns of a few hundred to a few thousand souls, because the smaller and less wealthy upper class in them lacked the means to hire numerous independent masters.

The Venetian data of 1587 permit the formulation of school attendance estimates. Attending formal schools were 4,595 boys and 30 girls.[3] With

[3]The teachers specifically mentioned twenty-seven girls with such terms as *putte, fiola, donzele,* and *creaturina,* plus one mixed group of eight pupils ("putti e putte"). For the latter, see ACPV, "Professioni di fede," fol. 176ʳ, Francescus de Fabretis; Baldo, 1977, p. 77. If one arbitrarily divides this group into three girls and five boys, the total number of girls is thirty. A word about counting girls in school. The Italian masculine collective nouns dominate and obliterate the sex of groups; e.g., *fanciulli* and *figliuoli* mean either boys or children of both sexes. Hence, it is possible that additional girls in school are hidden behind collective masculine nouns. On the other hand, since the teachers seem to have singled out the girls in their schools (because they were unusual?) with the above terms, it is not likely that many

the aid of the Venetian census of 1586, the rate of formal schooling (and achievement of literacy by this means) can be estimated by sex.

About 26 percent of the boys of school age (6 through 15) attended formal schools.

Only .2 percent of the girls of school age attended formal schools.

About 14 percent of boys and girls combined of school age attended formal schools.[4]

These figures count most but not quite all the boys and girls educated in Venice in 1587, for they omit three other groups of young people who received at least rudimentary vernacular schooling.

First, an undetermined number of lay girls lived and studied as long-term boarders in Venetian female monasteries. Nobles and wealthy commoners paid forty to sixty ducats annually for the privilege of having their daughters live a cloistered life for years before emerging to marry or remaining as professed religious (see ch. 4). The female monasteries were not boarding schools in either a Renaissance or a modern sense, because educating secular girls was not a convent's chief concern, and because each admitted only a handful of girls. Nevertheless, the female monasteries provided limited vernacular schooling to some wealthy Venetian girls.

Second, some informal schooling occurred both inside and outside the home. Mother, father, adult relative, or sibling might tutor the family's children. Girls forbidden to venture outside the moral safety of the home

---

girls have escaped notice. Other evidence supports the view that very few girls attended formal classes outside the home. Even if some girls have been missed in 1587, one doubts that it makes much statistical difference. By any measure the number of girls in formal schools was abysmally small.

[4]Fortunately, the Venetian government took a census in 1586. Beltrami, 1964, p. 82 et passim, provides the summary figures. The census counted 29,783 boys (putti) from the age of less than 1 year through 17, and 24,485 girls (putte) from less than 1 year through 17, in a total population of 148,637. (Renaissance censuses invariably enumerated more boys than girls for linguistic, social, financial, and possibly mortality reasons.) Obviously, Venice may have had more children of some ages than of others; the Great Plague of 1575–77 possibly created a dip in the age 9-to-11 group of 1586. But since dips or bulges are not known with certainty, it seems better to omit them than to guess about them in these calculations. It has been assumed that Venice had an equal number of children of each age from less than 1 through 17. Six through 15 was the school-age group; all but a handful of the pupils mentioned by teachers in ACPV, "Professioni di fede," were aged 6 through 15. Thus, it can be estimated that school-age children were $^{10}/_{17}$ (.58824) of the total. Hence, there were 17,520 boys of school age (29,783 × .58824) and 14,403 girls of school age (24,485 × .58824).

About 4,625 children (c. 4,595 boys and c. 30 girls) attended school in Venice in 1587. Hence, one can calculate that about 26.2 percent of school-age boys attended school (4,595 ÷ 17,520), while only about .2 percent of school-age girls attended school (30 ÷ 14,403). About 14.5 percent of boys and girls combined attended school (4,625 ÷ 31,923). For a discussion of some demographic issues raised here, see Mols, 1974; Herlihy and Klapisch-Zuber, 1978, pp. 332–36, 339–40, 563–68, 660–63; and Herlihy and Klapisch-Zuber, 1985, ch. 5.

for formal schooling may have been major beneficiaries of informal home schooling. Not all noble parents could afford convent boarding or a household teacher for their daughters, but society still expected girls from upper-class and prominent commoner families to be able to read and write in the vernacular. Maternal tutoring helped fill the gap between expectation and resources. A small number of boys from middle-class and artisanal backgrounds probably also received informal tutoring from a family member or from co-workers and friends who could read and write.

Third, a larger number of children received external informal schooling from the Schools of Christian Doctrine, the catechism or Sunday schools that taught religion, reading, and writing to both boys and girls on Sundays and holidays throughout the year (see ch. 12).

Adding estimates of the number of girls boarding in convents, plus boys and girls who received informal schooling either in the home or from the catechism schools, to the known number of pupils in formal schools gives a more complete picture of basic literacy in Venice. The distribution of the population by classes also helps in estimating a literacy figure. The Venetian census of 1586 indicated that 4.3 percent of the population (both sexes) were nobles and 5.1 percent (both sexes) enjoyed citizen status, a special hereditary status that raised citizens above commoners and entitled them to hold some state offices.[5] Nobles and citizens together comprised 9.4 percent of the population. As always, the census indicated more male than female nobles and citizens, roughly 55 percent male and 45 percent female.[6] Hence, about 4.2 percent (.094 × .45) of the population were females of noble or citizen status. If all but a handful of noble daughters, a very large majority of the citizen girls, and a few daughters of wealthy commoner merchants received convent schooling or home tutoring, another 4–5 percent of the female population achieved literacy in these ways. In addition, one may guess that another 1 percent of boys of all classes received home tutoring.

Although no numbers for Venetian catechism schools of the 1580s are available, evidence from other cities demonstrates that thousands of children, more or less evenly divided between the sexes, attended these schools. For example, Milanese catechism schools enrolled 7,000 boys and 5,800 girls in 1599, when the city's population was about 200,000.[7] One can confidently estimate that Venetian catechism schools in 1587 enrolled 2,000 to 3,000 boys and probably many more, plus the same number of girls. However, it is not likely that all girls and boys attended regularly enough, or were apt enough, to learn rudimentary reading and writing from this sporadic instruction. If one estimates that another 1,000 Venetian

[5]Beltrami, 1964, p. 72.
[6]Ibid., p. 81.
[7]Tamborini, 1939, pp. 323–26.

TABLE 2.2
Estimated Venetian Literacy, 1587
(in percentages)

Source of Literacy	Boys	Girls
Attendance in formal schools	26.0	0.2
Informal home tutoring (estimate)	1.0	2.0
Boarding in convents		3.0–4.0
Schools of Christian Doctrine	6.0	7.0
Literacy by sex	33.0	12.2–13.2
Literacy, sexes combined		23.0

girls and 1,000 Venetian boys learned rudimentary reading and writing skills at the Schools of Christian Doctrine in 1587, it means that another 7 percent of the girls and another 6 percent of the boys acquired basic literacy. The formal schooling rate and the estimated informal schooling rate added together yield a comprehensive basic literacy estimate (table 2.2).

Comparing Venetian schooling and literacy with that in other Renaissance societies is very difficult for the lack of data. Still, the estimated Venetian male literacy rate of 33–34 percent in 1587 is close to the estimated male schooling rate of 28–33 percent for Florentine boys aged 10 to 13 in 1480 (see ch. 3). The diocese of York may have had 20 to 25 percent male literacy and a literacy rate for both sexes of 15 percent in 1530.[8] Urban Venice and Florence in relatively wealthy and commercially developed Italy ought to have had a higher literacy than rural and poorer England, and probably did.

The Venetian and Florentine literacy estimates, despite their tentativeness, conform to our knowledge of the social structure of Renaissance society. All male nobles, professional men, and merchants of at least middling status probably could read and write well; their livelihood depended on it. Certainly almost all females of the nobility and the majority of wives and daughters of professional men and merchants acquired at least rudimentary vernacular literacy. The extent of schooling and literacy among the other 90 percent of the population—petty merchants, the many different kinds of artisans, laborers, soldiers, fishermen, peasants, servants, and the destitute at the bottom of society—is much more difficult to determine. Nevertheless, a societal literacy figure de-

[8]Moran, 1985, pp. 223, 225. Other studies of literacy in the early modern period deal with northern Europe in later centuries and must use different sources, making comparison difficult. The literature is too large to list here; see the bibliographical surveys of Graff, 1983; Houston, 1983; and P. Grendler, 1988c.

pends on guessing the extent of basic literacy of males and females in this large group. Probably the overwhelming majority of the females in this bloc of the population could neither read nor write; certainly, contrary evidence is hard to find. On the other hand, possibly a substantial minority of the males in this bloc possessed literacy.

Impressionistic evidence supports the view that a good number of male artisans possessed basic literacy. In the late 1580s, the Procurators of St. Mark asked for bids for interior construction on the Libreria Vecchia, begun over fifty years before by Jacopo Sansovino and finally nearing completion. Master carpenters, windowmakers, and wallers bid to build stairs, windows, and interior walls and do other work between 1589 and 1591. Seventeen artisans wrote out and signed their bids, while five, who presumably could not write, had their bids prepared by third parties.[9] This small sample suggests that a large majority of master artisans could write. The construction industry in fifteenth-century Florence exhibited a similar pattern.[10] It is possible that functional literacy existed among a broad part of the masculine population in Italy during the High Renaissance.[11]

CURRICULA

The data from 1587 reveal additional information about teachers and curricula (table 2.3). A teacher's description of his school, including the texts taught, determines the classification. A Latin teacher most often called his school a grammar or Latin school (*schola di grammatica*); or he stated, for example, "Io insegno grammatica a vinti scolari" ("I teach Latin to twenty students"). *Grammatica* meant Latin grammar and ancient Latin literature. A teacher might call his school humanistic; he claimed to teach *humanità, i fondamenti dell'humanità, lettere humane,* or *rethorica.* Here, *humanità* meant the same as *grammatica;* indeed, teachers sometimes used the terms interchangeably: "i fondamenti dell'humanità o della grammatica."[12] In every case, the teacher taught Latin grammar and literature with

[9]Those who could write followed a formula—"Io Pasqualin de betin marangon . . . "—and signed their names. (A *marangon* was a carpenter.) The carpenters and others who could not write had a third party prepare unsigned bids with a formula that avoided the use of "Io" or "Noi." I have omitted one bid the identity of whose author, the artisan or a third party, is not clear. Finally, the sample is limited to master artisans and permits no surmises about the literacy of lower artisans. ASV, Procuratori di San Marco de supra, Bu. 68, fascicolo 2, fols. 33ʳ–63ʳ.

[10]Goldthwaite, 1980, p. 419, writes about the artisans of the quattrocento Florentine construction industry as follows: "They were certainly literate—most artisans in Florence were." Also see pp. 313, 416. Goldthwaite does not clarify whether he means master artisans or all artisans.

[11]This is the belief of A. Petrucci, 1978, esp. pp. 183–86; and A. Petrucci, ed., 1982, p. 9.

[12]ACPV, "Professioni di fede," fol. 15ʳ. Carefully drafted educational documents, such as Venetian Senate legislation establishing *sestiere* schools and Jesuit *ratii studiorum,* distinguished

TABLE 2.3
Enrollment in Latin and Vernacular Schools in Venice, 1587

Type of School and Curriculum	Number of Teachers	Enrollment
Independent—Latin	129	c. 1,220
Independent—Latin with Greek[a]	6	60
Independent—Latin with logic and philosophy	21	260
Independent—Latin with limited vernacular reading and abbaco	4	110
Church—Latin	13[b]	322
Communal—Latin	5	188
Teachers without schools—Latin[c]	10	0
Subtotal: Latin teachers	188	
Subtotal: Enrollment in Latin schools		c. 2,160 (47%)

continued

Source: ACPV, "Professioni di fede."

Note: About 90 percent of the active teachers gave enrollment figures. However, some offered approximate figures (for example, 40 to 50), and those with large schools tended to round off numbers to the nearest five or ten. When a teacher gave no enrollment figure, an estimate based on the average known enrollment for his type of school was assigned. The table presents precise figures for the sake of clarity, but the figures cannot be deemed absolute. Nevertheless, the overall numbers and the distribution among different kinds of schools cannot be far from reality. Baldo, 1977, pp. 11–13, gives a total enrollment figure of 4,481.

[a]This figure includes five independent masters who taught a few *zaghi* (the Venetian word for boys studying to become priests) in addition to lay boys. Hence, five teachers have been counted twice.

[b]One church school master who taught a little Greek to the older pupils in his school has been counted in the "Church—Latin" category. ACPV, "Professioni di fede," fols. 134[v]–135[v], Francescus Grossa; Baldo, 1977, p. 63.

grammar manuals, elementary Latin readers, and the classics of antiquity.

A small number of teachers added additional subject matter to the classical Latin curriculum. Approximately sixty boys learned classical Greek. The limited interest in Greek contrasts sharply with the preeminent role previously played by Venice in Greek printing and with Venice's continuing role in Greek manuscript collecting and copying in the late sixteenth century.[13] Apparently neither the presence of a large colony of

---

between grammar (lower level) and humanities (upper level) Latin schools. But many people used the terms interchangeably in informal speech and writing.

[13]M. Grendler, 1980, esp. pp. 407–10.

TABLE 2.3
Continued

Type of School and Curriculum	Number of Teachers	Enrollment
Independent—vernacular reading, writing, abbaco, and accounting with limited elementary Latin grammar	45	c. 1,970
Independent—vernacular reading and writing with limited elementary Latin grammar	12	330
Independent—vernacular reading and writing	15	165
Teachers without schools—vernacular	3	0
Subtotal: Vernacular teachers	75	
Subtotal: Enrollment in vernacular schools		c. 2,465 (53%)
Total number of teachers	263[d] (258)	
Total enrollment		c. 4,625

[c]Thirteen teachers made professions of faith but were not teaching. Some had recently arrived in Venice and had not yet found teaching employment, others pursued other careers, and still others offered no explanation. Yet, they described themselves as Latin and vernacular teachers to the point of listing the texts that they would teach. There seems to be no reason to exclude them from this table.
[d]As mentioned in note a, five teachers have been counted twice.

Greeks and Cretans in Venice nor the Republic's commercial contacts with the eastern Mediterranean stimulated much interest in the language of ancient Greece. A minority of teachers added some logic and philosophy to the standard Latin humanistic curriculum.

A single teacher, a priest at the patriarchal seminary, taught elementary Hebrew to an unknown number of seminarians. He did not teach very much Hebrew: an hour a day from "a simple text from the book of Genesis and the psalms of David" ("el semplice teste del libro del genesis e i salmi di David").[14] Venice in the first half of the century boasted the most impor-

[14]ACPV "Professioni di fede," fols. 302[r–v]; Baldo, 1977, pp. 28, 78–79.

tant Hebrew press in Europe; although much reduced because of anti-Jewish sentiment, it still published in the 1580s and 1590s.[15] But because Italian humanists did not call for the study of Hebrew, the language did not become part of the syllabus.

Finally, four independent Latin schools added abbaco or vernacular reading to the standard Latin curriculum. One teacher stated that he taught *humanità e abbaco* to twenty students in order to get more pupils: while many wish to learn abbaco, only a few want to study the humanities, he lamented.[16] Another independent teacher did the same with greater results. Francescus Gambarutius, a 48-year-old clergyman from Siena who had taught for sixteen years in Venice, taught the standard Latin curriculum plus two vernacular texts, Bonsignore Cacciaguerra's *Lettere spirituali* and Antonio de Guevara's *Vita di Marco Aurelio*.[17] None of these four schools taught a truly integrated Latin and vernacular curriculum; each simply added a little abbaco instruction and vernacular reading to the Latin classics. Overall, 80 percent of the students in the Latin stream followed an exclusively classical Latin curriculum, 3 percent added Greek, 12 percent added logic and philosophy, and a final 5 percent added a little abbaco and vernacular reading.

The other 53 percent of Venetian pupils attended vernacular schools. The vast majority of these schools taught "lezer, scriver, abbaco et quaderno" ("reading, writing, abbaco, and [how to keep an] account book") or "lezer e scrivere e abbaco e far conti" ("reading and writing and abbaco and accounting or bookkeeping"). A smaller number of vernacular schools taught reading and writing but not abbaco and accounting. The vernacular schools taught a standard group of vernacular religious and secular textbooks, plus writing and the mathematical and accounting skills needed for the world of commerce.

Almost all the vernacular schools also taught the rudiments of Latin grammar, probably just the contents of an elementary manual. They did not go further into Latin reading. This brief instruction in Latin grammar gave future merchants and artisans a very limited introduction to the language of the legal, ecclesiastical, and professional worlds above them. A longing to participate in the Latin culture so praised by humanists helps explain why students at vernacular schools memorized rules of grammar. They would at least be able to recognize a few words and inflected forms. But grammatical drill alone could not prepare students to join the Latin world. At best it facilitated the transfer of a boy from the vernacular to the

---

[15]On the Hebrew press, see P. Grendler, 1977, pp. 89–93, 140–45, 255; and P. Grendler, 1978. On the Jewish community, see *Venezia ebraica*, 1982.

[16]ACPV, "Professioni di fede," fols. 161ʳ–162ʳ; Baldo, 1977, pp. 64–65, Angelus de Nigris.

[17]ACPV, "Professioni di fede," fols. 174ᵛ–175ᵛ; Baldo, 1977, pp. 66–67.

Latin stream, if he changed schools before he forgot what he had learned of Latin grammar. The vernacular schools made no attempt to· teach an integrated curriculum. Latin and vernacular schools remained separate and distinct.

TEACHERS

Approximately 115 (circa 44 percent of the total) Venetian teachers conducted independent Latin schools all across the city in their own houses or rooms rented for the purpose. Francescus Gambarutius, mentioned earlier, had the largest Latin school, with fifty-five to sixty pupils.[18] Antonius Figarius, a 65-year-old clergyman from Verona who claimed to have taught for fifty years, instructed forty-four or forty-five pupils with the aid of his *nipote* as *ripetitore*.[19] A teacher who was a near-namesake of a famous humanist led the third largest Latin school: Aeneas Piccolominens (Piccolomini), a 42-year-old layman from Siena, taught a broad humanistic curriculum to twenty pupils in the morning and fourteen different pupils in the afternoon.[20] Surely his famous humanistic name helped attract students and secure for him an honored place in Venetian life; he delivered funeral orations for doges in 1595 and 1605.[21] The vast majority of Latin independent masters taught fewer students: the average enrollment was twenty-three pupils, an appropriate number for one master.

Another forty-five teachers taught Latin as household tutors. A handful of vernacular masters, who taught reading and writing but not abbaco, also acted as household tutors. None of the instructors of the complete vernacular curriculum of reading, writing, abbaco, and bookkeeping acted as a household tutor, because parents who had the means to hire a tutor wanted their children to acquire a Latin education rather than commercial skills. Household tutors lived in the pupils' home or came daily to instruct a handful of students. These tutors, including the numerous clergymen among them, moved from house to house throughout their professional lives. They were not family chaplains who taught on the side; nor were they clerical relatives needing sinecures. For example, from his arrival in 1570, Vincenzo Bibione, a 43-year-old cleric from Campania, taught continuously in three different Venetian households. In 1587 he

[18]ACPV, "Professioni di fede," fols. 174ᵛ–175ᵛ; Baldo, 1977, pp. 66–67. I give the names of teachers as found in the documents, despite inconsistencies and the occasional mixing of Latin and Italian.

[19]ACPV, "Professioni di fede," fols. 92ᵛ–93ᵛ; Baldo, 1977, pp. 54–55, for some of this material.

[20]ACPV, "Professioni di fede," fols. 115ᵛ–116ᵛ; Baldo, 1977, pp. 58–59. I do not know how closely related he was to Pius II or the scholar Alessandro Piccolomini (1508–78).

[21]Da Mosto, 1966, pp. 380, 389, 708.

taught five noble sons, the oldest 13 years of age, of Paolo and Zuanne Nani.[22]

Some teachers combined the roles of household tutor and independent master. For example, Scipio Dianus, a 36-year-old layman from Calabria, taught three sons of the noble Girolamo Mocenigo and five other pupils "outside the house."[23] Presumably he taught the other five pupils in a neighborhood school or like setting. A resident tutor might not restrict his instruction to the children of the family. Luchas Guadagnoli, a clergyman from Arezzo aged 44, had been living in the house of the noble Zaccaria Priuli for nine years. He taught Priuli's four sons plus five non-noble pupils.[24] They could have been day students recruited by the teacher, commoner relatives of the Priuli, or children of employees of the Priuli. Financial reasons undoubtedly explained the dual teaching roles. Eight or nine pupils provided more income than three or four, and if noble parents could not pay an adequate stipend, income from additional pupils was necessary.

Boarding schools had played a key role in propagating the *studia humanitatis* in the fifteenth century but did not loom large in sixteenth-century Venice. Only two existed in 1587: a 41-year-old Florentine Dominican friar taught the Latin curriculum to seven boarding students and four or five day students, and a 63-year-old Venetian layman taught Latin and abbaco to three boarding students and twenty-six or twenty-seven day students.[25] Boarding schools run by the religious teaching orders would become important again in the seventeenth century.

The forty-five independent reading, writing, abbaco, and bookkeeping schools enrolled an average of 45 pupils each, making them much larger than the Latin schools. Blasius Pellicaneus, a 32-year-old married man from Treviso who had been teaching in Venice for eight years, conducted the largest such school—indeed, the largest school in Venice—for 143 pupils. A 23-year-old layman served as his *ripetitore,* but one suspects that additional help was needed.[26] Another vernacular reading and abbaco school had 120 pupils,[27] and six others enrolled 70 to 80 students.[28]

---

[22]ACPV, "Professioni di fede," fols. 1ʳ⁻ᵛ; Baldo, 1977, pp. 44–45. One cannot always easily differentiate between a household tutor and a neighborhood master. When a teacher said that he lived in the house of a noble, this usually signified that he was a household tutor. But he sometimes meant only that he rented (and lived in) a house owned by a noble. One must look to other evidence for clarification, and accept the possibility of making mistakes.

[23]ACPV, "Professioni di fede," fol. 187ʳ.

[24]Ibid., fols. 61ʳ⁻ᵛ; Baldo, 1977, pp. 50–51, for part of this information.

[25]ACPV, "Professioni di fede," fols. 258ʳ–261ʳ, Iulianus Caponus (Capponi) and Giovanni Battista Contarini. Although Contarini bore a Venetian noble name, he was not a nobleman.

[26]Ibid., fols. 136ʳ–138ʳ, Pellicaneus and Philippus Passagnoli; Baldo, 1977, pp. 60, 62.

[27]ACPV, "Professioni di fede," fol. 5ʳ, Hieronimus Ciprii; Baldo, 1977, p. 44.

[28]ACPV, "Professioni di fede," fols. 20ʳ (Iohannes Lionnegro), 205ᵛ (Hieronimus a

Although the student population was divided almost equally between Latin and vernacular streams (47 percent and 53 percent respectively), the student-teacher ratio differed considerably—12.5:1 in the Latin stream and 34:1 in the vernacular schools.[29] The substantial number of Latin household tutors and the absence of household tutors in the vernacular stream made the difference.

Forty-two of the forty-five masters of the vernacular reading, writing, abbaco, and bookkeeping schools were laymen, sometimes with close ties to the commercial world. One such teacher, aged 66, had been a marketing agent for the principal butchers of the city from 1549 to 1572 before turning to teaching.[30] Bartholomeus Partenus, aged 45, taught a school for future wine merchants and kept the books for various nobles, merchants, and others. He had little formal learning beyond his mathematical and accounting skills. When asked if he had any prohibited books, Partenius responded that he owned only two titles, the *Epistole e Evangeli* and the *Little Office of Our Lady*, texts read by young children in the schools.[31]

Teachers of all ages conducted classes. The oldest, an 87-year-old clergyman who also served as chaplain to an *ospedale*, taught Latin to four to six boys in order to keep busy rather than for monetary gain.[32] The youngest masters were two 18-year-old laymen. The first, who had assumed direction of his aging father's school, taught Latin to between twenty-two and twenty-four students. All we know about the second is that he taught abbaco to three students.[33] Overall, 32 percent of Venetian teachers were 18 to 30 years old; 26 percent were aged 31 to 40; 24 percent were aged 41 to 50; and 18 percent were aged 50 or older.[34] It is impossible

---

Lignamine), 206ᵛ (Aloysius Lioni), 232ᵛ (Iohannes a Lignamine, the father of Hieronimus), 246ʳ (Ioseph de Thomasiis), 291ᵛ (Rochus q. Hieronimi); Baldo, 1977, pp. 46, 70, 72, 74, 78. However, Baldo, p. 46, mistakenly records the enrollment of Lionnegro's school as twenty rather than seventy.

29The ratios are derived by dividing the 2,160 pupils in Latin schools by the 173 active Latin teachers and the 2,465 pupils in the vernacular stream by the 72 active vernacular teachers. They should be seen as estimates rather than as absolute figures. In particular, they do not take into account the possibility of additional *ripetitori*, especially in the abbaco schools. Only two *ripetitori* professed their faith: Philippus Passagnoli, the assistant to Pellicaneus (mentioned in n. 26), and Georgius de Redulphis, who assisted another Latin teacher and taught as a household tutor in his own right. ACPV, "Professioni di fede," fols. 101ᵛ–102ᵛ; Baldo, 1977, p. 57. Three other masters mentioned that they had *ripetitori* but provided no further information beyond giving the age of one *ripetitore* as 18. Ibid., fols. 29ᵛ–31ᵛ, 33ᵛ–34ᵛ, 93ʳ; Baldo, 1977, pp. 49, 55.

30ACPV, "Professioni di fede," fols. 55ʳ⁻ᵛ, Iocomus Bricola; Baldo, 1977, p. 51.

31ACPV, "Professioni di fede," fols. 169ʳ–170ʳ; Baldo, 1977, pp. 64–65.

32ACPV, "Professioni di fede," fols. 312ʳ–314ʳ, Raynaldus Valerio; Baldo, 1977, pp. 80–81, gives part of this information.

33ACPV, "Professioni di fede," fols. 263ᵛ–264ᵛ (Iohannes f. Franceschi), 300ᵛ–301ᵛ (Francescus de Grottis); Baldo, 1977, pp. 77, 79.

34These data are from Baldo, 1977, p. 20.

to verify ages as reported by teachers. Furthermore, the distribution may be slightly distorted by the tendency of some to exaggerate their longevity.[35]

Throughout the period from 1300 to 1600, teachers frequently found posts beyond their birthplaces. The birthplaces of Venetian masters were as follows:

Venice: 39%

Venetian state (Italian mainland and Adriatic outposts): 28%

Other parts of Italy and Sicily: 32%

Foreign lands (one each from England, France, and Spain): 1%[36]

Some teachers had taught elsewhere and had moved about a great deal. Anianus de Salvis, a 68-year-old layman from Siena, had previously taught for eighteen years in the Milanese state. Indeed, he had held an appointment—whether for teaching is not clear—in the house of Cardinal Carlo Borromeo before coming to tutor in a Venetian noble house.[37] A 36-year-old Calabrian layman had taught for ten years in Perugia and Rome, had both taught and studied philosophy at Padua for four years, and then had moved to Venice in 1585.[38] Antonius Adriani, a 33-year-old priest from Ancona, had previously taught members of the Malatesta family, landowners and warriors in the Romagna, and had also taught in Padua before moving to Venice in 1585. In Venice he conducted in his home an independent Latin school for twenty-five students.[39]

A variety of reasons brought teachers to Venice. Ambition played a role: Pomponius Tranquillus, a 30-year-old layman from the Abruzzi, had come in order to make more money (*far mazor lucro*) and to publish his new teaching method, which he did not describe.[40] The numerous Venetian presses offered supplementary employment less available elsewhere; for example, a Neapolitan clergyman taught Latin to ten pupils and worked as a corrector for a press.[41] At least one teacher came in order to begin a second career. A Bolognese layman had studied medicine at the University of Bologna but had been barred from becoming a physician because of an unspecified infirmity. He had just moved to Venice in 1587

[35]Herlihy and Klapisch-Zuber, 1985, ch. 6, esp. pp. 163, 171.

[36]See Baldo, 1977, pp. 17–19, for more details. One caution: when the documents provide no information on birthplace or background, Baldo concludes that the teacher is a Venetian, a reasonable but not infallible conclusion to draw.

[37]ACPV, "Professioni di fede," fol. 121ᵛ; Baldo, 1977, pp. 58–59, for some of this information.

[38]ACPV, "Professioni di fede," fols. 187ʳ⁻ᵛ, Scipio Dianus.

[39]Ibid., fols. 193ʳ⁻ᵛ; Baldo, 1977, pp. 68–69.

[40]ACPV, "Professioni di fede," fol. 293ᵛ; Baldo, 1977, pp. 19, 79.

[41]ACPV, "Professioni di fede," fols. 248ʳ⁻ᵛ, Ascanius Guidoto.

but had not yet started a Latin school.[42] Some teachers had been forced to leave their homes. The "cursed Spaniards" ("maledette spagnoli") had driven one teacher from his native town of Barletta in the Kingdom of Naples.[43] The sole teaching Englishman in Venice had fled Elizabethan religious persecution.[44] And Hieronimus Florius, a 30-year-old clergyman from Spalato, had been banished by his bishop because of "the weakness of the flesh." In 1587 he taught reading and writing to six students in Venice.[45]

The documents provide little information on the education of the teachers, because the patriarch's representative did not ask. Nevertheless, at least five teachers held university degrees, and another six claimed university training. Five teachers named the University of Padua as their place of study, one mentioned the University of Bologna, another named the Collegium Germanicum in Rome, and the rest did not specify.[46] This does not preclude the possibility that other teachers studied at universities. In addition, some clerical teachers may have received university-level training in theology or philosophy from *studia theologiae*.

A majority of all the teachers in Venice—62 percent—were clergymen.[47] Clergymen tended to teach Latin, while laymen taught in the vernacular schools: 80 percent of the Latin school masters were clerics, and 75 percent of the vernacular stream teachers were laymen. Again household tutors explain part of the difference—80 to 90 percent of them were clergymen. That laymen would teach in the vernacular literature, abbaco, and accounting schools seems logical. These schools trained boys to enter the world of commerce, to which some vernacular school masters had strong ties. Clerics, on the other hand, learned Latin but lacked much access to the lay professions (such as law, medicine, government, and the notariate) requiring Latin. Hence, some of them gravitated to the remaining profession open to those with Latin—teaching. Parents may have preferred clerical teachers in the belief that priests would exert a more beneficial moral influence on the young than would laymen. Perhaps clerical masters charged lower fees than laymen who needed to support families. But most

[42]"Io son stato in studio à Bologna per voler deventar medico ma li medici mi hanno prohibito per esser infermo et pero d'agosto in qua son venuto à Venezia et me ho deliberato de voler tenir schola de grammatica ma anchora no llo le trova." Ibid., fol. 78r, Venturas a Christianis.

[43]Ibid., fol. 190v, Giovanni Cafagno; Baldo, 1977, p. 19.

[44]ACPV, "Professioni di fede," fols. 261r–262v, Balduinus Flerus; Baldo, 1977, p. 77.

[45]Spalato is the modern Split on the Adriatic coast of Yugoslavia. ACPV, "Professioni di fede," fol. 266r; Baldo, 1977, pp. 20, 77.

[46]ACPV, "Professioni di fede," fol. 28r–29r, 31v–33r, 52v, 78r, 94r–95r, 132r–133v, 151r–v, 187v, 188v, 269r–270r, 322r–323r; Baldo, 1977, pp. 49, 51, 57, 61, 69, 77, 81, for some of this information.

[47]This is the figure in Baldo, 1977, p. 20, with which I concur.

impoitant, clerical teachers were available, because many priests, instead of following strictly ecclesiastical careers, became educators.

The Tridentine decree ordering the establishment of diocesan seminaries added to the teaching corps. Venice had two seminaries, the patriarchal seminary, which opened in the autumn of 1579, and the ducal one of 1581.[48] Fourteen former seminarians, aged 19 through 25, taught school in 1587. Two led *sestiere* clerical schools with enrollments of up to forty pupils (see below), while the other twelve served as independent masters or household tutors.[49] The bishop of nearby Treviso ordered his seminarians to take employment as teachers after six years of study but before ordination;[50] Venetian seminarians may have been under a similar obligation. Whether obliged to do so or not, these young men joined the ranks of independent clerical masters; many probably never returned to ecclesiastical careers. The Italian clerical population continued to grow in the seventeenth and eighteenth centuries until it far surpassed the number of available benefices. Then even more priests became teachers.

CHURCH SCHOOLS

About 322 boys studied in Venetian church schools in 1587. These schools for boys intending to become clergymen (*zaghi*) came in different forms.

The school for the *zaghi* of San Marco provided Latin training for the boys attached to the famous church. Although possibly founded during the pontificate of Eugenius IV, the school is first mentioned in a notice from March 1456, when Father Anthonius, a canon and *rector scolarum* of St. Mark's, made a will leaving ten ducats to support four young clerics at St. Mark's. They were expected to study Latin for three years and singing (*in cantu*) for one. When the first quartet finished their studies, a new group of four pauper *zaghi* should follow, a pattern to be repeated in perpetuity. A second teacher (*rector scolarum*) resident at St. Mark's witnessed the will.[51] Hence, the school had one teacher if the witness replaced a dying Father Anthonius and two if the witness and Father Anthonius taught simultaneously.

The St. Mark's school for *zaghi* can be continuously documented from 1479. In that year it hired Francesco Diana to teach. A layman, Diana had substituted in late 1450 and early 1451 for one of the two masters at the Scuola di San Marco, the humanist chancery school.[52] Diana's profes-

[48]Tramontin, 1965.
[49]ACPV, "Professioni di fede," fols. 35ᵛ, 36ʳ, 44ᵛ, 45ᵛ, 49ᵛ, 74ʳ⁻ᵛ, 79ʳ, 83ʳ, 129ʳ⁻ᵛ, 131ᵛ–132ᵛ, 134ʳ⁻ᵛ, 177ᵛ–178ᵛ, 285ʳ–286ʳ, 314ʳ–315ᵛ; Baldo, 1977, pp. 49, 51, 53, 55, 59, 61, 67, 79, 81.
[50]Liberali, 1971, pp. 81, 162.
[51]Bertanza and Dalla Santa, 1907, p. 327, 8 March 1456, for the text of the will.
[52]Sforza, 1870, pp. 394, 403–4; Segarizzi, 1915–16a, p. 643.

sional activities between 1452 and 1479 are unknown; perhaps he taught as an independent master. At the school for *zaghi* he received a salary of twenty-five ducats plus ten more to rent a house, which may have doubled as a school. A stream of successors taught at the school through 1726 and perhaps beyond.[53]

The masters at St. Mark's taught a rich humanistic curriculum to the *zaghi*. Father Marc'Antonio Zambon, aged 24 and newly appointed to the post, taught thirty-five to forty-five boys in 1587. Although Zambon did not give his pupils' ages, Zambon's instruction suggests that they ranged in age from 6 or 7 to the mid-teens. He divided his school into four classes. Five *putti* (little boys) learned to read and write in the first class, while the next class studied Latin grammar, Terence, and the catechism. Zambon instructed the third class in more Terence, Ovid's *Metamorphoses*, Horace, Caesar's *Gallic Wars,* and Latin grammar. He led the fourth and most advanced class through book one of Cicero's *Epistulae ad Atticum*, more Horace and Ovid, plus Plautus's *Aulularia*.[54] Only the *zaghi* of St. Mark's among all the schoolboys in Venice read the sometimes racy Roman comedian. Although expected to teach Greek as well, Father Zambon did not do so.[55] A second master instructed the older *zaghi* in Greek grammar and reading.[56]

Another 185 or more young clerics attended five church schools under the direction of the patriarch in 1587. Patriarch Antonio Contarini (1508–24) founded these schools. Citing the necessity for boy clerics to be educated in letters and good morals, the patriarch appointed a priest to teach all the *zaghi* in the *sestiere* (civil administrative district) of Castello. The priest would receive a salary of forty ducats plus lodging for his teaching.[57] Patriarch Contarini then expanded the program to six church

[53]ASV, Procuratori di San Marco de supra, Bu. 89, fascicule 1: "Maestro di Grammatica delli Chierici ò Zaghi." This is an unpaginated bundle of materials with a list of the masters from 1479 through 1726. It also contains contracts beginning with that of Diana of 22 May 1479. Five of the first six masters were laymen; priests dominated from 1587 onward. The average tenure was over twelve years. Salaries plus allowances were 35, 40, and 42 ducats through 1586, and 80 or 100 ducats from 1587 through 1628. This is a church school because it was attached to a church and it educated clerics. Nevertheless, state officials, the Procurators of St. Mark, oversaw its affairs, because San Marco was canonically the doge's private chapel.

[54]ACPV, "Professioni di fede," fols. 317r–319r. His appointment, also in 1587, is noted in ASV, Procuratori di San Marco de supra, Bu. 89, "Maestro di Grammatica."

[55]"Il Precettor delli Zaghi habbi cura oltre de insegnarli le bone lettere greche et latine. . . ." ASV, Procuratori di San Marco de supra, Bu. 89, "Maestro di Grammatica," 12 July 1587.

[56]ACPV, "Professioni di fede," fols. 134v–135v, Francescus Grossa; Baldo, 1977, pp. 62–63.

[57]The following description is based on ACPV, Bu. 580, "Maestri de' sestieri de S. Polo et S. Croce," a bundle of unpaginated documents, 1524 through 1620. Baldo, 1977, pp. 31–34, and 89–94, summarizes and prints some of the documents.

schools, one for each of the six *sestieri* in the city. Pope Clement VII endorsed the schools, and the next patriarch confirmed them in 1525. Through the sixteenth century and beyond, these church schools trained boys who wished to become priests.

When a teaching vacancy occurred, the parish priests of the *sestiere* deputized a committee of their number to search the city for suitable candidates; they then chose the master by secret ballot. A representative of the patriarch oversaw the election in order to prevent irregularities. All the parishes and some monasteries in a *sestiere* were assessed to pay the master's salary and other expenses. For example, twelve parishes and one monastery in the *sestiere* of Cannaregio paid 4 to 18 ducats each for a total of 74 ducats in 1592. And fourteen parishes in the *sestiere* of San Marco paid 1 to 20 ducats each for a total of 114 ducats to support the master there in 1597. The teacher chose the *ripetitore* and paid him from his salary. The master might locate the school anywhere within the boundaries of the *sestiere*, with one exception. Patriarch Girolamo Querini (1524–55) decreed that the school for the *sestiere* of Castello must be located at the patriarchal cathedral church, San Pietro di Castello, at the extreme eastern tip of the city. Schools in the other *sestieri* might move about. Querini also reduced the number of *sestiere* church schools from six to five by combining the schools for the *sestieri* of Santa Croce and San Polo, the two smallest *sestieri* in area and population. The combined populations of Santa Croce and San Polo normally only equalled the population of one of the other four *sestieri*.[58]

Patriarch Francesco Vendramin (1605–19) slightly modified the organization of the *sestiere* church schools in 1613.[59] The pastors of each *sestiere* henceforth had to meet every second year to confirm or replace the incumbent teacher. Salaries were raised to one hundred ducats for the masters and twenty ducats for the *ripetitori*. Because teachers had complained about difficulties in collecting their salaries, the patriarch ordered pastors in each *sestiere* to choose a treasurer to collect and disperse funds. He also asked students to help pay the teachers' salaries, if they were able. Finally, the patriarch added visitations: two priests in each *sestiere* would visit the school monthly in order to ensure that the young clerics attended regularly and that the teachers followed curriculum directions.

In this way the hierarchy placed the training of boys intended for the priesthood on a systematic basis. The church viewed the boys somewhat as apprentices to the clerical life: they studied in school and assisted parish priests in their duties. Indeed, Patriarch Vendramin in 1613 ordered pastors not to impose on the boys to the extent that they would miss many

[58]Beltrami, 1964, pp. 72–73.
[59]Vendramin's rules are printed in Baldo, 1977, pp. 95–101.

classes.[60] The organization of the *sestiere* church schools exhibited the Venetian preference for local decision making and financial responsibility in church affairs. Just as Venetian householders elected parish priests, so the pastors chose a schoolmaster who would train their eventual successors. The approach ensured local participation and a supply of priests drawn from the community. At the same time, the local beneficiaries had to bear the costs. The *sestiere* church schools continued to educate future clergymen long after Trent decreed the establishment of seminaries.

All five *sestiere* church schools functioned in 1587. The school for the *sestiere* of San Marco enrolled 55 boys, that of Cannaregio 36 to 40 boys. The school for the *zaghi* of Dorsoduro had 30 pupils, and the masters of the other two schools gave no enrollment figures.[61] If the last two had at least 30 pupils each, the five *sestiere* church schools combined enrolled 185 or more in 1587. The teachers mentioned the ages of only two pupils, a boy of 6 and another of 8 or 9. The teaching program confirms that the majority of the students were aged 14 and under: it consisted of much grammar drill, the *Disticha Catonis* and Vives' *Colloquia* for beginning Latin reading, plus Vergil, Cicero's *Epistulae ad familiares,* and a little material from other classical texts. It was the standard Latin curriculum for the first six to eight years of school.[62] The pupils also studied the catechism, but they studied no additional religious works.[63] In short, the *zaghi* followed exactly the same humanistic curriculum as did lay students.

Masters aged 22, 24, 32, 55, and 70 taught in the church schools. All five were clerics of at least subdiaconate rank; the two youngest had been students at the patriarchal seminary. The 70-year-old master had held his post for four years; the tenure of the others is unknown. They did not mention any *ripetitori*. Although the posts were not reserved for the clergy, it appears that parents preferred that clergymen teach their sons. A lay teacher related that he had been the master of the church school for the combined *sestieri* of Santa Croce and San Polo five or six years previously, but that he had been forced to relinquish the post after six to eight months

[60]"Comettano che ogn'uno delli chierici attendi alla chiesa fin l'hora della scola; che poi ritenendone due per li servicii della chiesa gli altri vadino a scola, et questo facciasi per settimana o per giornata. . . ." As quoted in Baldo, 1977, p. 97.

[61]ACPV, "Professioni di fede," fols. 38ʳ–39ᵛ (Ioseph de Lanzonibus), 79ʳ–80ʳ (Iohannes Maria Bevilaqua), 129ʳ⁻ᵛ (Sanctus Pisens), 221ʳ–222ʳ (Iohannes Maria), 236ʳ–237ᵛ (Bernardinus de Ambrosiis); Baldo, 1977, pp. 48, 54, 58, 72, 74.

[62]The church schools followed the same curriculum as did other schools; see chs. 7–9 for a discussion of the Latin curriculum. Patriarch Vendramin's guidelines of 1613 continued the same syllabus: the *Disticha Catonis,* Vives, Aesop's *Fables,* Cicero's letters, Vergil's *Eclogues,* and Caesar's *Commentarii*. Baldo, 1977, p. 96.

[63]One master taught the *Christias* (1535), a vergilian Latin epic poem on the life of Christ by Marco Girolamo Vida (1485–1566). ACPV, "Professioni di fede," fol. 236ᵛ; Baldo, 1977, p. 75.

because some noble fathers did not wish to send their sons to him to be prepared for clerical careers.[64] His statement suggests that parents believed that a clergyman could better instruct their sons and, perhaps, help smooth the way for ecclesiastical preferment, a consideration never far from the minds of Venetian nobles sending their sons into the church.

Other boys intending to become clergymen did not attend schools reserved for them, but studied alongside lay students. A priest living in the church of San Basegio (Basilio) taught twenty pupils, including "all the zaghi" of that church, in his nearby school.[65] He did not say how many of the twenty were zaghi. Another priestly schoolmaster taught three zaghi from the local parish church and six to eight lay pupils.[66] A clerical tutor in a noble household also taught without payment a zago at the nearby church of San Vio.[67] A fourth clerical teacher taught, in addition to other pupils, a handful of zaghi at the Ospedale degli Incurabili, a place for the care of victims of syphilis and a center for much charitable work in which the zaghi may have participated.[68] A vernacular master taught singing to the zaghi of the church of Santa Maria Formosa.[69] This might have been a choir school or, perhaps, just a choir.

Finally, the two Venetian seminaries enrolled a number of boys below the age of 16. Only two seminary teachers are documented in 1587, the first a layman who taught Latin grammar, Vergil, and Cicero to twenty-four pupils at the ducal seminary.[70] He assigned composition exercises according to the capabilities of the students, but only agreement exercises to two little boys. The priest who taught Hebrew, mentioned earlier, was the other.[71] The two seminaries probably enrolled sixty or seventy pupils of pre-university age.[72]

Zaghi preparing for the clerical life comprised about 7 percent of the scholastic population. With the exception of those at the two seminaries, zaghi followed no predetermined ecclesiastical path in their preparation for ordination. They lived at home, attended a variety of schools, and studied

[64]"sono cinque o 6 anni ch'io hebbi le sestere S. croce [e] S. polo et de ho tenuto da 6 o otto mesi et padri alcuni gentellomini non volevano mandar i suoi fioli per aver dei zaghi, fu sforciato lasciar esse sestiere." Punctuation has been added. ACPV, "Professioni di fede," fols. 86ᵛ–87ʳ, Eneas Pucietus.

[65]Ibid., fols. 7ʳ–9ʳ, Iohannes Baptista Angaranus; Baldo, 1977, pp. 44–45.

[66]ACPV, "Professioni di fede," fols. 167ʳ–168ᵛ, Marcus; Baldo, 1977, pp. 64–65.

[67]ACPV, "Professioni di fede," fols. 220ʳ–221ʳ, Iohannes Vitus Lariza.

[68]Ibid., fols. 145ᵛ–146ᵛ, Emidius Lisius; Baldo, 1977, pp. 60–61, but without the details. On the Ospedale, see Pullan, 1971, pp. 233–38 et passim.

[69]ACPV, "Professioni di fede," fols. 12ʳ–13ʳ, Lionellus Pinus; Baldo, 1977, pp. 44–45.

[70]ACPV, "Professioni di fede," fols. 131ʳ–ᵛ, Gratia Maria Gratius; Baldo, 1977, p. 60.

[71]ACPV, "Professioni di fede," fols. 302ʳ–ᵛ, Sebastianus Taliapetra; Baldo, 1977, p. 78.

[72]The two seminaries had a combined enrollment of about 110 students in 1581 but seemed to be losing students. Hence, it can be estimated that they enrolled between 60 and 70 pupils aged 15 and younger in 1587. Tramontin, 1965, p. 375.

the same Latin humanistic curriculum that lay boys did. The custom of preparing for the priesthood outside the walls of a seminary predated the sixteenth century and endured long after Trent. Only after 1593 did a majority of priests (but not all) receive *some* seminary training in the diocese of Novara (adjacent to Milan), when a reforming bishop and follower of Carlo Borromeo led the diocese.[73] One suspects that far fewer priests received seminary training in unreformed dioceses. In Lyon, bishops did not require clerical aspirants to attend the seminary until the late seventeenth century.[74] And some candidates for the priesthood still completed all their studies in local Latin schools in eighteenth-century Spain.[75]

The close integration of church and society explains why future clergymen received the same education as laymen during the Renaissance: if church and lay society were two branches of one tree, the same education would serve both future lay leader and cleric. A humanistic education helped a priest to advance. Boys had to learn a great deal of Latin in order to enroll in a university and study canon law, a sure path to preferment. In similar fashion, popes and bishops, like princes and republics, wanted servants capable of drafting a letter in Ciceronian Latin or delivering an oration that followed the norms of classical rhetoric. However, the lack of formal religious content in humanistic education may have contributed to the neglect of spiritual matters characteristic of some parts of the Renaissance church. The education of priests did not change until the Jesuits and other teaching orders of the Catholic Reformation added prayer, religious devotions, and theological training to the humanistic curriculum when educating priests.

SESTIERE SCHOOLS

About 4 percent (circa 188 pupils) of students attended communal schools in Venice in 1587. The Republic moved toward communal education very slowly, over a long period. It began by supporting the education of individual civil servants for pragmatic reasons. For example, in 1336 it provided subsidies for some ducal notaries to attend school.[76] And in 1375 the state doubled the salary (from ten to twenty ducats) of another ducal notary attending school, on the grounds that his additional education would improve the operations of the chancery and that he had a wife and family to support.[77]

[73]Deutscher, 1981, p. 305.
[74]Hoffman, 1984, pp. 74–79.
[75]Callahan, 1984, p. 17.
[76]Rossi, 1907, p. 773.
[77]Bertanza and Dalla Santa, 1907, p. 138, September 1375(?).

In the following century the needs of the chancery led indirectly to the founding of a famous humanistic school. In 1443 the government chose a dozen boys at least 12 years old to serve as ballot boys in the Great Council. They gave out the balls used for voting, carried voting boxes, and generally made themselves useful to this large and fundamental organ of the Venetian government. Viewing these boys as future secretaries and notaries, the government made provision for their intellectual training by giving each a stipend of ten ducats with which to learn "grammar, rhetoric, and other subjects appropriate to the chancery and to write well."[78] The decree's mention of rhetoric confirmed that La Serenissima, like other city-states, wished its chancery officials to be humanistically trained. Since the Great Council met only on Sundays, the boys were expected to attend the school of their choice the rest of the week, paying the masters with the ten ducats provided.

Some boys, however, took the money but did not attend classes. So the Republic in 1446 created a school by appointing a master to teach these youths and others from the chancery "grammar, rhetoric, and other subjects." The master would live at or near Piazza San Marco and receive one hundred ducats, with the rent for his quarters to be deducted from his salary. The Republic reduced the stipends of each of the boys (now sixteen in number) by five ducats in order to help pay the master's salary. The government appointed Filippo di Federighino da Rimini, a citizen of Venice but not an important humanist, to be the first teacher. Thus the Scuola di San Marco began.

The Republic soon expanded the school. In 1453, 1457, and 1463, it increased the number of youths employed in the councils of government and eligible to attend the Scuola di San Marco. When the number reached fifty-three in 1486, the state reduced it to thirty.[79] The government added a second master in 1460 with the appointment of Gian Mario Filelfo to teach poetry, oratory, and history. This second lectureship then became a more advanced and distinguished post of humanities and Greek held by some major humanists, including George of Trebizond, Giorgio Valla, and Marco Musuro. These men helped the Scuola di San Marco earn an excellent humanistic reputation and a position of prominence in the eyes of contemporaries and future historians. Lesser figures normally held the

---

[78]"grammaticam, rethoricam et alias scientias aptas ad esercitium cancellarie ac bene scribere." As quoted from the original by Segarizzi, 1915–16a, p. 641. Segarizzi, 1915–16a, pp. 640–43; Della Torre, 1902, pp. 10–15; and Sforza, 1870, pp. 403–5, quote the acts of the 1440s and 1450s establishing the school. VC, Ms. P D C 2250/VIII, provides copies of important acts and appointment notices. Ross, 1976, is the indispensable guide through the complex story. Also see Paternoster, 1883, pp. 12, 14–16, 18; Labalme, 1969, pp. 96–106; Nardi, 1971, pp. 31–43, despite some errors; and Branca, 1973.

[79]Labalme, 1969, p. 100.

first lectureship, for grammar and rhetoric. They continued to fulfill the school's original purpose by training youths for chancery positions, as the appointment notices proclaimed.

The government remained content with this limited communal schooling for some time. Then, in the middle of the sixteenth century, at a time of heightened concern for the intellectual and spiritual life of the city during the tenure of Doge Francesco Donà (1545–53), the Senate went further. On 23 March 1551, it passed a comprehensive law to provide more schools. The preamble justified the measure in civic terms.

In every well-founded city, which by the grace of God and the prudence of our forefathers our city is, every effort must be made to train the young people in a praiseworthy manner in order that they do not rot through idleness, but growing up well-trained, they can be useful and an ornament to the Republic, to themselves, and to their families. Hence, there being in this our city a very thriving and most numerous youth, it must be arranged that they be given the opportunity to undertake the study of good letters so that, in this way, they can reach the desired end.[80]

But, the Senate continued, there is only one public professor of the humanities teaching at the Scuola di San Marco, quite far away for many pupils. Moreover, many youths cannot profit from his instruction for lack of teachers of *grammatica*,[81] "which is the foundation and beginning of all studies of letters." In order that all might earn, we order the Riformatori dello Studio di Padova (the magistracy which oversaw the University of Padua and Venetian intellectual life generally) to appoint "as soon as possible" four more "good and skilled professors of the humanities" to accompany the two existing ones, Francesco Robortello and Giovita Ravizza (Rapicio). Each of these four new humanists will receive salaries of up to two hundred ducats. Since Robortello already teaches at San Marco, Ravizza and the four new appointees should distribute themselves

---

[80]"In cadauna città bene instituta come per la gratia di Dio, et per la prudentia delli maggiori nostri è questa nostra, si deve poner ogni opera, che la gioventù di quella sia laudevolemente essercitata si che ella non si marcisca nell'ocio, acció che crescendo ben disciplinata, possa poi esser di utilità & ornamento alla Repubblica à se stessa et alli suoi. Onde essendo in questa nostra città una floridissima, et numerosissima gioventù, si deve procurare che li sia data commodità di far opera alli studij delli buone lettere; accio che per tal via possa pervenire à quel fine che si desidera." ASV, Senato Terra, R. 37, fols. 126ʳ⁻ᵛ. I have modernized the punctuation. The law can also be found, sometimes with minor orthographical changes, in various manuscripts, including VC, Ms. P D C 2250/VIII, document 17; and VM Ms. Italiani, Classe VII, 1847 (9617), fols. 264ʳ–265ᵛ. Baldo, 1977, pp. 102–3; and Boldrini, 1904, pp. 152–54, print it from manuscript sources.

[81]Although the city had numerous independent grammarians, it lacked communal grammarians, because the Scuola di San Marco offered only upper-level instruction. That is the meaning of this phrase.

through the other five *sestieri* of the city. The Riformatori must also appoint six new "maestri di grammatica," one for each *sestiere,* at sixty ducats per annum to teach grammar.

It is interesting to note that, earlier, the Senate had spoken of only one professor of the humanities, Robortello. The reason for the confusion is that the Senate saw Robortello teaching at a more advanced level than that at which Ravizza taught. The Senate wished to support four more humanists to teach standard Latin grammar and rhetoric, as Ravizza was doing. Indeed, Robortello spent much of his career at universities, and Ravizza did not. Robortello (Udine 1516–Padua 1567) taught at Lucca and Pisa before winning the humanities plus Greek lectureship at the Scuola di San Marco in 1549 at the high salary of 220 ducats. A few months after the Senate law of March 1551, he moved to the University of Padua, where he remained except for three years at the University of Bologna. He published a commentary on Aristotle's *Poetics* (1548) which ushered in the age of Italian literary criticism. He also published works in history and rhetoric.

Ravizza (Rapicio in Latin, 1476–1553) was born at Chiari, midway between Brescia and Bergamo. He had a career typical of successful communal masters. Beginning as a *ripetitore* at Chiari in 1493 at 30 ducats per annum, he became a master at Caravaggio in 1499, communal master at Bergamo from 1508 through 1523 with an initial salary of 75 ducats, communal master at Vicenza from 1524 to 1532 at 100, later 135, ducats, and moved to Venice with some kind of communal appointment in 1532. From 1538 he held the lower of the two lectureships at the Scuola di San Marco at 150 ducats, and in 1543 received Venetian citizenship. Ravizza published orations, a rhetorical work, poetry, psalm paraphrases, inaugural academic lectures, and a pedagogical treatise.[82]

The Senate would raise the money for the salaries of four new humanists and six grammarians through new taxes. It required all benefice holders to pay .5 percent of the income from benefices (whether once only or annually was not stated). Auction houses must assess buyers one soldo per ducat (that is, $\frac{1}{124}$ of the ducat of account) on the sale prices of buildings and goods.[83] The Senate also strongly urged, but did not require, the clergy to support the schools financially. In the eyes of the Senate, the clergy might put their money to better use by supporting the state *sestiere* schools, open to clerics and laymen alike, rather than church *sestiere* schools. The Senate concluded with a typically Venetian attempt to in-

[82]ASV, Senato Terra, R. 32, fol. 148r, which indicates that Boldrini, 1904, pp. 69–70, was slightly incorrect on the citizenship. Nevertheless, Boldrini, 1904, is the basic study; also see Mantese, 1964, pp. 758–59.

[83]The government issued further instructions for the collection of this money on 5 August 1552. ASV, Collegio, Notatorio, R. 28, fol. 112r.

volve neighborhood leaders in the fate of the schools. Visitation committees composed of two nobles and one citizen from each parish (*contrada*)
would urge the boys in their parishes to attend the schools and would visit
the schools. They must report their findings to the Riformatori dello
Studio di Padova and another magistracy. The Senate passed the law by a
vote of 133 in favor, 34 opposed, and 30 abstentions, substantial but not
overwhelming endorsement by Venetian legislative standards.

The 1551 law marked a much greater Venetian commitment to education at substantially higher cost than in the past. Indeed, the *sestiere* schools
offered free education.[84] In the past the Venetian government had proclaimed a civic vocational goal—training boys for the chancery—as the
justification for spending money on education. Now it added good morality, self-fulfillment, and the future health of the state. Although the Senate
opened the schools to all, it intended them mostly for the sons of nobles
and original citizens. The Senate wanted more communal schooling for
the elite because the Venetian constitution reserved all legislative and
executive offices to the nobility and most chancery posts to original
citizens. The Senate held the typical Renaissance republican belief that
only properly trained future leaders guaranteed the survival of the state.

Nothing is known about noble opinion favoring the communal *sestiere*
schools, largely because the records of Senate debates do not survive.
Nevertheless, one of the teachers at the Scuola di San Marco had broadly
hinted at the desirability of state support of education. In 1544 Ravizza
published his oration inaugurating the academic year 1543–44, *De praestantia earum artium quae ad recte loquendi, subtiliter disputandi et bene dicendi
rationem pertinent* (On the excellence of those arts which lead to correct
speech, subtle disputation, and good pleading).[85] Addressed to his students, the "young scribes of the Republic of Venice," the oration praised
the *studia humanitatis* as the keys to unlock the treasures of antiquity and the
indispensable means to carry on civic life. In the course of his praise of
grammar, Ravizza approved examples of state support for schools in the
ancient and medieval world. The great Julius Caesar had given Rome
grammarians, rhetors, and professors of all the liberal arts. The emperors
Antoninus Pius and Septimus Severus had supported grammarians and
rhetors from the public treasury and exempted them from taxes. Constantine had extended the policy of public support of education to the free
cities of Italy, that is, those not directly subject to imperial rule. The
emperor Charlemagne had encouraged schools. These examples of state
support for education by great rulers of the past, combined with repeated

---

[84]Although the 1551 law did not indicate whether or not students would pay fees, the
Senate in 1567 and 1578 explicitly forbade teachers to accept any payment from pupils. See
below.

[85]Ravizza, 1544. See Boldrini, 1904, pp. 97–102, for a summary.

declarations of the usefulness of education to society, pleaded for greater Venetian support of education.

Ravizza returned to the theme of state support for education with the publication of a pedagogical treatise, *De liberis publice ad humanitatem informandis* (On public education of children toward humanity), dedicated to Doge Francesco Donà and Marino Giustiniani, one of the three nobles who had proposed the law establishing *sestiere* schools to the Senate.[86] It carried the date of June 1551; clearly Ravizza published the treatise to mark the law of 23 March 1551. Most of the treatise elaborated a pedagogical blueprint full of practical details of curriculum, teaching practice, library, pupil deportment, and the physical facilities of a school. Ravizza even urged that the school provide a toilet for the pupils, the first mention of such a practical detail in Renaissance pedagogical literature.

In the last chapter, Ravizza discussed the responsibility of the government for education. He urged the city to promote the education of its people for moral reasons. In a well-constituted city (*in civitate bene morata*), the magistrates should make provision to educate the citizens from earliest childhood to despise vice and to pursue virtue. Learning "good letters" opened the way to every honest habit; even the crudest and most ignorant spirits (*rudes animos*) could learn from the sentences and examples of the ancients. This was the standard humanistic belief that *bonae litterae* produced good men, but with a major difference: Ravizza placed most of the responsibility for bringing about the desired end on the magistrates rather than on parents. He charged the magistrates with electing academically qualified and morally upright teachers. Magistrates must also ensure that no teacher had more pupils than he could handle. Finally, Ravizza wanted the city to establish a school visitation committee chosen by parents and relatives of the pupils to uncover problems in the schools. However, authority to dismiss teachers should remain in the hands of the magistrates.

Ravizza had held these beliefs for years; indeed, he had presented this same treatise under a different title to the communal government of Bergamo in 1523. It is likely that he had been urging these policies on his Venetian noble acquaintances for some time, and now seized the opportunity to publish his work.

Thus, the Venetian Senate committed itself to much greater communal education. It decreed the founding of an additional four humanities and six grammar schools, all free of charge to the pupils. The state would pay relatively generous salaries to the ten new masters. The Senate especially wished to expand communal education at the lower level, so that a student

[86]It was published in Venice, 1551, and reprinted in Ricci, ed., 1790, pp. 7–42, the edition used here. On the work and the circumstances, see Boldrini, 1904, pp. 40–59, 110–11; and Gerini, 1897, pp. 124–48.

might progress from a *sestiere* grammar school to the humanities schools, and finally to advanced instruction with Robortello at the Scuola di San Marco. Or the student would go on to the University of Padua. It was an ambitious program.

Unfortunately, the government did not live up to its commitment. The Riformatori dello Studio di Padova gave new meaning to the phrase "as soon as possible" by waiting several years before trying to make the new appointments. On 2 July 1556 the Riformatori wrote asking Robortello, now teaching at the University of Padua, for his recommendation for a master to fill a *sestiere* humanist post. Another letter, of 2 December 1557, spoke of four humanists for the *sestieri* to be appointed.[87] The letters did not describe these as replacement appointments. Eventually some humanists, but no grammarians, were appointed. What had happened?

A new Senate law of 4 November 1567 explained that the six grammarians had never been appointed because the funds raised for the purpose were insufficient.[88] Consequently, the humanist schools had borne little fruit: the lack of grammar schools had left the students unprepared for the next level. Hence, the Senate now decreed the establishment of four (rather than the original six) grammar schools to teach beginning Latin. The four humanists and four grammarians would teach together; that is, a humanist and a grammarian would teach in the same location "for the convenience of the pupils." The four schools, each with a humanist and a grammarian, would be scattered across the city, two on each side of the Grand Canal, to be accessible to all six *sestieri*. The Senate lowered humanists' salaries to 150 ducats but raised the grammarians' stipends to 80. It added 20 ducats for rent money, presumably for each of the four locations. The Senate explicitly forbade the teachers to accept payment of any kind from the pupils. Finally, the Senate laid down curriculum prescriptions. The humanist must teach a Ciceronian text, to be named by the Riformatori, in the morning, and Vergil, Terence, or Horace in the afternoon. Every week he must receive and correct a Latin epistle from each pupil. Grammarians would teach Donatus, Guarino's *Regulae,* and agreement exercises.

The law of 1567 finally implemented the *sestiere* school system. It also clarified the schools' status. The curriculum directions and the lowered salary for the humanists clearly indicated that these were primary and secondary Latin schools. The Senate then instructed the Riformatori dello Studio di Padova to select four grammarians and one humanist.[89] The

---

[87]These and other letters are found in ASV, Riformatori dello Studio di Padova, F. 63, no foliation.

[88]I cite the law from VC, Ms. P D C 2250/VIII, document 23. The vote was 147 in favor, 10 opposed, and 9 abstentions.

[89]ASV, Collegio, Notatorio, R. 37, fol. 17ᵛ, 2 November 1567.

appointments were of unlimited duration, although the Senate never stipulated this. Venetian *sestiere* teachers held on to their posts tenaciously except during the Great Plague of 1575–77. The government had to appoint four new humanists and two new grammarians between December 1575 and January 1580 to replace one teacher who had died and to fill another five unexplained vacancies.[90] Like many other Venetians, the five teachers had probably fled the city. The Republic's ability to find replacements even during the plague testifies to the posts' desirability.

Stability then returned and lasted well into the seventeenth century. Baldo Antonio Penna taught as an independent master in Venice from about 1564 until his appointment as *sestiere* humanist for Cannaregio in 1576, a post he still held in 1587. He claimed to have taught more than five thousand Venetians by that time.[91] Girolamo Bardi of Florence (b. circa 1549), a priest and monk of the Camaldolese Order of Hermits, was appointed humanist for the *sestiere* of Dorsoduro in February 1577 and still held that post in July 1587.[92] Lodovico Paolini began as grammarian for the *sestieri* of Santa Croce and San Polo circa 1580 and still held the post in 1600 or 1601.[93] Salaries remained at the level fixed by the Senate in 1567 through the 1640s, with minor variations. The *sestiere* masters tended to follow the pattern of other Venetian teachers in these decades: about half were non-Venetians, and the majority were priests.[94] But they were better educated than the majority of teachers: three humanists and one grammarian of the seven identifiable *sestiere* masters in 1578 held university doctorates.[95]

Additional instructions from the Senate in 1578 obligated each humanist to teach a lesson from Cicero's *Epistulae ad familiares* in the morning and Terence or a similar book in the afternoon. He must also assign and correct two letters or compositions from each student every week. The grammarian should teach the principles of grammar, including the declensions of nouns and conjugations of verbs. These were minimum requirements, however, which both humanists and grammarians considerably exceeded.[96] As time passed, the grammarians increasingly became assistants to the humanists. In 1614 the Riformatori dello Studio di Padova ordered the grammarian to come to school before the humanist and to remain after

[90]Ibid., R. 42, fols. 32ᵛ, 91ʳ, 100ʳ, 200ᵛ; R. 44, fol. 65ᵛ.

[91]Ibid., fol. 100ʳ; ACPV, "Professioni di fede," fols. 191ʳ–192ᵛ.

[92]ASV, Collegio, Notatorio, R. 42, fol. 200ᵛ, 16 February 1576 mv (=1577); ACPV, "Professioni di fede," fols. 302ᵛ–305ʳ; Baldo, 1977, pp. 78–79.

[93]See his undated (but 1600 or 1601) letter in ASV, Riformatori dello Studio di Padova, F. 419. Also see ACPV, "Professioni di fede," fols. 180ʳ–181ᵛ; Baldo, 1977, pp. 66–67.

[94]See a series of pay vouchers and other materials through 1654 in ASV, Riformatori dello Studio di Padova, F. 235 and F. 236.

[95]VM, Ms. Italiani, classe VII, 1847 (9617), fol. 263, "Copia tratta del Zornal de grammatici." Baldo, 1977, p. 104, first noticed and printed this document.

[96]ACPV, "Professioni di fede," passim, amply demonstrates this.

he left. The humanist would teach for two hours in the morning and another two hours in the afternoon. The grammarian must serve as his *ripetitore,* helping the students to recite and repeat the lessons taught by the humanist.[97]

A few *sestiere* masters pursued scholarly careers outside the classroom. Bardi, the humanist for Dorsoduro, was a historian who recounted the past glories of Venice. He published, in the vernacular, a universal history, the tale of the legendary but fictitious naval victory over the forces of Emperor Frederick I Barbarossa in 1177, and a study of the paintings in the ducal palace which narrated the triumphs depicted and the lessons to be learned. He also claimed in 1587 to be writing a history of the popes.[98]

Another *sestiere* humanist published extensively in Latin on medical and humanistic topics. Fabio Paolini (Udine 1535/44–Venice 1605), a clergyman, studied humanities, Greek, philosophy, and medicine at Padua, taking degrees in the last two. He practiced medicine in Venice before becoming a teacher circa 1580. He held the post of humanist for the *sestieri* of Santa Croce and San Polo in 1587. He later lectured on Greek at the Scuola di San Marco, lectured on Latin authors to the notaries' guild, and taught Greek and Arabic medical writers independently. His long list of publications included a commentary on Cicero's *De oratore* (published 1587) and his own *De doctore humanitatis* (1588), which drew a distinction between the true humanist, who mastered all the humanities, and the grammatical pedant of limited ability. Paolini also translated into Latin Aesop's fables (1587), commented on Vergil (1589), Thucydides (1603), Avicenna (1609), and Hippocrates (1604), and wrote a medical work, *De viperis* (1604).[99]

Sestiere humanists played other roles in the intellectual life of Venice. Two of them served as press censors. From 1562 on, each manuscript to be printed had to be read by three readers: the inquisitor or his designate, a public reader, and a ducal secretary.[100] Fabio Paolini censored books as public reader in the 1580s and 1590s, and Baldo Antonio Penna did the same in 1587.[101] Public readers received a fee for each manuscript based on the number of pages read.

Although open to all, the communal *sestiere* schools undoubtedly had

---

[97]The 1578 and 1614 prescriptions are found in VC, Ms. Cicogna 3160, no foliation, and printed in Baldo, 1977, pp. 105–6.

[98]"fo adesso scrivo le vite de Papi." ACPV, "Professioni di fede," fol. 303ᵛ; Baldo, 1977, pp. 78–79. Also see Bouwsma, 1968, pp. 224–27; and *STC Italian,* p. 71.

[99]ACPV, "Professioni di fede," fol. 170ᵛ; Liruti, 1780, pp. 353–72; Avesani, 1970.

[100]P. Grendler, 1977, pp. 151–58.

[101]"et son salariato da S. Marco nel sestier de canaregio ad condition de reveder i libri che vano in stampa che non ci sia cose contra la fede o contrario [?] i Principi. . . ." ACPV, "Professioni di fede," fol. 191ʳ, Penna. For Paolini, see P. Grendler, 1977, pp. 151n, 156.

more pupils from the nobility and original citizenry than from the ranks of commoners. Lodovico Paolini, grammarian for Santa Croce and San Polo, stated that he taught the sons of nobles, citizens, and commoners.[102] But in 1612, a *sestiere* humanist boasted that he taught the sons of the city's principal nobles and citizens.[103] The caste structure of Venetian society almost guaranteed that the sons of the city's political elite would benefit the most from free communal education.

The Venetian *sestiere* schools never realized their full potential because the government refused to fund them to the level of the original plan. Nevertheless, they lasted through the 1640s and probably beyond.[104] Like all communal schools in the Renaissance, they had a significance greater than their enrollment numbers. They manifested the state's interest in pre-university education and, to a limited extent, its leadership in curricular matters. Here, as in other towns and centuries, communal schools reflected the values of the state. Venetian state involvement in education shows that the patriciate viewed schools primarily as a training ground for civil servants and secondarily as a place to teach good morals and wisdom to future leaders.

[102]". . . appresso 100 scolari, cosi nobili et cittadini, come populari à quali tutti io insegnava gratis." ASV, Riformatori dello Studio di Padova, F. 419, undated letter of 1600 or 1601.

[103]Ibid., F. 168, undated letter of October 1612 of Don Gironimo Vendramin.

[104]I have followed their fortunes through 1650 but not beyond.

CHAPTER THREE

Florentine and Roman Schools in the High Renaissance

lmost all Italian cities and towns about which information is available had a mixture of independent, church, and communal schools in varying proportions between 1300 and 1600. These schools taught both the Latin and vernacular curricula. The Venetian data permitted a very close study of the distribution of pupils and teachers among the three kinds of schools and the two curricula, plus a calculation of estimated schooling and literacy rates. Although current knowledge does not permit such a comprehensive look at schooling in other important Italian cities, it invites comparisons of some aspects of their schools. Florence probably had schooling and literacy rates similar to those of Venice, while Roman communal and independent schools functioned much like those in other Italian cities. Roman communal authorities made a greater effort to certify and inspect the schools (but not the church schools) of the city. The similarities show that the schools of the High Renaissance displayed an overall unity through the northern half of the peninsula. The variations confirm their individuality and the importance of local conditions.

VILLANI'S STATISTICS OF 1338

In his famous passage describing Florentine schools circa 1338, the chronicler Giovanni Villani wrote: "We find that 8,000 to 10,000 boys and girls are learning to read. There are 1,000 to 1,200 boys learning abbaco in six schools. And those who study grammar and logic in four large schools are 550 to 600."[1] In other words, 9,550 to 11,800 boys and girls in a total

---

[1]"Troviamo ch'è fanciulli e fanciulle che stanno a leggere, da otto a dieci mila. I fanciulli che stanno ad imparare l'abbaco e algorismo in sei scuole, da mille in milledugento. E quegli che stanno ad apprendere la grammatica e loica in quattro grandi scuole, da cinquecentocinquanta in seicento." Villani, 1844–45, vol. 3, bk. 11, ch. 94, p. 324. In some editions this is ch. 93.

population of about 120,000 attended school.[2] If Villani's count is correct, 37 percent to 45 percent of the school-age population (ages 6 through 15) of both sexes attended school. Since so many more boys than girls attended formal schools outside the home, one must conclude that a large majority, probably nine-tenths, of the Florentine pupils were boys. Hence, Florence had a male schooling rate of 67 percent to 83 percent, according to Villani.[3] If so, Florence in 1338 educated boys at approximately three times the rate Venice did in 1587, and twice the rate Florence did in 1863–64.[4] If Villani's statistics are correct, Florence in 1338 had a male schooling rate probably higher than that in any other European town or city for centuries.

The way to test Villani's figures is to examine the individual parts of his statement in light of what is known. If the details that make up the whole fail to convince, then the whole fails.

Florence never had more than six active abbaco schools at any time between 1300 and 1500. The Florentine population precipitously dropped as a result of the Black Death and recurrent plagues, and the city had only three or four abbaco masters in the late fourteenth century and five or six in the middle of the fifteenth century.[5] Hence, Villani probably correctly counted the number of abbaco schools.

He vastly inflated the enrollments of the abbaco schools, however. Florentine abbaco schools enrolled 25 to 40 students each in the late Trecento and early Quattrocento, exactly what might be expected in a single school with one master, as abbaco schools were structured.[6] Venetian *combination* schools had average enrollments of 45 in 1587. Indeed, one Venetian combination school taught beginning reading and writing, Latin grammar, advanced vernacular reading, abbaco, and bookkeeping to 143 pupils aged 6 through about 14. The curriculum and age spread of the pupils of Venetian combination schools were far broader than those of Florentine abbaco schools. The latter taught only abbaco for about two

[2]Herlihy and Klapisch-Zuber, 1978, p. 176; Herlihy and Klapisch-Zuber, 1985, pp. 68–69. Their population estimate is a little higher than that of other historians. See Goldthwaite, 1980, p. 33.

[3]These school attendance estimates for 1338 are extrapolated from the distribution of the Florentine population by age and sex in 1427. In that year, boys aged 6 through 15 comprised 11.82 percent of the total population, and boys and girls combined made up 21.65 percent of the population (Herlihy and Klapisch-Zuber, 1978, pp. 660–63). Imposing these percentages on a Florentine population of 120,000 in 1338, one finds 14,184 boys, and 25,980 boys and girls combined, aged 6 through 15. Hence, the 9,550 to 11,880 boys and girls in school were 36.76 percent to 45.42 percent of the school-age population in 1338. If 90 percent of the students were male, then 8,595 to 10,620 boys aged 6 through 15, or 67.33 percent to 83.19 percent of the male population aged 6 through 15, attended school in 1338. Of course, these are only estimates.

[4]Fiumi, 1953, pp. 239–41, who rejects Villani's figures.

[5]Van Egmond, 1976, pp. 87–88.

[6]Ibid., pp. 105–6, on the basis of limited evidence.

years to boys between the ages of 10 or 11 and 13 to 15. Twenty-five to 40 students seems an appropriate number for this narrow, intensive training. Florentine abbaco schools with their limited curriculum and restricted age clientele could not possibly have enrolled as many as 200 students.

The enrollment figures for the four large grammar and logic schools raise similar doubts. Venetian independent Latin schools educating pupils of all ages had an average enrollment of 23 students in 1587; the largest had 55 to 60. Fifteen Genoese Latin schools for pupils of various levels of accomplishment, but mostly younger pupils, had an average enrollment of 31 students in 1501.[7] Upper-level Renaissance Latin schools, as the Florentine grammar and logic schools were, had even smaller enroll-ments, never upwards of 150 students. Villani's enrollment figures contra-dict the Renaissance pattern of one school, one teacher. That is, a school consisted of a teacher who taught, perhaps with the aid of a *ripetitore,* only as many students as he could handle. Renaissance teachers did not teach one class among many in a large building with several rooms until the religious order schools appeared in the late sixteenth century. Then Jesuit Latin schools teaching students of all ages and employing several teachers had enrollments of 150 and more students.[8]

Finally, Florence would have required an enormous number of teachers to make Villani's schools function, if one accepts Villani's enrollment figures. Florence would have needed 500 to 600 teachers to instruct 9,550 to 11,800 pupils, given the Italian pattern of single schools with relatively low teacher-student ratios.[9] Five or six hundred teachers would have left numerous traces in the city's archives. However, scholars have had diffi-culty locating a handful of teachers, a fact that casts grave doubt on the accuracy of these figures.[10] Even if Florentines valued education more

---

[7]Massa, 1906, pp. 320–27.

[8]Jesuit and other religious order schools had enrollments of 150 and more students, the bulk of them in elementary grades, in the second half of the sixteenth century and in the seventeenth century. See ch. 13.

[9]This is an extrapolation based on Venice in 1587, where 245 active teachers taught circa 4,625 pupils.

[10]If Florence had 500 to 600 teachers, pedagogy would have been the eighth- or ninth-largest occupation in the city in 1338. But this was not the case in 1427, a year for which information is available (Herlihy and Klapisch-Zuber, 1985, p. 128). Indeed, only 12 teachers, 2 of them abbaco masters, appeared in the Florentine *catasto* of 1427 (personal communication from David Herlihy). Even if many teachers were omitted from tax records because they lacked taxable assets or were tax-exempt clergymen, it is unlikely that 500 to 600 teachers could escape notice. A diligent search for Florentine teachers found only 27 abbaco masters in Florence between 1300 and 1500 (Van Egmond, 1976, p. 88). Clearly Florence had more teachers than the number documented, but not enough to support a pedagogical establish-ment of the size Villani described. But then, how many pupils did Florence have in 1338? A guess extrapolated from Venetian data suggests about 3,000, one-fourth to one-third the figure Villani conjectured.

highly than other Italians (a dubious assumption), Villani's figures cannot be correct.

FLORENTINE SCHOOLING IN 1480

Another set of documents makes possible an estimate of the Florentine male schooling rate in 1480, when the Florentine government ordered the preparation of a new *catasto,* a comprehensive survey of the persons and their status, the assets, and the liabilities of every household in Florence. Taxes were assessed on the basis of the *catasto.* The Florentine government had first used this system for raising revenue in 1427.[11] Now, in 1480, the government prepared for the last Florentine *catasto* with a new tax law, which demanded to know the occupation and annual salary of each masculine member of the household.[12] This encouraged heads of households to mention boys in school, because a student was an unproductive mouth to feed who drained money from the household through school fees. A household supporting students probably paid lower taxes.

The 1480 *catasto* provides a great deal of information about boys from the middle and lower ranks of taxpayers who attended formal schools outside the home. It offers less information on the schooling of the sons of the very wealthy, possibly because the few lire or florins spent on their education did not reduce the tax on households worth thousands of florins. Nevertheless, wealthy boys universally attended school: proof can be found elsewhere or inferred from other sources. The *catasto* declarations listed some, but probably not all, of the household tutors, and they omitted children learning informally from parent, sibling, or relative at home, because this information had no financial implication.[13] The *catasto* declarations omitted some younger students and made no mention of the education of girls. Communal officials demanded to know the value of a girl's dowry, not the content of her mind. Like society, the law assumed that a girl would not attend a formal school or earn a salary outside the home.

Despite its lacunae, the 1480 *catasto* furnishes a great deal of information about Florentine schooling in 1480, far more than the isolated bits from the 1427 *catasto.*[14] Armando Verde has published all the relevant parts of the 1480 *catasto* declarations which mention students or from which schooling can be inferred. An analysis of the declarations yields the accounting in table 3.1.

[11]On the *catasto,* see Roover, 1966, pp. 23–31; Herlihy and Klapisch-Zuber, 1978, chs. 2 and 3; Herlihy and Klapisch-Zuber, 1985, ch. 2.
[12]The following discussion is based on Verde, 1973–77, vol. 3:1005–10.
[13]Here is a rare exception: "Giovanni, legie la tavola in chasa; d'età d'anni 6." Ibid., p. 1042.
[14]Herlihy and Klapisch-Zuber, 1978, pp. 563–64.

Florentine schooling looks like a smaller version of Venetian schooling. Florentine boys between the ages of 4 and 17 studied reading and writing, Latin, and abbaco. Some followed the Latin curriculum, others the vernacular syllabus. A minority prepared to become clergymen. A noticeable feature of this picture of Florentine schooling is that more boys aged 10

TABLE 3.1
Florentine Boys in School, 1480

Age	Total in School	=	Alla scuola[a]	+	Leggere[b]	+	Abbaco[c]	+	Gram- matica[d]	+	Chierico[e]
4	5		5		0		0		0		0
5	23		16		7		0		0		0
6	41		29		11		1		0		0
7	82		48		34		0		0		0
8	61		36		22		2		0		1
9	86		38		42		3		0		3
10	121		59		48		12		1		1
11	129		41		45		38		1		4
12	154		43		50		52		6		3
13	122		30		18		58		5		11
14	96		26		15		41		4		10
15	58		18		5		28		3		4
16	30		6		3		9		2		10
17	13		3		0		6		1		3
18	4		1		0		1		0		2
No age given	6		4		0		2		0		0
Totals	1,031	=	403	+	300	+	253	+	23	+	52

Source: Verde, 1973–77, vol. 3:1011–1202. The count, the analysis, and the table are mine, however. Following Verde, I have tried to omit boys attending the Faculty of Rhetoric and Poetry, the Florentine university. Nevertheless, some 16-, 17-, and 18-year-olds counted in the table may have been university students. I have also omitted the four daughters, aged 12, 9, 7, and 5 (Alessandra), of Chancellor Bartolomeo Scala, who hired a male tutor for them (p. 1141).

[a]Such expressions as "va alla schuola," "alla isquola," "sta alla squola," meant that the boy attended school without indicating what kind of school. Occasionally a declarer called a school a bottegha: "Iachopo mio figliuolo sta alla bottegha a legiere; d'età di anni 12." Verde, 1973–77, vol. 3:1030.
[b]"Va a leggere," "istà a legiere," or "impara a scrivere e legere" usually meant learning to read and/or write, that is, early elementary schooling.
[c]Any reference to abbaco, such as "sta all'abacho" or "va all'abacho," meant that the boy attended an abbaco school.
[d]A mention of grammatica, such as "sta a 'mpara grammatica," meant that the boy studied in a Latin school. Of course, many more boys studied Latin than the twenty-three whose fathers used the term grammatica. A good number of boys who "va alla schuola," and possibly a few who "va a leggere," studied Latin. The declarations lack precision at times.
[e]Such statements as "cherico, va alla scuola," "sta per cherico," "è chericho e istudia," and "studia per essere prete" meant that a boy lived at home while he studied the Latin curriculum in order to become a clergyman.

through 14 were in school than younger boys. Part of this unbalance comes from the obvious underreporting of younger boys in school. Another aspect of Florentine education is that many boys aged 11 through 14 studied abbaco rather than Latin.

The schooling of Niccolò and Totto Machiavelli, viewed through their father's diary, brings the Florentine statistics to life.[15] On 6 May 1476, Bernardo wrote in his diary that Niccolò, born 3 May 1469 and just turned 7, had begun school with "Maestro Matteo, maestro di grammatica, sta a piè del ponte a Santa Trinità di qua, a imparare a leggere il Donatello." That is, Niccolò went to study with Master Matteo, whose school was located at the foot of the bridge of Santa Trinità, on the other side of the Arno, in order to learn Latin grammar. Bernardo agreed to pay Matteo della Rocca (d. 1480), a communal master listed on the university roll,[16] five soldi per month plus twenty soldi at Easter. On 5 March 1477, Niccolò changed schools; he began to study Latin grammar with an independent master named Batista di Filippo dalla Scarperia at a different location. Bernardo gave no reason for the change.

On 3 January 1480 Niccolò again switched schools, now studying abbaco with Maestro Piero Maria.[17] Bernardo agreed to pay "one large florin" (that is, a florin worth about six lire instead of four) for the entire abbaco course. On the same day, Niccolò's younger brother Totto, aged 5, began school in order to learn to read (imparare la tavola, the ABC primer), presumably with another teacher. Niccolò began the abbaco course at the age of 10 years and 8 months and completed it twenty-two months later, when he was 12 years and 6 months old. Then, on 5 November 1481, Niccolò and Totto, the latter now about 6 years and 10 months old, went to study with another communal Latin master, Paolo da Ronciglione.[18] Niccolò studied the Latin classics (Nicolò fa de' latini), and Totto studied Latin grammar (Totto impara il Donato). Bernardo recorded a payment of nine soldi eight dinari "for the fire" (to heat the school) and a tip of six soldi for the teacher.

Another Florentine boy followed a similar scholastic path with less happy results. Guerrieri dei Rossi, born in 1485, went to school to learn to

---

[15]For excerpts from Bernardo Machiavelli's diary and some explanations, see Verde, 1973–77, vol. 2:535–37.

[16]Ibid., pp. 488–89.

[17]This may have been Piero Maria Calandri (1456–after 1519). Van Egmond, 1976, p. 407; Van Egmond, 1981, p. 96.

[18]See Verde, 1973–77, vol. 2:535–36. Two final comments on Machiavelli's education. First, Verde believes that he must have learned some Greek because humanistic schools always included Greek. The evidence suggests the opposite, that they seldom included Greek. Second, although no evidence exists that Machiavelli enrolled in a university, it seems likely that he would at least have audited some lectures on the classics at the Florentine faculty of rhetoric and poetry.

read at the age of 4 years and 4 months. He also studied writing, elementary arithmetic, and Latin grammar with two other teachers and a *ripetitore* in the next five years. His father sent him to abbaco school when he reached 9 years and 7 months. He left at the age of 13 years and 7 months to work for a merchant. When Guerrieri was fired eight months later, his father tried to send him back to abbaco school, but the boy refused. His father found another job for him, which lasted until the authorities arrested him on an unspecified morals charge. Guerrieri died at the age of 19.[19]

Giannozzo Manetti (1396–1459) offered a happy contrast. He learned vernacular reading and writing, but little or no Latin, then studied abbaco, which he mastered in a few months. At the age of 10 he began work at a bank. After a few months he took charge of the *cassa,* that is, petty accounts, and went on to a successful career as a merchant. But at the age of 25, he left it for letters, beginning with an intensive study of Latin grammar followed by the classics. He succeeded in becoming a major humanistic scholar.[20]

These and other examples highlight a difference between Florentine and Venetian schooling. While Venetian boys learned abbaco over a period of years in combination schools teaching vernacular reading and writing, a little Latin grammar, plus abbaco and bookkeeping, Florentine boys learned abbaco in intensive courses lasting about two years.[21] They normally did this between the ages of 11 and 15; this partially explains the age distribution of Florentine abbaco students in table 3.1. Machiavelli interrupted his Latin studies for an abbaco school and then returned to the Latin curriculum. Other Florentine boys went directly from the abbaco school into an apprenticeship or the work force.

Approximately 28 percent of boys aged 10 through 13 attended formal schools in Florence in 1480.[22] This figure can be extended to the entire age cohort 6 through 14, because a boy could not study abbaco or Latin at 12

[19]Klapisch-Zuber, 1984, pp. 766–68.
[20]See *Commentario della vita di Messer Giannozzo Manetti* by Vespasiano da Bisticci, in Garin, ed., 1958, p. 297. See Edler, 1934, p. 18, for other Florentine boys who studied abbaco.
[21]Goldthwaite, 1972. For more on abbaco, see ch. 11 herein.
[22]Florence had a population of about 41,590 in 1480 (Herlihy and Klapisch-Zuber, 1978, p. 183; Herlihy and Klapisch-Zuber, 1985, p. 74). We do not know what percentage of the population consisted of boys aged 10 through 13, because the 1480 *catasto* has not been studied for demographic purposes. However, 4.49 percent (1,660) of the Florentine population in 1427 consisted of boys aged 10 through 13 (Herlihy and Klapisch-Zuber, 1978, pp. 660–63). If this masculine age cohort composed 4.49 percent of the population in 1480 as well, there were 1,867 boys, of whom 526 were in school. Hence, 28.2 percent of Florentine boys aged 10 through 13 attended formal classes in 1480. Demographic patterns in 1480 and 1427 may have differed; nevertheless, this is the best available comparison. The reader is reminded again that Renaissance schooling and literacy rates noted herein and elsewhere can only be informed estimates.

unless he had learned to read and write earlier. The schooling rate should be increased slightly to take into account schoolboys not counted in the *catasto* plus those who learned through informal tutoring. A somewhat conservative overall literacy (reading and writing) estimate of 30 percent to 33 percent seems reasonable for the Florentine male population in 1480. Thus, Florence in 1480 and Venice in 1587 shared similar male schooling and literacy figures.

ROMAN SCHOOLS

An analysis of schooling in Rome further illuminates the educational picture in the High Renaissance. Ruled by a clerical monarch, Rome derived its importance and much of its income from its position as the capital and administrative center of an international church. Although differing from Venice and Florence in almost every way, Rome had the same mixture of communal, independent, and church schools. Indeed, it had more communal schools than the two commercial republics, which relied overwhelmingly on independent schools.

Rome's communal teachers, the *maestri dei rioni*, taught in the administrative districts (*rioni*) of the city. The city government appointed and paid the *maestri dei rioni* through the university. The origins of the *maestri* are unknown. Boniface VIII may have established them when he founded the Studium Urbis, the University of Rome, in 1303, but nothing is known until 1458. In that year a *maestro del rione* petitioned the pope for an increase in salary.[23] *Maestri* then appeared on the earliest extant payment records of the Studium. Those of 1473–74 list payments to twenty-two *maestri dei rioni*. However, twenty-two *maestri* may not have taught simultaneously—some masters may have replaced others during the year. The records of 1482–84 list payments to fourteen.[24] By the sixteenth century, the number of *maestri dei rioni* had stabilized at thirteen, one for each of the thirteen *rioni* in the city. In 1514 the first extant roll of the University of Rome listed the names of ten *maestri* and their *rioni*, plus three vacancies to be filled.[25] Each *maestro* earned fifty florins. When Pius IV added the *rione* of Borgo Pio in the 1560s, the number of *maestri dei rioni* rose to fourteen.[26]

In the early sixteenth century, two Roman teachers escaped anonymity through their poetry. Giulio Simone Siculo, *rione* master for Trastevere, won a university lectureship in rhetoric for feast days and holidays in 1513 because his Latin verses pleased Leo X.[27]

[23]Pelliccia, 1985, pp. 52, 429–30.

[24]Chambers, 1976, pp. 68–69, 75–76, 78–79, 89–102; Dorati da Empoli, 1980, pp. 142–45; Lee, 1984, p. 145.

[25]Printed in Renazzi, 1803–6, vol. 2:239; also see vol. 2:34–35, 78.

[26]Ibid., p. 138.

[27]Gnoli, 1938, p. 364.

Another teacher, however, earned immortality through "his" Latin verses. Shortly after 1500, schoolboys began to hang humorous and mistake-ridden Latin verses on a battered ancient statue in the center of Rome on the feast day of St. Mark the Evangelist, the twenty-fifth of April. They named the statue for a schoolmaster, who may have been unpopular, living a few feet away. Before long the practice became a minor spring academic festival, as passers-by came to read, laugh at, and copy the best and worst of the schoolboy efforts. At the end of the feast day, schoolboy hordes stoned the poor schoolmaster statue who "wrote" such bad Latin verse. Others imitated the students. Before long this statue and another "wrote" and held up to public gaze barbed political comments, gossip, and attacks on high officials all year long. In 1509 an enterprising Roman printer collected and published the year's verses, attributing his volume to *Mastro Pasquino,* the statue.[28] Annual volumes preserving as many as three thousand lines of the year's most pungent poetry followed. And "pasquinade" became a part of Western culture and language. The fate of the luckless teacher who gave his name to the genre is unknown.

Aside from the scholastic high jinks of *Mastro Pasquino,* the *rione* schools probably rose and fell with the University of Rome through most of the first half of the sixteenth century, because funds to pay the salaries of the *maestri dei rioni* came from the same city tax on imported wine which supported the university. Unfortunately, academic fortunes were often bad.[29] The Studium closed during the Sack of Rome in 1527 and did not reopen until circa 1539. The operations of the *rione* schools very likely were tied to the functioning of the university.

The *rione* schools received a boost in 1543 when the city government vowed to make a greater effort to educate Rome's youth. *Rione* leaders (*caporioni*) lamented that few students profited from studies because of the inadequacy (*poca sufficienza*) of the schoolmasters; they resolved to elect "learned and good men [to be] masters of the schools of the rioni."[30] The 1548 university roll, the first extant after 1514, set aside 700 florins—50 for each of twelve *maestri dei rioni,* and 100 for the master of the *rione* of San Eustachio, a senior teacher with undefined supervisory authority over the others.[31] The continuous existence of the *maestri dei rioni* can be documented from this date.

The *maestri dei rioni* survived a grave threat at mid-century. On 22 February 1551, the Society of Jesus opened the Collegio Romano, the famous school that became the heart of Catholic intellectual renewal. The

[28]Ibid., pp. 166–76.

[29]Ibid., pp. 363–64; Renazzi, 1803–6, vol. 2:90, 95.

[30]ASCR, Registro di Decreti di Consiglio e Magistrati e Cittadini, Credenzone I, vol. 36 (1515–57), fol. 444ᵛ, 8 October 1543. Pecchiai, 1948, pp. 393–94, quotes the essential phrases. However, he incorrectly believes that this act marked the beginning of the *maestri dei rioni.*

[31]It is printed in Renazzi, 1803–6, vol. 2:248.

sign over the door of the Collegio Romano made the threat plain: "Schola [*sic*] de Grammatica, d'Humanità e Dottrina Christiana, gratis." Whereas the *rione* schools extracted fees from most students, and independent masters charged all, the Collegio Romano taught for free. Its enrollment quickly grew. The acutely unhappy *maestri dei rioni* and independent masters vented their anger by breaking into the Collegio Romano and disrupting classes in January 1552. They also attacked the Jesuits as too ignorant to teach. The latter responded by issuing a challenge to a disputation. In October 1552 Jesuit instructors and *maestri dei rioni* disputed for three days in grammar, rhetoric, Greek, and Hebrew. According to contemporary accounts written by Jesuits, the Jesuits routed the *maestri dei rioni*.[32]

Routed and threatened with the loss of livelihood, the *maestri dei rioni* and independent masters, nevertheless, survived because the Jesuits changed pedagogical direction. Although initially intending to teach all ages, levels of preparation, and social classes, the Jesuits soon concentrated on more advanced students, clerics, and the wealthy. From its founding, the Collegio Romano admitted only students who already could read and write and, preferably, had begun Latin.[33] This threshold still admitted too many weak students or students whose parents lacked commitment to their sons' education, in the eyes of the Jesuits. The instructor of the lowest class (elementary Latin grammar), complained in 1557 that his students frequently missed two or three days at a time.[34] The majority of parents were poor, and they cared little about their children's lack of progress, he lamented. The founding in 1552 of the Collegium Germanicum, a Roman residence for wealthy German and Italian boys aged 14 and older, channelled more attractive students to the Collegio Romano.[35] The Jesuits raised the minimum age and proficiency required for admission to all their schools and tacitly resolved to attract a majority of wealthy, upper-class students. The Collegio Romano became more and more a secondary- and university-level institution whose teachers concentrated on philosophy and theology.

In the end, Roman teachers and the Collegio Romano served different constituencies. The *maestri dei rioni* and independent masters taught ABC beginners, elementary Latin students, a few advanced students, and those

---

[32]Villoslada, 1954, pp. 19–24, 26–28; Tacchi Venturi, 1951, vol. 2, pt. 2, pp. 378–82.

[33]MP, vol. 1:95 (n. 3), 285, 526, 530, 537–38, 558, 575.

[34]"Maestro Renato dice che li suoi discepoli vano male, perché molti stano dui tre giorni che non vengano alla schola, et perché li parenti delli più sono poveri, non hano cura delli suoi figliuoli." MP, vol. 2:429.

[35]Tacchi Venturi, 1951, vol. 2, pt. 2, pp. 385–93; Scaduto, 1974, pp. 325–33; MP, vol. 1:111, vol. 2:874, 938, 966. There is a great deal of additional information on the Collegium Germanicum in MP, vol. 2:318–419, 799–1004.

who wanted to learn vernacular reading and abbaco. Although teaching these students was less rewarding intellectually and financially, such students existed in large numbers. Undoubtedly the Roman independent and *rione* masters lost some wealthy and advanced students, especially those wishing to become clergymen, to the Collegio Romano. But they may have retained others who did not wish to undergo the rigorous and rigid Jesuit program.

The Roman teachers made their peace with the Collegio Romano. By 1557 they were attending classes there. A Jesuit instructor wrote that various adults, including "public and private teachers" ("maestri publici et privati"), attended his afternoon class on Cicero, Caesar, and the poets. The teachers tended to leave after the lecture; if they stayed, they did not want to be questioned in class or to have their compositions corrected publicly. The Jesuit obliged by correcting their compositions with them in private.[36] One can imagine that the Roman teachers feared that news of their mistakes would get back to students and parents to cause ridicule and student defections. Still, the teachers' presence at the free classes of the Collegio Romano showed their eagerness to learn.

The city government required the *maestri dei rioni* to educate the poor children of the *rione* for free, but permitted the *maestri* to impose fees on other students. The origin of the obligation is unknown because of the lack of early records. Nor is it known how many poor children a *rione* teacher taught or was expected to teach. Nevertheless, this aspect of communal education generated a good deal of controversy. The city government expected the *maestri dei rioni* to teach the poor without charge in exchange for their salaries. Some *maestri* believed that the government did not pay them adequately for teaching the poor, and they evaded the obligation. Without poor students, they had more room for fee-paying pupils. Parents, who viewed free education as a limited right, then protested to the government over its loss.

An official report of the 1560s argued that the failure of *maestri dei rioni* to teach the poor without charge came from their low salaries. The "poverissimi" *maestri dei rioni* lacked sufficient income even to pay the rent on their school quarters. To make up the difference, the *maestri* demanded fees from the poor students, who, unable to pay, dropped out. The report recommended that the government give the *maestri dei rioni* supplementary funds to pay the rent on their schools. In return, the *maestri* should be

---

[36]"Et perché in questa classe vengono huomini et massime maestri publici et privati, li quali si partono fornita la lettione, o se restano, non vogliono essere publicamente interrogati, né mostrare le compositioni, ma questo vogliono far in privato, se gli deve offerire, et esortarli che lo faccino come vogliono, perché cosi se mantengono." The writer is Ioannes Roger (c. 1522–79), who taught various courses at the Collegio Romano. MP, vol. 2:431, and vol. 2:463 for the same in the academic year 1561–62.

required to teach gratis all students in the *rione* who produced certificates of poverty signed by their parish priests.[37]

The financial recommendation probably went unheeded, because the issue erupted again in 1610. By this date the law clearly stated that each of the fourteen *maestri dei rioni* must "teach for free all the poor in his *rione.*"[38] But parents charged that some *maestri dei rioni* ignored their obligation: one located his school outside the *rione;* another wandered about the city instead of teaching; and a third concentrated on his singing career. How can the poor learn under such circumstances? they asked. "Poor widows and other destitute persons" had as their only alternative sending their "poorly clothed" (*mal vestiti*) offspring far across the city to the distant free school of the Piarist Fathers.[39]

The *maestri dei rioni* presented their side of the issue. They acknowledged that "poor widows" and "families burdened with debts" could pay only small fees "and rarely." But the *maestri* received only thirty scudi per annum, which barely paid the rent of their schools; they begged for higher salaries.[40] The government did not raise their salaries,[41] and some *maestri* continued to ignore the obligation to teach the poor.

The problem remained insoluble because of the attitude of the leaders of Renaissance cities toward education for the poor. Rome made a greater effort to educate the poor than other cities: it funded fourteen schools distributed across the city and insisted that they teach the poor. But the commune educated the poor for charitable motives, not because it saw educating them as an obligation or a contribution to the public good. Moreover, the commune insisted that poorly paid *maestri dei rioni* teach the poor. The commune's leaders refused to accept that they were asking the

[37]ASVa, Miscellanea Armadio XI, 93, fols. 34ʳ–35ᵛ, "Considerationi per la congregatione del Studio." The unsigned and undated report is addressed to the congregation of cardinals charged with overseeing the university. Internal evidence suggests a university official as author and the 1560s as the date.

[38]"Fuor dello Studio ci sono li Maestri di Rioni in numero 13 li quali sono obbligati leggere, et insegnare gratis à tutti li poveri del suo Rione, hanno di provisione ciascheduno Scudi 30 l'anno, mà il Decano Scudi 40." From an anonymous *relazione* of 1623 on the university in ASR, Archivio della Università di Roma, R. 83, fol. 26ʳ.

[39]See two petitions of 1610 in ibid., R. 71, fols. 9ʳ, 10ʳ. The second petitioner lived in Rione Campitelli, near the Tiber River, perhaps 800 to 900 meters distant from the Piarist school at San Pantaleo. See ch. 13 for the Piarist schools (Scuole Pie).

[40]Petition of "Li quattrodici maestri de' Rione di Roma" to the pope, 1610, in ibid., R. 71, fol. 13ʳ.

[41]Several sources confirm that the *maestri dei rioni* received thirty scudi and the deacon forty through the first half of the seventeenth century. See ASCR, Registro di Decreti di Consiglio e Magistrati e Cittadini, Credenzone I, vol. 31 (1600–1611), pp. 282–84, 16 January 1610. For the salaries in 1628, 1630, 1640, and 1646, see ASR, Archivio della Università di Roma, R. 94, "Delle Copie dei Ruolli . . . dal 1539 fino al 1783," fols. 71ʳ–72bisʳ, 85ʳ, 152ʳ, 191ʳ. Many rolls are missing.

maestri dei rioni to act against their own interests. Nothing changed as long as the leaders of society saw educating the poor—indeed, educating the bulk of the population—as optional paternalistic charity toward the lower classes that were denied a significant role in the life of the commune. A different attitude only evolved in later centuries.

COMMUNAL SUPERVISION OF ROMAN SCHOOLS

In the first half of the seventeenth century, the Roman commune anticipated the future; it began to bring communal and independent schools under the supervision of the state.

The commune began to examine and certify teachers for competence, the first such exercise in Italy. The rector of the University of Rome and later the senior *rione* master (called the deacon) began in 1614, or slightly earlier, to examine teachers.[42] The examiner issued printed licenses testifying that the named teacher possessed good character, that he had made his profession of faith, and that he was competent to teach various subjects. Every year seventy to eighty-five instructors underwent examination. Members of the regular clergy, such as the Jesuits and Piarist Fathers teaching in schools of their orders, did not need to submit to examination. Some household tutors, *ripetitori,* and a few others also skipped the examination, perhaps to avoid paying the fee. But all other teachers, especially the independent and *rione* masters who drew their students from the general public, underwent certification.

The permissions to teach show that Roman schools, like those in other Italian cities, taught the Latin and vernacular curricula, albeit in proportions different from those elsewhere. A substantial number of elementary teachers taught reading and writing only (*arti legendi et scribendi*). The largest group of masters were licensed to teach "reading, writing, and Latin" ("legendi, scribendi, atque grammaticam docendi facultatem"). The examiner sometimes reduced this to "reading, writing, and introductory Latin" ("legendi, scribendi et prima rudimenta grammaticae"). A few teachers were permitted to add the more advanced humanities to the standard reading, writing, and Latin: "ac humanitatem docendi." One teacher passed an examination in "grammaticam, humanitatem, et rheto-

---

[42]The documents hint that the teacher examinations may have begun two or three years before 1614; they continued through the century. The licenses to teach (called *patenti*) were small printed forms with places for the name of the teacher, the subjects that he might teach, and the date to be filled in. The rector sometimes threatened to punish those who failed to undergo examination, but the documents offer no clues about the form and content of the examination. This and the following two paragraphs are based on the *patenti* and other documents in ASR, Archivio della Università di Roma, R. 71, fols. 23ʳ–411ᵛ. Rome's population varied between 99,000 and 126,000 in the first half of the seventeenth century (Cerasoli, 1891), but not enough information is available to estimate the schooling rate.

ricam."[43] And one learned teacher, a Spoleto priest serving as chaplain at a
Roman church, wished to open a school in his rooms to teach reading,
writing, abbaco, Latin, and Greek. He passed examinations in all.[44]

All the above masters taught the Latin syllabus, much as their colleagues in other cities did. Only a handful of Roman teachers obtained
licenses to teach abbaco, and then only in conjunction with other subjects.
Of course, permission to teach such elementary mathematical functions as
addition, subtraction, multiplication, and division may have been tacitly
included with licenses to teach reading and writing. But no Roman master
obtained a license to teach bookkeeping. Roman schools offered little
abbaco education beyond that found in the Scuole Pie (see ch. 13). It
appears that Roman schooling reflected the city's character, and Rome was
a curial rather than a commercial city.

The effort to bring schools under state supervision continued in 1646
when the rector of the university ordered the deacon of the *maestri dei rioni*
to inspect "all the schools of Rome." The deacon did not visit the religious
order schools or household tutors, however. As might be expected, he
found a few teachers incapable of maintaining discipline in the classroom.
More important, he discovered that four *maestri dei rioni* deceptively
evaded their obligation to teach the poor for free. One *maestro del rione* had
divided his school sign into two parts: a clearly visible lower half, which
listed the subjects taught, and an almost invisible upper half, containing
the obligatory "pro regione gratis," tucked away near the roof.[45]

After the inspection, the rector of the University of Rome promulgated
comprehensive regulations for the conduct of Roman schools.[46] All teachers, including substitutes and *ripetitori,* had to be certified and to make
professions of faith. Lay teachers had to be at least 30 years old; no
minimum age was required of priests. The *maestro del rione* had to teach all
the poor of the *rione* who presented certificates of poverty from their parish
priests. He might establish his school anywhere in the *rione.* Independent
masters had to locate their schools at least 100 *canne* (rods of about 2 meters;
hence, about 650 feet) distant from the *rione* school and 40 rods (about 260
feet) beyond the next independent school. All teachers were forbidden to
steal each other's students under pain of the loss of the license to teach.

Several regulations imposed norms of good behavior and pedagogical
conduct on all teachers. The rector would warn any teacher whose immoral behavior scandalized his students or the public. If the teacher
persisted in his immorality, he would lose his school. A teacher might not

[43]ASR, Archivio della Università di Roma, R. 71, fol. 65ʳ, 23 January 1618.
[44]Ibid., fol. 300ʳ, 20 January 1648.
[45]Ibid., fols. 295ʳ–296ʳ. He did not say how many schools were inspected. In November
and December 1651, the deacon inspected seventy-one schools. Ibid., fols. 329ʳ–338ʳ.
[46]Ibid., fols. 297ʳ–299ʳ. Also see Pelliccia, 1985, pp. 456–58.

leave his school in order to take his pupils around Rome during school hours; nor could he teach prohibited or "worldly" (*profani*) books. He must not enroll adults or pupils who disrupted the classroom. All teachers had to examine their students on the catechism once a week and take them to confession once a month. The 1646 regulations concluded by promulgating a fee schedule to be followed by all teachers.[47]

For reading the alphabet or primer: 15 soldi per month

For reading smoothly syllable by syllable: 20 soldi

For simple reading and writing: 30 soldi

For declining and conjugating: 40 soldi

For learning arithmetic for accounting: 50 soldi

For Latin from the beginning of active verbs through all the rules: 50 soldi

For learning any lesson on Cicero or other authors: 60 soldi

Teachers did not become wealthy on this fee schedule. Giovanni Battista Papirio taught twenty-eight boys in his independent school near Piazza Navona in 1636.[48] Had he been teaching ten years later, he would have earned the following monthly amounts: 60 soldi from four boys learning the alphabet, 220 soldi from eleven boys who were syllabizing, and 300 soldi from ten boys learning to read and write. One pupil had begun to conjugate and decline (40 soldi), and another did more advanced Latin grammar and simple reading (50 soldi). Only one boy did more advanced work, studying Cicero's *Epistulae ad Atticum* (60 soldi). Hence, the teacher would have earned 730 soldi per month, which amounted to 60 scudi in an academic year of eleven months or 70 in twelve months.

These regulations indicate that the city of Rome in the first half of the seventeenth century exercised closer supervision of the city's schools than earlier Renaissance governments had. Communes of the fourteenth, fifteenth, and sixteenth centuries oversaw communal schools but ignored the rest. The Catholic Reformation alone does not explain the closer Roman state supervision, because the supervision was lay rather than ecclesiastical, and more concerned with academic accreditation than with

---

[47]"Tassa che devono pagare li scolari anticipatamente alli mastri per la loro mercede.

Per leggere l'alfabeto, seu Santa Croce ogni mese 15.

Per leggere compitando, et scorrendo 20

Per leggere e scrivere semplicemente 30

Per diclinare, e cogniugare 40

Per impare l'abbaco in scriptis 50

Per latinare tanto dalla prima delli attivi quanto di tutte le regole 50

Per intendere alcuna letione di Cicerone o altri Autori 60."

Although no monetary unit is given, it must be soldi. Ibid., fol. 299ʳ.

[48]Ibid., fol. 144ʳ, 10 April 1636. The listing of exactly what each pupil was studying makes this document unusual. The Roman scudo was worth about sixty soldi at this time.

moral behavior. Seventeenth-century governments exhibited paternalistic concern for all their subjects, so long as people did not try to climb up a rigid social ladder. Limited seventeenth-century state supervision of schools pointed to the eighteenth-century Enlightenment, when the state strongly intervened in the name of school reform.

The same Roman mixture of *rione,* independent, and church schools continued to the fall of the papal state, with one major difference: many more girls attended school by the middle of the nineteenth century. The Italian census of 1871 revealed a literacy rate of 57 percent (both sexes) in the Roman population of 248,000, a rate considerably above the 31 percent literacy rate for Italy as a whole at that time.[49]

[49]Casalini, 1932, p 19.

CHAPTER FOUR

Girls and Working-Class Boys
in School

 limited number of girls plus some boys from artisan backgrounds attended school. Female teachers, another minority,
helped teach. These were exceptions in a school organization
designed to serve upper- and middle-class males.

WHAT SHOULD GIRLS LEARN?

Leonardo Bruni (1370–1444) addressed his humanistic manifesto *De
studiis et litteris liber* (written 1423–26) to a noble lady, Battista Malatesta.
Bruni argued that a girl should study the ancient classical and Christian
authors in order to learn grammar, rhetoric, poetry, history, moral philosophy, and how to become virtuous.[1] Bruni omitted only public oratory
and disputation, considered unbecoming and impractical for women.
Otherwise, his program followed exactly the *studia humanitatis* proposed
to and followed by boys in the Latin curriculum.

Ludovico Dolce (1508–68), a prolific vernacular author, offered a
nuanced view of female education which took into account different social
levels and roles in his *Dialogo della institutione delle donne* (1545).[2] Dolce
rejected what he termed the common opinion of the majority, who viewed
learned women with suspicion because they believed that learning led to
loss of chastity. He offered numerous examples of ancient and modern
learned women. Girls should read "little holy books" ("libretti santi") full
of good teaching, and write down good precepts, always in the vernacular.
But women did not have to learn as much as men. A man must learn many

[1]Baron, ed., 1969, pp. 5–19; and the English translation in Bruni, 1987, pp. 240–51. For
the date, see Baron, 1966, p. 554 n. 23.

[2]At least five editions (1545, 1547, 1553, 1559/60, and 1622) are known. I cite Dolce, 1559,
pp. 12ᵛ–19ᵛ. The work is not original, because Dolce rewrote Juan Luis Vives' *De institutione
feminae christianae* (1523) for an Italian audience and conditions. Dolce lacks a modern
biography.

subjects so that he can act for the good of the republic, his prince, and his friends. A woman ruled only herself, her children, and her home. She will not teach school or "dispute," that is, participate in an academic disputation.

Dolce made an exception for the woman who must "govern a kingdom." She should learn the whole Latin humanistic curriculum, including history and "all of Cicero." On the other hand, Dolce did not insist that she learn Greek, because he did not wish "to place such a heavy weight on the shoulders of women." She should also read the major vernacular authors, such as Dante, Petrarch, and Pietro Bembo, and she should read Castiglione's *Il cortegiano* but not Boccaccio's *Decameron*. Nevertheless, Dolce cautioned a woman destined to rule not to study so hard that she neglected her husband or the running of her household.

Both Bruni and Dolce linked the *studia humanitatis* to public roles.[3] Since a woman could not attend university, hold a position as lawyer or civil servant, or become a clergyman, she should not follow the Latin curriculum. The few women who would become civil rulers could and should study a nearly complete humanistic program of studies. Dolce added reading in major vernacular authors, because the vernacular had come of age since 1525. But the rest of the female population needed only the learning appropriate to a woman's role as wife and mother.

Fra Sabba Castiglione (1480–1554), the founder of a school for the poor in Faenza, described the ideal education for the majority of upper- and middle-class girls and explained its rationale. Which young man does not want to marry a girl who can read and write well? he asked rhetorically. She should be able to read Dante, Petrarch, Boccaccio, and similar vernacular authors; if not, she will be seen as a "rustic," as having been "poorly brought up," and as being of little account. Girls should be praised for reading good books: the Bible, the *Little Office of Our Lady*, saints' legends, the *Vite dei Santi Padri*, and other spiritual and religious works. Girls should not be lauded for reading *La vita nuova* of Dante, the sonnets and *canzoni* of Petrarch, the *Decameron*, *La Fiammetta*, and *Il Filocolo* of Boccaccio, and similar lascivious and dishonest works. She should not be applauded for knowing how to write "saucy rimes" and "love letters," but for writing what was necessary, honest, and appropriate to an "honorable woman."[4]

Sabba Castiglione sought to temper what he judged to be excessive emphasis on gentility at the expense of virtue in the education of noble and

---

[3]So did Erasmus in his discussions of female education. See Sowards, 1982.

[4]Sabba Castiglione, 1554, pp. 95[r–v]. Also see F. Petrucci, 1979; Scarpati, 1982, pp. 27–125; and Zama, 1920, pp. 71–82, for his school. I have not used *La institutione di una fanciulla nata nobilmente*. *L'institution d'une fille de noble maison* (Anvers, 1555) of Giovanni Michele Bruto, an Italian Protestant exile, because I doubt that it had much Italian influence or reflected Italian conditions.

wealthy commoner girls. He complained that fathers and mothers made every effort to teach their daughters singing, playing an instrument, "and like vanities," in order that they might be considered "courteous, refined, and well bred." His recommendations demonstrated that the higher ranks of society considered vernacular reading and writing to be desirable accomplishments for girls.

Other theorists echoed Sabba Castiglione's views in their own ways. Agostino Valier or Valerio (1531–1606), Venetian nobleman and cardinal and bishop of Verona, frequently exhorted women to read good, spiritual books in his four tracts advising women (published in 1575 and 1577). He had very conventional, that is to say, limited, views on women's role. Mothers should teach their daughters to be silent and to keep the needle and spindle going; male spiritual advisors should monitor women's reading. But Valier assumed that women could read, and he endorsed reading as a path to virtue.[5]

Another conservative clerical pedagogical theorist outlined the expectations and the limits that society imposed on female learning. Silvio Antoniano (1540–1603), in his *Dell'educazione cristiana e politica de' figliuoli* (first edition 1584), wrote that girls of noble status destined to become mothers of eminent families should know how to read and write well, and should understand elementary arithmetic. Girls of middling status should learn to read and to write a little, and girls of humble and poor station should be able to read books of prayers. Antoniano endorsed vernacular reading and writing; he did not approve of girls learning "languages," that is, Latin and Greek. Nor should a girl learn "pleading and writing poetry" (Latin oratory and poetry); the vain female sex must not reach too high. A good father should be content that his daughter recited the *Little Office of Our Lady* and read saints' lives and other spiritual books. A girl should attend to sewing, cooking, and other female activities, leaving to men what was theirs.[6]

Despite the differences in tone, these pedagogical theorists articulated the same opinion: a girl should acquire vernacular reading and writing skills appropriate to her expected role as virtuous and practical spouse and mother. Upper-class girls needed to be able to read and write well, and perhaps to keep accounts, in order to fulfill social expectations and to manage a household. Girls lower on the social ladder needed less learning. Those at the bottom should be able to read prayers or, more accurately, to recite aloud prayers learned by rote. A girl ought not acquire Latin learning, because she had no public role to play.

---

[5] I cite an edition that includes all four tracts: Valier, 1740, pt. 2, pp. 25–26; pt. 3, pp. 21, 38; pt. 4, pp. 29, 31–32, 37. For similar views from other contemporary treatises, see Secco, 1973, pp. 153–59.

[6] Antoniano, 1852, bk. 3, ch. 46, pp. 425–26. For his life, see Prodi, 1961.

FEMALE TEACHERS

Italy, like France and England, had a limited number of women teachers.[7] The presence of female pedagogues in Italy between 1300 and 1600
would seem, at first glance, to contradict the limited educational role
assigned to women. A closer look shows that they were the exceptions
that "proved the rule. Some female teachers, especially in the fourteenth
century, taught Latin. But the majority, particularly in the later Renaissance, taught only an elementary vernacular curriculum.

The earliest notice comes from Florence in 1304. A certain Clemenza,
wife and "teacher of boys" ("doctrix puerorum"), signed a contract to
instruct a boy in beginning reading (*legere Psalterium*), Latin grammar
(*Donatum*), and *instrumenta et scribere*, the preparation of Latin notarial acts
with their formulas and abbreviations. Her pupil went on to become a
notary, a leading merchant, and holder of high political office.[8] This boy
from the Florentine merchant elite could have studied with any number of
male teachers, but his parents placed him with a woman, a testimony to
her ability and high standing.

Other female teachers appeared in several cities and towns. Siena had a
female teacher in 1307.[9] Francesco di Marco Datini, the merchant of Prato,
recorded in 1401 the payment of a gold florin to the lady who taught his
daughter, aged 9, to read.[10] In Modena, the wife of a grammarian contracted to teach two boys in 1406.[11] A lady named Ursa was rector of a
girls' school in the district of Sant'Angelo in Venice in 1409.[12] Lucia, a
Venetian widow, made a will leaving small sums of money to her pupils in
general (*scolarum suarum*), as well as sums to three specific girls, described
as *discipulabus suis* and *sue discipule,* in 1413.[13] In 1480, a 5-year-old Florentine boy learned to read from "mona Chosa."[14] A female teacher taught

---

[7]See the rules of 1357 for Parisian teachers, who included school mistresses (who should
teach only girls), in Thorndike, 1971, pp. 239–41. For England, see Orme, 1973, pp. 54–55;
and Moran, 1985, p. 70.

[8]Debenedetti, 1906–7, pp. 333, 344.

[9]Ibid., p. 341 n. 3.

[10]Origo, 1963, p. 199.

[11]Bertoni and Vicini, 1904–5, pp. 169, 201.

[12]". . . Ursiam retricem [*sic*] scolariarum S. Angeli et magistrum Guielminum rectorem
scolarium." Bertanza and Dalla Santa, 1907, p. 266, 23 September 1409. I interpret *scolariarum*
to mean girls and *scolarium* to mean boys.

[13]"Domina Lucia uxor q^m sir Natalis Sisti . . . ordinat testamentum suum in hac
forma. . . . Item reliquid unicuique *scolarum suarum* soldos XX. . . . Item reliquid *discipulabus suis* silicet Mariecte et Benedicte pro qualibet medium ducatum. Item reliquid *sue
discenti sive discipule* Clare filie Manulii ducatos duos." Ibid., p. 280, 26 August 1413. Italics are
those of Bertanza and Dalla Santa.

[14]"Agnolo di Tommaso, va a leggere cho' mona Chosa; d'età d'anni 5." Verde, 1973–77,
vol. 3:1027.

girls in Vicenza in 1496.[15] A Florentine father noted in his diary payment to a female teacher, Mona Dianora, who taught reading to girls in 1513. His daughter Maddalena, learned to read from her.[16] The civil government of Turin ordered all teachers, including "the mistresses who teach reading and sewing to little girls" ("le maestre che insegnano a leggere e a cucire alle bambine"), to make professions of faith in 1566.[17] A lady named Marieta opened a school in Venice in late 1585 or early 1586. She taught a group of eight boys and girls vernacular texts, elementary Latin grammar, and a little abbaco; her neighborhood independent school enrolling both boys and girls was very unusual. After teaching for more than a year, she turned the school over to her brother, Francesco de Fabretis, because she was about to get married.[18] One wonders if she ever returned to teaching.

Verona tax records document female teachers in three centuries. The first female teacher appeared in documents of 1382 and 1383; about twenty other female pedagogues made tax declarations between 1409 and 1595.[19] The majority were termed *magistra puerorum* (teacher of boys) or *magistra da scolla* (schoolteacher) in the documents; they did not carry the more elevated titles of some male teachers, *grammaticus* or *retoricus*. Three of the women teachers taught girls: Onorata in 1465 was a *magistra puellarum,* as was Tadea, aged 63 in 1469, while Maddalena, the 18-year-old daughter of a widowed teacher, taught girls (*insegna alle putte*) in 1555.[20] The Veronese female teachers included one wife, at least two widows, and three or more young, unmarried women; the marital status of the rest is undetermined. Their ages ranged from 18 to 87. Their tax declarations indicated a low economic level: all but one of the women teachers paid zero to six *soldi,* the lowest amounts of those paying taxes, and one was described as *povera* and *paupera*.[21] Male elementary teachers paid eight to ten *soldi* on the average, grammarians ten to fifteen, and members of other learned professions, such as notaries, physicians, and lawyers, much more.[22] Two women

[15]Mantese, 1964, p. 754.

[16]"A M(on)a Dianora ch' ensegnia legiere alle fanciulle presso a la volta di Ghuicciardini, grossoni X d'ariento le demo chontanti per avere insegniato legiere i libricino o parte d'esso alla Maddalena nostra figliuola, portò lli Gismondo nro fanciullo." Archivio di Stato, Firenze, Carte Strozziane, ser. 4ª, n. 418, Ricordanza di Tommaso di Iacopo Guidetti, fol. 61ᵛ, 21 June 1513. I am grateful to Anthony Molho for this reference.

[17]As quoted in Bettazzi, 1928, p. 338.

[18]ACPV, "Professioni di fede," fols. 276ʳ–277ʳ, Francesco de Fabretis; Baldo, 1977, pp. 21, 76–77.

[19]C. Garibotto, 1921, pp. 7, 9, 15–47 passim. Female teachers appear in the *estimi* of 1409, 1456, 1465, 1469, 1492, 1545, 1555, 1572, 1584, and 1595.

[20]C. Garibotto, 1921, pp. 36, 43, 17.

[21]"Isabeta maistra da scola povera," aged 45, supported daughters of 12, 9, and 5 years of age and a sister-in-law. She apparently paid no tax in 1570. Described as "paupera," she paid five soldi in 1572. C. Garibotto, 1921, p. 30.

[22]Tagliaferri, 1966, pp. 123–25.

teachers made tax declarations in successive *estimi,* that is, the valuations of assets on which the amount of the tax was calculated. Donna Francisca, *magistra scollarum,* paid five *soldi* in 1456 and again in 1465, and the widow Serena remitted five *soldi* in 1572 and in 1595.[23] This suggests that Francisca and Serena, like most male teachers, pursued teaching as a career, not as a temporary occupation. Probably the women teachers supported themselves entirely, or supplemented the family income, by teaching, almost always at the elementary level.

The percentage of the Veronese teaching corps that was female can be roughly estimated by extrapolating from the tax data. The Commune of Verona imposed *estimi* with its tax assessments twenty times, approximately once every decade, from 1409 through 1595.[24] No women teachers appeared in half of the *estimi.* Four different *estimi* listed a single female pedagogue, three *estimi* named two women teachers, those of 1465 and 1572 recorded three female teachers, and the *estimo* of 1558 registered five women teachers. The two women teachers appearing in the tax records of 1545 composed 9 percent (two of twenty-three) of the teachers listed; in 1555, the female pedagogues composed 24 percent (five of twenty-one) of teachers. But the tax records failed to include all teachers; for example, they omitted clergymen who lived and taught in households. Those who had very few assets, a category that included some teachers, also escaped taxation. Verona, a provincial center of 46,000 people in 1545,[25] obviously had more than twenty-three teachers in 1545 and twenty-one in 1555. If Verona had as many teachers for its population as Venice in 1587, it had seventy-six active teachers in 1545.[26] Hence, female pedagogues probably composed a small fraction, perhaps one-tenth, of those teaching at any one time in the fifteenth and sixteenth centuries.

Women continued to teach in the seventeenth century. Venetian census records mentioned two female teachers in 1633, six in 1642, and four in 1670. "Giulia" in 1633 and "Paula vedoa" in 1670 taught young girls (*putte*); the sexes and ages of the students of the others are unknown. Three of the women taught vernacular reading (*insegna a lezer*); the others taught school (*tien scola* or *maestra di scuola*).[27]

The presence of female pedagogues through four centuries and in several towns and cities suggests the educational pattern and the exceptions. Although men made up a very high percentage of teachers, a few

[23]C. Garibotto, 1921, pp. 19, 24.

[24]Tagliaferri, 1966, p. 20 table 1.

[25]Ibid., p. 49 table 7.

[26]Venice in 1587 had 245 active teachers in a population of 148,600, that is, .0016487 of the population. Multiplying this figure by the 46,000 people in Verona in 1545 suggests that Verona had 76 teachers.

[27]I owe this information taken from ASV, Sanità, to Peter Burke. Records survive for only five (of six) *sestieri* in the census of 1633, four *sestieri* in 1642, and one in 1670.

women did instruct, just as a few women became physicians (but without university degrees) in Renaissance Italy.[28] Female teachers were exceptions in a male profession. Yet their existence, even in small numbers, proves that some women were educated throughout these centuries: female teachers had to learn before they could teach. Thus, female literacy and learning did not fall below a certain, admittedly low, level.

FEMALE PUPILS

The majority of female students came from the upper and middle classes and studied the vernacular curriculum, sometimes with women teachers. A significant minority of girls studied the Latin humanities, usually with male household tutors.

A few fifteenth-century girls received excellent Latin educations. Isotta Nogarola (1418–66), Cassandra Fedele (1465–1558), Laura Cereta (1469–99), and others learned Latin well. They acquired local and sometimes wider reputations, partly because they were women in a man's field. The life of Alessandra Scala (1475–1506) illustrates the lives of the others. She began her studies at home when her father, the Florentine chancellor Bartolomeo, hired a household tutor for his four daughters.[29] She later studied privately with Angelo Poliziano, earning high praise for her facility in classical Greek. At the age of 18 Alessandra played the title role in a performance of Sophocles' *Electra* in her father's house; Poliziano and others lauded her rendition. After the tragic death of her husband, a Greek soldier-poet, in battle in 1500, she entered a convent. She left very little writing behind when she died.[30]

Most members of fifteenth-century Renaissance society could not comprehend learned women.[31] Those favorably disposed saw them as prodigies, whereas others viewed them with hostility. Indeed, these girls did differ greatly from the norm in many ways. Born into aristocratic or wealthy professional families, they enjoyed very strong support from loving fathers and received private tutoring. They blossomed intellectually in benign circumstances, but found it difficult to exercise their talents beyond the paternal home. When they addressed Latin letters and orations to outsiders in bids for recognition, as often as not they suffered rejection or the frustration of being ignored. Lacking support from the larger world, the majority of these Latin learned women discontinued their studies after marrying or entering a female monastery. They had acquired impractical skills for their sex.

[28]Park, 1985, pp. 71–72; Lenzi, 1982, pp. 205–6.
[29]Verde, 1973–77, vol. 3:1141.
[30]Ibid., pp. 36–37; A. Brown, 1979, pp. 210–12, 245–47.
[31]See Labalme, ed., 1984; Rabil, 1981; King and Rabil, eds., 1983; Jardine, 1983.

Although societal attitudes remained basically the same in the sixteenth century, external circumstances lowered the barriers to recognition for learned women. First, printing became widespread and relatively inexpensive. A woman could now have her works published; she did not have to rely on an exchange of letters with a famous humanist to achieve recognition. Second, after about 1525, the learned world accepted Italian as a language worthy to bear lofty and elegant thoughts on some subjects. This simplified matters for women denied Latin educations; even with limited training, a gifted woman could write well in the vernacular. Finally, the period from about 1530 to about 1560 saw Italian society, especially literary circles, become more open than it had ever been, or would be again for some time.[32] During the age of Pietro Aretino and the adventurers of the pen, learned women experienced fewer difficulties. Vittoria Colonna, Tullia d'Aragona, Veronica Franco, Veronica Gambara, Gaspara Stampa, and Laura Terracina wrote and published vernacular prose and poetry. Not all of them had the advantages of high birth and wealth; the prostitutes Tullia d'Aragona and Veronica Franco enjoyed acclaim despite low birth and immodest occupation.

The life of Modesta da Pozzo (1555–92), who published under the pen name Moderata Fonte, illustrates some of the conditions for a learned woman after the middle of the sixteenth century. The daughter of a Venetian citizen who held a legal post with the government, Modesta was orphaned at a very young age. Her grandparents placed her in a convent, where she displayed a prodigious memory and a gift for recitation. When she returned to her grandparents' home at the age of 9, her grandfather provided her with books and encouraged her to study and to write poetry. She learned Latin from her older brother. Every day when he returned from his Latin school, he showed her what he had learned. With her quick mind and retentive memory, she learned in this second-hand way to read Latin very well and to write it adequately. She also wrote vernacular poetry, could do arithmetic, played the lute and the ancestor of the harpsichord, sang, and sewed. She later married a Venetian citizen and legal official, and gave birth to four living children, dying at the birth of her second daughter at the age of 37.[33]

Unlike some learned women of the fifteenth century, Modesta continued to write after marriage. Her major prose treatise, *Il merito delle donne,* appeared posthumously in 1600 with a dedicatory letter by one of her daughters. A dialogue carried on by seven women of different ages and statuses, the work applauded a woman's worth independent of men with a

[32]See P. Grendler, 1969a, ch. 1.

[33]All the information on her life comes from the biography of her written in 1593 by her brother-in-law, the historian Giovanni Nicolò Doglione, and published in Fonte, 1600, pp. 1–7. Labalme, 1981, pp. 84–92, is the indispensable guide to her life and works.

variety of arguments and examples. Although not primarily concerned
with schooling, the treatise made three points about female education.
First, few girls from the lower classes had the opportunity to learn: "How
many servant girls do not know how to read, how many peasant and
plebian women?"[34] Second, men either exhibited little interest in ensuring
that women received educations or prohibited them from learning on the
grounds that literacy led to loss of virtue. (Modesta did not suffer from
either of these disadvantages.) Third, if given the opportunity to study,
women would surpass men in learning. Another Venetian woman writer,
Lucrezia Marinella (1571–1653), made the same points in her treatise, also
published in 1600.[35]

Moderata Fonte and Lucrezia Marinella accurately described the situation for the majority of women, those who did not enjoy strong male
support or reach learned heights. Most girls who studied acquired only the
education deemed appropriate and useful to women: vernacular reading
and writing plus, at times, elementary Latin grammar or a little arithmetic. In particular, women were expected to read, and probably did read,
simple vernacular religious and secular texts. For example, a fourteenth-
century translator of an exposition of the *Epistole e Evangeli,* the pericopes
read in daily mass, stated that he had translated it "especially at the petition
of women" ("che io habbia facto questo spetialmente a petitione di femine").[36] A fifteenth-century widow, probably a Florentine, had a scribe
prepare a manuscript book for her own consolation and for that of her
daughters after the death of her husband. Presumably they read the book.
The manuscript book contained various religious and secular texts: the
first twenty chapters of the *Fior di virtù;* a miscellany of religious materials
including the Ten Commandments, the Apostle's Creed, and advice on
how to make a good confession; and pious legends. These materials were
staples of the vernacular curriculum (see ch. 10). The manuscript also
included brief words of advice from "a wise mother" to her daughter upon
becoming a bride and portions from Petrarch's *Triumphs.* Later, another
woman owned this manuscript.[37]

[34]"Quante serve, che non sanno leggere, quante contadine, e femine plebee sono. . . ."
Fonte, 1600, pp. 144 (quote)–145; also see p. 29.

[35]Marinella, 1601, pp. 32–34. First published in Venice, 1600, Marinella's *La nobilta et
l'eccellenza delle donne* appeared in expanded versions in 1601 and 1621. See Labalme, 1981, pp.
92–98, for her life and writings.

[36]*Epistole e Evangeli,* 1495 (Hain 6643), sig. a2ᵛ. Authorship is attributed to Fra Simone da
Cascia (Simone Fidati, 1295–1348), the translation to Fra Giovanni da Salerno (1317–88). The
work went through numerous manuscript and early printed copies. The *Epistole e Evangeli* in
this version and others was a standard textbook in the vernacular schools.

[37]"Questo libro affatto scrivere mona ghostantia donna fu d benedetto cicciaporci el quale
alibro affatto fare per consolatione dellanima sua e secondariamente a chonsolazione delle sue
figliuole." FN Ms. Nazionale II.II.89, fol. 144ʳ. The manuscript is written in a fifteenth-
century humanist hand (chancery formal). On fol. 1ʳ is the name of a later fifteenth- or

Girls studied at home with a tutor and sometimes with a female teacher; very seldom did they study in neighborhood independent schools taught by men. The female teachers with their pupils mentioned earlier and a few others illustrate the point. The names of a handful of female pupils appeared in Venetian and Florentine notarial and other records in the fourteenth and fifteenth centuries, unaccompanied by information on what they studied. For example, "Marchesine . . . a scolis" and "Nicolota filia quondam d. Marie a scollis" appeared in Venetian records in 1348. A Venetian *magister Andrea rector scholarum* won a judgment against his daughter, "Lucia scolara," in 1405.[38] A Genoese exception proves the rule that girls almost never appeared in independent schools. A series of documents listed the names of about five hundred students in seventeen Genoese independent schools between 1498 and 1500. Only one pupil, Catharinetta, the daughter of a barber, was a girl. She and her brother read *Donatus* syllable by syllable; that is, they studied elementary Latin grammar.[39]

The approximately thirty female pupils uncovered by the Venetian survey of 1587 followed a pattern. The majority were daughters of nobles, they studied at home with teachers who came to them, and they learned at an elementary level. For example, one teacher stated, "I am called to teach six maids at home [how] to read and write and the catechism."[40] About twenty of the thirty girls had noble blood; thirteen of the thirty were intended for the convent. The largest group consisted of ten convent-bound girls who assembled in a noble house to learn reading from a teacher who came to them. A few more girls studied with household tutors across the city. The words used to describe many of them (*putte, puttina, creaturina*) suggest that the majority were very young. Most of the girls studied elementary reading and writing. Several read the *Little Office of Our Lady;* although it was a Latin book, teachers normally used it as a primer and prayer book to be memorized. The exceptions to the scholastic pattern were two girls reading the breviary, which required more Latin, and the handful of girls attending the mixed school belonging to Marieta, and later to Francesco de Fabretis, mentioned earlier.

Some girls, possibly a substantial fraction of those who received educations, studied as long-term residents in female monasteries. The origin of

---

sixteenth-century female owner: "Questo libro e di mᵃ lucreza dj nicᵒ di gunta figola dj bnedeto."

[38]Bertanza and Dalla Santa, 1907, pp. 44 (14 May 1348), 46 (4 June 1348), 250–51 (4 February 1404 mv). For Florentine students, see Bec, 1967, pp. 385–86.

[39]"Item Catharinetta et Petrinus filii magistri Ioannis tonsoris de bernardis donatum legens syllabicandum." Massa, 1906, p. 321, 4 June 1500.

[40]"et son chiamando à insegnar à sei donzele in casa à lezer et scrivere et la dotrina cristiana." ACPV, "Professioni di fede," fol. 281ʳ; the other references to girls in school are on fols. 30ᵛ, 68ᵛ, 74ʳ⁻ᵛ, 100ᵛ, 194ᵛ, 227ʳ, 235ᵛ, 273ᵛ, 276ᵛ–277ʳ (school of Francesco de Fabretis).

the practice is unknown, but by the fourteenth century Florentine fathers often sent motherless daughters, probably with a sum of money, to the monastery to be raised.[41] In a typical situation, a widower placed his young daughter in a female monastery until he remarried; he then brought her back to the family home. Or he placed a motherless girl in a convent until she married. In 1453 a Florentine widower put his two daughters, aged 11 and 13, in a female monastery. He expected to remove them four years later because he had dowries for them and, he said, "I want them to marry." Once in the convent, a girl was subject to the rules, including cloister. If she left even temporarily, she could not return. The Florentine term for the practice, *serbanza* ("in reserve" or "put aside" to be used on another occasion), exactly described the girl's destiny. She spent years in the female monastery until her father decided that she should rejoin the world. She emerged with virginity intact, spiritual training, domestic skills, and a limited vernacular education.

Shortly after the Council of Trent, the papacy issued regulations that made the female monastery more like a strict boarding school. Female monasteries might accept secular girls, that is, girls who did not profess vows, as boarding-school pupils under several conditions. The superior had to grant permission, and the girl could not bring along a maidservant. She had to observe the convent's rules (including cloister), and if she once left, she could not return. Of course, upon leaving one convent, she could go to another. Local regulations often established minimum and maximum age limits (typically 7 and 25) and the number of girls that each female monastery might accept. Parents paid high fees, such as thirty-five to forty-two ducatoni (worth ten to twelve lire each) per annum in Cremona in 1593 and thirty scudi per annum in Siena in 1600.[42]

Carlo Borromeo, archbishop of Milan, issued more stringent regulations for the archdiocese of Milan in 1566. The "lay girls . . . present for education" ("putte secolari . . . al presente per causa di educatione") in the female monasteries had to be at least 10 but not older than 15 years of age, must observe cloister, would pay at least thirty gold scudi per year, and had to leave after one year.[43] Why he imposed the last rule is not clear. In any case, his rules were eased over time: the minimum age dropped to 7, and the girls stayed several years. The curriculum remained a very simple one of reading, writing, work, and prayer. Lay girls boarded in the Milanese female monasteries through the seventeenth and eighteenth centuries.[44]

[41]Klapisch-Zuber, 1984, pp. 777–78, 790 n. 78, found seventeen examples between 1358 and 1528. Two girls were 3 years old, one was aged 6, and the rest were between 9 and 16.

[42]Marcocchi, 1966, pp. xlv–xlvi; Marcocchi, 1974, p. 65. For Siena, see Masetti Zannini, 1982, p. 359.

[43]*Ordinationi*, 1566, pp. 44–47.

[44]Chinea, 1953, pp. 104, 111, 114, 124–25.

Venetian girls, especially daughters of nobles, also lived and studied in female monasteries. Patriarchal inspections carried out between 1560 and 1627 revealed that at least nine of the twenty-five to twenty-seven female monasteries of the city boarded "putte à spese" ("girls at their own expense") at one time or another.[45] One visitor called the girls "le figliuole accetasse à spese per educazione" ("girls accepted at their expense for education").[46] The remaining sixteen to eighteen convents may also have boarded lay girls—the inspectors only mentioned the girls when criticizing their behavior. The girls tended to come from noble families, because only the wealthy could afford the fees of forty to sixty ducats annually.[47] There were exceptions: one convent boarded the daughter of a *fattore* (an employee of some kind) for free.[48] The inspectors complained that the girls did not remain in their own quarters, but ran around the convent, made excessive noise, slept in the nuns' cells, and disrupted routine. They also groused that family members, in violation of regulations, chatted with the girls at windows and doors and outside of hours. These complaints confirmed that families remained in close touch with their daughters.

In general, six to twelve girls between the ages of 7 and 16 lived and learned in typical female monasteries with thirty to one hundred nuns, lay sisters, and novices, all across Italy. For example, a dozen female monasteries in Cremona boarded from three to twenty-two girls each in 1593.[49] Sixteen female monasteries in Siena boarded an average of eight girls each in 1600.[50] A female monastery in Faenza boarded an average of ten girls through the sixteenth and seventeenth centuries, charging twenty scudi for each girl in 1594 and higher fees in the next century.[51]

[45]The Venetian patriarchs imposed several visitations of inspection of the female monasteries between 1560 and 1627. Results are found in four unnamed packets of documents in ACPV which I have labelled "Visite alle monasteri di monache" and the dates. For evidence of boarding girls, see "Visite alle monasteri di monache, 1560–1589," fols. 6ᵛ, 10ᵛ, 37ᵛ, 79ʳ; "Visite . . . 1592–1596," fols. 138ᵛ, 158ᵛ, 159ᵛ, 168ᵛ–169ʳ, 184ᵛ, 192ʳ, 515ʳ⁻ᵛ, 538ʳ, 616ʳ, [638ʳ⁻ᵛ]; "Visite . . . 1609–1618," no pag., reports on San Girolamo, Ognisanti, San Servolo, and San Iseppo; "Visite . . . 1620–1627," no pag., reports on Santa Marta and San Girolamo.

[46]ACPV, "Visite alle monasteri di monache, 1609–1618," report on San Iseppo, 19 August 1618.

[47]The few names found were usually those of Venetian noble families: Balbi, Morosini, Pisani, etc.

[48]ACPV, Visite alle monasteri di monache, 1592–1596," fol. 515ʳ, San Iseppo, 8 November 1595. San Iseppo had seventeen boarding girls and seventy-seven nuns and lay sisters at this time. Unfortunately, the reports do not give enough figures to make possible an estimate of the total number of "putte à spese" in Venetian convents.

[49]Marcocchi, 1966, p. xlvi.

[50]Masetti Zannini, 1982, pp. 358–61. For other examples, see pp. 349 (Chieri), 365 (Alatri), 369 (Valenza and Florence). For two convent schools for girls in Turin in 1586, see Sassi, 1880, p. 17.

[51]Zama, 1938, pp. 72–81.

The girls learned only vernacular reading and writing, sewing, and singing. Few progressed further, because families did not demand rigorous academic training for their daughters. Even if the families had wanted the girls to learn more, the nuns were ill equipped to teach them more.[52] A convent could only provide teachers from the permanent members of the community, professed nuns who were subject to cloister and not allowed to go outside for study. Moreover, too few girls lived in each female monastery for a strong scholastic environment to develop except under unusual circumstances. The female monasteries were less schools than communities of women and girls who lived, sewed, and prayed together.

The arrangement reaped obvious benefits to the female monasteries. The boarding-school fees must have brought badly needed income to many of the small, poor convents that dotted the landscape of urban and rural Italy. The girls also brought youthful joy and energy to the communities. Indeed, ecclesiastical inspectors sometimes found that the girls created too much excitement, as they ran around the monastery, dressed in men's clothing, and chattered with the nuns.[53] The boarders also helped convents to grow. After spending their formative years in this protected and happy environment, some girls gladly professed vows and remained.

But not every girl benefited from the convent experience. Not knowing any other life and subtly pressured by family and nuns, some girls took vows that they later bitterly regretted.[54] Nor did a cloistered existence necessarily prepare girls for secular adult life. Teen-age girls thrust into aristocratic marriages immediately after leaving the convent must have found the adjustment very difficult.

Nevertheless, whether the girls rejoined the secular world or professed vows, they had a much better chance of learning than their sisters outside the convent. Although it is impossible even to estimate numbers, it is apparent that numerous noble and wealthy commoner girls studied in convents. Few girls lower on the social scale learned this way, because only wealthy parents could afford the high fees. The overall result is clear: it is very likely that all daughters of nobles and a good number of wealthy

---

[52]The problem was not illiteracy. Seventy-six percent (290 of 383) of the nuns in the female monasteries of Cremona, and 22 of 44 nuns in nearby country convents, could write, according to the inspector's report of 1593. Marcocchi, 1966, pp. xli–xlii.

[53]Ibid., p. xlvii.

[54]Arcangela Tarabotti (1604–52), a Venetian girl tricked by her father into becoming a nun at the age of 16, bitterly denounced the practice in her writings. See Labalme, 1981, pp. 98–104; and Zanette, 1960. The story of Gertrude, who spent eight years as a boarder in a convent and then professed vows as a result of her family's pressures, in Manzoni's *I promessi sposi*, ch. 9, is based on the story of Sister Virginia Maria de Leyva (1575–1650). See A. Manzoni, 1977, pp. 278–93; and Leyva, 1985.

commoner girls received limited vernacular schooling, in the convent or by other means.

Maternal tutoring in families of some social status increased the rate of female vernacular literacy. Not all middle- and upper-class families could afford household tutors or the fees of female monasteries, or wanted to send their daughters away. When social custom barred girls from attending a neighborhood independent school filled with boys, maternal tutoring helped to fill the gap. Sabba Castiglione strongly urged mothers to teach their sons "and especially their daughters" how to read, at least enough to read clearly the Office, psalter, and other devout and holy prayers.[55] Modesta da Pozzo taught her two sons and a daughter to read and write in Latin, to sing, and to play the viola da gamba.[56]

Limited parental tutoring may have taken place among artisans, as well. Two sixteenth-century Venetian teachers published home teaching manuals to help parents teach their children reading, writing, and arithmetic. Giovanni Antonio Tagliente, best known for his writing manuals, published his *Libro maistrevole* (Teaching book or Skillful book) in Venice in 1524. With this book, he assured readers, you can teach your young son, daughter, or friend how to read very well.[57] Domenico Manzoni, a teacher of reading, writing, abbaco, and bookkeeping, published his home-teaching manual, *La vera et principal ricchezza de' giovani, che disiderano imparar ben legere, scrivere, et abaco* (The true and principle riches of youth, who wish to learn to read well, write, and [do] abbaco), in Venice in 1550. He exhorted parents to seize this opportunity to teach their children at low cost (the price of the book). He promised that teaching one's children reading, writing, and abbaco would bring satisfaction to the parents and make the children useful and virtuous.[58] Both authors stressed several times that they intended their books for the poor. Artisans and others without much money could learn to read and write, and could teach

---

[55]"Deve la virtuosa, & buona moglie essere molto diligente & sollecita, in creare, & ammaestrare li figliuoli, & massimamente le fanciulle, le quali usi ogni diligentia, ogni studio, et ogni opera, acciò imparino à leggere almeno, tanto quanto li basta à leggere distintamente l'ufficiolo, il saltero, & altre divote & sante orationi. . . ." Sabba Castiglione, 1554, p. 115ᵛ.

[56]Doglione's biography in Fonte, 1600, p. 5.

[57]"Sapientissimi lettori, & voi carissimi auditori, questa e una opera nuovamente composta, & stampata, laquale insegna a ciascheduno che sappia leggere, ad insegnare al suo figliuolo et figliuola, o vero amico, che niente sapino leggere, talmente che ciascheduno potra imparare et etiam le donne grandi, et piccole, che niente sanno potranno imparare a leggere. . . ." Also: "Dico a te lettore che desideri de insegnare al tuo figliuolo, o vero alla tua figliuola, over al tuo amico." G. A. Tagliente, 1524, sigs. aiiʳ, aiiiᵛ. For more on this book and its author, see chs. 6 and 11 herein.

[58]"havendola principalmente fatta per quelli che non hanno cosi commodità di poter andar alla schola. . . ." "Adonque sarà vostro offitio di abbracciar il bene & il thesoro, che per cosi poco pretio vi è offerto prendendolo per ammaestrar i figliuoli vostri. . . ." Manzoni, 1550, sig. aᵛ.

others, especially their children, they argued.[59] Notwithstanding the pro-
motional tone of such comments, authors would not have written, nor
printers published, these books if some parental tutoring of daughters and
sons did not occur.

Certainly some mothers tutored their sons and daughters, but the
number is impossible to determine.[60] Middle- and upper-class families,
even if fallen on hard times, were more likely than artisans to possess the
skills and motivation to enter into home tutoring. A middle- or upper-
class girl who learned to read and write could create a literary cell by later
teaching her daughters, nieces, and granddaughters. Such a mother also
wanted to make her daughters more attractive potential marriage partners
by teaching them reading and writing. Mothers in working-class and poor
families, by contrast, had to break the shackles of illiteracy in trying
circumstances. An artisan mother probably had little free time to teach her
daughter, and the daughter had few years in which to learn before being
sent out to work as a servant girl.

Finally, if nothing else was possible, the working-class daughters of
illiterate mothers might learn a little reading and writing on Sundays and
holidays in the schools of Christian Doctrine which sprang up after 1540
(see ch. 12) or in a handful of charity schools. Eleonora of Austria (d. 1611),
duchess of Mantua after 1584, established and supported such a school in
Mantua. In it two women teachers taught the catechism, reading (but not
writing), and sewing to girls aged 7 to 12 who presented certificates of
poverty from their parish priests. However, the school would not accept
"undisciplined" and "unteachable" girls. The pupils had to bring catechism booklets (to be used as reading primers as well) and sewing materials; otherwise, the school was free.[61] This very elementary day school for
poor girls had about ninety pupils in the mid-1590s.[62]

Social status and wealth, more than anything else, determined whether
or not a girl received an education. Probably all noble and wealthy commoner girls learned to read and write. Middle-class girls had some oppor-

[59]". . . quanto sia necessaria cosa alli figliuoli di ciaschuno padre, che siano della etade
della bona discretione che non habbiano el modo de andar lungamente a schuola per imparare
a leggere il suo bisogno et simelmente agli Artesani & altre donne, che niente sanno, io qui
seguentemente per zelo di Carita et per commune beneficio voglio dare una regula, di
amaistramento a ciascheduno che sapi leggere che con la presente opera sapera insegnare a
leggere alli putti. . . ." G. A. Tagliente, 1524, sig. aiiir.

[60]See Klapisch-Zuber, 1984, p. 771, for a fifteenth-century Florentine mother who taught
her son the alphabet and elementary reading.

[61]See "Ordini et regole della Sereniss. Madama Eleonora Arciduchessa d'Austria, &
Duchessa di Mantova, per la scuola delle fanciulle povere, la quale ella instituì in Mantova," in
Possevino, 1604, pp. 146–50. I wish to thank J. Patrick Donnelly for bringing this source to
my attention.

[62]"La Serenissima Duchessa di Mantova Leonora [sic] d'Austria, a questo fine instituì una
schuola di figliuole, al numero di novanta. . . ." Carbone, 1596, p. 132.

tunities to learn, and poor and working-class girls had few possibilities. Only a handful of girls of any class attended neighborhood independent schools;[63] even the few girls who did go outside the home often studied with female teachers of limited learning. Almost all girls learned under household tutors, in female monasteries, through parental tutoring at home, or at the Schools of Christian Doctrine. Girls learned vernacular reading and writing almost exclusively. They did not study the Latin curriculum, because most males judged Latin learning to be impractical and unsuitable for girls.

WORKING-CLASS SCHOOLBOYS

Wealth and social class also played the key roles in determining whether boys attended school and the kind of education they received. Practically all sons of nobles and wealthy merchants, and sons of professionals such as lawyers, physicians, notaries, high civil servants, university professors, and pre-university teachers, attended school, usually a Latin school.[64] Many boys from the next rank of society, master craftsmen and major shopkeepers, also attended school. Lower on the social ladder were petty artisans and shopkeepers and employees in large industries; some of their sons received schooling. Even conservative educational theorists endorsed education for boys of humble birth. Silvio Antoniano believed that all boys, even the lowest, should learn at least reading, writing, and arithmetic. Antoniano did not endorse education as a means of upward social mobility; he urged "poor fathers" to send their sons into "manual occupations" ("arti manuali"). Nevertheless, he believed that a rudimentary education would prove useful throughout life.[65] A variety of sources demonstrate that some sons of artisans and other poor boys went to school.

Boys from artisan, shopkeeper, and industrial worker families received educations in Florence in 1480. Sons, brothers, and *nepoti* (nephews or

[63]This changed in the second half of the seventeenth century, at least in Rome. At that time the eternal city had numerous neighborhood reading and writing schools for girls taught by women, both as free communal schools with funds provided by the papacy and as independent schools. See Pelliccia, 1980, and Pelliccia, 1985. In general, seventeenth-century Italian girls enjoyed greater educational opportunity than had girls in earlier centuries. It is ironic that Renaissance girls received little schooling even though humanists strongly endorsed female education. By contrast, the Catholic Reformation through its charitable activities provided more educational opportunity for girls even though its pedagogical theorists wished to limit girls' schooling.

[64]Here is a rare exception. A wealthy Florentine father stated in 1480 that his 16-year-old son had not wanted to learn to read and write. "Tommaso suo figliuolo, el quale nonn'à voluto imparare a. leggere nè a scrivere et è in villa; d'età d'anni 16." Verde, 1973–77, vol. 3:1202.

[65]Antoniano, 1852, bk. 3, ch. 45, p. 423; ch. 67, p. 465.

grandsons) of bakers, beltmakers, butchers, cabinetmakers, cobblers, doubletmakers, petty employees of the commune, flax workers, gold-beaters, small merchants and shopkeepers (*merciai*), saddlemakers, tailors, woolworkers, and members of other crafts and industries attended school.[66] Some schoolboys came from families of the working poor. For example, Madonna Chaterina, aged 50, the widow of a mattressmaker, had eight children. The five oldest sons, aged 21, 19, 17, 15, and 13, worked as mattressmaker, hosiers, and shopkeeper's assistants, earning modest annual salaries of 10 to 50 lire each, for a total annual family income of about 22½ florins. The family had net assets of 19 florins. The only daughter, aged 8, had no dowry, a clear sign of poverty. Nevertheless, the second-youngest son, a boy aged 9, attended school. The youngest son, aged 5, did not.[67] Probably the five working sons made it possible to send the sixth to school, although with nine people to feed, clothe, and house, it could not have been easy.

Other Florentine families of the working poor managed to send boys to school. One such family consisted of a mother and four sons. The eldest, aged 25, was a woolworker; the next two sons, aged 22 and 20, worked as threadjoiners in the silk industry when they could find work. The family had no net assets. Yet, the youngest son, aged 12½, attended school in 1480.[68] An extended family of eleven in similar circumstances did the same. The grandfather, a butcher aged 80, headed the family of wife, son and daughter-in-law, five granddaughters without dowries, and two grandsons aged 10 and 5. Although the family had no net worth, it managed to send the 10-year-old boy to school.[69]

The ranks of craftsmen and shopkeepers with a little more money offer additional examples. A Florentine barber worked for an annual salary of 30 florins on which he supported his wife, elderly mother, and two children. He sent his son, aged 12, to school. The 8-year-old daughter had a dowry of 100 florins based on investments in the state-run dowry fund, and the family's net worth totaled 234 florins, making the family not poor but far from rich.[70] Many other Florentine households of similar financial status sent their school-age sons to school. A cobbler supported a wife, seven children, and a niece. He had no net assets, although his two oldest girls, aged 14 and 12, looked forward to dowries of 200 florins each. This modest family managed to send three boys, aged 9, 7, and 5, to school.[71]

The sons of shopkeepers, artisans, and industrial workers attended school in other cities, as well. A Genoese master taught fifty-seven pupils

[66]See Verde, 1973–77, vol. 3:1011–1202 passim.
[67]Ibid., p. 1030.
[68]Ibid., p. 1018.
[69]Ibid., pp. 1012–13.
[70]Ibid., p. 1018.
[71]Ibid., p. 1052.

whose fathers included a baker, banker or bank employee, barber, boat-maker, druggist, miller, muleteer, papermaker, manufacturer, two shoe-makers, two shopkeepers, a spinner or threadmaker, a tanner, several weavers, and several woolworkers in 1498.[72] A Roman independent master of 1636 had a school of twenty-eight boys, including two sons of a tailor and three sons of a notary, the only parental occupations listed.[73]

Since working-class parents and schoolboys did not leave behind statements indicating why they sacrificed in order to learn, one must rely on the comments of the pedagogical theorists and common sense to explain their motivations. First, boys studied in order to improve their vocational possibilities. An employee who could read, write, and count made himself more useful to his employer; an educated craftsman or shopkeeper might earn additional income and more easily defend himself against fraud through his reading and abbaco skills. Education at least removed one obstacle and may have aided upward mobility slightly in a hierarchical age.[74] Second, working-class boys wished to ape their betters, who were always speaking, writing, and computing. Thanks to education, the leaders of Renaissance society wrote detailed laws, recorded complicated financial transactions, committed to paper their commercial and marriage arrangements, wrote speeches, and kept diaries. One must assume that their social inferiors also longed to do these magical deeds with pen and paper. Third, some Italians must have taken seriously the argument of the pedagogical theorists that education contributed to moral and spiritual improvement: one could then read edifying books. Finally, education led to reading for pleasure. The boy who went to school for a sufficient period of time could read chivalric romances, racy *novelle,* and exotic travel literature.

All of the boys mentioned above paid for their schooling; other poor and working-class boys received free education. Although the majority of state schools obliged pupils to pay fees to supplement the master's salary, a few communal schools offered free schooling. The communes of Turin, Ivrea, and Pinerola in Piedmont forbade their communal masters from charging fees in the fifteenth century.[75] Arezzo also moved toward limited free schooling in the second half of the fifteenth century. In 1450 the commune appointed an abbaco teacher on condition that he not accept fees from his students. In 1456 Arezzo changed the regulations for the students

[72]Massa, 1906, pp. 325–26, under Simon Arada de Clavaro. Unfortunately, the occupational listing does not indicate the father's position—employee or master employing others—within the craft.
[73]ASR, Archivio della Università di Roma, R. 71, fol. 144ʳ.
[74]For a more qualified assessment of the effects of literacy on social mobility, see Cressy, 1980, p. 189.
[75]Gabotto, 1895, p. 280.

of the communal grammarian: sons of Aretine taxpayers might study for free, but foreigners and residents of the *contado* who did not pay taxes to the commune had to pay fees.[76]

Communal regulations required masters on university rolls in Bologna and Rome to teach a handful of poor boys for free. Some independent teachers did the same. A Genoese independent teacher taught four boys for free—three brothers of servants and a poor boy whose name he did not know—in a school of thirty-five in 1498.[77] These poor boys shared the classroom with sons of nobles, notaries, soldiers, spice merchants, abbaco teachers, and a potter. Other Genoese teachers also taught children gratis or reduced the fee *pro amore Dei* in 1498.[78] Whether they did so spontaneously or in conformity with communal regulation is unknown.

Although never the norm, free communal education became slightly more available in the sixteenth century. In an attempt to resurrect its schools after years of suspension caused by frequent wars, the Commune of Brescia in 1545 appointed two teachers to teach a limited number of poor boys (*pueros pauperculos*) free of charge. The subsequent history of this free education is unknown.[79] A similar initiative began and failed within a few months in Bassano del Grappa (in the Veneto). In the spring of 1590 the commune opened a free vernacular reading and abbaco school to be taught by a master who also served as communal accountant. But the commune dismissed him from his accounting duties in August 1590, and probably from teaching as well, for nothing more is heard of this free school.[80]

The small, politically independent city of Lucca provided more free schooling in proportion to its population than any other commune. In the first half of the sixteenth century, Lucca permitted its six communal Latin teachers to accept only voluntary payments from their pupils. In 1574 the commune made the schools completely free. None of the six communal teachers (who shortly became seven) might accept payments of any kind from the pupils, under threat of a fine for violators. The teachers were required to post signs indicating that the schools were free: "Scola del Magnifico Comune dove s'insegna senza pagamento alcuno."[81] In 1621 Lucca began to help poor boys attend school by giving them money to buy books, clothing, and shoes. Cold and rain would no longer keep the poor out of school, read the decree. The commune gave moral and practical

[76]Black, 1987, pp. 185–86.
[77]"Tres fratres servorum amore dei, nihil. Quidam pauperculus cuius presens nomen ignoro, nihil." Massa, 1906, p. 322, students of Antonius Syllanus.
[78]Ibid., pp. 321, 327.
[79]Zanelli, 1896, p. 21.
[80]Chiuppani, 1915, pp. 131–32.
[81]Barsanti, 1905, pp. 51–54, 175–76, 233–34.

reasons for its extraordinary action: poor boys without schooling ran the risk of falling into vice; if they learned to read, they could support themselves through a trade.[82]

A very few endowed schools gave free schooling to the poor. In 1374 a Treviso confraternity donated the use of a house to a teacher for his classes on condition that he teach twenty-five poor students chosen by the confraternity. Other Treviso confraternities made similar arrangements for the instruction of small numbers—eight, ten, or twelve—of poor or orphaned boys in the first half of the fifteenth century.[83] Fra Sabba Castiglione established in Faenza in 1536 a free Latin school for thirteen poor pupils, the number intended to commemorate Christ and the twelve apostles. By 1540 the school had expanded to enroll additional pupils, who paid a capon at Christmas, a hen at carnival, and a dozen eggs at Easter. The school continued to exist until 1825.[84] In Naples, Lucio Giovanni Scoppa (c. 1480–1555), a grammarian, founded in 1543 a Latin school in which a master and a *ripetitore* taught up to a hundred poor boys without charge. Scoppa apparently financed the school partly through the profits on the sale of his textbooks, which included a comprehensive grammar manual, an epitome for beginners, an anthology of classical commonplaces, and a Latin-Italian phrase book. His free school endured at least one hundred and fifty years.[85] In the small Piedmontese town of Vercelli, private contributions made possible the establishment in 1564 of a free elementary school, attached to a hospital, for the poor.[86] Yet, unlike England, Italy had very few endowed schools. The vast majority of Italian confraternities engaged in other charitable and social activities, and individual donors gave their money elsewhere. The situation did not change until the Catholic Reformation.

The Renaissance church offered some free education for working-class boys if they intended to become clergymen. Church schools and seminaries were not free to all, but usually made provision for students who were unable to pay. As noted earlier, fifteenth-century cathedral schools gave free education to a small number of poor boys seeking ordination. In this way the church became a means of educational and social advancement; Michele Ghislieri, a peasant's son who became Pope Pius V (1566–72), presented a spectacular (and unique) example.

Silvio Antoniano commented on the church's role in promoting educational opportunity and social advancement. Poor fathers should send their sons to work, he wrote, because these boys were more suited to manual

[82]Ibid., p. 54.
[83]Serena, 1912, pp. 60–61, 75.
[84]Zama, 1920, pp. 71–79.
[85]N. Barone, 1893.
[86]Bettazzi, 1928, p. 36.

labor than to mental application. But there were exceptions; like "a flower in the desert," a poor boy might have a natural disposition toward something more noble. He went happily to school, learned more quickly than others, loved books, and disliked the "humble crafts" ("arti vili"). If the teacher confirmed that the boy possessed superior intelligence, a penniless father need not despair, because seminaries taught the sons of the poor "through charity." Antoniano meant that the Tridentine legislation ordered seminaries to accept those who could not pay. But, Antoniano reminded his readers, only those who wished to become priests might follow this path.[87]

After Trent, the seminaries did become a means of educational opportunity and social advancement for sons of artisans, shopkeepers, and others. In Venice, boys chosen for the patriarchal seminary (called the Gregoriano, founded in 1579) had to be at least 12 years old and of legitimate birth. In addition, preference went to those with superior reading, writing, and Latin skills, and the capability of becoming "useful to the Church of God."[88] The criteria were elastic enough that the successful entrants of the 1580s and 1590s came from a very broad cross-section of Venetian society: sons of flax workers, jug sellers, old clothes and rag dealers, painters, shoemakers, tailors, and weavers, as well as noble boys, attended the seminary.[89] Seminary training followed by ordination meant a rise in social status for some of these boys.

Those who studied for free came from diverse backgrounds, but it is very difficult to know from what part of the social and economic spectrum came the majority of such boys. Because communal Latin schools were intended to train future leaders and civil servants, it is likely that many of their students, including those who studied without payment, came from noble, merchant, and professional ranks. Even the poor boys may have been sons of impoverished nobles. On the other hand, some of the boys who benefited from free education emerged from the ranks of artisans, shopkeepers, and the poor in general, despite the formidable social barriers. Scattered evidence of paternal occupations, plus the words and actions of governments (such as the Luccan initiative to provide books and shoes for poor pupils), indicates this.

Whether they paid for their education or not, many male members of the working classes became literate. Familial tutoring and, after 1540, the Schools of Christian Doctrine also contributed to male literacy. An unusual piece of evidence suggests that some male members of all professions

---

[87]Antoniano, 1852, bk. 3, ch. 67, pp. 465–67.

[88]ASV, Procuratori di San Marco de supra, Bu. 158, fascicolo 1, "Alunni del Seminario," fol. 20ʳ, 19 April 1580.

[89]ASV, Procuratori di San Marco de supra, Bu. 158, fascicolo 2, "Alunni per il Seminario," fols. 4ʳ–5ʳ, 8ʳ–16ᵛ, for 1580, 1584, 1587, and 1591.

could read or write. The widow Maddalena operated a pork butcher shop (*pizzicheria*) in Trastevere, Rome, between 1523 and 1537. Because Maddalena could not write, the men with whom she did business made debit and credit entries in her account book. For fifteen years, a boatman, cheesemakers, druggists, innkeepers, porters, shopkeepers, suppliers, tradesmen, and their employees, plus, from higher ranks, property owners, notaries, and a priest, wrote in her account book. Ninety-six of the 102 people who made entries could write. Each occupation of this sample had at least one literate member. Ninety-five of Maddalena's customers and others wrote in the vernacular; a dozen of these included a Latin word or formula as well.[90] It is impressive evidence for broad male literacy.

Even though the noble, the wealthy merchant, and the professional ranks inevitably provided the bulk of the schoolboy population, some sons of the working poor and others at the lower end of the social scale either found the funds to attend school or benefited from the limited amount of free education available in the Renaissance. Despite the difficulties, working-class boys had greater opportunity to learn than almost all girls.

[90]A. Petrucci, 1978.

THE LATIN CURRICULUM

Curriculum revolutions are rare occurrences. Education resists change so successfully that Western civilization has witnessed only a handful in three millennia. The Greeks and Romans established the earliest known form of Western education. After the ancient rhetorical curriculum fell with Rome, medieval men created a new education based on logic and Christianity which retained a few elements of Greco-Roman education. A third educational revolution occurred during the Italian Renaissance, when pre-university schooling based on a thorough grounding in the Latin and, to a lesser extent, the Greek classics began. The Italian humanists and the northern humanists who followed established the studia humanitatis to train students in eloquence and wisdom. A Latin education based on the classics became the norm for the sons and a few daughters of the elite, and those from the middle class who hoped to rise, in Italy in the fifteenth century and the rest of Europe in the sixteenth century. The humanist educators succeeded so well that the Latin humanistic curriculum lasted until well into the twentieth century.

The early Italian humanists sought in the classics of antiquity an eloquent Latin style and advice on how to live. This moral advice and eloquence for the public life appealed to the intellectual, political, and economic elite of the Italian city-states, just as it had attracted their predecessors in ancient Greece and Rome. The transition from Middle Ages to Renaissance through Petrarch, Bruni, Valla, and others is essentially the development and acceptance of Renaissance humanism. The less dramatic but equally important story is how Renaissance humanism became institutionalized through Italian primary and secondary schools. Between 1400 and 1450 the curriculum of the Latin schools changed from medieval to Renaissance.

CHAPTER FIVE

The Coming of the *Studia Humanitatis*

THE LATE MEDIEVAL LATIN CURRICULUM

either the "Renaissance of the twelfth century," a northern phenomenon, nor the "pre-humanism" or "proto-human-ism" prevalent in northern Italian legal circles around 1300 had any discernible impact on Italian schooling, especially pre-university education. Instead, fourteenth-century Italian schoolchildren followed a normative medieval curriculum that consisted of reading medieval authors and a few ancient poetic classics (or portions of them) and learning to write formal letters according to the principles of *ars dictaminis*.

Medieval grammarians and rhetoricians left lists of preferred authors and books, so-called curriculum authors, to be used in the schools.[1] These texts taught Latin, imparted rules of grammar, and inculcated Christian morality. Probably no teacher or school used every book on the lists; rather, each teacher constructed a syllabus from them.

The first group of curriculum authors and books consisted of elementary texts.[2]

Donatus—the *Ars minor,* an accidence and limited syntax manual to be memorized. It is attributed to Aelius Donatus, the fourth-century Roman grammarian and teacher of Jerome.

Cato or the *Disticha Catonis*—a collection of moral sayings compiled in late antiquity with additions in the early Middle Ages, but attributed to Cato the Censor (Marcus Porcius Cato, 234–149 B.C.).

---

[1]The term comes from Curtius, 1963, pp. 48–54.

[2]This list is a composite one based on the evidence in Manacorda, 1914, vol. 2:338–77; Thorndike, 1971, pp. 141–43, 169, 246, 304; Garin, ed., 1958, pp. 91–103; Curtius, 1963, pp. 42–45, 48–54, 260–64; Bolgar, 1964, pp. 197–200, 208–23; and Orme, 1973, pp. 88–93, 102–5. Baebler, 1885, provides excerpts from and information on many of the grammars and glossaries.

Liber Aesopi or *Aesopus*—Aesop's animal fables, which may have been written by Gualterus Anglicus, chaplain to Henry II of England, in the second half of the twelfth century.

Ecloga Theoduli or simply *Theodulus*—an anonymous tenth-century work in which "Pseustis" or "Liar" and "Alithia" or "Truth" engage in a poetic contest. Pseustis recites stories from mythology, and Alithia counters with Old Testament examples and, naturally, vanquishes her foe.

This group of books included an elementary Latin grammar and readers that taught good morality.

Next, the student advanced to a series of more difficult grammars, glossaries, and dictionaries. The *Doctrinale,* an extremely long (about 2,650 hexameter lines) Latin grammar in verse, was written circa 1199 by a French teacher, Alexander de Villedieu. The most famous textbook of the Middle Ages, the *Doctrinale* dealt with the parts of speech, syntax, quantity and meter, and figures of speech. A sample verse illustrates its approach and usefulness.

> Rectis as es a dat declinatio prima
> atque per am propria quaedam ponuntur Hebraea,
> dans ae diphthongon genetivis atque dativis.
> am servat quartus; tamen en aut an reperimus,
> cum rectus fit in es vel in as, vel cum dat a Graecus.
> rectus in a Graeci facit an quarto breviari.
> quintus in a dabitur, post es tamen e reperitur.
> a sextus, tamen es quandoque per e dare debes.
> am recti repetes quinto, sextum sociando.

> The first declension nominative ends in *as, es, a,*
> But certain Hebrew proper nouns in *am.*
> The genitive and dative end in the diphthong *ae,*
> The accusative in *am,* but *en* or *an* for nominative *es* or *as,*
> Or when the Greek gives [nominative] *a*
> (the nominative of the Greek in *a* makes short *an* in the accusative).
> The vocative is *a,* but *es* makes *e;*
> The ablatives are also *a* and *e* when the nominative ends in *es.*
> But nominative *am* remains the same in both the vocative and ablative.[3]

This verse explained the singular endings for all possible first-declension nouns. Indeed, the unrivalled completeness of the *Doctrinale* helped account for its popularity and longevity—it lasted longer into the Renais-

[3]Reichling, 1893, ch. I, p. 8, ll. 29–37.

sance than any other medieval curriculum text except *Donatus* and *Cato*.[4]
  Other books in the second group included the following.

Papias or *Elementarium doctrinae rudimentum*—a word list in alphabetical order which also attempted to explain genders, declensions, and other grammatical material, written c. 1050 and attributed until recently to a certain Papias from Pavia. Scholars now believe that *Papias* is part of the title of the work, and the author remains unknown.

Derivationes or *Magnae derivationes*—an etymological lexicon that included compounds, derivatives, and roots of words, written by Hugutio of Pisa, bishop of Ferrara, who died in 1210.

Graecismus—another metric verse grammar, written by Évrard de Bethune before 1212.

Catholicon—a large glossary with grammar, written c. 1286 by Giovanni Balbi, a Genoese Dominican.

  The student also continued to read books that inculcated good morality as well as Latin.

Tobias—a verse book of morality written by a French scholar, Matthew de Vendôme, c. 1185.

Prospero or *Ex sententiis Augustini*—a series of epigrams taken from Augustine's works by St. Prosper of Aquitaine, c. 400–460.

Chartula—the first word of a verse treatise, *De contemptu mundi*, attributed to the Cluniac monk Bernard of Morlaix, c. 1140.

Facetus—a verse manual of good manners which may be the work of the Englishman John of Garland in the first half of the thirteenth century.

Eva columba—the first two words of a Christian morality poem called the *Dittochaeum*, attributed to the Roman Christian poet Prudentius of the fourth century.

Physiologus—also known as the *Tres leo naturas* from its first three words, a Christian morality poem by an unknown Italian teacher of the eleventh or twelfth century.

  Medieval teachers also taught a few classical authors and books.

Vergil—70–20 B.C., possibly the most famous poet in history and the author of the *Aeneid, Eclogues,* and *Georgics*.

---

[4]See Reichling, 1893, for the critical edition. On pp. clxix–ccciii, Reichling lists 267 fifteenth- and sixteenth-century printings of the *Doctrinale*, of which only 46 (17 percent) were Italian imprints. The printing of other medieval curriculum authors, except Donatus and Cato, followed the same pattern. They were often published in the rest of Europe but seldom or never in Italy.

Ovid—43 B.C.–A.D. 18, Roman love poet and author of *Ars amatoria,* *Metamorphoses,* the *Fasti, Tristia,* and *Epistolae ex Ponto,* the last elegies written during his banishment.

Statius—c. 40–96, a Roman epic poet much influenced by Vergil whose best-known work was the epic *Thebaid,* the story of Thebes told with much reference to mythology.

Lucan—39–65, Roman poet best known for his *Pharsalia,* an epic historical poem describing the war between Caesar and Pompey.

Boethius—Roman statesman and author, c. 480–524/25, who wrote *De consolatione philosophiae* and other works before being executed by Theodoric the Ostrogoth.

Medieval scholars and teachers often called this canon of textbooks collectively *auctores* (authors), and the teacher who taught them an *auctorista* ("authorist").[5] Sometimes they gathered together in manuscript (and later in print) eight of the shorter works and called them *Auctores octo.*[6] The *Auctores octo* were *Cato, Theodulus, Facetus, Chartula, Liber parabolarum* (a book of verse proverbs attributed to Alain de Lille, d. 1203), *Tobias, Aesopus,* and *Floretus,* a religious poem.

Although predominantly medieval and Christian, the curriculum authors included a minority of Roman classical authors. Almost all were poetical; Donatus, the *Catholicon,* and Boethius (half-prose, half-poetry) stand out as exceptions. Medieval teachers and scholars probably preferred poetry for its presumed mnemonic value and because "poetry teaches truth" in the traditional conception. The *auctores* mixed together pagan and Christian, classical and medieval, Augustan and late classical, original works of imaginative literature and pedagogical manuals, epic poem and glossary, without distinction. Teachers seem to have valued all *auctores* equally; all taught language and good morality. Many of the *auctores* written in the Middle Ages exhibited a "manufactured" quality. They were not original works of literature borrowed for classroom use, or even works strongly based on original usage, but texts written to display rules of grammar, etymology, or morality.

Students went on to *ars dictaminis,* the theory and practice of writing prose letters, a key part of late medieval education.[7] *Ars dictaminis* developed in response to a need. As the number of political and religious authorities—emperor, kings, princes, barons, city councils, pope, cardinals, and bishops—grew, the demand for public correspondence expanded. Secretaries had to write more letters to different kinds of authori-

[5]Curtius, 1963, pp. 261–62; Billanovich, 1965, pp. 143–55.
[6]Garin, ed., 1958, p. 92; Orme, 1973, pp. 103–4.
[7]The following is based on Banker, 1971 and 1974; J. Murphy, 1981, pp. 194–268; Faulhaber, 1978; Ward, 1978; and Witt, 1982, 1983a, and 1986.

ties, and the letters' composition had to take into account a complex hierarchy of political and social relationships between writer and recipient. Hence, the need for manuals that would instruct secretaries and notaries in the principles of composition and provide them with examples to imitate. Alberic of Monte Cassino, a Benedictine monk, perhaps wrote the first treatise on *ars dictaminis* about 1087. Numerous other manuals and teachers followed in the next two hundred to three hundred years.

Ars dictaminis took principles for letter writing from Cicero's *De inventione* (written when he was 19) and the pseudo-Ciceronian *Rhetorica ad Herennium,* written at about the same time. The manuals taught a highly technical method of writing according to formulas. Letters consisted of five major parts: *salutatio* or salutation, which had to be very carefully calibrated according to the hierarchical positions of addressee and writer; *benevolentiae captatio,* the securing of good will by ordering the words in such a way as to win the approval of the recipient; *narratio,* the presentation of the matter under discussion; *petitio* or request; and *conclusio* or conclusion. Discussion of each of the five major sections could expand into numerous subdivisions, especially the discussion of the *salutatio,* which often occupied the major part of an *ars dictaminis* course or treatise. The *salutatio* section considered a very long list of potential recipients; each different higher authority had to be saluted correctly, an essential step in securing the desired end, in the view of the *dictatores.* An *ars dictaminis* manual also listed numerous phrases, lines, even entire letters, to be copied; indeed, it might consist entirely of a collection of model letters.

Ars dictaminis exemplified the typical medieval tendency to organize and classify an intellectual activity according to logical and hierarchical principles, and then to supply answers for all possible contingencies. It taught the rhetoric of formal public letters and rejected spontaneous and familiar expression. The *dictatores* favored a preceptive method based on rules, rather than imitation, which was preferred by the humanists. In similar fashion, fourteenth-century grammarians favored speculative grammar, an attempt to base language on a logic of meaning. Although primarily a university subject, and especially important at Bologna, *ars dictaminis* was taught in some advanced schools by communally hired masters. More important, *ars dictaminis,* like speculative grammar, embodied a late medieval Scholastic approach to learning which colored pre-university education, as well.

A few examples illustrate Italian education in the fourteenth century and the first decade of the fifteenth century. In 1326 a Savona father hired a Genoese master to instruct his two sons in various *auctores,* namely the *Disticha Catonis, Liber Aesopi, Prospero, Chartula,* and "summa," probably the *Summa artis notariae* (c. 1256) of Rolandino de' Passeggeri (d. 1300).[8]

---

[8]Petti Balbi, 1979, pp. 61–62, 131, 149.

Another student, Giovanni Conversino da Ravenna (1343–1408), who became an important teacher in his own right, described in later life his early training.[9] Between 1349 and 1353, when he was 6 to 10 years old, he lived in a boarding school in Bologna. After the primer, he read a group of unnamed poetical works (possibly *Aesopus, Eva columba, Physiologus,* and *Chartula*) followed by the *Disticha Catonis, Prospero,* and Boethius. He read no classics at this stage. In the spring of 1359, when he was 16, Giovanni Conversino went to the University of Bologna, where he heard lectures on the *Bononiannatus,* a well-known *ars dictaminis* treatise written by Giovanni di Bonandrea (c. 1245–1321), a famous teacher at Bologna. In the second half of his course, the young Giovanni Conversino attended lectures on the *Rhetorica ad Herennium.*

Giovanni Dominici (1357/8–1419), a Florentine Dominican cardinal, diplomat, and fiery opponent of the emerging humanistic studies, confirmed the curricular pattern. In his *Regola del governo di cura familiare* (written 1401–3), Dominici contrasted the wicked learning of the classics with the good learning of the past, by which he probably meant his own schooling in Florence in the 1360s and 1370s. At that time, Dominici wrote, students first learned the primer ("salterio") and "holy doctrine," that is, the standard prayers found in the primer. They then learned the "morality of Cato" (*Disticha Catonis*), the "inventions of Aesop," the "doctrine of Boethius" (*De consolatione philosophiae*), "good knowledge of Prospero taken from St. Augustine" (*Ex sententiis Augustini*), "philosophy from *Eva columba* or the *Tres leo naturas*" (*Physiologus*), "and a little versified Holy Scripture from the *Aethiopum terras*" (part of *Theodulus*).[10]

Although Dominici rejected the classics, late-fourteenth-century Italian schools included those classics beloved by medieval educators, albeit without making a distinction between them and medieval texts. In 1386 the Commune of Chioggia hired a new communal master and permitted him to charge his students supplementary fees on a graduated schedule. Unlike most schedules, this one listed the titles of the classroom texts and their ranking in the syllabus. After the lowest level of elementary Latin grammar came *Aesopus, Prospero,* Ovid's *Heroidum epistulae,* and Boethius. Pupils at a higher level studied "tragedies, Vergil, Lucan, Terence, and similar poets and authors," although the fees were the same as for those studying *Aesopus* and so on.[11] Moreover, one suspects that the pupils read only selections, perhaps in *florilegia.* This fee schedule, repeated in

[9]The following is based on Giovanni Conversino's autobiography, *Rationarium vite* (probably written 1396–1400), printed in Sabbadini, 1924, pp. 12–13, 23–24, 132. Garin, ed., 1958, pp. 106–11, quotes key sections of the *Rationarium vite.* See Conversino da Ravenna, 1980, pp. 13–30, for a good summary of Giovanni's life.

[10]For the text, see Varese, ed., 1955, pp. 27–28; or Garin, ed., 1958, p. 72. On Dominici, see Denley, 1981.

[11]"et volentibus audire tragedias, virgilium, lucanum, terentium, et similes poetas et

1397, indicated that late Trecento pedagogues taught certain classics. But the curriculum made no distinction between the classics and medieval textbooks, between Vergil and *Prospero*. Perhaps most important, poetical works dominated the curriculum. Classical Latin prose, such as in the letters, orations, and philosophical treatises of Cicero, was conspicuous by its absence.[12]

A final example further confirms the pattern. In 1410 the Commune of Faenza advertised for a teacher: "unus bonus magister et expertus in grammatica et in arte dictaminis."[13] The combination of grammar and *ars dictaminis* indicated a typical late medieval curriculum.

THE HUMANISTIC ALTERNATIVE

The humanists savagely attacked the medieval curriculum authors. Petrarch, as usual, started it: "In my childhood when all the others gaped at *Prospero* or *Aesopus,* I pondered the books of Cicero."[14] Lorenzo Valla and other humanists followed with sharp attacks on medieval learning in general and the curriculum authors in particular, a well-known polemic that need not be followed here.[15] A new group of Italian intellectuals imbued with enthusiasm for classical studies found the intellectual training inherited from the late Middle Ages inadequate and objectionable.

The humanists next offered a new vision in place of the old. In an effort to win elite public opinion to their cause, they wrote pedagogical treatises that advertised the rosy promise of the new studies. Pier Paolo Vergerio (c. 1368–1444) wrote the first and most important of these, *De ingenuis moribus et liberalibus studiis adulescentiae* (On noble customs and liberal studies of adolescents), in 1402 or 1403 in Padua.[16] Born in Capodistria, Vergerio studied at Padua, taught at Florence and Bologna, studied under Manuel Chrysoloras at Florence, returned to Padua at the end of 1399, went to Rome in 1405, and finished his career in obscurity in the service of

---

auctores ultra esopum, prosperum, ovidium, heroidum et boetium duc. IJ in anno pro quolibet." Bellemo, 1888, pp. 49–50.

[12]Although concerned with university level instruction and, perhaps, overstating the importance of the classics in the medieval curriculum, Wieruszowski, 1971, esp. pp. 589–627, contains much useful information on the teaching of the classics in thirteenth- and fourteenth-century Italy.

[13]Zama, 1920, p. 55. For additional information on mid- and late-*Trecento* Latin schools confirming the above, but without lists of textbooks, see Zanelli, 1900, pp. 9, 16–21, 25, 30–32, 115, 118; and Barsanti, 1905, pp. 109, 112, 211, 212.

[14]"Ab ipsa pueritia, quando ceteri omnes aut Prospero inhiant aut Esopo, ego libris Ciceronis incubui." *Senili* XV.1, as quoted in Garin, ed., 1958, p. 91.

[15]See Garin, ed., 1958, pp. 91–92, 103–4, for some of the humanistic attacks on the curriculum authors. For one of Valla's attacks, see ch. 7 herein.

[16]The fundamental study is Vergerio, 1934, pp. xi–xxx, for his life. For Vergerio and civic humanism, see Baron, 1966, pp. 126–34. On his birth date, see Baron, 1977, pp. 602–4, 614–25.

King Sigismund of Hungary. He addressed the work to Ubertino da Carrara (1390–1407), whom Vergerio probably tutored at one time, the third son of a one-time ruler of Padua. *De ingenuis moribus* far transcended its origins, becoming the most frequently copied and reprinted Renaissance pedagogical treatise before the works of Erasmus. More than one hundred fifteenth- and sixteenth-century manuscripts of *De ingenuis moribus* can be found in Italian libraries, and more than thirty Italian incunabular printings are known. It enjoyed similar diffusion in northern Europe.[17]

Vergerio sought to foster good character and learning in youths, and to celebrate education in general and humanistic studies in particular.[18] In the first part of the treatise, Vergerio set forth the importance of good character: the son of a prince should be disciplined, active, modest, moderate in pleasure, and free of indulgence and vice. Vergerio proclaimed an ideal close to the moderate and rational Stoic ethic of antiquity. The longer part of the treatise celebrated "liberal studies," those studies appropriate to a free man, in the phrase borrowed from Seneca (*Epistles* 88.2). They developed the individual's mind and body, bringing him to a high pitch of virtue and wisdom. Vergerio mentioned a large group of traditional and new studies. He gave pride of place to history, moral philosophy, and eloquence, a novel and significant emphasis.

Vergerio strongly praised liberal studies as preparation for the civic life.

Hence, for those with noble minds and those who must involve themselves in public affairs (*in publicis rebus*) and the community (*communitate*), it is useful to study history and moral philosophy. . . . From moral philosophy we learn what it is appropriate to do, while from history we extract the examples to follow. The one sets forth the duties of all men and is suitable to each person. The other narrates to us what has been said and done, teaching what we must do and say on various occasions. To these two disciplines, if I am not wrong, comes next a third, eloquence, also part of the civil science (*civilis scientiae*). . . . With eloquence, instead, one learns to speak gracefully, with gravity, in order to win over the hearts of the multitude.[19]

Rather than developing further the notion that the *studia humanitatis* prepared men for the active life, Vergerio went on to the *trivium* and *quadrivium,* and then the professional disciplines of law, medicine, and theology. He also recommended and discussed physical training for the future prince. The celebration of traditional subjects along with the appeal for the *studia humanitatis* underlined the transitional and mixed nature of Ver-

---

[17]Robey, 1980, pp. 56–57.

[18]For the Latin text see Vergerio, 1917, pp. 95–154. Garin, ed., 1959, pp. 57–112, provides an Italian translation, and Woodward, 1963, pp. 93–118, a free English translation. My interpretation depends on my own reading of the text but has been influenced by Garin, 1957, pp. 127–32, and Robey, 1980.

[19]For the Latin, see Robey, 1980, p. 30. The translation is mine.

gerio's treatise—not surprising, given the date of composition. Nevertheless, Vergerio enunciated themes, especially the link between the *studia
humanitatis* and the civic life, which future humanists and pedagogues
approved of and echoed.

Other humanists sought to persuade parents and princes that humanistic studies built character, taught eloquence, and trained future leaders of
society. Leonardo Bruni followed with *De studiis et litteris liber* (1423–26).
Then came Aeneas Silvius Piccolomini (1405–64) and his *Tractatus de
liberorum educatione* (1444), Maffeo Vegio (1407–58) and his *De educatione
liberorum* (composed 1445–48), and the *De ordine docendi et discendi* (1459) of
Battista Guarini (1435–1505).[20] These and other works offered a very
general program of studies and emphasized that humanistic studies prepared students for life.

Pedagogical treatises made very effective propaganda for the emerging
new curriculum by stressing the ideology, the purpose and promise, of
humanistic studies. Possibly Guarino Guarini of Verona (1374–1460)
promised the most. In letter after letter, Guarino told parents, princes,
students, and former students that they would become virtuous, eloquent,
learned, and successful leaders of society if they devoted themselves to
humanistic studies. In 1419 he pointed out to his friend Gian Nicola
Salerno (1379–1426), the *podestà* of Bologna, how humanistic studies had
prepared him to meet the challenge of his duties.

I understand that when civil disorder recently aroused the people of Bologna to
armed conflict you showed the bravery and eloquence of a soldier as well as you
had previously meted out the just sentence of a judge. . . . You therefore owe no
small thanks to the Muses with whom you have been on intimate terms since
boyhood, and by whom you were brought up. They taught you how to carry out
your tasks in society. . . . Hence you are living proof that the Muses rule not only
musical instruments but also public affairs. . . . How much then must we prize
this learning and praise those arts with which one educates the future ruler of the
state. And if he possesses justice, benevolence, prudence, and modesty, all will be
able to enjoy the fruit, and the benefit, as usual, will be spread among all. But if
these philosophic studies train a private citizen, it is not the same thing, for they dry
up and help only him alone.[21]

Guarino skillfully adapted his message to his reader. To an aging
Venetian patrician, he praised "liberal studies and disciplines" for the

[20]For the Latin texts and Italian translation, see Garin, ed., 1958, pp. 146–69 (Bruni), 198–
295 (Piccolomini), 434–71 (Battista Guarini). For free English translations of the treatises of
Bruni, Piccolomini, and Guarini, see Woodward, 1963, pp. 118–78. For the text of Vegio's
treatise, see Vegio, 1933–36. Also see Horkan, 1953.

[21]Guarino, 1967, vol. 1:263, letter of 19 September 1419; also Garin, ed., 1958, pp. 326–29.
For the first half of the quoted section, I follow the English translation of Grafton and Jardine,
1982, p. 53; the rest is mine. On Salerno, see Cavedon, 1983.

comfort and intellectual stimulation that they brought to old age.[22] To 12-year-old Ludovico Gonzaga, then attending the school of Vittorino da Feltre, Guarino promised that the books of the ancients offered better advice than the adulation of courtiers.[23] Guarino spread his message even if he had to flatter the princeling outrageously. Further letters in praise of humanistic studies can be found in the writings of Guarino and other early humanists who sought to win the approval of aristocratic public opinion for their new educational program. Of course, they also believed in their message.

An important discovery provided strong ancient support for a new education combining eloquence and moral philosophy for the civic life. In September 1416, Poggio Bracciolini discovered the complete text of Quintilian's *Institutio oratoria*. Previous scholars had had to make do with partial texts. He immediately communicated the news to Leonardo Bruni, who rapturously hailed the discovery.[24] Quintilian became the revered authority behind every humanistic pedagogical treatise through the next century and a half. Quintilian supplied a synthesis of pedagogical practice and rationale which the humanists used to explain and justify their rejection of medieval rhetoric specifically and medieval education generally.[25] In the preface to book 1, Quintilian wrote:

My aim, then, is the education of the perfect orator. The first essential for such an one is that he should be a good man, and consequently we demand of him not merely the possession of exceptional gifts of speech, but of all the excellences of character as well. For I will not admit that the principles of upright and honourable living should, as some have held, be regarded as the peculiar concern of philosophy. The man who can really play his part as a citizen and is capable of meeting the demands both of public and private business, the man who can guide a state by his counsels, give it a firm basis by his legislation and purge its vices by his decisions as a judge, is assuredly no other than the orator of our quest.[26]

Further support came in 1421, when Bishop Gerardo Landriani found at Lodi a manuscript of five Ciceronian works including the complete text of *De oratore*, missing for centuries. Written circa 55 B.C., some thirty years after *De inventione* and the pseudo-Ciceronian *Rhetorica ad Herennium*, *De oratore* presented Cicero's mature reflections on rhetoric. In it he dismissed *De inventione* as the imperfect effort of youth.[27] Going beyond the didactic prescriptions and disembodied rules of *De inventione* and *Ad Herennium*,

[22]Guarino, 1967, vol. 1, pp. 136–38, letter of 1417; Garin, ed., 1958, pp. 319–23.
[23]Guarino, 1967, vol. 1, pp. 397–402, letter of 8 June 1424; Garin, ed., 1958, pp. 334–43.
[24]Sabbadini, 1914, pp. 381–407.
[25]J. Murphy, 1981, pp. 357–63.
[26]*Institutio oratoria* I. preface.9–10, in Quintilian, 1966–69.
[27]*De oratore* I.2.5.

Cicero wrote a wide-ranging dialogue on character, civic duty, philosophy, and rhetoric.

With the full Quintilian and *De oratore,* the humanists had an arsenal of ancient support for what they already believed: that fourteenth-century rhetorical teaching and the formulas of *ars dictaminis* were too narrow in scope and restrictive in content. They focused excessively on formal hierarchical relationships and the limited subject matter of a letter while ignoring the larger dimensions of the orator in society. In the judgment of the humanists, medieval rhetoric viewed the letter writer as a technician with an ample file of examples to copy; the humanist educators wanted wisdom and variety as well as technique. They now sought ancient prose authors to teach in the classroom.

THE REDISCOVERY OF CICERO

The late medieval curriculum did not teach ancient prose authors as models of style. Medieval instructors taught poetic classics such as Vergil, and used ancient rhetoric manuals such as Cicero's *De inventione* and the *Rhetorica ad Herennium,* to inculcate the techniques and terminology of rhetoric. But they did not use an ancient prose author as a standard of excellence to be imitated. Not only did late medieval pedagogues evince no interest in teaching an eloquent Latin style based on ancient prose, but they lacked a suitable model. The letters and other prose works of Seneca were widely available, but medieval scholars mined them for moral precepts instead of imitating their style.[28] Perhaps the lack of form, inconsistent style, and experimental nature of Seneca's prose alienated medieval teachers.[29] The emerging humanistic curriculum needed a standard of correct and eloquent classical prose to substitute for *ars dictaminis* and late medieval Latin prose generally. The rediscovery of most of Cicero's letters and orations, either unknown or ignored in the Middle Ages, gave the humanists such a model.

Petrarch made the first Ciceronian discoveries, the oration *Pro Archia* at Liège in 1333 and the *Letters to Atticus* in Verona in 1345.[30] Boccaccio found the *Pro Cluentia* in 1355. Above all, Coluccio Salutati instituted the search that uncovered the *Epistulae ad familiares* in 1392 at Vercelli. This became the most important discovery for the curriculum.

[28]Reynolds, 1965, esp. pp. 112–15.

[29]Duff, 1960, vol. 2:179–86.

[30]The story is still best followed in Sabbadini, 1914, who provides a wealth of extracts from contemporary sources so that the reader can follow the path of discovery and experience the excitement. Also see Sabbadini, 1967; and Reynolds and Wilson, 1974, pp. 116, 118, 120–23; and Bracciolini, 1974, for English translation of some of the letters announcing the discoveries.

When the papal court moved to Constance for the council there (1414–17), the Italian humanists who accompanied the court had a splendid opportunity to ransack northern monastic libraries for classical texts. They had great success. In 1415 Poggio Bracciolini found in the monastery of Cluny in Burgundy a very old manuscript, perhaps from the eighth century, of Cicero's orations which included the previously unknown *Pro Roscio Amerino* and *Pro Murena,* as well as *Pro Cluentio, Pro Milone,* and *Pro Caelio.* In the summer of 1416, Poggio found at St. Gall Asconius's *Commentary* on five of Cicero's speeches, as well as the complete Quintilian and other works. In the summer of 1417, Poggio found in France and Germany eight more previously unknown speeches of Cicero's: *Pro Caecina, Pro Roscio comoedo, De lege agraria* i–iii, *Pro Rabirio perduellionis reo, In Pisonem,* and *Pro Rabirio Postumo.* The Ciceronian discoveries reached a climax in 1421 when Landriani found *De oratore* and *Orator* (available before only in partial copies) and the previously unknown *Brutus.*

The humanists made these discoveries of previously unavailable Ciceronian texts and more complete versions of known ones in less than a century, with the bulk of the finds made between 1392 and 1421. The Renaissance found Cicero with his ornate style, simplified Greek philosophy, conception of the orator, and involvement in the legal and political affairs of the Roman Republic more congenial than any other classical prose author. Petrarch held Cicero in high esteem, although he found Cicero's fatal plunge into political intrigue after the assassination of Caesar (documented in the *Letters to Atticus*) unacceptable. Later humanists admired Cicero's combination of eloquence and politics. Leonardo Bruni wrote a biography of Cicero, his *Cicero novus* of 1415, as did Gasparino Barzizza between 1416 and 1421. Humanist scholars spent much time integrating Cicero's works and life into the emerging humanist world view in the early Quattrocento.[31]

The Ciceronian discoveries and the accompanying flurry of scholarship would have had a major impact on the Renaissance in any case. That they occurred precisely at the moment when educators found the medieval curriculum wanting, and were constructing the new, meant that Cicero permanently shaped the Italian Renaissance. In simplest terms, the humanistic educators substituted the letters and orations of Cicero for the medieval *auctores* in their schools. Cicero became the orator in the new curriculum of orators, poets, and historians.

Guarino inserted Cicero's epistles and orations into his school at an early stage of his pedagogical career. He commented on *Pro Roscio Amerino,* praising Cicero as a teacher of life and language, when teaching at Venice (1414–19). He continued to teach the orations when he moved to

---

[31]This is a well-known story. See, in particular, Baron, 1938b; Baron, 1966, pp. 121–29; and Fryde, 1980. For Barzizza, see Mercer, 1979; and Pigman, 1981.

Verona, where he lectured on *Pro Murena*. In April or May 1419, when Guarino initiated his independent school in Verona, his prolusion (inaugural lecture) went as follows.

In the same manner, for the first libations of studies to be tasted in these years, I have chosen not difficult orations nor bitter topics of this art, but rather a certain easy and very clear way of speaking which, enticing the reader, may be useful and delightful by its very agreeable order of words and gentle weight of the sentences. I have gathered together some letters of Cicero in which this style of pure and very elegant speech is expressed.[32]

Indeed, Guarino compiled an anthology of fifty of Cicero's letters and made the *Epistulae ad familiares* a fundamental part of his lower-division instruction. The term *Epistulae ad familiares* as a collective title for a large group of Cicero's letters to diverse correspondents (excluding Atticus) came into existence in the first two decades of the fifteenth century and entered common usage about 1430, possibly as a result of the letters' introduction into the school curriculum.

More than thirty years later Guarino looked back and praised the difference that the use of Cicero as a model for Latin style had made. His son Niccolò had found some of his father's youthful letters and laughed at their bad Latinity. You linger over some Latin words lacking any suitability for expression, Guarino wrote him in 1452. I am happy for the way you judge your father's style, but not for this reason am I embarrassed at what I wrote long ago. You are fortunate to have grown up in these blessed new times. For until our times, humanistic studies lay prostrate in a dark night, and writing had lost every splendor of elegance. Italy did not have Cicero, "the greatest authority of the Latin language," as a mirror and example for its discourse. But now, the admiration and imitation of Ciceronian language by itself constitutes a notable cause of progress. For, after a long pause, Italy finished saturating herself with *Prosperos, Eva columbas,* and *Chartulas,* which had taken Cicero's place, producing a horrible and uncultured barbarity in speaking and writing. In those times, one would have been praised for a happy style if one wrote

Vobis regratior, quia de concernentibus capitaniatui meo tam honorificabiliter per unam vestram litteram vestra me advisavit sapientitudo.

I rethank you because your wisdomness advisified me so honorifically through one letter of yours about concerning my captaindom.[33]

---

[32]"Eodem modo ad prima studiorum delibamente his annis propinanda non difficillimas orationes non asperos artificii locos sed facile quoddam et planissimum dicendi genus delegi, quod suavissimo verborum ordine et leni sententiarum pondere lectorem alliciens prosit atque iuvet. Nonnullas enim decerpsi Ciceronis epistulas, in quibus ille puri et facetissimi sermonis stilus exprimitur. . . ." Sabbadini, 1914, pp. 32, 52–59, quote on p. 58.

[33]Guarino, 1967, vol. 2:581–84, quote on p. 582, letter of 30 August 1452; also Garin, ed., 1958, pp. 416–21. I am grateful to Erika Rummel, who suggested this translation.

If you find improprieties and errors in my old writings, Guarino concluded, the fault lies in the corrupt usage of former times.

An English translation cannot convey how awful the sentence is, with its grammatical mistakes, artificial suffixes, non-classical usage (*capitaniatui, honorificabiliter, sapientitudo*), repeated *v* sounds, and lack of rhythm. Could Guarino really have written such a dreadful sentence before the advent of humanism? Whether he did or not, the sentence vividly conveyed his judgment on late medieval Latin before the adoption of Cicero as a model.

Guarino correctly assessed the importance of Cicero to humanistic education. Schools need a canon of works and authors to compose the unchanging literature curriculum and to serve as a model for style.[34] Cicero's prose, especially the letters and orations, became canonical in Italian Renaissance Latin schools. Students learned to write like Cicero, and Ciceronian style became the standard.[35] Eventually it became such a severe and rigid standard, and its proponents became so filled with pedantic excesses, that Erasmus found Italian Ciceronianism an easy target for barbed scorn in his *Ciceronianus* (1528).

GREEK

Greek completed the arch of humanistic studies. Western medieval scholars knew very little Greek. They did not yearn to read Greek masterpieces in the original language, and even had they wished to learn Greek, very few competent teachers existed to instruct them. Petrarch caressed his Homer manuscript but made no great effort to acquire Greek, partly because he loved ancient Latin culture more. On the other hand, Petrarch did proclaim his desire to learn Greek. In this, as in so many other matters, later humanists followed his lead. They also began to realize how much Roman civilization owed to the eloquence and wisdom of Hellas.

The first real opportunity to learn Greek came when Salutati invited Manuel Chrysoloras to come to Florence to teach.[36] Mutual needs brought them together. Chrysoloras (1350–1415), a wealthy and highly placed figure at the Byzantine court, wished to secure Western support for Constantinople against the coming onslaught of the Mongols and Turks. Salutati desperately wanted to bring someone from Constantinople to

[34]Curtius, 1963, ch. 14, esp. pp. 247–48, 259. For Guarino's use of Cicero in his school, see Sabbadini, 1964b, pp. 36–37, 59–65, 84–86; and Battista Guarino's *De ordine docendi et discendi* in Garin, ed., 1958, pp. 452–59, 462–65; and in Woodward, 1963, pp. 169–72.

[35]For a recent assessment of the importance of Ciceronian style to the Renaissance, see D'Amico, 1983, pp. 123–43.

[36]For this very brief summary of a large topic, I have relied on Cammelli, 1941; Weiss, 1977, esp. chs. 1, 11, 14, and 15; Setton, 1956; Reynolds and Wilson, 1974, pp. 105–7, 130–41; and Monfasani, 1976.

teach Greek competently. Chrysoloras's trip accomplished Salutati's pedagogical purpose and more.

In his teaching in Florence between 1397 and 1400, Chrysoloras brought to the West the best of Byzantine approaches to Greek. He taught his pupils to abandon the medieval literal translation of Greek to Latin in favor of a literary and rhetorical approach that emphasized fidelity to meaning and style. He wrote a Greek grammar, *Erotemata,* to help Italians (Guarino prepared an abridgment of it that spread widely). Finally, the humanists' affection for Chrysoloras's learning and humanity magnified the impact of his teaching. Guarino, in particular, never tired of singing his praises.

Spurred by Chrysoloras's example, Italians went to Constantinople. Guarino was there between 1403 and 1408, his expenses paid by a Venetian noble. Guarino lived in Chrysoloras's household, imbibed Chrysoloras's pedagogical methods, translated Greek to Latin, and perfected his Greek. Upon his return to Italy, Guarino added Greek to his teaching in Florence (1410–14), Venice (1414–19), and elsewhere. The cultural interchange continued. Francesco Filelfo (1398–1481) also went to Constantinople, where he married a Greek noblewoman before returning to Italy. In or about 1416, George of Trebizond (1395–1472/3) came to Italy, where he had a long and influential career training future Italian humanists in Greek, rhetoric, and dialectic.

The contributions of Italian scholars expert in Greek to Renaissance learning are well known. In addition, Greek had a symbolic importance: nothing better expressed a commitment to the *studia humanitatis* than glowing statements about the riches to be unlocked through a knowledge of classical Greek. Communes and parents pledged themselves to the new learning by hiring a master to teach Greek with other subjects. But the number of humanists fluent in Greek—other than the genuine experts— and the number of students learning Greek may have been small. One doubts if many more learned Greek elsewhere in the late fifteenth or sixteenth centuries. However, the call to learn Greek, a talisman promising almost magical benefits, had great power to win converts to the *studia humanitatis.*

THREE FAMOUS TEACHERS

Vergerio, Guarino, and other early humanists rejected medieval *auctores* and subjects in favor of the *studia humanitatis.* They looked to Quintilian and Cicero's *De oratore* for inspiration, wished to substitute Cicero's letters and orations for the *ars dictaminis,* and insisted on the importance of Greek. These innovations marked a major intellectual change.

The humanists next had to provide new schools and teachers to implement humanistic studies. A trio of pedagogical pioneers won the support of a few political leaders who sent their sons and a handful of daughters to

be instructed. The new humanistic schools, especially the humanistic
boarding schools, became the schools of choice for sons of princes, nobles,
and wealthy commoners in northern Italy. Indeed, the boarding-school
experience reinforced the new curriculum. The initial establishment of the
studia humanitatis in the schoolroom took approximately twenty-five
years, with the key developments occurring between about 1420 and 1430.

The teaching career of Gasparino Barzizza (1360–1430), especially in the
Paduan period, between 1407 and 1421, marked a transition from medieval
to Renaissance schooling. The son of a minor noble and notary, Gasparino
was born at Barzizza, an estate in the hills about eighteen miles northeast of
Bergamo. He studied grammar and rhetoric with Giovanni Travesi da
Cremona at the University of Pavia between 1387 and 1392, and received
his arts degree (*laurea*) in 1392.[37] By 1396 he was teaching at a pre-
university level in Bergamo; in 1404 he appeared as a university lecturer in
grammar and "authors" (*auctores*) at Pavia alongside his former teacher. He
served as an independent master to several patrician families in Venice for
several months in 1407 until appointed in October of that year to teach "in
Rhetoricis et Moralibus (Auctoribus)" at the University of Padua at a
salary of 120 ducats per annum. For fourteen years Barzizza lectured at the
university and taught other students at home, where he lodged and
boarded up to twenty youths at a time. In 1421 he returned to the University of Pavia, where he helped edit the Ciceronian manuscripts discovered
by Bishop Landriani in Lodi. He lectured at the University of Bologna
from the autumn of 1426 until 1428, and returned to Pavia to die in 1430.[38]

Barzizza endorsed humanistic scholarship while clinging to medieval
authors and methods.[39] He showed a keen interest in the prose masterpieces of Latin antiquity, warmly greeted the new discoveries, and helped
edit them. He particularly loved and taught the works of Cicero. Although trained in speculative grammar, he rejected it in favor of grammar
based on ancient usage. At the same time, much of his teaching remained
traditional. He relied on such medieval *auctores* as Balbi, Hugutius, and
Alexander de Villedieu. Although proclaiming the importance of Greek,
he learned very little of the language. And he wished to reform rather than
discard *ars dictaminis*. Even though his teaching did not become completely
humanistic, Barzizza communicated his love of the new studies to a large
number of influential students who spread his enthusiasm.

After Barzizza came Guarino, whose schools, pupils, and patrons did
much to advance the *studia humanitatis* in these years. Born Guarino
Guarini in Verona in 1374, he studied in Verona, Venice, Padua, and
possibly elsewhere, before opening his first school in Verona, probably in

[37]On Travesi (c. 1350–1418), see Rossi, 1901.
[38]Mercer, 1979, pp. 24–28, 38–39, 44–45, 132–37.
[39]Ibid., passim. Pigman, 1981, sees Barzizza as somewhat more humanistic than Mercer.

the 1390s.[40] After he returned from Constantinople, he began his second pedagogical career in Florence in 1410. In July 1414 he moved to Venice, where he opened an independent school with boarding students. His pupils included Francesco Barbaro (1390–1454) and Bernardo Giustiniani (1408–89), Venetian patrician statesmen and humanistic scholars. While in Venice, Guarino wrote his *Regulae grammaticales,* which enjoyed great success (see ch. 7). By the end of 1417 Guarino wished to leave Venice, possibly because the Venetian constitution barred non-Venetians, even very learned ones from nearby Verona, from holding high chancery positions. After angling for a post in the Roman curia and considering a return to Florence, Guarino married a wealthy Veronese woman at the end of 1418 and moved to Verona in the spring of 1419 to open an independent school. He prospered in Verona. Pupils from leading Veronese families filled his school, and his marriage brought him a villa in Valpolicella, a few miles outside of Verona. When the plague arrived in the summer of 1419, Guarino and his pupils retired to Valpolicella, where the region's famous wine helped wash down the lessons.

The elite of Verona warmly received Guarino's pedagogical efforts. In May 1420 the Commune of Verona appointed him "to lecture in rhetoric, to teach the *Epistles* and *Orations* of Cicero, and other means that lead to eloquence, as well as other authors that are pleasing to the listeners and useful to all the adolescents and adults of the city and district of Verona."[41] The commune awarded him a five-year appointment at the high salary of 150 gold ducats and allowed him to continue to teach independently for additional fees.

The appointment can be seen as the formal inauguration of pre-university humanistic education. Verona's leading citizens appointed a famous humanistic pedagogue to teach Cicero's *Epistles* and *Orations,* quintessential texts of the *studia humanitatis,* at substantial public expense. If a symbolic date for the beginning of Renaissance Latin education is sought, 1420 may be considered to be it.

Guarino taught in Verona for ten years, producing a steady stream of humanistically trained pupils including the Venetian patrician and scholar Ermolao Barbaro (c. 1410–71), who came to him in 1421. When the commune did not wish to renew Guarino's *condotta* in 1425, possibly because of the teacher's lengthy absences from the city, a student spoke eloquently on his behalf to the city council and praise flooded in from abroad. The commune renewed the *condotta.* Guarino moved to Ferrara in

---

[40]The following is based on Sabbadini, 1964a and b; Woodward, 1968, pp. 26–47; Garin, 1967, pp. 69–106. For an iconoclastic view, see Grafton and Jardine, 1982.

[41]". . . elligerit Rhetoricam legere, Epistolas et Orationes Tullianas et alias facultates que ad elloquentiam pertineant docere et alia que fuerint auditoribus placita et utillia omnibus adolescentibus et maioribus civitatis et districtus Verone." Printed in Garin, ed., 1958, p. 486.

1430 to become tutor to Leonello Este (1407–1450), designated successor to Duke Niccolò III. Just as the Veronese communal appointment of 1420 indicated civic approval, so this post signalled princely approbation for the *studia humanitatis*. And when in 1435 Guarino's pupil Leonello Este married Vittorino's student Margherita Gonzaga, humanists must have felt that their efforts to win over the ruling class to the *studia humanitatis* had been crowned with success.

Guarino's appointment at Ferrara had advantages for both the humanist and the Este rulers. Guarino became the tutor and confidante to a young prince who became ruler in 1441. Guarino also received an impressive salary; in 1435, when he became a public lecturer, his salary was 300 ducats. And he became an academic "star" in the revivified University of Ferrara in 1442. When Guarino died in 1460, Duke Borso and the commune of Ferrara erected a magnificent church monument to Guarino which was intended to rival Bruni's monument in Florence.

Guarino, in turn, conferred distinction on the Este city and court. In the view of Ludovico Carbone (1435–82), a pupil of Guarino's who delivered the teacher's funeral oration, Guarino single-handedly brought humanistic studies to Ferrara. Before Guarino's arrival, the Ferrarese knew no Cicero, scarcely mentioned Caesar, Sallust, and Livy, lacked the first principles of Latin grammar, could not interpret the poets, and dared not open their mouths for their ignorance of rhetoric, according to Carbone.[42] Even if Carbone exaggerated Ferrara's former cultural barrenness, it is clear that Guarino added considerable intellectual luster to the city. He attracted many pupils from Italy and abroad, and induced leading humanists to visit Ferrara. He graced court marriages with Latin epithalamia and defended princely rule in a celebrated debate (1435) with Poggio Bracciolini on the subject of Caesar's role in ancient Rome.[43]

In his long pedagogical career, Guarino taught numerous future princes, civil servants, and teachers. He sought out the powerful everywhere he taught and maintained friendly relations with them after moving on. They, in turn, kept coming to his school. For example, in 1452 a Venetian youth submitted a petition to the Venetian government. He had left his post as a ballot boy in the Great Council in order to go to Ferrara "to study oratory under that most learned man Guarino of Verona." Having returned to Venice, he wished to regain his former post and to be favorably considered for the first notary vacancy in the chancery. The government granted his request.[44] Guarino also taught several members of the impor-

---

[42]Carbone's oration is printed in Garin, ed., 1952, pp. 382–417, especially pp. 390–91.
[43]For Guarino's part of the exchange, see ibid., pp. 314–77.
[44]"ad studendum in arte Oratoria sub doctissimo viro Guarino Veronensi." The youth's name was Lodovico fu Giovanni de Bonisio. ASV, Collegio, Notatorio, R. 8, fol. 161ʳ, 18 June 1452. I owe this reference to the kindness of Susan Connell.

tant Strozzi family of Florence, the son of Poggio Bracciolini, Janus Pannonius (Joannes de Csezmicze, 1434–72) and other Hungarians, several English students, and even the famous preacher San Bernardino da Siena for three months in Verona in 1422 and 1423. Those destined to become humanistic teachers, such as Martino Rizzoni and Gian Pietro da Lucca, also studied with Guarino.

Vittorino (Rambaldoni) da Feltre (1373 or 1378–1446/7) completed the trinity of pioneering humanistic schoolmasters. The son of a notary, Vittorino was born in Feltre, a small town in the foothills of the Dolomites about sixty miles north of Venice.[45] Vittorino spent the years from about 1390 to 1415 in Padua, where he sat at the feet of Giovanni Conversino da Ravenna, taught Latin in an independent school, obtained a degree in arts in 1410, became a servant in the house of a mathematics teacher to pay for mathematical instruction, and later tutored in that subject. He went to Venice in 1415 to learn Greek from Guarino of Verona and especially from George of Trebizond. In turn, Vittorino taught Latin to Trebizond and won the undying affection of the volatile Greek.

Vittorino returned to Padua in 1419 to teach independently. In 1421 he succeeded Barzizza in the chair of rhetoric at the University of Padua and also conducted a boarding school in his home. But Vittorino never coveted university or chancery posts, preferring to shape the minds and character of youngsters. Hence, in 1422 he abandoned his chair in order to return to Venice to direct his own independent school with boarders. An unfortunate incident probably caused him to leave: the Venetian government sentenced a cousin of Vittorino's to prison, later exile, for treasonous speech against the state.[46] A man of immense rectitude and sensitivity in matters of family honor—later he paid the considerable debts of some worthless relatives—Vittorino must have felt stained by his cousin's disgrace and unable to remain in Venice. Hence, he accepted the invitation of Marquis Gianfrancesco Gonzaga to come to Mantua to establish a school for his several children and others of the court.

Vittorino moved to Mantua in the middle of 1423 and taught at his famous school, the *Casa Giocosa* (Pleasant or Merry House), for the rest of his life. Vittorino devoted his energies to his students rather than to his own studies. Indeed, his devotion to their best interests led him to support his pupils in the face of princely anger on occasion. Vittorino insisted that all the students, including the Gonzaga children, live in simple surround-

---

[45]A large bibliography, which cannot be listed in its entirety here, exists on Vittorino da Feltre. Contemporary biographies and descriptions of his school are found in Garin, ed., 1958, pp. 504–718. Also see Platina, 1948. Good summary accounts are found in Woodward, 1963, pp. 1–92; *Mantova. Le Lettere*, 1962, pp. 5–52; and the papers in *Vittorino e la sua scuola*, 1981.

[46]Nardi, 1971, p. 48.

ings within the Casa Giocosa, thus making it exclusively a boarding establishment (for as many as seventy students at its height). He taught the children of the Gonzaga, other princely, noble, and wealthy commoner students from Mantua and beyond, plus as many as forty poor students (boarded at his own expense) at one time. Vittorino accepted students aged 4 to about 20; they stayed between one and ten years. Possibly the majority entered between the ages of 12 and 14 and studied four to six years, making the Casa Giocosa mostly a secondary school.

Vittorino taught future princes, prelates, humanists, and schoolmasters. Federigo II da Montefeltre (1422–82) studied with Vittorino from 1434 to 1436. Taddeo de' Manfredi, *signore* of Imola, and Gilberto da Correggio also learned under Vittorino. The future prelates included Gregorio Correr and Pietro Balbo of Venice, Giovanni Andrea de' Bussi, bishop and commentator on Livy, and Battista Pallavicini from Rimini. Niccolò Perotti and Lorenzo Valla studied with Vittorino, as did the lesser humanists and schoolmasters Ognibene Bonisoli and Gian Pietro da Lucca. Guarino Guarini and Francesco Filelfo sent their sons to Vittorino, while Theodore Gaza and George of Trebizond helped Vittorino teach. The Casa Giocosa enrolled at least three girls, two Gonzaga daughters and Barbara of Brandenburg (1422–81), who came to Mantua as the 12-year-old intended bride of Ludovico Gonzaga. Possibly only girls of the Gonzaga family attended, for there is no evidence of other female pupils.

The boarding-school experience compounded the teachers' influence over students and considerably aided the spread of the *studia humanitatis*. Boarding schools had medieval roots; as noted in chapter 1, a Genoese father sent his 5-year-old son to one in 1221. Professors at the University of Bologna conducted them in the first quarter of the fourteenth century. A student came to the university and lived with a professor. The student attended the professor's public lectures at the university and received private instruction from him at home. Before long, younger students not yet ready for university classes also boarded with a professor.[47] By the last quarter of the fourteenth century, the boarding school run by a relatively well known pedagogue who did not necessarily live in a university town had become common, although not nearly as common as other forms of schools. For example, Giovanni Conversino da Ravenna conducted boarding schools at Conegliano from 1371 to 1373, at Padua from 1392 to 1404, and in Venice from 1404 to 1406.[48] Teachers operated boarding schools for personal financial gain as well as for the education of youths. To be sure, operating a boarding school involved heavy responsibilities and expenses: a large house, food, domestic assistance for cooking and housekeeping, and teaching assistants who had to be paid. But the finan-

[47]Zaccagnini, 1926, pp. 72–73.
[48]Mercer, 1979, pp. 15–16.

cial rewards could be substantial: Barzizza's fees reached the very high figure of forty gold ducats annually (it is not known if this figure was typical).[49]

Barzizza probably had a total of about seventy boarding students in his fourteen years at Padua; if each remained three to five years, about twenty resided there simultaneously. Leon Battista Alberti (1404–72), who studied with Barzizza between 1415 and 1418 before going on to study law at Bologna, must have been Barzizza's most famous boarder. Barzizza also taught Francesco Filelfo in 1416 and 1417, and George of Trebizond, probably in 1416. But the vast majority of his pupils were not future humanists but northern Italian aristocrats. Carlo Alberti, brother to Leon Battista, boarded with Barzizza, as did boys from the princely Malaspina family, members of the Barbaro, Correr, Loredan, Trevisan, and Zeno patrician families of Venice, boys from the Castiglione and other noble families of Lombardy, some students from the middle class of professionals, and a handful of foreigners, including Alfonso of Portugal. Barzizza's pupils often later studied at a university and then pursued one of three kinds of careers. Some took their places in the ruling circles of government and the church. Others became lawyers and physicians. And a third, non-aristocratic, group of students taught school.[50]

Barzizza set the example; Guarino and Vittorino made the boarding school an essential component in the lives of the governing class and a prime means of spreading the *studia humanitatis*. Certainly humanistic boarding schools catered to the elite: sons of princes, nobles, and professionals, plus a few bright but poor students supported by the master, lived with an eminent teacher who trained their minds and shaped their character. The humble Italian term for attending a boarding school, *stare a dozzina* (to be a boarder), or the casual *a dozzina* (to board) seemed inadequate to the humanistic educators.[51] Barzizza called his school a *gymnasium*, that is, a Greek public school.[52] And Guarino, with his usual mix of classical ideals and shrewd sense of public relations, called his a *contubernium*, a common dwelling, implying comradeship, intimacy, and intellectual exchange.[53]

---

[49]Ibid., p. 106. In a letter to a male relative, possibly an uncle, of a student, Guarino seemed to imply that the cost of his boarding school at Verona in 1423 was also "forty pieces of gold [ducats?]." "De re pecuniaria vero parva sane cura; nec me aurei XL movent; vestra imprimis omnium rectissima voluntas movet, cui ut morem geram incredibiliter ardeo." Guarino, 1967, vol. 2:366, letter of 1 June 1423, Verona.

[50]Mercer, 1979, pp. 106–7, 121–24, 168.

[51]*Grande dizionario della lingua italiana*, 13 vols. (Turin, 1961–86), 4:994.

[52]Mercer, 1979, p. 106.

[53]For example, on 6 October 1418, Guarino wrote to a friend, Paolo de Paolinis, then a professor at Florence, inviting him to join him in his boarding school in Venice. Guarino promised neither fine food nor luxurious accommodations, but intimacy and companionship with Guarino and his students in the joyful common enterprise of learning. In the middle of

Master and student sought to forge a lifetime bond in the years that they lived and learned under the same roof. The boarding-school experience might generate stronger and more intimate ties than existed between parent and child. A boy of 10 or 12 left his parental home to live in a pedagogical family. The master corrected the boy's lessons in the classroom, chided his manners at the table, and improved his morals everywhere.

The boarding school also nourished the humanistic curriculum. *Contubernium* and *studia humanitatis* complemented each other so well. Renaissance teachers wanted a group of studies to teach good morals and good literature. The boarding school needed a curriculum to train boys for leadership roles requiring wisdom and character more than technical skills. The humanists believed that they could recreate in the boarding school a miniature ancient world whose youthful inhabitants would become responsible and upright leaders of society. The presence of the boarding school as the ideal learning environment helps explain why Renaissance pedagogical literature insisted that the teacher must be good as well as learned, and that an affective bond must unite teacher and student. It also explains the almost pathetic eagerness to believe that these privileged boys would grow up to be just rulers immune to the corrupting influences of power and wealth.

The boarding school became in integral part of the maturation process for the sons of the wealthy and powerful in Western civilization. In this setting the privileged learned Latin and Greek, how to share authority with their peers, and how to command the rest of society. The line from Vittorino's Casa Giocosa to Thomas Arnold's Rugby and the prep schools and highly selective private colleges and universities of North America is a direct one.

During the Renaissance, the boarding school helped propagate the *studia humanitatis,* for the ethos of the elite quickly becomes the goal of the middle class. Obviously few non-noble parents and not all nobles could afford to pay forty ducats per annum to send their sons to Guarino's *contubernium.* Nor did many Italian communities have princes with the financial resources to found court schools. But parents and communal councils could hire humanistic schoolmasters to teach the new curriculum in their own household or town. Their sons might study in local independent and communal schools the same *studia humanitatis* pursued by Gonzaga princelings in the Casa Giocosa, if they had the right teachers. Humanists and parents next had to establish the new Latin curriculum across a broad range of northern Italian towns.

---

his elegant invitation, Guarino wrote: "Utinam tibi tam aurum argentumque polliceri possem, quam iocundum contubernium amoenumque convictum." Guarino, 1967, vol. 1:205.

THE ESTABLISHMENT OF THE *STUDIA HUMANITATIS*

Guarino and Vittorino founded schools that trained the sons of the ruling class and future humanists. Convinced of the importance of an education based on the orators, poets, and historians, graduates of the schools of Guarino and Vittorino spread the knowledge of the *studia humanitatis*. When these "old boys" reached positions of authority, they chose other pupils of the famous pedagogues, classmates of lower social rank who had become teachers, to instruct their sons. Guarino and Vittorino helped by recommending their former students for teaching posts. In the way that influence works, humanistically trained masters gained teaching positions and implemented the new curriculum. Humanistic education became established in the 1430s, 1440s, and 1450s, especially in towns within the orbit of Guarino and Vittorino. The *studia humanitatis* soon spread throughout northern and north-central Italy.

Numerous fifteenth-century humanists held elementary and secondary school teaching posts. The most ambitious and gifted men went on to become university professors, chancery secretaries, advisers to princes, and curial officials in Rome. Those who published little or lacked the good fortune to win the favor of the powerful remained in the elementary and secondary schools and solidified the triumph of the *studia humanitatis*.

The careers of students of Barzizza, Guarino, and Vittorino who became teachers illustrate the process. Martino Rizzoni, born circa 1404 in Verona, probably came from the middle ranks of society. He and his brother attended Guarino's school in Verona until their father died in 1424. Because Rizzoni had to earn a living, Guarino found him a post as tutor to a noble family in Venice. When Rizzoni complained that his noble pupils had little interest in studying and that the family treated him like a servant, Guarino encouraged him to persevere. He also persuaded Rizzoni's employer to raise the tutor's salary. Guarino continued to watch over Rizzoni's career, and Rizzoni performed minor scholarly tasks for his mentor. By 1432 Rizzoni had returned to Verona (Guarino having left); there he married and taught as an independent master for the rest of his life. His rising tax payments suggest that his school prospered. He also joined the scholarly circle around Ermolao Barbaro (probably a classmate in Guarino's school), who served as bishop of Verona from 1453 to 1481. Like other humanistic schoolmasters, Rizzoni wrote and delivered a number of nuptial orations and a grammatical work (now lost). He died in 1488.[54]

Ognibene Bonisoli (Omnibonus Leonicenus) also helped spread the *studia humanitatis* through his teaching and writing. Born about 1412 in the

---

[54]Marchi, 1965–66. Guarino's twenty-four surviving letters to Rizzoni and one of Rizzoni's letters are found in Guarino, 1967, vols. 1 and 2.

small town of Lonigo about fifteen miles south of Vicenza and twenty-five miles west of Padua, Ognibene moved to Mantua as a child.[55] There he studied with Vittorino da Feltre in the Casa Giocosa, possibly as an indigent pupil supported by the master, from about 1423 to about 1433. His schoolmate Ludovico Gonzaga remained Ognibene's friend long after becoming ruler of Mantua. After completing his schooling, Ognibene went to the Council of Basel, and then to Vicenza, where he ran an independent school and married in or about 1436. He served Ludovico Gonzaga between 1436 and 1438 and taught independently in Treviso in 1440. Ognibene won a communal mastership at the relatively young age of about 29 when the Commune of Treviso appointed him in January 1441 "to teach grammar and read rhetoric and whichever authors the students require" for five years at a salary of fifty ducats per annum.[56] The mention of rhetoric plus his background and scholarly activity confirm that Ognibene taught the *studia humanitatis*.

Ognibene accepted a communal mastership at Vicenza in 1443. In the next few years he declined offers to join the Venetian chancery and to become the tutor of Galeazzo Maria Sforza, future ruler of Milan (from 1466 to 1476). But when in 1449 Ludovico Gonzaga asked him to come to Mantua to tutor his eldest son and heir, Federico (d. 1484), and to assume leadership of the Casa Giocosa, Ognibene accepted. He remained in Mantua for four years, teaching the historian and humanist Bartolomeo Sacchi (il Platina, 1421–81), among others. Ognibene returned to his post as communal master of Vicenza in 1453 and remained there until his death in 1474. He won the affection of his students for his benevolence and pedagogical skill.

Like Vittorino, Ognibene supported and taught poor pupils at his own expense. Unlike Vittorino, he wrote extensively, becoming a prolific editor, commentator, and translator of the ancient historians, orators, and poets. He translated Plutarch's *Lives* and works of Xenophon and John Chrysostom from Greek to Latin. A course of study on Quintilian led him to edit the *Institutio oratoria* (printed in Venice, 1471). He edited and commented on *De oratore, De officiis,* and various orations of Cicero, plus the *Rhetorica ad Herennium.* He commented on Sallust and Valerius Maximus among ancient historians, Juvenal, Persius, Ovid, and Lucan among the poets. Finally, he wrote *De octo partibus orationis* (printed in Venice, 1473, followed by at least three more incunabular editions), a Latin grammar based on Priscian.

[55]For the following, see Serena, 1912, pp. 68–72, 142, 327–30; Sansonetti, 1952, pp. 171–74; and Ballistreri, 1970. The fifteenth-century biographers of Vittorino usually mention Ognibene; see Garin, ed., 1958, pp. 604–5, 672, 675.

[56]". . . Grammaticam docere, legereque Rectoricam, ac quoscunque auctores reguisierant audientes. . . ." Serena, 1912, p. 68.

By editing and commenting on basic Latin texts used in the schools, Ognibene produced "pedagogical" scholarship. He prepared simple, unadorned paraphrase-commentaries eminently suitable for the classroom. For example, in his commentaries on Sallust and Valerius Maximus, Ognibene briefly identified historical personages, and gave the meaning, often with synonyms, of all nouns and verbs, plus many other words in the text. But he did not present grammatical, rhetorical, etymological, or allegorical explanations. Ognibene gave only enough information to enable teachers and students to read and understand the text literally.

Ognibene's editions, usually ignored by scholars, filled a need at an important point. Between about 1460 and 1490, humanists produced relatively accurate editions, accompanied by brief commentary, of the classical texts used in the schools. Ognibene and others did the pioneering work of preparing readable versions purged of the worst mistakes of medieval copyists. Although Ognibene's generation knew little of textual criticism, they gave the humanistic movement basic reading editions (soon to be printed) upon which later scholars might improve.

Ognibene's career typified the way humanism spread. He acquired mastery of his subject and met the political and economic elite of northern Italy in Vittorino's school. He then taught for four years as a court tutor, two to five as an independent master, and almost thirty as communal master. The civic leaders of Treviso and Vicenza hired him to teach; Gonzaga and Sforza princes wanted him as tutor. Ognibene did not forsake local schools for the court, chancery, or university, despite his considerable scholarly accomplishments. Nevertheless, through his teaching, scholarship, and contacts with the powerful, he aided the spread of the humanistic curriculum.[57]

A strong interest in the humanities for vocational purposes also aided the growth of the *studia humanitatis*. Over the course of the century, princes and governments, especially the most important in the peninsula, came to want their secretaries and other civil servants to be trained in the humanities. The Venetian Republic founded the Scuola di San Marco in 1446 because La Serenissima wanted humanistically trained secretaries. Rome offers another good example.[58] After a few humanists such as Leonardo Bruni and Poggio Bracciolini found positions in the Roman curia in the

[57]One might cite other teachers as well. Antonio Baratella (c. 1385–1448) studied with Barzizza, then taught as an independent and communal master at Padua, Pirano, Venice, Belluno, and Feltre (Ziliotto, 1963). Giorgio Valagussa of Brescia (1428–64) studied with Guarino at Ferrara, became tutor to the sons of Duke Francesco Sforza of Milan, and composed a Ciceronian phrase book with Italian translation for school use and other works (Resta, 1964). Gian Pietro da Lucca, discussed below, was another.

[58]For employment and advancement opportunities for humanists in the papal curia, see D'Amico, 1983, ch. 1 and p. 67.

first decade of the fifteenth century, many others followed. Applicants with humanistic training had a clear edge in securing employment there from the pontificate of Nicholas V (1447–55) onward.

Thus, a humanistic education helped individuals climb the social ladder. The expanding Roman curia and other chanceries wanted more and more secretaries, abbreviators, and other officials who were well grounded in classical Latin and could write the new humanistic scripts (see ch. 11). The posts carried good salaries in their own right and might lead to higher preferment, if the humanist also possessed diplomatic skills and political support. At the very least, a curial or secretarial post offered a secure living and improvement in the family's fortunes.

Such employment and opportunities and the example set by the governments of Florence, Rome, and Venice encouraged parents and communal councils to hire humanistic masters. Parents living far from the metropolitan centers also wanted their sons to have the humanistic training that made advancement possible. One suspects that few youths trained in *ars dictaminis* and unfamiliar with Cicero's epistles found chancery positions after 1450. Individuals did not need to have law degrees—although such degrees helped—to secure chancery positions, but thorough training in the *studia humanitatis* beginning in elementary school was a necessity.

As communal councils and parents hired humanistic schoolmasters, the *condotte* (contracts between employer and teacher) reflected the change in curriculum. The *condotte* used new terminology to describe the curriculum and listed the teachers who gave effect to it. Masters were expected to teach the Latin orators, poets, and historians, or grammar, rhetoric, and poetry, plus Greek at times. Eventually the *condotte* specified which ancient authors and books must be taught. The terminology of medieval learning—*auctores, ars dictaminis,* speculative grammar, *Eva columba, Doctrinale,* Boethius, and so on—disappeared. Not being able to sit in their classrooms of long ago, we will never be certain that these teachers taught differently from their medieval predecessors. But a change in terminology indicated a commitment to the new curriculum. And if the new teachers were followers of Guarino and Vittorino, we can be sure that they taught the *studia humanitatis.*

The lack of a strong ecclesiastical or state presence in pre-university education facilitated the switch to the new humanistic curriculum. Some bishops would have resisted the reading of more pagan authors had they exercised jurisdiction over communal and independent schools. In like manner, church schools, had they been numerous, might have been a formidable force for scholastic inertia. Instead, only a few clergymen (Giovanni Dominici was one) opposed the reading of pagan authors as morally corrupting. Humanists answered that the ancient poets led readers to virtue through their stories of adultery and vice, and humanists carried public opinion (see ch. 9). Since the church as an institution had very few schools and possessed no influence over communal and independent schools, it took no position. The same might be said for princes and republics, who only interested themselves in the few schools and teachers they supported. The lack of overall church and state control over schools allowed individual masters, parents, and city councils to make changes freely and quickly.

The change from medieval to Renaissance schooling can be seen in the extant teacher *condotte* of towns with ongoing communal schools. In 1376 the Commune of Spoleto (in Umbria) hired a master to teach "correct speech, speculative grammar, logic, and strict rhetoric," a typical late medieval curriculum.[59] Spoleto continued to hire masters to teach grammar or *in gramaticalibus et poesi* in the early fifteenth century (1427). In 1432, a change occurred: the commune hired Pietro da Tolentino to teach grammar, poetry, and oratory (*pro scolis in gramaticalibus, poesi quoque et oratoria facultate in civitate gerendis*).[60] In the absence of additional information we cannot be certain that an unknown teacher in a small town far distant from the humanistic centers of the Veneto or Florence inaugurated a humanistic curriculum at this early date. Nevertheless, the appointment notice signalled the beginning of change.

In 1371 Lucca appointed a certain Antonio da Volterra to teach. The commune described his scholarly accomplishments: he has a doctorate in grammar and logic from Bologna, is an excellent "authorist" (*auctoristam optimum*), and is expert in philosophy.[61] The combination of grammar, logic, *auctores,* and philosophy indicated a medieval curriculum.

In 1453 the Commune of Lucca wished to join the humanistic movement by offering a communal mastership to Giovanni Pietro d'Avenza, also called ·Gian Pietro da Lucca. Born in 1404 in Avenza, a tiny hamlet about twenty-five miles north of Lucca, Gian Pietro studied with Francesco Filelfo for a short time in Florence, with Vittorino in Mantua, and with Guarino in Ferrara.[62] He then taught school, possibly in Brescia, certainly in Verona and Venice. His scholarship included a grammar for school use, orations in which he strongly argued for the *studia humanitatis* as the key to cultural and civic formation, and extensive study of the works

---

[59]". . . nostrae civitatis pueros et juvenes per excellentes Magistros disciplinarum praesertim recte loquentis gramaticae speculative loycae intentisque rhetoricae volumus erudiri. . . ." Fausti, 1943, p. 32.

[60]Ibid., pp. 34, 106.

[61]"Et alias habuit in commissione de conducendo pro lucano cumuni [sic] unum peritissimum virum qui doctoratus est in Bonomia in gramaticalibus et logicalibus, auctoristam optimum et in philosophia peritum et aliis facultatibus. . . ." Barsanti, 1905, p. 212. Antonio da Volterra taught at Lucca from 1371 to 1379, but nothing more is known about him. Barsanti, 1905, p. 240.

[62]See Sforza, 1870; Segarizzi, 1915–16a, p. 643; Barsanti, 1905, pp. 122–24, 175, 241; Labalme, 1969, p. 98; Ross, 1976, p. 562; Cortesi, 1981a and b; Marchi, 1981, p. 291.

of Caesar and Livy. In 1450 he won the important appointment of master at the Scuola di San Marco, making him the second master to teach there. After an interval of illness in which another master substituted for him, Gian Pietro began at the Scuola di San Marco in 1451 teaching liberal studies (*ad legendum studia liberalia*).[63]

Now, in 1453, the Luccans offered Gian Pietro the opportunity to return home. They offered him one hundred ducats (the same salary he earned in Venice), plus permission to collect supplementary fees, to come to Lucca to teach "oratorical arts, poetry, and letters" ("in magistrum artis oratorie, poesis et literarum").[64] Gian Pietro turned them down. The persistent Luccans renewed the offer in 1456, describing the appointment now as "rhetoric and oratorical art, poetry, and Greek and Latin letters" ("rhetoricam et artem oratoriam, poesim et licteras [*sic*] grecas atque latinas").[65] Gian Pietro accepted the offer, but he died in 1457, before he could have had much influence. Nevertheless, Lucca had joined its schools to the humanistic movement.

The Latin schools of other northern Italian towns also became humanistic by the middle of the fifteenth century. In 1446 Foligno appointed a communal master to teach "the rules of grammar, poets, historians, and books appropriate to the ability of the pupils" ("in legendo regulas gramaticales, poetas, historicos et libros convenientes secundum qualitatem auditorum").[66] In 1444 or 1449 the Commune of Treviso in the Venetian Dominion hired Filippo da Reggio "to teach grammar to boys and youths in the city of Treviso and to lecture on poetry and rhetoric to all who wish to attend." Moreover, the commune required Filippo "on feast days to lecture publicly on the art of oratory and such authors as his audience desire."[67] In 1459 the Commune of Recanati for the first time described the duties of the communal master as "teaching grammar, rhetoric, and poetry" ("legere grammaticam, rhetoricam et poesim").[68] And in Modena, also in 1459, a teacher bought a house with the money that he had earned "from lecturing and teaching in schools grammar, the poets,

[63]See the document printed in Sforza, 1870, p. 403.
[64]Document printed in ibid., p. 404.
[65]Document printed in ibid., p. 406.
[66]Zanelli, 1899, p. 103.
[67]". . . ad docendum gramaticam pueros et adolescentes in Civitate Tarvisii et legendum poesiam et rethoricam omnibus audire volentibus." "Item dictus magister Philipus singulis diebus festivis teneatur legere publice artem oratoriam et auctores pro libito auditorum." Serena, 1912, pp. 331, 332. For an English translation, see Thorndike, 1971, pp. 339, 340. There is some confusion about the date of the contract and when Filippo began teaching. Serena, 1912, pp. 74, 331, states that he began teaching in 1449; Thorndike gives the date as 1444. The document appears to be a contract of 1449 which repeated the original date and language of an offer that Filippo first declined in 1444.
[68]Borracini Verducci, 1975, p. 131.

rhetoric, and humanistic authors" ("ex exercitio legendi in scolis et docendi gramaticam, poetas, rethoricam et humanitatis auctores").[69]

Foligno, Treviso, and Recanati were not important towns by any
definition in the fifteenth century or later. Yet, by the 1450s, they had
humanistic communal masters. If such small and obscure towns had
adopted the *studia humanitatis* by the 1450s, it is very likely that the
majority, possibly a large majority, of northern and north-central Italian
towns taught the humanistic curriculum in their communal schools by the
middle of the century. Communal schools had a significance greater than
their numbers, because they embodied the educational preference of the
town's leaders. Independent teachers could not have been far behind
communal masters. The humanists had won.[70]

The humanistic curriculum also moved south, although at a slower
pace. Aldo Manuzio (Aldus Manutius) recalled his early Latin education in
the preface to his Latin grammar of 1501, addressed to teachers. Do not
force children to memorize anything except the best authors, Aldo admonished. Of course they must learn inflections by heart, but do not force
children to memorize the grammar book. I had to do this as a child, and I
forgot everything in a hurry. In the time that students struggle to learn
such things as grammar exercises, they could more easily and with greater
profit memorize something of Cicero and Vergil. I regret that I could not
do this as a child, but had to memorize a stupid work of verses of
Alexander on grammar (the *Doctrinale* of Alexander de Villedieu).[71]

Manuzio first saw light of day circa 1450, perhaps slightly earlier, in
Bassiano, a tiny provincial hill town about fifty miles south of Rome. That

---

[69]Vicini, 1935, p. 69. Arezzo also appears to have made the transition to a humanistic
curriculum at this time. Guglielmo di Giovanni da Francia taught as the communal grammarian there from 1440 to 1447, from 1458 to 1465, and from 1473 until his death in 1477.
Guglielmo wrote Latin verse in a humanistic manner and demonstrated a knowledge of
classical antiquity. It is likely that he taught the *studia humanitatis*. Black, 1987, pp. 218–19.

[70]A change in terminology shows that the *studia humanitatis* came to some universities at
about this time. In 1435 students at the University of Pavia petitioned the Duke of Milan to
hire Baldassar Rasinus to teach the *studia humanitatis:* "For in this city there are many youths
who are exceedingly eager to cultivate those studies which they call humanist (*istis studiis, que
humanissima vocant*) if they might have a wise preceptor of the art of oratory and the sweetness
of sacred poetry. . . . Wherefore, most humane prince, since here in our midst is the eminent
man Baldassar Rasinus, most famous in the art of speaking, who from earliest years has
devoted himself to humanistic studies (*studiis humanitatis*). . . ." *Codice diplomatico*, 1971, vol.
2, pt. 1, p. 347; for the English translation, see Thorndike, 1971, p. 312. In 1440–41, the
University of Bologna appointed Giovanni Lamola (c. 1407–49), a former student of both
Guarino and Vittorino's, "Ad lecturam rethorice et poesie et studiorum humanitatis."
Dallari, 1888–1924, vol. 1:15.

[71]"Aldus Manutius Romanus literarii ludi magistris" of June 1501, in Manuzio, 1501, sigs.
Aʳ–A2ʳ and reprinted in all subsequent editions that I have examined. The preface also
appears in Manuzio, 1975, vol. 1:39–40, vol. 2:224–26.

Bassiano lacked a humanistic instructor in the late 1450s or early 1460s is not surprising. Aldo probably received no humanistic training until he moved to Rome (at an unknown date). There he studied with Gaspare da Verona (c. 1400–1474) and Domizio Calderini (1446–78) either at the University of Rome or in an elementary or secondary school.[72]

But some provincial towns south of Rome boasted humanistic masters by the early 1470s. Had Aldo been born a few years later in nearby Velletri, twenty-five miles closer to Rome than Bassiano, he could have studied with an excellent humanistic teacher. By 1473 Antonio Mancinelli (1452–1505), a well-known humanistic pedagogue and author of Latin grammar textbooks, had opened a humanistic school in Velletri.[73] Aldo was a little unlucky in his birthplace.

By the end of the fifteenth century, probably nearly all Latin schools in Italy were humanistic and commonly called "schools of oratory, poetry, and grammar" ("scole in arte oratoria, poesi et gramatice").[74] Detailed curriculum prescriptions made the humanistic direction even clearer. For example, the Commune of Lucca in 1499 ordered its communal teachers to teach daily "a grammatical author, an historian, an orator or a book of epistles, a poet, and the rudiments of Greek" ("uno autore grammatico, uno historico, uno oratore overo uno libro di epistole, uno poeta et li erotimati greci").[75] Lucca renewed these instructions in 1524, 1546, and 1574, in identical or very similar words.[76]

A few remnants of medieval schooling lingered. In 1498 the Commune of Pistoia instructed its communal master to teach grammar, rhetoric, *arte oratoria,* poetry, and Greek, but also "something or part or all of speculative grammar," if the pupils so wished.[77] In the following year the commune ordered the master to teach daily the *Doctrinale* of Alexander de Villedieu, in addition to the standard Cicero and Vergil.[78] Moreover, almost all humanistic schools retained *Donatus* and the *Disticha Catonis* for teaching beginning Latin grammar and reading.

These were small exceptions. Italian pedagogues had effected a curricu-

[72]Lowry, 1979, pp. 48–49.
[73]Sabbadini, 1878. See ch. 7 herein for more on Mancinelli.
[74]From a Luccan communal decree of 1492 in Barsanti, 1905, p. 214.
[75]Printed in ibid., p. 215.
[76]Ibid., pp. 220, 225–27, 232.
[77]"Item acciò che gli scolari introducti habbino ridocto et possino volendo come a loro parà imparare a fare pistole, versi, arte oratoria, ortografia, grecho e qualunque cosa o parte o tucto di gramatica speculativa, provviddeno et hordinorono che decto Maestro principale sia tenuto fare residentia alla Scuola. . . ." *Capitoli* for the communal masters of 1498 printed in Zanelli, 1900, p. 145. The rest of the *capitoli* makes amply clear the humanistic orientation of the Pistoia schools.
[78]"Teneatur dictus magister legere in dictis suis scolis doctrinale et nullomodo omictere. . . ." *Capitoli* of 1499 printed in Zanelli, 1900, p. 147; also see p. 76. Like the instruction, the document employed medieval rather than classical orthography.

lum revolution, one of the few in the history of Western education, in the relatively short time of about fifty years—1400 to 1450. They solidified their triumph by 1500. Boethius, *Graecismus, Facetus, Theodulus,* and the rest of the curriculum authors gave way to Cicero, Terence, and Caesar. The *studia humanitatis* replaced *ars dictaminis.* The *auctorista* disappeared; the humanist took his place.

CHAPTER SIX

Learning the ABCs with Hornbook and Primer

hether destined for the Latin or the vernacular curriculum, a child first had to learn to read. No educational revolution occurred at the primary level. A Renaissance schoolboy learned to recognize the letters of the alphabet, then to read syllables, words, and sentences, in the same way that Greek, Roman, and medieval schoolboys had done.[1] Italian pupils continued to learn in this way for centuries after the Renaissance.

TAVOLA AND SALTERIO

The hornbook and primer lay at the heart of the process of learning to read.[2] Late medieval and Renaissance Italians almost always described the earliest stage of reading in terms of the reading matter used. Teacher contracts and fee schedules often referred to la tavola or tabula (board, table, or tablet), la carta (card or paper), or il quaderno or quaterno (notebook). For example, a contract dated 1386 described the beginning stage as teaching "boys from the board all the way to Donatus" ("pro pueris a tabula usque ad donatum").[3] Donatus, of course, meant elementary Latin grammar. A 1377 contract in Vigevano described beginners as those "reading the alphabet and notebook" ("legentes alphabetum et quaternum").[4] An early-fifteenth-century fee schedule for the communal master of Volterra called the earliest stage "reading the card" ("a scolaribus legentibus

---

[1]For excellent descriptions of how Greek and Roman children learned to read, see Marrou, 1964, pp. 210–18; Bonner, 1977, pp. 165–80; and Falanga, 1979. Also see Quintilian I.1.24–37. Although little is known, it is very likely that medieval schools followed the same methods.

[2]For convenience I differentiate between the hornbook (la tavola, la carta, or il quaderno) and primer (il salterio), even though not all Renaissance Italians used the terms precisely.

[3]Bellemo, 1888, p. 49.

[4]Fossati, 1902, p. 163.

142

carta").[5] Fifteenth-century Piedmontese teacher contracts used these terms interchangeably to describe the initial stage: "scolares de pagina sive de carta," "scolares de quaterno," or "legentes tabulam."[6]

La tavola, la carta, and *il quaderno* meant a single sheet or card displaying the letters of the alphabet and, as space allowed, a series of syllables and a prayer or two.[7] Indeed, Italians in the late sixteenth century defined *la tavola* or *la carta* as the sheet of paper that teaches reading.[8] The card always began with a cross—this was a deeply engrained custom. An accounting master explained in 1540 that his students should label the first account book with the cross rather than with *A,* because as children we learned to read the alphabet from primers that began with the cross.[9]

La tavola is the hornbook in English, a small wooden board into which letters have been carved or onto which a piece of paper with the alphabet and other matter has been attached. A thin sheet of transparent horn— hence the name—was placed over the paper to protect it from children's fingers.[10] Hornbooks frequently had a handle so that the child might hold the hornbook with one hand while he traced the letters with the other. One of the frescoes of Benozzo Gozzoli's splendid cycle on the life of St. Augustine in the church of San Agostino in San Gimignano depicts little Augustine at the age of 5 or 6 holding a hornbook without a handle (illustration 1). Another fifteenth-century painting of Augustine with a hornbook depicts him at an older age (illustration 2). Other hornbooks, with and without handles, appeared in woodcuts and engravings in Italian printed books.[11]

Italians also described the initial stage of learning to read as "reading the psalter." In 1248 a Genoese banker hired a teacher to teach his two sons

[5]Battistini, 1919, pp. 34–35.

[6]Gabotto, 1895, pp. 275, 328, 335, 341, 346.

[7]Tuer, 1979, pp. 5–6 et passim. In addition to presenting a great deal of information on and illustrations of the hornbook, the first edition includes sample facsimile hornbooks. Also see Lucchi, 1978, pp. 597–601, whose analysis differs slightly from mine.

[8]"Abecedaria, tabella, la carta, ò il foglio, over s'impara à legere." "Elementaria tabella, la tavoletta da imparare l'A.B.C." The quotes are found in the two 1597 editions of *Ianua,* sigs. A19ᵛ, A20ʳ (both editions), listed in Appendix 1; they are repeated in the 1611 *Ianua,* sigs. A19ᵛ, A20ʳ, also listed in Appendix 1.

[9]". . . e pero è costume fra noi christiani, di segnare li primi libri di quel bel segno di santa croce, dal quale ancor nelli primi et teneri anni ad imparar di leggere l'alphabeto cominciasti. . . ." D. Manzoni, 1540, sig. † 5ᵛ. Because a Greek cross preceded the alphabet in almost all hornbooks and primers, later Italians, especially those in seventeenth-century Rome and Lombardy, called the primer *la Santa Croce.* See ASR, Archivio della Università di Roma, R. 71, fol. 299ʳ, as quoted in ch. 3, n. 47; the notes of Don Carlo Trivulzio which accompany MT Ms. 2163; and Toscanella, 1568a, p. 3.

[10]Eventually the English term *hornbook* meant any kind of alphabetical tablet, ABC book, or primer. Tuer, 1979, pp. 5–6.

[11]Ibid., pp. 155–61 and p. 390 for John Florio's 1598 Italian and English definitions of the hornbook.

1. Little St. Augustine holding a hornbook. Detail from Benozzo Gozzoli's cycle (1465) in the church of San Agostino, San Gimignano.

2. St. Augustine being taken to school by his parents. A hornbook on a string dangles from his arm. School of Sanseverino, fifteenth century, in the Pinacoteca Vaticana.

how to read well the psalter (*scient legere bene salterium*) before they went on to Latin grammar.[12] Clemenza, the Florentine female teacher of 1304, first taught her pupil "to read the psalter" ("legere psalterium").[13] A Venetian inventory of books of 1445 included "a little psalter for boys" ("un psalterio picolo da puti").[14] The psalter had several pages containing the alphabet, syllables, a group of prayers, sometimes but not always a few psalms, and perhaps limited additional material (see below). A *psalter* is a *primer* in English. Sixteenth-century teachers usually made a distinction between *la tavola* and *il salterio*. Genoese teachers of 1500 listed separately pupils learning *la tabula* and those learning *il salterio*.[15] Venetian pedagogues in 1587 stated that they taught *la tavola* (also *la tolla, la tola,* and *la toletta*) or *il salterio*, or both.[16]

Stationers (*cartolai*), who copied and sold manuscript books and writing materials, prepared and sold hornbooks and primers. The 1426 inventory of a Florentine *cartolaio* included nine quarto- and octavo-sized hornbooks, another ten of unspecified size, one unbound primer, and twelve quires of paper to be used for primers and elementary Latin grammars.[17] Another Florentine stationer in 1476 had a primer bound in parchment plus twenty-nine bundles or packages of hornbooks, and another seventy-five packages of sheets of paper not yet turned into hornbooks.[18] Obviously hornbooks, primers, and elementary Latin grammars constituted a significant part of a stationer's business.

But no manuscript hornbooks have survived, and only one manuscript primer is known: Trivulziano ms. 2163, "Libretto dell'Iesus."[19] Prepared about 1496 for the boy prince Massimiliano Sforza (1491/2–c. 1530), the son of Lodovico il Moro Sforza and Beatrice Este, the small, lovely, illuminated manuscript of ten leaves presents the alphabet in capital and lower-case letters, the Pater Noster, Ave Maria, Symbolum Apostolorum, invocations to the Holy Cross (Crux christi salve me. Crux christi deffende me. Crux christi protege me), the Miserere, and the Salve Regina—all standard primer content (see below). It also includes Italian verses addressed to the young prince and copious illustrations. Mas-

[12]Reynolds, 1937, p. 256. Also see Massa, 1906, p. 173 n. 1; and Cecchetti, 1886, p. 363.
[13]Debenetti, 1906–7, p. 333; see p. 339 for other Florentine examples.
[14]Cecchetti, 1886, p. 362.
[15]"De psalterio scolares decem in circa. De tabula circa totidem." Massa, 1906, pp. 320–22, 326 (quote).
[16]ACPV, "Professioni di fede," fols. 9ʳ–329ʳ passim; Baldo, 1977, pp. 45–81 passim.
[17]"3 alfabeti di fogli reali," i.e., paper 305 × 220 mm. "6 alfabeti di fogli mezani," paper 255 × 170 mm. "10 carti da fanciulli." "Saltero da fanciulli sciolto." "12 quaderna di carte da salteri et Donadelli." De la Mare, 1972, p. 244.
[18]"Uno saltero da fanciulli di charta pechora." "Ventinove colli scripti per tavole da fanciulli." "Sectantacinque colli bianchi non scripti da tavole da fanciulli." Martini, 1956, p. 61.
[19]MT Ms. 2163.

similiano's primer survived as a work of art; the little boy probably never used it.

Soon the printing presses began to produce hornbooks and primers. The press at the monastery of San Jacopo a Ripoli (active 1477–83?) in the outskirts of Florence printed in 1480 a "salteruzzo da fanciulli" to sell for three, four, or five soldi.[20] In 1488 a Pisan stationer had six "reading tablets for children on good paper."[21] The 1497 inventory of the stock of printed books of a recently deceased Bolognese printer and bookseller listed forty-four primers.[22] Unfortunately, no Italian incunabular hornbook or primer has survived.[23] Printers produced them in numerous press runs that have disappeared without trace. Classroom use of these inexpensive little booklets and single sheets of paper practically guaranteed destruction.

Fortunately, a handful of printed primers from the second half of the sixteenth century have survived. A primer published in Perugia, 1578, gives a clear idea of contents.[24] A small octavo (20 × 14 cm. with cropped margins), the Perugian primer contains twelve pages printed in gothic type, with red and black ink, and several woodcuts. The primer has no title page; the first page begins with the words *Jesus Maria,* a large cross, and the alphabet (illustration 3). Next follow five lines in two columns of a series of syllables using all five vowels: *Ba be bi bo bu, Da de di do du, Ga ge gi go gu,* and so on. Then comes the Pater Noster entitled "Oratio Dominicalis." The following pages present (in Latin) the Ave Maria, a grace before meals, the Confiteor, a few psalms, the canticle of the Blessed Virgin Mary (Magnificat . . . , Luke 1:46 ff), the canticle of Simon (Nunc dimittis servum tuum Dominum, Luke 2:29 ff), Miserere mei Deus, the Apostles' Creed (called Symbolum Apostolorum), Salve Regina, the beginning of the Gospel according to John (In principio erat verbum . . .), and some of the prayers and responses exchanged between priest and acolyte or congregation at mass.

The Perugian primer contains woodcuts of the twelve apostles, one for each of twelve sections of the Symbolum Apostolorum. Sixteenth-century primers depicted the apostles in order to express pictorially what an anonymous fifteenth-century Florentine put into words: "Peter says, I

[20]Nesi, 1903, pp. 45–46; Noakes, 1981, pp. 31–32.

[21]"tavole da leggere per fanciugli [*sic*] di carte buone." Verde, 1973–77, vol. 3:751.

[22]"Santerii [*sic*] da puti, n. 44." Sorbelli, 1942, pp. 327–28. Other inventories of bookstores and private collections of the fifteenth and sixteenth centuries often listed psalters without a qualifying description such as "da puti." Some of these may also have been primers rather than liturgical works.

[23]A possible northern European incunabular primer is Hain *13532: *Psalterium puerorum.* Per Erhardum Ratdolt, Augsburg, no date. 16 pp. in gothic type. Incipit: "Iesus. Maria," followed by the alphabet and Pater Noster.

[24]Perugia primer, 1578. Colophon: Perusiae, apud Petrumiacobum Petrutium. NYPL Spencer Coll. Ital. 1578.

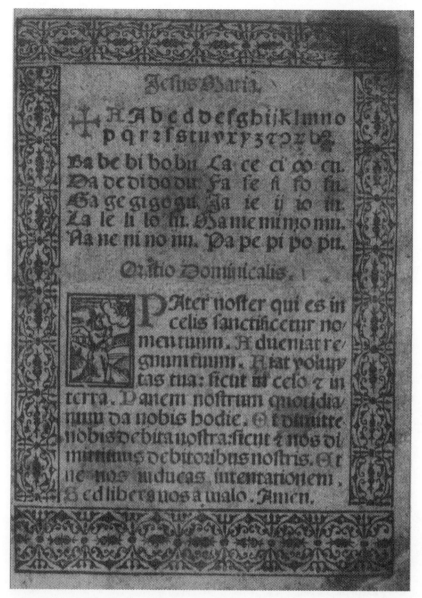

3. First page of a primer. No title. Colophon: Perusiae, apud Petrumiacobum
Petrutium. 1578. NYPL Spencer Coll.

believe in God the Father Almighty. . . . Andrew says, And in Jesus Christ, His only Son, our Lord."[25] The manuscript expressed in simplified form the fourth-century legendary explanation of the origin of the creed. Before going their separate ways to proclaim the gospel, the apostles met together and agreed to make a brief sign (*symbolum*) of their future preaching, each contributing a part. This compilation of the thoughts of the twelve became the believers' faith, the Symbolum Apostolorum or Apostles' Creed.[26]

A longer Bolognese primer of 1575 added catechetical material: *Psalterio per putti principianti con la Dottrina aggionta*.[27] This is a small octavo (20.3 × 14.8 cm.) of thirty-two pages printed on vellum mostly in Gothic type, with red and black ink, in Latin and Italian. It contains several illustrations. The title page indicates that it is both a primer for beginners (*putti principianti*) and a catechetical manual (illustration 4). The first page contains a crucifixion woodcut, the alphabet preceded by a cross, the words of the sign of the cross, the Pater Noster, and the Ave Maria (illustration 5). Succeeding pages present in Latin the Symbolum Apostolorum with woodcuts of the twelve apostles, prayers for vespers, the Confiteor, psalms, hymns in honor of Mary (Ave Maria Stella, Magnificat), the canticle of Simon, prayers and responses for mass, and the beginning of the Gospel of John. It lacks only the syllables of standard primer content.

Then follows a section entitled "Christian Doctrine for beginners as ordered by Cardinal [Gabriele] Paleotti, Bishop of Bologna." This second part of the primer lists typical catechetical material: the words of the sign of the cross, the Ten Commandments, seven sacraments, seven capital sins, seven gifts of the Holy Spirit, and so on. Next come exhortations on religious and public conduct such as, Go to confession at least once a month, and Remove your hat when speaking to persons deserving respect. The Bolognese primer finishes with an episcopal decree of 15 October 1575 ordering all teachers in the city and diocese of Bologna to teach the catechetical matter in the book. This copy printed on vellum obviously survived because it was a commemorative copy not intended for schoolroom use. More modestly printed combination primer and elementary catechism booklets that served both regular schools and the Schools of Christian Doctrine in the last third of the sixteenth century also survive (see ch. 12).

Using a primer written in Latin, or Latin and Italian, to teach students who will later follow either the Latin or the vernacular stream appears strange and unworkable to twentieth-century readers. Why not teach all

[25]"questi sono i dodici articoli della fede i quali compostono i dodici apostoli. Piero dixe: Credo in dio padre omnipotente. . . . Andrea dixe: Et in Jesu Cristo. . . ." FR Ms. 1716, "Trattato della Dottrina Cristiana," fols. 2ᵛ–3ʳ.

[26]F. Murphy, 1967, p. 433.

[27]*Psalterio*, 1575.

4. Title page of *Psalterio per putti principianti con la Dottrina Christiana aggionta.* In Bologna per Alessandro Benaecio, 1575. BA 16. Q. IV. 29.

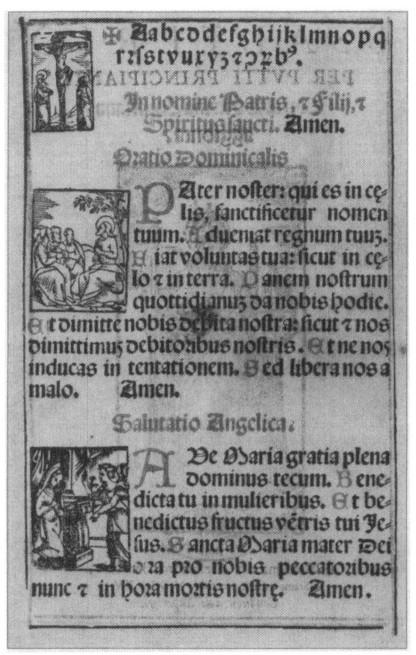

5. Verso of title page of *Psalterio per putti principianti con la Dottrina Christiana aggionta*.

Fab.feb.fib.fob.fub.   Fac.fec.fic.foc.fuc.
Fad.fed.fid.fod.fud.   Faf.fef.fif.fof.fuf.
Fag.feg.fig.fog.fug.   Fal.fel.fil.fol.fõl.
Fam.fem.fim.fom.fum,   Fan.fen.fin.fon.fun.
Fap.fep.fip.fop.fup,   Far.fer.fir.for.fur.
Fas.fes.fis.fos.fus.   Fat.fet.fit.fot.fut.
Gab.geb.gib.gob.gub.   Gac.gec.gic.goc.guc.
Gad.ged.gid.god.gud.   Gaf.gef. gif. gof.guf.
Gag.geg.gig.gog.gug.   Gal.gel.gil.gol.gul.
Gam.gem.gim.gom.gũ.   Gan.gen. gin. gon.gun.
Gap.gep.gig.gop.gup: Gar.ger.gir.gor.gur.
Gas.ges.gis.gos.gus.   Gat.get.git.got.gut.
Hab.heb.hib.hob.hub.   Hac.hec.hic.hoc.huc.
Had.hed.hid.hod.hud.   Haf.hef.hif.hof.huf.
Hag.heg.hig.hog.hug.   Hal.hel.hil.hol.hul.
Ham.hem.him.hom.hũ.   Han.hẽ.hin. hon.hun,
Hap.hep.hip.hop.hup.   Har.her.hir.hor.hur.
Has.hes.his.hos.hus.   Hat.het.hit.hot.hut.
Iab.ieb.iib iob.iub.   Iac.iec.iic.ioc.iuc.
Iad.ied.iid.iod.iud.   Iaf.ief.iif.iof.iuf.
Iag.ieg.fig.iog.iug.   Ial.iel.fjl:iol.iul.
Iam.iem.iim.iom.ium.   Ian.ien.fjn.ion.iun.
Iap.iep.fip.iop.iup.   Iar.ier.fjr.ior.iur.
Ias.ies.fis.ios.ius.   Iat.iet.ijt.iot.iut.
Lab.leb.lib.lob.lub.   Lac.lec.lic.loc.luc.
Lad.led.lid.lod.lud.   Laf.lef.lif.lof.luf.
Lag.leg.lig.log.lug.   Lal.lel.lil.lol.lul.
Lam.lem.lim.lom.lum.   Lan.len.lin.lon.lun.
Lap.lep.lip.lop.lup.   Lar.ler.lir.lor.lur.
Las.les.lis.los.lus.   Lat.let.lit.lot.lut.

mab.meb.mib.mob.mub. mac.mec mic.moc.muc.
Mad.med.mid.mod.mud·Maf.mef.mif.mof.muf.
Mag.meg.mig.mog.mug.Mal.mel.mil.mol.mul.
Mam.mẽ.mim.mom.mũ.Man.mẽ.min.mõ·mũ.

Map.mep.mip.mop.mupMar.mer.mir.mõr.mur,
Mas.mes mis.mos.mus.Mat.met.mit.mot.mut.
Nab.neb.nib.nob.nub.   Nac.nec.nic.noc.nuc.
Nad.ned.nip.nod. nud.   Naf.nef.nif.nof.nuf.
Nag.neg.nig.nog.nug.   Nal.nel.nil.nol.nul.
Nam.nẽ.nim.nom.num.   Nan.nen.nin.non.nun.
Nap.nep.nip.nop.nup.   Nar.ner.nir.nor.:nur.
Nas.nes.nis.nos.nus,   Nat.net.nit.not.nut.
Pab.peb.pib.pob.pub.   Pac.pec.pic.poc.puc,
Pad.ped.pid.pod.pud.   Paf.pef.pif.pof.puf.
Pag.peg.pig.pog.pug.   Pal.pel.pil.pol.pul.
Pam.pem.pim.pom.pũ.   Pan.pen.pin.pon.pun,
Pap.pep.pip.pop.pup.   Par.per.pir.por.pur.
Pas.pes.pis.pos.pus.   Pat.pet.pit.pot.put.
Quid quod.   Qual.quel.gl.quã.quẽ.
Quan.quen.quin.   qp.ãs.ãs.qs.quos.quit,
Rab.reb.rib.rob.rub.   Rac.rec.ric.roc.ruc,
Rad.red.rid.red.rud.   Raf.ref.rif.rof.ruf.
Rag.reg.rig.rog.rug.   Ral.rel.ril.rol.rul.
Ram.rem.rim.rom.rum.   Ran.ren.rin.ron.run,
Rap.rep.rip.rop.rup.   Rar.rer.rir.ror.rur.
Ras.res.ris.ros.rus.   Rat.ret.rit.rot.rut.
Sab fed.fid.fod.fud.   Sac.fec.fic.foc.fuc.
Sad.fed.fid.fod.fud.   Saf.fef.fif.fof.fuf.
Sag.feg.fig.fog.fug.   Sal.fel.fil.fol.ful.
Sam.fem.fim.fom.fum.   Sãn.fen.fin.fon.fun,
Sap.fep.fip fop.fup   Sar.fer.fir.for.fur.
Sas.fes.fis.fos.fus.   Sat.fet.fit.fot.fut.
Tab.teb.tib.tob.tub.   Tac.tec.tic.toc.tuc.
Tad.ted.tid.tod.tud.   Taf.tef.tif.tof.tuf.
Tag.teg.tig.tog.tug.   Tal.tel.til.tol.tul.
Tam.tem.tim.tom.tum.   Tan.ten.tin.ton.tun.
Tap.tep.tip.top.tup.   Tar.ter.tir.tor.tur.
Tas.tes.tis.tos.tus.   Tat.tet.tit.tot.tut.
                                           b ij

6. Syllables from Aldo Manuzio, *Institutionum grammaticarum libri quatuor*. Venetiis, 1549. Colophon: In aedibus Francisci Bindonei & Maphei Pasini. Mense Aprilis.

students with an Italian primer, and later use a Latin primer to instruct students beginning the Latin curriculum? The bilingual (Latin and Greek) educational tradition of ancient Rome probably decided the issue long before the Renaissance. Tradition exerts its greatest influence at the most elementary phase of education; more than likely, the format of the Latin, or Latin with limited Italian, primer had been established centuries before and could not be altered. The enormous influence that Latin exerted in culture and society through the church, the government, and the legal profession further encouraged teachers to force 5 year olds and 6 year olds to memorize Latin words and prayers. The lack of prestige of the regional vernacular languages discouraged teachers from drafting and using Italian primers. Finally, teachers might justify using a Latin primer on the grounds that it taught future vernacular students the prayers read at mass, and prepared future Latin students for their studies.

The practical difficulties of using a Latin primer were not great. Of all the Romance languages, Italian most closely resembles Latin in sound and pronunciation. Both employ open vowels and pronounce vowels and most consonants in the same way. In Italian, every syllable has one vowel, and in Latin, every syllable has either a vowel or a diphthong. Latin has twenty-three letters (omitting *j*, *u*, and *w* of the twenty-six-letter English alphabet), and modern Italian has twenty-one letters (plus *j*, *k*, *w*, *x*, and *y* borrowed from other languages). In the fifteenth and sixteenth centuries, before modern Italian had fully developed, the letter differences were fewer; Venetian, for example, used the letter *x*. Both Latin and Italian normally accent the first syllable in two-syllable words, the penult in three-syllable words, and the antepenult in words of more than three syllables. The strong oral pedagogy in which children heard, spoke, memorized, and finally read further minimized the difference between Latin and Italian at this level. One sixteenth-century teachers' manual said that the instructor might begin with Latin or Italian in teaching reading.[28] This summarized the Renaissance view. The complexities of language came later.

Although primers and hornbooks usually appeared as self-contained booklets or sheets of paper, their contents could be incorporated into another school text. Aldo Manuzio prefaced his Latin grammar with primer material, making it a combination primer and comprehensive Latin grammar. First published in 1493, and revised in 1501 and again in 1508, Manuzio's grammar had at least twenty-nine printings through 1586.[29] After the title page and author's preface, Aldo's grammar began with an invocation to Christ crucified: "In nomine Domini nostri Iesu Christi crucifixi." This was Manuzio's version of the cross that began all primers. Then followed the alphabet and four or five pages of syllables (illustration 6), more than in any of the primers. Then came the Pa-

---

[28]". . . togliendo molti membri di oratione ò volgare, ò latina, & segnando in essi le lettere, le sillabe, le dittioni, & l'orationi." Toscanella, 1562, p. 6ᵛ.

[29]The first edition (Venice: Andrea Torresano, 9 March 1493), IGI 6139, survives in a single copy now located (May 1986) in VM, Inc. V. 632. Scarafoni, 1947, first discovered it. It lacks sigs. A3–A6 (eight pages) but otherwise is in excellent condition. Examination of the page preceding those missing (A2ᵛ) and comparison with the 1501 edition show that the missing pages probably had much of the primer material and syllables found in the 1501 edition. Indeed, a cursory examination indicates that the 1501 edition differs little from that of 1493. Other known editions include the following, with the place of publication Venice unless otherwise indicated: 1508*, Florence 1510, Paris 1513, 1514*, Paris 1514, Florence 1516, Paris 1516, Florence 1519*, Cologne n.d. (1520?), 1523*, Paris 1524, 1526*, Paris 1531, Toscolano 1532*, 1533*, 1538, 1545*, 1549*, 1551*, 1558, 1559, 1561*, 1564*, 1568*, 1575*, 1576, 1585. I have examined the editions marked with an asterisk. Also see M. Grendler and P. Grendler, 1984, p. 13. A seventeenth-century Latin grammar also included vowels and syllables; see the 1636 *Ianua*, sig. Aᵛ, listed in Appendix 1.

ter Noster, Ave Maria, Symbolum Apostolorum, Ten Commandments, Salve Regina, beginning of the Gospel of St. John, prayers between priest and acolyte at the beginning of mass, Confiteor, and several psalms, all in Latin. The primer material occupied eight to twelve pages, depending on the printing format. Manuzio's *Institutiones grammaticae libri quatuor* taught the child how to read before introducing him to Latin grammar.

Vernacular school texts intended for other purposes also occasionally included primer material. The first section of Domenico Manzoni's *La vera ricchezza de' giovani* (1550), intended for the home teaching of reading, writing, and elementary abbaco, began with primer material in Italian and Latin.[30] The book opened with the cross and the alphabet printed four ways: gothic lower-case letters, gothic capitals, roman upper case, and italic lower case. Then followed the Pater Noster, Ave Maria, and Apostles' Creed, each in both Latin and Italian. The book then switched exclusively to the vernacular for the Ten Commandments, grace before and after meals, and *terza rima* poetry to explain and amplify the prayers. Manzoni presented the alphabet in three typefaces, and alternated roman and italic type, with the latter dominating, through the rest of his work, because he wanted readers to be able to read easily all the typefaces then in use.

Italian hornbooks and primers changed very little from the sixteenth through the middle of the nineteenth century.[31] They invariably began

[30]D. Manzoni, 1550, sigs. A2r–A6v.

[31]See the following *tavola* and primers.

A single sheet listed in the catalogue as "Abbecedario Santa Croce." Printing information at the bottom: In Prato 1826. Nella Stamperia di Vincenzo Vestri. BA 8, Didascalici Cart. IV.11. It is a single sheet of paper 30.5 × 22 cm., printed on one side only in roman type. In the upper corners are two small engravings of the elevation of the host at mass (left) and Christ at the Last Supper (right). The alphabet is listed twice between the engravings in normal order and backward, in two lines flanked by crosses. Next come two lines of syllables, some backward (*Ba be bi bo bu, Ab eb ib ob ub,* etc.), vowels in normal order and backward, six lines of Latin spiritual sayings and prayers, blessing before meals, a list of Italian nouns of food (pane, vino, olio etc.), and a line of arabic numbers (1 2 3 4 5 – 1,000).

Two printed twelve-page primers lacking title and dates are included with MT Ms. 2163: (1) In Milano, per Giuseppe Mazzuchelli, and (2) In Milano, Nella stampa di Antonio Agnelli. Don Carlo Trivulzio (1715–89), in his accompanying handwritten notes, dates them as "end of the sixteenth century," which is accepted by Lucchi, 1978, pp. 606–7. The dating cannot be correct, because no Milanese printers with these names were active at the time, and because typeface and layout are very different from those used in late-sixteenth-century schoolbooks. Sixteenth-century printers still preferred gothic, or gothic and roman, type, and antique layout for elementary schoolbooks. These primers appear in roman type and modern layout. I believe that they date from the late seventeenth or first half of the eighteenth century. Indeed, a certain Antonio Mazzuchelli printed in Milan between 1671 and 1690.

Also see the following:

ABBICCIDARIO PER USO DEI FANCIULLI, E DELLE FANCIULLE . . . edizione seconda. In Milano, 1760, Presso Gianbatista Bianchi, 24 pp. Price information: "Si vendono legati in cartone soldi sette e mezzo di Milano." Copy: MA SC.C.11.16.

with the cross and the alphabet, sometimes followed by syllables. Then came prayers, always beginning with the Pater Noster, which might be printed in divided syllables to facilitate reading: *Pa ter nos ter, qui es in cae lis.* Then came the rest of the usual selection of prayers, canticles, psalms, and responses at mass. The books sometimes contained numbers: 1 through 100 plus selected larger numbers in hornbooks, a whole page with tables of numbers in primers. Hornbooks and primers continued to be written in both Latin (especially the prayers) and Italian, with the latter gradually dominating as time passed. The title pages of eighteenth- and nineteenth-century primers sometimes boasted that the primer taught both Latin and Italian beginning reading—undoubtedly a legitimate claim. The printing format remained small octavo or duodecimo, between twenty by fifteen and seventeen by ten centimeters. Engravings replaced woodcuts. Hornbooks continued to be a single sheet; primers might be twelve, sixteen, or twenty pages long, as in the sixteenth century, or longer (forty-eight to sixty-four pages). The title *Salterio* gradually gave way to *Abbecedario,* although some primers had no title page. Prices remained low: 7.5 soldi for a twenty-four-page primer in Milan in 1760 and 1 lira for a sixty-four-page primer in Venice in 1807.

Hornbooks and primers varied little from country to country. All those issued in Italy, the British Isles, France, and Germany, whether manuscript or printed, whether in Latin, the vernacular, or both, had the same contents.[32] Sixteenth- and seventeenth-century primers began with the

---

NUOVO SALTERIO OVVERO REGOLE UTILISSIME PER ISTRUIRE I FAN-CIULLI a ben sillabare e facilmente leggere . . . terza impressione . . . PER USO DELLE SCUOLE. In Venezia 1798. Presso Gio: Valerio Pasquali in Rio terrà S. Marcuola. 64 pp. BA 6, Scienze Sociali, Istruzione, Caps. E.2.n.1.

(No title). Colophon: In Faenza 1806. Presso Michele Conti. 16 pp. RCas Misc. 569.1.

NUOVO SALTERIO OVVERO REGOLE UTILISSIME PER ISTRUIRE I FAN-CIULLI . . . quarta impressione . . . In Venezia 1807. Presso Gio: Valerio Pasquali, 64 pp. Price information: "Il presente libro legato vale L 1." The book is identical to the 1798 edition above. BU A.V. Caps. 292.43.

ABBECEDARIO con una raccolta di massime, proverbj, favolette morali e colle tabelle della cognizione delle lettere, del compitare, sillibare, e del leggere, e del leggere per uso delle scuole normali, edizione riveduta e corretta. Como 1809. Dalla Tipografia Eredi Caprani. 64 pp. BU A.V.Caps. 295.3.

ABBICI de' fanciulli ad uso delle scuole d'Italia. Modena, Presso Gem. Vincenzi e Comp. 1810. 56 pp. BU A.V.Caps. 298.19.

[32]I have examined the following English, French, and German hornbooks and primers:

English

NNC, Plimpton Ms. 258: an early fifteenth-century English ms. primer of 16 pages on vellum.

Revised STC, 19.6: An 8-page printed primer. London, Richard Lant, no date but c. 1545. IU.

Revised STC 21.9 (formerly 13813). A large printed sheet (28.4 × 11.3 cm.) probably intended to be divided into two hornbooks. Aberdene, E. Raban, [1622]. NNPM.

A very small silver hornbook probably of the late seventeenth century. NNPM, E.8.B.

cross and the alphabet, usually followed by syllables and always the same initial prayers. Schoolchildren in Catholic Italy and France, in Protestant Germany and England, learned to read from the same kind of traditional hornbook and primer.

LEARNING TO READ

The organization of hornbook and primer indicated the steps involved in learning to read. Writing in the academic year 1564–65, the Jesuit prefect of studies at the Collegio Romano described what a beginners' class did.[33] First, the pupils read aloud and learn the alphabet. Next, they begin to join letters together into syllables such as *ba, be,* and so on. Third, they begin to read fluently from the primer, called the *Santa Croce.* Next, having learned the Ave Maria, Pater Noster, Credo, and Salve Regina, they write the alphabet. Fifth, they read a vernacular book and learn to write through copying practice on lined or unlined paper. Finally, they go on to study Latin grammar, recite from memory the little catechism, and learn to count, add, subtract, and divide a little.

This description and other contemporary testimony confirm that instructors faithfully followed the organization of the primer.[34] A severely analytical view of language had long ago determined this method. The ancient Greeks had broken language down into its smallest parts: sentence, word, syllable, and letter. Learning to read meant reassembling the parts;

For additional hornbooks and primers printed in the British Isles, see *Revised STC* 17.7 through 22.5.

French
A French primer of six leaves printed in Latin with some French headings. Probably printed in Paris between 1520 and 1530. NNPM, E.2/47/A.

German
Tabulae abcdariae pueriles. A sixteenth-century printed hornbook sheet, 36.2 × 21 cm., in Latin. NNPM, E.2/45/A/XVIe.

Also see Tuer, 1979, passim.
[33]*Eorum qui tantum legunt vel scribunt*

1. Qui alphabetum tantum legunt.
2. Qui iungere literas incipiunt, ba, be, etc., aut etiam syllabas.
3. Qui legere continuo tractu incipiunt, ut sanctam †, etc.
4. Qui scribunt alphabetum, quibus omnibus docetur *Ave, Pater, Credo, Salve.*
5. Qui legunt librum aliquem vulgari sermone, et scribunt continue ex exemplo, ductis lineis vel etiam non ductis.
6. Qui legunt latine, ut Donatum seu rudimenta, et discunt memoriter doctrinam christianam parvulam; et hi etiam poterunt discere practicam arithmeticam, numerare, addere, subtrahere, partiri aliquousque.

MP, vol. 2:560. The author is Jacobus Ledesma (1524–75), a Spanish Jesuit who taught at, and in 1562 became prefect of studies at, the Collegio Romano.
[34]See Toscanella, 1562, pp. 6ᵛ–7ʳ; and Vives, 1908 (his *Colloquia* of 1538), dialogue 5, p. 18.

pupils acquired discrete bits of information in separate steps and later combined them.[35]

Children began by reciting the alphabet aloud. Teachers set about the task of teaching the letters of the alphabet through a variety of methods. For example, a Genoese teacher of 1286 used wax tablets to teach the letters of the alphabet.[36] A teacher might leave much of this drill to the *ripetitore* if he had one. Students next associated sounds with letters by pointing to them in hornbook or primer and saying the letter sound aloud, paying particular attention to vowels. Because primers and hornbooks often presented the alphabet in upper case and lower, and in more than one typeface, pupils learned a variety of letter forms.

Renaissance teachers, like the ancient Greeks and Romans before them, assigned high priority to learning syllables and using them in reading. The Greeks had developed the alphabet by permitting letters to represent sounds, abandoning the use of pictures drawn to represent things and actions.[37] As a result, Greek, Latin, and Italian became syllable-oriented languages whose letters and syllables almost always show consistency in sound and orthography, and whose words divide easily into syllables. (By contrast, English demonstrates many inconsistencies in sound and spelling, and is more word oriented). Hence, Italian Renaissance teachers gave much attention to syllabification. Indeed, syllabification was important enough to penetrate into at least one teacher contract despite its elementary status and lack of a word equivalent in Latin. In 1414 a Genoese teacher arranging with a colleague to split teaching duties excluded from the agreement "the teaching of *babinbabo.*"[38]

Aldo Manuzio stressed the importance of teaching syllables in a strong statement immediately following the syllables in the primer part of his Latin grammar. Certainly there are those who laugh at this, he wrote, but I have decided to teach pronunciation and orthography, to be accomplished through teaching syllables well.[39] A boy should learn how to divide the

[35]For an excellent discussion of Renaissance pedagogical methodology and psychology, see Strauss, 1978, chs. 3, 4, 5, and pp. 176–77, 188–90.

[36]Petti Balbi, 1979, p. 56.

[37]See Mathews, 1966, pp. 2–6.

[38]". . . usus est legere autores, loycam et alia extraordinaria et docere babinbabo. . . ." Petti Balbi, 1979, p. 153; also see pp. 62–63.

[39]Erant qui haec rideant tanquam perquam rudia, certo scio. Sed nos & ad pronuntiationem, & ad orthographiam facere arbitramur. Nam si bene didicerit puer quot syllabarum sint dictiones, easque tum in libro, tum ad digitos syllabatim connectere, nec scribet, pronuntiabitque caelli caellorum, & allius allia alliud per germinum ll ut plurimi solent, nec ubi una esse debeat consonans, duas ponet, nec ubi duae unam. Quod si sub litterarii ludi magistro, cum essent parvuli didicissent ad digitos pluria verba syllabatim tractare, quod fieri in Latio assolet, non toties & scribendo & loquendo Barbarismum facerent. Sed rideat ille vel ille quandiu libuerit, si prosum rudibus, non facio pili.

Manuzio, 1501, sig. A2ᵛ. This is a slight revision of the statement found in the 1493 edition, sig. A2ᵛ; the latter is quoted in full by Bateman, 1976, p. 232 n. 22.

word into syllables, pointing them out with his fingers, and then connecting them. For if a boy has learned well the number of syllables in words, he will neither spell nor pronounce "caeli, caelorum, alius, alia, aliud," with double *l—ll*—as many do, and put two consonants where there should be only one, and vice versa. If students learn this under the guidance of a schoolteacher while young, they will not commit barbarisms in writing and speaking.[40] Aldus finished as he had begun: although some may laugh at me for discussing this minor matter, I care not a whit so long as I am useful to the ignorant. Aldus made his argument on his own authority in the 1493 and 1501 versions of his grammar. In his final revision (1508), he cited the "highest ancient Latin and Greek grammarians" in support of the careful study of syllables.[41]

Giovanni Antonio Tagliente took teacher and pupil step by step through learning to read in his home teaching manual, *Libro maistrevole* (1524). He accompanied his explanation with amusing patter that included flattering references to the pupil. You must teach the dearest student how to recognize letters, Tagliente began. The student should point them out with a stick or pointer until he can name them all, forward and backward. When the virtuous scholar can identify all the letters of the alphabet, teach him what is a letter, what is a syllable, and what is a word. The prudent scholar should next learn syllables. Suppose that a man ill in bed has a great thirst and wishes to call his good wife whose name is Madalena. But because of his suffering, he lacks breath. He should learn to call her name slowly and in parts, putting a little emphasis on each part: *Ma da le na.* These are syllables, each a part of a word.[42]

The intelligent scholar is now ready to learn all the other syllables; after studying them for a few days, the skillful learner will know how to read. Tagliente listed the alphabet and the five vowels, explaining that every syllable has a vowel. He went on through a full page of two-letter sylla-

---

[40]This passage is close to Quintilian I.5.6.

[41]"Imitati autem summus antiquos & graecos & latinos grammaticos discant igitur pueri, quot syllabarum sint dictiones. . . ." Manuzio, 1508, sig. A8ᵛ. Twentieth-century research on reading points out that we learn and speak phonemes rather than syllables. Phonemes are single speech sounds represented by the same symbol, such as the *r* sound in *bring, red,* and *round*. English is composed of about forty phonemes. Discernible phonetic differences result when two phonemes are combined. Learning syllables really means learning combinations of phonemes.

[42]"E gli uno infermo in letto, il quale ha grande passione nel suo core, et si ritrova solo & ha gran sete, & vorria chiamare la sua massara che ha nome Madalena, et per la passione che lha nel suo core, gli manca lo fiato, et non puo chimare Madalena, ma else [sic] inzegna a chiamare Madalena in piu parti chel puo, e dice cosi, Ma da le na, cioe prima el chiama Ma et poi da et poi le et poi na, che vien haver chiamata Madalena in quatro parti & ad ogni parte si ha posato uno poco, adonque diremo che tanto viene adire una syllaba, quanto una parte duna parola. . . ." G. A. Tagliente, 1524, sig. A4ᵛ. I retain Tagliente's idiosyncratic spelling and punctuation. Also see Schutte, 1986.

bles. Note well, obedient scholar, Tagliente continued, that these are all the two-letter syllables in the world. With them one can read all the nouns composed of combinations of two-letter syllables, such as *Ni co lo.* "Natural reason" explains this happy state of affairs.[43]

Having learned to read all the two-letter syllables, the dearest scholar should learn all the three-letter syllables, such as *ban ben bin bon bun,* all the four-letter syllables, such as *bran bren brin bron brun,* and all the five-letter syllables, such as *schia schie schii schio schius.* After learning six pages of syllables, the good scholar was ready to read words composed of two two-letter syllables: *Ie su, Ro ma.* Tagliente went on to three-syllable nouns such as *ro ma no,* four-syllable nouns such as *to de schi no* (in Venetian; *tedesco* [German] in standard Italian).[44] Next followed long phrases comprised of two brief phrases: "Gaspare da Roma, de dare," and "Gasparino da Napoli, de havere." Although the pupil had not yet read sentences, Tagliente informed the eager student that he might begin to compose epistles and gave some examples. Finally the studious disciple was ready to read verse sentences. Tagliente presented vernacular moralistic couplets similar to those of the Latin *Disticha Catonis.*

> se brami una virtù presto imparare
> Buon precettor, et degno, devi cerchare.
>
> If you desire virtue quickly to learn,
> a good worthy teacher, you must discern.[45]

Like the primer, Tagliente's teaching manual stopped here. It did not go on to teach grammar. Rational and well organized, Tagliente moved step by step from the smallest piece to the whole: letter, syllable, word, phrase, and sentence. Learning to read meant identifying and assembling the building blocks of language. Classroom teachers followed the same path as Tagliente, because the primer's organization pointed to it.

The syllabus of the primary class of the Collegio Romano indicates that pupils next began to write. Again they moved from the smallest part to the whole. Students first wrote out the letters of the alphabet;[46] one can visualize little boys tracing the letters on the hornbook, then writing rows

---

[43]"Come saria adire, Ni, co, lo, guarda che ritroverai dove dice, ni et poi ritroverai dove dice, co et seguendo ritroverai dove dice lo che fara nicolo, & cosi ritroverai scritto ogni altro nome italiano del mondo de syllabe de doe lettere, & a ben che tu sapi leggere, et scrivere, forsi mai piu tu non intendisti questo simile amaestramento & ragioni tratte dalla ragione naturale, et anchora a te lettore ti puo essere accaro ad intendere." G. A. Tagliente, 1524, sig. B3r.

[44]Ibid., sig. C4r.

[45]Ibid., sig. E2v. The translation is mine, with apologies for forcing the rhyme.

[46]"Impararai adunque prima a formar ben tutte le lettere della [sic] alfabeto dipoi accompagnando le insieme fa fabricarai le parole." D. Manzoni, 1550, sig. A7v.

of *As*, rows of *Bs*, and rows of *Cs* across a sheet of paper.[47] After letters and probably syllables, the pupils wrote words. They probably first copied words in the primer and then others supplied by the teacher.

How much time did the initial stage of elementary school, encompassed within the pages of the primer, require? Even with a time-consuming pedagogy based on oral repetition, memorization, and copying, it must have gone fairly quickly for the majority. A 6- or 7-year-old child can memorize the contents of a twelve- to sixteen-page primer in a few weeks and a longer combination primer and catechism in a few months.[48] Children not yet ready to learn need more time; progress at this age depends greatly on a child's readiness. Surely within a year the majority of Renaissance pupils had completed the first stage of learning and reached the great watershed: Latin or the vernacular. The young learner either began the long climb toward a mastery of Latin or perfected his vernacular reading skills and studied abbaco.

This pedagogy for teaching beginning reading had significant advantages. Above all, it was effective and thorough. The endless drill of voice, eye, ear, and hand guaranteed that the students memorized the rudiments of reading and writing. An imaginative teacher might devise ways to vary the learning process in order to make it even more effective. The children might sing and shout the alphabet, or march around the classroom as they chanted syllables and the Pater Noster. Competition might be used to encourage good performance.

Thoroughness and rigidity also constituted the chief disadvantage. Renaissance teaching at this beginning level was inefficient and time-consuming. Teachers took a typically analytical and methodical approach to teaching reading, even though children (and adults) often learn intuitively: the eye and the mind skip ahead once principles are grasped. Moreover, group memorization failed to take into account different rates of learning. Did teachers insist that all students progress at the same rate, or did they divide the class into fast and slow learners? The Piarist Fathers who taught elementary reading and writing to masses of pupils at the end of the sixteenth century developed techniques for teaching students who progressed at different rates (see ch. 13). As always, much depended on the number of pupils in the classroom and the teacher's skills.

The traditional approach of learning letters, syllables, words, and sentences developed by the Greeks and used by the Romans, Renaissance Italians, and everyone else for centuries began to come under attack in the

[47]This is exactly what my son, aged 6, did when enrolled in *prima elementare* (first grade) in a Florentine public school in 1971.

[48]The *prima elementare* class that my son attended in 1971 had one reader of sixty-four pages. Within three months he had memorized it so well that he could repeat any page on command. Renaissance primary schools worked toward this degree of thoroughness.

late eighteenth and especially the nineteenth century. A few French and German educational reformers, followed by Americans in the nineteenth century, argued for learning to read by the "word method," a broad term encompassing several approaches using the word, rather than the letter or syllable, as the beginning of reading.[49] Users of the word method taught children the meaning and pronunciation of a word and then analyzed its constituent parts (letters and syllables). They might teach children the pronunciation and meaning of groups of words without doing a phonetic analysis. A common twentieth-century approach to learning English reading puts simple familiar words into sentences immediately: "See Jane run." When the student understands the pattern, he goes on to more difficult and less familiar sentences, accompanied by limited analysis of the constituent parts (letters, syllables, and words). This approach takes advantage of a child's experience; he learns to recognize the words for known objects and actions. Analysis follows. The word method has come under attack in the late twentieth century for lacking thoroughness and failing to give students an understanding of the principles of phonetics and grammar.

Reading may be the most complex and sophisticated skill to be learned in childhood.[50] It involves coordination between eye, mind, and page; it involves recognizing symbols for sound and meaning, coordinating motor movements of the eyes, learning very complex rules, using memory and experience, interpreting information, and finally, applying previous learning to new words and sentences. All these things have to be done almost simultaneously in order for a person to read well. Despite a great deal of research, how children learn to read remains partially a mystery now, as it was in the Renaissance. Whatever the strengths and weaknesses of the traditional method, Renaissance children succeeded in mastering this wondrous skill.

[49]Mathews, 1966, chs. 4, 5, 6, 7.
[50]Gibson and Levin, 1975, summarize much of what is currently known about reading.

CHAPTER SEVEN

Grammar

sidore of Seville (c. 570–636) offered this definition of grammar: "Grammatica est scientia recte loquendi et origo et fundamentum liberalium litterarum" ("Grammar is the science of speaking correctly and the origin and foundation of the liberal arts").[1] Numerous medieval men repeated Isidore's definition. For example, the city council of Lucca justified its expenditure of funds to appoint three communal grammarians in 1371 as follows: "Verum quod gramaticalis scientia est origo et fundamentum omnium virtutum et scientiarum . . ." ("Indeed, because the science of grammar is the origin and foundation of all virtues and sciences . . .").[2] "The science of grammar" expressed the basic medieval view that grammar analyzed language.

The Renaissance saw it differently. Niccolò Perotti wrote in late 1468: "Grammatica est ars recte loquendi recteque scribendi, scriptorum et poetarum lectionibus observata" ("Grammar is the art of speaking and writing correctly, observed in the reading of writers and poets").[3] Perotti enunciated the Renaissance view that grammar was the art of correct expression based on the usage of ancient authors. Although possibly inspired by Quintilian or later classical grammarians,[4] Perotti's definition

---

[1]*Origines* or *Etymologia* I.5.1, as quoted by J. Murphy, 1981, p. 74 n. 110.

[2]Barsanti, 1905, p. 212.

[3]Quoted from the autograph manuscript (Vaticanus Latinus 6737) of Perotti's *Rudimenta grammatices* by Percival, 1981, p. 237. All the incunabular editions that I have examined include it: Copinger 4682; Goff, *Third Census*, P-317; Hain 12675; and Hain-Copinger 12688*.

[4]See Quintilian, *Institutio oratoria* I.4.2–4. Various statements from ancient or medieval grammarians may also have influenced Perotti, if he knew of them. "Grammatica quid est? Scientia interpretandi poetas atque historicos et recte scribendi loquendique ratio. . . ." *Audacis de Scauri et Palladii libris excerpta*, in Keil, 1880, p. 321, ll. 6–7. Audax, whose dates are unknown, may have been a medieval grammarian. "Grammatica est scientia recte scribendi et enunciandi interpretandique poetas per historiam formatam ad usum rationemque verborum. . . ." Aemilius Asper, *Ars grammatica*, in Keil, 1868, p. 547, ll. 6–8. Aemilius Asper probably flourished in the late classical period. "Grammatica est specialiter scientia exercitata

162

seems to have been original. Numerous Renaissance grammar manuals repeated it or gave slight variations of it.[5]

The contrasting definitions of Isidore and Perotti articulate the difference between Middle Ages and Renaissance. The humanists sought to restore pedagogical grammar to its ancient roots by eliminating medieval manuals and speculative grammar, and replacing them with new elementary and comprehensive grammar manuals expressing their conviction that grammar must be based on ancient usage. However, closer inspection shows that Renaissance teachers retained one medieval manual and included medieval grammatical theory in their new books. In the end, a distinctive Renaissance grammatical tradition combining old and new emerged.

THE MEDIEVAL GRAMMATICAL TRADITION

The Middle Ages inherited from the Greco-Roman world pedagogical or descriptive grammar, that is, grammatical study that prepared the student to write and speak correctly.[6] The pupil learned rules, based on examples of good Latin, which taught him how to form and combine words for correct and, eventually, elegant expression. Not an end in itself, pedagogical grammar prepared the student for composition and the study of literature. A manual of the principles of correct usage became the standard method of communicating pedagogical grammar and served to transmit classical grammar to the Middle Ages.

Aelius Donatus, a fourth-century Roman grammarian who taught Jerome, wrote two of these manuals and became the most famous grammarian of all time. His smaller work, *De partibus orationis ars minor* (The lesser art concerning the parts of speech), usually called *Ars minor,* had enormous success. It discussed the parts of speech and the main declensions and conjugations. Donatus's larger work, the *Ars maior,* was less successful; only book 3, *De barbarismo,* circulated in the Middle Ages. It defined such errors as *barbarismus* (the use of an unacceptable foreign word or phrase) and *soloecismus* (a grammatical fault in the construction of a sentence).

---

lectionis expositionis eorum quae apud poetas et scriptores dicuntur, apud poetas, ut ordo servetur, apud scriptores, ut ordo careat vitiis." Diomedes, *Ars grammatica,* bk. 2, in Keil, 1857, p. 426, ll. 6–8. Diomedes was a well-known fourth-century Roman grammarian. Finally, Valla's emphasis on the usage of the ancients (see below) may have influenced Perotti.

[5]For example, the majority of printed editions of Guarino's *Regulae* featured the quote.

[6]A very large bibliography on ancient and medieval grammar exists; a few studies with good bibliographies that have been particularly helpful are representative. For the ancient background see Bonner, 1977, chs. 14 and 15. On Donatus, see Holtz, 1981. Also see, for general information, Scaglione, 1970, with the review article by Percival, 1975a. On medieval grammar, see Baebler, 1885; Bonaventure, 1961; Bursill-Hall, 1978; Thomson, 1983; and Huntsman, 1983.

Priscian's *Institutiones grammaticae,* another comprehensive grammar, had greater success in the Middle Ages than the *Ars maior.* Priscian, who taught in Constantinople in the first part of the sixth century, wrote a work of eighteen books. The first sixteen, called *Priscianus maior,* dealt with morphology (the internal structure and forms of words) and phonology (phonetics or speech sounds). The last two, called *Priscianus minor,* discussed syntax. Priscian approached grammar semantically, defining words according to what they signified or the qualities they possessed rather than their formal functions. For example, Priscian stated that a noun indicated a substance and had the quality of acting; he did not define a noun in terms of accidence of case, number, and gender. In his eighteen books, Priscian explored in leisurely fashion the main roads and many byways of Latinity, collecting illustrative specimens to lay before the eyes of the reader. Grammarians did not use Priscian's cumbersome work in the classroom, but they ransacked it for their own manuals.

The treatises of Donatus and Priscian set the tone for medieval pedagogical grammar; medieval grammarians had little knowledge of other ancient grammars. Donatus and Priscian made it possible for pupils to learn and scholars to study Latinity. Eventually medieval scholars wrote new texts that continued the basic approach of pedagogical grammar. The *Etymologiae sive origines* of Isidore of Seville collected a storehouse of etymologies for Latin words, some erudite and nearly correct, others fanciful. Later medieval grammarians composed verse grammars on the theory that rhymed definitions and explanations were easier to learn. Such works served as intermediate and advanced textbooks. The student began with Donatus's *Ars minor* and then might study the *Graecismus* or the *Doctrinale,* where he learned a great deal of syntax by memorizing the endless hexameters.

Medieval grammarians not only continued classical pedagogical grammar, but also struck out in new directions with speculative grammar.[7] With the reintroduction into the West of the logical works of Aristotle in the early twelfth century, medieval man possessed the tools to inquire into the nature of language and to relate his discoveries to reality itself. Some ancient grammarians had studied language philosophically, but their analysis had not been transmitted to the Middle Ages along with late classical pedagogical grammar. The new approach came to be known as speculative grammar, because grammar or language mirrored (*speculum* is the noun) the structure of the universe. It rose in the twelfth century and flourished in the second half of the thirteenth century and the first half of the fourteenth century, before some philosophers began to doubt its epistemological foundations. Contemporaries called its practitioners *modistae* because they used the term *modus* (mode or process) to explain

[7]See Robins, 1951, pp. 75–90; Bursill-Hall, 1971; and Pinborg, 1982.

the links between existence, understanding, and language. The *modistae* coined such terms as *modus essendi* (actual existence), *modus intelligendi* (mode of understanding or mental existence), and *modus significandi* (mode of signifying or understanding through language).

In speculative grammar, the structure of reality is the ultimate foundation of grammar. Real things exist and possess various qualities or modes of being. The mind through the modes of understanding apprehends these qualities. Then the mind endows vocal noises with modes of meaning, that is, the quality or power of signifying the reality. Words are the surface manifestation of reality and reflect the way that the mind comprehends reality. Words signify the qualities of things; the word *homo* must behave grammatically according to the qualities that are in man.

The mode that specifies a relation is the link between words. Two word forms can be combined into speech when a congruent relationship exists between the modes of the two words; that is, a semantic feature of one depends on the semantic features of the other. For example, *homo* and *currit* can be combined, because the noun *homo* has the mode of substance—it is something—and the verb *currit* (runs) has the mode of changeability. Hence, modal congruity between the two exists. The substance can act: "man runs."[8] Speculative grammar could be much more complicated than this simple example.

Speculative grammar flourished in northern France, Flanders, Germany, Denmark, and England, the lands of its chief scholars and teachers. It had less influence in southern France, Spain, and Italy. A few fourteenth-century Italians followed speculative grammar on the eve of the Renaissance. In 1391 the Commune of Pavia appointed Giovanni Travesi(o) to teach speculative grammar at the University of Pavia.[9] Gasparino Barzizza, who had studied with Travesi at Pavia, knew the writings of the *modistae,* but he omitted speculative grammar from his own teaching.[10] And the terminology of the *modistae* occasionally appeared in the grammatical works of the humanists.[11] Finally, as noted earlier, the Commune of Pistoia in 1498 authorized a master to teach speculative grammar if the pupils wanted it.[12]

Overall, Italian Renaissance humanists viewed speculative grammar as a wrongheaded Scholastic enterprise that foolishly tied language to dialectic. The humanists' sweeping rejection of medieval logic made it impossible for them to see any value in linking grammar to being. The humanists also abhorred the technical, unclassical and, hence, "barbarous" Latin

[8]The example is derived from Pinborg, 1982, pp. 259–60.
[9]Rossi, 1901, p. 25.
[10]Mercer, 1979, pp. 48, 56.
[11]Percival, 1975a, pp. 239–40.
[12]Zanelli, 1900, p. 145.

of the speculative grammarians. Literary men who did not see the point of speculative grammar, the early Italian humanists learned grammar to read the classics and to become eloquent. Nothing more. They instinctively preferred pedagogical grammar, but not necessarily medieval pedagogical grammar. Before long they began to find fault with the manuals of their medieval predecessors.

THE BEGINNING OF RENAISSANCE GRAMMAR

In the early fifteenth century, humanists struck out in new grammatical directions. The first humanistic pedagogues pledged themselves to the standards of ancient Latin but did not reject medieval pedagogical grammar. Gasparino Barzizza, in his Paduan teaching (1407–21), divided Latin grammarians into three groups: (1) ancients, especially Varro (116–27 B.C.); (2) "the moderators of pristine antiquity," that is, grammarians from Quintilian in the first century through Priscian of the early sixth; and (3) "moderns," who included every major medieval pedagogical grammarian from Isidore of Seville through Alexander de Villedieu as well as Barzizza's contemporaries Manuel Chrysoloras and Guarino of Verona.[13] Barzizza apparently knew at first hand the works of most of the grammarians from all three groups—no small achievement. He assigned greatest authority to "the moderators of pristine antiquity": Quintilian, Donatus, and the others could judge Latinity best by reason of their chronological position. He ranked the "moderns" lower because, with the exception of Chrysoloras and Guarino, they lacked Greek and therefore had no access to the roots of Latin.

In his classroom teaching, Barzizza focused on ancient practice while accepting some medieval pedagogical grammar. His teaching on orthography, diphthongs, and punctuation became the best-known part of his grammatical instruction. Barzizza, like Guarino, argued in favor of the classical spelling of *mihi* and *nihil* instead of the medieval forms *michi* and *nichil*. Barzizza revived the diphthongs *ae* and *oe* which medieval Latin had dropped in favor of the monophthongs *e* and *o*.[14] He also laid particular emphasis on punctuating correctly in order to clarify the rhetorical import of passages. Barzizza tried through such basic changes to recapture an accurate understanding of classical Latin. Reform of spelling and punctuation preceded reform of literary expression.

Barzizza believed that grammar came from the usage of antiquity, and that grammatical training prepared students to read the ancient classics. He carefully studied and preferred ancient Latin, but he did not repudiate

---

[13]Mercer, 1979, ch. 4.

[14]Also see Ullman, 1960, pp. 24–26, 53, 70–72, 81, et passim. With the notable exception of Bruni, humanists adopted classical usage in these matters. See Baron, 1968, pp. 219–23.

completely the learning of his youth in the 1370s and 1380s. He accepted medieval grammarians, consulting *Papias,* Hugutius, and others when necessary. His blended pedagogy of old and new which favored innovation strongly influenced masters in the Veneto and nearby regions.

Renaissance grammar really began with the appearance of the *Regulae grammaticales* of Guarino of Verona, written in Venice and first mentioned in a letter of January 1418.[15] Guarino's *Regulae* kept some traditional content, purged other material, and presented the whole in an innovative format. The combination had enormous influence in the Italian Renaissance.

Guarino's *Regulae* began with a very brief discussion of the four parts of grammar: letter, syllable, word, and sentence or speech (*littera, syllaba, dictio, oratio*), a fourfold division to be found in ancient and medieval sources and endlessly repeated in the Renaissance.[16] Guarino next analyzed the eight parts of speech in conventional terms by listing attributes. He discussed them in the order of noun, verb, participle, pronoun, preposition, adverb, interjection, and conjunction, the order of fourteenth-century Italian grammars.[17] Guarino did not conjugate and decline but went directly to verbal syntax, that is, the construction of sentences according to the rules governing the use of verbs. Indeed, Renaissance grammarians always made the verb the point of reference for the discussion of syntactical construction.

Guarino described how to form the first-person singular in the present tense and active voice of a verb, *amo.* He called such a verb a "simple, active verb" and explained that the subject of a simple active verb should be in the nominative case and the object in the accusative case. He then made a sentence: "Ego amo Petrum." Guarino manufactured a sentence to illustrate his point rather than taking one from a classical source. Next, he

---

[15]"Has quidem Regulas ad Christophorum meum mittere opus habeo. . . ." Guarino, 1967, vol. 1:180, letter 98 of 19 January 1418, Venice.

[16]My analysis is based on examination of the printed editions listed in Appendix 1 plus the secondary literature. Although the original manuscript has not been located, and the text began to undergo emendation almost immediately, the content remained consistent enough for this summary to be made. In my discussion of the grammars of Guarino and other authors, I try to provide a historical account that pays particular attention to the texts used. Space does not permit textual comparisons or full analysis of grammatical points. The basic studies on Guarino's *Regulae* are Sabbadini, 1964b, pp. 38–58; Percival, 1972; Percival, 1975a, pp. 238–40; and Percival, 1976 and 1978. Three studies that put Guarino's teaching into a broader context are Garin, 1967, pp. 69–106; Scheyen, 1973; and Grafton and Jardine, 1982.

[17]The question of the sources for the *Regulae* is a complex one. Sabbadini, 1964b, pp. 39–46, and elsewhere, argued that Guarino based the *Regulae* on the *Ianua* in particular, the *Doctrinale,* Priscian, and Francesco da Buti. Percival, 1972, concludes that while Guarino may have used these sources, it is not clear that he did so directly. He questions the existence of a direct link between *Ianua* and the *Regulae,* and he points to other possible Italian late medieval texts. Percival also points out that Guarino departed from his sources in significant ways.

listed several common verbs guided by this syntactical rule (*amo, diligo, fero, porto, lego, canto*, etc.) in four principal forms (*amo, amas* [*sic*], *amavi, amatum*), and gave the Italian meaning of each (*per amare*—to love). Finally, he added a three-line verse to help the student learn and memorize the verbs and the rule just explained. The use of a mnemonic verse was, again, a typically medieval feature; indeed, Guarino probably borrowed some of the verses from medieval grammars. Guarino followed the same procedure each time he described a subclass of verbs (active, passive, deponent).

The medieval concept of "government," the notion that "the verb governs all the nominal expressions in the sentence including the subject,"[18] lay at the heart of Guarino's approach to verbal syntax. Government assumed that the sentence has its parts in the "natural order" of subject, verb, and object. The verb then exercises semantic influence on the nominal expressions to its left and right. Hence, the noun at the left of the verb denoting the performer of the action becomes the agent (*persona agens*), and the noun at the right which undergoes the action becomes the patient (*persona patiens*). Guarino relied on medieval Italian grammarians, the *Doctrinale*, and especially Priscian for his basically medieval syntactical description. Whether he knew Priscian directly or through intermediary sources is not clear.

Guarino's *Regulae* concluded with a series of short discussions on a variety of grammatical topics: adverbs of place, heteroclite nouns (irregularly declined nouns), comparative and superlative adjectives, orthography, and so on. Anonymous editors often appended his *Carmina differentialia*, poetic couplets that gave examples of synonyms, homonyms, and *differentiae* (words that differ only in nuance, for example, *metus-timor*—fear), to manuscript and printed versions of the *Regulae*. Guarino's classroom instruction also included study of diphthongs, some orthography, and metrics, but the *Regulae* did not include them.[19]

Guarino broke with the past in several ways.[20] The first, obvious, point is that he wrote his own manual. He must have found the previous texts wanting, a significant conclusion in itself. Second, he purged much medieval syntactical material. For example, he did not use such common medieval grammatical terms as *suppositum* for subject and *appositum* for predicate, and he generally simplified. Since Guarino knew well the medieval tradition, his decision to purge indicated a partial rejection of the past. And he eliminated a great deal: the text of the *Regulae* was only one-fourth to one-third as long as most medieval manuals. Fifteenth- and sixteenth-century printed editions usually contained thirty-six, forty, or

[18]Percival, 1975a, p. 237.
[19]Sabbadini, 1964b, pp. 47–52, 79–82.
[20]Some of the following was suggested by Percival, 1976, pp. 77–78.

forty-eight pages in a small octavo format (15 × 10 cm.). Guarino handled in a few sentences material to which medieval grammarians devoted pages. Purgation became revolutionary when compared with the normal medieval and Renaissance habit of accretion. For example, commentaries on texts grew as scholar after scholar added glosses without eliminating previous matter. Guarino's grammar liberated the student from some of the grammatical details and complex terminology that medieval students had to learn. Third, Guarino innovated through reorganization. In a field in which the body of fundamental material changes little, Guarino's organization of the content seems more direct and streamlined than that of his predecessors. This admittedly is a subjective judgment, but the format of the printed editions supports the judgment.

Humanists and teachers approved of Guarino's *Regulae*. About forty surviving manuscripts are known,[21] as well as at least forty-six Italian incunabular printings.[22] Another twenty-seven sixteenth- and seventeenth-century Italian printings have been located.[23] The known surviving post-1500 printings are probably only a small part of the total number of editions issued. Editors added new material, another sign of approval. Imitations appeared, as did versions that falsely claimed to be the *Regulae* (see below). Teachers and pupils used Guarino's text continuously through the first half of the seventeenth century. Given the strength of tradition in the field of Latin grammar, Guarino's achievement in writing a widely adopted new manual testified to his importance. The *Regulae* alone confirmed his stature as a major pedagogical force of the Renaissance.

The decade between 1410 and 1420 proved to be an important one for Renaissance Latin grammar. Guarino wrote the first Renaissance treatise on diphthongs probably in 1415 and his grammar by 1418. Barzizza composed the first version of his work on orthography between 1417 and 1421.[24] A few years earlier, Poggio Bracciolini and Niccolò Niccoli had begun to develop the new humanistic scripts, formal and cursive, in which they adopted classical usage in orthography and diphthongs (see ch. 11). Teaching correct (that is, classical) orthography, punctuation, and grammar signalled the humanists' intention to restore Latin to its classical form. Although retaining much of medieval pedagogical grammatical practice, the humanistic pedagogues initiated a new approach.

Neither Barzizza nor Guarino proclaimed a sharp break with the medi-

---

[21]See Percival, 1978, p. 242 and p. 251 n. 4.

[22]See Hain 8105 through 8125; Copinger 2809 and 2811; Reichling 202, 203, 544, 545, 1747; Reichling Supplement 84; IGI 4529, 4533, 4534, 4536–41, and 4539a. Percival, 1972, pp. 282–83, lists three more incunables in the Bodleian Library of Oxford University not listed in the above catalogues. I have examined Hain 8108 and 8111; IGI 4536, 4541, and 4539a.

[23]See Appendix 1.

[24]Mercer, 1979, p. 49.

eval past, but the iconoclastic Lorenzo Valla (1407–57) did. Although not a
classroom manual, his *Elegantiarum linguae latinae libri sex* (Six books of the
elegances of the Latin language) helped change the study of grammar.[25]
The prefaces—really manifestoes—to the six books praised ancient Latin
and ancient culture and condemned medieval Latin and its culture. Valla
saw language as the foundation of civilization; if men could recover
elegant ancient Latin, they might then reform the liberal disciplines,
jurisprudence, theology, and the rest of culture.

Grammar made the difference. In the preface to book 2, Valla rejected
the view that grammatical continuity linked late antiquity and the early
Middle Ages.[26] He praised the three major grammarians of very late
antiquity, Donatus, Servius (probably first half of the fifth century), and
Priscian. But only "stutterers" followed. First came Isidore of Seville, the
most presumptuous of the lot, who, knowing nothing, pretended to teach
everything. More ignoramuses followed: Papias, Évrard de Bethune and
his *Graecismus,* Hugutius, Giovanni Balbi and his *Catholicon,* and "Aymo"
(probably Aimeric of Angoulême and his *Ars lectaria,* a treatise on quantity
and accent written 1086), and others not worth mentioning. These grammarians taught less than nothing; they rendered scholars in school more
stupid than the ignorant at home, in Valla's judgment.

Valla saw an absolute rupture between classical elegance and medieval
barbarity. Medieval men had irretrievably lost classical Latin in the sixty or
seventy years between Priscian and Isidore of Seville, and the ensuing
eight hundred years had made matters worse. Only a comparable break
with medieval Latin would restore pure Latinity, according to Valla.

Having condemned medieval pedagogical grammar, Valla devoted his
very large book to reconstructing good Latinity on the basis of ancient
usage. In his 475 chapters, Valla presented several thousand examples of
correct and incorrect Latin, discussing forms of words, etymology, orthography, syntax, and semantics. The beginning, book 1, chapter 1,
presents a good example of the content and approach. Entitled "De
nominibus, quorum ablativi plurales exeunt in abus" ("Concerning nouns
which end in *-abus* in the ablative plural"), the chapter began as follows:
"Deus, dea, deabus, dicimus; divus, diva, divabus non dicimus. Item, in
quibusdam alijs, ut filius, filia, filiabus; non privignus, privigna, privig-
nabus" ("We say god, goddess, by the goddesses; deity, she-deity, but we
do not say by the she–deities. The same for these others: son, daughter, by

[25]Three good recent studies on the *Elegantiae* are Marsh, 1979; Martinelli, 1980; and De
Caprio, 1984. Also see the brief remarks by Percival, 1975a, pp. 254–56.
[26]The text of the preface is most conveniently given with Italian translation in Garin, ed.,
1952, pp. 602–3.

the daughters; stepson, stepdaughter, but not by the stepdaughters").[27]

Valla made a grammatical point.[28] Some nouns, notably the feminine *dea* and *filia*, use the older, uncommon suffix *-abus* in the ablative plural in order to distinguish them in that form from the ablative plural of the corresponding masculine nouns. Hence, one uses *deabus* rather than *deīs*, which is the same as the ablative plural (*deīs*—by the gods) of the masculine *deus*. However, the ancients limited the use of *-abus* to *deabus* and *filiabus*. They normally used the regular suffix *-īs* for the feminine ablative plural unless both sexes were mentioned together and the writer needed to differentiate between them by using *-abus* and *-īs*. Valla went on to give other examples, pointing out that one did not use *dominabus, animabus,* and so on. Then he cited a classical example, the salutation of a letter from Cicero to his wife and daughter (*Ad fam.* XIV. 14): "Cicero tamen ad uxorem & filiam scribens 'Duabus animis suis' dixit, non 'animabus'" ("However, Cicero writing to his wife and daughter said 'His two dear hearts' (*animis*), not *animabus*"). Valla concluded the chapter with a typical pugnacious declaration: "Sed ego de usu loquendi disputo, non de abusu" ("But I weigh the use of speech, not the abuse").

In this and more erudite examples, Valla reconstructed classical Latin. He began by savagely condemning medieval linguistic variations and language scholarship. He particularly enjoyed demolishing mistaken etymologies. He then offered a correct Latin based on the best ancient authors, those who flourished in the two centuries between Cicero's birth in 106 B.C. and Quintilian's death in c. 100.[29] Valla used the inductive method; he observed, then derived from his observations principles of good usage. Above all, he presented hundreds, perhaps thousands, of quotations from classical authors to prove his points. Frequent historical examples from the best authors, especially Cicero, Caesar, Sallust, Livy, and Quintilian, became an organic system that yielded "elegant" Latin that filled the ear with sweet sounds. Frequency of usage helped determine his standard; he rejected obscure and uncommon words even if Cicero had employed them. His standard of excellence depended on a very wide knowledge of the sources and *ratio*, his judgment of what seemed historically, culturally, and philosophically true.[30] He proposed a standard more difficult to achieve than the Ciceronianism eventually adopted by the majority of Italian teachers. Valla did not write a pedagogical manual, but

[27]For the sake of convenience, I am using my own copy—L. Valla, 1543, p. 13—for all three quotes. I have slightly modernized the punctuation and capitalization. The same can be found in L. Valla, 1962, p. 5.

[28]Allen and Greenough, 1931, paragraph 43e, p. 19, explains the point.

[29]De Caprio, 1984, pp. 180–81.

[30]Martinelli, 1980, p. 62.

his *Elegantiae,* with its knowledge, its acuity, and its vehement rejection of medieval Latin, proclaimed principles that greatly influenced other Renaissance grammarians.[31]

GRAMMAR MANUALS IN THE CLASSROOM

Guarino and Valla did much to establish the Renaissance approach to grammar. After them, Renaissance grammarians wrote manuals that combined (1) ideological rejection of medieval pedagogical texts, (2) proclamation of the principle that classical usage constituted the standard of excellence, sometimes with accompanying quotations to serve as examples, and (3) retention of a considerable amount of medieval grammatical theory, but not speculative grammar. In a sense, Renaissance grammarians combined Valla's ideology with Guarino's moderate practicality.

Latin style meant so much to fifteenth-century humanists. A good Latin style expressed *humanitas,* a combination of lofty culture and excellent education. As John D'Amico writes, "The cultivation of a fine Latin style to a great extent defined culture, and this language could concilitate a variety of ideas and traditions to form a cultural unity."[32] The humanists preferred the Latin of the golden age of the late republic and early empire over the Latin of another ancient period, or medieval Latin. One attained a good Latin style by imitating the ancients. But within the broad canon of imitation, some room for disagreement existed. Poggio Bracciolini argued for a Ciceronian style, and Valla for a more eclectic Latin based on a range of the ancients, in a celebrated debate of 1451 and 1452.[33]

On a practical level, humanists of the fifteenth century taught good Latin by writing manuals of grammar and rhetoric. Seldom have the intellectual leaders of a historical period so occupied themselves with elementary tasks the way the Quattrocento humanists who wrote grammar textbooks did. A few need to be mentioned. The humanist and university professor Gaspare da Verona (c. 1400–1474), who studied with Guarino at Verona, around 1450 wrote his *Regulae grammaticales,* a syntax manual modeled on Guarino's work but adding figures of speech derived from the *Graecismus.*[34] It circulated in manuscript before first appearing in print in Milan (1475), and it had at least two more printings. Around 1450 Ognibene Bonisoli wrote an elementary morphology manual, *De octo partibus orationis liber,* which appeared in print in 1473 and had at least four

---

[31]For other fifteenth-century Italian humanistic condemnations of medieval grammatical texts, see the quotations gathered by Garin, ed., 1958, pp. 91–92, 103–4.

[32]D'Amico, 1983, p. 124.

[33]Martinelli, 1980.

[34]See FR Ms. 4039. For incunabular printings, see Reichling 1527–29 and IGI 4178–80. Also see Percival, 1981, p. 235.

more printings in the 1470s and one in 1506.[35] Ognibene's grammar explained at length word forms that the printed versions of Guarino's *Regulae* briefly explicated with primitive paradigms. Ognibene's grammar did not quote from ancient Latin authors, but it did employ limited Greek to explain Latin.

Niccolò Perotti wrote the second most important fifteenth-century grammar after Guarino's. Born in Sassoferrato (in the Marches) of noble parents, Perotti (1429–80) studied with Vittorino da Feltre and Guarino before becoming an apostolic secretary in 1455.[36] Named archbishop in 1458, Perotti carried out diplomatic missions and governed Viterbo (1464–69), Spoleto (1471–72), and Perugia (1474–77) for the papacy. He also pursued an extremely active scholarly career as editor of Martial and Pliny and translator of numerous Greek works, especially Polybius and Epictetus, into Latin. He wrote the *Rudimenta grammatices* (finished in 1468, printed in 1473 with about sixty more incunabular editions)[37] and the *Cornucopiae* (left unfinished at his death, published in 1489, followed by at least twenty-three editions by 1536).[38]

The first humanistic comprehensive grammar, Perotti's *Rudimenta grammatices* had three parts: (1) definitions of the parts of speech followed by elementary morphology, (2) syntax, and (3) a treatise on letter writing.[39] Several times longer than Guarino's *Regulae,* Perotti's grammar was meant to be used throughout a student's career. The work began with primer material of alphabet, Ave Maria, Pater Noster, and Apostles' Creed. Perotti employed the catechetical format for the rest of the book, beginning with questions illustrating his pedagogical principles: What is the first sign of intelligence in boys? Memory. What is the second? Imitation.[40] Thus Perotti emphasized *imitatio,* so dear to the humanists. Perotti then proceeded to the parts of speech and inflections, giving vernacular translations of some Latin words. Perotti organized verb inflections into regular arrangements of columns and rows of the inflected parts, an early use of paradigms (medieval grammars did not employ paradigms). Throughout his work Perotti borrowed from the ancient grammarians Donatus and Priscian and from medieval Italian grammars, especially the *Ianua* (see below). He used artificial sentences to illustrate grammatical

[35]Hain 10022–26; IGI 7001–4. I have examined Hain 10024/IGI 7002 (Padua, Bartolomeo Valdezoccho, 14 January 1474) and Ognibene, 1506. All but one printing appended Ognibene's treatise on metrics.
[36]For Perotti's biography, see Mercati, 1925; and Kristeller, 1981.
[37]See Hain 12635 through 12696; and Percival, 1986.
[38]See Hain 12697 through 12707 for some of the editions.
[39]I have briefly examined Hain 12646, 12674–75, 12678, and 12688*, Copinger 4682, and Goff, *Third Census,* P-279a, P-280, P-317. Above all, see Percival, 1981, who analyzes the work on the basis of the autograph ms. Vaticanus Latinus 6737.
[40]Hain 12675 (Cremona, 26 August 1486), sig. A2ᵛ.

points as had medieval grammarians and Guarino, but he also took examples from ancient authors. Perotti wrote a comprehensive manual that mixed old and new.

In his *Cornucopiae,* a very detailed commentary on two works of Martial, Perotti explained every word through numerous quotations from a large number of Latin and Greek authors. Thanks to the exhaustive index that preceded the work, the *Cornucopiae* served as a comprehensive dictionary and encyclopedia of classical Latin. Teachers borrowed from it when commenting on ancient works.

The availability of the ancient works of Donatus and Priscian, medieval texts such as the *Doctrinale,* and the new humanistic grammars gave teachers a variety of manuals from which to teach. It is difficult to determine which of them Quattrocento schools most often used, because teacher contracts which have been found did not specify the grammar text to be taught. Nevertheless, fragmentary evidence suggests that the humanistic grammars found favor almost immediately. In 1432 a schoolboy named Maffeo Valaresso copied out a grammar manual showing Guarino's influence, perhaps through a teacher who had studied with Guarino. Valaresso, who came from the Veneto, had an ecclesiastical career in Rome before becoming archbishop of Zara (or Zadar) on the Dalmatian coast in 1450. He died there in 1496.[41] In 1471 a communal master at Sarzana (in Liguria, south of Genoa) taught Guarino's *Regulae.*[42] A wealthy Florentine boy of the late Quattrocento used a manuscript grammar prepared for him: "Regole di Palla figliuolo di Bernardo Rucellai, e degli ami." The title and content of this verbal syntax manual prepared for Palla di Bernardo Rucellai (1473–1543) showed Guarinian influence.[43] Other wealthy boys had manuscript grammars entitled "Donatus," although they were not necessarily the famous fourth-century text.[44] And medieval grammars continued to circulate.

Sixteenth-century teachers and pupils had a much wider choice, thanks to the great expansion of printing and lower book prices. Which grammars did they prefer?

IANUA

Sixty-seven teachers stated that they taught *Donato, Donado, Donà,* or *Donao,* according to the linguistic and orthographic preferences of speaker

---

[41]VC Cicogna Ms. 59, as described by Segarizzi, 1915–16b.

[42]Petti Balbi, 1979, p. 121.

[43]FR Ms. 720, a small octavo vellum manuscript of twenty-four leaves written in Latin. On Rucellai, see Kent, 1977, p. 308 et passim.

[44]For example, there is an apparently uncatalogued fifteenth-century manuscript grammar of thirty-eight leaves (including the *Disticha Catonis*) bound with the incunable FN Landau-Finaly Inc. 49. It was written by "Petrus Honestus" for the sons of Gregorio

TABLE 7.1
Latin Grammars and Elementary Latin Texts Taught by Venetian Teachers,
1587–1588

	Number of Teachers
Grammars	
"Donatus"	67
Donato al senno	8
Guarino, *Regulae grammaticales*	8
"Le regole" (probably Guarino's *Regulae*)	12
Despauter, "La grammatica"	4
Alvares, *De institutione grammatica*	3
"Valla" (probably an epitome of the *Elegantiae*)	2
Cafaro, *Grammatices epitome*	2
Manuzio, *Institutiones grammaticae*	1
Elementary Readers	
Disticha Catonis	21
Vives, *Colloquia sive linguae Latinae exercitatio*[a]	39
Liber Aesopi	2

Source: ACPV, "Professioni di fede."

[a]I include references to "Essercitation dela lingua latina" because this is a vernacular translation of the title of Vives' work, and because no other book seems to match the title.

and scribe. *Donato* in the Italian Renaissance meant either the *Ars minor* of Aelius Donatus or "elementary grammar manual" in general.[45] Renaissance teachers tended to use the term specifically. As indicated in table 7.1, they differentiated between the text of Donatus and those of Guarino and other grammarians. Moreover, publishers issued a large number of printings of a manual carrying the name of Donatus. Hence, it appears that at least a large majority of the teachers who stated that they taught *Donatus* really did use the famous late Roman text.

But the text that circulated under the name of Donatus was not the historical *Ars minor*, but a late medieval text of Italian origin. The pseudo-Donatus carried the title *Aelij Donati grammatici pro impetrando ad rempublicam litterariam aditu: novitijs adolescentibus grammatices rudimenta quae aptissime dedicata* (The rudiments of grammar of Aelius Donatus the grammarian, the approach to entering the republic of letters for beginners to whom it is most fittingly dedicated). Even more important, manuscript

---

Piccolomini, probably a Sienese noble. The grammar is neither Donatus's *Ars minor* nor the *Ianua*, but a fairly comprehensive morphology and syntax combined. How many other manuscript grammars can be found in Italian libraries is difficult to conjecture.

  [45]For dictionary definitions of *Donato*, see Carlo Battisti and Giovanni Alessio, *Dizionario etimologico italiano.* 5 vols. (Florence, 1951), 2:1380; and *Grande dizionario della lingua italiana*, 13 vols. (Turin, 1961–86), 4:943.

and printed versions of the pseudo-*Donatus* always prefaced the grammatical material with an eight-line verse. Indeed, this verse substituted for a title if the manuscript or printed book lacked one.

Ianua sum rudibus primam cupientibus artem
    Nec sine me quisquam rite peritus erit.
Nam genus et casum speciem numerumque figuram
    His quae flectuntur partibus isinuo.
Pono modum reliquis quid competat optime pandens
    Et quam non doceam dictio nulla manet.
Ergo legas studiumque tibi rudis adice lector
    Nam celeri studio discere multa potes.

I am the door for the ignorant desiring the first art;
    Without me no one will become truly skilled.
Because I teach gender and case, species[46] and number, and formation
    in their parts, which are inflected.
I put method into the remaining parts of speech, explaining what agrees the best.
    And no use of the word remains that I do not teach.
Therefore, unskilled beginner, read and dedicate yourself to study,
    Because you can learn many things with rapid study.[47]

Renaissance Italians, even in the late sixteenth century, believed this book to have been the authentic *Ars minor* of Donatus. For example, the encyclopaedist Tommaso Garzoni (1549–89) in his discussion of grammarians and their manuals referred to "il Ianua sum rudibus del Donato" ("the 'I am the Door for the Ignorant' of Donatus").[48] Although some humanistic scholars probably knew otherwise, the rank and file of Italian teachers and writers identified this other manual as the authentic *Ars minor*.

However, the two works bore little resemblance to each other. After the introductory exhortation, the pseudo-*Donatus* began with a series of questions:

Poeta quae pars est? nomen est. quare est nomen? quia significat substantiam et qualitatem propriam vel communem cum casu. Nomini quot accidunt? quinque. quae? species genus numerus figura et casus.

---

[46]*Speciem* refers to the origin or derivation of a word. Hence, "species" or "kind" seems the best translation.

[47]The verse is found in all *Ianua* printings. The translation is mine. The following discussion is based on the *Ianua* texts examined and can be conveniently followed through the text of GW 8998 (Pavia: Franciscus Girardengus, 8 November 1481), most of which is printed by W. Schmitt, 1969, pp. 74–80.

[48]Garzoni, 1601, p. 90. His work *La piazza universale* first appeared in 1585, to be followed by editions of 1586, 1587, 1589, 1592, 1595, 1599, 1601, 1610, 1617, 1638, and 1665. Garzoni gave evidence of extensive knowledge of contemporary and ancient grammarians in his humorous discourse "De' grammatici et pedanti," in Garzoni, 1601, pp. 86–93.

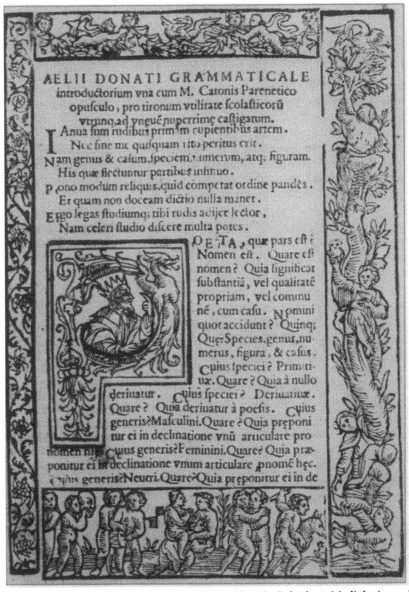

7. Title page of *Aelii Donati grammaticale . . . (Ianua)*. Colophon: Mediolani, apud Franciscum Paganellum, 1597. MT H 1898/1.

The *Ars minor* of Donatus began quite differently.

> Partes orationis quot sunt? Octo. Quae? Nomen pronomen verbum adverbium participium coniunctio praepositio interiectio.
>
> DE NOMINE
>
> Nomen quid est? Pars orationis cum casu corpus aut rem proprie communiterve significans. Nomini quot accidunt? Sex. Quae? Qualitas comparatio genus numerus figura casus.[49]

The noun had five attributes according to the spurious work and six according to the authentic *Ars minor*. The differences persisted the length of the two works. Both used the catechetical method, but organization, examples, and sometimes terminology varied.

Sabbadini recognized in 1896 that this grammar manual differed from the historical *Ars minor* of Donatus.[50] Adopting the medieval custom of naming a textbook for its first word, Sabbadini called it *Ianua*. Historians of grammar have called it that ever since. Some incunabular and other catalogues recognize the difference and list *Ianua* and the *Ars minor* separately.[51] But the majority of inventories, especially library catalogues, do not distinguish between the two.

The Italian Renaissance learned from *Ianua;* the rest of Europe used *Donatus* (i.e., the *Ars minor*). At least thirty-eight incunabular printings of *Ianua* or its close variants, the *Donatus melior* of Antonio Mancinelli and the *Donato al senno,* but only ten printings of the historical *Donatus,* appeared in Italy.[52] Eight of the latter ten were joint publications with other ancient grammars, such as the *Ars maior* of Donatus or the *Ars grammatica* of Diomedes, suggesting an intended readership of scholars rather than teachers and students.[53] By contrast, more than three hundred incunabular

---

[49]For the Latin text with English translation, see Donatus, 1926, p. 28. For a comprehensive study, see Holtz, 1981.

[50]Sabbadini, 1964b, p. 43.

[51]GW, vol. 7, col. 661, very briefly notes that they are two different works. It calls *Ianua* "Donatus, *Ars Minor (Rudimenta grammatices).*" The entries give incipits of the *Ianua* verse and the text proper ("Poeta quae pars est?") so that one can distinguish between *Donatus* and *Ianua.* IGI lists *Ianua* as "Donatus, Aelius. Rudimenta gramatices" (see nos. 3551–62) and the authentic *Donatus* as "Donatus, Aelius. De octo partibus orationis." However, other printed catalogues and all library catalogues that I have examined list *Ianua* as *Donatus;* the catalogues' authors were apparently unaware of the difference.

[52]The thirty-eight Italian incunabular printings of *Ianua* or its variations are: (1) Twenty-seven printings of the *Ianua:* GW 8987–94, 8997–99, 9002–15, 9017, and IGI 3551–53, 3553a, 3555, 3557, 3558. I have examined GW 8994, 9002, 9007, and 9014. W. Schmitt, 1969, pp. 74–80, prints the text of GW 8998. (2) Seven Italian incunabular printings of the *Donatus melior* of Antonio Mancinelli: GW 9018–24; IGI 3555a, 3558a, 3559–61. And (3) four Italian printings of the *Donato al senno:* GW 9025–28; IGI 3562.

[53]See GW 8818 and 8908; the latter begins with the *Ianua* verse but then becomes Donatus's *Ars minor.* I examined the copy in VM Misc. 1375.2. Also see the following print-

printings of *Donatus* or close variants, but only six printings of *Ianua,* were published in the rest of Europe.[54]

The divergency between Italy and the rest of Europe continued, and perhaps became greater, after 1500. Thirty-eight different Italian printings of *Ianua* and its close variants from the sixteenth and seventeenth centuries have been located.[55] But post-1500 Italian printings of *Donatus* are extremely difficult to find. Finally, when Italian grammarians began to write their own elementary manuals, they elaborated on, or borrowed from, *Ianua* rather than Donatus's *Ars minor* (see below). Even Perotti who, unlike his contemporaries, knew and used *Donatus,* borrowed much more from *Ianua.*[56]

Since the origins of *Ianua* remain unknown, one can only speculate on how Italy came to prefer *Ianua* to *Donatus.* Early medieval Italian grammarians probably inherited *Donatus* from ancient Rome. Then, at some point in the eleventh, twelfth, or thirteenth century, when most medieval school texts were written, an Italian grammarian composed *Ianua.* Either he or a later copyist placed Donatus's name on the manuscript and appended the *Disticha Catonis.* The earliest surviving manuscript may be FN Magliabechianus I 45, ff. 1r–15v, followed by the *Disticha Catonis* in the same hand on ff. 15v–21r. Scholars do not agree on the date of this manuscript, their conjectures ranging from the eleventh to the fourteenth century.[57] Another manuscript has been ascribed to the thirteenth century, and several came from the fourteenth and fifteenth centuries.[58] As time passed, *Ianua* dominated and *Donatus* dropped from sight in Italy. *Ianua* shared some characteristics of grammars written by the fourteenth-century Francesco da Buti from Pisa and Folchino dei Borfoni from Cre-

---

ings of two or more ancient grammars that included the *Ars minor.* GW 966, 8399, 8401–4, 9031–32. I have examined 8401 and 9032.

[54]For the incunabular printings of Donatus or versions fairly close to the original *Ars minor* appearing outside of Italy, see GW 8674–8817, 8819–8907, 8909–86. GW, vol. 7, cols. 582–584, notes that the *Ars minor* printed in the Renaissance was not quite the original text but a late medieval variation. Nevertheless, it was much closer to the original Donatus than *Ianua.* For the six non-Italian incunabular printings of *Ianua* see GW 8995–96, 9000–9001, 9008, and 9016.

[55]See Appendix 1.

[56]Percival, 1981, pp. 245–46, 257, et passim.

[57]I have examined the manuscript but hesitate to venture an opinion when experts differ so much.

[58]For a list of some manuscripts, see W. Schmitt, 1969, pp. 50–51. I have examined two others as well: VM, Mss. Latini, Cl. XIII, 8 (3937), 20 folios containing *Ianua* and the *Disticha Catonis* in a fifteenth-century hand on vellum; and NNC, Plimpton Ms. 138, 22 folios containing *Ianua* and the *Disticha Catonis* with a little interlinear Italian translation in a fourteenth-century *littera rotunda* hand on vellum. W. K. Percival first identified the latter manuscript as *Ianua.* The first pages of both manuscripts present the *Ianua* verse followed by a large capital *P* (for *Poeta*) colored in red. Fifteenth- and sixteenth-century printers often exactly followed this first-page format in their printed versions.

mona.[59] But their works were not the same as *Ianua* and, most important, they did not prosper in the age of print. The earliest surviving printed *Ianua* is GW 8987 (Rome: Sweynheim and Pannartz, 1470).[60] As is always true with elementary grammars, the surviving manuscripts and printed editions are undoubtedly only a small fraction of the number produced.

A morphology, *Ianua* defined, explained, and listed inflections, which are the changes of form which Latin words undergo in order to indicate case, number, tense, mood, and voice. The *Ianua* proceeded catechetically; the beginning of the text (cited above, "Poeta quae pars est?") was typical. "Poet is what part [of speech]? It is a noun. What is a noun? That which signifies proper or common substance and quality by means of case. How many accidents [or attributes] does a noun have? Five. What are they? Species, gender, number, figure, and case."

The questions and answering definitions continued. According to *Ianua,* nouns had two species, which were primitive (the stem or root word, such as *mens*—mind) and derivative (a noun derived from the stem by adding a prefix or suffix, such as *mentio*—mention or hint). Of course, the composition of words is part of semantics, not morphology, but the *Ianua,* in medieval fashion, mixed the two. *Ianua* continued: the genders were masculine, feminine, neuter, common, inclusive, uncertain, or "promiscuous," that is, signifying both sexes.[61] Number was singular or plural. "Figure" meant the composition of a noun, whether simple (*iustus*—just), *composita* or compound (*iniustus*—unjust), or *decomposita* (derived from a compound noun, such as *iniustitia*—injustice). Again this was semantics, derived from Priscian.[62] The fifth accident was the familiar one of case: nominative, vocative, genitive, dative, accusative, and ablative.

Ianua employed the same method of classification and definition for the other seven parts of speech: verb, participle, pronoun, preposition, adverb, interjection, and conjunction. This order came from Priscian, not Donatus, who employed a different listing.[63] Like nearly all medieval and Renaissance grammars, *Ianua* considered the participle—but not the adjective—a part of speech.[64]

---

[59]On *Ianua* and the medieval Italian tradition, see W. Schmitt, 1969, passim; Sabbadini, 1964b, pp. 42–44; and Percival, 1972; 1975a, pp. 233–37; 1976, pp. 74–77; 1978, pp. 245–49; and 1981, pp. 234–37.

[60]W. Schmitt, pp. 52–53.

[61]Modern grammars note these complexities but do not try to resolve them by means of multiple classifications. For example, modern grammars state that a noun of uncertain sex, such as *parens* (parent) is either masculine or feminine according to the context, i.e., whether father or mother is meant, and go no further. Allen and Greenough, 1931, paragraph 34.

[62]W. Schmitt, 1969, p. 58.

[63]Percival, 1981, p. 239.

[64]Most Renaissance grammars followed the medieval tradition of dividing nouns into substantive and "adjectival" nouns. Sixteenth-century manuals ingeniously explained the difference. A substantive noun signified an individual or general body or thing. An adjectival

After defining attributes, the *Ianua* presented inflections, again through explanatory phrases: "Nominativo hic poeta. Genitivo huius poetae. Dativo huic poetae." Manuscript versions of *Ianua* lacked paradigms, and Renaissance printings of the work did not add them. Editors and printers remained remarkably faithful to the medieval manuscript format of *Ianua*.

A handbook of condensed definitions for students, the *Ianua* explained discrete bits of Latinity. It lacked mnemonic devices such as jingling verses, and relied on the catechetical method to aid memory. It neither discussed syntax nor presented sample sentences. Like Guarino's *Regulae,* the *Ianua* separated the teaching of the rudiments of grammar from the teaching of literature. Despite its austere, abstract nature, the *Ianua* prospered during the Renaissance while other medieval manuals, such as the *Graecismus,* disappeared.

Obviously, part of the reason was that many Renaissance pedagogues thought *Ianua* to be the famous *Ars minor* of Donatus. But tradition also explained *Ianua*'s continuing popularity. Teachers had been using it since the fourteenth century or earlier, and pedagogues have always valued tradition, especially at the elementary level. They seldom change methods and textbooks, because they feel comfortable with the tried and true, and because education includes passing on tradition. With *Ianua* they could teach the textbook of their own youth. Parents also valued tradition as a sign that teachers upheld standards. Parents could look on benignly as their progeny learned the same material from the same text that they had mastered. Indeed, some students brought textbooks from home. One Venetian teacher reported in 1587 that the students brought to school "i Donadi" and other books that fathers and mothers wanted them to learn.[65] Upholding tradition reduced expenses, because parent, child, and sibling could study the same book until it wore out. Teachers and students used *Ianua* because it had been used before. They would stop only if humanists denounced the text, and this did not happen.[66]

---

noun had to be "added to" a substantive noun to have meaning. For example, the adjectival noun *felix* fails to indicate who or what is happy and has little meaning. But *felix homo* has meaning. If one can place a word thought to be an adjectival noun next to a substantive noun and the resulting phrase has meaning, both are correctly used. *Res bonus* is perfectly understandable as "good thing," while *Deus res* and *Alexander res* are nonsensical, because they combine two substantive nouns. See Toscanella, 1568a, pp. 15, 262; and Priscianese, 1540, sigs. Aa7v–Aa8r. Although continuing to define an adjectival noun as above, some sixteenth-century grammars began to use the term *adjective* and came closer to viewing it as an independent part of speech. Nevertheless, the tradition of viewing the adjective as a noun lasted well into the twentieth century in Latin grammars written by Italians. See Mantovani, 1950.

[65]"I portano i Donadi, Fior de virtù et de questi Orlandi Furiosi che ghe da i padri et le madri che debbano imparar." Statement of Bernardinus Fiozetto, in ACPV, "Professional di fede," fol. 173v; Baldo, 1977, p. 67; also see "Professioni di fede," fol. 205v; Baldo, 1977, p. 71.

[66]I do not know of any humanistic denunciations of *Ianua* or the *Ars minor* of Donatus. On

Ianua also flourished because it provided the content that teachers wanted in an arrangement suiting their purposes. An elementary textbook at any time and in almost any field is a work of organization first and content second, because introductory content seldom varies much from textbook to textbook. *Ianua* presented the same declensions and conjugations that students had been learning for hundreds of years and would learn for hundreds more. It also defined the parts of speech before moving on to grammatical exercises and elementary reading. And *Ianua* presented this material in a considerably shorter package than other medieval grammars.

It is ironic that Renaissance humanists and teachers who proclaimed their emancipation from medieval learning taught elementary Latin grammar with a medieval manual and in a medieval way. But the contradiction was more apparent than real, and was limited in its effects. Elementary medieval pedagogical grammar, especially the breaking down of language into its smallest parts and then labeling each word form according to grammatical categories, had been ancient before it became medieval. Although different books, *Ianua* and Donatus's *Ars minor* followed the same approach. The real break between medieval and Renaissance instruction occurred immediately after the students had finished the *Ianua* and *Disticha Catonis*. Renaissance students did not go on to medieval verse grammars such as the *Doctrinale,* but read Vives' *Colloquia* and, above all, Cicero and Vergil. Renaissance humanists and teachers viewed grammar as a tool for the study of ancient literature.

DONATUS MELIOR, DONATO AL SENNO, AND VERNACULAR LATIN GRAMMARS

Humanists and pedagogues of the first half of the Quattrocento established the grammatical curriculum and manuals (Guarino's *Regulae* and the *Ianua*). After the pioneers came pedagogues who, while remaining faithful to the teaching of their predecessors, made grammatical instruction slightly more accessible to their pupils. Children in ancient Rome already knew Latin in a rudimentary fashion; their Italian Renaissance descendants did not. Hence, a few grammarians in the late Quattrocento began to introduce a little Italian into the grammar manuals. In the sixteenth century, other grammarians wrote whole grammars in the vernacular.

Exactly when the first scribe introduced a handful of Italian words into the standard *Ianua* text is unknown, but at least one fourteenth-century manuscript had a little interlinear Italian.[67] Fifteenth-century manuscript

---

the contrary, Valla praised Donatus, Servius, and Priscian in general terms in the preface to bk. 2 of the *Elegantiae*. See Garin, ed., 1952, p. 602.

[67]See NNC, Plimptom Ms. 138.

and printed versions of Guarino's *Regulae* sometimes added an Italian word in order to give the Italian meaning of a Latin verb, for example, *amo, amas amavi amatum—per amare*. Whether Guarino himself inserted a little Italian into his manual is impossible to determine. In any case, printed editions of the *Regulae* used Italian very sparingly, only to define an occasional word. Perotti in his *Rudimenta grammatices* added Italian translations of the inflected forms of *poeta*.[68] In 1487 Antonio Mancinelli published his version of *Ianua*, which went a little further.

The career and publications of Antonio Mancinelli offer a good example of the development of grammatical instruction in particular, and of humanistic teaching in general, in the last quarter of the fifteenth century, after the pedagogical giants had passed from the scene.[69] Born in 1452 in Velletri, twenty-five miles south of Rome, Mancinelli studied at Pisa and earned a degree in civil law at Perugia and a degree in medicine at Padua. In 1473 he began teaching in Velletri, possibly as a communal master. He taught there through 1485, writing textbooks, marrying, and fathering eight children to whom he gave classical names: Marta, Prisca, Porfirio, Pindaro, Quinto, Festo, Aquilino, and Tito. In demand as a teacher, Mancinelli taught in other towns, probably at increasingly higher salaries: Rome from 1486 to 1491, Fano circa 1491, Venice in 1492, back to Velletri as communal master in 1494, Orvieto in 1498, and Rome again in 1500. He died in 1505.

Mancinelli wrote approximately twenty short pedagogical works, including grammars, rhetorical manuals, and commentaries, almost all intended for younger students, according to his prefaces. The rhetorical works included the *Versilogus*, which discussed rhetorical *figurae* with etymologies in hexameter verses, and *Scribendi orandique modus* in two parts, which presented phrases and sentences drawn from ancient authors for use in letters and orations. He wrote commentaries on the first twenty-four lines of the *Disticha Catonis* and on the *Rhetorica ad Herennium*. In the latter he defended the authorship of Cicero. Mancinelli wrote *Speculum de moribus et officiis*, a treatise on virtue in imitation of *Cato*, for one of his sons. Another *Versilogus* taught the quantity of syllables and meter. The short grammatical works included two epitomes of Valla's *Elegantiae* (see below) and a series of syntax manuals and lexicons.[70]

---

[68]Percival, 1981, p. 243.

[69]The only study on Mancinelli is Sabbadini, 1878. This was Sabbadini's first publication, written while he was teaching, like Mancinelli before him, at the *liceo* in Velletri.

[70]They included the *Summa declinationis* and *Spica declinationum et genera*, both of which discussed morphology; *Declinationis lexicon*, an etymological, historical, and mythological explanation of the words declined in the two previous works; *Regulae constructionis*, which conjugated verbs and dealt with syntax; *Spica praeteritorum et supinorum*, which conjugated supines, etc.; and *Thesaurus de varia constructione*, an alphabetically organized discussion of the syntax of common verbs.

In 1487 Mancinelli published his *Donatus melior,* which was *Ianua* with limited but systematic vernacular translation of the inflected Latin phrases: "Indicativo modo tempore presenti: ego amo. *io amo.* tu amas. *tu ami.* ille amat. *quello ama*"[71] (italics have been added to differentiate the Italian from the Latin). In the dedicatory letter of 1 December 1487 addressed to three of his sons, Mancinelli opined that a little vernacular explanation would lighten the burden of learning Latin grammar.[72]

Teachers apparently approved. *Donatus melior* appeared in eight incunabular printings, always in Italy.[73] Printers usually issued *Donatus melior* with two other works, Mancinelli's *Catonis carmen de moribus,* which commented on the first twenty-four lines of the *Distichs* of Cato by means of paraphrase, synonyms, and analogous passages from ancient authors, and *De arte libellus,* which taught grammar by listing a series of statements on *littera, syllaba, dictio, oratio, nomen,* and so on culled from ancient authors, especially Diomedes and Priscian. Sixteenth-century printers added at least six more editions of *Donatus melior, Catonis carmen de moribus,* and *De arte libellus* combined, all but one appearing in the first twenty years of the century.[74]

Mancinelli devoted his considerable energy to refining and teaching the grammatical and, to a lesser extent, the rhetorical part of the Latin curriculum. He concentrated on the lower end of the syllabus: morphology, syntax, and Cato. He demonstrated his humanistic approach by making extensive use of quotations from the ancients and limited use of Greek. And he introduced a little vernacular translation into the *Ianua* text. His career and works demonstrated the strong commitment of his generation to humanistic grammatical and rhetorical instruction for the young. Mancinelli won no fame as orator, secretary, editor, or author of original humanistic treatises. He prospered as a teacher of grammar who helped younger students with his manuals. In turn, practically every sixteenth- and early-seventeenth-century assessor of the grammatical scene praised him. Even Erasmus mentioned him in his *Ciceronianus* (1528).[75]

Donato al senno (Donatus to wisdom) went further. It initially added a tiny amount of Italian translation to *Ianua* and then developed into an interlinear bilingual *Ianua.* The earliest surviving printed version appeared in Venice in 1492 (GW 9025), printed with the *Disticha Catonis;* this was followed by three more incunabular editions (GW 9026–28), also in Venice. Incunabular editions of the text proclaimed its bilingual nature immediately by giving a vernacular translation of the *Ianua* verse: ". . . ego Donatus *mi Donado* sum *son* Ianua *la porta* rudibus *ali scholari novi*

---

[71]*Donatus melior* (Milan, 18-V-1501), sig. B7ᵛ. See Appendix 1 for full citation.
[72]*Donatus melior* (Milan, 18-V-1501), sig. A1ᵛ.
[73]See GW 9018–21, 9021bis–24.
[74]See Appendix 1.
[75]Erasmus, 1986, p. 418.

Aelij Donati grammatici eruditissimi adolescentibus candidissima litterarum fundamenta.

I anus sum rudibus primam cupientibus artem.
Nec sine me quisquam rite peritus erit.
Supple ego Donatus io Donato, sum, io sono.
Janua, la porta, rudibus, alli scolari novi, cupientibus, che si
deranti primam artem, la prima arte liberale, cioe la Gram-
matica. Nec quisquam, ne alcuno, erit, sara, peritus, amaestrato, rite, di-
rittamente, sine me, senza me.
Nam genus, e casum, speciem, numerum, atque figuram.
Dis, que flectuntur, partibus insinuo.
Nam perche, in sinuo, io mostro con desterita, genus, il genere, e casum, e
il caso, speciem, la specie, numerum, il numero, atque figuram, e la figura, bis
partibus, in quelle parti, que, le quali, flectuntur, sono declinate.
Pono modum reliquis, quid competat ordine pandens.
Et, quam non doccam, dictio nulla manet.
Pono, io assegno, modum, il modo, reliquis, alle altre parti, pandens,
mostrando, ordine, per ordine, quid competat, quello che convenga.
Et nulla dictio, e nessuna dittione, quam, la quale, non doccam, io non in-
segni, manet, rimane.
Ergo legas, studiumque tibi rudis adijce lector,
Nam celeri studio discere multa potes.
Ergo, dunque, o rudis lector, o novo lettore, legas, legi, e adijce, aggion-
gi, studium, lo studio, tibi, a te.
Nam, perche, potes, tu puoi, discere, imparare, multa, cose assai, celeri stu-
dio, con pronto studio.

P O E T A Que pars est? nomen est, quare est nomen?
quia significat substantiam, e qualitatem propriam, vel communem, cum casu. Nomini quot accidunt? quinque. que?
Species, Genus, Numerus, Figura, e Casus. Deus cuius speciei? primitive. quare? quia a nullo derivatur. Poeta cuius speciei? derivative. quare? quia derivat a poesis,
Poeta cuius generis? masculini quare? quia preponitur ei in declinatione vnu articulare pronome hic. Musa cuius generis? feminini. quare? quia preponitur ei in declinatione vnum articulare pronomen hec.
Templum cuius generis? neutri. quare? quia preponitur ei in declinatione vnum articulare pronomen hoc. Aduena cuius generis? communis. quare? quia preponuntur ei in declinatione duo articularia

8. Verso of title page of *Donato al senno con il Cato volgarizato*. . . . In Milano, 1570.
Colophon: Mediolani per Iacobum Girardonium, ad instantiam D. Matthaei Besutij. MB ††.5.28.

cupientibus *desideranti* primam artem *la prima arte"*[76] (the Italian has been italicized). After translating the opening eight-line verse, incunabular editions added only a little more Italian, chiefly to translate inflected word forms. In the sixteenth century the text gradually became a completely bilingual interlinear work, as did the *Disticha Catonis* when the two were printed together. Although lacking a title in the incunabular era, the bilingual *Ianua* became *Donato al senno* by the middle of the sixteenth century.[77] At least eleven surviving sixteenth- and seventeenth-century printings, almost always accompanied by the *Disticha Catonis,* are known.

Donatus melior and *Donato al senno* simply added less or more vernacular translation to a Latin grammar. Only later did a Latin grammar written in Italian first appear, an anonymous *Grammatica latina in volgare* (Verona, 1529) sometimes attributed to Bernardino Donato of Verona, who taught as communal master and independently in Verona, Parma, and Vicenza in the 1530s and early 1540s. He also published on Plato and Aristotle. The work was a fairly standard comprehensive morphology and syntax manual of 285 pages in a small octavo format. The author made a simple claim in his letter to the readers: learning Latin through the vernacular would be easier and less boring than learning it through Latin.[78] The difficulty of learning Latin barred many persons from the *boni arti* and sciences; indeed, no other branch of learning had such "sour and odious" beginnings, he lamented. Why shouldn't we teach Latin in the vernacular when all the other arts are learned in this way? he asked. Apparently few agreed with him, for the work had no further printings.

A few years later, Francesco Priscianese, a Florentine grammarian, published another comprehensive Latin grammar in the vernacular, *Della lingua Romana* (1540). Priscianese argued that the instructor must use a language that is "known and familiar" to explain one that is "unknown and strange."[79] Some say that writing a Latin grammar in the vernacular is a grave mistake; I reply that modern grammarians who imitate ancient grammarians by writing in Latin err gravely, Priscianese wrote. Even those grammarians who write grammars in Latin still teach in the *volgare,* he continued. Since they teach in Italian, composing a grammar in Latin is ostentatious. Some argue that if grammarians wrote in Latin, the language

---

[76]I cite the edition of Venice, 29-IV-1508, sig. A1r. See Appendix 1 for full citation.

[77]*Donato al senno con il Cato* appears on the title pages of all the editions of 1570 and later located. See Appendix 1 for a list of printings.

[78]*Grammatica latina in volgare,* 1529, sigs. A2r–A3v. On Donato, see Biadego, 1895. I have been unable to locate Giuseppe Biadego, *Bernardino Donato grecista veronese del secolo XVI.* Nozze Fraccaroli-Rezzonica (Verona, Franchini, 1895).

[79]Priscianese, 1540; it is a comprehensive grammar of 600 pages. Priscianese pleaded his case in two introductory letters, sigs. iir–viir, and a postscript, sigs. Oo4r–Oo6v. I have also examined a reprint of Venice, Giovan Maria Bonelli, 1553; printings of Venice 1550 and 1567 may also exist.

would be more universally understood. Yes, but only "with the greatest difficulty and effort, as experience shows," Priscianese replied. Youths first have to understand some Latin to read a Latin grammar; if they can, they have no need of Latin instruction. Since all teachers instruct in the vernacular, I am simply making their task easier, Priscianese concluded.

Priscianese saw Latin as a dead language and opined that it should be treated as such.[80] His title page and frequent references to the "Roman" language, and his lamentation that his century had lost the original pronunciation of Latin, underlined the point. He emphasized the distinction between "Roman" of the ancient world and Tuscan of the sixteenth century. His final argument, that one could not understand one's native language without a knowledge of "Roman," must have been one of the earliest uses of this favorite argument of Latin teachers ever since.

Priscianese returned to the subject a decade later in his elementary manual, *De' primi principii della lingua Latina, overo il Priscianello* (1550). In the preface Priscianese announced that his small book would be better for little children because *Donatus* was too dry and difficult for beginners. The latter treated the material in such a complex and strange way that no one could understand it without interpretation. But, Priscianese continued, I have written my little book in a language that can be understood by almost everyone (he meant that nearly all Italians could read his Tuscan).[81] The booklet of forty-six pages was a standard *Ianua* manual written in Italian. It had two reprints.

Orazio Toscanella (d. 1579) published a Latin grammar written in Italian in 1567, with reprints in 1568, 1575, 1580, 1588, 1594, and 1626. In his letter to the reader, Toscanella explained that he wished to accommodate himself to "the capacity of rude intellects" rather than to "the learned."[82] He may have meant that he wished to help merchants and tradesmen who lacked the opportunity to spend years in a Latin school. Toscanella wrote a comprehensive grammar that covered standard material in the usual order. Lazzaro Bonamico (1477/8–1552), a strict Ciceronian, wrote in Italian a Latin grammar that was published in 1562 and reprinted five times between 1563 and 1581 under the name of another author.[83]

Priscianese's comment that an Italian child had great difficulty understanding grammars written in Latin because of their unfamiliar language,

[80]Italian humanists were inconsistent on this point. On one hand they saw Latin as the embodiment of the culture of a historically distant ancient Rome. But they also tried to recapture Rome's glory through a living Latin purified of its medieval corruption. See D'Amico, 1984, pp. 351–52.

[81]Priscianese, 1552, pp. 3–4, for the preface. *STC Italian*, p. 539, lists other editions of Venice 1550 and 1553.

[82]Toscanella, 1568a, sig. **vii^v.

[83]Bonamico and Paleario, 1567. On Bonamico, see Avesani, 1969; on Aonio Paleario (1503–70), see Caponetto, 1979.

austere content, and abstract organization certainly rings true to a twentieth-century observer. Yet, only a handful of Renaissance grammarians wrote grammars in Italian, and the majority of grammar manuals remained in Latin. Teachers preferred Guarino's *Regulae* or the *Ianua,* or other grammars written in Latin. At most they used *Donatus melior* or *Donato al senno,* which added some or much interlinear vernacular translation. The vernacular grammars did not succeed in entering very many classrooms. The centuries-old tradition of learning Latin from a Latin manual continued in the Renaissance. Not until the eighteenth century did almost all Italian grammarians write Latin grammars in the vernacular.

How, then, did teachers teach and students learn in the classroom? Priscianese's statement that instructors used Italian to teach Latin had to have been true. Despite the urging of humanists and the rules of the Jesuits that only Latin be used in the classroom, instructors explained Latin grammar to Italian children in Tuscan, Venetian, Roman, or another vernacular. Prodigious memorization of the manual did the rest.

THE RENAISSANCE GRAMMATICAL TRADITION

By the end of the sixteenth century, the Italian Renaissance had its own grammatical tradition with its own canonical grammars, above all the new *Regulae* of Guarino and the medieval *Ianua.* They guaranteed authenticity and stability to the Renaissance grammatical tradition. It may seem paradoxical to assert that a definite Renaissance tradition existed when so many manuals circulated. Nevertheless, Renaissance humanists and teachers shared the view that grammar prepared students to read ancient literature, and they rejected all medieval pedagogical grammars except *Ianua,* which many thought to be Donatus's *Ars minor.* They preferred *Ianua,* Guarino's *Regulae,* and the grammars that followed their lead. Indeed, other Renaissance grammars seldom departed significantly from the norms of Guarino and *Ianua.* Finally, teachers and scholars recognized and praised a select list of grammarians who embodied the new Renaissance grammatical tradition.

Teachers sometimes taught both *Ianua* and Guarino's *Regulae.* A teacher in 1524 stated that students wishing to learn Latin should study "la tavola, il salterio, il donato, le regole," and other Latin books, according to the ancient custom.[84] In 1567 the Venetian Senate ordered the four publicly supported *sestiere* grammarians to teach *"Donatus"* (i.e., *Ianua*) and Guarino's *Regulae.*[85] And in 1587, two Venetian independent masters stated that

[84]"Se questi tali debbeno imparare la tavola, lo salterio, lo donato, le regole, & altri libri grammaticali, secondo lo antiquo solito. . . ." G. A. Tagliente, 1524, sig. A2ᵛ; see sig. A2ʳ for a nearly identical statement.

[85]"Sia parimente provisto per detti Reformatori di quattro maestri, i quali abbino a tener

they taught both *Ianua* and Guarino's *Regulae*.[86] Despite some overlapping content, the two grammars could profitably be used together by teachers because *Ianua* concentrated on morphology while the *Regulae* paid most attention to verbal syntax, with sections appended to many printings on one or more of the following subjects: adverbs of place, heteroclite nouns, orthography, synonyms, and homonyms. Indeed, three joint printings have come to light: Rome: Apud Victoriam Elianum, 1575; Rome: Apud Antonium Facchettum, 1595; and Rome: Typis Vitalis Mascardi, 1638.[87] All three paired editions presented *Ianua* (with Cato) and the *Regulae* in that order. It is appropriate and, somehow, comforting that the pedagogical leader of the early Renaissance and the anonymous medieval author of *Ianua* joined hands to teach Latin.

The Jesuits also taught *"Donatus"* and Guarino's *Regulae* after failing to introduce with any success the grammar of Despauter (see below) to Italian schoolboys. When the Jesuits began teaching in Italy in the mid-Cinquecento, they used Despauter, probably because they had learned from this text in Paris. But pupils and parents from Messina, Bologna, Ferrara, Florence, Modena, and Perugia vehemently protested: they preferred the traditional grammars that they knew.[88] Fearing loss of enrollment, the Jesuits adopted *Donatus* (more than likely *Ianua*), Guarino's *Regulae,* and occasionally other grammars.[89] The Jesuits often used *"Donatus"* as a beginners' conjugation and declension manual and added the *Regulae* for syntax in the second class.[90] They also began the quest for a new Jesuit manual. After three Jesuits failed to write a satisfactory one, the Portuguese Manoel Alvares published his in 1572 (see below). Most Jesuit schools across Europe had adopted it by the end of the sixteenth century.[91] Until then, the Jesuits had to conform to the Italian Renaissance grammatical tradition that preferred *Ianua* and Guarino.

Grammarians and teachers continued to proclaim their allegiance to *"Donatus"* (*Ianua*) and Guarino, and the grammatical tradition that they embodied, by reprinting and revising the works. Marco Antonio Bonciari

schola di grammatica . . . insegnar debbano il Donato, le regole di Guarino, dar latini et concordantie. . . ." Senate law of 4 November 1567 in VC Ms. P D C 2250/VIII, document 23.

[86]". . . Regule de Guerin, el Donado et ghe insegno a far concordantie. . . ." ACPV, "Professioni di fede," fol. 264r, Iohannes f. Franceschi; Baldo, 1977, p. 77. Also see ACPV, "Professioni di fede," fol. 270v.

[87]See Appendix 1 for full citations.

[88]Farrell, 1938, pp. 440–44.

[89]For the use of *"Donatus"* in Italian Jesuit schools, see MP, vol. 1:23, 95, 137, 168, 410, 456, 529; vol. 2:14, 90, 177, 560; vol. 3:555; for the use of Guarino's *Regulae,* see MP, vol. 1:410, 456, 479, 574; vol. 2:14, 90, 520, 533, 560, 572, 581, 589, 598; vol. 3:282.

[90]See, for example, how the Collegio Romano used *"Donatus"* and Guarino's *Regulae* in the academic year 1564–65. MP, vol. 2:560.

[91]Farrell, 1938, pp. 444–54.

(1555–1616), who was born near Perugia and spent much of his adult life teaching in the seminary there, was a Latin poet, fervent Ciceronian, correspondent with most of the major Italian scholarly figures of his age, rhetorician, and grammarian. He published *Donati et Guarini grammatica institutio* in Perugia in 1593.[92] Bonciari presented in tandem slightly revised versions of *Ianua* and the *Regulae,* the latter with a separate title page: *Guarinus sive introductio ad latinam linguam. A M. Antonio Bonciario collecta, & ad puerorum usum accommodata.* Bonciari followed traditional norms: he wrote in Latin with the exception of some few vernacular translations of vocabulary words and had the book published in the customary small format of about ten by fifteen centimeters. Bonciari remained reasonably faithful to the *Ianua* and *Regulae* texts but added explanatory *notae* for students and *admonitiones* for teachers. His work had numerous printings, probably ten or more, by the middle of the seventeenth century.

Grammarians also proclaimed their allegiance to "Donatus" and Guarino by placing the names of their illustrious predecessors on texts that had little or nothing to do with them. For example, an anonymous, undated grammar appearing in Modena in the third quarter of the sixteenth century bore the title *Donatus diligenter recognitus.* A work of forty-eight pages in the usual small format, it had fourteen pages devoted to morphology but did not follow *Ianua.* The second section, of twenty-six pages, carried the title "Rudimenta constructionis regulae Guarini diligenter recognitae, et auctae." It discussed verbal syntax and showed some Guarinian influence but was not Guarino's text.[93] A Genoese grammar of 1638 intended for the Piarist schools proclaimed itself to be an abbreviated version of Guarino's *Regulae.*[94] But it was neither Guarino nor short.

Italian grammarians of the seventeenth century looked back to the period 1400 to 1600 as a golden age of pedagogical grammar. They recalled those glorious days and drafted an honor roll of grammarians that began with "Donatus" and moved immediately to Guarino and others of the Renaissance. Naturally, they lamented that contemporary grammarians failed to measure up to the giants of the past.

Girolamo Urbani, a teacher, made this point in his defense of Donatus and Guarino published in 1615. Urbani attacked an unnamed grammarian for "improving" *Donatus* (i.e., *Ianua*) and the *Regulae.* Asserting *Donatus* to be full of errors, the "improver" had published a corrected version with his own annotations entitled *Donatus expurgatus.* Urbani verbally spanked

[92]I have examined the following editions: Bonciari 1603, 1620a, 1620b, 1623, and 1651. For the biography, see Negri, 1969.

[93]*Donatus diligenter recognitus.* Mutinae. Colophon: Ex Officina Gadaldina. Various printers named Gadaldino were active in Modena from 1555 through about 1590. From the clean layout and roman type, I would put the printing in the 1550s or 1560s.

[94]Pseudo-Guarino, 1638.

him: Donatus and Guarino were fine grammarians whose texts should be left alone. In addition, Urbani explained the grammatical tradition by listing his honor roll of great grammarians: Donatus, Guarino, Mancinelli, Manuzio, Despauter, Alvares, and Bonciari. "Lesser grammarians" such as Valla also contributed.[95] This little polemical work makes an important point: despite the multiplicity of manuals, teachers recognized and respected a central Renaissance grammatical tradition.

In the middle of the seventeenth century, another grammarian and teacher, Giovanni Battista Corradi of Monsampolo (near Ascoli Piceno), voiced similar sentiments in his very long (eight hundred pages) rambling grammatical treatise entitled *Elio Donato Romano . . . overo di tutta la grammatica Latina e volgare* (Rome, 1654), written in both Italian and Latin. He modeled his work on that of Bonciari, making it a combination of *Ianua* and Guarino's *Regulae,* the latter with a separate title page: *Delle introduttioni grammaticali di Guarino Veronese ripatriato.* But Corradi added comments on previous grammarians, instructions to teachers, and much new material. He lamented that contemporary grammatical instruction did not measure up to that of the past; teachers ought to use the pristine works of "Donatus" and Guarino. He longed for the days when beginning students used the elementary manuals of "Donatus" and Guarino with their "large characters" (i.e., the printings with large semi-gothic type of the period c. 1470 to c. 1550).[96] Corradi lamented that some teachers of his generation did not always know that Guarino the father, rather than Battista the son, had written the *Regulae,* that "book of gold." In the course of his lengthy work, Corradi praised Lorenzo Valla, Perotti, Mancinelli and his *Donatus melior,* Aldo Manuzio and his grammar, Aonio Paleario ("un altro Tullio d'eloquenza"), and Bonciari several times.[97] Corradi understood and respected the normative tradition of Italian Renaissance pedagogical grammar.

The Venetian teachers of 1587 who did not use *Ianua* or Guarino usually taught other grammars from the tradition. Four teachers used "La grammatica del Spauterio," as noted in table 7.1. Ioannes Despauter or Despauterius (Jan Van Pauteren, c. 1460–1520), a Flemish humanist, wrote

[95]Urbani, 1615, sig. A4ʳ, for the list of grammarians. I have not identified the book under attack.

[96]Corradi, 1654, sig. A10ʳ⁻ᵛ. This was the third edition. The author proudly related how the first edition appeared in 1646 and sold 1,500 copies in three years (sig. A8ᵛ), so he followed with a second edition of 1649, and then with this third edition, with an introductory letter of 3 December 1653. Corradi probably taught in Rome, because he addressed his book to Roman youth. He also published a Latin rhetorical work: Corradi, 1653. But nothing more is known of him.

[97]The references to the grammarians are in Corradi, 1654, sig. C1ʳ, pp. 200, 520, sig. C1ᵛ, pp. 358, 53, respectively. I use both signatures and page numbers because of the complex organization of the work.

three grammar manuals: *Syntaxis* (1511), a morphology called *Prima pars grammaticae* (1512), and *Rudimenta* (1514). A combined edition entitled *Commentarii grammatici* appeared in 1537. These and his other works on epistolary style, metrics, and orthography were frequently reprinted, especially in the Netherlands and France, but had less influence in Italy. Three teachers indicated that they used the grammar of Emmanuel Alvarus, that is, Manoel Alvares (1526–83), a Portuguese Jesuit who in 1572 published *De institutione grammatica,* a comprehensive manual covering rudiments, morphology, syntax, and metrics. It employed mnemonic verses, vernacular glosses, and discussion of the views of ancient and Renaissance grammarians. Alvares published an abridged edition in 1583.[98]

Two Venetian teachers said that they taught "Valla," probably Valla's *Elegantiae* in one of the epitomes or abbreviated versions, because of the length and unsuitability for classroom use of the original.[99] Several epitomes circulated. Bonus Accursius published a brief one in 1475 which went through numerous editions.[100] In the 1490s Antonio Mancinelli prepared two epitomes for classroom use: *Elegantiae lima,* which amplified many of the rules propounded by Valla, and *Elegantiae portus,* a compendium of Valla's material organized alphabetically.[101] Erasmus wrote the best-known epitome, *Paraphrasis seu potius epitome . . . in elegantiarum libros Laurentij Vallae* (1529, with many reprints).[102] Two teachers stated that they taught the grammar of "Capharo," that is, Girolamo Cafaro (Capharus) of Salerno, a sixteenth-century teacher at Cortona and Venice who wrote textbooks on grammar, epistolary style, metrics, and orthography, plus a dictionary and Latin poetry. His short elementary manual, *Grammatices epitome* (first edition 1545), was devoted mostly to verbal syntax and showed Guarino's influence.[103] Finally, one teacher reported that he used Aldo Manuzio's *Institutiones grammaticae libri quatuor.*

The grammars mentioned by Venetian teachers in 1587 hardly exhausted the list of available manuals. Because the sixteenth-century press made printing relatively cheap and the schools guaranteed some sales, numerous grammarians wrote texts. Only a few need be mentioned. Stefano Plazon, the Venetian teacher who operated a very successful

---

[98]See Alvares, 1575; and Farrell, 1938, pp. 446–54. I have not seen E. Springhetti, "Storia e fortuna della *Grammatica* di Emmanuele Alvares," *Humanitas* 13–14 (Coimbra, 1962).

[99]It is possible, but not likely, that they meant the *Grammatica* (published 1514) of Giorgio Valla of Piacenza (1447–1500), holder of the chair of poetry and rhetoric at the Scuola di San Marco from 1485 until his death. It is a large and comprehensive manual that may not have been reprinted: G. Valla, 1514.

[100]See Hain, 57, 58*, 59*, 60*, 61*, 62, 63*, 64, 65, 66.

[101]Sabbadini, 1878, pp. 33–34.

[102]For a listing of the many editions of the work, see van der Haeghen, 1961, pt. 1, pp. 152–53; and M. Grendler and P. Grendler, 1984, pp. 18–19.

[103]See Cafaro, 1560; for Cafaro's biography, see Parenti, 1973.

school for the sons of patricians in the 1520s until his personal transgressions brought the school down, wrote a comprehensive grammar that had five or more printings. Entitled *Donatus,* the work began with the *Ianua* verse and appended the *Disticha Catonis,* but it offered more. Plazon expanded the morphology and syntactical rules found in small manuals and added orthography and other matter to produce a comprehensive work of nearly three hundred pages. Plazon constantly stressed the humanistic approach and links to the ancients as, for example, in his definition of grammar: "Quid est grammatica? ars congruè loquendi, recté scribendi, poetas, historicos, & caeteros authores enarrandi perspicué rationem, & usum complectens."[104] Elsewhere in the work Plazon listed Greek letters and borrowed illustrative sentences from Pliny, Vergil, Valerius Maximus, and others.

More common than comprehensive grammars were smaller works, such as the syntax manual *De constructione octo partium orationis libellus* written by William Lily (1468?–1522), the first master to teach at St. Paul's School in London, and revised by Erasmus. The Lily-Erasmus text first appeared in print in 1514, to be followed by about eighty more printings in northern Europe. Italians also published and used the book; it first appeared in Florence in 1519 and had at least eighteen more Italian printings in the sixteenth century. The text appeared under Erasmus's name until the mid-1550s and under Lily's name later in Italy, when the Index of Prohibited Books banned Erasmus's works. However, Italian Jesuit schools taught the work as late as the academic year 1564–65.[105]

Local teachers, such as Cristoforo Saxo of Perugia and Lucio Giovanni Scoppa of Naples, also wrote syntax manuals in the sixteenth century.[106] Equally humble grammarians wrote morphology manuals: Gianfrancesco Boccardo (called Buccardus Pylades) of Brescia early in the sixteenth century, Lorenzo Clarenzio toward the end of the century, and Alessandro Sole, who taught for thirty-three years in Ferrara, in the seventeenth

[104]Determining how many revisions and printings of the work appeared is difficult because of the conflicting claims by the works themselves. *STC Italian,* p. 525, lists a printing of Venice, 1542, which claimed to be the third edition. I have examined the following printings: Plazon, 1557, which claimed to be both second and fourth edition (see sig. E4ᵛ for the quote); Plazon, 1565, claimed to be a second edition; Plazon, 1574, claimed to be second edition in the title and third edition elsewhere; Plazon, 1578, claimed to be a second edition revised by Raffaele Bovio, who in his dedicatory letter of 18 September 1578 linked Guarino and Plazon (see sig. A2ᵛ). All the printings examined appeared in the usual format of about 10 × 15 cm.

[105]For lists of Italian printings of the Lily-Erasmus work, see van der Haeghen, 1961, pt. 1, pp. 60–63; M. Grendler and P. Grendler, 1976, p. 17; and especially M. Grendler and P. Grendler, 1984, pp. 5–6, 9 (nn. 29–31), and 13. Two Italian imprints under Lily's name only are Lily-Erasmus, 1564, and 1570. For its use in Italian Jesuit schools, see MP, vol. 1:97, 138, 168, 438–39; vol. 2:333, 589, 591; vol. 3:282.

[106]Saxo, 1562; Scoppa, 1616.

century.[107] Many more Renaissance grammars can be found in Italian libraries. Most of these Latin works tended to be short texts (about 48 pages) in a small format (about 10 × 15 cm.). They usually resembled *Ianua* somewhat if morphology manuals and Guarino's *Regulae* if primarily syntactical works.

These authors labored in obscurity. In the fifteenth century major figures such as Guarino, Perotti, and Manuzio composed grammars. After 1500 no major or middle-ranking Italian humanist published a grammar text. Instead, primary and secondary school teachers and persons whose careers are unknown to us wrote manuals that exhibited little originality. They revised, amplified, and embroidered previous works, because the Renaissance grammatical tradition was set. Just as medieval grammarians developed a curriculum based on the *auctores,* so the Renaissance had its pedagogical grammatical tradition, and it permitted little deviation.

GRAMMATICAL DRILL AND ELEMENTARY READING

A sixteenth-century pedagogue briefly described the duties of a grammar teacher. He begins by defining letter, syllable, word, and speech. He must then explain the noun, how it is divided (into substantive and adjectival nouns), and its declensions. Then he teaches the verb: into how many parts it is divided and its conjugation and "construction" (i.e., syntactical use). The grammarian does the same for the other parts of speech, and he initiates the explanation of grammatical figures.[108] Based on the pages of numerous Renaissance grammar manuals, this exactly described classroom procedure. Teachers and students followed the path laid out for them by *Ianua* or another manual.

Immediately after learning the ABCs, students began to memorize the parts of speech and their inflections. One pedagogical adviser put it this

---

[107]Boccardo, 1508; Clarenzio, 1591; and Sole, 1623. In his letter to the readers, Sole stated that he had learned from the Jesuits and had taught for thirty-three years. He intended his work, now in its third printing, for beginners. See sig. A2r–v.

[108]Toscanella, 1559, p. 43. Aonio Paleario offers a similar description: "L'ufficio del grammatico, come poco dinanzi dicevano, è insegnare con la lingua, che ha propria, & che è commune a lui, & a scolari conoscere le parti dell'oratione, & variare, ò declinare, come voi dite le parti declinabili, & congiungere attamente le parole insieme, sempre havendo l'essempio avanti de i buoni autori, ne fidarsi mai di regole di grammatico alcuno, & dichiarando li scritti latini colla lingua volgare, insegnare la significatione propria di ciascuna parola, & essercitare i giovani, tutta via in far loro tradurre qualche epistola, ò altra cosa latina in volgare. . . ." *Dialogo intitolato il grammatico overo delle false essercitationi delle scuole,* in Bonamico and Paleario, 1567, sig. *3r. For additional information on classroom procedure, see a teacher-student contract of 1405 in Venice that read ". . . me dive insignare li octo parte de la grammatica e y compertin e relatin e y superlatin e y partitimi [*sic*] e distributivi e y reditivi e le figury che sia exeminato, . . ." in Bertanza and Dalla Santa, 1907, pp. 253–54; and Battista Guarini's *De ordine docendi et discendi* in Garin, ed., 1958, pp. 442–45.

way: "Teach your children to recognize the nouns, verbs, and other parts of speech, and to "vary" [i.e., inflect] those parts of speech that must be varied, and to recognize their accidence."[109] Teachers did this by following the order of the elementary manual. As a Venetian pedagogue wrote, "For the youngest who cannot be more than eight years, I teach *il Donato* and the catechism which they learn by heart."[110] Teachers often described this stage as teaching the "principles" ("i principii") or "beginnings" of Latin, and the students were called "i putti principianti," literally "beginning boys" or "beginners."[111] Teachers also described this initial stage as "Latinizing [or making Latin] by the rules" ("latinano per le regole"), which meant memorizing the inflected forms of the parts of speech and other elementary matter.[112] Teachers noted the precise stage in learning the rudiments that their pupils had reached. One Venetian teacher stated that he had a pupil 6 years old "who memorizes all the nouns, pronouns, and verbs at first."[113] Another teacher taught the "actives, passives, and futures" (i.e., the inflected forms of verbs in the active and passive voice and future tense) to an 8 year old and a 10 year old.[114] The young learners went on to more complicated rudiments when they were ready. A group of 7 year olds and 9 year olds "Latinized" active, passive, deponent, and impersonal verbs, and learned the comparative forms of adverbs and adjectives.[115]

Pupils beginning the study of Latin at the Jesuit school at Messina in 1551 followed the same pattern.[116] Immediately after learning to read, the class of beginners began to recite *Donatus* from memory. They practiced declining nouns and conjugating verbs with vernacular explanation (presumably the Italian meaning of the verbs). Older students helped drill the beginners, and one can easily visualize the class loudly reciting in unison. Then the students began to learn the *Rudimenta* of Despauter—"not all of it, but the most necessary part." For the next several days the students

[109]"Insegnato che havete a vostri fanciulli a conoscere i nomi e verbi, & l'altre parti dell'orazione, & variare que si variano, et conoscere i loro accidenti. . . ." Paleario, *Il grammatico*, in Bonamico and Paleario, 1567, sig. *6r-v.

[110]"Alli piu pizoli che non possono esser da 8 anni li leggo il Donato et la dotrina cristiana la qual imparano a mente." ACPV, "Professioni di fede," fol. 1r.

[111]Corradi, 1654, p. 217.

[112]"altri latinano per le regole." ACPV, "Professioni di fede," fol. 99v. Also see the definition of "latinare" in *Grande dizionario della lingua italiana*, 13 vols. (Turin, 1961–86), 8:809.

[113]"che impara à mente tuti i nomi pronomi et verbi nel principio. . . ." ACPV, "Professioni di fede," fol. 79r.

[114]". . . insegno li latini attivi, passivi, et venturi. . . ." Ibid., fol. 10v, Lionellus Pinus; Baldo, 1977, p. 45.

[115]"Li facio latinare alcuni per li attivi, passivi, deponenti, impersonali, comparativi." ACPV, "Professioni di fede," fol. 26r, Lucas Parmisius; Baldo, 1977, p. 47.

[116]MP, vol. 1:95–97. The beginning grammar class at the Collegio Romano followed the same pedagogy in 1564–65; see MP, vol. 2:535–37, ll. 449–64, 491–519.

wrote out "substantives" (i.e., "substantive nouns"), which were succeeded by "adjectival nouns." Other simple written exercises followed.
The class alternated these written exercises with further recitation of
Donatus from memory, "so as not to forget it." This process continued for
an indefinite period, certainly months.

Renaissance educators believed very strongly in repetition and memorization throughout the learning process, but especially at the beginning
stage. One Venetian teacher said that his pupils learned *Donato al senno* "by
heart and no other way, because they are very young."[117] Others echoed
this sentiment.[118]

A psychology of learning inherited from the ancient world lay behind
the emphasis on repetition and memorization.[119] Renaissance pedagogues
viewed children's minds as blank wax tablets on which anything written
deeply enough would endure until death. Or, to use another analogy,
young minds were empty storehouses from which information stocked
during childhood could be brought out on demand in later life. Indeed,
educators believed that early learning lasted longest. Renaissance pedagogues never worried that the child's memory would become saturated;
on the contrary, they believed that constant practice enlarged the memory's capacity. Guarino put this point forcefully in 1425: I will repeat "and
repeat again, and recommend many, many times" (a line from Vergil) that
you must exercise the student's memory. Give him something to memorize, and pay more attention to repetition than to explanation.[120] Rep-
etitious drill ensured the thorough memorization of the elementary rules
of Latin grammar. Most ancient, medieval, and Renaissance pedagogues
held a mechanistic view of the mind's operation which encouraged memorizing discrete pieces of Latinity, such as inflected forms and definitions.
The well-stocked memory fed bits of correct Latin to the intellect, which,
according to this view, constructed sentences.

The careful, repetitive, and cumulative drill went on and on. After
memorizing the parts of speech and their inflections, students began to
assemble the pieces of Latin. Students wrote out phrases of two or more
words in agreement, an exercise called "doing concordances" ("concor-

[117]"Donao a seno et a mente et non altro perche sono putti pizoli." ACPV, "Professioni di
fede," fol. 229ʳ.
[118]For other statements that students memorized the grammar manual and the catechism,
see ibid., fols. Iᵛ, 48ᵛ–49ʳ, 57ʳ–58ʳ, 79ʳ, 142ᵛ, 150ʳ–ᵛ, 183ᵛ, 194ʳ, 205ᵛ, 220ʳ; Baldo, 1977, pp.
45, 51, 61, 63, 69, 71.
[119]See the discussion in Strauss, 1978, pp. 81–83, 153–55.
[120]"Unum. tibi repetam 'repetensque iterumque iterumque monebo' [Vergil, *Aeneid*
III.345] ut puerorum memoriam exerceas; quaedam memoriae mandent, ut Virgilii versus
magis frequentes quam multos." Letter to Martino di Matteo Rizzoni of 28 October 1425
Verona, in Guarino, 1967, vol. 2:498; and Garin, ed., 1958, p. 344.

dantie")—in actuality, agreement exercises.[121] Students combined a substantive noun and an adjectival noun in various cases, for example, *homo bonus, hominis boni, homini bono*. They might add the relative pronoun: *poeta elegans cuius, poetae elegantes quorum. O poeta elegans a quo*.[122] A verb might be added to make a phrase: *bonus vir amat*. Students everywhere did these exercises. In the Jesuit school at Messina, the students daily had to "make a composition," which was not a theme, but phrases of noun, adjective, verb, and relative pronoun in agreement.[123] The teacher fed students new vocabulary to expand their stockpile of agreements. Teacher and students also continued to recite from memory the elementary manual so as not to forget the basic rules. All this Latin drill occupied most of the day. On Saturdays, teacher and students reviewed the week's work.

One can see the benefits of this repetitive approach. Teachers wanted to lay an absolutely secure foundation. Ceaseless drill in declining and conjugating, plus repeating from memory the definitions and syntactical rules from the grammar manual, probably implanted the principles so firmly that students could not forget them had they wanted to. Agreement exercises ensured that correct standard phrases came tripping off tongue or pen without thought. To the charge that this pedagogy emphasized memory and facility more than understanding, a Renaissance teacher might have replied, "Yes, and so much the better!" Renaissance Latin training sought to develop linguistic facility, the ability to deliver conventional classical sentiments easily and correctly. Even at this most elementary level teachers looked forward to the end result, which was a very high level of Latin facility and eloquence. Fixing the rudiments into the student's memory so thoroughly as to make them an instinctive part of his mind marked the first step.

After intense drill in the fundamentals, the students began to read Latin with the *Disticha Catonis*.[124] Initially compiled in late antiquity by an unknown author, the text circulated under the name of Cato the Censor (Marcus Porcius Cato, 234–149 B.C.), reputedly the author of precepts of practical wisdom for his son. Early medieval copyists probably added lines. It became a favorite medieval schoolbook; from the tenth century onward, the *Disticha Catonis* circulated as one of a group of school texts that included *Theodulus, Chartula, Facetus, Tobias, Aesopus, Floretus,* and *Alani parabolae*.[125] However, in late medieval Italy, Cato—but not the

---

[121]"alcuni fanno concordantie. . . ." ACPV, "Professioni di fede," fol. 99ᵛ. For additional statements, see fols. 194ʳ, 205ᵛ, 216ᵛ, et passim; Baldo, 1977, pp. 69, 71, 73.

[122]This example comes from Corradi, 1654, pp. 217–18, but various grammar manuals describe or mention agreement exercises.

[123]MP, vol. 1:97.

[124]Of course, students continued to study grammar and to write out exercises as well.

[125]Boas, 1914.

other *auctores*—joined *Ianua;* when and why is unknown. The marriage lasted: a large majority of surviving manuscripts and printed editions of Italian provenance include both. The *Disticha Catonis* usually occupied nine to twelve pages in the standard forty-eight-page duodecimo or sextodecimo printed volume of *Ianua* and Cato. The *Disticha Catonis* also appeared alone or with a commentary after the invention of printing.[126]

The *Disticha Catonis* alone of the medieval *auctores* survived humanistic scorn, probably because its language and content appeared to be classical.[127] In a short preface, "Cato" addressed his son: Since so many men live badly, I wish to offer good counsel so that you might live honorably.[128] Read my precepts and fashion from them a rule for life. The text itself consisted of five parts. Part I presented fifty-six very brief proverbs: *Deo supplica* (Pray to God), *Parentes ama* (Love your parents), *Cognatos cole* (Cherish your kinfolk), *Coniugem ama* (Love your wife), *Pugna pro patria* (Fight for your country), *Iracundiam rege* (Control your temper), *Pauca in convivio loquere* (Say little at banquets). It is likely that a medieval editor added the introduction and part I to the main body of distichs that followed.

The main body of the text consisted of four short books of forty, thirty-one, twenty-four, and forty-nine verse couplets. Each couplet was composed of twelve to fifteen Latin words. Short introductions stressing that the couplets taught virtuous living prefaced books 2, 3, and 4. The couplets presented advice of worldly prudence and good morality that especially emphasized filial piety, friendship, caution, forbearance, and patience with one's lot in life. Ancient Greek and Roman authors, notably Ovid, Horace, Cicero, Seneca, Plutarch, and Juvenal, were the sources for the distichs, which manifested no obvious Christian influence. Typical of the style and content was I.10:

> Contra verbosos noli contendere verbis:
> Sermo datur cunctis, animi sapientia paucis.
>
> Try not with words the talker to outdo;
> On all is speech bestowed: good sense on few.[129]

---

[126]I have not gone into this further because the discussion would be lengthy. Suffice it to say that commentators usually addressed children and tried to reinforce the moral and social messages of the distichs.

[127]Italian Jesuit schools also used the *Disticha Catonis* as the first Latin reader in the 1550s and 1560s. See MP, vol. 1:421, 456, 479; vol. 2:506, 535, 564, et passim.

[128]While various versions of the text exist, I follow the common text that appeared in most Italian manuscripts and printed editions. For the critical edition of the common text, see Cato, 1952. For a Latin edition with facing English translation, see Cato, 1922.

[129]I follow the English translations in Cato, 1922, but have modernized them slightly when paraphrasing.

Admonitions of worldly prudence predominated, followed closely by maxims exhorting virtuous social behavior. If you cannot give your sons riches, teach them trades so that they will survive (I.28). Be prepared to take advantage of opportunity (II.5). Be wary of the promises of others (I.13). If you must appear as a witness, favor your friend, but keep your good name clear (III.3). Conceal your shameful deeds lest others make things worse by open criticism (II.7).

The distichs emphasized practical experience throughout; wisdom acquired through life outweighed knowledge from books (III.1 and 18; IV.48). Some of the distichs were wary and worldly-wise: Repay the man who is smooth in speech but false at heart in his own coin (I.26). Help even those whom you do not know, because friends won in such a way are very precious (II.1). A Stoic hue colored many: Scorn wealth if you wish to be happy (IV.1). Bear poverty patiently (I.21). Never give rein to your lust (IV.10). Some were mildly misogynous: Do not choose your wife for her dowry, nor keep her if she spoils your life (III.12; also III.20 and 23). They were pagan rather than Christian: Do not fear death lest it kill the joy of living (I.22; also II.3; III.22; IV.22). Do not inquire about the gods above earth because mortal man should limit himself to mortal concerns (II.2).

No wonder Renaissance pedagogues liked Cato. Students learned to read classical Latin while imbibing good advice based on ancient sources. Other medieval *auctores* provided good moral and social advice based to some extent on the classics, but few had the classical appearance, content, and conciseness of the *Distichs*. The book presupposed the reader to be a boy (not a girl) who would become an adult participant in civic and private affairs. Hence, he needed advice on worldly conduct from the ancients. Renaissance men believed that ancient pagan authors offered better and more eloquent advice for life in the world than did Christian authors—so long as pagan wisdom did not contradict Christian morality. The distichs of Cato met this criterion admirably.

Thirty-nine Venetian teachers in 1587 taught the *Colloquia sive linguae Latinae exercitatio* of Juan Luis Vives (1492–1540). Born in Valencia, Vives spent most of his adult life in England and the Netherlands, where he wrote treatises on the education of women, against medieval dialectics, in favor of poor relief, against war, and in support of humanistic education generally. He published the *Colloquia* in 1538 to help students learn Latin. The dialogues won enormous favor and continued to be published and taught for two hundred years and more. Venetian teachers used Vives' *Colloquia* either as an alternative to the *Disticha Catonis* or in combination with Cato.

The *Colloquia* consisted of twenty-five dialogues ranging in length

from about thirty to one hundred lines of Latin.[130] Vives dedicated the
book to the 11-year-old Prince Philip of Spain, the future Philip II. Most
dialogues had three or four speakers and presented scenes from middle-
and upper-class schoolboy life. The dialogues combined realism and humor in order to teach Latin, especially vocabulary for ordinary actions and
objects, plus good manners and morality. Good humor pervaded the
whole. Vives brought a sense of moderate decency and an understanding
of youthful high spirits to the dialogues. Pupils must have found Vives'
sprightliness a welcome relief from the relentless adult moralizing of the
Disticha Catonis and the high-minded seriousness of Vergil and Cicero.

The first dialogue, "Surrectio matutina" ("Getting up in the morning"), had three characters, Beatrix the maid and two boys. It began as
follows.

Beatrix: May Jesus Christ wake you from your dreams of vice. Boys, are you ever
going to wake up today?
Eusebius: I do not know what has fallen over my eyes. I seem to have them full of
sand.
Beatrix: That is always your morning song, a very old song. I will open both the
wooden and glass windows, so that the morning will strike your eyes. Get up!
Get up![131]

Dialogue 2 consisted of an exchange of morning greetings between the
boys and their parents. In the third, they went off to school. In the fifth,
they had an elementary reading lesson. Other dialogues dealt with boys'
games (cards, dice, etc.) and banqueting, which turned into a discussion of
food and table manners. Schoolboy humor permeated the dialogues. For
example, the seventh dialogue included this description of an ignorant
master: "The schoolmaster of the Straight Street [*vicus rectus*] school who
smells worse than a goat, and instructs his three-penny classes in his
school, which abounds in dirt and filth, pronounced three or four times
volucres [fleeting things, or birds] with the accent on the penultimate. I
really was astounded that the earth did not swallow him up instantly."[132]

The dialogues included numerous puns and a good deal of humor.
They introduced real persons, such as Vives himself and Prince Philip,
who became a participant in dialogue 20, "Princeps puer" ("The young
prince"). In it "Morobulus" ("Foolish Counsellor") and "Sophobulus"
("Wise Counsellor") alternately advised Philip. Morobulus told Philip
that princes rode horses, flirted with girls, danced, bore arms, and played

[130]The text is found in Vives, 1964, vol. 1:280–420. I have also used a Latin-Italian edition,
Vives, 1753; and an English translation, Vives, 1908. A large bibliography on Vives exists; the
standard biography is Bonilla y San Martin, 1929, and Watson, 1971, is particularly useful.
[131]Vives, 1908, p. 1. I have slightly modernized Watson's translation.
[132]Ibid., p. 36. Quintilian I.5.28, also discussed where the accent should fall in *volucres*.

cards. Sophobulus, by contrast, gave Philip standard Renaissance mirror-of-princes advice: reward good and punish evil, take counsel from wise men, and so on. Vives interjected bits and pieces from ancient authors by linking them to current events. For example, in dialogue 8, a mention of what the Spanish discovered in "India" led to a reference to Pliny, who wrote about the very high trees of India. Vives also condemned medieval school texts and dialectical disputations.

Vives' text equalled or surpassed in popularity two other Renaissance school dialogues, Erasmus's *Colloquia* (first edition 1516) and Mathurin Cordier's *Colloquiorum scholasticorum libri iiij ad pueros in sermone Latino paulatim exercendos* (1564).[133] All three combined good Latin and good morals with schoolboy realism, but Italian teachers probably preferred Vives' *Colloquia* to the other two for religious reasons. Cordier and his work were overtly Protestant. Erasmus fell under suspicion as a precursor of the Reformation, and his *Colloquia* were condemned by papal *Indices librorum prohibitorum* of 1554, 1559, and 1564.[134]

With Vives' *Colloquia* the grammatical or preparatory phase of the humanistic curriculum ended. The whole grammar program from *Ianua* through the *Disticha Catonis* and Vives prepared students to read the classics. To be sure, teachers and students probably did not suddenly drop Cato and Vives to begin Cicero and Vergil; good pedagogy opposes decisive breaks. But overall, humanists and teachers made a distinction between the lower school, where students learned their ABCs and the rudiments of Latin, and the upper school, where they studied rhetoric, poetry, and history based on the ancient classical authors.

Renaissance humanists and teachers transformed the study of grammar. Medieval men began with the rudiments, and then progressed to more complex grammatical study through such works as the *Doctrinale,* and to an examination of the nature of language itself through speculative grammar. Renaissance teachers proceeded differently. They began with study of the rudiments, often with a medieval text and some medieval theory. But they skipped the more elaborate study of grammar in favor of reading the classics. Renaissance men saw grammar as a tool for language users, not as an independent field of inquiry. Of course, a Renaissance

[133]On Cordier (1479–1564), see Le Coultre, 1926.

[134]See M. Grendler and P. Grendler, 1976, pp. 2–6. Jesuit schools also used Vives' dialogues until Loyola in the 1550s objected to them as "disonesti" ("dishonest" or "immoral"). It is hard to imagine what Loyola found objectionable—possibly the boys playing cards and throwing dice in dialogue six? Other leading Jesuits disagreed and sometimes advised Jesuit schoolmasters to continue to use Vives' text. Nevertheless, it gradually faded from the Jesuit curriculum. See MP, vol. 1:97, 138, 410, and esp. 438–39, 557–58, 581; vol. 2 passim.

pupil did not leave behind the study of grammar when he began to read Cicero; grammatical analysis helped him to understand Cicero's meaning. But grammar had a lower place in the *studia humanitatis* than it had held in the medieval liberal arts. Grammar became a preparation for higher studies, and grammarians lesser figures who taught children.

CHAPTER EIGHT

Rhetoric

THE ADVANCED HUMANISTIC CURRICULUM

fter a student had mastered the rules of Latin grammar and
had read elementary Latin texts, he advanced to the rest of the
authors and texts composing the *studia humanitatis*. Although
it is difficult to speak of a lower division and an upper division
in Latin schools consisting of a single teacher and ten to thirty pupils, it is
clear that pedagogues saw grammar as preparatory to the higher studies of
rhetoric, poetry, and history. *Ianua*, Guarino, Cato, and Vives laid the
foundations for Cicero, Vergil, Terence, and Caesar. These upper-level
subjects and authors were the heart of the humanistic curriculum.

Teachers had a very large number of classical authors from which to
choose when drafting a syllabus. Indeed, Quattrocento pedagogical theorists enthusiastically prescribed wonderfully ambitious programs of study.
Battista Guarini laid out a comprehensive syllabus in his *De ordine docendi et
discendi* (1459), based, he claimed, on the practice of his father and other
teachers. The student should commit to memory the letters of Cicero in
order to achieve an easy writing style, plus study other texts of Cicero.
The pupil should learn the poetry of Vergil by heart, and study Horace,
Plautus, the *Thebais* of Statius, and the *Metamorphoses* of Ovid, as well. He
should read the *Tragedies* of Seneca for moral wisdom, Terence's plays and
Juvenal's *Satires* for elegance of speech, Justinus and Valerius Maximus for
history and examples of virtue, Pomponius Mela, Solinus,[1] and Ptolemy
for geography and astrology, plus the *Ethics* of Aristotle and unnamed
works of Plato. Students must also learn Greek thoroughly, beginning
with Chrysoloras's *Erotomata*, followed by Homer. The mature student
should read independently Aulus Gellius, Macrobius's *Saturnalia*, Pliny's
Natural History, and Augustine's *De civitate Dei*. He should also read the
commentaries on the texts of the curriculum. And throughout his study,

---

[1]Solinus (third century A.D.) wrote *Collectanea rerum memorabilium* based on the geographical and medical sections of Pliny the Elder's *Natural History*.

he must set down in notebooks "sentences suitable for the subject matter."[2]

Within his very broad curriculum prescriptions, Battista Guarini gave pride of place to Cicero's epistles and Vergil's poetry. Students should read other authors and texts but memorize Cicero's letters and Vergil. The students would acquire elegance of style, purity of language, and profundity of thought from Cicero, and the understanding of poetic meter and syllabic feet from Vergil, according to Battista Guarini.[3]

What an ambitious curriculum! How could ordinary students accomplish all of this by the age of 16 or 18? Even more important, how could an average teacher learn such a large number of texts well enough to teach them competently? Guarini Senior had studied numerous ancient texts over a very long and productive lifetime, but he did not teach them simultaneously.

Teachers solved the problem by creating a standard curriculum consisting of a handful of texts to be taught extremely thoroughly. Teacher contracts of the middle of the fifteenth century directed pedagogues to teach subjects (grammar, rhetoric, poetry, and history) rather than specific authors and texts. By the end of the century, curriculum directives ordered teachers to teach a single author or text in each of the humanistic disciplines. For example, Lucca in 1499 directed its communal masters to teach daily "*a* grammatical author, *a* historian, *an* orator or *a* book of letters, *a* poet, and the rudiments of Greek" (emphasis added). The commune repeated these instructions in 1524.[4] Then in 1546 it named the ancient texts to be taught: Cicero's *Epistulae ad familiares* and Vergil's *Aeneid*.[5] In 1566 Lucca directed an upper-level humanist to teach Cicero for oratory, Vergil for poetry, Livy or Sallust for history, and Homer for Greek.[6] In similar fashion, the Venetian Senate in 1567 instructed the publicly paid *sestiere* humanists to teach Cicero in the morning, and Vergil, Terence, or Horace

---

[2]"Nec sint solum a praeceptore audire contenti, sed qui in auctores commentaria scripserunt et probati sunt, eos ipsimet perlegant et radicitus, ut aiunt, sententias et vocabulorum vim annotent. Novas ipsi sententias et ad rem accommodatas exquirant." I cite the edition of *De ordine docendi et discendi* from Garin, ed., 1958, pp. 448–71, quote on p. 460.

[3]"Sub idem tempus et in Ciceronis epistulis declamabunt, ex quibus stili tum elegantiam tum facilitatem et sermonis puritatem ac scientiarum gravitatem adipiscentur; quas si memoriae mandaverint mirificos postea fructus in scribendi promptitudine percipient." Also see "Quapropter Virgilii carmina memoriae mandent ut ad omnem syllabae quantitatem optimi poetae auctoritate nitantur et exemplo; declamare autem etiam in his oportebit, ut assiduitate pedum numerum etiam solo verborum cantu annotent." Text in Garin, ed., 1958, pp. 452, 448.

[4]"Item, che epsi [*sic*] maestri siano tenuti et obligati legere in le loro schuole, tra la mattina et il dì, uno autore grammatico, uno historico, uno oratore overo uno libro di epistole, uno poeta et li erotimati greci." Barsanti, 1905, pp. 215, 220.

[5]Ibid., p. 224.

[6]Ibid., p. 178.

in the afternoon, the exact text to be chosen by the governmental bureau directly responsible for the schools.[7] In 1578 the Senate ordered its humanists to teach Cicero's *Epistulae ad familiares* in the morning and Terence or an equivalent text in the afternoon.[8]

Although these directives constrained only a small number of communal masters, the guidelines reflected a pedagogical consensus among almost all teachers, including the very numerous independent masters. A scrutiny of the ancient Latin authors and texts (excluding grammar manuals and the elementary readers listed in table 7.1) taught by the 258 Venetian teachers in 1587–88 clearly indicates which authors and books composed the core curriculum for rhetoric, poetry, and history, and which texts were added for spice and variety (see table 8.1).

In the wake of the triumph of the *studia humanitatis* in the middle of the Quattrocento, teachers reached a new curriculum consensus. After an intensive study of the grammar manuals and elementary reading texts, students learned one author or text thoroughly for each of the three upper-level subjects—rhetoric, poetry, and history. They most often learned Cicero's letters for rhetoric, Vergil for poetry, and Caesar, Valerius Maximus, or Sallust for history. Some teachers taught additional authors, especially Terence, Horace, and Ovid. Students also learned to write Latin prose through unflagging practice at composing letters on set themes. And they learned moral philosophy by paying constant attention to the moral content of all the texts read. A new canon of authors had replaced the medieval syllabus. This chapter describes the teaching of rhetoric, and chapter 9 discusses the rest of the humanistic curriculum.

FROM MEDIEVAL TO RENAISSANCE RHETORIC

Nothing so marked the difference between the Middle Ages and the Renaissance as the revival of classical rhetoric. Medieval scholars had placed grammar and logic at the center of learning and expression. They had little interest in the whole of classical Latin rhetoric and ignored its cultural associations. Medieval rhetoricians dismembered ancient rhetoric, preserving only the parts that contributed to the skills they prized, especially the arts of preaching, memory, poetry, and letter writing (*ars dictaminis*). They retained discrete technical elements such as definitions of rhetorical figures. Medieval writers developed a highly logical intellectual system and a technical, scientific language in which to express it. But they abandoned classical rhetoric's fusion of thought and expression within a unified cultural and ethical vision of society, or at least, Renaissance humanists thought so.

[7]VC, Ms. P D C 2250/VIII, document 23.
[8]Baldo, 1977, p. 105.

TABLE 8.1
Latin Classics Taught by Venetian Teachers, 1587–1588

	Number of Teachers
Cicero	
Unspecified	55
Epistulae ad familiares	50
"Epistulae"	19
Epistulae ad Atticum	1
De officiis	8
Orationes	6
Pro M. Marcello	1
Partitiones oratoriae	3
De amicitia	1
Paradoxa Stoicorum	1
Pseudo-Cicero, *Rhetorica ad Herennium*	17
Total	162
Vergil	
Unspecified	82
Aeneid	7
Bucolica	4
Georgica	1
Total	94
Terence (unspecified)	46
Horace (unspecified)	36
Ovid	
Heroides	9
Unspecified	3
Metamorphoses	1
Total	13
Aristotle (in Latin translation)	
Rhetorica	6
Organon	2
Categoriae	2
Politica	1
Total	11
Caesar	
Commentarii or *De bello Gallico*	9
Unspecified	1
Total	10
Valerius Maximus, *Facta et dicta memorabilia*	7
Sallust, *De Catilinae coniuratione* and *Bellum Iugurthinum*	5
Flavius Josephus, *De antiquitate Judaeorum*	2
Livy, *Ab urbe condita libri*	1
Plautus, *Aulularia* (The pot of gold)	1

Source: ACPV, "Professioni di fede."

The transition from late medieval rhetoric to a revival of classical rhetoric occurred at the end of the fourteenth century and the first two decades of the fifteenth century.[9] In 1393 Pier Paolo Vergerio delivered in Padua a funeral oration that may have been the first completely classical oration since the end of antiquity. His epideictic oration praising the deceased Francesco da Carrara il Vecchio was firmly classical: Vergerio organized his oration according to classical norms, employed classical rhetorical figures, and paid a great deal of attention to style (*elocutio*). The humanist praised the dead ruler's good actions in order to foster admiration for Carrara and to move the listeners, including Carrara's son and successor, to emulate the dead man.

Late medieval oratory had been syllogistic rather than persuasive. When eulogizing a prince, the late medieval orator might enunciate a theme taken from Scripture about the greatness of princes and then demonstrate that the dead lord possessed greatness. The medieval orator presented a logical, deductive proof; he tried to convince through reason rather than move the emotions. The other orations (besides Vergerio's) at Carrara's funeral lacked stylistic ornamentation but added many appeals to authority. In other words, a clear theme, syllogistic reasoning, limited attention paid to style, and an appeal to authorities characterized the late medieval oration. Classical form, the use of ancient rhetorical figures, concentration on style, an attempt to move the listener, and a call to civic action—all these identified the Renaissance oration.

Vergerio continued his efforts to create a new oratory by delivering other orations in classical form. In a celebrated letter of 1396, he outlined his views, based on classical precepts, on oratory.[10] Vergerio argued that an oration should exhibit balance and harmony, and that congruence between content and expression would make an oration persuasive. He proposed Cicero as the single model for speakers. Then in his *De ingenuis moribus* (1402–3), Vergerio argued that oratory, along with moral philosophy and history, should be the core of the humanistic curriculum. Over the next twenty years the classicizing funeral oration became more common, as Gasparino Barzizza, Leonardo Bruni, Francesco Barbaro, and others followed Vergerio's lead. Thanks to such oratorical examples, the rediscovery of Quintilian and more of Cicero's orations, and the general enthusiasm for antiquity, classicizing rhetoric became securely established.

[9]Monfasani, 1976, p. 261 n. 80, wrote that the history of Quattrocento rhetoric has yet to be written. That statement remains true, although Monfasani, 1988, which appeared just as this book went to press, is a step toward such a history. What follows is a sketch that mentions a few important figures and textbooks that contributed to the teaching of rhetoric. Above all, see McManamon, 1982. Also see Seigel, 1968, esp. pp. 3–30, 200–225; Kristeller, 1979, pp. 211–59, 312–27; O'Malley, 1979; and the papers in *Renaissance Eloquence*, 1983.

[10]McManamon, 1982, pp. 6–9.

Antonio Loschi (1368–1441) seems to have written the first humanistic rhetorical treatise, *Inquisitio super undecim orationes Ciceronis,* a commentary on eleven of Cicero's orations, in Pavia between 1390 and 1396.[11] Medieval rhetoricians had paid little attention to Cicero's orations, partly because they were mostly unavailable.[12] Gasparino Barzizza continued the revival of ancient rhetoric by commenting on the *Rhetorica ad Herennium,* emphasizing Cicero's works in his teaching, and writing a short treatise on word order and prose rhythm entitled *De compositione* (written in 1420 and later revised). He often followed Quintilian and classical norms in *De compositione,* maintaining, for example, that the verb should go at the end of a clause. The *Doctrinale,* by contrast, insisted on the order of nominative, verb, adverb, accusative, and so on (verses 1390–96).[13]

Guarino of Verona did not write a treatise on rhetoric, but he taught from and commented on the *Rhetorica ad Herennium,* which he believed to be Cicero's work. He also integrated into his teaching rhetorical precepts from Quintilian, Cicero, Vergil, and other ancient authors. He liked to teach rhetorical principles by means of examples drawn from ancient writers, including poets and dramatists. For example, he showed how the long narration of Simo concerning his son's love for a young lady in Terence's *Andria* (act I, scene I, lines 70–136) conformed to the rules of classical rhetoric. Finally, Guarino affirmed the social utility of rhetoric. All the other arts and disciplines needed rhetoric's aid: the military art needed rhetoric in order to inflame the soldiers, politics needed the help of rhetoric in order to inspire respect for institutions, and philosophy needed rhetoric to make abstruse material attractive.[14]

George of Trebizond published the first comprehensive humanistic rhetoric, his *Rhetoricorum libri V,* in late 1433 or early 1434. His work mattered for two additional reasons: it argued strongly for the civic utility of rhetoric, and it greatly influenced future Renaissance rhetorical works. In his introduction, George defined rhetoric as "the civil science by which we speak in civil questions with the assent, as much as possible, of the listeners" ("Rhetorica est civilis scientia qua cum assensione auditorum quoad eius fieri potest in civilibus quaestionibus dicimus").[15] Here and elsewhere Trebizond strongly underlined the civil vocation of rhetoric. His message that rhetoric had civil utility and that its subject matter was anything of social interest put rhetoric into the mainstream of Quattrocento intellectual life. Trebizond united the ancient view of rhetoric—of Cicero and Quintilian—with the Renaissance belief that academic training should prepare the student for the active life.

[11]Sabbadini, 1964b, pp. 59–60; Monfasani, 1976, pp. 265–66.
[12]Monfasani, 1976, pp. 245 (n. 9), 257 (n. 62).
[13]Mercer, 1979, p. 93.
[14]Sabbadini, 1964b, pp. 61–65, 93–96.
[15]Quotation and translation from Monfasani, 1976, p. 267.

In the body of his treatise, Trebizond reached several conclusions significant for future Renaissance rhetorical education. Trebizond followed ancient rhetorical teaching by reuniting the five parts of rhetoric (invention, disposition, style, memory, and division) which medieval rhetoricians had separated. He also included material from Hermogenes of Tarsus (fl. A.D. 75), the major authority in the Byzantine rhetorical tradition. Trebizond strongly emphasized stylistics (*elocutio*). In his view, style separated man from beast by giving expression to man's reason. Since style perfected man, rhetoric became the *ars humanitatis*. At the same time, Trebizond, like Vergerio, realized that substance of thought preceded elegant expression. Finally, Trebizond viewed Cicero as the highest model of Latin prose, and illustrated his text with examples taken from Cicero's orations. But like Cicero, he believed that the orator had to adapt to the situation, even if this meant occasionally breaking the rules of rhetoric. Future Italian teachers of rhetoric substantially agreed with Trebizond in all these points, although their own treatises might not cite Trebizond.[16] By the 1430s the leaders of the humanistic revival had enunciated a new view of rhetoric to be taught in the Latin schools.

When Renaissance rhetoric entered the classroom, it changed somewhat. Vergerio had emphasized primary rhetoric, that is, the actual speech for a specific occasion, rather than secondary rhetoric, the application of rhetorical techniques to the writing of a text that probably would not be delivered orally.[17] Ancient Rome preferred primary rhetoric for the public life, partly because of the inconvenience and scarcity of books (often papyrus rolls). The Middle Ages emphasized secondary rhetoric as taught in the *ars dictaminis*. Renaissance humanists, in turn, asserted the superiority of primary rhetoric when they revived ancient ways. But when rhetoric descended from the rarefied air of humanistic manifestos to enter the classroom, secondary rhetoric regained its primacy for practical reasons. Few Italian schoolboys would grow up to become princes, ambassadors, or court humanists declaiming formal orations. But many boys would write letters and other prose treatises as secretaries, diplomats, civil servants of many kinds, and members of the ecclesiastical bureaucracy. The same held true in private life: few middle- and upper-class men would orate, but all would have to write letters. Hence, while humanistic teachers proclaimed the primacy of oratory for the civic life and delivered a few orations as a semiofficial condition of employment, they mostly taught the secondary rhetoric that met the needs of the majority of their students.

The emphasis on secondary rhetoric became clear as soon as the human-

---

[16]Ibid., pp. 261–99. Italians wrote a number of treatises on rhetoric, especially in the sixteenth century. But following this aspect of Renaissance rhetoric would take us away from pre-university pedagogy.

[17]Kennedy, 1980, pp. 4–5.

istic pedagogues began to write rhetoric textbooks. Barzizza taught letter writing and composed model letters heavily based on Cicero's *Epistulae ad familiares* for students to imitate. His anthology of letters enjoyed wide success in Italy and north of the Alps subsequently.[18]

A few years later a lesser-known teacher composed a phrase book that had wide use. Stefano Fieschi (Fliscus) was born in Soncino, sixty kilometers east of Milan, about 1400. He studied with Barzizza, perhaps as a youth and certainly as an adult in 1429 and 1430. Fieschi served as secretary to an Italian bishop in France from 1424 to circa 1428. He held the post of chancellor in the town of Ragusa, a Venetian possession in Dalmatia, in 1441. Next he taught school in Ragusa, from 1444 to 1459. In the following year he conducted an independent school in Venice, and died by November 1462, probably in Venice. Fieschi had ample experience as teacher and secretary to write *De prosynonymis* or *Synonyma sententiarum* in Venice in 1437, plus other works of grammar and rhetoric.[19]

In his preface Fieschi explained that he had written the book as an aid to "boys and youths" ("pueri & adolescentes") wanting to learn to write eloquent letters and orations while avoiding "barbarisms."[20] The book provided a large supply of sentences that could be inserted into letters and, to a lesser extent, orations. It began with sentences appropriate to the *exordium* (introduction) of a letter or oration. Fieschi gave the sentence in Italian and then its Latin equivalents; he started with a simple sentence, then proceeded to sentences of greater complexity and more sophisticated meaning. The expression "May God be our support" illustrates the book's method.

> Iddio sia in nostro adiutorio. [Italian]
> Deus nos adiuvet.
> Deus sit nobis propitius.
> Deus nobis res nostras secundet.
> Deus causas nostras ex voluntate prosperet.
> [Plus many more.][21]

Fieschi proceeded to expressions appropriate to different parts of typical letters. For example, he offered the expression "I will love you forever" as a strong affirmation of affection or good will.

> Io te amo senza fine. [Italian]
> Finem nullum facio mi Cicero in te amando.
> [I will love you forever, my Cicero.]

---

[18]Mercer, 1979, pp. 96–98.

[19]Mazzuconi, 1981; and Bertanza and Dalla Santa, 1907, pp. 328, 329. The book also appeared under other titles.

[20]Fieschi, 1534, sig. A1ᵛ.

[21]Ibid., sig. A2ʳ.

Amori nostro nullum profecto finem impono.

Nostram benevolentiae coniunctionem sempiternam fieri cupio.

Nostram amicitiae affinitatem immortalitati conservari desidero.[22]

Many other variations followed. The student could write an entire routine
letter by copying or slightly adapting the given sentences. Much of the
Latin appeared to be "middle style," suitable for the majority of letters.
Elaborate Ciceronian hortatory periods did not appear. Instead, Fieschi
provided reasonably straightforward statements, especially those protest-
ing good will, which any secretary would have to churn out in large
number. Fieschi probably relied on his own experience as secretary in
compiling the *Synonyma sententiarum*.

The book had great success. It survives in at least twenty-one manuscripts, thirty-eight incunabular printings, and a smaller number of sixteenth-century editions. Dutch, French, German, and Spanish readers
used it in versions adapted for them.[23] Those who wished to learn to write
letters in classical style, such as students preparing for employment as
secretaries and civil servants, could read Fieschi's textbook with profit.
Fieschi sought to replace the *ars dictaminis* manual with his own classicizing
manual. Indeed, inserting the name Cicero into the sample sentences
advertised that the book participated in the new humanistic rhetoric.
Fieschi dropped the elaborate salutations calibrated according to the many
possible relationships between writer and recipient, and the numerous
forms of address found in *dictamen* manuals. He gave the book a less
schematic organization as he progressed from one sentiment to another.
And he wrote basically classical sentences.

But the book did not meet high humanistic Latin standards. Fieschi
knew Cicero and Terence but possibly not a great deal more.[24] He did not
claim to have borrowed his sentences from classical sources. Its simplicity
and its place as one of the first phrase books of humanistic rhetoric made
the *Synonyma sententiarum* successful.

Other teachers wrote similar textbooks that more strongly reflected the
new rhetorical standards. Giorgio Valagussa was born in Brescia or nearby
in 1428 and died in Milan in 1464. He studied with Guarino at Ferrara in
1448 and in his boarding school before embarking on a teaching career that
took him to Venice in 1451 and Pavia later. He then taught as an independent master in Milan until the Sforza ruler hired him in about 1456 to teach
four of his sons. At this time Valagussa compiled his *Elegantiae Cicero-*
nianae, a book of phrases and constructions (with vernacular translation)
taken from Cicero's letters. He intended it for the use of his pupils and the

[22]Ibid., sig. A2ᵛ.
[23]Mazzuconi, 1981, pp. 276–77. See GW 10000 to 10037 for the incunabular editions.
[24]Mazzuconi, 1981, pp. 272–73.

secretaries at the Milanese chancery. Several printed editions followed.[25]

To diffuse the principles of classical rhetoric, pedagogues also wrote textbooks. Antonio Mancinelli, for example, wrote *Scribendi orandique modus* (1493) for his students at Velletri. The book offered definitions and explanations taken from classical sources of the various kinds and parts of letters, but offered little material for orations. Mancinelli patiently explained the purpose of letters in simple terms: a letter might announce one's affairs, describe distant events, or faithfully record one's thoughts for others. Following Cicero, *Ad fam.* II.4.1, Mancinelli defined three kinds of letters: informative for someone absent, intimate and humorous (*familiare et iocosum*), and austere and serious (*severum et grave*).[26] Through this textbook Mancinelli reduced the elaborate corpus of classical rhetoric seen in the *Rhetorica ad Herennium,* Cicero's *De oratore,* and George of Trebizond's *Rhetoricorum libri V* to a few basic principles for students and, possibly, elementary-level teachers to learn.

With such humble rhetoric textbooks, fifteenth-century teachers taught classical rhetoric in a way that met the needs and limited skills of their students. Teachers did not neglect primary rhetoric, but they devoted more attention to secondary rhetoric.

CICERO

Cicero's name frequently surfaced in Quattrocento rhetorical works. That was no accident, because Cicero's prose dominated Italian Renaissance rhetorical instruction. As they taught rhetoric, teachers followed three paths. First, they taught the principles of rhetoric from classical manuals, especially the *Rhetorica ad Herennium* but also others, such as Aristotle's *Rhetorica* when it became available in the sixteenth century. Second, they articulated the civic purpose of rhetoric. And, above all, teachers taught prose composition by training their students to imitate classical models that medieval teachers had not known or had ignored. Cicero's writings played a key role in all three activities.

Venetian teachers in 1587–88 used the books named in table 8.2 to teach rhetoric.[27] Unlike other rhetorical works popular in the Middle Ages whose importance diminished in the Renaissance, the *Rhetorica ad Herennium* continued to be influential. An unknown author wrote it circa 86 to 82 B.C. Jerome believed Cicero to be the author, and this belief persisted through the Middle Ages. Medieval writers called the *Rhetorica ad Heren-*

---

[25]Resta, 1964, pp. 38–42.

[26]Mancinelli, 1493, sig. A3ʳ.

[27]Although teachers seldom said in so many words that they taught rhetoric with Cicero's texts, poetry with Vergil's books, etc., the curricular function of individual titles is quite clear. The more detailed Jesuit school documents did explicitly indicate the pedagogical uses of the texts in table 8.2.

TABLE 8.2
Rhetoric Texts Taught by Venetian Teachers, 1587–1588

	Number of Teachers
Principles of rhetoric	
Rhetorica ad Herennium	17
Aristotle, *Rhetorica*	6
Cicero, *Partitiones oratoriae*	3
Castellesi, probl. *De modo loquendi* and *De sermone Latino*[a]	1
Total	27
Art of letter writing	
Cicero, *Epistulae ad familiares*	50
———, *Epistulae ad Atticum*	1
———, "Epistulae"	19
"Cicero" (possibly *Ad fam.*)	55
Manuzio, *Eleganze*[b]	1
Total	71 (126?)[c]
Oratory	
Cicero, *Orationes*	6
———, *Pro M. Marcello*	1
Total	7

Source: ACPV, "Professioni di fede."

[a]The teacher referred to "il cardinale Adriano," i.e., Cardinal Adriano Castellesi (1458–1522?), a major Roman humanist and Ciceronian. He published *De modo loquendi* (1507), a phrase book based mostly on Cicero, and *De sermone Latino* (1516), a brief history of the Latin language which praised the Golden Age, i.e., the century between the maturity of Cicero in c. 80 B.C. and the death of Livy in A.D. 17. The two works often appeared together in sixteenth-century imprints. Anastasius Iusbertus, the master who used Castellesi, taught an unusually rich group of texts that included Aristophanes in Greek, Cleynaerts's Greek grammar, a logical work, and Valla, in addition to the standard Caesar and *Epistulae ad familiares*, to thirteen noble and citizen youths. ACPV, "Professioni di fede," fol. 43ʳ; Baldo, 1977, pp. 49, 51. For Castellesi, see D'Amico, 1983, pp. 16–17 et passim.

[b]The teacher meant the *Eleganze insieme con la copia della lingua toscana e latina . . . utilissime al comporre nell'una e l'altra lingua* of Aldo Manuzio the Younger (1547–97), a Latin-Italian phrase book first published in Venice, 1558. Aldo's father, Paolo, probably helped him write it. ACPV, "Professioni di fede," fol. 23ʳ.

[c]The figure is at least 71 and may be as high as 126. It depends upon how many teachers who stated that they taught "Cicero" meant that they taught Cicero's letters.

nium "Rhetorica nova" or *"Rhetorica secunda"* in order to distinguish it from Cicero's *De inventione* (called *"Rhetorica vetus"* or *"prima"*).[28] Valla may have doubted Cicero's authorship, and Raphael Regius in 1491 definitely did. Nevertheless, many Renaissance men continued to attribute the work to Cicero through the end of the sixteenth century. Ognibene Bonisoli

[28]*Rhetorica ad Herennium*, 1954, pp. vii–xxxvii. Also see J. Murphy, 1981, pp. 19–21, 365–74; and Ward, 1978 and 1983.

edited the *editio princeps* of Venice, 1470. At least twenty-eight incunabular editions followed in Italy.

A well-organized technical synthesis of ancient teaching, the *Rhetorica ad Herennium* provided the catalogue of rhetorical definitions that Renaissance instructors wanted. Books 1 and 2 covered much the same ground as Cicero's *De inventione;* book 3 discussed memory and delivery of an oration. Book 4, nearly as long as the first three combined, treated style. It listed the three levels of style of classical rhetoric: grand, middle, and plain (IV.8.11). All three should demonstrate taste (*elegantia*), artistic composition (*compositio*), and distinction (*dignitas*). To help the writer or speaker achieve *dignitas,* book 4 defined and explained at length forty-five figures of speech (*verborum exornationes*) and nineteen figures of thought (*sententiarum exornationes*). Book 4 had the most significance for the Renaissance.

The figures began with *repetitio* (beginning successive phrases with the same word), and included were such familiar figures as antithesis and interrogation, as well as less well known ones such as frankness of speech (*licentia*), understatement (*diminutio*), comparison (*similitudo*), and simile (*imago*). The Renaissance in particular loved the *sententia* (maxim), which the *Rhetorica ad Herennium* defined as "a saying drawn from life, which shows concisely either what happens or ought to happen in life" (IV.17.24). "Furthermore, the hearer, when he perceives that an indisputable principle drawn from practical life is being applied to a cause, must give it his tacit approval." The text went on to caution that maxims should be used "only rarely, that we may be looked upon as pleading the cause, not preaching morals" (IV.17.25). Renaissance men completely ignored this admonition, because they wanted to preach good morals.

The *Rhetorica ad Herennium* continued to be used and taught long after the authentic *De oratore* became available, because pedagogues viewed them as works of different purpose for different readers: the *Rhetorica ad Herennium* taught rules to students, *De oratore* imparted wisdom to the learned.[29] Teachers could have used them sequentially. However, the *Rhetorica* served in the classroom, whereas *De oratore* became inspiration and authority for the civic and cultural conception of Renaissance rhetoric.

When teachers taught composition in the classroom, they proposed ancient models as examples of correct and eloquent style to be imitated. They saw no other way to re-create the standards of antiquity. But antiquity offered a large number of Latin authors and several styles; which should be followed? A lively debate ensued; should writers cultivate an eclectic, individual style or follow Cicero? Proponents of eclecticism or Quintilianism, so called because Quintilian argued for a Latin style based

---

[29]"percioche Cicerone nell'Oratore parla solamente à dotti, & presuppone, che si sappino le regole generali dell'arte Oratore, il perche non si potrete raccorre quel frutto, che fareste havendo letta la Retorica." Toscanella, 1575, p. 38.

on the reading and copying of a variety of the best authors, believed that language was not fixed but must evolve in order to respond to new circumstances. By contrast, Ciceronians put their trust in an unchanging style based on close study and imitation of Cicero's periodic sentence structure and vocabulary. The fifteenth and early sixteenth centuries witnessed some famous exchanges: Poggio Bracciolini for a Ciceronian style against Valla the eclectic; Paolo Cortesi in favor of strict Ciceronianism against Angelo Poliziano, who argued for eclectic imitation; Pietro Bembo, who imitated Cicero against Gianfrancesco Pico, who preferred an innate personal style free of imitation. Erasmus in his *Ciceronianus* of 1528 wittily and savagely attacked Roman Ciceronians, and Ciceronians across Europe replied in kind.[30] These debates illuminated major cultural issues at the heart of Renaissance humanism: whether or not Latin should be (and could be) a living language; the nature of cultural and linguistic authority; the degree to which Renaissance men had equalled or surpassed ancient achievements; the standards for prose expression; the relationship between a man's writing style and his personality; and, finally, the link between style and societal values.

The importance of the issues and the stature of those who debated them would suggest that a consensus could not be reached. Yet, the majority of humanists, or at least those engaged in teaching, preferred Ciceronianism from the beginning. As early as 1395 Coluccio Salutati outlined a periodization of the history of Latin prose literature which judged the age of Cicero to be the golden age of Latin eloquence.[31] Barzizza and Guarino favored Cicero. Indeed, Cicero's victory was almost inevitable for several reasons. Cicero produced much more literature that survived than any other Roman author. His career as Roman senator and his repeated observations on honor, family, and *patria*—the ideal of the citizen-philosopher—greatly attracted Renaissance humanists. Cicero further benefited from the growth of the papal court in the late fifteenth and sixteenth centuries, because papal humanists and secretaries were Ciceronians to a man.

Above all, teaching correct and elegant expression required having a standard against which to judge the efforts of learners. Ciceronian prose, with its alternating flowing periods and short dramatic statements, and its uniform vocabulary, could be learned by all. Bright students learned quickly, slower ones by long study and diligent imitation. Great creativity was not required in either case. Even more important, any teacher could

---

[30]The basic bibliography is Sabbadini, 1885; Scott, 1910; Angelo Gambaro's introduction to Erasmus, 1965; D'Amico, 1983, pp. 123–43; and D'Amico, 1984, pp. 355–59 et passim.

[31]Salutati, the first to reach this conclusion (still accepted today), wrote in a style more Senecan than Ciceronian. Born in 1331, Salutati received pre-humanistic training and never completely abandoned the *ars dictaminis*, speculative grammar, and etymology of his youth. Later humanists followed Salutati's literary judgment rather than his prose example. See Witt, 1983b, pp. 254–59.

teach Ciceronian style. It satisfied the universal need for a clear authoritative standard that teachers could teach, students learn, and society accept. Ciceronianism did not satisfy creative geniuses like Valla and Erasmus, but it suited the rest very well.

It is impossible to overestimate the importance of Cicero as a cultural and literary model in the Italian Renaissance. To quote a recent authority, "His writings defined the fundamental concept of *humanitas,* i.e., the knowledge of how to live as a cultivated, educated member of society."[32] A fine Latin style expressed *humanitas,* and in the opinion of the overwhelming majority of Italian humanists and teachers, Cicero had the best style. They taught his works, imitated his prose, used his vocabulary, and cherished his wisdom. Ciceronian dictionaries and phrase books helped student and teacher achieve their aims. Almost all teachers were Ciceronians, in that they taught Cicero's prose, though some more strictly than others.

Although they possessed the full Ciceronian corpus except for the undiscovered *De republica,* Italian Renaissance men, like their predecessors, concentrated on part of it. Different eras preferred different works of Cicero. The *De officiis* had great influence in the early Middle Ages through its adaptation by St. Ambrose in a guide for medieval clergymen and laymen, the *De officiis ministrorum,* and through the propagation of Ciceronian moral views in compilations such as the twelfth-century *Moralium dogma philosophorum.* Ambrose, Jerome, and others saw not the active Roman politician but the Stoic sage who advocated *otium,* or withdrawal from the world in order to contemplate the world philosophically.[33] In thirteenth- and fourteenth-century Italy, Cicero of the *De inventione* and the *Rhetorica ad Herennium* attributed to him dominated through the teaching of *ars dictaminis.* The letters and *De oratore* attracted minimal attention. As Bolgar put it, "The familiar missives of Cicero . . . offered little guidance to a diplomat addressing an archbishop, or to a lawyer concerned to elucidate some question of feudal right. Nor had they any information to give on the thorny subject of current social usage."[34]

In contrast, Italian Renaissance schoolmasters set great store by the letters, admired the orations, continued to use the *Rhetorica ad Herennium,* and paid less attention to the philosophical Cicero, that is, the Stoic Cicero who advised on life's duties in *De officiis, De amicitia, Paradoxa stoicorum, De finibus bonorum et malorum,* and *Tusculanae disputationes.* One might have expected schools to give a prominent place to *De officiis,* in which Cicero outlined to his son, a student, the duties of a Roman gentleman. Cicero

[32]D'Amico, 1983, pp. 123–43, quote on p. 124.
[33]Baron, 1938b, pp. 77–80; Curtius, 1963, pp. 522–27; Bolgar, 1964, p. 197; and Wilkinson, 1982, pp. 263–64.
[34]Bolgar, 1964, pp. 214–15; also see J. Murphy, 1981, pp. 106–23.

asserted a life of public service to be worthier than a life of retirement; he discussed social relationships and the importance of propriety, self-control, and virtue. While northerners such as Erasmus found *De officiis* of great interest, Italian schoolmasters paid less attention to it and other Ciceronian philosophical works, probably because these works did not provide practical examples of letter writing.

The earlier Middle Ages admired the Stoic, withdrawn sage; the Italian High Middle Ages taught the Cicero of rhetorical rules and definitions; Italian Renaissance Latin schools embraced the public man of *De oratore* and taught the letters. Each age used the most important ancient author according to its own priorities.

THE *EPISTULAE AD FAMILIARES* AS PROSE MODEL

Medieval teachers and the prehumanists of the early fourteenth century knew only two ancient letter collections, those of Seneca the Younger to Lucilius, and the first hundred letters of Pliny the Younger. Medieval men did not follow ancient epistolary models; at most, they slightly imitated Seneca's somewhat disconnected, jerky, antithetical, and epigrammatic sentences. But Quintilian severely criticized Seneca's style, and the Renaissance rejected Seneca as a prose model.[35] As Francesco Priscianese wrote in 1540, one should flee Seneca's style as vehemently as one ought to embrace his ethics.[36] The Renaissance had an alternative, Cicero's two great letter collections. As mentioned earlier, Petrarch discovered the *Epistulae ad Atticum* in 1345, and Salutati instigated the search that uncovered the *Epistulae ad familiares* in 1392. Practically every humanistic pedagogical theorist believed that a child could learn a good Latin style by studying and imitating the *Epistulae ad familiares*.[37]

A short discussion may help to clarify what the Renaissance found so attractive about Cicero's prose. Latin expresses the relations between words by inflection, which is a change in the forms of words in order to indicate grammatical categories such as number, case, gender, and tense. Function and meaning emerge through them. Since inflection defines the relationship of the words to each other, Latin permits, even encourages, variety in the word order of a sentence. It makes possible the Ciceronian period that postpones the verb and full meaning to the end of the sentence. English and most modern Western languages employ little inflection and rely heavily on a word order of subject, verb, and object to express

---

[35]Quintilian, *Institutio oratoria*, X.1.125–31. Sabbadini, 1922, p. 65; Duff, 1960, vol. 2:179–88; Curtius, 1963, p. 50; Bolgar, 1964, p. 423; Reynolds, 1965.

[36]". . . & l'opere di Seneca, se lo stile di questo Autore non fosse tanto da fuggire, quanto la disciplina da seguitare." Priscianese, 1540, sig. vᵛ.

[37]For one example among many, see Piccolomini, 1560, p. 109.

grammar and meaning. Although English prose does not permit extensive use of periodic sentences, Milton wrote this splendid one in *Paradise Lost* II.1–5:

> High on a throne of royal state, which far
> Outshone the Wealth of Ormus and of Ind,
> Or where the gorgeous East with richest hand
> Showers on her kings barbaric pearl and gold,
> Satan exalted sat.[38]

Cicero's well-known periodic style might be defined as using techniques of syntactical, logical, and rhetorical suspension in order to set up an anticipation that the conclusion of the sentence resolved.[39] Cicero typically employed a subordinate clause to express an expectation resolved through antithesis or conclusion. "If" leads to "then"; "since" implies "therefore." Cicero and other classical writers often arranged clauses in their order of thought; cause preceded result, purpose came before act. For the periodic style to succeed, the author must signal what is to follow in the long, complex sentence. Cicero did this in a variety of ways: *non solum . . . verum etiam, non quod . . . sed,* the use of *tam, ita,* or *sic* followed by an *ut* and a subjunctive clause. The predicate tended to bear the structural weight of the Ciceronian period. Often, but not always, he postponed the verb to the end. He tried to close the period with a pleasing succession of long and short syllables: "quod scīs nihil prodest, quod nescīs multum obest" ("What you know is of no use, what you do not know does great harm," Cicero, *Orator,* 166).[40] Medieval Latin writers, by contrast, took little advantage of opportunities to write periods.

Cicero formed a thought, had his periodic structure in mind, and swiftly organized the parts to create the desired effect. He described his own working habits in *Orator* 200: "The outline of the thought is no sooner formed in the mind than the words begin to muster; and these the mind, the swiftest thing there is, immediately distributes so that each one falls into its proper place in the ranks, and the orderly line of words is brought to a close now with one, now with another rhythmical pattern."[41] As one scholar put it, there is an "orderly and well-disposed placement of words, phrases, and clauses that flow rhythmically through minor resolutions to a well-rounded conclusion, frequently orchestrated by a set cadence."[42]

Cicero's periods were predictable in overall structure but full of internal surprises. Periodicity based on parallelism, antithesis, and balance would

[38]As quoted in Allen and Greenough, 1931, p. 399.
[39]I am following closely the excellent analysis of Cicero's periodicity of Gotoff, 1979.
[40]Allen and Greenough, 1931, p. 400.
[41]As translated and quoted by Gotoff, 1979, p. 64.
[42]Ibid., p. 65.

become boring unless handled with variety and imagination. Cicero had these in abundance; he used every kind of imbalance, asymmetry, and surprise that he judged the reader or listener could bear. He achieved his purpose through a very skillful use of prose rhythms and cadences, and by blending the individual units of thought into an integral whole.

Periodicity is the best-known aspect of Cicero's style, lending it impressive dignity and form. But periodicity did not dominate his letters, and it appeared only in restricted form in some orations and the philosophical treatises. Cicero also frequently used simple declarative sentences, impassioned short pleas, direct address, rhetorical questions, and practically everything else in the rhetorician's arsenal.[43] Probably the variety, range, and content of his prose mattered more than periodicity in making him a prose model to the Renaissance. Cicero often wished to convey a noble sentiment through appropriate words in a structured style that contained enough surprise to move reader or listener. Cicero succeeded admirably in suiting tone to content, words to sense.

The *Epistulae ad familiares* best embodied Cicero's union of content, form, and variety. After Cicero's death, someone, possibly his secretary Tiro, collected and edited these 426 letters to friends, members of his family, associates, and political figures, plus a few replies. An attempt was made to group them according to purpose and subject. The early letters of book 1 were political missives, book 4 contained mostly letters of condolence, book 13 was given over to 79 letters of recommendation, book 14 had Cicero's letters from exile to his wife and daughter, and book 15 dealt with his governorship of Cilicia. Letters to and from a single correspondent were sometimes grouped together. The letters dated from 62 B.C., when Cicero was 44 years old and at the height of his fame, to 43 B.C., a few months before his murder by order of Octavian (Augustus).

The letters exhibited a great variety of style, tone, and content. In places Cicero wrote in the most pathetic tones; elsewhere he cheerfully described the amusements of the city to a friend in the country. He addressed political missives arguing his case for a triumph as a reward for his successful proconsulship, and he vented his frustration when a lesser man obtained the honor through political influence. He passed on written instructions about mundane domestic details to his servants, and he discussed his campaign to get his worthless son-in-law to pay the dowry owed his daughter. His letters provided models for very many occasions.

Throughout Cicero displayed his wonderful, lofty, full, elegant, complex, and variegated style, which seemed to rise effortlessly from the content of his message. His way with words lent weight (*gravitas*) to anything he said, however conventional. His style made every sentiment seem lofty, and the Renaissance loved it. Practically every letter demon-

43Ibid., p. 56.

strates the point. For example, he addressed letter 22 of book 6 to Cn.
Domitius Ahenobarbus, son of an aristocrat who had fallen at the hand of
Antony. Domitius wished to join the remnants of Pompey's army in Spain
in order to battle against the Triumvirs and to avenge his father. In lofty
and grave words, Cicero advised him to desist:

. . . oro obtestorque te pro vetere nostra coniunctione ac necessitudine proque
summa mea in te benevolentia et tua in me pari, te ut nobis, parenti, coniugi
tuisque omnibus, quibus es fuistique semper carissimus, salvum conserves; in-
columitati tuae tuorumque, qui ex te pendent, consulas; quae didicisti, quaeque ab
adolescentia pulcherrime a sapientissimis viris tradita, memoria et scientia com-
prehendisti, iis hoc tempore utare; quos coniunctos summa benevolentia plurimis-
que officiis amisisti, eorum desiderium, si non aequo animo, at forti feras.

. . . therefore I implore and conjure you in the name of our old association and
friendship, and of the abundant good will I bear you and you equally bear me;
preserve yourself for me, for your mother, your wife, and all your family, to whom
you are and have ever been most dear. Think of your own safety and that of those
near to you, who depend on you. Make use now of what you have learned, those
admirable teachings handed down by the wisest of mankind which from youth up
you have absorbed into your memory and knowledge. Bear the loss of persons
bound to you by good will and good offices, signal in measure and number, if not
with equanimity, then at any rate with fortitude.[44]

The message was unexceptional: do not get yourself killed. But the
reasons advanced were lofty and philosophical (consider your duty to
others, bear your father's death with fortitude) and the words sonorous
and grave.

His letters also provided numerous examples of what one scholar calls
"the grand, impetuous manner, throbbing with emotive words."[45] In
book 14, letter 3, Cicero from exile began a letter to his wife, Terentia, with
the following words:

Accepi ab Aristocrito tres epistulas, quas ego lacrimis prope delevi. Conficior enim
maerore, mea Terentia, nec meae me miseriae magis excruciant, quam tuae ves-
traeque. Ego autem hoc miserior sum, quam tu, quae es miserrima, quod ipsa
calamitas communis est utriusque nostrum, sed culpa mea propria est.

I have received three letters from Aristocritus, and almost blotted them out in
tears. I am overwhelmed with grief, dearest Terentia; and my own distresses do not
torture me more than yours and your family's. But my wretchedness is greater
than yours (and yours is bitter enough) because, while we both share the disaster,
the blame for it is mine and mine only.[46]

[44]For the Latin, see Cicero, 1958–60, vol. 1:516, 518. I give the English translation of
Shackleton Bailey in Cicero, 1978, vol. 1:378, letter 221 in his numbering.
[45]Wilkinson, 1982, p. 238.
[46]The Latin comes from Cicero, 1958–60, vol. 3:190; the English from Cicero, 1978, vol.
1:32, letter 9.

The emotional tone carried this mixture of the conventional and the unexpected. Cicero began matter-of-factly by acknowledging the three letters received, but he surprised the reader with the arresting statement: "I have blotted them out with my tears." Having set this desperately pathetic mood, he continued in the same vein. In the third sentence he accepted full responsibility for the misfortune by means of a relatively simple but effective period that employed balance, rhythm, and antithesis.

Medieval letter writers followed *dictamen* manuals that provided *formulae* for salutation, petition, closing, and everything else. They learned to write very formal letters that emphasized harmonious relationships between members of the social hierarchy. Even personal letters between friends and relatives followed the *dictamen* rules for public correspondence. Hence, private correspondence became depersonalized and lacked the emotions and personal meditations of the age.[47] Similarly, rhetoric based on the *De inventione* of Cicero and the *Rhetorica ad Herennium* only taught men to classify the parts of letters and to label rhetorical figures. Was it any wonder that, compared with Trecento rhetoric, Cicero's corpus of letters had enormous impact? Here was a great letter writer who used rhetorical devices in a highly sophisticated and powerful way to express moving personal views. Cicero supplied what was missing from previous rhetoric: a living, breathing set of letters of the highest quality from which to learn.

The human situations and civic values that filled Cicero's letters clinched their primacy for the Renaissance. The letters taught not only practical rhetorical skills, but personal morality in a social context. Cicero the letter writer was a committed participant in the political and personal affairs of upper-class Roman life. The Italian elite acted similarly, while middle-class Italians would write about public affairs as secretaries to the high. Humanistic pedagogical writers stressed the civic and moral values to be learned from Cicero's letters. Orazio Lombardelli (1540/45–1608) of Siena made this point. A private teacher, then communal master, and finally professor of humanities from 1599 at the University of Siena, Lombardelli wrote grammatical works, vernacular literary criticism, and copious advice to young students. In the works of advice he asserted that one should compose Latin letters in imitation of Cicero.[48] Like many other humanistic pedagogical writers, he urged students to compile a notebook of notable sentences: "The sentences of Cicero and of Terence in Latin . . . are important for speaking well and good composition. The proverbs come into use daily, the similes and maxims serve as instruction for life. Words open up the understanding of the authors. The examples from history fit into arguments and discourses, and very much teach how to

---

[47]Witt, 1983a, pp. 21–23.

[48]Lombardelli, 1594, p. 19ᵛ. For brief biographical information on Lombardelli, see Volpicelli, ed., 1960, pp. 598–99.

live."[49] Practically every book of pedagogical advice recommended that students devote part of Saturdays and holidays to copying out and memorizing *sententiae* (maxims) from particularly important texts such as the *Epistulae ad familiares*.[50]

LEARNING TO WRITE LIKE CICERO

Teachers wished to train students to write in ways appropriate to almost any situation and with a variety of words. They reached their goal through four closely related classroom procedures. First, the student read under the teacher's direction Cicero's letters. Then teacher and student analyzed one or more Ciceronian letters for content, form, and vocabulary. From this the student learned the different kinds of letters, their purposes, their different styles, and the appropriate high, middle, or low words to be used.

Orazio Toscanella, teacher and pedagogical writer, described in detail the method of teaching Cicero.[51] Probably born circa 1520, Toscanella claimed that he descended from a Florentine abbaco teacher, Luca di Matteo (1356–c. 1435). Toscanella's immediate family lived in the Polesine, the plain of the Po in the Venetian state. In 1554 Toscanella held a teaching post in Castelbaldo, a tiny village about fifty kilometers southwest of Padua. He then taught as communal master in nearby Lendinara from 1559 to about 1566. After earlier visits and publications had paved the way, Toscanella moved to Venice circa 1566 where he became a *poligrafo*, one who supported himself by writing, translating, and editing for the

---

[49]"Le frasi di Cicerone, e di Terenzio in latino, e del Bembo, e del Tolomei in volgare, giovano a ben parlare, e ben comporre. I proverbi vengono a uso giornalmente. Le similitudini, e gli apotegmi servono a l'istruzion de la vita. I vocaboli apron l'intelligenza de gli autori. Gli esempi d'istorie cadon ne' rationamenti, e discorsi, e molto insegnano a vivere." Lombardelli, 1594, p. 12ᵛ, carrying the date 6 July 1575.

[50]See, for example, Toscanella, 1562, p. 8ᵛ.

[51]For Toscanella's life, see Bongi, 1890–97, vol. 2:219–25; Artese, 1983a and b; and Bolzoni, 1983. For Luca di Matteo, who wrote an abbaco treatise, see Van Egmond, 1976, pp. 387–88, and 1981, pp. 74, 248, 264–65. On the *poligrafi*, see P. Grendler, 1969a, pp. 11–14, 17–19, 65–69. Toscanella's works included the following, published in Venice unless otherwise indicated: *I modi più communi con che ha scritto Cicerone le sue epistole* (1559); *La Retorica di M. Tullio Cicerone a Gaio Herennio ridotto in alberi* (1561, 1566); *Precetti necessarii . . . sopra la grammatica, poetica, retorica, historica, topica, loica* (1562, 1567); *Prontuario di voci volgari et latini* (1565); *Modo di studiare le epistole famigliari di Cicerone* (1566, 1568); *Ciceroniana epitheta* (Antwerp: C. Plantin, 1566); a translation of Quintilian (1566); *Osservationi sopra l'opere di Virgilio* (1566, 1567); *Institutioni grammaticali volgari et latine* (1567, 1568, 1575, 1580, 1588, 1594); a translation of Rudolph Agricola's *De inventione dialectica* (1567); *Quadrivio* (1567); a translation and adaptation of Plutarch's *Lives* in two volumes (1567, 1568); *Arte metrica facilissima* (1567); *Dittionario volgare e latino* (1568); *Armonia di tutti i principali retori, et migliori scrittori degli antichi, e nostri tempi* (1569); *Bellezze del Furioso di M. Lodovico Ariosto* (1574); *Discorsi cinque* (1575); *Oratio Ciceronis pro Milone examinata* (1576).

Venetian presses. Toscanella concentrated on pedagogical works in Italian and Latin; he prepared teachers' manuals, study guides, and textbooks, plus translations and commentaries on the standard Latin curriculum authors, especially Cicero. He published more than twenty books between 1559 and 1579. Toscanella made his will on 19 January 1579, and died in March or April of that year. His frequent advice on teaching Cicero, supplemented by other sources, informs the following discussion.

The obvious first step was to read Cicero. In order to decipher the meaning of a Ciceronian sentence with its complex word order, the young student could rearrange the words to express directly the meaning. He could do this easily by labelling each word with consecutive letters of the alphabet according to Italian (and English) word order.

A	E	F		G	H		I		K	L	
Ego	omni	officio,	ac	potius		pietate		erga	te,		

C		B		D		P	M	O		N	
caeteris		satisfacio		omnibus;	mihi	ipse	nunquam	satisfacio.	(*Ad fam.* I.1)[52]		

One can translate by following the letters of the alphabet: "I satisfy all the others with every duty, and more, with piety toward you; myself I satisfy never." Understanding the meaning, one can translate the sentence in a way that better captures Cicero's style: "In any such dutiful, or rather affectionate regard as I show you, I satisfy the world; myself I can never satisfy" (Loeb translation). This learning device was so obvious and useful, one can surmise that students have always used it.

Having read one or more letters of Cicero, teacher and students began to analyze them. Using Cicero's *Ad familiares* as the textbook of examples, and relying on ancient and Renaissance rhetoric manuals for labels, a teacher might explain that Cicero had composed twenty-four different kinds of letters: accusatory, advisory, annunciatory, celebratory, congratulatory, consoling, excusatory, persuasive, recommending, and so on.[53] Then the teacher would define and explain each type. For example, he might explain that an excusatory letter was a letter of excuse and explanation whose purpose was to deny a deed or justify an error. The letter writer might deny the accusation by refuting the charges, giving examples, and adding lamentations about the corrupt times or the common peril posed by wicked accusers. If the purpose was to explain, justify, or apologize for the error, the letter writer might write that he had committed the deed through *pietas,* for the love of father, mother, brother, religion, or *patria.* Or he might write a letter that explained and excused the deed for reasons

[52]The example comes from Toscanella, 1575, p. 20; also see Toscanella, 1562, pp. 2ʳ⁻ᵛ.
[53]Toscanella, 1559, p. 8. However, Toscanella, 1575, p. 6ʳ, listed only nineteen kinds of letters.

of necessity—it occurred because of youth or age, poverty or infirmity, perhaps ignorance.[54]

Teacher and student then analyzed a letter such as *Ad fam.*I.1. In the letter of 56 B.C., Cicero from Rome wrote to his devoted friend Publius Lentulus Spinther, proconsul of Cilicia, to explain why the Senate had failed to give Lentulus the charge of restoring the king of Egypt to his throne. As proconsul of the nearest Roman province in Asia Minor, Lentulus was the logical choice; moreover, he wanted the assignment. But the powerful Pompey also sought this opportunity to command Rome's legions and to win glory. Cicero tried to persuade the Senate to give Lentulus the mission that was rightfully his. But the Senate, fearing to offend either candidate, shelved the matter. Now Cicero had the unhappy duty of explaining his failure, a painful task because Lentulus had persuaded the Senate to recall Cicero from exile the year before.

The teacher began his analysis of the letter by explaining the historical circumstances, identifying the chief characters, expounding on a consul's duties, and presenting a brief biography of Cicero.[55] The teacher might find this historical information in ancient works, such as Livy, or in a modern text. Next he classified the letter as excusatory because Cicero tried to excuse himself for failing to bring Lentulus's affair to a successful conclusion. The teacher then fitted the letter into a larger rhetorical context. He pointed out that the Greeks had identified three rhetorical genera: demonstrative, deliberative, and judicial. Cicero's letter was judicial, because excusing oneself was a form of defense. Rhetorical theory further recognized several methods of defense or excusing; Cicero used transferral of blame to others (see *Ad Herennium* I.15.25, for a definition). Cicero wrote that Pompey was powerful, that the Egyptian king favored Pompey and had given bribes to get his way, that the consul Marcellinus had been angry with Lentulus and refused to support his cause, and that Cicero's known friendship with Lentulus had rendered Cicero's advocacy suspect. The teacher's analysis concluded that Cicero had transferred the blame to the Senate that had failed to act properly.

After discussion of classification and content, the teacher proceeded to an internal analysis of the letter. The teacher noted the parts: salutation, introduction, narration, petition, and conclusion. He instructed students to keep in mind the hierarchical relationship between correspondents, that is, whether the recipient was superior, equal, or inferior in rank to the writer. Lentulus was Cicero's equal or his better by a slight margin. Cicero subtly humbled himself while maintaining his dignity in order to show his respect and devotion to Lentulus. The opening two sentences demon-

[54]Toscanella, 1566, pp. 69–81.
[55]The following comes mostly from Toscanella, 1575, pp. 6–19. See also Toscanella, 1562, pp. 9ʳ⁻ᵛ.

strated this: "In any such dutiful, or rather affectionate, regard as I show you I satisfy the world; myself I can never satisfy. Such is the magnitude of your services to me, that when I think how you gave yourself no rest in what concerned me until you had fully achieved your purpose, while I have no such success on your behalf, I feel that life is embittered to me." This approach showed "noble humility," in the judgment of the teacher.

The teacher then explained a few aspects of Cicero's *elocutio* or style: how Cicero used individual words, two-word combinations, and infinitives. The teacher noted from the letter some examples of how Cicero achieved his famous harmony. For example, in paragraph 3, Cicero wrote successive phrases with the same ending sounds (*ut exercitum religio tollat, te auctorem senatus retineat*). He also employed cadences, patterns of long and short syllables, which concluded in words with similar sounds and the same case (*exulceratis . . . exagitatis* in paragraph 4).

Although the analysis of *elocutio* in this example was relatively brief, Renaissance teachers commonly devoted a great deal of attention to style. They knew well Cicero's three kinds of rhetoric: high, middle, and low (*Orator* 20–21.69–70). Although originally formulated to identify three kinds of oratory, Cicero's high, middle, and low rhetoric served as pegs on which to hang wide-ranging instruction in the mysteries of style applicable to letters, as well. Teachers explained that high, middle, or low style should be employed according to the subject matter.[56]

High or serious style

matters of war	governments	"enormous	victory
peace	of republics,	excesses"	defeat
religion	kingdoms,	counsel	rebellion
states	empires, etc.	jurisdiction	conspiracy
	princes	philosophy	
	captains		
	magistrates		

Middle style

private matters	private honor	individual	anything per-
management	disputes	friendships	taining to
of affairs		individual	persons nèi-
private gains		hostilities	ther *signori*
and losses			nor lowly

Low or humble style

woods and	peasants	waters
forests	villages	animals
shepherds		

[56]Toscanella, 1566, pp. 53–54.

Words could also be classified as high, middle, or low according to the style to which they belonged.[57]

High-style words are
serious   illustrative   splendid
sonorous   grand   ancient

Middle-style words are
clear   brief
mild   temperate

Low-style words are
low
new

Renaissance teachers explained at length the three levels of style. They offered examples of words appropriate to each style and tried to define the differences. According to Toscanella's manual, *dilectio* was a low word, *amor* a middle word, and *caritas* a high word.[58] All three meant "love," but *amor* had more force than *dilectio,* and *caritas* greater force and significance than *amor.* To convey the differences in English, one might translate *dilectio* as "affection," *amor* as "love," and *caritas* as "high esteem and love." Similarly, *medicamentum* was a high word because it had greater force than *remedium.* Both meant "remedy"; the greater significance of *medicamentum* came as much from its greater length and sonority as from its meaning. One might translate *medicamentum* as "medicine" and *remedium* as "relief" in an effort to convey the difference. *Laurus,* a high word, had greater weight than *triumphus,* a middle word. Although both probably should be translated as "triumph," *laurus* had greater significance because it was based on the laurel wreath placed on the brows of victors in ancient Greece and Rome. It evoked the enormous honor and prestige of the laurel wreath ceremony so beloved of the humanists. *Triumphus* lacked these connotations; it came from the Roman triumphal procession but did not evoke the laurel.

Teachers classified words through a combination of meaning, circumstances, and sound. Such words as *miserum* (wretched or pitiable), *calamitosum* (ruinous), *horribile* (terrible or horrible), *divina vis* (divine force), *incredibiliter* (incredibly), were all high words, because they conveyed high subject matter. One also judged high words by sound: high words contained many vowels (except *u* and *i*), many consonants (especially *r*), and doubled consonants.[59] In addition, whole groups of words partook of high style, such as illustrative words that created a portrait. Plain words

[57]Ibid., p. 54.
[58]The examples in this paragraph are taken from ibid., p. 163.
[59]Ibid., pp. 161–62.

only attempted to make the meaning clear, while descriptive words made one understand and "almost see" the thing. In Toscanella's view, the following passage, from Cicero's *Verrines*, II.5.62.161, consisted of illustrative words: "Ipse inflammatus scelere & furore in forum venit, ardebant oculi, toto, ex ore crudelitas eminebat" ("Then he made for the marketplace, on fire with mad and wicked rage, his eyes blazing, and cruelty showing clearly in every feature of his face").[60]

Very sonorous words were also high words. The writer had to judge the sonority of an individual word. For example, *moderatio* (moderation) had greater sonority than *modestia, tempestas* (time or season) more sonority than *tempus*. Generally speaking, those words that had a fuller sound were more sonorous, especially words using *a, o,* and *r*. Even some one-syllable words possessed great sonority: *ros* (dew or moisture) and *bos* (ox or cow).[61]

Plain or clear and sweet words were appropriate to the middle style. Plain words had the following characteristics: a precise and clear meaning, plus the same meaning in various usages through the eight parts of speech. They were in frequent use, were neither too long nor ambiguous, had a clear pronunciation, and left nothing necessary unsaid. Sweet or mild words tended to exhibit the same sounds, syllables, and endings, and to flow gently into each other. Examples were *Doctus eras? at non studueras.* (You had been taught? But you had not studied.) Words ending in *-ni, -it,* and *-tem* were typical mild words: *nullum vidi legentem* (I saw no one reading), *venit, vidit, vicit* (he came, he saw, he conquered). Antonyms that had similar sounds were typical sweet words: *difficile-facile* (difficult-easy), *otium-negotium* (idleness-activity), *fidenter-timide* (boldly-timidly).[62]

Low style appeared in familiar or domestic letters. These letters dealing with everyday matters should be written with such words that anyone, however ignorant, could hope to understand. The writer should use the words that nature taught, those imbibed with mother's milk and used daily at home. One could add a few adroit sentiments of courtesy, just as one sprinkled sugar on food. A familiar letter could discuss diverse matters, but the writer must finish one thing before starting another so as to avoid the hint of artifice. Despite their low subject matter, familiar letters had to be written carefully and thoughtfully; a familiar letter should resemble a serene cloudless sky, open and clear. Cicero's *Epistulae ad Atticum* provided excellent examples for imitation. To depart from these examples was perilous, to follow Cicero the most certain path, advised Toscanella.[63] Teachers probably spent little time on low words, those that

[60]Ibid., p. 165. Toscanella, as usual, did not give the reference; I thank Erika Rummel for locating it. Cicero, 1948–53, vol. 2:645, for the English translation.

[61]Toscanella, 1566, p. 164.

[62]Ibid., pp. 166–67.

[63]Ibid., p. 56.

signified lowly things. Diminutives and words including the vowel *u* were typical low words: *tenella* (tender or delicate), *munusculum* (small present), *humilis* (low), and *exilitas* (thinness).[64]

All this analysis and rhetorical study, plus the use of Cicero's letters as models, had as its goal teaching students to write with richness and variety. The student learned how to make a point in a variety of ways with different combinations of words, syntactical diversity, and an assortment of rhetorical figures. Teachers and textbooks demonstrated at length how the student might do this.

The teacher might begin with the statement "Cicero wrote that friendship is a gift of God." He then explained different ways of writing it by putting Cicero into the nominative case: *Cicero scripsit; amicitiam donum esse Dei.* Or the genitive: *Ciceronis sententiam esse scimus, quod amicitia est donum Dei* (We know that it was a sentence of Cicero that friendship is a gift of God). Or the dative case: *Ciceroni placuit scribere, amicitiam esse donum Dei* (Cicero was happy to write that friendship is a gift of God). The accusative: *Ciceronem scripsissem volunt, amicitiam esse donum Dei* (They maintain that Cicero wrote that friendship is a gift of God). Vocative case: *O Cicero sapienter scripsisti: amicitiam esse donum Dei* (Oh Cicero, you wisely wrote: friendship is a gift of God). And so on.[65] This kind of rhetorical variation put to practical use the endless grammatical drill and agreement exercises of the grammar school.

The student could also achieve variety through the use of synonyms. For the verb *scribere,* he might substitute *conscribere* (write or compose), *prodere* (bring forth, produce), *ponere* (to lay down, establish), and *tradere* (to hand down, record).[66] Hence, he could pen the following variations:

> Conscripsit Cicero, amicitiam donum Dei esse.
> Cicero wrote: friendship is a gift of God.
>
> Cicero prodidit, amicitiam esse donum Dei.
> Cicero brought forth that friendship is a gift of God.
>
> Romanae eloquentiae pater posuit, donum Dei esse amicitiam.
> The father of Roman eloquence laid down that friendship is a gift of God.
>
> Traditum fuit a Cicerone, donum Dei amicitiam esse.
> It was recorded by Cicero that friendship is a gift of God.

Further, the student could find in one of the many Ciceronian dictionaries many two-word combinations to substitute for *scribere,* such as *literis consigno* and *historiae mando.* Then he could write:

[64]Ibid., p. 162.
[65]Ibid., p. 177.
[66]Ibid., pp. 177–80.

Consignavit literis Cicero, amicitiam esse donum Dei.
Cicero attested in his letters that friendship is a gift of God.

Historiae mandavit Cicero, amicitiam esse donum Dei.
Cicero charged history: friendship is a gift of God.

Or the student might use an idiomatic expression such as *dicere bene* (to speak well):

Bene dixit Cicero; amicitiam esse donum Dei.
Cicero spoke well: friendship is a gift of God.

All this and more could be done without making recourse to more elaborate rhetorical devices. Two examples of the numerous rhetorical devices that the Renaissance student learned will suffice. He might use the rhetorical figure of extreme brevity or *brachilogia*, in which the statement was delivered in such a brief, clipped, and authoritative way as to close off debate:

Amicitiam esse donum Dei. Dixit, scripsit, testatus est Cicero.[67]
Friendship is a gift of God. Cicero has spoken, written, born witness.

Or he might adopt the rhetorical figure of *iracundia*, that is, the pose of anger that the listener might have the insolence to doubt the speaker's word:

Ergo tu omnium ignorantissimus negare audes Ciceronem scripsisse, amicitiam esse donum Dei?[68]
Therefore, you of all men the most ignorant dare to deny that Cicero wrote, friendship is a gift of God?

Thus students learned Ciceronian verbal facility and grammatical dexterity.

WORDS AND THINGS

The words that a student learned to manipulate were not reality; they signified reality. Teachers were expected to keep the real world in mind and make it the goal of instruction. The student had to learn "things," that is, content, which often consisted of maxims of advice to guide his life and to include in his letters and speeches. The student practiced writing letters whose content embodied what the Renaissance saw as reality.

The humanists from the beginning believed that they discussed and taught "things not words." Leonardo Bruni made this point as early as the

[67]Ibid., p. 187.
[68]Ibid., p. 195.

1420s. In the prefatory section of his *De studiis et litteris,* he advocated true learning, which was "expertise in letters united with the knowledge of things" ("quae litterarum peritiam cum rerum scientia coniungit").[69] By *things,* Bruni meant the moral facts and principles that should govern men's lives. *Things* also meant practical experience in the world, which might be acquired through history as well. "Things not words" became a humanistic commonplace repeated in one form or another for two centuries.[70] Toscanella linked things to words by explaining that words were not arbitrary names but proceeded from the things that they named. Just as clothes were measured and cut to fit bodies, so words fitted things.[71] Hence, high, middle, and low words derived their validity from subjects, experiences, and persons who were high, middle, and low.

This meant in practical pedagogical terms a belief in a bond between curriculum and life. Teachers stated that they trained students for practical experience; they taught students to write and speak in ways that kept the real world of practical affairs and moral decisions in mind. A teacher should demonstrate how the student-writer might relate his letter to the real circumstances—persons, situations, goals, and dilemmas—of life. To be sure, these "real circumstances" were the adult roles of men of affairs or secretaries to princes, roles that students hoped to assume. And students were expected to learn from the ancient world; classical Rome was as "real" as fifteenth-century Italy.

In this way, students learned content as well as form. For example, a common type of letter which probably every child learned to write was the letter of duties, a formal letter in which the writer advised the recipient—son, father, servant, master, youth, or prince—of the obligations imposed on him by his station in life. Such letters became samplers of humanistic moral and social advice. For example, according to Toscanella, a letter defining the duties of a prince should include the following admonitions: the prince should defend the Christian faith, build hospitals, observe the laws, refrain from tyrannizing his subjects, reward the good, punish the wicked, and act in such a way as to be loved rather than feared.[72] Machiavelli took delight in inverting such dutiful commonplaces, and the social critic Anton Francesco Doni (1513–74) mocked them by pointing out that a prince would not be a prince if he did not do as he pleased.[73] Machiavelli and Doni shocked and amused their readers because the letter

[69]Baron, ed., 1969, p. 6.

[70]Garin, 1957, pp. 225–28; P. Grendler, 1971, p. 452.

[71]"perche le parole sono state trovate per le cose; & non le cose per le parole; & precedono le cose, poi seguitano le parole; & si come le vesti sono proportionate ai corpi, cosi le parole alle cose. . . ." Toscanella, 1566, p. 174.

[72]Toscanella, 1559, pp. 39–41.

[73]P. Grendler, 1969a, pp. 79–80.

detailing a prince's duties had been so relentlessly taught in school and so often elaborated in humanistic treatises that readers instantly recognized the inversion and mockery.

At the same time, composing sample letters on duty or other serious subjects constituted instruction in content (*res*) as well as practice in literary form (*verba*). Teachers encouraged a focus on moral content in a variety of ways. For example, a teachers' manual advised that students might perform an exercise in order to learn how to develop and expand a letter on a serious subject. The assignment was to write a letter on "love." The student should take a sheet of paper and write in the center the theme: love. Then he should write around the margins of the paper all those benefits gained through love: honor, peace, benevolence, favor, accord, preservation of life, security, liberty, and so on. Having written out the names of the benefits in some connected fashion, the student could then expand on those benefits and themes in ways appropriate to the circumstances and the correspondent.[74] Thus, the student learned how to develop his thought from a central concept to related ones. He also learned and repeated the benefits of love.

Students also learned moral content from rhetorical study by jotting down in the ubiquitous notebook the maxims and concepts found in their reading. They did this for Cicero's *Epistulae ad familiares* and the other texts studied. As always, maxims collected in the notebook were expected to be useful for style and for life; they would help the student to write gracefully and to become wise.[75]

To complete their training in prose composition, students wrote a great many practice letters. Students might begin writing Latin letters at the age of 12 and continue for years. In 1425, Guarino of Verona endorsed letter writing as an exercise. Writing to a former pupil now teaching, he advised him to introduce his eldest pupil to writing letters. The teacher should give a student themes that illustrated syntax rules so that from the beginning the pupil might learn to express himself coherently and gracefully, Guarino advised.[76] The Commune of Lucca directed its masters to give students a daily theme in the vernacular to translate into a Latin letter or oration.[77] Venetian schoolmasters in 1587 constantly assigned letters or

[74]Toscanella, 1566, pp. 54–56.
[75]Toscanella, 1575, pp. 17–18.
[76]"Ludovicum iam epistulis consuefacias interque themata constructionum regulas permisce, ut pariter et ornate et congrue dicere incipiat et consuescat." Letter to Martino Rizzoni of 28 October 1425, Verona, in Guarino, 1967, vol. 1:498; also in Garin, ed., 1958, p. 344, with Italian translation.
[77]"Item, che dicti maestri ogni giorno di ciascuna septimana siano tenuti dare theme vulgare alli scholari per fare epistole et orationi in latino." *Capitoli* of 8 January 1499 in Barsanti, 1905, p. 215. The commune repeated this direction in 1524. Ibid., p. 220.

orations to be translated into Latin.[78] Such letter-writing exercises built on
the agreement exercises that students had done earlier.

The teacher might organize a series of letters around a central theme,
with the letters crafted to simulate reality and to make it possible to use
classical vocabulary. For example, a group of letters might assume that the
youth was visiting a nearby city and sending back reports of what he had
seen. In one such series, the exercise letters assumed that the student,
possibly a Florentine, had gone to visit Arezzo for two years. Each letter to
be translated into Latin contained an account of Aretine life and customs
about one hundred words long. The first one, of 29 April 1534, began with
a description of the pretty, garlanded girls of Arezzo, and ended with a
caution that one must flee these maidens who tempted one's virtue in
springtime. Moral admonition was such an integral part of Renaissance
pedagogy that teachers could not be expected to pass up any opportunity
to teach good morals. Later letters in this series imitated political missives
and on such subjects as the Senate's actions, the deeds of magistrates, and
even pirate threats. The student copied down the vernacular version from
his teacher, wrote out his translation, and then entered a fair copy of his
corrected Latin translation into an exercise book to be preserved for future
reference. Indeed, in this particular letter-exercise book, the first Latin
translations were written in an awkward, somewhat immature hand that
became more fluid and adult in the course of two years.[79] Another Florentine letter-exercise book of 1590 contained seventy vernacular epistles to be
translated.[80]

Teachers were expected to correct these compositions diligently. But a
seventeenth-century pedagogical writer entered a sensible caution. Teachers should correct every infelicitous or incorrect expression and make sure
that students used only grammatical and rhetorical figures found in the
ancients. But do not correct everything at once, he cautioned, lest you
discourage the student. Correct one thing now, something else at a later
date. And do not correct so harshly that the student will come to hate you

[78]"et li propongo poi orationi in vulgar et epistole da redur in latino." ACPV, "Professioni
di fede," fols. 126ᵛ–127ʳ. Also see fols. 15ʳ, 31ᵛ, 65ᵛ–66ʳ, 150ʳ, 159ᵛ, et passim; Baldo, 1977, pp.
47, 49, 53, 59, 63, 65, et passim.
[79]FN Ms. Nazionale II - 158. "Ioannes Angloriensis" translated the letters dated 29 April
1534 through 30 May 1536. A few letters were not translated into Latin.
[80]FN Ms. Nazionale, II.IX.69. This manuscript is clearly labelled an exercise book:
"Libro di pistole vulgari rivoltate in latino et date da mz. Gio. Bat. Conti mio maestro
cominciate a scrivere . . . a di 19 di Maggio 1590 in Fiorenza. . . . Ad usum Bernardi de
Salvestris fu Inquilini, Florentiae Apud Plateam Antinoream." Although the exercise book
leaves space for translation, only the first letter has been rendered into Latin. Also see FN Ms.
Nazionale, II - 111, an anonymous sixteenth-century exercise book with short (ten-line)
vernacular statements and Latin translations on such subjects as how good the school is.

and, consequently, to abhor good letters.[81] This pedagogue recognized that the twin goals of fluency and correctness according to classical standards might be reached in stages.

RHETORIC AND LIFE

Renaissance teaching of prose composition had roots in the *ars dictaminis* but differed significantly. Above all, Cicero's own prose, not his abstract rhetorical theory enunciated in the *De inventione* and codified in the *Rhetorica ad Herennium*, became the foundation. This lent the undertaking a concreteness, variety, and vivacity that the *ars dictaminis* manuals lacked. Second, Renaissance pedagogy relied slightly less than medieval pedagogy on careful and comprehensive organization of the art of letter writing. Renaissance teachers substituted a looser organization for the long list of categories of medieval letterwriting. Renaissance rhetoricians did not worry so much about composing the exact salutation appropriate to pope, emperor, clergyman, friend, father, or other recipient. Indeed, the textbooks of the Renaissance did not provide exact salutations. Rather, they emphasized the subject matter, which was often viewed as lofty concepts and values widely applicable to man in society. A concern for uniting form and content dominated. Moreover, the Renaissance approach depended little on the logical categories that seemed to underlie so much late medieval intellectual endeavor. Having scorned medieval dialectic, Renaissance humanists organized their teaching of prose composition in ways that reflected their effort to unite rhetoric and life.

A view of the union of learning and life lay behind the techniques of prose composition and maxims of advice. The Renaissance saw culture and society as two parts of a whole. *Verba* were linked to *res* in a rational, ordered universe of civic society composed of people with different duties to perform. Oral and written communication gave life to this civic society; as Angelo Poliziano argued, the word educated, improved, and renewed. Civil society formed itself and acted, usually for the better, through rhetoric.[82] Learning to write letters about the duties attendant on one's station in life, honor and *patria,* winning favors and avoiding losses, expressed the reality in which humanists and pedagogues believed. Teachers taught a style of communication which expressed the ideals of Renaissance society, not the sometimes brutal, irrational reality. Pedagogues urged students to copy into notebooks maxims that expressed the positive values of this world. Proverbs, maxims, and commonplaces articulated the *res* of the world. Humanists and teachers did not accept that high ideals

[81]Corradi, 1654, pp. 226–27.
[82]Garin, 1961, pp. 128–29.

were found only in books, any more than they believed ancient Greece and Rome to be irrelevant. Classical texts were not reserved for the scholar but were given to those who lived and worked in society, because the works were seen as useful.

It can be objected that Renaissance Latin education built on a utopian dream, because the majority of students would never become citizen orators who would apply the moral wisdom of Cicero to the greater good of the *patria*. Reality was not necessarily rational, men not very often in control of their own destiny. Fortune lifted them up or cast them down, as the age's most perceptive observers noted. And possibly the majority of men and women did not try very hard to act knowingly, but were content to be shoved hither and yon by fate. It did not matter. Education always involves utopian dreaming or, at least, lofty assumptions that students will step from the classroom into an orderly world that can be comprehended and managed to some degree by one's learning.

CHAPTER NINE

The Rest of the Latin Curriculum

POETRY

enaissance pupils studied ancient poets in order to learn metrics and style, and to enjoy the rhythms and words of poetry.
They also hoped to acquire knowledge of men, events, and
nature, and to be stimulated to acts of virtue. The schools
read Vergil above all, plus Terence, Horace, and Ovid to a lesser degree.
Teachers and students perpetuated much of a rich medieval approach to
poetry. But they also innovated by reading the ancient poets exclusively
and by raising poetry to the status of an independent subject in the
curriculum.

Medieval men did not view poetry as one of the seven liberal arts, but as
a branch of philosophy and theology.[1] They learned from the ancient
world that the poet was sage, teacher, educator, and philosopher, and they
added theologian. The poet penetrated divine mysteries. Medieval scholars used allegory, the basis of most of their poetical interpretation, to
unlock poetry's wisdom.

Medieval men also believed poetry to be a subsection of grammar and
rhetoric. As Matthew of Vendôme in his *Ars versificatoria* (c. 1175) argued,
verse was metrical discourse. It married beautiful words and flowers of
intelligence. Neither the counting of feet nor syllabic quantity, but the
elegant union of words and expression, created poetry, in his judgment.[2]
Hence, the study of poetry was part of the broader study of grammar and
rhetoric and included analysis of words and concepts. Matthew of Vendôme offered information on metrics and quoted examples from Horace
and Ovid, but overall, he and other medieval scholars viewed poetry as
style, and carried on extended discussions of grammatical figures and
rhetorical tropes. In similar fashion, Alexander de Villedieu dealt with

[1]See Curtius, 1963, chs. 8, 9, 11, and 12; and J. Murphy, 1981, ch. 4.
[2]J. Murphy, 1981, pp. 163–68.

quantity and accent as part of a very large grammatical universe encompassing syntax, etymology, figures, and much else.[3]

Medieval schools taught some ancient poets, notably Vergil, Ovid, Statius, and Lucan, as curriculum authors. Vergil exerted a powerful attraction, especially outside the classroom. The Roman poet inspired Dante, and the *Aeneid* gave rise to a rich allegorical tradition. Even a popularized Vergil in the form of vernacular romances stirred readers.[4] But medieval pedagogues did not bequeath to the Renaissance a strong tradition of schoolroom study of ancient poetry. Sabbadini concluded that medieval men taught ancient poetry badly because they did not understand metrics very well. He particularly criticized the inadequate treatment of syllabic quantity in the *Doctrinale*.[5]

The Renaissance raised poetry to the status of a separate discipline within the *studia humanitatis*. Beginning in the middle of the fifteenth century, curricular directions specified that masters must teach grammar, rhetoric, poetry, or history. For example, the Commune of Treviso in the 1440s directed the communal master "to teach grammar . . . and to lecture on poetry and rhetoric to all who wish to attend."[6] Other communes gave similar directions.

In the same middle years of the Quattrocento, universities established chairs of poetry and rhetoric. For example, Cristoforo Landino taught "poetry and oratory" at the Florentine *studio* from 1452 through 1497.[7] The joining of poetry and rhetoric showed medieval influence but also marked an advance in status for poetry over the *trivium* of grammar, rhetoric, and dialectic. Poetry's stock further rose when the eminent Landino began to lecture on the *Aeneid* in the academic year 1462–63. He also taught Horace, Juvenal, and Persius.[8] Poetry had not received such attention in medieval universities.

The humanists wished to teach only the ancient poets. But first they had to refute the charge that the pagan poets corrupted readers. Petrarch, Boccaccio, Salutati, and Quattrocento humanists argued that underneath the surface accounts of lust and violence, the ancient poets taught love and virtue. They borrowed arguments from the *Exhortation to Youths as to How They Shall Best Profit by the Writings of Pagan Authors* of St. Basil the Great (c. 330–79) and added their own.[9] The humanists argued that the church fathers had approved of and loved the pagan poets. Jerome and Plato, who

---

[3]Ibid., pp. 149–50.
[4]Comparetti, 1896. However, the author offers very little information on the medieval pedagogical use of Vergil.
[5]Sabbadini, 1922, pp. 67–69.
[6]See ch. 5, n. 7 for the quote.
[7]Verde, 1973–77, vol. 2:174–77. Also see Ibid., 2:26–29, 260–61.
[8]Field, 1978.
[9]See P. Grendler, 1977, pp. 64–66; Ronconi, 1979; and Robey, 1984.

had banished poets from the republic, meant to condemn only a few wicked poets, not the majority, in the view of the humanists. Poetry corrupted only those already inclined toward evil. It benefited everyone else, not least by teaching eloquence. Above all, poetry taught and inspired good habits and virtue. Poetic depictions of evil invoked horror in the reader and a preference for noble goods of the soul.

The humanists prevailed, and Renaissance schools taught only ancient poetry, with very few precautions. Pedagogical theorists sometimes warned against certain works of, or passages in works of, such poets as Ovid and Juvenal. Even the Jesuits altered little. The moralizing verse poems of the Middle Ages, such as *Eva columba, Chartula,* and *Prospero,* disappeared from the curriculum. Vergil, Terence, and Horace took their place.

Some fifteenth-century humanists used allegoresis to interpret poetry, but not in the same way their medieval predecessors had. In humanistic allegoresis, poetry taught secular goodness—moral advice for the man who must make his way in this life—rather than Christian theology. Cristoforo Landino (1425–98) presented the most important moral allegory of the period, an interpretation of the *Aeneid,* in his university lecturing, in his *Disputationes Camaldulenses* of 1472, and in his commentary on Vergil of 1488. In his preface to the commentary, Landino explained: "Vergil's poem portrays every kind of human life, so that there is no class, age, sex, or, finally, no condition which could not learn from it the entirety of its duties."[10] Landino interpreted the poem as the story of Aeneas's progress out of sensual pleasure (beginning in Troy) and into the civic life (his visit to Carthage, where he loved Dido). Landino judged the civic life to be praiseworthy in itself but also a preparation for higher things. Thus, Aeneas went on to found Rome, which Landino interpreted as entering into the highest plane of the contemplative life. Landino's allegorical interpretation of the *Aeneid* as a complete guide to secular virtue exercised great influence.

To be sure, a few variations developed within the dominant pattern of a secular moral interpretation. Most Renaissance allegorists saw Dido in book 4 as a temptress, a personification of lust who seduced Aeneas from his duty.[11] But not all. Maffeo Vegio, the most conservative and religious of the Quattrocento humanistic pedagogical theorists, presented a more sympathetic interpretation of Dido as a female ruler who strayed from civic duty. At first she performed her duties as queen of Carthage magnificently, but then she succumbed to her passion for Aeneas and neglected her

[10]"Maronis poema omne humanae vitae genus exprimit, ut nullus hominum ordo, nulla aetas, nullus sexus sit, nulla denique conditio, quae ab eo sua officia non integre addiscat." Kallendorf, 1983, pp. 525–26, for both the Latin and the English translation. Indeed, this paragraph is based on Kallendorf's article.
[11]Ibid., pp. 541–42.

people. Just as Aeneas served as an allegorical example for boys, so Dido became a lesson to girls.

By similar token, in Dido he strives to teach women, too, . . . by what rational counsels they ought to order their lives, motivated either by the reward of being praised or by fear of dishonor and pitiful ruin. For what woman is not moved by Dido's example and set on fire with zeal for goodness, as she hears how earnestly the queen devoted herself to the task of establishing walls for her great city, regulating institutions and laws for the people in a spirit of justice, and, even though her husband was dead, won high renown and reverence for herself and inspired fear in her neighbors by keeping her faith and marriage vows. And yet, contrary to understanding, she fell madly in love with her guest, a stranger, gave up the building of her city and the rule of her people, spent her time in such pursuits as merrymaking and feasting, and in the end, forsaken by her lover, in grief and affliction, bereft of all hope, resolved to compass her own death?[12]

Other prominent humanists and educators judged that poetry taught virtue without allegory. They saw poetry as a literal teacher of virtue and experience for the secular life. Pier Paolo Vergerio emphasized the secular nature of the poet's call to virtue without making recourse to allegory: the poet kept alive the imperishable memory of great human deeds of the past and moved men to emulation.[13] Vittorino da Feltre, who introduced his pupils to Vergil when they were at a tender age and taught several ancient poets to students of all ages, presented moral precepts without allegory and mined poetry for *sententiae*.[14]

The humanists searched poetry for eloquence, as well. Vittorino taught poetry for the rhetorical figures and *copia,* or fullness of style. Landino, a rhetorician as well as allegorist, identified rhetorical figures and explained difficult passages. Like their medieval predecessors, Renaissance pedagogues taught poetry grammatically and rhetorically, but Renaissance pedagogues taught with more sophistication, because of their greater understanding of ancient literature. Poetry enjoyed an independent existence in the Renaissance curriculum, a position that the numerous Cinque-

---

[12]. . . ita per Didonem feminas etiam, quibus vitam rationibus instituere deberent vel praemio laudis vel metu infamiae ac tristissimi demum interitus . . . admonere studuit. quae nam enim audiens illam condendis tantae urbis moenibus intentissime vacantem, iuraque et leges populis iustissime moderantem, marito etiam extincto fidem ac pacta tori conservantem, cum summa laude sua et veneratione finitimorumque omnium timore, non eius exemplo moveatur atque ad virtutis studium magnopere incendatur; contra vero intelligens novi eam hospitis amore insanientem, ab extructione urbis gubernationeque populorum cessantem, lusibus tamen et conviviis indulgentem, derelictamque ab amante demum, dolentemque et affligentem sese, de perditaque omni spe, mortem etiam ultro sibi consciscentem. . . .

Vegio, 1933–36, bk. 2, ch. 18, p. 87, ll. 17–29. The English translation is taken from Brinton, 1930, p. 27, and has been slightly modified.
[13]Robey, 1984, p. 15.
[14]Ibid., pp. 18–19.

cento treatises on poetics strengthened,[15] and it also maintained its links with grammar and rhetoric.

Poetry's descent from theology to secular ethics had another consequence: humanists viewed poetry as a combination of sound morals and descriptive learning. Leonardo Bruni made this case eloquently. Ancient poetry teaches not only principles of moral philosophy, but knowledge of life and nature in the broadest sense, including practical experience, he wrote, arguing that Homer had brilliantly portrayed generalship and military valor. Bruni quoted the *Aeneid* VI.724–32, a passage linking man to the natural world, to demonstrate that Vergil surpassed all philosophers in unveiling the mysteries of nature.[16]

Bruni went on to explain poetry's profound and delightful appeal. Men heed the poet's call because poetry pleases, yielding a delight that is the fruit of the deep harmony between poetry and mankind. He obviously had in mind Horace's dictum that poetry both teaches and delights (*Ars poetica*, 333). Children memorize poetry easily, and even uneducated men express themselves in poetry, because of the deep affinity between human nature and the poetic form.

When I consider our studies, I find a knowledge of the poets to be necessary before all others, because of their utility of which I have spoken, for their broad understanding of many things, and for the splendor of their style. Of all the studies, this does not take time away [from important things]: one learns the poets in childhood when it is almost impossible to occupy oneself with anything else, and they remain fixed in our memory through their sonorous elegance, following us always and returning to our minds without need of books; we think of them even when attending to other matters.

That it is our nature to incline toward poetry, I believe, can be seen in the fact that uncouth and wholly unlettered men, so long as they have wit, delight in composing harmonies and rhythms in their own rough way. And although the same things could be said more easily in prose, they believe that they have composed something worthy to be heard if they succeed in expressing it in poetic meter. . . . Only this do I wish to make clear: by nature we are disposed to poetry more than to any other literary genre, and it is the source of the greatest utility and delight; he who lacks poetry cannot be considered liberally educated.[17]

[15]Weinberg, ed., 1970–74, has edited them.

[16]Bruni's *De studiis et litteris liber* (1422–29), found in Baron, ed., 1969, pp. 5–19, and pp. 14–16 for poetry. Garin, ed., 1958, pp. 146–69, reprints the Latin text with an Italian translation; see pp. 158–61 for the above material on poetry.

[17]Mihi vero studia haec nostra intuenti in primis necessaria videri solet poetarum cognitio, cum propter utilitatem, de qua supra dixi, variamque multarum rerum notitiam, tum ob sermonis excellentissimum nitorem. Praeterea nihil est ex omnibus studiis, quod minus nobis auferat temporis; nam et addiscuntur in pueritia cum aliis fere vacare non possumus, et inhaerent memoriae ob rotundam concinnitatem et peregrinantur una nobiscum et sine libris ultro recursant, ut vel aliud agens hoc etiam agas. Quanta vero sit naturae ipsius ad poeticam convenientia, vel ex hoc patere arbitror, quod vulgo inerudit homines, quamvis litterarum doctrinaeque expertes, tamen, si

Orazio Toscanella presented Bruni's message that poetry is vivid description that moves men. The poet "mirrors the nature of men, animals, the forces of earth, all things."[18] In poetry the reader sees the fire of burning cities, the blood of the fallen, the clash of arms, Toscanella wrote. Through its impact on the soul, poetry spurs virtue, checks vice, and reforms human habits, he concluded. In other words, poetry describes life, and these powerful descriptions move men to do good deeds. To help the reader appreciate and use Vergil's descriptions, Toscanella composed a descriptive lexicon. Under a series of alphabetical headings (*abbandomento* [abandonment], *abbracciamenti* [embraces], *accampamento* [encampment of an army], *accompagnamento* [accompaniment], etc.), Toscanella defined the action, indicated how the poet described it, and listed passages (in Latin) from the *Aeneid* as illustrative examples. He did this without brandishing grammatical or rhetorical terms.[19] A student might easily locate and borrow for his own use Vergil's powerful, moving descriptions.

POETRY IN THE CLASSROOM

Renaissance students most often studied Vergil among the ancient poets.[20] But pedagogical theorists, communal school guidelines, and classroom teachers did not indicate which works of Vergil or how much of them were to be taught. Printed editions intended for school use (i.e., inexpensive small octavo or duodecimo imprints with little or no commentary) included all three of the authentic works: the *Aeneid*, the *Eclogues* or *Bucolics,* and the *Georgics.* The Aldine Press of Venice issued at least twenty-one such collective editions between 1501 and 1587. Other publishers also issued collective editions.[21]

Students read more than one work of Vergil but not necessarily complete texts. For example, pupils in the Jesuit school at Messina in 1551 began with the *Eclogues* at about the age of 12, then progressed to books 6

---

ingenio valent, ea ipsa, qua possunt, ruditate sonitus quosdam et rhytmos efficere delectantur. Etsi queant eadem solutis verbis dicere commodius, tamen ita demum aliquid dignum auditu se perfecisse putant, si illa numero rhytmisque incluserint. tantum illud intelligi volo: nos natura magis ad poeticam duci quam ad aliud genus litterarum et esse in ea utilitatem plurimam et delectationem et ingenuitatem, cuius qui expers sit minime liberaliter eruditus videatur.

Garin, ed., 1958, pp. 162, 164. The translation is mine, prepared before the one in Bruni, 1987, pp. 246–47, appeared.

[18]"Egli specolò la natura de gli huomini, de gli animali, le forze dell'erbe, di tutte le cose." Toscanella, 1574, dedicatory letter, sigs. *2ʳ–*3ᵛ, quote on *2ᵛ.

[19]Toscanella, 1567c.

[20]For an overview of Vergil in the Renaissance, see Zabughin, 1921–23.

[21]This is based on my examination of about twenty sixteenth-century Italian imprints of Vergil in the library of the University of Illinois at Urbana-Champaign; plus Renouard, 1953, passim; Camerini, 1962–63, passim; *STC Italian,* pp. 729–32; and Mambelli, 1954.

and 7 of the *Aeneid* at age 13 or 14.[22] A Jesuit syllabus of 1565 expected more. The grammar classes were to read *Eclogues* 1, 4, and 5; the humanities class was expected to read books 1, 10, 11, and 12 of the *Aeneid;* and the rhetoric class should read the *Georgics* and books 2, 6, and 8 of the *Aeneid*. Students were also expected to read selections from Terence, Horace, and Ovid, plus additional classical authors.[23] This 1565 syllabus may have represented a goal rather than have been a report of what was achieved. Communal and independent schools followed the same pattern of selective reading: teachers concentrated on certain books of the *Aeneid* and added what they could from the rest of the Vergilian corpus.

Ancient Roman schools taught poetry in two stages. In the lower or grammar school, students read aloud and memorized passages intended to elevate young minds and to implant good expression in youthful ears. In the upper or rhetorical school, teacher and student scanned poetical texts, paying close attention to syllabic quantity, grammar, and rhetorical figures. They also commented on the text at this stage.[24]

Renaissance schools followed the ancient pattern to some extent. Orazio Lombardelli, Sienese teacher and pedagogical writer, advised the young student to study poetry for moral reasons first. He should read and memorize poetical works because they contained good precepts and great deeds of the ancients. The child would then strive to imitate these honorable deeds, in Lombardelli's view.[25] The teacher may have added elementary exposition on the moral significance of the lines at this stage. But more extensive commentary, with or without allegory, would be postponed.

Then the pupils studied metrics, the skill of measuring the pattern of long and short syllables, in order to understand and appreciate the construction of Latin verse. As a Venetian teacher stated in 1587, "I teach a lesson on metrics (*arte metrica*), that is, about verse."[26] He meant that he taught his students to scan Latin poetry. Renaissance schools restored a skill that had been mostly lost during the Middle Ages. A brief description may help explain what was taught.

[22]Letter of Hannibal du Coudret of 14 July 1551, Messina, in MP, vol. 1:97, 100, 101. Coudret reported what teachers actually accomplished.

[23]MP, vol. 2:210, 211, 214, 215, 216. See also Bolgar's estimate of the number of lines of Latin which students in English Renaissance schools might have read in an academic year. Bolgar, 1955.

[24]Bonner, 1977, chs. 16 and 17.

[25]"gli mette avanti principalmente l'opere de gli eccellenti poeti, acchioche gli legga, e impari a mente. dove sono assaissimi ammaestramenti; e vi son lodati i fatti de gli antichi valent' huomini: acchioche il fanciullo, accesso d'emulazione, imiti l'onorate imprese de' maggiori." Lombardelli, 1594, p. 4ʳ.

[26]"Leggo una lezion dell'arte metrica cioè del verso." ACPV, "Professioni di fede," fol. 193ᵛ, Antonius Adriani; Baldo, 1977, p. 69.

The beauty of Latin poetry depends on quantity, that is, on the weight or length of syllables.[27] Much English poetry, by contrast, relies heavily on accent and rhyme for its beauty. Syllables in Latin are classified as long or short, with the long syllable usually considered to be equal to two shorts. Syllables containing a long vowel or a diphthong, and syllables containing a short vowel followed by certain clusters of consonants, are long. Syllables consisting of a short vowel followed by no more than a single consonant are short. With very few exceptions the quantity of the syllables in a Latin word is fixed. The fixed quantities make it possible to organize complex patterns of "longs" and "shorts."

Some of the most common Latin meters consist of regular measures of approximately equal time. The dactylic hexameter, the commonest of all, consists of six dactyls (– ◡ ◡), although a spondee (– –) may be substituted for a dactyl, since spondees and dactyles were considered metrically equivalent (two shorts equal one long). The so-called lyric meters are usually more complex and cannot be divided into regular patterns of recurring feet. Hexameters are divided at approximately the midpoint of the line by a short pause between words, known as the caesura. Students learning to scan the hexameter must mark the quantities of the syllables and indicate the position of the caesura. Scansion of the first line of Vergil's *Aeneid* illustrates the point:

Ārmă vĭ / rūmquĕ că / nō // Trō / iǣ quī / prīmŭs ăb / ōrīs

Thus, one needs to know not only the various metrical patterns but also the quantities of Latin words. The rules for recognizing the quantity of a syllable are simple. But the student must know the quantity of the vowel in order to determine whether a syllable is long or short. Unfortunately, clear rules do not exist; only long practice enables the student to comprehend the quantity of the vowel in the syllable. Hence, teachers in the Renaissance did not begin the study of meter until students had acquired a sufficient mastery of Latin, which might take three to five years. For example, Jesuit schools of the 1550s did not introduce *ars metrica* until the fourth class, the first of the humanities school, following the three classes of the grammar school.[28]

Students learned the rules from a teacher or grammar manual. Comprehensive Latin grammars devoted much space to *ars metrica*. For example,

[27]The following is based on Allen and Greenough, 1931, pp. 401–27; and Drury, 1982.

[28]"interpretanda ars metrica et exercenda: ad cuius proprium est poesim exercere, tametsi in superiori [classe] legi possit ars metrica ac simplici exercitio tractari." P. Hieronymus Nadal, S. I., "De studii generalis dispositione et ordine" of 1552. MP, vol. 1:139. This was a very early attempt to draft a constitution for Jesuit schools by Nadal (1507–80), who had been the first rector of the Jesuit school at Messina (Sicily), 1548–52. It is typical of Jesuit school practice of the 1550s and 1560s. It should also be remembered that students might spend more than a year in a single class.

Manuzio devoted all of book 4 of *Institutionum grammaticarum libri quatuor,* about 40 percent of the total volume, to it. He began with a long section on feet ("De pede in metro") and proceeded to discuss numerous intricacies of syllabic quantity: how syllables are long or short, how diphthongs affect length, how to evaluate first, middle, and ultimate syllables. He went through numerous kinds of verses and lines: hexameter, pentameter, and so on. Aldus provided numerous quotations from Vergil, Terence, and other Latin poets, plus Homer and additional Greek poets in the original, as illustrations.[29] But he gave few general rules and offered inadequate guidance on the very difficult question of the quantity of vowels. Tosca-nella followed the same procedure in simpler fashion in his textbook, *Arte metrica facilissima,* of 1567. He defined verse, feet, quantity, accents, cae-surae, and so on. Proceeding more slowly than a grammar manual, Toscanella's text gave examples, most frequently drawn from the *Aeneid,* and added vernacular explanations.[30]

Battista Guarini made the case for memorization. Students should memorize some verses of Vergil in order to learn the quantity of every syllable on the basis of the authority and example of the greatest poet. It is also very important that they declaim the lines in such a way that the rhythm of the words draws out the rhythm of the feet, he wrote.[31] Toscanella used memorization in another way: he gave the student some nonsense verses to fix the long and short syllables in the memory.[32]

Giovanni Battista Corradi summarized the pedagogy of scansion. Since verse consists of letters, syllables, and feet, the teacher should concentrate on these, he wrote. Begin by teaching students to measure the lines. Teach them the rules of syllables for several days, then show them how to scan ancient verse. When students have learned the rules of quantity and have acquired some experience, the teacher should give them scrambled verse to set right. Ultimately students will learn more from the ancients them-selves, with the help of a few modern grammar manuals such as those of Despauter and Aldo Manuzio, Corradi concluded.[33]

It does not appear that learning how to write Latin verse was a normal part of poetry instruction. To be sure, some students learned to write Latin verse well. Maffeo Vegio, for example, had already written much Latin verse by the age of 15, and composed a thirteenth book to supplement the *Aeneid* at the age of 21.[34] Occasionally Jesuit teachers asked students to

[29]See Manuzio, 1549.

[30]Toscanella, 1567b.

[31]"Qua propter Virgilii carmina memoriae mandent ut ad omnem syllabae quantitatem optimi poetae auctoritate nitantur ex exemplo; declamare autem etiam in his oportebit, ut assiduitate pedum numerum etiam solo verborum cantu annotent." Battista Guarini, *De ordine docendi et discendi,* in Garin, ed., 1958, p. 448.

[32]Toscanella, 1567b, pp. 55^{r-v}.

[33]Corradi, 1654, pp. 776–78, 811.

[34]Brinton, 1930, pp. 9 et passim.

compose Latin verses for holiday celebrations or as an alternative to prose composition.[35] But practice in writing verse did not have a regular place in the Jesuit curriculum. Overall, pedagogical theorists did not mention teaching verse composition, and teachers did not report that they taught it.

THE PARAPHRASE-COMMENTARY

The heart of teaching for much of the curriculum in the Latin school was the paraphrase-commentary. A great deal of Renaissance instruction on individual texts of different subject matter proceeded through detailed commentary. The teacher read, paraphrased, and explained the text word by word.

The paraphrase-commentary came from the ancient world. Commentaries written by late Roman grammarians, such as Servius's commentary on Vergil and Donatus's commentary on Terence, served as examples. Priscian's bulky paraphrase-commentary on the first twelve lines of the *Aeneid* also became a historical model.[36] By the time of the Renaissance, the paraphrase-commentary served the student from his first serious reading of a text through university studies. The teacher might offer a simple paraphrase to 12 year olds, to be followed by more comprehensive treatment in the secondary school. The university professor commented at length on the basis of his own research, while the degree candidate wrote down as complete a set of notes as possible to serve his future needs.

The teacher began his commentary by paraphrasing the text with numerous synonyms in order to ensure that the student thoroughly understood every word. He then discussed grammatical, rhetorical, etymological, and philological points, sometimes launching a lengthy discussion from a single word. He might explain the word's derivation, note its Greek origin if necessary, and present passages from other ancient texts which contained the word. He explained unfamiliar persons, places, and customs, thereby deepening the student's historical, geographical, and mythological knowledge of the ancient world. And he presented an allegorical-cum-moral interpretation of the text. The student took notes.

The paraphrase-commentary provided methodological unity in Latin education from elementary school through university training. A student's knowledge grew as successive teachers instructed using the same approach. The paraphrase-commentary also served scholars and teachers well, because each commentator might add additional rhetorical figures, ancient parallels, and interpretative lessons. Commentators seldom if ever deleted scholarship. Printing made it easier to preserve the old and to add new learning. Indeed, sixteenth-century editions of standard classical

[35]MP, vol. 1:101; vol. 2:91, 246, 535, 563.
[36]Marrou, 1964, pp. 375–77; J. Murphy, 1981, pp. 139–40.

authors often surrounded a few lines of text with waves of commentary in small type. The original text became a tiny island of text lost in an endless sea of erudition.

The paraphrase-commentary began modestly. A sixteenth-century pedagogue defined paraphrasing as repeating the passage "with other words, sometimes less, sometimes more, sometimes an equal number [in order to] convey gracefully the same meaning as the author."[37] The teacher paraphrased a passage in Latin synonyms to make sure that the pupils fully understood every word.

The opening lines of Vergil's *Aeneid* (I.1–3) read as follows:

> Arma virumque cano Troiae qui primus ab oris
> Italiam fato profugus, Laviniaque venit
> litora, . . .

> Arms I sing and the man who first from the coasts of Troy,
> exiled by fate, came to Italy and Lavinian shores:

Here is one teacher's paraphrase:

Ego Virgilius, cano, id est canto, arma, id est bella, que, pro &, virum, scilicet Aeneam illum hominem fortissimum, qui, id est Aeneas, primus, id est ante alios, profugus, id est exul, fato, id est deorum praeordinatione, venit, accessit Italiam, pro in Italiam, ab oris, id est a regionibus, Troiae illius provinciae, & civitatis in Phrigia.

I, Vergil, sing, that is, I recite poetry about arms, that is, wars, *que* means and, the man, namely Aeneas, that bravest of men, who, that is, Aeneas, first, that is, before the others, was a fugitive, that is, an exile, by fate, that is, because of the preordination of the gods, came, approached, Italy (for: toward Italy), from the coasts, that is, the region of Troy, that province and city in Phrygia.[38]

---

[37]"con altre parole alle volte meno, alle volte più, alle volte pari dire leggiadramente il medesimo senso dello autore." Bonamico and Paleario, 1567, *Il grammatico*, sig. *2ᵛ. Born at Veroli near Rome in 1503, Paleario (Antonio della Paglia) studied in Rome and taught in Siena before assuming the humanities lectureship, the highest post in the Luccan communal school system. He held it from 1546 through 1554 (see Barsanti, 1905, pp. 141–61, 224–25). He taught in Milan from 1555 until arrested for heresy in 1567. The Holy Office condemned him as a relapsed heretic; Paleario was hanged and his body burned in Rome in 1570. Paleario wrote Latin orations, a treatise on the family, and religious works. Caponetto, 1979, is the standard modern biography.

[38]Bonamico and Paleario, 1567, *Il grammatico*, sig. *verso. A word about this source. In the dialogue, "Aonio" and "Maestro Giovanni Grammatico" discussed pedagogical practice in primary and secondary schools. "Aonio," speaking for Paleario, argued for strict imitation of golden age Latinity for paraphrasing. When "Maestro Giovanni Grammatico" offered the quoted paraphrase as a sample of his teaching, "Aonio" criticized it for departing from the words of Vergil. He did not reject paraphrasing; indeed, the whole dialogue assumed paraphrasing to be the basic pedagogical tool. Later "Maestro Giovanni Grammatico" offered additional sample paraphrases, two of Cicero's *Ad familiares* I.1.1, and another of the *Aeneid* I.1–3. They were very similar to the first. Here is the second sample paraphrase on

When translated into the native language of the listeners (English here), the paraphrase seems redundant. But young students learning Latin probably welcomed an exposition full of synonyms. Paraphrasing had other pedagogical advantages: it clarified the text, underlined meaning, and taught vocabulary within a literary context rather than by means of lists of words. Paraphrasing presented different uses of words and helped the student to understand and memorize the verse. Few students aged 10 to 16 were likely to have learned Latin so well as to have found paraphrasing unnecessary.

After paraphrasing came grammatical, rhetorical, philological, historical, and interpretative analysis of the text. One teacher called this method teaching by means of "Latin glosses," meaning that teachers explained or glossed every word of the text.[39] After the paraphrase the instructor might continue his instruction on the beginning of the *Aeneid* as follows:

Arma: arms precisely are war instruments, but he has put *arma* in place of *bella*, that is, wars, because arms are used, and that is a Latin figure called *Tropus metonymia*.[40] Cicero does the same where he says *cedant arma togae bella paci* because in peacetime one wears the toga, and in time of war one bears arms, and therefore it is a metonymical trope.[41]

The preceding sample is from an edition of the *Aeneid* with extended paraphrase-commentary prepared by a Venetian teacher for the benefit of other teachers. Giovanni Fabrini (or Fabbrini) was born in Figline Valdarno (near Florence) in 1516.[42] He studied in Florence, spent several years in Rome, and moved to Venice to teach about 1547. The references to Venetian nobles, who had been his students, sprinkled through the prefatory letters to his works argue that he taught independently in Venice from just before mid-century until his death, probably in 1580.[43] Most important, he published editions with extensive paraphrase-commentary of the

---

Vergil: "Ego cano, ludo, modulor, meditor arma, proelia, gesta, facta; que, pro &, atque, item, quoque, necnon; virum, troiugenam, troem, Archisiadem; qui primus, ante omnes, ante alios, prae omnibus; venit, profectus est, adivit, tetendit; fato, ineluctabili voluntate deorum, numinibus imperantibus, ordine sempiterno; Italiam." Bonamico and Paleario, 1567, *Il grammatico*, sig. *3verso*. "Aonio" criticized this one for prolixity.

[39]"quel modo nel legger & dichiarare le lettioni latine colle chiose latine." Ibid., sig. *6recto*.

[40]Metonymy is the use of one term to indicate a kindred thing or action.

[41]"[Arma] arma propriamente sono strumenti bellici, ma ha posto arma a scambio di bella, cioè, guerre, che co l'arme si fanno, & è una figura latina, che si chiama Tropus metonymia. il medesimo fa Cicerone, dove dice cedant arma togae, bella paci, e pone arma per le guerre, e toga per la pace, perche al tempo di pace se usa la toga, & al tempo di guerra s'usano l'armi: & però è Tropo metonymia." Vergil, 1581, p. 3ᵛ.

[42]Sarri, 1939–41, is the basic source.

[43]Ibid., pt. I, pp. 623–24, speculates that a *sestiere* humanist of 1576 named "Fabri" was Fabrini. However, the humanist for Dorsoduro turns out to be one Federico Fabri. ASV, Collegio, Notatorio, R. 42, fol. 200ᵛ, 16 February 1576 m.v.

four curriculum authors that the Venetian Senate in 1567 ordered taught in publicly supported *sestiere* schools: the *Aeneid* (first edition 1568), Cicero's *Epistulae ad familiares* (first edition 1561), Terence (first edition 1548), and Horace (first edition 1566). In other words, teachers might find the requisite material to teach their classes in Fabrini's commentaries. Teachers probably found these editions attractive for two reasons. First, they were comprehensive. Fabrini does not seem to have exhibited any originality, but he diligently gathered mounds of information from other commentaries. Second, following the Latin paraphrase, the running commentary explaining the Latin text and linking citations from other Greek and Latin authors to the text being studied was in Italian. Teachers could comprehend and use the commentary with relatively little effort. All four of these editions went through numerous printings in the sixteenth and seventeenth centuries.[44]

To continue with the example from the *Aeneid:* Fabrini went on to suggest a Greek root for *arma* as well as to mention other rhetorical tropes found in the first few lines. Later he offered a geographical note:

Troiae: Troy is a region of Asia and Ilium is the city of Troy, but he puts the province for the city, as one might put Italy for Rome. The poets do this often, as Juvenal does . . . [a phrase from Juvenal follows].[45]

Shortly thereafter he explained the meaning of *vir:*

virum: vir signifies excellent man, which Aeneas was, who was full of every virtue, and it is derived from *vis,* that is, from the excellence of the soul and not from virtue. But *virtus* derives from *vir.* Therefore in the fourth book of this work he says *Multa viri virtus animo, multusque recusat gentis honos.* Nevertheless, sometimes one takes *vir* for male, and sometimes for husband . . . [a quotation from Terence follows].[46]

After a few lines came a geographical and political lesson relevant to Venetian students:

And one should know that before Aeneas came to Italy, Italy had as its boundary the Rubicon River, that is in the territory of Cesena, and today is called the

---

[44]The known printings are: Vergil (1568, 1575, 1581, 1588, 1597, 1604, 1609, 1623, 1641, 1654, 1672, 1675, 1683), Cicero's *Ad familiares* (1561, 1576, 1598, 1611), Terence (1548, 1556, 1558, 1567, 1575, 1580, 1594), and Horace (1566, 1573, 1587). All are Venetian imprints. The list is based on Sarri, 1939–41, passim; Mambelli, 1954; and my own additional research.

[45]"[Troiae] Troia è una regione de l'Asia; & Ilium è la città di Troia, ma pone la provincia per la città, come sarebbe porre Italia per Roma. e questo spesse volte fanno i Poeti, e però Iuvenale. . . ." Vergil, 1581, p. 3ᵛ.

[46]"[virum] vir significa huomo eccellente, quale era Enea, che era pieno d'ogni virtù. & è detto à vi, cioè de la eccellenza de l'animo, e non da virtù, ma virtus è detta da viro. e però nel quarto libro di questa opera egli disse: Multa viri virtus animo, multusque, recusat gentis honos. nondimeno qualche volta virum si piglia per maschio: e qualche volta per marito, però Terentio. . . ." Ibid.

248

The Latin Curriculum

Piffatello [i.e., Pisciatello] River. The country north of the Rubicon, which is Venetian territory that one calls "the Venices," was called Cisalpine Gaul, and not Italy.[47]

Then a grammatical note:

Italiam: he should have said *ad Italiam,* because for names of provinces one puts a preposition with the accusative . . . when signifying motion to place . . . nevertheless in the majority of cases they (the poets especially) change this rule, and the orators also do this.[48]

Eventually the commentary came to the "allegorical and moral meanings" of the opening lines:

He writes that Aeneas is born in Troy. For Troy we must understand the first age of man, in which not reason but the senses dominate. And therefore in that age each person places the highest good on pleasures, not attending to anything except the body, not taking any account of the soul, but he knows well that one must pay more attention to the soul because it is important and perpetual. . . . But when he comes to a more mature age, then the mind begins to be illuminated by the light of reason, at which time, the intellect having been illuminated, it begins to recognize good from evil, and then man begins to walk in the right path. Aeneas, therefore, is born in Troy to show that he was in the first age and could not recognize good from evil, but reason having been awakened in him, he leaves Troy, and begins to think of going to Italy, that is, the civil and holy life.[49]

This allegoresis which viewed the *Aeneid* as a study in the ages of man went on at length. It was not original, for humanists commonly identified Troy with the sensual life. The civic life allegory came, without acknowledgment, from Landino.[50]

Fabrini spent four hundred lines commenting on every conceivable

---

[47]"E da saper, che gia innanzi, che Enea venisse in Italia, l'Italia haveva per confino il fiume Rubicone, che è nel territorio di Cesena, che oggi si chiama il Piffatello. il paese, che è dal Rubicone in la verso settentrione, dove è il paese Venetiano, che si chiamano le Venetie, si chiamava Gallia Cisalpina, e non Italia." Ibid.

[48][Italiam] doveva dire ad Italiam, perche i nomi de le provincie, significando moto a luogo si pongono co la prepositione . . . nel accusativo. . . . nondimeno il piu de le volte (i Poeti massimamente) confondano questo ordine, & ancor gli oratori fanno questo." Ibid.

[49]Fa che Enea nasca in Troia. per Troia noi debbiamo intendere la prima età de l'huomo, dove non domina punto la ragione, ma il senso, è però in tale età ciascuno pone il sommo bene ne piaceri, non attendendo ad altro, che al corpo, de l'animo non facendo conto alcuno, se bene egli sà, che si debbe attendere piu a l'animo, per essere immortale & perpetuo. . . . Ma quando poi egli è venuto ne la età piu matura, allora la mente comincia ad essere illustrata dal lume de la ragione, per lo quale illuminato l'intelletto comincia a conoscere il bene dal male, & allora l'huomo comincia a caminare per la via diritta. fa adunche nascere Enea in Troia, per mostrare, che egli era ne la prima età, e non poteva conoscere il bene dal male, ma svegliata in lui la ragione, si parte da Troia, e comincia a pensare d'andare in Italia, cioè la vita civile, e santa.

Ibid., p. 4ᵛ.

[50]Kallendorf, 1983, p. 536.

aspect of the initial seven lines of the *Aeneid*. This may seem excessive to modern readers. But here was the beginning of the most famous Latin poem of all time, and any teacher would want to establish his authority at the outset through an impressive display of erudition.

The rest of the commentary continued at close to this fulsome length. As a recent study noted, each word of the original text became the subject of a "full-scale dictionary article," and the paraphrase-commentary as a whole a kind of encyclopaedia of ancient literature and history.[51] When delivered by a dedicated teacher, the commentary became a detailed, knowledgeable, affectionate guide to ancient language, history, and culture. It also compensated for the fact that Renaissance students studied a limited number of texts, and sometimes only parts of these. Exhaustive paraphrase-commentary partially filled the lacunae.

Not all printed commentaries were as comprehensive as Fabrini's. For example, a Brescian publisher issued in 1573 an edition of Vergil's *opera* with *scholia* attributed to Maffeo Vegio. In his preface to "the young student," the publisher called the *scholia* brief but useful. The much abbreviated commentary—simply brief marginal notes—omitted the paraphrase and presented a limited amount of information and interpretation. A short comment on the opening lines of the *Aeneid* conveyed the notion that the wars and voyages of Aeneas were an example of the journey of our civic and private lives; the poet depicted the heroic life through battles and taught us to abhor impiety.[52] Very brief additional notes referred to other works and identified a few rhetorical figures. Other printings charted a middle course between the extended paraphrase-commentary and minimal *scholia*. For example, a number of sixteenth-century Aldine editions of the classics gave eight to twelve lines of text and twenty to twenty-five lines of commentary in smaller type on a single duodecimo-sized page. This type of edition omitted the paraphrase but gave rhetorical and other information in condensed form.[53]

What did the student do as the teacher delivered the paraphrase-commentary? He wrote down the paraphrase interlineally on his printed or handwritten copy of the text. He added the names of rhetorical tropes in the margins. And, above all, he copied into his ubiquitous notebook phrases of vivid descriptions and moral *sententiae* pointed out by his teacher. The student then memorized as much as possible. When he had to

---

[51]Grafton, 1981, p. 48. This article and Grafton, 1977, explain well the role of the paraphrase-commentary.

[52]"cum duplex sit operis huius argumentum, bella Aeneae, & navigatio: per navigationem civiles & privatae vitae exemplum exubet [= exhibet], bellis herovam [= heroicam] vitam adumbrat, monet impietatis suspitionem." Vergil, 1573, p. 104, sigs. *1v–*2v, for the preface. Some punctuation has been added to the quote.

[53]Vergil, 1576, and Vergil, 1580, are typical examples.

write a composition, he drew on his notebook and memory for phrases, tropes, and moral lessons to include. At the Saturday oral examinations, he also regurgitated what he had learned during the week. Finally, Vergil's stirring lines—*Arma virumque cano*—stayed with him for the rest of his life.

TERENCE, HORACE, AND OVID

Three other ancient poets held a secondary position after Vergil in Latin schools. For example, in 1587 forty-six Venetian instructors taught Terence, thirty-six taught the works of Horace, and thirteen taught some Ovid. But they taught them more for their style and as sources of moral philosophy than for their verse.

Born a slave in Africa, Publius Terentius Afer (195?–159 B.C.) left for posterity six urbane comedies of manners.[54] Based on Greek plots, the plays dealt with the unhappy separations and joyful reunions of lovers. Terence portrayed domestic conflicts between father and rebellious son, aristocratic youth and courtesan, master and slave; all conflicts were settled in a happy conclusion. The braggart soldier, the parasite, the miserly parent, and the sharp servant made appearances. Virtue did not always escape unsullied, but moderation never lost. Those who pursued extreme courses of action, such as the father who attempted to force his son into an unwanted marriage, received their comeuppance gracefully. Terence's humane comedies of manners in polished verse induced more smiles than laughs.

Medieval scholars and teachers did not know Terence nearly as well as they did Vergil.[55] In contrast, Renaissance teachers from the beginning gave Terence a prominent pedagogical role. Barzizza greatly favored Terence, lecturing on his comedies and compiling excerpts from his works and insisting that students do the same. Barzizza frequently referred to the good moral content of Terence's works. He also judged Terence to be a master of poetic style and a source for correct orthography.[56] In similar fashion, Guarino preferred Vergil and Terence to all other ancient poets. He saw Terence as a supreme stylist, a teacher of good morals, an important source of rhetoric, and a major text for education in the early years. Guarino also habitually cited Terence in his letters.[57]

Sixteenth-century editors, commentators, and even translators praised

[54] I use the Loeb edition: Terence, 1912. For rapid surveys, see Duff, 1960, pp. 148–59; and Gratwick, 1982, pp. 116–27.

[55] See Sabbadini, 1897; Bolgar, 1964, pp. 125, 189, 197, 413, 423, 430; and *Texts and Transmission*, 1983, pp. 412–20. I have been unable to locate Umberto Bucchioni, *Terenzio nel Rinascimento* (Rocca S. Casciano, 1911).

[56] Mercer, 1979, pp. 57, 81–82, 96, 99, 107, 109.

[57] Sabbadini, 1964a, pp. 144–47; Sabbadini, 1964b, pp. 36, 55, 63, 80, 143, 144, 149, 204; Guarino, 1967, passim.

Terence as a teacher of good style and good morals.[58] The editor of a 1542
translation argued that the reader would find in Terence's words "dottrina,
elegantia, inventione, arte, & ottimo stile."[59] The editor of a 1612 translation went further: the comedies were a mirror of habits and a teacher of
virtuous living, because prudence and humanity moderated actions. One
learned rhetorical figures, ways of speaking, conceits, and even humor
from this poet of the pure and polished style. Overall, the comedies
offered a portrait of truth, examples of good habits, and commonplaces of
virtue and vice to remember.[60]

Terence's skill in turning a phrase accounted for some of his appeal to
the Renaissance. His comedies abounded with well-chosen words that
elegantly expressed proverbial wisdom. These became enduring adages:
"Fortes fortuna adiuvat" ("Fortune favors the brave," *Phormio* I.4.203);
"Homo sum: humani nil a me alienum puto" ("I am a man; nothing
human is foreign to me," *The Self-Tormenter* I.1.77). The Renaissance
schoolboy was expected to write these phrases down in his notebook.

A phrase book underlined the point. Entitled *Locutioni di Terentio over
modi famigliari di dire* . . . (Sayings of Terence or easy ways of speech . . .),
the book offered Latin quotations organized under various headings. The
compiler, Aldo Manuzio the Younger, promised the reader that he would
acquire "purity of style and abundance of conceits to ornament" his
writings which would be useful whatever his station in life.[61]

Nevertheless, some attacked the ancient poets generally and Terence in
particular as corrupters of youth. During the Lenten season of 1450, a friar
preaching in Ferrara denounced the reading and teaching of the ancient
poets, especially Terence. He then wrote to Guarino, the most important
pedagogue in the city. Guarino responded with a long and warm defense.
He argued that one studied poetry in order to understand theology better;
hence, poetry aided religion. Guarino defended Terence as a good moral
influence, asserting that his speeches, such as the father's dissection of
his son's life in *Andria* (I.1.35–38), gave good moral advice for sons
everywhere. When Terence described sinful actions, one should condemn
the person or vice described, not the writer, Guarino declared. Should
one burn the Evangelist because he told us that Judas betrayed Christ?
Guarino appealed to Quintilian, who wrote that knowledge of evil was

[58]One finds such encomia, often linked to youthful studies, in the prefatory matter of
most sixteenth-century printings of Terence.
[59]Undated letter of Giovan Battista da Borgofranco, in Terence, 1542, sig. A1v. Obviously he had in mind a broader concept of style than Latinity only, which one could hardly
learn from a translation.
[60]Dedicatory letter of 20 October 1612, Rome, and letter to the readers, of Bartolomeo
Zannetti, in Terence, 1612, sigs. *2r–*8v.
[61]". . . purità di stile, et copia di concetti, che ornando gli scritti vostri, possa esser di
servizio al publico, nel carico, al quale vise te dedicati." Manuzio the Younger, 1585, sig. a2v.

necessary in order to defend what was right (III.8.43).[62]

The issue resurfaced in the sixteenth century. Ignatius Loyola thoroughly distrusted Terence, especially his apparent tolerance of fornication. An attempt at expurgation did not satisfy Loyola, and he banned Terence from Jesuit schools in 1553. Not all Jesuits agreed. After Loyola's death in 1556, Terence made a limited return to Jesuit schools, either in expurgated form or in toto but restricted to "mature" students. Further moral concerns drove him from the classroom for good in the 1570s.[63]

One Venetian teacher volunteered in 1587 that while he had taught Terence's comedies during the previous carnival season, he would not do so in the future.[64] Perhaps Terence's portrayals of young aristocrats who consorted with prostitutes and impregnated virgins alarmed some people. Piero Vettori (1499–1585) in 1565 tried to disarm critics by stressing that the libidinous deeds that created the situations in Terence's plays resulted in good, honest actions in the end.[65] Despite the barrage of humanistic assertions that Terence taught virtue, printed commentaries did not draw out moral lessons but confined themselves to expository paraphrase, grammatical analysis, and explanation of unfamiliar persons and terms.[66] Some instructors developed the moral lessons orally. The editor of a new Aldine printing (1570) of the *Comoediae,* who claimed to have spent years teaching Venetian youths, made this point. One must explain orally to boys that Terence develops virtue. His ingenious artifices and situations engender delight and teach good habits to the young, he wrote.[67]

Renaissance schools also taught Horace. The son of a freedman from

[62]Letter 823 of 7 April 1450 in Guarino, 1967, vol. 2, pp. 519–32, esp. ll. 331–77 for the defense of Terence. For an Italian translation, see Garin, ed., 1958, pp. 395–417, esp. pp. 411, 413, on Terence. The Loeb edition of Terence gives the above citation as I.1.62–66.

[63]Tacchi Venturi, 1951, pp. 604–7. MP, vol. 1:138, 168, 298–99, 438–39, 528–29, 557, 581; MP, vol. 2:425, 520, 534, 561, 589, 703, 742; MP, vol. 4:577.

[64]"Lessi questo carneval passado le comedie de Terentio, ma adesso non le leggo più." ACPV, "Professioni di fede," fol. 201ᵛ; Baldo, 1977, p. 71.

[65]"Ut taceam maiores virtutes ab ipso acceptas: quaemadmodum cum Graecus ille fingat in meretriciis amoribus adulescentium libidinem exerceri solitam, nec feminae ingenuae pudicitiam expugnatam arte ulla in scaenam referri, si quando tamen virgini civi stuprum infertur, numquam non inde nuptias nasci solitas: ut ex principio illo malo turpique res bona atque honesta proficiscatur." Letter of the editor, Piero Vettori, of 17 May 1565, Florence, in Terence, 1565, sig. *4ʳ.

[66]Obviously this is a tentative statement. Nevertheless, examination of two editions with extensive commentary (Terence, 1524 and 1567), plus several editions with limited commentary, supports the point.

[67]"Sed inter caetera mihi animo semper insedit, ut quae facerent ad Ethicen, ea obiter attingerem: ita tamen, ut quanto hic, ex vulgi sententia, Comoedia periculosior est, tanto ibi magis in locis vitiorum, ac virtutum communibus explicandis viva voce apud pueros elaborandum putem: & sic cum Methodico sermonis artificio, reique iucunda festivitate bonos mores teneris auditorum, lectorumque animis distillandum." Letter of Vincenzo Cardato of 1 October 1569, in Terence, 1570, p. 5ᵛ.

Apulia, Q. Horatius Flaccus (65–8 B.C.) studied in Rome and Athens, and then joined the republican army after Caesar's assassination in 44 B.C.[68] After the defeat at Philippi in 42, the impoverished young man made his peace with the regime and began to write verses in order to secure patronage. He wrote odes and epodes, plus satires and epistles, calling the latter two forms collectively *sermones,* that is, chatty essays in verse. Horace used a variety of forms but avoided the heroic epic form of Vergil. At different times he tried to amuse and to inspire; love and wine alternated with admonitions to live the good life of moderation. He praised civic virtue and celebrated bucolic nature.

Scholars in the Middle Ages knew and used Horace, although not so intensely or so often as they did Vergil.[69] The early Renaissance, however, accorded Horace little pedagogical importance. Barzizza practically ignored him in his teaching, and Guarino paid him little attention.[70] Only Vittorino da Feltre and his circle among the early humanistic pedagogues made much use of Horace, but he was always considered subordinate to Vergil.[71] This pattern endured through most of the fifteenth century, probably for two reasons. With their vision of an education preparing boys for the public life of service to the state and devotion to the common good, the humanistic teachers of the first half of the fifteenth century directed their attention to the works that had an immediate, obvious relevance, especially the letters of Cicero and the poetry of Vergil. Second, like their medieval predecessors, they lacked full knowledge of ancient poetic meter. Only after Niccolò Perotti published his *De generibus metrorum* in 1453 did they begin to appreciate the subtleties of Horace's meters.[72]

Horace later became important. The *editio princeps* of his works appeared in Venice circa 1470 (Hain 8866); most incunabular and sixteenth-century printings included the whole corpus in an octavo volume of moderate size. Landino followed with the first commentary on Horace in 1482. While preferring Vergil, Landino praised Horace for his wisdom, style, polished verse, and good morals. Three other commentaries, including one by Antonio Mancinelli in 1492, shortly appeared, and this group of four became the standard *scholia* to Horace. Avoiding the allegoresis applied to Vergil, Renaissance commentators on Horace confined themselves to grammatical, rhetorical, and poetical analysis. Horace steadily assumed a larger role as the Renaissance progressed, as Ludovico Ariosto and Pietro Bembo, among others, imitated his Latin po-

[68]Duff, 1960, vol. 1:363–98; Rudd, 1982, pp. 370–404.
[69]Curcio, 1913, chs. 1 and 2; Curtius, 1963, *ab indice;* Bolgar, 1964, *ab indice.*
[70]Mercer, 1979, does not have a single reference to Horace. For Guarino, see Sabbadini, 1964b, pp. 36, 79.
[71]Curcio, 1913, pp. 41–43.
[72]Ibid., pp. 50–52; Mercati, 1925, pp. 25, 27, 29.

etry.[73] His *Epistula ad Pisonem* (also called *Ars poetica*), with its analysis of different kinds of poetry and its dictum that poetry should please and instruct, influenced many.

Sixteenth-century pedagogues taught Horace as a model of good style and a conveyer of good morals. They used the term *artificium* (art or skill; *artificio* in Italian) when explaining his craft. For example, Toscanella published *Libro primo de gli artifici osservati . . . sopra l'orationi di Cicerone, sopra Virgilio, le ode d'Oratio, & le comedie di Terentio . . .* (Book one of the skills observed . . . in the Orations of Cicero, in Vergil, the Odes of Horace, and the Comedies of Terence . . .) in 1568. In his analysis, Toscanella explained how Horace conveyed his message and the means (fiction, fable, affirmation, negation, etc.) employed. Toscanella did not scan Horace's meters or use technical rhetorical terms to describe Horace's style, but he explained how Horace suited words to thought. Toscanella presented a general rhetorical analysis that demonstrates, once again, how closely the Renaissance linked poetry and rhetoric.[74] Elsewhere Toscanella presented in paradigm form a summary of the *Ars poetica*.[75] Giovanni Fabrini in 1566 summarized the view that moral philosophy could be taught through Horace: "Horace's intention is to bring man to perfection, filling him with those moral virtues that make him perfect, in effect rational and, as a consequence, blessed."[76]

Publius Ovidius Naso (43 B.C.–A.D.17), from an equestrian family in the Abruzzi, wrote the famous and racy *Ars amatoria,* additional poems called *Fasti* and *Tristia,* the epic poem *Metamorphoses,* the *Heroides,* and other works.[77] His works had an immense diffusion in medieval culture and schools; even the *Ars amatoria,* properly allegorized, appeared in the classroom.[78] But his importance as a curriculum author declined in the Renaissance. Neither Barzizza nor Guarino laid great stress on Ovid. Nor, for that matter, did Vittorino da Feltre. Only thirteen Venetian teachers taught Ovid in 1587: one taught the *Metamorphoses,* three did not name a work, and nine taught the *Heroides.*

The *Heroides* or *Heroidum epistulae* comprised twenty-one verse letters, although modern scholars doubt the authenticity of up to seven of them. Each presented a self-contained essay of artful hortatory verse in the form of a letter. A woman lamented a lover's absence or deplored his perfidy or

[73]Curcio, 1913, pp. 68–71, 84–85, 101–3, 140–41.

[74]Toscanella, 1568b, passim. Also see Toscanella, 1562, p. 9ʳ; Toscanella, 1567a, pp. 68ʳ–83ᵛ.

[75]Toscanella, 1562, pp. 73ʳ–80ʳ.

[76]"l'intention d'Oratio è ridurre l'huomo a la perfettione empiendolo di quelle virtù morali, che lo fanno perfetto, & in effetto rationale, e per conseguente beato." Horace, 1566, sig. a3ʳ.

[77]See Duff, 1960, vol. 1:422–45; Kenney, 1982, pp. 420–57.

[78]Wilkinson, 1955, pp. 366–98; Curtius, 1953, *ab indice;* Bolgar, 1964, *ab indice.*

bemoaned the consequences of love. Penelope expressed anxiety for her husband's welfare and longed for his return. Hermione begged her cousin to rescue her from an unhappy marriage. Phyllis sounded the note of innocence betrayed, and three other women expressed bitterness at their desertion. Canace despaired because her father had discovered and punished her for her passion. Ovid borrowed the characters and subject matter mainly from Greek sources, but he endowed the letters with his own acute psychological perception of feminine feelings.

Renaissance pedagogues taught the *Heroides* for style and moral exhortation.[79] The letters taught the reader how to behave correctly and with dignity in the face of perfidy and misfortune. They claimed to express the personal feelings of historical characters caught in human dilemmas, a combination that the Renaissance could not resist.

HISTORY

The Renaissance's most original curricular innovation was teaching history.

Ancient Roman schoolmasters did not teach history or expound on historians in class. Quintilian and others referred to *historia, historiae,* and *enarratio historiarum,* but they meant explaining the story (*historia*) behind an allusion in a poetic text.[80] This could mean that the teacher identified genuine historical figures, located a tribe or mountain, or supplied the genealogy of a character. But most often *enarratio historiarum* meant explaining the myths behind poetry. A Roman schoolboy especially had to learn the myths of the gods. He did not analyze the historical progression of Rome by reading Livy and other historians; nor did he study historical figures as examples to emulate.

Medieval men, including Italians, had even less interest in history as a subject. They ignored the ancient historians; for example, only a handful of references to Caesar can be found before the fourteenth century.[81] Other ancient historians fared only slightly better. Late medieval Italians used Valerius Maximus's *Facta et dicta memorabilia* as a source for their ever-popular treatises on virtues and vices (see below). But they had little or no interest in ancient history as history. The Middle Ages were profoundly unhistorical.

Petrarch initiated the Renaissance appreciation of history. He saw history as biography and a source of examples; hence, he wrote two historical collections, *De viris illustribus* and *Rerum memorandarum libri IV.* Petrarch

---

[79]See, for example, the brief introductions to each letter by Remigio (Nannini) Fiorentino in Ovid, 1555, passim.

[80]Quintilian I.8.18; Marrou, 1964, pp. 377–78; Bonner, 1977, pp. 237–39.

[81]V. Brown, 1976, pp. 89–91.

had moral, aesthetic, and critical aims: he wished to improve the reader's virtue, to set before him an example of good style, and to give true information about the past.[82] History came of age in the first half of the fifteenth century. Bruni, possibly the first modern historian, demonstrated how to write political history dealing with such themes as liberty and the growth of the state in such a way as to preclude the fables found in chronicles. Lorenzo Valla, with his keen eye for anachronism, demonstrated history's revolutionary potential. And Cicero gave history the final stamp of approval in his De oratore II.9.36: "Historia testis temporum, lux veritatis, magistra vitae, vita memoriae, nuntia vetustatis" ("History is the witness of the times, light of truth, teacher of life, life of memory, and announcer of the past"). Practically every discussion of the nature of history from the 1420s onward cited Cicero's bromide.

The humanistic pedagogues repeatedly endorsed history. Guarino praised it as useful and pleasurable. History's examples from the past enable a youth to acquire the experience and wisdom of an old man; the descriptions of events, battles, and places give pleasure, he wrote.[83] Vittorino da Feltre commended Livy, Sallust, and Caesar for their style and eloquence. He also taught Valerius Maximus for the variety and richness of the episodes, although disapproving of the man as a servile flatterer.[84] The pedagogical treatises echoed these points and added others. Bruni advised students to read Livy, Sallust, Tacitus, Curtius, and especially Caesar.[85] Aeneas Silvius Piccolomini exhorted the young heir to the throne of Bohemia and Hungary to read illustrious ancient historians, not barbarously written medieval chronicles full of lies and fables.[86] Battista Guarini urged the study of Roman historians in order to learn the customs, laws, institutions, and varying fortunes of men.[87]

As a result of such high praise, history found a place in the studia humanitatis. Communes decreed that the upper-level Latin master must teach "a historian" along with a grammarian, an orator, and a poet. Although humanists and historians viewed Caesar, Sallust, and Livy as the best models, teachers did not completely follow their judgment. As table 8.1 indicates, Venetian schoolmasters taught Caesar and Sallust but practically ignored Livy.[88] They put in his place Valerius Maximus.

There were great differences among Caesar, Sallust, and Valerius Maxi-

[82]Sabbadini, 1922, pp. 75–77; Kohl, 1974.

[83]Sabbadini, 1922, pp. 77–79.

[84]See the various accounts of Vittorino's teaching found in Garin, ed., 1958, pp. 546, 632, 686.

[85]Ibid., pp. 156, 158.

[86]Ibid., p. 270.

[87]Ibid., p. 454.

[88]The reason is not clear. Possibly Livy's rich prose proved too difficult for students to master. Or it may have been that he marked a transition from golden age Latinity to the silver

mus. The best-known work of Gaius Julius Caesar (100–44 B.C.) was his commentary on the *Gallic War,* his military campaigns in Gaul from 58 to 52 B.C.[89] The Caesarian corpus also included commentaries on the *Civil War* (covering the years 49 and 48 B.C.), the *Alexandrian War* (48 and 47 B.C.), the *African War* (47 and 46 B.C.), and the *Spanish War* (46 and 45 B.C.). Although Caesar wrote only the first seven books (of eight) of the *Gallic War* plus the *Civil War,* the five histories remained together through the manuscript era, and were generally printed together until the nineteenth century. *De bello gallico* provided a straightforward annalistic account. The third-person narrative soberly imparted a great deal of information on military affairs and some on politics. Even though Caesar wrote his two books for the public record and to further his ambitions, he gave the appearance of objectivity. He understated his own role and seldom made overt judgments about men and events.

By contrast, Sallust filled his histories with moral judgments. He openly advocated patriotism and loyalty to the state while condemning those who, in his view, fell into corruption, vice, and treason. Plebeian, senator, and governor, Gaius Sallustius Crispus (c. 86–c. 35 B.C.) wrote two major accounts of Roman politics and·war, the *Bellum Catilinae* and the *Bellum Iugurthinum,* between circa 44 and circa 40 B.C., as well as the *Historiae,* which survive only in fragments.[90] A few other, very brief, pieces, some of them spurious, also survived. Nearly all Italian printed editions in the Renaissance included all of the above in one volume. Sallust wrote lively histories full of analysis of causes and psychological insight. He frequently used the device of putting speeches narrating the causes for actions into the mouths of historical figures; these freely denounced Roman nobles for their corruption. Sallust's prose—brief, jerky, sometimes colloquial, full of novelty and variety—contrasted with Caesar's uniformity and Cicero's stately periods.

Valerius Maximus may have been a rhetoric teacher, but nothing is known of his life except that he wrote the *Facta et dicta memorabilia* between A.D. 30 and 37.[91] This silver age work is a compilation of deeds and sayings illustrating virtues and vices. Each of the nine books presents short Roman and foreign (mostly Greek) historical anecdotes, up to ten or twelve lines long each, to illustrate virtues and vices. Book 1 discusses religion, omens, prodigies, and marvels; book 3 describes intellectual and moral qualities such as bravery, endurance, and degeneracy; book 9 illustrates luxury, lust,

age. Renaissance schools avoided teaching such silver age authors as the two Senecas, the two Plinys, Quintilian, Tacitus, and Suetonius. Only Valerius Maximus of the silver age sneaked into the curriculum.

[89]Duff, 1960, vol. 1:291–302; Ogilvie, 1982; V. Brown, 1976.

[90]Duff, 1960, vol. 1:303–9; Goodyear, 1982.

[91]Duff, 1960, vol. 2:54–66.

cruelty, avarice, and hatred. Valerius drew his material from a wide variety of chiefly historical sources, but he paraphrased, embellished, or otherwise revised them so as to make the stories fit his format. He moralized constantly but also revealed himself to be an apologist for Caesarism. He adopted a complicated, pompous style full of artifice in his effort to make his material yield *sententiae*.

CAESAR, SALLUST, AND VALERIUS MAXIMUS IN THE CLASSROOM

Renaissance pedagogues invariably began by defining the nature of history: its utility, form, style, and goals. Practically every preface to an ancient historical text quoted or alluded to Cicero's dictum; this usually led to the promise that a youth of few years might acquire the experience of centuries through history.[92] Then he would make wise decisions as an adult statesman. Less frequently the editor pledged that the examples of bravery and rectitude found in the historical work would generate good character in the reader.[93]

Pedagogical discussions of history also repeated the distinction among annals, ephemerides, and history made by Aulus Gellius in *Attic Nights* V.18. According to the teachers, annals chronicled events year by year, month by month, and day by day. Ephemerides indicated a brief daily journal of events, a diary. But history was a well-written, ordered, and true narration of deeds that illuminated causes.[94] Humanistic pedagogues rejected annals and ephemerides in order to emphasize their own distance from medieval historical naiveté, even though annals were still produced and read.[95]

Teachers wanted their students to grasp the distinct characteristics of history. The preface to an early-sixteenth-century edition of Sallust grandly assumed that young readers would write history, and listed a series of principles entitled *Viginti praecepta pro historica lege ac stilo pueris animadvertenda* (Twenty precepts of historical law and style to be observed by boys). The historian should not write falsely, nor suppress evil for the

---

[92]For two typical examples, see the preface of 1504 by Josse Bade (Jodocus Badius Ascensius) in Sallust, 1521, sig. AA3ʳ; and the undated prefatory letter of Paolo Manuzio in Caesar, 1571, sig. a2ʳ.

[93]"Le sentenze morali, e memorevoli, di Gaio Sallustio Crispo. Utilissime à formar la vita honesta e laudevole." A heading to a section in Sallust, 1564, p. 197.

[94]See Bade's preface in Sallust, 1521, sig. AA3ʳ; and Toscanella, 1567a, pp. 1ʳ⁻ᵛ.

[95]See, for example, the chronicle of Fra Jacopo Filippo Foresti, which went through many fifteenth- and sixteenth-century printings. *STC Italian*, p. 273; see P. Grendler, 1969b, pp. 165, 167–68, 170, for other examples. From the 1540s through the 1590s the Venetian government ordered "Annali" to be prepared. Still in manuscript, they have been a boon to historians ever since.

sake of reward. Second, he should not use a reverse order of narration, but follow the chronology of events. The precepts continued: avoid digressions and rhetorical ornaments except those in orations in the text. Do not use obsolete or archaic words. Write briefly, because brevity pleases and instructs effectively. Avoid writing in verse or meter, because history is not poetry. Use a uniform, appropriate, "middle" style, but make sure that the speeches placed into the mouths of historical persons fit the individual and circumstances. And so on.[96] The same or similar guidelines for writing history appeared in a teaching manual.[97]

After considering such preliminary remarks, teachers and pupils turned to the reading and study of Caesar, Sallust, and Valerius Maximus. Since no ancient or medieval commentaries on Caesar existed, the humanists had to create the commentary tradition, and with it the teaching approach, from nothing. Guarino of Verona, plus Gasparino Barzizza and his son Guiniforte, also a teacher, made brief marginal annotations on manuscripts of Caesar in their possession, but did not write commentaries. However, Raimundus Marlianus compiled a geographical index that was printed with Caesar's *opera* in Venice, 1477 (Hain-Copinger 4215*), and accompanied practically every succeeding printing in the Renaissance. By the end of the fifteenth century, some historical and geographical information commonly accompanied the text. In the sixteenth century the Swiss scholar Henricus Glareanus (first edition 1538) and Aldo Manuzio the Younger (first edition 1571) wrote full commentaries.[98]

The commentary tradition of Caesar consisted almost exclusively of geographical and historical information. For example, editions of Caesar's *De bello gallico* conscientiously identified the peoples and places in Gaul and then explained their modern names and inhabitants. They informed the reader where the city of Lyon and the Pyrenees Mountains were located and gave the distance between them. They identified and placed geographically the various tribes that Caesar fought. Indexes in some editions listed the modern French, German, Italian, and Spanish equivalents of the peoples, cities, rivers, and mountains mentioned by Caesar.[99] Textbook editions also sometimes presented pictures and explanations of Caesar's bridges, military devices, and the like.

The note accompanying the famous beginning of Caesar's *De bello gallico* turned the passage into an ancient and modern geography lesson. The note informed the reader that Gaul was usually divided into Cisalpine and Transalpine Gaul. Cisalpine Gaul is now called Lombardy, and ex-

[96]Sallust, 1521, sigs. AA3r–AA4r.

[97]Toscanella, 1567a, pp. 2r–6v.

[98]V. Brown, 1976, pp. 92–96. I have examined Raimundus's geographical index in Caesar, 1482; Hain-Copinger 4218*.

[99]Caesar, 1571, sigs. ttt1r, ttt5r. The same material can be found in many other editions.

tends north to the Alps and south to the Rubicon River, which flows into the Adriatic Sea. Venetians and Milanese live in Lombardy, but various ancient tribes lived there in Caesar's time. The note cited Livy, Strabo, and other ancients as authorities.[100]

When Caesar began to discuss Britain, a similar note told the reader that Great Britain was an island also called England. Those born on the island lived in the interior part, whereas those who came across the sea first as robbers, and then settled to cultivate fields, lived on the coast. The island was a thousand miles in size and had been colonized by Germans, Scots, and Picts. It had no cities of any size. Instead, undisciplined, wild peoples came out of the woods and forests to attack unsuspecting victims.[101]

Another note informed the reader about London: "London, the most important town in England, full of banks and trades, has many people. Caesar does not mention this, but Tacitus does. The episcopal city in which are contained kings, princes, the Senate, people, and merchants of England, is located in the province of Canterbury."[102] And so on.

As these examples indicate, students learned modern as well as ancient geography and history from Caesar's works. One early-sixteenth-century translator offered a justification for the contemporary emphasis. Readers of Caesar's works should learn of provinces, cities, rivers, seas, islands, mountains, fortresses, and the habits, opinions, governments, wars, and diverse religions of various peoples, for two reasons: first, "the Gauls" and the Germans have filled "our Italy" with the clash of arms and various tumults, and second, today we have commerce with so many peoples and nations.[103]

On the other hand, commentaries on Caesar omitted the grammatical, etymological, and rhetorical information that loomed so large in the teaching of poetry and rhetoric. This omission followed logically from the prescription that history's style had to be straightforward and unadorned; rhetorical analysis was unnecessary according to this point of view. Nor did the commentaries draw moral lessons from Caesar's works, although teachers may have added a little of this orally. Overall, students learned ancient and modern geography and history from Caesar.

[100]Caesar, 1569, p. 304^v.

[101]Ibid., p. 275^r.

[102]"Londinum, opidum in Anglia insigne, copia negotiatorum, & mercatuum maxime celebre. Non memorat Caesar, sed Tacitus. Civitas est Episcopalis in qua Angliae Reges, Principes, Senatus, Populi, & Mercatores continentur, in Provincia Cantuariensi sita." Caesar, 1482, sig. v4^r; the same is found in Caesar, 1571, p. 608.

[103]"perche havendo gia piu volte Egalli [sic: i Galli] come Egermani [sic: i Germani] ripiena questa nostra Italia di strepiti darme, di rumori & di varii tumulti, non me parso fuori di propositio, che li huomini cosi per questo, come pel commertio, che noi habbiamo hoggi con tali popoli & nationi, habbino mediante questa nostra traductione di quelli luoghi & provincie notitia." Preface by the translator, Dante Popoleschi, in Caesar, 1518, sig. 4^r.

The teaching of Sallust adhered more closely to instruction in poetry and rhetoric. The *Bellum Catilinae* told the story of an internal Roman conspiracy centering on the infamous Catiline, and the *Bellum Iugurthinum* described a North African rebellion. Sallust turned them into vivid histories of intrigue and struggle full of discussions of patriotism and corruption, trust and betrayal. He often invoked fortune, and he delivered numerous moral judgments.

Sallust's preface to the *Bellum Catilinae* began

Omnis homines qui sese student praestare ceteris animalibus summa ope niti decet ne vitam silentio transeant veluti pecora, quae natura prona atque ventri oboedientia finxit.

It behooves all men who wish to excel the other animals to strive with might and main not to pass through life unheralded, like the beasts, which nature has fashioned groveling and slaves to the belly.[104]

An edition of 1521 with commentary attributed to Lorenzo Valla, Ognibene Bonisoli, and Josse Bade informed the reader that "Omnis homines" meant that Sallust addressed all men, that the phrase was plural in number, and that the sentence was in the active voice. *Student* came from *studere*, which meant to apply the mind with great will to a task.[105] And so on.

A teacher who paraphrased the text and explained Sallust's meaning did not have to develop moral lessons from historical behavior, because Sallust did it for him. A little later (II. 5), Sallust stated that a ruler's insolence led to a change in fortune for princes:

But when sloth has usurped the place of industry, and lawlessness and insolence (*superbia*) have superseded self-restraint and justice, the fortune of princes changes with their character.[106]

The comment on *superbia* explained:

Superbia, licentia est. Licentia in pace generat superbiam principibus, ut quisque facit pro libidine quod voluerit.

Insolence is an aspect of license. License in peacetime breeds insolence in princes so that each man does what he wants according to his pleasure.[107]

The commentary continued in this vein, not going beyond Sallust's text in its meaning.

Thus, the teaching of Sallust followed the conventional pattern of paraphrase-commentary, albeit with limited grammatical and rhetorical explanations. Such instruction did not provide the geographical and his-

---

[104]As quoted and translated in Sallust, 1971, p. 3.
[105]Sallust, 1521, p. 1ʳ.
[106]Sallust, 1971, p. 5.
[107]Sallust, 1521, p. 3ʳ.

torical information that accompanied the study of Caesar, perhaps because Sallust's works provided little opportunity for this. Teachers could and did offer abundant moral and political explanation, because Sallust did. But the commentaries did not go beyond Sallust to, for example, add allegoresis. And when Sallust made no moral or political judgments, commentators also refrained from making them. In short, humanists and teachers saw history as different from poetry or rhetoric and adjusted their paraphrase-commentaries accordingly. They respected the differences between subjects and texts. They taught Caesar as a source of ancient and contemporary geographical and military/political lore, and Sallust as a purveyor of political morality.

Seven Venetian pedagogues taught Valerius Maximus in 1587, a figure that put him behind Caesar but ahead of Sallust in schoolroom popularity. The single Venetian teacher in 1587 who volunteered a reason stated that he taught Valerius Maximus for "history."[108] Jesuit schools of the 1550s and 1560s also called Valerius Maximus a historian and taught him as that, although less often than they taught Caesar, Sallust, or Livy.[109] There is no doubt that masters viewed Valerius Maximus as a historian, even though his collection of close to a thousand anecdotes lacked chronological coherence.

The Renaissance inherited from the Middle Ages an enthusiasm for Valerius Maximus. Culled from a variety of sources and organized into a catalogue of virtues and vices, the work attracted men from the fourth century onward. Medieval treatises on virtues and vices imitated Valerius Maximus to greater or lesser degree; other authors borrowed stories and *sententiae* from the work. Petrarch, in *Rerum memorandarum libri*, used Valerius Maximus as model and source. Giovanni Boccaccio may have prepared one of the several Italian translations of Valerius Maximus which circulated. The work's popularity continued undiminished into the Renaissance.[110]

Quattrocento humanistic paraphrase-commentaries on Valerius Maximus originated in, and were intended for, the classroom. An early one appeared under the name of Ognibene Bonisoli da Lonigo, although modern scholars doubt his authorship.[111] Oliviero da Arzignano (1440?–

[108]"et Valerio Massimo de extraordinario per le instorie [*sic*]." ACPV, "Professioni di fede," fol. 23ʳ, Nicola Brunus; Baldo, 1977, p. 47. "*Instorie*" is an obsolete form of "*istorie*," which in the plural means "history." See *Grande dizionario della lingua italiana*, 13 vols. (Turin, 1961–86), 8:611–12.

[109]MP, vol. 2:534, 558, 590, 611, 641, 737.

[110]Schullian, 1984, is the basic study on the *fortuna* of Valerius Maximus in the Middle Ages and Renaissance. Casella, 1963; and M. Grendler, 1973, pp. 40–42 et passim, document his influence on Tre- and Quattrocento vernacular writers.

[111]Valerius Maximus, 1482 (Hain-Copinger 15786). Schullian, 1984, pp. 360–64, doubts Bonisoli's authorship, as do other scholars.

c. 1495), a pupil of Bonisoli's who also taught at Vicenza, published in Venice, 1487 (Copinger-Reichling 5928), an extensive paraphrase-commentary that became the standard.[112] Its introductory matter emphasized the classroom orientation: Oliviero stated in his preface that adolescents should learn to love virtue and avoid vice from history. He judged Valerius Maximus to be most useful for that purpose.[113]

Oliviero's *scholia* and the one attributed to Bonisoli followed the standard paraphrase-commentary form as adapted to historical texts such as Sallust. They explained with paraphrase, synonyms, and elaboration every noun and verb in Valerius, and many other words, as well. Historical personages, events, and classical sources for the episodes were identified; sometimes quotations from other ancient authors expanded points. But the commentaries offered very little grammatical, rhetorical, or etymological analysis, despite Valerius's sometimes complex language. Nor did they draw parallels with the present or add to Valerius's pervasive moralizing. Valerius Maximus might be seen as a moral philosopher, but Renaissance schools treated him as a historian.

MORAL PHILOSOPHY

Renaissance pedagogues neither taught a separate subject called moral philosophy nor read specific texts for that purpose.[114] Instead, they extracted moral lessons from curricular texts. Practically any story of a virtuous or wicked deed might serve as the springboard for a lesson in morals.

Some of Cicero's letters, and sections in Vergil, Sallust, and Valerius Maximus in particular, told graphic tales of good actions. But more often the teacher expected the student to write down in his notebook a maxim or commonplace found in the text that expressed a pearl of universal wisdom capturing the attention of intellect and will. Toscanella defined these "pearls" as sayings not limited to particular circumstances, but so heavy with meaning that they could be written in a variety of letters or spoken on formal occasions.[115] Commonplaces delivered in compressed form the great humanistic union of wisdom and style. Teachers demanded that students write them down. And they fondly expected that in the journey

[112]Valerius Maximus, 1487. See Schullian, 1984, pp. 364–74, for much information and a listing of eight incunabular and thirty-five Cinquecento printings. I have briefly examined sixteen incunabular and Cinquecento printings. On Oliviero, see Mantese, 1964, pp. 741–44.

[113]See the exchange of letters between Oliviero and the dedicatee, Bishop Pietro de' Bruti, in Valerius Maximus, 1487, no foliation.

[114]There is a possible exception. Eight Venetian teachers in 1587 taught Cicero's *De officiis*. Although the instructors gave no reasons, it is hard to imagine a purpose other than learning moral philosophy for reading this text.

[115]Toscanella, 1575, p. 17.

from text to notebook, speech, and letter, something would remain in the student's heart.

The classics taught good morality through imitation. The pupil read about a laudable action and copied down a maxim in order to fix the action in his memory. He was then expected to imitate the deed when the opportunity arose. At the minimum, he would be prepared to mention the honorable action at the appropriate time. Thus, Renaissance schoolboys learned virtue from the ancient past.

Humanists and teachers assumed the existence of universal ethical standards. Of course, with their finely honed sense of history they knew that the ancient world was not the same as the modern. Pedagogues transcended the differences by silently postulating a universal ethics, a kind of generalized Christian moral behavior (without theological underpinning) based on perceived civic similarities between the two societies. They believed that ancient pagan Romans and Greeks held basically the same moral views as contemporary Italian Christians, and that Roman orators, poets, and historians taught the same social and personal values as Catholic clergymen in Renaissance Italy, but without mentioning the Church.[116]

Schoolboys learned adult virtues. As always in the Renaissance, teachers saw children as small-sized adults to be shaped. Thus, good morality meant adult morality. Any schoolboy reading Cicero, Vergil, Terence, Horace, Ovid, Caesar, Sallust, and Valerius Maximus learned a good deal about human nature. He discovered the complexity, beauty, and occasional savagery of secular society, and something about the relations between the sexes—all adult matters.

The moral values imbibed from ancient texts fell within a fairly narrow range. Personal virtues included honesty whatever the cost, plus moderation in all things. The individual should bear adversity stoically. He learned to honor laws, institutions, and customs as well as persons. Social ethics consisted mostly of loyalty to family, friends, and *patria,* especially *patria.* Certain omissions also defined the morality learned: the classics seldom exhorted the reader to challenge the existing order for the sake of overturning an injustice, and then usually to right a personal wrong rather than to correct a general evil. The ancients did not exhort men to exhibit much concern for their social inferiors. Equality between men, or the sexes, had no place in the classical world and little in the Renaissance. Overall, the classics taught a boy to work respectfully for good within existing institutions. A conservative morality of discipline, fortitude, and respect prevailed.[117]

[116]Bruni makes this point strongly. See Baron, ed., 1969, p. 18; and Bruni, 1987, pp. 249–50, for an English translation. See also the comments of Grafton, 1981, pp. 51–52.
[117]The moral philosophy learned in the Latin schools is reminiscent of the ethical universe of Venetian humanism. See King, 1986, pp. 29, 31–32, 37–38, 174–76.

GREEK AND LOGIC

Teacher contracts and communal guidelines for fifteenth- and early-sixteenth-century schools seldom went beyond the standard subjects of the *studia humanitatis*. They might mention Greek, but they never included logic or formal philosophical study; these were not part of the *studia humanitatis*. In the late Cinquecento, however, some Venetian teachers added Greek or logic and philosophy to the curriculum.

The study of Greek in Quattrocento schools began with Manuel Chrysoloras, who introduced Byzantine teaching methods. For the benefit of his Italian pupils, Chrysoloras wrote out Greek inflections in a catechetical manual called *Erotemata* (Questions). By the end of 1417 Guarino produced an abridged version of the work.[118] Two other Byzantine émigrés, Theodore Gaza (1400–1475) and Constantine Lascaris (1434–1501), also wrote Greek accidence manuals, plus brief texts on syntax and the rules for nouns and verbs.

Printing speeded the diffusion of Greek teaching materials, which were still sketchy and written in Greek. Lascaris's grammar first appeared in print in Milan, 1476 (Hain 9920). Aldo Manuzio, the teacher-turned-publisher, did much for Greek pedagogy in a series of publications. He began by issuing the *editio princeps* of Gaza's grammar in 1495 (Hain *7500) and went on to publish composite volumes in 1495, 1502, and 1512. For these works, Aldo drafted new material. He explained the Greek alphabet, presented the Lord's Prayer and other simple material in Greek, gave Latin translations of Greek words, added syntactical material, and composed sample sentences. Aldo then added his new material to the works of Lascaris and issued the whole in a single volume. In the edition of 1512, Aldo produced a reasonably comprehensive manual for the teaching of Greek grammar, although it seems brief compared with his very long Latin grammar. Other editors followed Aldo's lead. Aldo also transferred a little of his introductory Greek material into his Latin grammar in order to affirm the link between the two ancient languages and, possibly, to entice readers to try Greek.

In the sixteenth century Nicolaas Cleynaerts (Clenardus, 1495–1542), a humanist and university teacher from Brabant, wrote the manual that became the standard classroom text.[119] His *Institutiones in linguam Graecam* (1530) replaced all the others and went through three hundred printings and more. Venetian Greek teachers mentioned no other grammar in 1587–88, and Jesuit schools across Europe also used Cleynaerts's manual. A

---

[118]See Guarino, 1967, vol. 2, p. 176; vol. 3, pp. 76–77. For the following discussion of the development of Greek grammars, see Sabbadini, 1922, pp. 17–27; and especially Grafton and Jardine, 1986, pp. 99–106. See Renouard, 1953, passim, for the relevant Aldine printings.

[119]See Bietenholz, 1985, for a brief biography; also see the works themselves.

TABLE 9.1
TABLE 9.1
Greek, Logical, and Philosophical Texts Taught by Venetian Teachers,
1587–1588

	Number of Teachers
Greek	
Cleynaerts, *Institutiones in linguam Graecam*	4
Isocrates, orations	3
Sophocles, *Oedipus tyrannus*	1
Aristophanes, unspecified	1
Total	9
Logic	
Aristotle, *Organon*	3
———, *Categoriae*	2
Toledo, *Introductio in dialecticam Aristotelis*	1
Agricola, *De inventione dialectica*	1
Kayser, *Dialectica*	3
Petrus Hispanus, *Summule logicales*	1
Total	11
Philosophy	
Aristotle, *De coelo*	1
———, *Politica*	1
Total	2

Source: ACPV, "Professioni di fede."

comprehensive grammatical work appearing in the usual textbook format of about ten by fifteen centimeters, it taught Greek by means of Latin explanation. Other scholars sometimes added *scholia*. Cleynaerts also published *Meditationes graecanicae in artem grammaticam* (1531); here he printed a Greek letter by Basil the Great and subjected it to close Latin paraphrase, grammatical analysis, and translation. Printers sometimes issued the *Institutiones in linguam Graecam* and the *Meditationes* together. Cleynaerts also wrote a widely used Hebrew grammar, *Tabula ad grammaticen Hebraeam* (1529).

Despite the efforts of Cleynaerts and his predecessors, Greek grammar manuals were still so concise, and the language so foreign, that teachers had to supplement the material in the manuals to enable students to grasp and remember the complicated rules.[120] And when the class was ready to read a Greek text, the teacher proceeded in the same careful fashion employed for the study of Latin works: summary of the content; grammatical, rhetorical, and lexical explanation of most words; a certain

[120]See the excellent discussion of classroom Greek instruction in Grafton and Jardine, 1986, pp. 107–21.

amount of allegorizing; and endless review. The class normally studied part, possibly only a small fraction, of a text.

In 1587–88, Venetian teachers taught very few Greek texts beyond the grammar.[121] Three taught the orations of Isocrates. An important ancient Greek orator, the Athenian Isocrates (436–338 B.C.) directed an influential school of rhetoric and philosophy. He was the master of the "set speech," the rhetorically correct and smoothly written package of conventional sentiments. He probably never delivered orally any of his lengthy orations, all of which exhibited balance, antithesis, alliteration, symmetry, and long periodic sentences. Isocrates set the standard for Greek rhetorical prose and influenced Roman oratory as well.

The works of Isocrates enjoyed great success in the Italian Renaissance because, like Cicero, Isocrates used rhetoric to inculcate the ideals of the *paideia*. The humane prince or council of patricians who respected the rights of subjects composed one part of the *paideia*. Free citizens who faithfully served the prince for the good of the commonwealth completed the ideal political society. The two orations taught in Venetian schools embodied these views: *To Nicocles* described the wisdom, moderation, justice, and gentleness that a good king must possess, and *Nicocles* discussed the obligations of citizens without losing sight of their rights.[122] The work of Isocrates offered a storehouse of well-turned phrases highly suitable for the mirror-of-princes genre that humanists loved.

The early humanists turned to Isocrates as soon as they became competent in Greek.[123] Guarino translated the *Nicocles* and another oration into Latin; Bernardo Giustiniani did the same for the *To Nicocles*. Printed editions of the Greek text of Isocrates' orations and letters appeared in the 1490s. Numerous Latin and Italian translations and commentaries on Isocrates followed in Italy and northern Europe in the sixteenth century, as his words became part of Renaissance civic discourse.

One Venetian teacher in 1587–88 taught the tragedy *Oedipus tyrannus* (often called *Oedipus rex*) of Sophocles (c. 496–c. 406 B.C.). Finally, a lone teacher taught an unspecified work by the comedian Aristophanes (c. 445– c. 385 B.C.), whose best-known plays were *Birds, Clouds, Frogs,* and *Lysistrata*. The availability of printed editions of most of the ancient Greek corpus, largely through the efforts of Aldo Manuzio and his associates, made the teaching of Greek literature much easier than it had been in the fifteenth century. Few Venetian teachers took advantage of the opportunity, however.

---

[121]The teachers specifically stated that they taught the Greek texts of Isocrates, Aristophanes, and Sophocles.

[122]See Isocrates, 1928–45, esp. vol. 1:ix–li; and Kennedy, 1985, pp. 509–14.

[123]Sabbadini, 1964b, pp. 125–26; King, 1986, pp. 168, 361, 377, 382, 417; and especially Gualdo Rosa, 1984, for the Renaissance *fortuna* of Isocrates.

Despite soaring humanistic praise for Greek as the key to recovering the ultimate riches of the ancient world, the study of Greek lingered at the periphery of the Latin syllabus.[124] Bruni and Marsilio Ficino in the Quattrocento and a larger number of university professors in the Cinquecento became excellent Greek scholars. But Greek failed to find a secure place in the curriculum, because it only served the needs of Latin culture. The majority of Renaissance men absorbed Greek philosophy through Latin translations and commentaries prepared by a few experts. Competence in Greek remained the province of scholars, not the goal of schools. Mastering Greek did not seem worth the effort to the vast majority of Italian schoolboys, teachers, and parents. The rhetorical, civic, and ethical content of the classical world that the Renaissance loved so well was more easily found in Rome than in Greece. Ancient Rome was more "relevant" than Hellas.

None of the twenty-one teachers who added logic to the humanistic curriculum gave a reason or explained how they taught. Indeed, ten of them simply stated that they taught logic (*"lezer logica"*) and did not mention the text. Despite the paucity of information, the few texts named (see table 9.1) suggest that Venetian instructors followed the two main paths of Renaissance logic, the Aristotelian and the humanistic. Aristotle's *Organon* contains the six parts of his dialectical corpus: *Categoriae, De interpretatione, Analytica priora, Analytica posteriora, Topica,* and *Sophistici elenchi.* Three teachers indicated that they taught the *Organon* (presumably part of it, perhaps in an epitome), and two that they taught the *Categoriae.* Another teacher taught the Aristotelian logical textbook (published in 1561) of the Spanish Jesuit Francesco de Toledo (1532–96). A leading figure in late-sixteenth- and early-seventeenth-century Scholasticism, Toledo taught philosophy (1559–63) and theology (1563–69) at the Collegio Romano, and wrote additional commentaries on Aristotle and Thomas Aquinas. The six teachers who taught the logical works of Aristotle and Toledo shared in the period's continuing enthusiasm for this part of the Aristotelian corpus.[125] Nevertheless, Aristotelian dialectic lost some of its medieval intricacy when taught in the Renaissance.

Four teachers taught humanistic logic with two of the most popular textbooks in this tradition, the *De inventione dialectica* of Rudolph Agricola (1444–85) and the *Dialectica* (1532) of Johann Kayser (Caesarius, 1460–1551).[126] Agricola began his book while studying in Italy between 1469 and

[124]I came to this conclusion some time ago and am happy to see it confirmed by Grafton and Jardine, 1986, p. 119.

[125]For a brief overview of Aristotle in the Renaissance, see C. Schmitt, 1983.

[126]For the following, see Risse, 1964; Vasoli, 1968, pp. 147–82, 249–77; Ashworth, 1974 and 1982; and Jardine, 1982. Italian Catholic teachers could not use the humanistic logical textbooks of Philip Melanchthon or Peter Ramus (1515–72), a French Calvinist, after the appearance of the Tridentine Index of 1564.

1479; it circulated in manuscript until finally printed in 1515. Taking a cue from Renaissance rhetoric, writers of textbooks in humanistic logic treated everyday ratiocination, *inventio* (the selection and organization of material), and topics (the classification of arguments, especially less formal ones, according to their appropriateness for a variety of purposes). They emphasized persuasion and probability while relegating syllogism to a lesser position. By contrast, medieval dialecticians had given pride of place to syllogistic reasoning. Agricola and the other humanistic logicians tended to see logic as a branch of rhetoric and to offer logical training that complemented rhetoric. The Middle Ages, on the other hand, had subordinated rhetoric to logic. Finally, one teacher taught the *Summule logicales* of Peter of Spain (1210/20–77), a famous medieval work that continued to serve as a university text in the sixteenth century.

Two external academic influences, one local and the other international, probably help to explain the relatively large number of students learning logic and Aristotelian philosophy in pre-university schools in sixteenth-century Venice. First, the local Scuola di Rialto (often called the school of philosophy) taught logic and the works of Aristotle. Begun circa 1408, the school served as a counterweight to the humanistic Scuola di San Marco. By the early sixteenth century, the Venetian Senate usually appointed to the Rialto school's single chair a Venetian patrician known for his Aristotelian studies or expertise in logic. Indeed, sometimes the Senate designated the appointment as "for logic."[127] Young pupils who expected to attend lectures at the Scuola di Rialto at a future date would wish to prepare themselves in secondary schools. Hence, logic and Aristotelian philosophy continued to exert some influence in Venetian schools, possibly more than in schools in other Italian cities.[128]

Second, Venetian schools, and possibly schools elsewhere in Italy, participated to a limited degree in the European revival of logic in the second half of the sixteenth century. Pupils in Jesuit schools, for example, went on to logic (plus philosophy and theology) if they completed the Jesuit curriculum. The Jesuits helped promote the Scholastic revival of the late sixteenth and early seventeenth centuries at the university level;[129] some of this interest in logic and Aristotle at the university level inevitably trickled down to secondary schools. Logic remained a peripheral subject compared to the *studia humanitatis*, but it did play a limited role.

Locally, in Venice, approximately 13 percent (24 of 183) of the Latin teachers in 1587–88 went beyond the standard humanistic curriculum in order to give their students a broader education; indeed, they taught a

[127]See Ross, 1976, pp. 529–32, 557, 561–66; Nardi, 1971, pp. 3–98.

[128]For the reliance of Venetian humanism on Aristotle, see King, 1986, pp. 98–99, 154, 175, 182–84, 189–90, 224–25, 234, 241, *et ab indice*.

[129]See C. Schmitt, 1985, pp. 11–27.

program reminiscent of the curricular dreams of the Quattrocento pedagogical theorists. They did more than just append one more author; they
added both Greek and logic (as 4 masters did), or several authors and texts,
to the standard syllabus of *Ianua*, Cicero, Vergil, and Terence.

A few examples illustrate the point. Francescus Grossa, the clerical
instructor for advanced pupils at the choir school of San Marco, taught the
Epistulae ad familiares, Caesar's *Commentaries*, Terence, and Horace's *Odes*
from the standard humanistic curriculum. He also taught Cicero's orations, Toledo's *Introductio in dialecticam Aristotelis*, Cleynaerts's grammar,
and Isocrates' orations.[130] One might expect this richer curriculum at the
government-sponsored choir school with its handpicked student body.
But some independent masters also offered more than the standard *studia
humanitatis*. Domenicus Barchinus, a clergyman-tutor to a noble household, taught the usual *Epistulae ad familiares*, but also Cicero's orations,
Aristotle's *Rhetoric* and *Organon*, and Cleynaerts's Greek grammar, to four
boys.[131] Aeneas Piccolominens conducted an independent school of
thirty-four pupils to whom he taught Cicero's *Ad familiares* and Horace in
the morning. After lunch he launched into Agricola's *De inventione dialectica*, Aristotle's *Politica*, Cicero's *Partitiones oratoriae*, and Terence.[132] His
namesake would surely have approved. Anastasius Iusbertus, a lay independent master, taught Cleynaerts and Aristophanes in Greek, the *Dialectica* of Kayser, the *Rhetorica ad Herennium*, an unspecified work of Valla's,
and Castellesi's *De modo loquendi*, in addition to the standard *Epistulae ad
familiares*, Caesar, and Horace, to thirteen boys drawn from the noble and
citizen classes.[133] Even if the above masters taught only brief selections
from this array of authors, the pedagogical range—grammar, rhetoric,
oratory, poetry, history, logic, and Aristotle in Latin, plus grammar and
literature in Greek—was impressive. Although the vast majority of pedagogues stuck to a fairly limited normative curriculum, a small minority of
teachers did much more.

This was the Latin stream. Beginning in the early fifteenth century, the
humanists rejected the late medieval curriculum in favor of a new one
based on the Roman and, to a very limited extent, the Greek classics of
antiquity. Through the course of the fifteenth century this curriculum
developed into the *studia humanitatis*. Further refinement yielded a normative syllabus consisting of a grammar manual, the *Disticha Catonis*, Vives'
Colloquia, plus endless exercises, in the elementary school. The upper
school taught Cicero's letters for rhetoric and Vergil for poetry; it often

[130]ACPV, "Professioni di fede," fols. 134v–135r.
[131]Ibid., fols. 126v–127r.
[132]Ibid., fols. 115v–116r.
[133]Ibid., fol. 43r.

added another poet (Terence, Horace, or Ovid) and perhaps a historian (Caesar, Sallust, or Valerius Maximus). A few pedagogues garnished the core curriculum with Greek, logic, or Aristotle. The Latin school taught schoolboys sufficient Latin to enable them to attend university or to pursue professional careers as civil servants and clergymen. It also expected to train wise and morally upright future leaders of society.

THE VERNACULAR
CURRICULUM

Those students not following the Latin curriculum attended vernacular schools. Boys on the far side of the social divide learned how to read, write, think, and count in Italian. They sought good moral example in vernacular books rather than in the Latin classics. They also learned how to live in this world and to strive for salvation in the next. Not aimed toward university study, the professions, or civic leadership, these boys graduated into the world of work. The vernacular schools prepared them by teaching commercial mathematics, bookkeeping, and writing skills. Less structured than the studia humanitatis, *the vernacular curriculum emerged from the practical experience and lay culture of the Italian merchant community of the later Middle Ages. Teachers added new texts from fifteenth- and sixteenth-century literature until the vernacular curriculum achieved a rich blend of old and new, religious and secular, learning.*

CHAPTER TEN

Italian Literature

n the late sixteenth century, Venetian vernacular schoolmasters taught a variety of Italian works. As is evident from table 10.1, the vernacular curriculum lacked the unity of the *studia humanitatis*. Latin schools began with a pseudo-ancient or humanistic grammar and proceeded to a series of texts drawn almost exclusively from the golden age of classical Latinity, a narrow range of about one hundred fifty years. The Italian curriculum, by contrast, came from the fourteenth, fifteenth, and sixteenth centuries. The Trecento produced a large number of curricular religious texts, but the catechisms came from the sixteenth century. Chivalric romances emerged from the late Middle Ages, to be joined by the *Vita di Marco Aurelio* and *Orlando furioso* of the Cinquecento. Whereas the Latin schools eliminated almost all medieval textbooks, the vernacular schools cheerfully used both medieval and Renaissance works.

The vernacular syllabus developed without any guidance from above. Not a single curricular directive exists, because humanistic pedagogical theorists ignored the vernacular schools. Communal governments supported them but did not tell their masters what to teach.

The books themselves provide the clues to the development of the vernacular curriculum: classroom texts were the books of adult vernacular culture. The large number of surviving fourteenth- and fifteenth-century manuscripts of vernacular curricular texts, often with evidence of lay ownership, points to their significance in adult culture. Moreover, inventories of the possessions of Italians who died in the fifteenth century often included copies of vernacular curriculum texts still in use in the sixteenth century. For example, household inventories of Florentines who died between 1413 and 1425 included the *Fior di virtù, Epistole e Evangeli, Le vite dei Santi Padri,* saints' legends, and "il libro si chiama Troiano in volghare"

275

TABLE 10.1
Vernacular Texts Taught by Venetian Teachers, 1587–1588

	Number of Teachers
Religious: Catechistic	
"Dottrina cristiana"	31
"il catechismo"	11
"La vita cristiana"	10
Canisius, *Catechism*	2
"laude"	1
Total	55
Religious: Liturgical	
Officiae Beatae Mariae Virginis	7
"sette salmi"	3
"officio dei morti"	1
Total	11
Beginning reader: *Fior di virtù*	43
Religious: Scripture	
Epistole e Evangeli	16
Religious: Hagiography	
Cavalca, *Vite dei Santi Padri*	2
Jacopo da Varazze, *Leggendario dei santi*	2
Baarlam e Josaphat	1
"La passione di Cristo"	3
"Vite dei diversi santi"	3
"Vita di San Francesco"	1
"San Domenicho"	1
Total	13

continued

and "cantarie," chivalric romances in verse.[1] These titles appeared again and again in inventories of the fifteenth and sixteenth centuries.[2]

These books migrated from home to school. One can surmise the beginning. During the educational expansion in the second half of the fourteenth century, teachers needed schoolbooks. But vernacular works specifically written for schoolroom use did not exist. To solve the problem, parents sent children to school toting the book or two of the household. Or the teacher brought his own copy. In either case the school found its textbooks in adult vernacular culture. Popularity brought certain titles to the classroom; tradition kept them there. When a new vernacular title

[1]Bec, 1984, pp. 150, 152, 153, 157, 159, 161. Unfortunately, Bec only reproduces inventory entries. He does not identify the titles and is unaware of their significance.
[2]Ibid., passim.

TABLE IO.I
Continued

	Number of Teachers
Religious: Meditational	
Thomas à Kempis, *Imitation of Christ*	4
Columbini, unspecified, probably *Lettere*	I
Cavalca, *Lo specchio della croce*	I
Cacciaguerra, *Lettere*	I
Total	7
Secular: Chivalric romances	
Ariosto, *Orlando furioso*	9
Terracina, *Discorso sopra Orlando furioso*	2
Andrea da Barberino, *Buovo d'Antona*	2
"libri di batagia"	6
"Guerre di Trogia"	I
Total	20
Secular: Pseudo-classical	
Guevara, *Vita di Marco Aurelio*	23
Secular: Miscellaneous	
Dolce, *Osservationi della volgar lingua*	I
Dolce, *Le trasformationi*	I
Guazzo, *La civil conversatione*	I
Petrarch, unspecified	I
"Lettere a diversi a stampa"	2
Total	6

Source: ACPV, "Professioni di fede."

achieved extraordinary success among the Latinless, it also joined the curriculum.

The migration from home to school, from adult reading to schoolroom use, continued throughout the Renaissance. In 1587 ten Venetian teachers stated that children brought books from home to read in school.[3] One teacher said, "They bring grammar manuals, the *Fior di virtù,* and these *Orlando furiosos* that their fathers and mothers want them to learn."[4]

[3]ACPV, "Professioni di fede," fols. 6ʳ, 63ʳ, 104ᵛ, 173ᵛ, 185ʳ, 205ᵛ, 209ʳ, 230ʳ, 231ʳ, 299ʳ; Baldo, 1977, pp. 53, 57, 67, 71, 73, 79. Books brought to school included chivalric romances (mentioned four times), *Fior di virtù* (three mentions), *Vita di Marco Aurelio* (two), "Donatus" (two), *Orlando furioso, Epistole e Evangeli,* a *salterio,* and an unnamed Petrarch.

[4]"I portano i Donadi, Fior de virtù et de questi Orlandi Furiosi che ghe da i padri et le madri che debbano imparar." ACPV, "Professioni di fede," fol. 173ᵛ; Baldo, 1977, p. 67.

Another stated that he taught the *"Fior di virtù, Marco Aurelio, Epistole et Evangeli* in Italian that they have at home."[5]

RELIGIOUS TEXTS

After the primer, vernacular reading began with the *Fior di virtù (Flower of Virtue)*, one of the most interesting medieval books of virtues and vices.[6] An unknown author, probably from northern or north-central Italy, wrote it between 1300 and 1323.[7] The consistent organization argues for a single author, and the lack of an ecclesiastical emphasis for a lay person. The book contained about forty prose chapters each given over to a single virtue or vice. Its Scholastic organization demonstrated the influence of Thomas Aquinas's *Summa Theologiae,* from which it borrowed and simplified definitions. Despite many apparent references to classical sources, the book presented only a very diluted ancient classicism. Instead, the author gathered stories and maxims from various medieval compilations such as the encyclopaedic *Speculum doctrinale* of Vincent of Beauvais (d. c. 1264) and Old Testament wisdom literature, again probably at second hand. It did not draw on the New Testament.

The book's popularity probably derived from its tight organization, vivid stories, and clear prose. The three main parts of each chapter are an animal legend, a series of maxims (in most cases falsely attributed to various classical, biblical, patristic, and medieval sources), and a story with human subjects, all illustrating the dangers of a vice or the rewards of a virtue. Chapter 34, "Intemperance," illustrates the pattern. The chapter begins with a short and simplified definition of intemperance drawn from the *Summa theologiae* of Aquinas. In the animal legend, the unicorn has such a taste for the company of young maidens that he frequently falls asleep in their arms, making it very easy for a hunter to capture him. Here the sentences against intemperance are mistakenly credited to Socrates,

[5]"Fior de virtù, Marco Aurelio, Epistole et Evanzelii vulgari che loro hano in casa. . . ." ACPV, "Professioni di fede," fol. 230ʳ; Baldo, 1977, p. 73.

[6]Discussion of catechetical instruction and the *Officium Beatae Mariae Virginis* has been postponed to ch. 12, because it fits more appropriately into the account of the Schools of Christian Doctrine.

[7]The author has not been identified. Some older studies and a few library catalogues attribute authorship to "Fra Tommaso" or "Fra Tommaso de' Gozzadini" (c. 1260–after 1329), a Bolognese notary who is supposed to have become a monk. But there are too many difficulties to accept this attribution with confidence. There is no evidence that Tommaso de' Gozzadini became a monk, and no information on any "Fra Tommaso." The secular emphasis of the work and the omission of some standard medieval monastic sources argue for lay authorship, but who it might have been remains a mystery. For a summary of the problems of authorship and dating, which can be done with assurance, see Segre and Marti, eds., 1959, pp. 883, 1107–9; and Corti, 1959, pp. 45, 49. The two fundamental studies are Frati, 1893; and Corti, 1959.

Plato, and Seneca. A vivid human story concludes the chapter. There once was the most virtuous maiden, Lacentina, who heard others speak of the pleasures of the flesh. Curious, she decided to sample them.

And she called one who was in love with her, and she slept with him many times. Having had this experience, she began to think about the abomination and horror of lust and about her great shame and about the fact that she had lost her maidenhood and that in no way would she be able to recover it. And she was so saddened by all this that she hanged herself by the neck.[8]

Some of the human stories present examples of heroic Christian virtue in which the protagonist performs an extraordinary act of self-denial or even self-mutilation in order to avoid sin. In chapter 39, a nun about to be violated by a nobleman asks him why. He answers that her eyes attracted him. She then claws them out and hands them to him; the stricken nobleman leaves without touching her (sig. B2ᵛ).

Not all chapters carried virtue defended to such an extreme, nor did the majority focus on sexual vice and virtue. Some recommended worldly wise social conduct. The book tried to teach the reader how to live in society prudently, even to the point of arguing that he must seize the advantage. In the chapter on anger the majority of the maxims did not condemn anger but advised prudence and self-control in one's own best interest (sigs. B8ᵛ–C2ʳ). And in chapter 12, apt criticism of a ruler brought a reward; this chapter exhibited the typical Italian belief that a well-turned phrase would deflect blame (sig. C4ʳ). The book proclaimed a good deal of Christian morality inspired by heroic saintly acts. But it carefully avoided doctrine, theology, praise of the religious life, and ecclesiastical matters and persons, except for an occasional monk or nun. The majority of human actors were lay persons.

The *Fior di virtù* strongly defended women against the charge of being an occasion of sin, an unusual stance for medieval virtue and vice literature. Chapter 7 states that those authorities who speak ill of women are mistaken and that the evils women commit are few in comparison with those perpetrated by men. The *Fior di virtù* argued that women exhibited much more reticence and suffered more in sexual matters than men. Every day they must defend themselves against the deceits and violence of man. The common charge that women often tempt men to lust has no foundation, the chapter concluded (sigs. B1ʳ–B2ᵛ).

The *Fior di virtù* played the same role in vernacular schools that the

---

8"& mando per uno suo amadore & dormi con lui più volte. & facta questa experientia, comincio a pensare [sopra] la abominatione & la puzza della luxuria & la sua grande verghogna: & pensando che ella havea perduta la sua virginità, & che per alcun modo non la poteva racquestare . . . e con tristo tanto che lei s'impiccho per la gola." *Fior di virtù*, 1949, sig. G3ᵛ; I also cite this edition in the text. No critical edition exists. Segre and Marti, eds., 1959, pp. 886–99, print selections from a Sienese manuscript.

Disticha Catonis did in Latin schools: it was a first reader that inculcated good morality. The major difference was that the *Disticha Catonis* offered classical morality and more extensive social advice. Teachers and parents obviously approved of the combination of stern Christian virtue and mildly prudent social advice on how to live in society found in the *Fior di virtù*, for it exists in a large number of manuscripts and its title frequently appears in inventories of private libraries of the fifteenth century.[9] It first appeared in print circa 1471, and fifty-six incunabular printings, some with vivid woodcuts, followed.[10] At least thirteen sixteenth-century and three seventeenth-century editions have also been found.[11]

The *Fior di virtù* came first, and other books, both religious and secular, followed in no discernible order. The only scriptural textbook was the *Epistole e Evangeli che si leggono tutto l'anno alla messa* (Epistles and Gospels that are read the whole year at mass). These books contained the canonical Epistles and Gospels, that is, the two pericopes (extracts) read daily at mass, the first drawn from the Epistles, the second from the Gospels. The pericopes tended to include well-known sermons and parables and scenes from the life of Christ, plus important passages from Paul's letters. Often the two were thematically related. Most pericopes had ten to fifteen verses, but those for Holy Week were considerably longer.

[9]Numerous manuscripts exist. Casini, 1886, pp. 154–59, lists thirty-eight; also see Bec, 1984, pp. 161, 181, 195, 206, 207. I have examined the following fifteenth-century manuscripts: FR Mss. 1702, 1711, 1729, 1763 (dated 1476), 1774; FN Fondo Principale II.II.89; VM, Ms. Italiani, Classe II, 17 (5192), dated 1404.

[10]For a list of the incunabular editions, see *Fior di virtù*, 1953, introduction. I have examined several.

[11]I have found and examined the following sixteenth- and seventeenth-century printings:

Venice, Zuan Batista Sessa, 3 February 1502. Copy: V Rossiana 7219.
Milan, per Lazarum de Turate, 20 November 1502. Copy: NNPM E-18-A.
Venice, Bernardin de'Vidali, 1504. Copy: MH Typ 525.04.393.
Florence, Hieronymo di Rugerii da Reggio ad instantia di Ser Piero da Pescia, 30 May 1505. Copy: FN Magl. 10.5.125.
Florence, Bernardo Zuechetta de Poveri ad istantia di Ser Piero da Pescia, 10 April 1511. Copy: MH Typ 525.11.393.
Venice, Alesandrum de Bindonis, 1517. Copy: BU Raro B 48[8].
Venice, Guilielmo de Fontaneto, 1522. Copy: Berg Mai 1, 1835.
Venice, Giovanni Padovano, 1545 (1544). MH Phil 9560.14*.
Venice, gli Heredi di Gioanne Padoano, 1558. V Capponi V.687 int. 4.
Milan, Vincenzo Girardoni ad instantia de Mattheo Besozzo, 1568. VM Misc. 1419.1.
Milan, Iacomo Maria Meda, 1588. MB E.I.173.
Viterbo, Appresso Agostini, 1622. RCas Misc. 1170.5.
Como, Amancio Frova, 1634. MA S.N.F.I.59.
Viterbo, il Martinelli, 1680. RAles N.g.133.f.2.

The *Fior di virtù* continued to be printed in the eighteenth century. Most sixteenth-century printings were in a small format (either 15 × 10 or 21 × 15 cm.), and had 80 to 100 pages and some illustrations.

The *Epistole e Evangeli* had deep medieval roots. For example, Fra
Simone da Cascia (Simone Fidati, 1295–1348) prepared a commentary that
often accompanied the work. So did Fra Giovanni da Salerno (1317–88),
who made an Italian translation of Fra Simone's commentary "especially
at the petition of women."[12] Their commentaries often accompanied
incunabular printings of the work. Printed editions usually borrowed the
pericopes from one of several available translations of the Bible.[13] Then
Remigio Nannini Fiorentino (1521–81), a Dominican friar and author who
lived in Venice, published in 1567 a new version of the *Epistole e Evangeli*
which added short commentaries. It became standard, enjoying at least ten
printings, possibly many more, in the sixteenth century, plus others in the
seventeenth century.[14] Unlike the short *Fior di virtù*, the *Epistole e Evangeli*
filled a book of two hundred to six hundred pages, depending on format,
additional matter, and illustrations.

One can imagine that reading the prescribed pericopes became a daily
school exercise. The *Epistole e Evangeli* played a dual role as schoolroom
reader and devotional book for home and at mass for several centuries.
Certainly its frequent appearance in private libraries and the number of
manuscripts suggest this.[15] Contrary to the charge of Protestant reformers
that Catholics neglected the Bible, the use of the *Epistole e Evangeli* shows
that Italian Catholics read the New Testament in this abbreviated liturgical
form.

[12]"che io habbia facto questo spetialmente a petitione di femine." *Epistole et Evangeli*, 1495
(IGI 3703), sig. A2v. I know of no studies on the *Epistole e Evangeli*. One must be content with
the remarks on pre-Reformation Italian translations of the Bible in Vaccari, 1952–58, vol.
2:378–90; and Foster, 1976, pp. 452–65.

[13]For the incunabular editions, see IGI 3690–3706; I have examined 3690, 3693, 3696,
3700, and 3703. I have also examined the following sixteenth-century editions:

Venice, Zuane Antonio & fratelli da Sabio ad instantia de Nicolo & Domenego dal Isus
    fratelli, 1542 del mese de zugno. Copy: MH.
Venice, Francesco di Alessandro Bindoni & Mapheo Pasini, 1533, del mese di Decembre.
    Copy: VCini.
Venice, Nicolo di Aristotile detto Zoppini, del mese di Novembrio, 1539. Copy: VCini.
Brescia, Lodovico Brittanico, 1540 del mese di Novembrio. Copy: Berg Mai.
Brescia, Damiano di Turlini, 1544. Copy: FN Guic. 23.2.43.
Florence, I Giunti, 1560 (1559). Copy: MH.
Venice, Francesco Ziletti, 1572. Copy: ICU.
Florence, I Giunti, 1578. Copy: MH.

[14]I am aware of the following printings of Nannini's version: 1567, 1569, 1570, 1575, 1582,
1583, 1588, 1590, 1598, and 1599, always in Venice. Bongi, 1890–97, pp. 253–54 et passim,
provides descriptions of six of these printings.

[15]For the appearance of the *Epistole e Evangeli* in Florentine private libraries, see Bec, 1984,
pp. 150, 178, 183–84, 186, 191, 198, 203, 207–9, 214–18, 220–21, 224, et passim. All these
entries refer specifically to "Vangeli e Pistole in volghare." Additional references on practically every page refer to "Vangeli in volghare," which might be the same thing.

Hagiographical books used as textbooks came next. Many of these were from the fourteenth century, because that century proved to be the greatest in the history of Italian literature for *volgarizzazione*. A work of *volgarizzazione* tried to capture the interest of readers through free translation. Vulgarizers manipulated the material, highlighting some features and diminishing others so as to produce a more persuasive work. They assumed that readers were more eager than reflective, readier to be moved than to study. One can only speculate whether the growth of vernacular schools in the Trecento created a larger audience for *volgarizzazioni,* or whether society's thirst to read stimulated an increase both in schools and in *volgarizzazioni.*

Fourteenth-century writers produced *volgarizzazioni* of books on many subjects but especially of certain kinds of religious texts. Scripture was one; Domenico Cavalca's *volgarizzazione* of the Acts of the Apostles may have encouraged the popularity of the *Epistole e Evangeli.* The translation and adaptation of Latin saints' lives had even greater importance. Through *volgarizazzione,* traditional hagiography became a kind of humane Christianity appealing to a wide spectrum of the population. The vulgarizer emphasized vivid action rather than theological discourse, miracles rather than grace-giving sacraments. Christian figures performed heroic deeds but expressed themselves in simple human speech and understandable emotions. Christ, Mary, and the saints naturally figured prominently in hagiography. But the vulgarizer cast them into a romantic environment of the distant past, an enchanted setting in which even horrible martyrdoms became infrequent and less frightful. The vulgarizer assumed the pose of the wide-eyed narrator of wondrous events.

Members of religious orders, more often Dominicans than Franciscans, wrote many of the religious works that became curricular texts. The Dominicans seem to have been closer in spirit to the urban merchants who now ruled northern and north-central Italy. Some fourteenth-century Dominicans gave up the theological lecture hall in favor of apostolates to the laity. Franciscans, by contrast, abandoned the streets that they dominated in the previous century in order to reenter convent cells, there to argue over the founder's vow of poverty. Franciscan poverty, whether strict or not, did not fit comfortably into the commercial world whence came the teachers and students of the vernacular schools.[16]

The schools used saints' lives as reading matter. While the Venetian teachers surveyed in 1587 were sometimes vague about which saints' lives they taught, two stated explicitly that they taught *Le vite dei Santi Padri* (Lives of the Holy Fathers), a famous medieval hagiographical work. The collection began with the lives of the desert fathers of Egypt, the first Christian anchorites. St. Athanasius (295–373), the patriarch of Alex-

[16]See Baron, 1938a.

andria, wrote them in Greek, and a certain Evagrio freely translated them into Latin circa 371. The stories of other saints' lives were added over the centuries until the work, called *Vitae Patrum,* became a large collection. Medieval and Renaissance Italians attributed authorship to St. Jerome. Domenico Cavalca (c. 1270–1342) translated the book into Italian between 1320 and 1342.[17] Born near Pisa, Cavalca entered the Dominican order and lived in and around Pisa, where he founded a home to redeem prostitutes. Cavalca wrote a series of original moral works in Tuscan. In addition, his *volgarizzazione* of the *Vitae Patrum* became a vernacular religious classic. He translated and rewrote the first long section, the lives of the desert fathers, but anonymous collaborators from his order probably did some or all of the rest.

A vivid episode prefaced the book.[18] During the severe persecutions of Emperors Decius (ruled 249–251) and Valerian (ruled c. 253–260), the Romans failed to break the spirits of the Christians in Egypt by fearful physical torments. Hence, they resolved to tempt them to renounce their faith. A young Christian was led into a delightful garden and made to lie down on a bed of feathers beneath an arbor. He was stripped and tied with chains of flowers. A beautiful prostitute came to tempt him; she roused his lust by embracing and fondling him. But remembering that God did not abandon his "knights," the young man bit his tongue off and spat it in her face as she bent to kiss him. By means of this sharp, distracting pain, the young man conquered his lust and remained faithful to his God. Early printed editions often illustrated the garden setting of the first episode.

Following the opening incident, which had little to do with what followed, the text began to narrate the story of Paul, the first hermit.[19] At the age of 16, he went into the Egyptian desert to await the end of persecution. There he found and lived in a large cave, complete with a clear spring and a palm tree, until reaching the age of 113 years. But his solitude did not last. Anthony, another holy man—a mere stripling of 90—learned from a vision that Paul lived a holier life. A centaur led him to find Paul, and after minor adventures, the two met. The crow who had daily delivered to Paul half a loaf of bread obligingly increased the ration to a whole loaf when Anthony arrived. The two holy men advanced in saintliness as a result of their meeting. When Paul died, two lions appeared to dig his grave with their claws. Anthony then returned to his monastery. The narrator closed with a sermon criticizing the rich and offering the example of Paul, who had lacked nothing, as a better model.

The second life, that of another St. Anthony (d. 356), the abbot who

---

[17]See Sapegno, 1952, pp. 549–54, 569–70; Tartaro, 1972, pp. 71–82, 149; Delcorno, 1979.
[18]Cavalca, 1915, vol. 1:21–22. Carlo Delcorno is preparing a critical edition; see Delcorno, 1977–78.
[19]Cavalca, 1915, vol. 1:22–31.

founded Christian monasticism, began immediately.[20] Born of noble and
religious parents in Egypt, Anthony as a young man entered the desert
when his parents died. Before leaving, he delivered his younger sister to a
convent, using the same method many medieval and Renaissance parents
did to dispose of girls. But Anthony did not live out his life in quiet
solitude; he traveled a great deal and experienced numerous adventures as
he warred with the devil and his hordes. The devil did not suavely tempt
Anthony but assaulted him with the sword. The narrator repeatedly used
the language and narrative style of chivalric romances to describe the
struggles. God called Anthony his "knight." When Anthony wondered
aloud why God had failed to rescue him in a particularly perilous battle,
God answered that he had wished to learn how "valiantly" Anthony
would fight. After Anthony proved his mettle in battle, God promised to
support him always. Adventure followed adventure, with periodic combats against the devil providing continuity, just as battles against the
archvillain did in chivalric romances. The story mixed realism with the
miraculous, as Anthony also cured the sick and exorcised demons. As he
had the life of Paul, the narrator interrupted this story for a didactic
sermon full of personal religious advice: say your prayers morning and
night, be humble, confess your faults to your spiritual fathers.

Cavalca created a work of popular hagiography that told exciting
stories of heroic saints. He avoided discussion of doctrine, sacraments,
grace, and ecclesiology in order to focus on the actions of these saints. He
offered vivid description but few rhetorical devices. The combination of
action and description reminds one of fourteenth-century fresco cycles,
which presented a series of encounters in romantic settings. Indeed, some
artists rendered episodes from the *Vite dei Santi Padri* into pictures. To aid
the narrative, Cavalca often borrowed the episodic structure and vocabulary of chivalric romances. From time to time Cavalca interrupted the flow
of action for simple spiritual instruction that reinforced the example of the
saints. The saints were humble enough that fourteenth-century tradesmen
and merchants might like them personally. And thanks to Cavalca's limpid
prose, the whole exuded the candor of a sincere soul.

Le vite dei Santi Padri had an immense *fortuna.* There were a large
number of manuscripts, nineteen incunabular printings, and at least
twenty-one sixteenth-century printings of the whole work.[21] The full or
nearly complete text contained three hundred to six hundred pages in its
common folio- or quarto-sized printings, very long for a classroom text.
But sections of the work, such as the life of one or a few saints, were also
copied and printed. And numerous writers pillaged it for their own books.

[20]Ibid., pp. 38–87.
[21]The basic bibliography is Cioni, 1962. I would like to add the following printing:
Venice, Fabbio [*sic*] & Agostino Zoppini fratelli, 1585. Copy FN Palat (14) X.1.7.29.

One cannot be certain how much of the *Vite dei Santi Padri* the two Venetian teachers used in 1587, or whether those who taught "vite dei diversi santi" also used parts of the *Vite dei Santi Padri*. One can be sure of the work's great influence and popularity.

Two other vernacular teachers stated that they taught "il legendario dei santi," probably the vernacular version of the *Legenda aurea* (composed 1260–67) of Jacopo da Varazze (Jacobus de Voragine, c. 1230–98).[22] Born at Varazze, about twenty miles east of Genoa on the Ligurian coast, Jacopo entered the Dominican order, taught youths and, later, theologians in a Genoese monastery, and eventually became archbishop of Genoa. The *Legenda aurea* presented about 180 chapters of saints' lives organized according to the liturgical year. Historically unreliable, the lives tried to foster devotion toward God and the saints by means of stories skillfully adapted to an unlearned readership. The work had enormous success in many languages. Translated into Italian in the middle of the fourteenth century, it became the *Leggendario dei santi* taught in Venetian schools.

One teacher taught the story of Barlaam and Josaphat, usually published in Italian as *La vita di San Josaphat convertito per Barlaam,* a Christianized version of one of the legends of the life of Buddha. Long after the Apostle Thomas had converted numerous Indians to Christianity, King Abenner still persecuted Christians in the third or fourth century, according to the legend. Then astrologers predicted that his son, Josaphat, would become a Christian. Abenner imprisoned Josaphat to prevent this; nevertheless, the hermit Barlaam chanced upon Josaphat and converted him. Eventually Josaphat shared the throne with his father and brought him to the true faith. Abenner abdicated in order to become a holy hermit in the desert, with Josaphat later following him. After Josaphat died, his tomb became the locus of miracles, and Barlaam and Josaphat entered the Roman martyrology.

The original text (probably in Arabic) was translated into Georgian, then Greek, and finally Latin in the eleventh century. The Latin version enjoyed wide diffusion in the West; Vincent of Beauvais included it in his *Speculum historiale* and Jacopo da Varazze in the *Legenda aurea*. Translations from Latin into Western vernacular languages followed.[23]

[22]See Petrocchi, 1978, pp. 53–54; and Reames, 1985, and the bibliographies therein. Jacobus de Voragine, 1969, is an English translation.

[23]See *Enciclopedia Italiana*, 36 vols. (Milan-Rome, 1929–39), 6:192–94; and Varanini, ed., 1965, pp. 465–69. It is a short work, about 80 pages in a 15 × 10 cm. format or 40 pages in a 21 × 14 cm. format. I have examined the following sixteenth-century Italian printings:

Venice, Per Ioanne Rosso da Vercelle, 24 December 1512. Copy: VCini 607.
Venice, Benedetto & Augustino de Bendoni [sic], 20 June 1524. Copy: VCini 608.
Venice, Augustino de Bindoni, 1539. Copy: NYPL Spencer Coll. Ital. 1539.
Venice, Daniel Bissuccio, 1606. Copy: V Capponi V.687 int. 7.

Three teachers taught "la passione di Cristo." This was probably the prose or poetic version of the section on the passion from a larger work, *Meditationes vitae Christi* or *Le meditazioni della vita di Gesù Cristo* in the *volgarizzazione*. Although the Renaissance attributed authorship of both the Latin and the Italian version to St. Bonaventure (1221–74), both are anonymous works coming from Tuscan Franciscan circles of the late thirteenth or early fourteenth centuries.[24] However, by the Quattrocento only the section on the passion from *Le meditazioni* circulated widely; twenty-nine of the thirty-one incunabular printings contained only the passion.[25] In addition, the Sienese layman Niccolò de Mino Cicerchia produced in 1364 a poetic version entitled *Passione di N. S. Gesù Cristo* which had numerous manuscript and printed editions. Nothing is known of Cicerchia except that he was a follower of St. Catherine of Siena. Hence, some sixteenth-century teachers might have taught "la passione di Cristo" in the prose version, and others might have taught Cicerchia's poem.[26] Both were dramatic narratives with extensive invented dialogue between a sorrowing Mary and a crucified Christ. The works underlined the human side of Christ's suffering in realistic and pictorial terms, and avoided theological discussion. Like the hagiographical textbooks, the books of the passion of Christ presented what one scholar aptly called "popular humanity" ("humanità popolaresca").[27]

Other teachers indicated more vaguely that they taught "lives of various saints" or individual saints' lives. They probably tapped the rich and varied assortment of anonymous *sante leggende* (holy legends) which circulated in the Middle Ages and Renaissance. These works narrated legendary events in the lives of Jesus, Mary, and the saints; a Marian legend, for example, might relate how Mary performed a good deed not mentioned in the New Testament. The legends were usually "sweet" stories of piety. Sometimes the legends offered assurance that, for example, the reader would not die without the opportunity for reconciliation with God. This easily became superstition, as in the legend that promised a woman about to give birth that if she were devoted to Mary and pinned a copy of the

[24]The basic work is Vaccari, 1952–58, vol. 1:341–78; also see Tartaro, 1972, pp. 144–48.
[25]Vaccari, 1952–58, vol. 1:344; GW 4767–97 for the incunables.
[26]I have examined the following sixteenth-century printings of the prose version:

Venice, Albertino de Lissona Vercellese, 12 June 1505. Copy: VCini 750.
Venice, no printer or date (but 1500 to 1515). Copy: VM Misc. 1018.4.
Bologna, Hieronymo di Benediiti, 1520. Copy: BA 16.Q.II.31.
Venice, Francesco Bindoni & Mapheo Pasyni, 15 August 1531. Copy: FN Palat. D.4.7.71.
Venice, Francesco Bindoni & Mapheo Pasyni, March 1537. Copy: MA LP 2144.
(No typographical information, but first half of the sixteenth century). Copy: FN Magl. 15.3.108.

For the text of Cicerchia's poem, see Varanini, ed., 1965, pp. 307–79.
[27]Sapegno, 1952, p. 542.

legend to her parturition bed, she would live through childbirth.[28] Many legends were written in verse, the ubiquitous *ottava rima* consisting of eight-line stanzas and a rhyme scheme of *a b a b a b c c*. Like the much better known hagiographical collections previously noted, the *sante leggende* carried medieval piety into the Renaissance.

The vernacular schools also used a few meditational religious works, which tried to inculcate good devotional habits, that is, lessons on how to worship and serve God through prayer and mental discipline. Four teachers stated that they taught the most influential and widely diffused European devotional book of the fifteenth century, the *Imitation of Christ* of Thomas à Kempis (c. 1379–1471).[29] Very different from the saints' lives or other Italian religious textbooks, the *Imitation of Christ* attempted to teach the reader the techniques of mental prayer, how to achieve rigorous control of himself, and to make Christ, rather than Mary and the saints, the center of meditation. It embodied the *devotio moderna*.[30]

The spirituality coming from the *devotio moderna* fostered by the Brethren of the Common Life in the Netherlands and northern Germany differed from that of late medieval and Renaissance Italy. The introspective northern *devotio moderna* appealed to the soul to conquer its weaknesses through methodical meditation. Italian spirituality took a warmer, more spontaneous and emotional approach to the spiritual life. It focused attention on the saints because their example moved the reader to do good. The *devotio moderna* emphasized contemplation, Italian spirituality good works. Italian spirituality also had stronger links to the liturgical life of Catholicism than did the *devotio moderna*.

Despite the differences, an Italian version of *devotio moderna* did appear in fifteenth-century Italy. A number of religious writers emphasized rever-

---

[28]I have examined three collections, beginning with twenty verse legends bound together as VM 2444.1. Segarizzi, 1913, pp. 311–14, briefly describes the first eleven. Although lacking titles and typographical information, they were probably published in the middle of the sixteenth century. Each legend has ten to sixteen pages. The first deals with Mary, the confession and penances of Mary Magdalene make up the third, and so on. Another such printed collection is FN E.6.5.2, forty-five "leggende, commedie spirituali e canzoni sacre," as the catalogue entry accurately describes them. Printed mostly in Florence between 1537 and 1633, they include legends of Sts. Albert and Basil, tales taken from the *Vite dei Santi Padri*, and much other material. V Capponi V. 687 collects thirteen legends, the majority printed between 1602 and 1616. Again they are anonymous, in verse, and range from eight to thirty-two pages each. Also see Battelli, ed., 1928, a fine collection based on many manuscript sources.

[29]Renaissance Italian printings attributed authorship to "Giovanni Gerson," i.e., Jean Gerson (1363–1429), chancellor of the University of Paris. Two modern Italian scholars have also argued that the author was "Giovanni Gersen," a thirteenth-century Benedictine. Neither claim has won much support. See Post, 1968, pp. 525–33.

[30]Although a large literature on the *devotio moderna* exists, Post, 1968, is the standard work. See pp. 521–36 for the *Imitation of Christ*.

ence toward Christ as an intellectual and volitional act in terms reminiscent of the northern movement. Whether or not they did so under the influence of the northern *devotio moderna* is difficult to determine.[31] In any case, the *Imitation of Christ* was the only foreign religious work widely read in Italy before the invasion of Spanish spirituality in the late Cinquecento. The first incunabular printing (in Latin) appeared in Venice, 1483, to be followed by eleven other incunabular printings in Latin and eleven in Italian.[32] The book continued to be frequently published, especially in Italian, through the sixteenth century and beyond.[33] And it found its way into a few vernacular schools.

Individual teachers used three other devotional and mystical texts. One taught an unnamed work by Blessed Giovanni Columbini, more than likely his *Lettere*. Columbini (c. 1304–67) was a Sienese merchant, member of the government, husband, and father until circa 1355, when he underwent a religious conversion. He then disposed of his goods and devoted himself to preaching. He gathered a group of disciples who became a religious order usually called the Gesuati. A mystic in the main line of Christian and especially Franciscan mysticism, Columbini expressed his desire for union with God in simple, warm, human terms in his letters.[34]

Another teacher taught Cavalca's *Lo specchio della Croce,* a devotional work that continued to be printed and read in the Cinquecento.[35] The master of a combined Latin and vernacular school taught the *Lettere spirituali* of Bonsignore Cacciaguerra. Born in 1495 in Siena, Cacciaguerra was a merchant who after suffering financial disaster became a secular priest. He lived in Naples and Rome, where, until he died in 1566, he frequented the circle around St. Philip Neri. Cacciaguerra wrote several mystical works; his *Lettere spirituali* (1563, followed by expanded versions) appeared at least ten times through 1588.[36]

The vernacular schools taught a cross-section of the available religious literature, but not in equal proportions. The *Fior di virtù* (more a moral

[31]See Petrocchi, 1978, pp. 125–54; and Pesce, 1969, vol. 1:268–75.

[32]See IGI 5107–11, 5115–16, 5121–22, 5124–25, 5127–38.

[33]The presses produced a very large number of printings of the *Imitation of Christ* in Italian. For example, Harvard University libraries hold twenty-two Italian printings of the sixteenth century and thirteen more of the seventeenth century. This is by no means all of them. I have examined the following editions: Venice, 1491 (Hain 9129); Florence, 1494 (Hain 9131); Venice, 1502; Florence, 1505; Florence, 1522; Venice, 1538; Venice, 1540; Venice, 1563; Venice, 1571; Florence, 1573; and Florence, 1574.

[34]See Sapegno, 1952, pp. 510–15; Tartaro, 1972, pp. 95–99; De Luca, ed., 1954, pp. 103–16, for four letters.

[35]For fifteenth- and sixteenth-century printings, see *STC Italian,* pp. 161, 636; and Bongi, 1890–97, passim.

[36]See De Maio, 1965.

than a religious work), scripture within the liturgical framework of the mass, and romantic hagiography dominated. Schools used meditational and devotional works less often, mysticism very seldom, and theology never. None of the works was written in what might be described as difficult Italian; indeed, several stood out for their simple, limpid prose. Fourteenth-century authors dominated; in this sense, vernacular schools remained faithful to their late medieval roots. The texts appealed to Christians of all kinds; even the texts written by clergymen addressed lay religious concerns as much as or more than clerical ones, an appropriate approach for the schools. Obviously, these books expressed adult religious culture.

The religious textbooks of the vernacular schools repeated themes from the mainstream of medieval Catholic spirituality. These books narrated stories of heroic saints, stressed deeds more than contemplation, and gave piety a human face, but they ignored doctrine and theology. By contrast, innovative humanistic scholars questioned Scholastic theological certitudes and had begun to approach God in new ways. The Latin schools under their influence taught ethics through classical reading rather than through hagiography. The two curricula implied some religious diversity: classical text and saint's life are not the same. But differences should not be exaggerated. One can agree with the humanists that the moral universes of Cicero and the saints were very similar. And Renaissance Latin teachers did not tell their students to make sacrifices to pagan deities. Still, subtle religious differences of attitude or nuance might exist between the graduates of Latin schools and the graduates of vernacular schools. This was one of several consequences of the cultural and social divide created by the two curricula.

Because the vernacular schools taught Trecento religious books, the late medieval devotional world of saints, prayers, and good works lived on in the sixteenth century for a significant part of the population. One wonders if the continuation of medieval piety in the vernacular schools prepared the ground for the Catholic Reformation, or at least helped create a receptive audience for renewal. Whatever the answer, the religious books of Renaissance vernacular schools perpetuated late medieval Italian spirituality.

CHIVALRIC ROMANCES

Some vernacular reading offered escapist entertainment rather than edification and good morality. After the earliest books, such as the *Fior di virtù*, the vernacular schools taught what the Venetian teachers called "libri de batagia," that is, "books of battles" or chivalric romances. Although teachers treated them as a genre, they did name two titles: *Buovo d'Antona* of Andrea da Barberino and *Orlando furioso* of Ludovico Ariosto. Another teacher mentioned a book on the "wars of Troy," another subject of romances. One Venetian teacher said that he taught these books to satisfy the parents. The pupils "bring to school books of battles, the *Orlando furioso,* and similar books," he said. He added with what may have been an attempt to justify himself: "I teach to the satisfaction of the fathers."[37]

Chivalric romances probably entered the classroom long before 1587. For example, Teofilo Folengo (1491–1544) inserted an episode suggesting this into his macaronic Latin poem *Baldus* (first edition 1517). Baldus as a little boy went off to school, where he made excellent progress for three years. But then he began to read chivalric romances: *I Reali di Francia, Buovo d'Antona, Altobello, Morgante, Orlando innamorato,* and others. Orlando and Rinaldo so intoxicated Baldus that he pummelled his teachers, wrecked the schoolroom, and ran off to become a knight.[38] Although the text did not explicitly state that Baldus read the romances as classroom assignments, the story suggests satirical exaggeration of schoolboy experience. If Folengo based the incident on his own reading as a student in Mantua and Ferrara, then schoolboys read romances around 1500.

A Florentine manuscript further supports the surmise that schools had used chivalric romances for some time. A copy of *I Nerbonesi,* a romance by Andrea da Barberino (see below), carried the following closing notice in the same hand as the text of the manuscript: "Copied by me, Barttolomeo di Iacopo di Barttolomeo Ghalli, Florentine citizen and banker, on this day the 23rd of January 1534; the original was badly lettered and in good part written by children, and it was poorly spelled out. I bought it from Salvi di Lorenzo Marochi and paid him the same day."[39] In other words, the adult banker made a fair copy of a children's book. Could the children have prepared the copy in school or for schoolroom use? In any case, chivalric romances played a role in school culture.

Three bodies of material provided the original sources for Italian romances: the Carolingian cycle centering on Roland and his comrades, the Arthurian matter, and ancient romances.[40] Little is known of the stories'

---

[37]"Per contentar i humori dei padri ghe ne sono anche che portano a schola libri de batagia, el Furioso et simil libri: io ghe insegno a satisfazion dei padri." ACPV, "Professioni di fede," fol. 209ᵛ; Baldo, 1977, p. 71.

[38]Folengo, 1958, bk. 3, ll. 86–120, pp. 90–93. Also see his *Orlandino* in Folengo, 1911, pp. 12–14 et passim.

[39]"Coppiati per me barttᵒ diacopo di barttolomeo ghallj cittadino e banchiere fiorentino questo dì xxiii di gennajo 1534; ella originale era male lettera e buona partte scritta di mano di fanciullj ch'era male chonpitata, quale achattaj da salvj di Lorenzo Marochi e detto dì gnene rendei." Punctuation has been added. From the last page of FN Ms. Nazionale II.VII.3, "Storie Narbonesi nella traduzione di Andrea da Barberino." See also Mazzatinti and Pintor, 1901, pp. 189–90.

[40]The scholarship on Italian chivalric romances is extensive but far from commensurate with the size and importance of this literature. I have found useful the following studies: Rajna 1872 and 1900; Foffano, 1904; Levi, 1914; Gardner, 1930; Russo, 1951; Dionisotti, 1959;

first appearance in the peninsula. Orlando (Roland) and other heroes of Roncesvalles (the battle of 15 August 778 in which Basque marauders wiped out a rear guard of French barons in the mountains of northern Spain) became known in several places in twelfth-century Italy. French pilgrims traveling through Italy in order to embark for the Holy Land from southern Italian ports may have brought the French romances with them. In similar fashion, signs of Arthurian romances appeared in a number of cities in northern and northeastern Italy, especially Padua, Pavia, and Treviso, but also in Cremona, Monselice, Ravenna, and Venice, in the twelfth century. Antiquity, especially the stories of ancient Greece revolving around Troy, provided the third cycle. The legends of antiquity never completely disappeared in Italy after the fall of Rome. Various towns, especially in northeastern Italy, boasted civic legends claiming that survivors of Troy had founded them. Classical and early medieval sources spread the tales of Jason, Medea, Achilles, Paris, and Helen, until they became heroes of chivalric romances.[41]

By the second half of the thirteenth century, Italian minstrels sang of the exploits of Orlando, Tristano, and Jason in the piazzas of northern and north-central cities. The minstrels appeared at set hours and in regular places, such as the piazza next to the church of San Martino del Vescovo in Florence and the arcade of the communal palace in Bologna.[42] Their songs found favor in civic life. The Commune of Siena paid a minstrel one hundred soldi for a ballad celebrating a Sienese military victory of 1255. Governments also rewarded troubadours who sang of peaceful occasions: in 1321 the Sienese Commune paid a minstrel for composing and singing a song celebrating the translation of scholars from Bologna to Siena. Troubadours performed at the dinners of the priors of Perugia in the late fourteenth century. In the following century they descended into the piazza below the Palazzo dei Priori to sing to the people. These recitations became regularly scheduled events in the public life of the city and were financially supported by the commune from 1461 onward.[43]

D. D. Branca, 1968 and 1974; Ragni, 1974. Various histories of Italian literature present good summaries: Bertoni, 1964, pp. 66–67, 79–92; Sapegno, 1952, pp. 600–618; Rossi, 1949, pp. 408–71; Battaglia, 1971, pp. 400–413. See also P. Grendler, 1988b. Cutolo, 1944, is the best bibliography of fifteenth-, sixteenth-, and seventeenth-century printings. Only a minority of the romances have been edited, most of these in the series *Collezione di opere inedite o rare dei primi tre secoli della lingua pubblicata per cura della R. Commissione pe' testi di lingua nelle Provincie dell'Emilia*. See vols. 2–3, 8–9, 11, 47–49, 71, 74, and 89, published in Bologna between 1863 and 1905. Good editions and anthologies are Andrea da Barberino, 1947; Mattaini, ed., 1957; Andrea da Barberino, 1972; and Segre and Marti, eds., 1959, pp. 533–735.

[41]See Gorra, ed., 1887; and Morf, 1892–95.
[42]Levi, 1914, pp. 1, 6.
[43]Ibid., pp. 6, 12, 14, 16.

Italians loved all three cycles but preferred the *chansons de geste* of Charlemagne's knights, or at least they wrote more romances based on the French tradition than any other. One can speculate on the reasons. The first epics of the French cycle mostly described battles against Saracens; gentle love came later.[44] Charlemagne as symbol of Christian unity and near-mythical military leader against the infidel exerted a nostalgic appeal to Italians long after the Holy Roman Emperors ceased to exercise any authority in the peninsula. Perhaps the straightforward action and unambiguous relationships of the Carolingian cycle were more entertaining than the perfumed magic of the Arthurian cycle.

Italian chivalric romances achieved maturity and a degree of independence in the latter half of the fourteenth and the first half of the fifteenth century. Italian authors reorganized the material inherited from French and Bretonnic sources into comprehensive sagas that unified previous stories and heroes. Whole new tribes of characters shared the stage with Roland, while the geographical setting expanded to embrace additional real and mythical lands. A common spirit animated classical, Carolingian, and Arthurian romances. The three traditions maintained their independence of characters; Tristano did not become a comrade in arms of Orlando's. But the wistful love of the Arthurian cycle softened the stern warriors of the Carolingian epics. Heroes and heroines behaved in much the same way in all three traditions, for all the romances alternated battles and *amours*. But epics full of the solemn pursuit of God's will or duty to sovereign gave way to novels of personal adventure. Heroes and heroines with individual personalities replaced knights of stylized virtue. Protagonists became more humanly attractive and psychologically familiar to readers. While much violence persisted, a cheerful optimistic spirit animated the romances, now often rewritten in good Tuscan prose. The key figure, the one who brought the late medieval and early Renaissance chivalric romance to culmination, was Andrea da Barberino.

Unlike most authors of romances who lived and died anonymously, Andrea da Barberino left some traces. Born circa 1370 as Andrea Mangiabotti or Magiabotti (a family from Barberino Val d'Elsa, about twenty miles south of Florence), Andrea lived in Florence. He listed his profession as *cantore* (minstrel) in tax returns, and enjoyed enough success to own the house on Via della Pergola where he lived, plus two farms. He died in 1431 or 1432.[45]

Two Venetian teachers mentioned *Buovo d'Antona*, Andrea's most popular work. It was book 4 of his cycle, *I Reali di Francia* (The kings of France), the narrative of a fictitious royal line that began with Constantine the Great of the fourth century and ended with Charlemagne of the eighth. *Buovo*

---

[44]Russo, 1951, pp. 45–51.
[45]Varanini, 1974; and Andrea da Barberino, 1972, p. 29, summarize what is known.

LIBRO CHIAMATO
BVOVO D'ANTONA,
NELQVALE SE CONTIENE
tutti gli suoi fatti mirabilmente che lui
fece, con la sua morte.

Nuouamente reuisto & corretto, & con diligentia aggion-
toui anchora alli suoi canti tutte le sue dechiaratione
molto piu giusto de tutti li altri uecchii,

IN MILANO,
Appresso Valerio Meda. 1579.

9. Title page of Andrea da Barberino, *Libro chiamato Buovo d'Antona.* . . . In
Milano, appresso Valerio Meda, 1579. MB Castiglioni 26/31.

d'Antona contained features typical of all chivalric romances as well as unique charms.

The story begins with the birth in Antona (i.e., Southampton, England) of Buovo, the son of Duke Guido (over 60 years of age) and Brandoria (about 14).[46] A faithful friend raises the infant Buovo in a village with better air about three miles from Antona. Three wet nurses, continuously available, suckle him for seven years. At the age of 10 he returns to his pleased father, who hires a master to teach him to read.

But all is not well in the household of Duke Guido. His young wife is very unhappy because the aged Guido has "little love for women" and seems reluctant to beget another son. Brandoria, vowing not to lose any more time, sends a message to the sons of a baron whom Guido had killed. Through her scheming, Guido is killed. Brandoria marries his 35-year-old murderer, who takes Guido's dukedom. She then gives birth to a son, Gailone of Maganza, a name taken from the line of archvillains who populate all the romances based on the French matter. Brandoria tries to poison Buovo, now 11, but he escapes.

This beginning illustrated an important reason for the popularity of Andrea's romances: the concrete details of life came directly from contemporary Italy. However fantastic might be the adventures, real life immediately surrounded the characters. Italian noble and middle-class families often removed a child from the parental household and gave him over to a wet nurse for two years and more. Buovo's father guarded against the perpetual anxiety of Renaissance parents that the wet nurse would lose her milk and the baby go hungry by hiring three of them.[47] A large age gap between elderly husband and very young wife characterized many upper-class Florentine marriages in the fifteenth century. The majority of wealthy males did not marry until their mid-thirties; upper-class girls often became brides at 15 and sometimes before.[48] Possibly Andrea's hint of Brandoria's sexual frustration evoked knowing nods from some members of the audience. And Brandoria's hostility to Buovo reflected the contemporary belief that a remarried widow would abuse or rob children of the first marriage of their patrimony.[49] Although Andrea exaggerated such details of life for artistic effect, this grounding in reality persisted throughout the work.

Having escaped his murderous mother, Buovo, disguised and denying his noble birth, is picked up by merchants. They take him to Asia Minor, where he is sold to the King of Armenia, who makes him into a servant.

[46]I use Andrea da Barberino, 1947.
[47]Ross, 1974, pp. 184–95.
[48]Herlihy, 1972, pp. 145–48.
[49]Ross, 1974, p. 201.

After five years of servitude, Buovo meets Drusiana, the beautiful and vivacious daughter of the king, and the two fall in love.

The courtship of Buovo and Drusiana, who are 16 and 14, is one of the happiest and artistically most successful interludes in the romance. After the stark drama of uxoricide, Andrea lightens the mood with the story of the two lively teenagers. Drusiana is spirited, bold, and likable, a delightful character. Buovo is handsome and brave, but very shy. So she pursues him. She arranges a dinner and dance, and orders Buovo (known as Agostino) to serve. When the music begins, she takes him by the hand and leads him to the dance. After two whirls, she asks him his story, and he tells her a sad, fictitious tale that he is the son of a miller and a washerwoman from far away. She cries and he cries. But then they revert to being playful teenagers: water is brought for washing before dinner, and Drusiana throws a handful in Buovo's face! He reddens but does not retaliate. She taunts him: surely you are the son of a miller, because when a girl throws water in your face, you don't throw back the whole basinful.[50]

Then follows a scene often noted by scholars. The members of the party are seated at the table, with Buovo one of the attending servants. Drusiana wants to kiss Buovo.

> She let fall her knife, and then leaned over and showed that she could not reach it. She said, "Agostino, get me that knife."
> Buovo bent over, and when he was under the table, she said, "Here it is!"
> And she grabbed him by the hair and the chin, and kissed him. She picked up the knife and stood up. Buovo emerged from under the table completely changed in color for shame, and Drusiana burning with love.[51]

But they cannot marry yet. Drusiana's father, the king, and his knights are taken in battle by Saracens. Buovo, armed by Drusiana, leads the rescue force. Before going into battle, Buovo reveals his identity, including the news that he is descended of Constantine, and the two plight their troth. Naturally, Buovo and his forces defeat a giant and win the battle. He frees Drusiana's father, who consents to the marriage.

Further perils threaten the pair. The defeated suitor for Drusiana plots against them. Through a ruse, he sends Buovo away to the area that is now Yugoslavia and Hungary, where Buovo is captured and sentenced to be hanged. But he again attracts the eye of a princess, the daughter of Buovo's would-be executioner. She begs her father to consign him into her hands

---

[50]Andrea da Barberino, 1947, bk. 4, ch. 10, pp. 306–8.

[51]"Ella si lasciò cadere il coltellino, e poi si chinava, e fece vista di non lo potere aggiugnere, e disse: 'Agostino, ricoglimi quello coltellino.' Buovo si chinò; e come fu sotto la tavola, ed ella disse: 'Vello qui!' e preselo pe' capelli e per lo mento, e baciollo, e prese il coltellino, e rizzossi. E Buovo uscí di sotto la tavola tutto cambiato di colore per vergogna; e Drusiana, tutta accesa d'amore. . . ." Andrea da Barberino, 1947, bk. 4, ch. 11, p. 308.

so that she may torture him. Instead she confines him in a tower and offers Buovo his freedom if he will marry her. He remains faithful to Drusiana and accepts his fate, which is death by starvation. But every night the girl sends him food attached to the collar of a dog. He remains a prisoner for three years and four months.

Back in Armenia, after waiting two years for Buovo, the king promises Drusiana, now practically an old maid of 16, in marriage to another. She reluctantly consents, but only if the suitor will wait another year for consummation. As the day nears when she must be delivered to the marriage bed, Buovo escapes the tower and rushes to the rescue. Disguised as a pilgrim, he arrives and begs her to flee with him. But Drusiana fails to recognize him. (Protagonists of chivalric romances frequently fail to recognize each other after lengthy absences, as improbable as it seems.) Then he uncovers the birthmark on his right shoulder carried by all members of the French royal line and shows her his sword and the ring given him by Drusiana. She is overjoyed; together they drug the man to whom she is promised and make their escape.

In the course of their escape, Buovo fights and kills various soldiers and guards, the secondary thugs whose bodies litter adventure stories of all centuries. Buovo and Drusiana consummate their marriage and the story plunges forward. The love interest recedes for many chapters while Buovo fights battles and either he or Drusiana escapes dire perils. Andrea continues to insert homely domestic details to promote audience identification. Buovo and Drusiana escape by horseback through the forest—forests seem endless in chivalric romances—even though poor Drusiana is eight months and fifteen days pregnant. The author interrupts to speak directly to his audience: oh think how miserable the poor girl was![52] Before long she gives birth to masculine twins. (The frequency of masculine twins in chivalric romances defies statistical probability.) Eventually Buovo returns to claim his dukedom and succeeds in a great battle against overwhelming odds. He kills his stepfather in battle. Buovo will not kill his mother, but he does insist that King Pepin condemn her to death. (Pepin the Short [714?–768], one of the historical personages introduced by Andrea, was a predecessor of Charlemagne.) She accepts her guilt, repents, and urges her second son, Gailone, to be a loyal subject to Buovo. She is then quartered, probably after being first executed by other means, although the text is not specific.[53] Chivalric romances did not spare women cruel punishment for heinous crimes.

After many additional perils are surmounted, Buovo, Drusiana, and their two sons are united in Antona, only this time it is Buovo who is

[52]"Ora pensi ognuno come poteva fare la misera Drusiana ch'era gravida!" Ibid., ch. 35, p. 350.
[53]Ibid., ch. 52, pp. 376–77.

rescued from a second marriage in the nick of time and initially does not recognize his wife and sons. For the reunion Andrea constructs a light-hearted scene full of embarrassment and laughter.[54]

After this interlude, many more adventures follow. Buovo sails up and down the Mediterranean, coming to the rescue of old comrades in arms with his special sword. His super horse Rondello, more than 25 years old, carries him to victory. Between adventures, Drusiana gives birth to eleven children. Buovo and Drusiana become grandparents and grow old grace-fully.

The author prepares for the end of his saga. Gailone, Buovo's half-brother, is taunted by evildoers for failing to avenge the death of his father. He plots to kill Buovo by sneaking up on him while Buovo kneels in prayer in a small country chapel. Andrea describes the foul deed in precise, pedantic detail: Gailone plunges his very sharp knife into the nape of the neck and through the throat in such a way that Buovo can not cry out. "And so died Buovo d'Antona, flower of the knights of the world in his time."[55] Gailone escapes to the Sultan of Babylonia and denies God and tramples on the cross. Drusiana comes upon the body of Buovo and expires of grief. With this ends the story of Buovo d'Antona, book 4 of *I Reali di Francia*—but not before the stage is set for the next saga.

Chivalric romances exhibited a number of qualities that made them attractive school texts. The borrowing of concrete details from contemporary life has been mentioned. In addition, some romances taught by example high standards of personal morality. Loyal knights, true lovers, and faithful spouses populated Andrea da Barberino's romances. His characters lived up to the ideals proclaimed by Italian merchants, who thought of themselves as loyal to family, city, and religion. Egregiously wicked villains, by contrast, suffered just punishments. Andrea's romances also skillfully maintained the appearance of history. Indeed, he cast his work in the mold of a dynastic chronicle in which real historical personages, such as Constantine the Great, Pope Sylvester I (314–335), and King Pepin, appeared. Historical personages served as fixed reference points around which Andrea's fabricated characters rode. He treated them all with a kind of pseudo-historical and geographical precision by naming dates and places. He absorbed some of the historiographical techniques of early-fifteenth-century Florentine humanism. Finally, his literary skill in alternating breathless action with charming personal interludes must have captivated his readers.

---

[54]Ibid., ch. 61, pp. 392–93.

[55]"Allora Gailone, vedendo bene affisato Buovo a orare, cavò fuori una coltella bene tagliente e appuntata, e di drieto per lo nodo del collo gliele ficcò, che passò insino dinanzi per la gola, per modo che gli non poté fare motto. E così morí Buovo d'Antona, fiore dé cavalieri del mondo al suo tempo." Ibid., ch. 79, p. 424.

When the chivalric romance passed into the High Renaissance of the late fifteenth and the sixteenth centuries, it diversified and became more complex. Unknown hands reworked some of the older romances into *ottava rima* poems without departing from their spirit and character. At the same time, learned poets from northern Italian courts transformed direct adventure stories into sophisticated works of art. As a result, Cinquecento readers in the classroom and out could choose from older prose romances, new poetical versions of traditional romances, and original chivalric poems.

Luigi Pulci (1432–84), from a Florentine noble family fallen on hard times, wrote *Morgante* (definitive edition 1483). Pulci retold the heroic deeds of Orlando and other knights loyal to Charlemagne. But he also introduced two comic figures of his own invention, Morgante the giant and Margutte the half-giant, who burlesqued chivalric ideals through their boasts and deeds. Pulci skillfully combined high tragedy and low comedy. Then Count Matteo Maria Boiardo (1441–94), a noble from Scandiano (near Modena and Bologna) and administrator for the Este princes, wrote *Orlando innamorato* (*Roland in Love*), left unfinished at his death. The poem described how Charlemagne's knights pursued Angelica, who exerted a magical attraction. Full of impossible loves, charms, spells, portents, and monsters, the poem wove a tapestry that jettisoned most of the honorable battles of previous romances.

Ludovico Ariosto (1474–1533), nobleman and courtier of the Este family of Ferrara, followed with *Orlando furioso* (1516; revised edition 1532).[56] Picking up the story where Boiardo left it, Ariosto allowed Orlando to lose his senses through love. The poem narrated the madness of Orlando, the courtship of Ruggiero and Bradamente, the war between Charlemagne and Agramante the infidel, as well as many lesser stories. *Orlando furioso* could be read on two levels. Like its chivalric predecessors, it functioned as an action story of combats and loves, warriors and ladies, and a conflict between good and evil. One could thoroughly enjoy the work on this level. But ambiguity and chance clouded the message, and things were not always what they seemed. Chivalric illusion contended with less courteous reality beneath a pervasive irony. Ariosto frequently upended the tradition with amusing results; he simultaneously honored and betrayed the genre, and he wrote a masterpiece. *Orlando furioso* entered the classroom, the only vernacular classic to win such approval. But whether teachers and students read it as popular romance, sophisticated poetry, or both, is difficult to determine.

---

[56]Although I have consulted only a small part of the enormous bibliography on *Orlando furioso,* I found Ramat, 1954, and Brand, 1974, particularly useful.

Two Venetian teachers in 1587 diverted their pupils from chivalric romances to morally upright *ottava rima* imitations. I teach the book of Terracina and some other works, the greater part spiritual books, to those who want to read *ottava rima,* declared one teacher.[57] He probably meant that he taught the *Discorso sopra il principio di tutti i canti d'Orlando furioso* of Laura Terracina (1519–c. 1570), a poetess from Naples.[58] First published in 1549, this work imitated and commented on Ariosto's poem, one of several such Cinquecento efforts. Terracina did this in an intricate fashion by inserting each opening stanza of Ariosto's cantos into every one of her own forty cantos, and then expanding on these initial lines. Since Ariosto in his introductory stanzas frequently discussed love, fidelity, vacillation, and so on in general terms, so did Terracina. Indeed, this permitted her to moralize much more than did Ariosto. Terracina tried to elevate and allegorize Ariosto's ironic and sometimes morally ambiguous lines.[59] This teacher may have substituted Terracina's *Discorso* and spiritual books for chivalric romances as a result of a strong personal commitment to the strait-laced Counter-Reformation. At least his training suggests this. Although a layman, he had studied at the Collegium Germanicum in Rome, the Jesuit boarding school that prepared priests to re-Catholicize Germany.[60]

Chivalric romances (including *Orlando furioso*) appeared in the curriculum because readers loved them. They did not build character, but they gave pleasure. Indeed, they must have come as welcome relief to children after the relentless moralizing of the *Fior di virtù* and like books. Chivalric romances occupied a central position in popular culture by the fifteenth century and possibly entered the vernacular curriculum at this time. Once arrived, they launched Italians on the wings of imaginative adventure for a flight that lasted centuries. Venetians, Neapolitans, and others still gathered in parks and similar public places to hear minstrels tell their stories of Buovo d'Antona, Orlando, and other heroes in the late nineteenth century and possibly well into the twentieth.[61]

[57]". . . quelli che vogliono imparar lettere d'ottava rima li facio imparar el libro del Terrazina e alcuni altri, ma la maggior parte tutti sono spirituali." ACPV, "Professioni di fede," fol. 151ᵛ, Johannes Baptista de Grimaldis; Baldo, 1977, p. 63.

[58]I use Terracina, 1564. It was reprinted at least a dozen times in the sixteenth century; see Fumagalli, 1912, p. 373. On Terracina, see Bongi, 1890–97, vol. 1:227–29, 269–70.

[59]Brand, 1974, pp. 186–87.

[60]ACPV, "Professioni di fede," fols. 151ʳ⁻ᵛ; Baldo, 1977, p. 63. See ch. 13 herein for the Collegium Germanicum.

[61]See the very interesting account of a minstrel from Chioggia who performed in the public gardens of Venice in Fusinato, 1883.

THE *VITA DI MARCO AURELIO* OF GUEVARA

Twenty-three Venetian teachers stated that they taught the "Vita di Marco Aurelio imperator" or simply "Marco Aurelio," making it the second most frequently mentioned title (after the *Fior di virtù*) in the vernacular curriculum in 1587. They referred to the *Vita, gesti, costumi, discorsi, lettere di Marco Aurelio Imperatore, sapientissimo filosofo, & oratore eloquentissimo,* the usual title for the Italian translation of the *Libro aureo de Marco Aurelio* of Antonio de Guevara (c. 1480–1545). Like their pedagogical colleagues elsewhere in Europe, Venetian teachers found this curious sixteenth-century work irresistible.

Guevara served Charles V as a courtier. Born in the province of Santander (north-central Spain) into an old noble family of modest means, Antonio first arrived at the court at the age of 12.[62] But he did not prosper; perhaps for this reason he became a Franciscan in 1505. Charles brought him back as court preacher to reward him for his services to the Crown during the revolt of the *Communidades* in 1521. Thereafter he served his monarch in Spain, Tunis, and Italy, discharging a number of political and administrative tasks in addition to preaching. The emperor appointed him court historian in late 1526, although Guevara never produced a history. He did receive several benefices, including the bishopric of Mondoñedo in Galicia in 1537. In later years Guevara devoted his time to administering his diocese and writing. He died in Mondoñedo on 3 April 1545.

Guevara began writing the *Vita di Marco Aurelio* in 1517 or 1518 when he first met the young King Charles I, not yet emperor.[63] Upon completion, the work circulated in manuscript for an indeterminate time before appearing in an unauthorized printing entitled *Libro aureo de Marco Aurelio: emperador y eloquentissimo orador* (Sevilla: Jacobo Cromberger, 27-II-1528).[64] Guevara immediately prepared a revised and much longer version, in effect producing a second, different, work entitled *Libro llamado relox de principes en el qual incorporado el muy famoso libro de Marco Aurelio* (Valladolid: Nicolás Tierri, 8-IV-1529). The two books enjoyed enormous popularity; more than two hundred printings, including Dutch, English, French, German, Italian, and Latin translations, appeared in the sixteenth and seventeenth centuries.[65] Guevara later published other courtly, historical, and religious works.

An abridged Italian translation of the *Libro aureo de Marco Aurelio* appeared in 1542.[66] A full, but somewhat free, new Italian translation

[62]A large body of secondary literature on Guevara exists. I have used Costes, 1925–26; Grey, 1973; Jones, 1975; and Redondo, 1976.

[63]Redondo, 1976, p. 466.

[64]Ibid., pp. 513–15.

[65]See the bibliographies listed at the end of Appendix 2 for the editions.

[66]For further information on the Italian translations and their printings, see Appendix 2.

appeared in Venice, 1544, attributed to Sebastiano Fausto da Longiano, a prolific if undistinguished author and translator for the Venetian vernacular presses. This version, 300 to 350 pages in the usual textbook format of about ten by fifteen centimeters, had at least twenty-one printings by the end of the century and five or more in the seventeenth century. This second translation became the school text used in Venice and no doubt other Italian towns.

Guevara wrote a fictional, very rhetorical book on Emperor Marcus Aurelius which pretended to be an authentic ancient biography. A brief prologue made this claim. In search of ancient wisdom, wrote Guevara, I found a reference praising an ancient book on Marcus Aurelius. After a long search, I found it in Florence among the manuscripts gathered by Cosimo de' Medici. I have translated this "golden book" of "sentences" whose wisdom should be held as tenaciously as princes cling to the gold of the Indies.[67] The account was completely fictitious, for Guevara did not visit Florence until 1536, years after writing the book.[68] At best, Guevara may have derived the idea of the book from the *Historia Augusta,* a series of ancient biographies of Roman emperors including a life of Marcus Aurelius attributed to Julius Capitolinus.[69] However, Guevara took very little from the *Historia Augusta.*

Guevara presented a loosely organized treatise of moral philosophy by means of the life and sayings of Marcus Aurelius. It began with a brief account of the emperor's ancestors, birth, and early life, then gave way to a series of tales embodying epideictic orations. An incident or a question might stimulate Marcus Aurelius to deliver long discourses full of moral and social advice and exhortation. The book did not proceed chronologically or follow a discernible logical progression, but skipped about freely. Guevara presented Marcus Aurelius in two guises: the ideal monarch austerely teaching virtue and dispensing justice, and the very human man burdened with a flighty wife, a disappointing son, foolish friends, and vindictive ex-mistresses.

Guevara told stories with an ancient Roman setting to give background and historical authenticity to the orations. For example, Guevara developed the context for a long exhortation on justice as follows. Marcus Aurelius and others had retired to the countryside to avoid a fever sweeping Rome. There they began to discuss the importance of justice in the state. To drive home the point, Marcus Aurelius narrated a tale of a barbarian, a rough and unlettered peasant from the Danubian frontier. Captured by the Roman army, he first told his story to the local Roman

[67]Guevara, 1572, sigs. a8r, a6v. The 1572 printing is a faithful reprint of the 1544 translation. I cite my own worn copy. The original vellum binding is ink stained and covered with simple arithmetical computations. It may be a battered survivor of Cinquecento schools.

[68]Redondo, 1976, p. 422.

[69]Grey, 1973, pp. 3–7; Jones, 1975, pp. 34–35; Redondo, 1976, p. 471.

governor and then to the assembled Roman Senate. In his speech the
peasant excoriated the Romans for taking the lands of others. He pas-
sionately defended liberty: we will leave our wives and slay our children
rather than live under the yoke of the Romans. He condemned the gross
wickedness that he had seen in Rome. He prophesied that just as the
Romans had cast the barbarians out of their rightful lands, so others would
drive the Romans out of Italy. And he finished with one of Guevara's
complex "sentences" summarizing the message: "Everything that the
wicked with their tyranny have gathered in many days I see the gods
taking from them in one; by contrast, all that the good lost over many
years, the gods will restore in an hour."[70] Unable to answer him, the
shamed senators honored the peasant, copied his speech, and sent honest
judges to the Danubian province.

The combination of a story within a story and placing the key message
in the mouth of a third party brought conventional moral philosophy to
life. The book delivered a great deal of mirror-of-princes advice: the prince
must dispense justice, avoid flatterers, reward the virtuous, defend widows, honor the gods, and so on. But Guevara usually managed to impart
his message within a human, personal context. The combination of mirror-of-princes content and novelistic approach probably accounted for the
book's popularity.

The book also doled out a great deal of moral and social advice applicable to commoners. One had to avoid occasions of dishonor; one should
meet death without dismay. A man must act in ways appropriate to his
age. The attractions of the flesh have their season but should be subordinated to reason when youth has passed.[71] Guevara kept interjecting vivid
stories to bring the messages to life. And he stayed within the confines of
ancient pagan morality. For example, Marcus Aurelius frequented prostitutes as a young man and took a concubine after his wife's death, but he
did not dishonor the wives of Roman citizens.[72] Guevara couched everything in personal terms and avoided abstract definitions of justice, wisdom, or fate. Concrete details of ancient peoples and customs lent verisimilitude.

Guevara employed a series of literary devices to create what he called
"high style."[73] A series of balanced clauses carried the message; often they
contrasted negative and positive behavior. Or the second half of the

---

[70]"che tutto quello che i non buoni con lor tirannia hanno adunato in molti dì, veggo gli
Iddii levarglili in un sol giorno, e pe'l contrario tutto quello che i buoni perderono in molti
anni, restituirlo gli Iddij in un'hora." Guevara, 1572, pp. 107–13, quote on pp. 108–9.

[71]Ibid., pp. 45–46.

[72]Ibid., pp. 296–300.

[73]"perche tante, e tante mature sentenze non si trovano nel tempo presente, ne tale, &
tanto alto stile conseguirono quei del tempo passato." Ibid., sig. a8[r].

sentence elevated a thought or action to a higher plane. To achieve balanced dualism, Guevara employed parallelisms, symmetry, solocon (the balancing of clauses of the same length), parison (the use of the same structure in such a way that noun corresponds to noun, adjective to adjective, through two clauses), repetition, and quasi-rhymes.[74] Most chapters reached a climax in a series of epigrammatic sentences of moral wisdom. Guevara's "high style" sometimes elevated ordinary sentiments or self-evident truths to the dignity of weighty *sententiae* that the Renaissance loved: "I have conquered many and today I am conquered by death";[75] "The love of the servant is the security of the master."[76]

The book frequently practiced epideictic oratory, the rhetoric of praise and blame.[77] A series of such speeches and letters dominated the book, as Marcus Aurelius praised or condemned behavior. Guevara even paired opposed vituperative speeches or letters for comic effect. For example, Marcus Aurelius and a Roman prostitute exchanged angry but imaginative letters of recrimination.[78] Epideictic oratory provided a continuity of approach and mood throughout the book; speeches of praise and blame must have seemed an efficacious device for instructing the young.

Personifying the message through the character of Marcus Aurelius permitted Guevara to indulge in a certain amount of thinly disguised discussion of contemporary manners and morals as he saw them. A speech by Marcus Aurelius purportedly narrating his own education became, in effect, a description of sixteenth-century schooling, plus a Renaissance exhortation to set letters above arms.[79] Marcus Aurelius also praised severity in the raising of offspring and stressed the importance of the teacher as moral example in humanistic terms.[80]

On the other hand, Guevara showed himself to be a vigorous, unpleasant misogynist in decidedly non-humanistic terms. Marcus Aurelius's long diatribe against his wife, Faustina, depicted her (and women generally) as childlike, contradictory, illogical, inconstant, perverse, vain, and much else.[81] While an oration of blame might be expected to engage in rhetorical excess, Guevara showed his true feelings by denying Faustina the opportunity to reply. Numerous other unanswered criticisms of women mark the book.[82]

Guevara created a pseudo-classical work. That is, the *Vita di Marco*

---

[74]Grey, 1973, pp. 17–22; Jones, 1975, p. 47; Redondo, 1976, pp. 197–215.

[75]"Ho vinti [*sic*] molti, & sono hoggi vinto dalla morte." Guevara, 1572, p. 168.

[76]". . . che lo amor del servo è la sicurezza del padrone." Ibid., p. 68.

[77]Hardison, Jr., 1962, pp. 29–42; O'Malley, 1979, pp. 36–42.

[78]Guevara, 1572, pp. 283–95.

[79]Ibid., pp. 16–17, 107.

[80]Ibid., pp. 40–48.

[81]Ibid., pp. 73–85.

[82]Ibid., pp. 49–51, 116–19, 123–38, 142, 146.

Aurelio purported to teach moral wisdom derived from the ancients without the grind of learning Latin. It pretended to be an ancient biography of a revered moral philosopher. Guevara remained faithful to his disguise by including many ancient Roman details, from street descriptions to anecdotes. Indeed, he interjected colorful episodes to maintain the fiction and to titillate, such as the story of a pagan people who sacrificed those over the age of 50 to the gods by burning them alive and eating their cooked flesh.[83] Guevara carefully avoided including Christian moral values and anachronistic references to post-imperial persons, events, or books. Just as the Latin humanistic schools taught moral obligation and eloquence by teaching the classics, so the vernacular schools might do the same through the *Vita di Marco Aurelio*. The pseudo-classical guise probably accounted for much of the book's extraordinary popularity across Europe.[84] A didactic work in an imaginative format could hardly fail to win approval.

The vernacular schools taught a rich and varied mix of medieval and modern, religious and secular, moralistic and escapist, books. Titles from the late Middle Ages, the Trecento in almost every case, were read, but so were Renaissance books. Some vernacular texts were overtly religious and Christian, but others taught secular morality, that is, the virtue, wisdom, and practical advice needed to live a good moral life while active in affairs. The chivalric romances, by contrast, entertained. The schools preferred a combination of didacticism and human interest that the *Fior di virtù* and the *Vita di Marco Aurelio* embodied in different ways. The vernacular schools taught only Ariosto's *Orlando furioso* among the classics of Italian literature, probably because parents and teachers saw it as a chivalric romance. Lacking authoritative voices telling them what to teach, the vernacular schools taught the books that adults read. These schools did not participate in the humanistic curriculum revolution, but followed the dictates of traditional vernacular culture.

Why did the vernacular schools fail to teach the masterpieces of Dante, Petrarch, and Boccaccio? Some immediate, practical reasons suggest themselves. Possibly teachers found Dante's *Divine Comedy* too abstruse and metaphysical for use as a school text. All the books used in the vernacular schools presented simple didacticism and human interest; Dante does not. Petrarch's *canzonieri* and sonnets offer imaginative love poetry, but not the love and adventure of the chivalric romances. Boccaccio's *Decameron*, full of ladies of easy virtue and monks whose behavior mocked their vows, was far too racy and immoral for use as a school text for children at any time, and especially during the second half of the

<hr>

[83]Ibid., p. 232.
[84]Grey, 1973, pp. 101–4; Huppert, 1977, pp. 84–85, 203.

sixteenth century. But most important, no one told the vernacular schools that they must or should teach these classics. Texts of lesser literary value earned their way into the curriculum through their popularity in vernacular culture. Dante, Petrarch, and Boccaccio did not.

CHAPTER ELEVEN

Learning Merchant Skills

he Venetian vernacular schools taught commercial mathematics, accounting, and writing as well as Italian literature. Teachers usually stated that they taught "leggere, scrivere, et abbaco" or "leggere, scrivere, abbaco et quaderno." This combination of subjects linked the vernacular schools to the commercial world of the later Middle Ages and Renaissance.

ABBACO

Italian international trading and banking companies transformed medieval trade and laid the foundations of city-state culture in the thirteenth century.[1] The merchants who created this commercial revolution employed new business techniques and mathematical skills to deal with money exchange, loans, partnerships, and the movement of goods over long distances. The pioneering merchants also had to train their employees and sons in sophisticated business mathematics if Italians expected to maintain their preeminence in international trade.

But neither classical mathematics nor the philosophical mathematics taught in medieval universities met their needs.[2] The Romans had little to offer. *De arithmetica* of Boethius (c. 480–524/25) included only elementary computations and philosophical number theory; nevertheless, it became a widely used medieval textbook through lack of competition. Greek mathematics remained mostly out of reach for linguistic reasons. Medieval universities taught arithmetic and geometry as parts of the quadrivium, but the approach, especially to arithmetic, focussed on number

---

[1]The basic short summary is Roover, 1942.

[2]For this summary, see Mahoney, 1972; Masi, 1983; Shelby, 1983; and the excellent summary of the triumphs and inadequacies of medieval mathematics in Rose, 1975, pp. 76–89.

theory that included the philosophical study of number, unity, equality, ratio, and proportion. That is, medieval university mathematicians sought to find harmonious relationships between numbers which might have significance for other disciplines. For example, medieval mathematicians studied the so-called perfect number, one whose dividends when added together equal the original number. Twenty-eight is an example; its dividends are 1, 2, 4, 7, and 14, and their sum is 28.[3] The obvious order, unity, and harmony appealed to medieval mathematicians who might then apply the principles to metaphysics and theology. But perfect numbers did not help merchants solve the disorderly problems of money exchange.

Medieval university mathematicians taught in Latin and used a series of texts distant from the merchants' world. They commented on Boethius and Euclid's *Elements of Geometry;* they studied the *Algorismus vulgaris* of Sacrobosco (John of Holywood, d. 1244 or 1256) and Alexander de Villedieu's *Carmen de algorismo* (c. 1202), which taught algorism as a means of locating movable feast days in the church calendar.[4] Medieval university geometry offered useful techniques for measuring heights, depths, and areas. But, again, its language was Latin and its primary focus a quest for harmony.

The merchants turned to a new, different mathematics called *abbaco,* elaborated in the Christian West by Leonardo Fibonacci (or Leonardo of Pisa, c. 1170–after 1240).[5] The son of a Pisan governmental official sent to direct the Pisan trading colony at Bougie, Algeria, Leonardo studied Arab mathematics in North Africa and on business trips to Egypt, Syria, Greece, Sicily, and elsewhere. Upon his return to Pisa circa 1200, Leonardo began to compose a series of Latin mathematical works which made him the most important Western mathematician between the fall of Rome and the Renaissance. He played a major role in establishing in the West the Hindu-Arabic numeral system first introduced about a century earlier; it replaced the cumbersome Roman numerals. Above all, he wrote *Liber abbaci* (1202, revised 1228), an encyclopaedia of practical mathematics adapted to the needs of merchants. Leonardo poured his extensive knowledge of Arab and ancient Greek mathematics into the book and added his own originality. The book earned him some fame in his lifetime, including an appearance before Emperor Frederick II, but it had little influence on medieval university mathematics. Nevertheless, he created the mathematics taught in the vernacular schools.

The Italian term *abbaco,* found in manuscripts, printed books, and school documents, did not mean a mechanical computing device. The

[3]See Masi, 1983, p. 150.
[4]For translated excerpts of some of these medieval texts, see Grant, ed., 1974, pp. 17–24, 94–114.
[5]Vogel, 1971.

Middle Ages inherited from the ancient world a simple abacus, a wooden reckoning board with raised edges within which wooden counters could be moved around, which Renaissance printed books sometimes illustrated.[6] But abbaco treatises did not assume the use of an abacus; instead, *abbaco* meant solving practical mathematical problems on paper.[7] Nor did *abbaco* refer to a single mathematical operation or technique. Abbaco used arithmetic, algorism (computing with numbers, especially decimals), algebra, and geometry, all based on the Hindu-Arabic numeral system, to solve business-related problems.[8] The nature of the problems, rather than the mathematical operations, unified abbaco.

Abbreviated vernacular versions of Leonardo Fibonacci's *Liber abbaci* began to appear toward the end of the thirteenth century; the oldest surviving abbaco treatise can be dated circa 1290.[9] Abbaco schools also made their appearance at about this time. A Veronese communal document of 1277 referred to "unum magistrum rationis abbachi," although the commune may not have made an appointment at this time. The Commune of Verona did appoint a certain "Maestro Lotto" from Florence as communal abbaco teacher in 1284.[10]

Many more abbaco schools followed in the fourteenth century. Tuscan teachers played a key role in the development and diffusion of abbaco; indeed, the majority of the identifiable abbaco authors and teachers of the Trecento and Quattrocento, including the handful of well-known ones, came from Florence.[11] The Florentines then taught others, as the Veronese appointment demonstrated. Only in the sixteenth century did non-Florentines, especially author-teachers from Venice and the Veneto, supplant the Florentines, at least in composing abbaco texts that had many printings.[12]

Abbaco schools could be found throughout northern Italy from the fourteenth through the sixteenth century. But the chronological position of abbaco within vernacular schooling varied. Florentines learned abbaco in specialized schools that taught only abbaco for about two years at the mid-point of schooling. Villani mentioned these schools circa 1338; ac-

---

[6]Bonner, 1977, pp. 182–87, including the illustrations.

[7]Van Egmond, 1981, pp. 5–6. This important work opens up the study of abbaco and abbaco teachers and should lead to a new appreciation of this relatively neglected field. Also see the numerous editions and studies of Gino Arrighi.

[8]Van Egmond, 1976, p. 17.

[9]This is FR Ms. 2404, "Livero del abbecho," as described by Van Egmond, 1981, pp. 156–57.

[10]Bolognini, 1896, pp. 10–11; also see E. Garibotto, 1923, p. 315.

[11]Van Egmond, 1981, passim.

[12]For example, Girolamo Tagliente, who taught in Venice, produced a text that had thirty-five printings, and Francesco Feliciano, who taught in Verona, wrote abbaco texts that had eighteen printings, in the sixteenth century. No Florentine abbaco master produced a work that matched these figures. See ibid., pp. 309–15, 334–44, for lists of the printings.

cording to him, boys studied abbaco after the reading and writing school and before going on to Latin grammar and logic (see ch. 3). This practice continued. Niccolò Machiavelli enrolled in an abbaco school at the age of 10 years and 8 months in 1480 and left at the age of 12 years and 6 months, completing the course in twenty-two months.[13] Almost all Florentine boys enrolled in abbaco schools in 1480 were between the ages of 11 and 14 or 15. A 1519 contract between an abbaco teacher and his assistant again demonstrated that Florentine abbaco schools taught commercial mathematics exclusively in a seven-stage curriculum that lasted two years or a little more.[14]

Masters in other Italian towns integrated abbaco into vernacular schools that taught reading, writing, abbaco, and sometimes bookkeeping together over many years. For example, in the fifteenth century the southern Tuscan commune of Volterra hired a *maestro d'abbaco* and charged him to teach abbaco and writing, plus reading to those who wanted to learn to read vernacular books instead of Latin.[15] In Verona a master taught "reading, writing, addition, subtraction, and accounting of every kind and other matter pertaining to mathematics" from the 1490s to the 1530s.[16] Venice also had comprehensive vernacular schools. In 1550 Domenico Manzoni, a Venetian abbaco teacher, published a self-teaching book for those who could not attend formal schools.[17] His textbook included the alphabet, syllables, vernacular words, elementary religious catechetical material, advice on the punctuation of vernacular prose, writing instruction, and abbaco. He put much of his school syllabus between the covers of the book. The Venetian abbaco teachers of 1587 repeatedly affirmed that they taught a combination of subjects to all ages. For example, one teacher stated that he taught reading, writing, abbaco, and accounting (*far conti*) to twenty-nine pupils aged 6, 7, 8, 10, and 12.[18]

Although an integral part of vernacular schooling, abbaco did not enter the Latin school curriculum on a regular basis. Some humanists recognized the importance of mathematics, and a few knew a great deal. But they seldom inserted mathematics into the curriculum. On the rare occasions when they did, they taught classical or medieval Latin mathematics.

[13]Verde, 1973; and Verde, 1973–77, vol. 2:535–37. For other examples of boys who studied abbaco at about this age, see Edler, 1934, p. 18.

[14]Goldthwaite, 1972.

[15]Battistini, 1919, pp. 29, 45 n. 140.

[16]". . . ivi insegnava leggere scrivere summare sottrarre e far conti d'ogni sorte et altro che appartiene alla matematica. . . ." Statement of 1533 describing the career of Francesco Feliciano by his nephew, Giacobbe dall'abbaco, as quoted in E. Garibotto, 1923, p. 324. Feliciano began teaching in the mid-1490s according to his own testimony; see Feliciano, 1536, sig. A1v.

[17]D. Manzoni, 1550, sig. av.

[18]ACPV, "Professioni di fede," fols. 104r–105r, Marinus Bonardi.

The humanistic pedagogical theorists saw mathematics as a quadrivium subject closely identified with medieval university schooling. Pier Paolo Vergerio in his *De ingenius moribus* (1402–3), which mixed together old and new views on education, praised arithmetic (described as the science of numbers) and geometry, because they offered certainty and delight.[19] He then went on to astronomy and natural philosophy. This view persisted. Alessandro Piccolomini (1508–78) in his *Della institutione morale* (1560) placed mathematics in the same philosophical context his medieval university predecessors had, that is, as a branch of natural philosophy which offered certainty through demonstrative logical proofs. Piccolomini saw mathematics and geometry within the framework of the quadrivium and made analogies with music and astrology. He recommended as texts the works of Euclid, Boethius, Archimedes, and "some parts" of Luca Pacioli. Most revealing was his recommendation that students postpone mathematics until the age of 14, two or three years before entering university.[20] He did not think it necessary for young children to learn the rudiments of mathematics, and he never mentioned how mathematics might solve practical problems.

Only Vittorino da Feltre of the great humanistic pedagogues had much interest in mathematics. Contemporaries narrated the story of how he studied mathematics privately with a master in Padua and became a household servant to pay for his tuition.[21] Vittorino studied Euclid (probably the *Elements of Geometry*) and possibly algebra as well, and later taught mathematics in his famous school in Mantua. But what kind of mathematics? The sparse available evidence mentions that he taught Euclid in the context of the quadrivium.[22] In other words, he probably taught exactly what he learned in Padua, traditional medieval university mathematics.

Leon Battista Alberti did recommend that children study abbaco. In *Della famiglia* (probably begun c. 1433 and finished in the early 1440s) he advised children to learn abbaco and some geometry for pleasure and utility. Students should then return to the "poets, orators, and philosophers."[23] Alberti had in mind the Florentine pattern of a two-year con-

[19]The English translation in Woodward, 1963, p. 108, is accurate enough. Also see the Italian translation in Garin, ed., 1959, p. 90.

[20]Piccolomini, 1560, bk. 4, chs. 16–17, pp. 159–66.

[21]Bartolomeo Sacchi (il Platina) tells the story in his *De vita Victorini Feltrensis commentariolus* (written 1461–65), in Garin, ed., 1958, p. 670. Also see Woodward, 1963, pp. 7–8.

[22]See the biographies of Sassolo da Prato, *De Victorini vita* (1443/44), and Francesco da Castiglione, *Vita Victorini Feltrensis* (c. 1469), as edited in Garin, ed., 1958, pp. 510, 526, 528, 536. Also see Woodward, 1963, pp. 42–43.

[23]"Apprendano dipoi l'abaco, e insieme, quanto sia utile, ancora veggano geometria, le quali due sono scienze atte e piacevoli a' fanciulleschi ingegni, e in ogni uso ed età non poto utile. Poi ritornino a gustare e' poeti, oratori, filosofi, e sopratutto si cerchi d'avere solleciti maestri, da' quali e' fanciulli non meno imparino costumi buoni che lettere." Alberti, 1969, bk. 1, p. 86.

centration on abbaco, a short interlude before returning to more intensive study of the Latin classics.

None of the other Italian pedagogical theorists mentioned mathematics. As a consequence, Latin schools almost always omitted mathematics and rejected abbaco completely. The Latin schools ignored abbaco because it added nothing to the social status and career goals of their students. The Latin schools sought to train society's leaders and the professionals (chiefly secretaries and lawyers) who aided them. Such men had no need to learn commercial mathematics, or so it was thought. Sassolo da Prato (1416/17–49), pupil and biographer of Vittorino, wrote in 1443 that many say that arithmetic should be left to artisans.[24] Although Sassolo noted that Vittorino rejected this view, it is clear that the majority held it. And even Vittorino did not teach abbaco.

The social gulf between the two academic streams limited curricular crossover. Vernacular schools might stretch upward to teach a little Latin grammar, but Latin schools did not stoop to teach the mathematics of tradesmen. Even the Florentine tradition of offering short intensive training in separate abbaco schools did not bridge the gap, but enabled Latin students to add abbaco if they wished. Of course, some of Italy's elite did engage in commerce. Then they hired clerks with abbaco training to compute for them or learned some of the skills themselves. Society did not expect the elite to learn abbaco as an integral part of their youthful education. Vernacular abbaco had no chance of winning a place in the curriculum of Latin eloquence.

ABBACO CLASSROOM INSTRUCTION

The manuscripts and printed texts, fourteenth through sixteenth centuries, indicated classroom instructional content. Indeed, some sixteenth-century printed abbaco books explicitly stated their intent to instruct children bent on commercial careers.[25] The books did not necessarily follow one organizational scheme or use identical mathematical problems (although some repeatedly appeared), but they did teach all or most of the same material.

[24]"Arithmeticam opficibus relinquendam dicens." In Garin, ed., 1958, p. 510, and repeated on p. 526. Van Egmond, 1976, pp. 137–38, has not found any links between Florentine abbachists and humanists.

[25]See Borghi, 1501, sig. A2r; Calandri, 1518, sig. A2r; Feliciano, 1536, sig. Av; Ghaligai, 1552, sig. A2r; D. Manzoni, 1553, sig. Av; and Clavius, 1586, sig. A5r. For the following discussion, I have also examined *Arte del abbacho* (Treviso, [Michele Manzolo or Gerardus de Lisa de Flandria], 10-XII-1478), GW 2674; G. Tagliente, 1520, plus the editions of Venice, 1557 and 1586; Giovanni Francesco dal Sole, *Libretto di Abaco* . . . (Colophon: Vinegia, per Francesco Bindoni & Mapheo Pasini, 1526 del mese di Magio); Giovanni Sfortunati, *Nuovo lume, libro di arithmetica* . . . , 1544 (Colophon: Venegia per Bernardino de Bindoni, 1545),

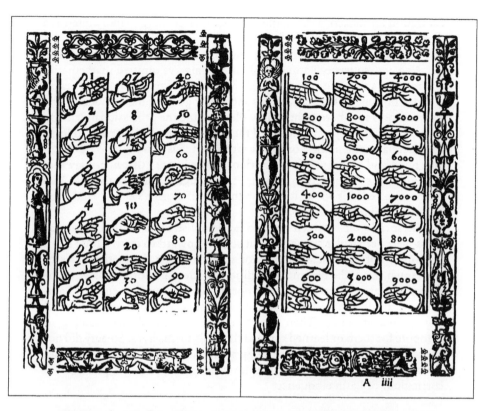

10. Finger reckoning from Filippo Calandri, *Pictagoris arithmetice introductor.* Colophon: Firenze per Bernardo Zucchecta, 1518, a dì XX di Luglio. Sigs. A3^v–A4^r. IU.

Abbaco books normally began with a discussion of Hindu-Arabic numeration and explanation of the place value of numbers. Sometimes books included a diagram in the form of a tall tapered figure with a larger base than apex called a *casteluccio* (little castle, although it looks more like a skyscraper to the twentieth-century eye) which demonstrated that one-digit numbers were smaller than two-digit numbers, which were smaller than three-digit numbers, and so on. Abbaco books also illustrated finger reckoning or notation, a system of keeping track of the intermediate steps

plus editions of Venice, 1561 and 1568; Pietro Cataneo, *Le pratiche delle due prime mathematiche* (In Venetia, appresso Giovanni Griffio, 1559), plus the edition of Venice, 1567; and Gemma Frisius, *Aritmetica prattica facilissima . . . in questa lingua ridotte Oratio Toscanella . . .*(In Venetia, appresso Giovanni Bariletto, 1567). Examination of the texts confirms the analysis of Van Egmond, 1981, pp. 15–26, and Van Egmond, 1976. Also see Franci and Rigatelli, 1982.

LIBRO

quale fi fa in quefto modo , che fi tra la proua della minor quantità della proua della magiore fendo pofsibile, & lo auanzo conuiene effer quanto la proua dello auanzo della fottrattion fatta , & quando la proua del minor numero di quella del maggiore trar non fi poteffe, allhora è neceffario aggiungere quel tal numero per ilquale fi fa la proua, cioè fe fi fa la proua del 7. aggiunger 7. & fi per 9. aggiunger 9. alla proua del numero maggiore & di detta congiuntione trarne la proua del minore, & fappi che tutti li numeri poffono effere proue, ma hoggi quefte del 9. & del 7. fono piu in ufo .

DEL MVLTIPLICARE DE' NVMERI.

MVltiplicare un numero per un'altro fecondo Euclide nel fettimo, è tante uolte pigliare il numero che fi deue multiplicare quante unità fono nel multiplicante, & per meglio fartelo intendere, dico che nel multiplicare bifognano 2. numeri, de' quali l'uno fi dice multiplicante, & l'altro multiplicando, cioè che fi deue multiplicare, & l'Algorifmo dice nel fefto capitolo, multiplicare un numero per un'altro è uoler trouare un altro numero che tante uolte contenga il multiplicando, quante unità fono nel multiplicante, & puofsi multiplicare il numero in fe medefimo, ouero in altro numero, & nota che quando fi multiplica un numero per un'altro, & faccia il detto numero, è neceffario quello effer multiplicato per unità come per il Megarenfe nel fettimo fi manifefta .

DEL MVLTIPLICAR A LA MEMORIA
detto uulgarmente Cafelle o Librettine.

M'A auantí che ne l operar con la penna ne le multiplicationi fi proceda è neceffario hauer quelle che bifognano a la memoria, e quanto piu fe ne imparaffe a mente tanto maggiormente giouarebbe al ragioniere o matematico , ma noi ne addurremo quelle che fon piu neceffarie & a le mifure e pefi piu commode, fenza lequali, non fi puo operar ne le ragioni .

PRIMO. 8

1	1	1
2	2	4
3	3	9
4	4	16
5	5	25
6	6	36
7	7	49
8	8	64
9	9	81
10	10	100
2	3	6
2	4	8
2	5	10
3	4	12
3	5	15
3	6	18
3	7	21
3	8	24
3	9	27
3	10	30
4	5	20
4	6	24
4	7	28
4	8	32
4	9	36
4	10	40
5	6	30
5	7	35
5	8	40
5	9	45
5	10	50

6	7	42
6	8	48
6	9	54
6	10	60
7	8	56
7	9	63
7	10	70
8	9	72
8	10	80
9	10	90
10	10	100
2	12	24
3	12	36
4	12	48
5	12	60
6	12	72
7	12	84
8	12	96
9	12	108
10	12	120
2	13	26
3	13	39
4	13	52
5	13	65
6	13	78
7	13	91
8	13	104
9	13	117
10	13	130
2	14	28
3	14	42

11. Multiplication tables from Pietro Cataneo, *Le pratiche delle due prime matematiche*. In Venetia, appresso Giovanni Griffio, 1567. Sigs. B3^v–B4^r. IU.

in long division and multiplication on the fingers. The student learned to bend and straighten fingers in his left hand in different ways to signify numbers, and he wrote the computation with his right hand.

Abbaco books next explained the arithmetical operations of multiplication and division with whole numbers, fractions, and the compound quantities involved in monies, weights, and measures. They did not usually explain addition and subtraction, probably leaving this to the teacher to do. The books often included multiplication tables (called *librettine*) to be memorized. Students memorized tables of 1 through 20, that is, 1 × 1 = 1, through 19 × 19 = 361, 19 × 20 = 380, and 20 × 20 = 400, plus some higher numbers up to 100. *Librettine* also included the multiplication of monetary units, so that students would commit to memory the multiples of monetary units in their different forms. Hence, the student memorized such operations as 1 denaro × 100 = 8 soldi and 4 denari (because 12 denari = 1 soldo).[26] The student also learned at this stage how to manipulate fractions and mixed numbers. By the time the student had completed this preliminary material, he had learned numeration, the four basic arithmetical operations, and reckoning on his fingers. He had also committed to memory a fairly extensive group of multiplication tables and elementary manipulation of the money system.

Having mastered this basic material, the student proceeded to the heart of abbaco, which was solving the mathematical problems of business. The ordinary abbaco book might contain four hundred problems and their solutions, of which the largest group by far were business problems of many kinds.[27] The business problems dealt with prices and products. For example, "a hundredweight of cloth sells for 10 lire; what are 7 *braccia* (arm's length, a unit of measure of about two feet) of this cloth worth?"[28] Money exchange problems asked the student to find the equivalent value of an amount of money in one monetary system in the money of another city. Measurement and weight problems were prominent, such as, "the Florentine pound gives 10½ ounces in Pisa, and the Pisan pound gives 11 ounces in Lucca; what does the Florentine pound give in Lucca?"[29] Barter problems appeared; for example, given their different values, how much wool should be bartered for its equivalent value in cloth? Partnership problems asked students to figure out how to divide the profits of a partnership: two men in a partnership earned 100 lire; the first had contributed 17 lire and the second 41 lire; what portion of the 100 lire should each receive? Interest and discount problems were common, and the search for the single payment with which to retire multiple loans was a staple exercise. The latter might be posed as follows. One man lent another these amounts: 230 lire on 2 April 1370, 150 lire on 15 June 1370, 272 lire on 18 August 1370, etc., all at the rate of 10 percent; the lender asked the borrower to pay back all the loans with interest on a single date, 1 October 1371; how much must he pay?[30] Finally, the business problems included alligation exercises to determine how much gold or silver to add or subtract to an existing metallic mixture so as to have the correct alloy with which to produce coins of a certain purity.[31]

The abbaco books also included lighter problems: "a fox is 40 paces ahead of a dog, and for every 3 paces the fox goes, the dog goes 5 paces; I

[26]Van Egmond, 1976, pp. 159–62.

[27]Van Egmond, 1981, pp. 15–16.

[28]Ibid., p. 21. Van Egmond has taken problems from abbaco manuscripts, either translating or restating them in briefer English form. Quotation marks here and below indicate that I am copying Van Egmond's English versions.

[29]Ibid., pp. 21–22.

[30]Ibid., p. 22.

[31]Ibid., pp. 22–23.

want to know in how many paces the dog will catch the fox."[32] These might be called "recreational problems," since their resolution mattered little in the real world. Other recreational problems might include number problems: "find me a number such that adding ½, ¼, and ⅕ of it plus three more makes 25."[33] These number problems might be elaborate and project verisimilitude:

There is a man who is very seriously ill and finally makes his will. He has a wife who is pregnant and leaves 1,000 lire to her in this manner: if the woman bears a daughter, ⅓ will go to the daughter for her dowry, and if she bears a son, ¾ will go to the son and ¼ to the wife. The good man died and the wife delivered twins, a son and a daughter. How much should each one have?[34]

Instruction included some theoretical discussion of geometry, such as the steps taken in the measurement of circumference, diameter, and area. But the books couched the problems in practical terms: find the height of a tower, the area of a field, the number of bricks needed to build a wall, and so on. Abbaco also might admit limited theoretical discussion of "the rule of the three" (proportions) and elementary algebra.

Abbaco pedagogy approached business problems in a literary, almost conversational, way and applied ad hoc eclectic methods. For example, an abbaco book might state a money exchange problem and explain its solution in narrative rather than symbolic terms.

A soldo of Provence is worth 40 denari of Pisa and a soldo imperiale is worth 32 of Pisa. Tell me how much will I have of these two monies mixed together for 200 lire of Pisa? Do it thus: add together 40 and 32 making 72 (denari), which are 6 soldi, and divide 200 lire by 6, which gives 33 lire and 6 soldi and 8 denari, and you will have this much of each of these two monies, that is 33 lire 6 soldi 8 denari for the said 200 lire of Pisa. And it has been done.[35]

A twentieth-century mathematics book would employ symbolism by substituting letters or symbols for the unknown quantities in order to derive an equation to solve the problem. Modern mathematics at the secondary school level concentrates on teaching a method (e.g., an algebraic equation or geometric theorem) applicable to all problems of a certain sort. The student must learn to recognize the type of problem and then apply the appropriate equation or theorem.

The Renaissance abbaco book stated the problem and its solution together, rather than deferring the solution to the back of the book. Moreover, it normally explained in a detailed narration all the steps needed to solve the problem. Only toward the end of the fifteenth century and in

[32]Ibid., p. 18.
[33]Ibid., p. 23.
[34]Ibid., p. 25.
[35]Ibid., p. 16.

the sixteenth century did abbaco books modify the narrative solution slightly in favor of a more streamlined "handbook" style, which laid out the mathematical calculations separately elsewhere on the page. These later abbaco books used slightly more symbolism as well.[36]

Teachers focussed on solving individual problems rather than developing an equation or rule applicable to a variety of mathematically similar problems involving different objects or matter. Abbaco books tended to provide a unique technique for each problem; even a slight change in the structure of a problem might necessitate a different approach.[37]

The abbaco book collected individual problems and their solutions for reference use. A teacher found in it the day's problems and solutions to teach; students copied down what the teacher explained. The slow, literary statement of the problem and solution may have helped the student to understand and remember. If he faithfully copied enough problems and solutions, he had his own abbaco book. When as an adult merchant, banker, or clerk he came across a problem that he could not solve, he looked into his student abbaco book to find an almost identical problem and applied its method. Joining problem and solution together made the learner's task easier.

In practice, abbaco relied on several mathematical methods, most of them relatively simple in principle but involving numerous steps. Abbaco very frequently used "the rule of the three," the elementary relation of proportionality which states that the product of the means equals the product of the extremes: if $A:B = C:D$, then $AD = BC$. If three values are known, the fourth can be found from the equation $A = BC/D$. Abbaco treatises often used the rule of the three to solve pricing and exchange problems that had three knowns and one unknown:

If twelve ounces of silver are worth 4 lire 10 soldi, what are 34 ounces of silver worth? . . . The thing that we want to know is the 34 ounces of silver, and that which is not the same is the 4 lire 10 soldi. Therefore, we multiply 34 times 4 lire 10 soldi which makes 153 lire, divide by 12, which gives 12 lire 15 soldi, and so much are 34 ounces of silver worth.[38]

In mathematical terms, this is a proportion problem as follows: 12 ounces are proportional to 4 lire 10 soldi as 34 ounces are to X. Therefore, X equals 34 times 4 lire 10 soldi divided by 12, or

$$X = \frac{34 \times 4\ \text{L}\ 10\ \text{S}}{12}.$$

[36]Van Egmond, 1976, pp. 268–74.
[37]Ibid., pp. 241–42.
[38]Ibid., p. 248.

One should keep in mind that 20 soldi equal 1 lira. Hence, the answer is: 153 lire (or 3,060 soldi) when divided by 12 equals 255 soldi, which is 12 lire 15 soldi.

Abbacists solved many problems by means of proportions which twentieth-century mathematicians would solve through other means. More often than not, the abbacists conceptualized a problem so that it could be stated and solved through the rule of the three. The method of proportions was so much a part of their mathematical mentality that Renaissance mathematicians applied it to fields such as mechanics and astronomy. Even Galileo and Newton used proportions.[39]

The abbacists also used a method that might be called ingenious reasoning, here used to solve this problem: "A master has a number of students such that if he received 2 soldi for tuition from each one of them he would have 20 soldi less than the rent; and if he received 3 soldi for tuition from each he would take in 40 soldi more than his rent. I ask: how much was the rent that the master paid, and how many students did he have?"[40] A twentieth-century algebra student might solve the problem with two simultaneous equations with two unknowns for the number of students and the rent amount. But the abbacist reasoned it through. When the master charged 2 soldi he had 20 soldi too few (or below the rent amount), and when he charged 3 soldi he had 40 soldi too much (or above the rent amount). When he increased the tuition by 1 soldo, the difference between the amounts below and above the rent was 60 soldi. Hence, he had to have had 60 students. And if 60 students paying 2 soldi each for tuition produced 20 soldi less than the rent, the rent must have been $2 \times 60 + 20 = 140$ soldi. The abbacist did not really apply a mathematical method, he resorted to ingenious reasoning.

The abbacists used another method called "the rule of the false" ("regola falsa"), which meant making a guess at the solution, and then using that guess to establish a proportion to solve the problem. For example, "50 lire earns 7 lire in 8 months and 12 days; . . . at what rate was the lire lent per month"?[41] (It should be remembered that Renaissance merchants usually stated interest as so many denari per lire per month rather than at an annual percentage.) To solve the problem, one proposes that the rate might be 5 denari per month. The interest on 50 lire for 8 months and 12 days would be 8¾ lire (5 denari $\times$ 50 = 250 denari per month $\times$ 7⅖ months = 2,100 denari = 8¾ lire). Next one establishes a proportion: if 5 denari per month earn 8¾ lire, a rate of how many denari will earn 7 lire per month? The proportion is 5:8¾ as X:7; $5 \times 7 \div 8¾ = 4$. The answer is that 50 lire

[39]Ibid., pp. 250–51.
[40]Ibid., p. 245.
[41]Ibid., pp. 253–54; pp. 254–56 for the solution.

loaned at an interest rate of 4 denari per month for 8 months and 12 days produces income of 7 lire. The method of "the rule of the false" could become much more complicated, for example, when the abbacist used two guesses (i.e., two unknowns) to establish a proportion to find the answer.

The abbacists did not often use algebra. Viewing algebra as an alternative, they sometimes gave an algebraic solution after solving the problem by another method. Then they did what all algebraicists do: substitute an unknown for the answer sought, write an equation, reduce the equation to one of the standard types for which a rule exists, and then apply the rule to the equation to find the answer. The available algebra techniques, fewer and less complex than modern ones, came ultimately from the ninth-century Arab mathematician Al-Khwarizmi. But the abbacists showed great ingenuity in applying their limited algebra to the solution of problems of considerable complexity.[42]

Renaissance students of abbaco did not learn any mathematics more complicated than what is taught in twentieth-century North American secondary schools. The techniques did not include advanced algebra and calculus (which had not yet been developed). Nevertheless, abbaco presented quite difficult mathematics for boys aged 11 to 14 or 15, and the individual problems and solutions could be longer and more complex than those found in twentieth-century high school texts. Abbaco taught the mathematics needed to carry on Renaissance commerce; its limitations were those of the business world it served. Within these limits abbaco taught mathematical skills of considerable ingenuity and utility.

Abbaco treatises taught students to solve numerous problems dealing with interest-bearing loans, and they did not mention the ethical and religious objections that canonists and theologians raised.[43] Major Italian theologians in the middle of the fifteenth century still permitted only certain kinds of interest-bearing loans. For example, St. Bernardino of Siena (1380–1444) and St. Antonino of Florence (1389–1459) reaffirmed traditional Scholastic teaching that defined usury as "any excess whatsoever above the principal of a *mutuum,* or loan, exacted by reason of the loan itself."[44] They did permit earning money through bills of exchange in which payment (including an additional amount) would be made in the future in a different currency. They also accepted investment into a profitable partnership, seeing it not as a loan but as a contract involving potential loss. But St. Bernardino and St. Antonino, who lived in commercial cities, distrusted the taking of interest as a threat to salvation, and surrounded it with restrictions. Some merchants were also troubled, even

[42]Ibid., pp. 217–21, 256–70.
[43]Ibid., pp. 181–82.
[44]Roover, 1967, p. 28. A vast literature on this subject exists.

though they had studied abbaco and had loaned and borrowed throughout their lives. At death's door they made pious donations as restitution for usury.

The abbaco treatises tacitly assumed the moral acceptability of interest-bearing loans by repeatedly presenting problems in which the student calculated the payment of principal and interest due as a result of a loan. One wonders if the Latin-educated and university-trained theologians who wrote treatises condemning usury ever read the vernacular abbaco manuals, which assumed that all loans earned interest. Merchants learned as boys through abbaco instruction the de facto conclusion that taking interest in a variety of circumstances was licit. They must have been disconcerted when theologians told them not to do it; their moral confusion is understandable. The dichotomy demonstrates, once again, the chasm dividing Latin learning and vernacular culture. Separate educational streams made it easier for different groups of society to ignore each other.

Despite the vast difference in subject matter, abbaco pedagogy and the teaching of Latin grammar and the classics exhibited methodological similarity. Teachers and students of both focussed on individual points and problems, and seldom generalized. Latin students learned Latin grammar with textbooks that relied on a verbal, almost conversational, approach with a minimum of paradigms and rules to explain inflections and other grammatical matters. Abbaco students learned to solve individual problems by means of a step-by-step discussion of the problem. The Latin student learned a series of precise examples of usage; the abbaco student learned how to solve individual problems. The Latin student learned a variety of ways to write the same sentiments, sometimes just rearranging the words into different grammatical constructions. The abbaco student moved from problem to very similar problem. Both the Latin student and the abbaco neophyte relied heavily on memorization. The Latin student copied down *sententiae* to insert into letters and speeches; the abbaco student accumulated a book of examples for future use. The same approach and mentality underlay Latin and vernacular schooling.

DOUBLE-ENTRY BOOKKEEPING

The Venetian vernacular schools also taught *quaderno* (literally "ledger") or *far conti* (accounting), that is, double-entry bookkeeping.

The Italian merchants who pioneered and controlled European commerce and banking also developed double-entry bookkeeping as a tool of management control.[45] The earliest surviving medieval business records

---

[45]Roover, 1974; also see R. Brown, 1905, pp. 93–135.

came from Genoa in 1157; a step-by-step development followed. By the early fourteenth century, merchants in several Italian centers had fused classification procedures dependent on dual entries into accounting systems that various scholars have regarded as double-entry. Nevertheless, only an account book of 1340 from Genoa has been accepted by all scholars as fully meeting the requirements of double-entry. The practice then rapidly expanded and added sophistication in fifteenth-century Italy. The first explanation of double-entry bookkeeping appeared in print in 1494, Luca Pacioli's "Particularis de computis et scripturis" (Details of accounting and recording). It introduced beginners to the subject rather than explaining the full range of contemporary Italian accounting. The rest of Europe did not use double-entry until the treatises of Pacioli and others introduced them to the art in the sixteenth century.

Born in Sansepolcro (Umbria) in north-central Italy, Pacioli (c. 1445–1517) moved to Venice as a young man and taught abbaco and bookkeeping to the three sons of a Venetian merchant between circa 1464 and 1470.[46] He then embarked on an itinerant career of teaching mathematics at numerous Italian universities. He found favor with princes, and also worked with Piero della Francesca and Leonardo da Vinci. In Venice, 1494, he published his mathematical encyclopaedia, *Summa de arithmetica, geometria, proportioni et proportionalità,* which included sections on theoretical and practical arithmetic; the elements of algebra; monies, weights, and measures in Italian states; the treatise on double-entry bookkeeping; and a summary of Euclid's geometry. Not a very original thinker, Pacioli summarized available information and added material from little-known sources. His *Summa* became a point of departure for future mathematics, especially algebra.

Although reprinted only once, as part of the 1523 edition of his *Summa,* Pacioli's treatise guided the modern history of bookkeeping. The first half of Domenico Manzoni's *Quaderno doppio col suo giornale* (possible first edition of 1534, followed by six reprints)[47] copied or paraphrased Pacioli, and the rest of the book added new examples. Europeans outside of Italy followed either Pacioli or Manzoni for centuries, for simple double-entry

    [46]Jayawardene, 1974; and Rose, 1975, ch. 6 et passim.
    [47]R. Brown, 1905, p. 120, states that the first edition appeared in 1534, followed by six others. I have examined the following editions, which, despite the different titles, are basically the same book: *Quaderno doppio col suo giornale* (Venetia, Comin da Trino di Monferrato, luio, 1540); *Quaderno doppio* (Vinegia, Comin da Trino, 1554); *Libro mercantile col suo giornale & alfabeto per tener conti doppi* (Venetia, Comin da Trino, 1565), Colophon: 1564; *Giornale doppio segnato* (Venetia, Comin da Trino, 1573). I have also examined another accounting textbook: Giovanni Antonio Tagliente, *Luminario di arithmetica* (n.p. and no printer, but Venice, 1525), Copy: CU. For excerpts and translations from Pacioli, Manzoni, and other texts, see Geijsbeek-Molenaas, ed., 1914.

bookkeeping has changed little since the fifteenth century.[48]

Pacioli began by affirming that he would use "the system of Venice" (p. 26);[49] indeed, he employed many Venetian names and examples. Pacioli first explained how to take inventory: make a very detailed list of everything possessed or owned down to minor household effects. Then he described the three account books: the *memoriale* (memorandum book), *giornale* (journal), and *quaderno* (ledger). A merchant recorded in rough form each transaction as it happened in the *memoriale*. He listed the monies involved in any form; later he would rewrite the amounts into a money of account. At the end of the day the merchant analyzed each entry in the memorandum book in order to transfer the information to the journal as a debit and credit entry. The journal held the permanent chronological record of all transactions. Each *giornale* entry listed the pertinent details: merchandise; number, weight, or measure; value; the period within which goods were to be imported or exported; financial terms; and the people involved. Each journal entry had two notations: *P* (*per*-for), accompanied by the name or account to be debited, and *A* (*avere*-to have), the name or account to be credited.

The bookkeeper next posted a debit and a credit from each journal entry to the ledger. Unlike the journal, the ledger grouped entries according to the person or firm involved, the venture, the merchandise, or another criterion. The ledger held a comprehensive, analytical record of an individual's business affairs. When the bookkeeper had made the debit entry from the journal, he drew one line across the journal entry and wrote the letter signifying the appropriate ledger (ledgers were lettered consecutively beginning with a cross followed by *A, B, C,* etc., just as in the primer's alphabet) and the page where the entry had been posted. When the credit entry had been posted to the ledger, the bookkeeper drew a second line across the journal entry.[50]

Pacioli also explained more complicated entries, which recorded the partners, objectives, length of a partnership (often the time needed to

[48]For the European influence of Pacioli and Manzoni, see R. Brown, 1905, pp. 120–22, 125–31. I learned sufficient double-entry bookkeeping in a high school in Iowa in 1952 to keep the accounts of a small road construction business in the summer of 1954. What I learned and used was Pacioli's system.

[49]The Venetian system followed double entry with minor variations. Venetian accounting laid greater stress on venture accounting, that is, accounts dependent on the results of sea voyages and not closed into a profit and loss statement until completion of the venture. Hence, accountants might not cast a balance for several years (Roover, 1974, pp. 161–64). Page references in the text are to the English translation of Pacioli's treatise found in Brown and Johnston, 1963, which appends a photographic reproduction of the original 1494 edition. I have also examined the second edition: Pacioli, 1523, pp. 197ᵛ–210ᵛ.

[50]Lane, 1973, pp. 142–43, provides illustrations and explanations of journal entries.

complete a venture, such as the shipping and selling of merchandise), the employee involved, partnership shares, and the debits and credits to be assumed by each partner. Pacioli demonstrated how to keep different kinds of accounts, such as household expenses and business expenses. He described the entries for business trips, the preparation of a profit and loss statement from the ledger, the correction of mistakes, balancing the ledger, and closing an account. Pacioli (and Manzoni) gave numerous realistic sample entries based on current firms, places, and conditions. Throughout their instruction, Pacioli and Manzoni, and presumably the teachers, went into minute detail to ensure that students understood correct procedure. Indeed, much instruction simply focussed on getting the details right.

Bookkeeping was more than a technique for keeping track of transactions. It expressed the Renaissance merchant's almost naive belief that life would be profitable and good if he could organize rationally and record everything. In the preface to his *Quaderno doppio,* Manzoni promised to teach the student how to deal with the accounting associated with any large or small transaction involving merchandise, rents from *Terraferma* farmlands, other rents, the expenses of house or villa, wages, house construction, loan accounts, treasury matters, disputes, imposts, dowries, counterdowries, marriages, inheritance, and litigation.[51] Double-entry bookkeeping raised a tent under which Italians might gather all the financial and other details of the most important events of their lives.

In the course of his instruction, Pacioli gave additional advice on the conduct of business. He explained such minor matters as how to tie into a bundle all the letters from one year or a branch office (p. 101), and that one should tip the messenger who delivers letters to get good service (p. 99). One must obtain handwritten receipts in duplicate, he insisted (p. 79). Some of Pacioli's almost obsessive concern for minor details came from his conviction that the merchant's role, though difficult, was essential for society's survival. "Businessmen maintain Republics" (p. 100). "More skills are required to make a good businessman than to make a good lawyer" (p. 101).

Pacioli frequently voiced the Renaissance merchant's deep conviction that only through exercising great caution, eternal vigilance, and care for the slightest detail might he avoid disaster. "A businessman rightly resembles a rooster which is the most alert animal that exists, because . . . it keeps night vigils in winter and summer, never resting" (p. 33). "It is

[51]". . . ogni grande & picciolo negotio over traffico, si de mercantie, come di entrade di Terra ferma, de fitti, spese di casa, de vila, de salariadi, de concieri & fabriche di case, di camere dimprestidi, di rason di Cecca, de lotti, di tanse, de rason di dotta, contradotta, & maridazi, di heredita, & litegamenti, di saldar il libro, per reportarlo in un'altro libro nuovo, del modo & ordine, a redrizar scritture o libri mal tenuti, & de moltissime altre cose. . . ." D. Manzoni, 1540, sig. ii^v.

always a good idea to close your books each year, especially if you are in a partnership. As the proverb says, 'Frequent accounting makes for lasting friendship' ('ragion spessa amista longa')" (pp. 87, 135). "The businessman must understand things better than the butcher" (p. 57). "He who does business without knowing all about it, sees his money go like flies" (p. 75). And, finally, Pacioli expressed the universal lament: "All these precautions must be taken because of the bad faith of the present times" (p. 79).

Pacioli and the accounting masters initiated their young charges into the world of Renaissance business. This included exhortations to conduct business honestly. Just as Latin pupils learned good morality from the classics, and vernacular pupils the same from Guevara's *Vita di Marco Aurelio,* so accounting students imbibed good commercial ethics. Pacioli lamented the practice of keeping two sets of books in order to deceive: "Unfortunately, there are many who keep their books in duplicate, showing one to the buyer and the other to the seller. What is worse, they swear and perjure themselves on them" (p. 38). And he told his readers to begin each letter by invoking the name of Jesus, "in whose name all business should be transacted," through the sign of the cross (p. 100). Nevertheless, like the abbaco texts, Pacioli never raised the specter of usury, but assumed that interest would be given and received. Through double-entry accounting, the vernacular schools introduced boys to the vocabulary, techniques, and mentality of Renaissance commerce.

WRITING

Both vernacular and Latin schools taught writing. They did not necessarily teach the same script at first, because writing styles reflected different professional roles. After 1500 a tendency toward uniform writing grew.

The early humanists inherited from the thirteenth and fourteenth centuries gothic handwriting, a vertical script characterized by lateral compression, angularity, the overlapping of rounded letters, and much abbreviation. The Italian version of gothic (often called *rotunda*) presented a slightly less severe form by rounding the letters more. Petrarch and Coluccio Salutati wrote *rotunda* throughout their lives, but complained that it weakened their overburdened eyes.

The humanistic movement produced new scripts.[52] Petrarch and his followers found some classical texts written in older script notable for its beauty and clarity. This was Carolingian minuscule, a small, rounded, upright hand closely associated with the revival of learning under Charlemagne around 800. It had the lure of antiquity—humanists thought that it

[52]See Ullman, 1960, for the well-known story.

came from ancient Rome—and seemed easier to read than gothic script. In 1402–3 Poggio Bracciolini (1380–1459), a young notary and humanist, wrote out a manuscript for Salutati in a new script that borrowed features of Carolingian minuscule. Poggio rounded the letters more than in *rotunda,* used fewer abbreviations, and spaced the individual letters more regularly. Scribes followed his example, especially when copying classical texts.

In the early 1420s, Niccolò Niccoli (1364–1437), another Florentine follower of Salutati and a friend of Poggio's, began to copy manuscripts in another new script, which seemed to run across the page in a slanted way. Niccoli had invented humanistic cursive. It owed something to Carolingian minuscule and a great deal to Poggio's formal humanistic script, but it also retained some gothic elements. Although lacking the stately beauty of Poggio's formal humanistic script, Niccoli's script offered ease and swiftness in writing. Scribes and patrons increasingly preferred these two new hands in the next half-century. Cosimo de' Medici wanted manuscripts copied in the new hands, and book dealers such as Vespasiano da Bisticci promoted them. Aided by a disdain for things "gothic," the two humanistic scripts spread across Italy.[53]

Despite the new developments, humanistic pedagogical treatises barely mentioned writing.[54] Only Aeneas Silvius Piccolomini took up the matter. In *De liberorum educatione* (1450), he ridiculed King Alfonso I of Naples (1395–1458) for his signature resembling "a worm crawling over the paper." A young prince must learn to write legibly, whether he formed round, square, oblong, or slanted letters. Piccolomini noted the existence of two systems of writing, "antique" (Carolingian minuscule/humanistic) and "modern" (gothic). He preferred "antique" for its ease in reading, neatness, and alleged closeness to its Greek origins. But whichever script a child learned, he should copy a good example, Piccolomini concluded.[55] He probably avoided condemning gothic script in deference to northern sensibilities, for he intended his treatise for the boy-king of Bohemia and Hungary.

Schoolboys enrolled in Latin schools learned the humanistic scripts, because chanceries adopted them in the second half of the Quattrocento. Vatican secretaries and their counterparts in republics and princedoms across Italy wrote letters and kept records in the new scripts, which

[53]Other scripts, such as *bastarda,* modified or combined the major scripts and were used less frequently. Osley, 1972, p. 4, lists the names of scripts employed by Renaissance writing masters.

[54]Although Woodward's translation (Woodward, 1963, p. 125) of Bruni's *De studiis et litteris* mentions cursive script, Bruni only said that he would not discuss calligraphy here. See Garin, ed., 1958, p. 150.

[55]See the text in Garin, ed., 1958, pp. 272, 274. Woodward, 1963, pp. 152–53, provides an accurate English version.

acquired new names: chancery formal (*cancelleresca formale*) for Poggio's script, and chancery cursive (*cancelleresca corsivo*) for Niccoli's hand.[56] The latter dominated. Famous humanistic secretaries such as Jacopo Sadoleto and Pietro Bembo in Rome drafted letters for their masters in Ciceronian Latin and copied them out in chancery cursive.

Printers adapted humanistic hands to their needs when engravers cut types based on the two chancery scripts. Chancery formal became roman typeface as early as circa 1470. Italian printers preferred roman for incunabular editions of Latin classics and contemporary humanistic texts. A few years later, other engravers cut italic types based on chancery cursive for Aldo Manuzio and his imitators.[57] The two typefaces coexisted peacefully, although after 1530 Italian printers tended to prefer italic for vernacular books and roman for Latin works.

But not all schoolboys learned chancery cursive. Late medieval and Renaissance merchants used a script called merchant (*mercantesca* or *mercantile*) or merchant cursive (*mercantesca corsivo*). Merchant script appeared in the account books of Trecento Florentine bankers and merchants, but almost nothing is known about its development.[58] Later Italians frequently employed it for keeping accounts, writing letters and diaries, and preparing abbaco treatises, mostly in the vernacular. Elaborate and sometimes exaggerated descenders (the stroke below the line in such lower-case letters as *g* and *y*) signalled merchant. The descenders seemed to be a series of ships sailing across the page (see illustration 12). Ascenders (the top part of lower-case letters such as *b* and *d*) also exhibited more pronounced loops than chancery cursive. Other letters, such as *m* and *r*, reflected the gothic origin of merchant script. *Mercantesca* had its own distinctive and sometimes elaborate abbreviations for ducat, lira, and other monetary terms. Pupils studying abbaco in the fourteenth and fifteenth centuries obviously learned to write merchant script in order to serve their employers.

In an ironic turn of events, printing aided the teaching of writing. As technical advances made it possible to cut cursive script for the press, the engraver brought to a wider audience the skills of the vernacular schoolmasters. Sigismondo Fanti's *Theorica et pratica . . . de modo scribendi fabricandique omnes litterarum species* of 1514 initiated a series of printed manuals that taught writing through explanation and beautifully engraved examples.[59] Most authors of early writing manuals came from the ranks of

---

[56]D'Amico, 1983, p. 30, for Rome; Black, 1985, pp. 155–57, for Florence.

[57]Lowry, 1979, pp. 136–41.

[58]See the comments of Van Egmond, 1981, pp. 14, 43, et passim.

[59]The two basic studies are Casamassima, 1966; and Osley, 1972. Several of the writing books have been reprinted in handsome modern editions; see Morrison, 1929; *Three Classics of Italian Calligraphy*, 1953; and Harvard, 1981. I have also examined several sixteenth-century editions of the writing manuals.

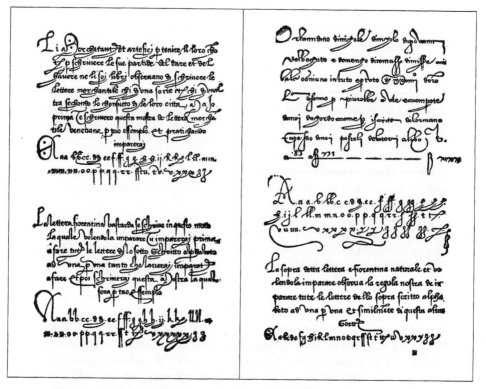

12. Writing examples from Giovanni Antonio Tagliente, *Lo presente libro insegna la vera arte delo excellente scrivere de diverse varie sorti de letere. . . . 1547.* Colophon: In Vinegia per Pietro di Nicolini da Sabio, 1548. IU.

abbaco teachers. Fanti advertised in his preface that he taught abbaco.[60] Domenico Manzoni, a teacher in Venice, wrote textbooks that taught writing, abbaco, accounting, and vernacular reading. Giovanni Antonio Tagliente, perhaps the best known of the writing masters who published in the 1520s, also emerged from the Venetian vernacular schools. Born between 1465 and 1470 in Venice, Tagliente tried to persuade the government to appoint him to teach writing to young chancery clerks.[61] The Venetians did not hire him directly, but gave him an administrative post that left him free to teach chancery boys and private pupils. Tagliente displayed the versatility of the vernacular master by publishing several writing manuals and an accounting textbook, plus collaborating in an

[60]Osley, 1972, p. 5.
[61]See ibid., pp. 15–16, for his biography.

undetermined way with a kinsman and former pupil, Girolamo Tagliente, in the preparation of the most frequently printed abbaco book of the sixteenth century.[62]

Writing manuals devoted most of their attention to teaching chancery cursive; space devoted to merchant script was limited. A Venetian teacher intending to instruct youths in both explained their status and functions. All sorts of people, including merchants, use chancery script, especially for writing letters, because it is "more beautiful to read and is shared by all," he wrote. One uses merchant script in ledgers, because it is difficult to counterfeit or falsify.[63] In other words, sixteenth-century Italians viewed chancery cursive as a script for general use, and limited merchant to specialized commercial application. One can be reasonably certain that Latin schools taught chancery cursive and that vernacular schools taught both chancery cursive and merchant, the latter in conjunction with abbaco and accounting.

Chancery cursive dominated Cinquecento correspondence and record keeping outside the merchant's ledger. Later in the century it took a turn for the worse. In 1560 Giovanni Francesco Cresci (c. 1535–1614) published his *Essemplare di più sorti lettere,* which taught a much more elaborate form of chancery cursive full of exaggerated ascenders and other frills. It won over the state bureaucracies of Italy by 1600 and spread abroad. Cresci inspired the mannered writing that makes research in seventeenth-century Italian records sometimes tedious.[64]

Classroom writing instruction involved several steps, some of them mechanical. The student had to learn to prepare a quill pen by trimming off the feathers and cutting the quill so as to make a point suitable for broad or narrow strokes. He had to choose the right kind of paper and learn to thin the ink.[65] Then he began to write. Renaissance teachers probably followed the pedagogy of ancient Rome.[66] The teacher wrote out the

[62]The book first appeared in 1515; I cite the second edition: G. Tagliente, 1520, sig. A2r. In some later printings examined, the reference to Giovanni Antonio Tagliente disappears. See Van Egmond, 1981, pp. 334–44, for a list of the editions.

[63]"Et avendo detto di sopra che i mercatanti (de i giudiciosi parlo) usano l'una et l'altra sorte di lettera, cioè la Cancelleresca et la Mercantile, non voglio restar di finir di dire per chi n'ha bisogno, che la Cancelleresca usano communemente nelle lettere missive, come più vaga à leggersi, et più commune à ciascuno. Et la Mercantile usan poi ne i libri, per esser molto più difficile à contrafarsi et massimamente à radersi et a falsare qualche parola. . . ." Domenico Manzoni, "Dell'alfabeto doppio come deve esser fatto et ordinato," which is appended to D. Manzoni, 1564, sig. M2r. A. Petrucci, 1978, p. 195 n. 40, first noted this comment.

[64]Osley, 1972, pp. 68–83. The introduction of highly acidic inks, which have eaten through the paper, is another problem.

[65]The writing manuals offered advice on these matters; also see the description in dialogue 10, "Scriptio," in Vives, 1908, pp. 71–73.

[66]Bonner, 1977, pp. 166–68.

alphabet, syllables, and words.[67] Then he put his hand over the child's hand in order to guide it through the unfamiliar motions. When the child could move his hand sufficiently well without external guidance, he practiced copying a model, first by tracing over a letter, then by making multiple repeated letters across the page. After learning to write one letter, he passed on to others. The student might write out the alphabet continuously, then write out syllables (*ba be bi bo bu*), and finally words. The teacher told students to write such round letters as *a, e,* and *o* in equal size; he gave instruction on the length of ascenders and descenders, which letters should be joined, and which separated.[68] After the student had mastered letters, syllables, and words, he copied longer texts. Printed writing books of the sixteenth century provided sample letters that teachers might write out for students to copy. When the student had mastered Italian or Latin sufficiently well, he could compose his own letters and copy them out in chancery cursive.

How long did it take to master a script? One writing master boasted that a gifted pupil could learn his version of chancery cursive in three months and the average pupil in five or six months. But pupils would need two or three years of hard work to learn chancery cursive from other writing masters, he claimed.[69] The master only hinted at the most important learning factors: the age and aptitude of the pupils and the learning conditions. His estimate of the time required by the pupils of other, lesser, masters seems realistic for all students. Very young pupils might need much time—months or a year and more—to master the smooth hand movements of chancery cursive. Consistent practice over several years might be needed to learn the script sufficiently well to embark on a chancery career.

Young people fortunate enough to attend formal schools for eight to ten years learned to write well. Boys and girls who attended formal schools for three to five years might learn to write either chancery cursive or merchant script adequately. But the semiliterate wrote a crude, eclectic script.[70] Those whose formal schooling ended after the primer or elementary writing stage, those who received irregular instruction in the catechism schools (see ch. 12), the beneficiaries of a little tutoring from relative or fellow worker, and the auto-didacts constituted the semiliterate. Their bits of writing—signatures, mistake-ridden words or phrases—might appear in capital letters exclusively or in an irregular combination of maius-

---

[67]"Pupil: Now give us a copy, if it seems good to you. Teacher: First the A B C, then syllables, then words joined together in this fashion. . . . Imitate these copies and come here after lunch, or even tomorrow, so that I may correct your writing." Vives, 1908, p. 74.

[68]Ibid., pp. 77–78.

[69]*Il secretario di Marcello Scalzini* (1581), as cited in Osley, 1972, p. 96.

[70]See the excellent discussion of the writing of the semiliterate by A. Petrucci, 1978.

cule and minuscule. Such writing might also mix together chancery cursive, merchant, and *rotunda* lettering.[71]

Ordinary printed books served as their writing models, a writing master noted. In the past, he said, many people used the forms of letters found in printed books, especially the lettering in choir books, missals, and psalters, when writing.[72] Moreover, old people lacking glasses, and women who did not know how to read well, used maiuscule letters extensively, again copied from printed books.[73]

A rudimentary eclectic script based on the typefaces in the books they read served the semiliterate. Their books—liturgical works, missals, the *Officium Beatae Mariae Virginis,* and primers with their alphabets, syllables, and prayers—usually appeared in semi-gothic[74] type or a mixture of semi-gothic and roman. Vernacular chivalric romances and elementary Latin grammars, especially the *Ianua,* also appeared in semi-gothic, or some mixture of semi-gothic, roman, and italic type, through the middle of the sixteenth century. Those lacking formal instruction laboriously copied the lettering of the books that circulated in their world. The printing press helped writing spread even among the barely educated.

[71]See illustrations 54, 76, 78, 157a, 179, 194, and 254 in A. Petrucci, ed., 1982.

[72]"Avanti questa nostra età non si scriveano, nè si usavano altre forme di lettere per ordinario, che quelle, che ne rappresentano hoggidi molte stampe, & particolarmente quelle, che al presente si costumano per libri da Choro, per Messali, & Salmi, della qual forma si veggono scritti infiniti libri in diverse parti dentro & fuori Italia." Scalzini, 1599, sig. B3r.

[73]". . . lettere antiche quadre, tonde, staccate, antichette tonde, queste tre servono per Privilegij, Officij, & particolarmente sono commode per quei vecchi c'hanno poca vista, ò non dedono senza occhiali, & per quelli, & quelle Donne che (non sapendo ben leggere) bramano sempre quelle forme di caratteri, che più assimigliano alle stampare, nelle quali hanno imparato a leggere Maiuscule. . . ." Ibid., sig. B1v.

[74]Semi-gothic seems the appropriate term for the typeface used in liturgical works, *Ianua* Latin grammars, and some vernacular titles of popular distribution. In the late Quattrocento and the early Cinquecento the original typeface based on *rotunda* lost some of its "gothic" qualities. It compressed less, eliminated most abbreviations and overlapping of letters, and allowed many letters to stand alone. While still obviously a gothic type, it moved closer to roman than did northern European "black letter" typefaces.

THE SCHOOLS OF THE
CATHOLIC REFORMATION

The men and women of the Catholic Reformation added new schools and pedagogical priorities to Renaissance education. Indeed, the Catholic reformers probably devoted more energy and resources to education than to any other religious or charitable activity. It all came from a single, original impulse, the desire to provide basic religious instruction in order to make men better in this life and to help them attain salvation in the next. The individuals and groups of the Catholic Reformation did not try to teach religion in isolation, but combined religious instruction with broader schooling. They taught vernacular reading and writing in free schools for the lower end of the population. At the top of the social ladder, they tried to mold the elite who pursued the Latin curriculum. Such diverse academic enterprises as the Sunday and holiday catechism classes for the poor and Jesuit boarding schools for nobles grew from the same desire to teach the doctrines of Catholicism. Not combating heresy, but the wish to reform morals and to save souls, motivated the educational reformers of the sixteenth century.

The move to expand education seems to have been a spontaneous impulse of the rank and file of Catholicism rather than the result of commands from above. Individuals such as the modest priest Castellino da Castello, the soldier turned ascetic Ignatius Loyola, and the founder of the Scuole Pie, José Calasanz, showed the way. Bishops and popes, nobles and civic leaders, followed. Most important, both rich and poor laymen made the new educational initiatives effective by sending their children to the new schools, by teaching in them, or by paying the bills. Schooling became more available in the late sixteenth century than it had ever been before. And it was more overtly religious.

CHAPTER TWELVE

The Schools of Christian Doctrine

hildren not destined to become clergymen or members of
religious orders probably received very little religious instruction prior to the sixteenth century. The hierarchy
seemed little concerned to provide religious instruction to lay
children. The activities of an exception, Bishop Nicolò Albergati (1375–
1444), elected bishop of Bologna in 1417, proved the point. In or about
1420, Albergati began to visit churches on holidays in order to teach the
elements of Catholicism to boys.[1] A schoolteacher and a few other laymen
accompanied him. By 1425 he had formed a twenty-four-member lay
confraternity of teen-age boys and adults to carry on the catechetical
instruction. The group soon split into separate confraternities, one for
adults and a second for youths aged 12 to 21. Mid-century statutes of the
latter confraternity exhorted its teen-age members to go out into the
streets every Sunday in order to teach the boys found there "la sancta
doctrina."[2] One wonders how many boys this small-scale informal effort
reached. Even less is known about the activities of the adult confraternity.
Bishop Albergati's initiative may not have had much lasting impact, partly
because he conceived it within the organizational framework and mentality of a small lay confraternity primarily concerned with other matters.

Quattrocento Latin schools did not provide very much religious instruction, either. Only Aeneas Sylvius Piccolomini among the humanistic
pedagogical theorists mentioned (briefly) religious training: "I assume, as
is proper for a Christian, that you have learned the Lord's Prayer, the Ave
Maria, [the preamble of] the Gospel of St. John, the Apostles' Creed, and
many other related matters: i.e., which are the capital sins, the gifts of the
Holy Spirit, the chief commandments of God, [and] the works of mercy.

---

[1]Mesini, 1981, pp. 242–51.
[2]"Et la domenica voi anderete a ensegnare la sancta doctrina conducendo con voi li pueri
che trovate per le strade." As quoted in ibid., p. 264.

These are the means of saving your soul and reaching heaven."[3] He then passed on to the *studia humanitatis*.

A contemporary account relates that Vittorino da Feltre took his pupils to daily mass and insisted that they confess and communicate, aid the poor, and observe the fasts of the Church. Since Vittorino knelt daily to recite the *Officium Beatae Mariae Virginis,* his princely pupils probably also knelt and prayed.[4] Aldo Manuzio prefaced his grammar manual with primer material that included the Pater Noster, Ave Maria, Apostles' Creed, Ten Commandments, Salve Regina, beginning of the Gospel of St. John, and other prayers.[5] These examples demonstrate that Quattrocento pupils learned the religious content of the primer. Boys and girls also acquired some general notion of Catholic belief by living in a society saturated with the ceremonies and traditions of Catholicism. But they apparently received no formal religious instruction beyond the prayers of the primer.

Stimulated by pious impulses, a few clergy and laymen began to offer religious instruction at the end of the Quattrocento. In 1473 Tommaso Grassi or Grasso, a wealthy Milanese merchant, made restitution for his usury by leaving in his will funds to hire five teachers to instruct 250 boys in reading, writing, abbaco, elementary Latin, and Christian doctrine.[6] These five schools seem to have become daily catechism schools, with writing and abbaco added in 1544.[7] They still functioned in 1591.[8] Two

[3]"Credimus te instructum esse, ut Christianum decet, orationem scire dominicam, salutationem beate Virginis, Johannis evangelium, symbolum fidei, collectas quoque plures, que sint mortis peccata, que sancti spiritus dona, que magni precepta dei, que opera misericordie, que denique salvande anime et in celum referende sit via." Piccolomini's *Tractatus de liberorum educatione* in Garin, ed., 1958, p. 226. I take "collectas quoque plures" to mean the collections or lists of virtues, sins, precepts, etc., found in elementary religious instructional material. Garin, ed., 1958, p. 227, and Woodward, 1963, p. 141, translate it a little differently.

[4]See the *Vita Victorini Feltrensis* (c. 1469) by his former pupil, Francesco da Castiglione (1434–84) in Garin, ed., 1958, p. 544.

[5]Manuzio, 1501.

[6]Tamborini, 1939, pp. 34–36; Castiglione, 1800, p. 16.

[7]The Confraternity of the Schools of Christian Doctrine (see below) apparently took over these schools and turned them into extended catechism schools that may have met daily. New regulations of 2 March 1544 established that the pupils should study four books: the "libretto," (i.e., the *Summario*), the primer, the *Interrogatorio,* and the *Little Office of Our Lady*. In addition, the new rules directed the schools to follow "il mode, e ordine" of "the schools that teach on the holidays for the love of God" ("Il modo, e ordine, che si hà da tenere nelle scole dove s'insegna le feste per l'amor de Dio"). See *Libretto,* 1567, sigs. A7r–v; repeated in *Libretto,* 1593a, sigs. A7r–v. The books of rules for the confraternities (*regole*), plus the *Summario* and *Interrogatorio* catechisms used in the Schools of Christian Doctrine, are listed in Appendix 3 rather than in the bibliography.

[8]Morigia, 1592, p. 407.

other attempts launched circa 1500 to catechize Milanese boys running the streets met with less success.[9]

Religious instruction next became a part of the developing Catholic Reformation. In the early 1530s the Venetian noble Girolamo Miani established orphanages for boys. Soon Miani and his orphans began to instruct large numbers of people on feast days.[10] Angela Merici (1470/75–1540) gathered young girls into her home at Desenzano in order to teach them the rudiments of Christianity.[11] In the above initiatives, catechetical instruction composed a segment rather than the sole activity of broad charitable enterprises.

Then Castellino da Castello began the Schools of Christian Doctrine, a movement devoted exclusively to religious instruction of the poor. Born between 1470 and 1480 at Menaggio on Lake Como, about forty miles north of Milan, Castellino may have come from an artisan family. Ordained a priest, he became a chaplain at a Milanese church; this is all that is known about him until 1536.[12]

In the fall of that year, Castellino and several lay associates founded the first School of Christian Doctrine. According to a popular account, on the Feast of St. Andrew (30 November), one of the numerous holidays on which work was suspended, a lay colleague of Castellino's went out into the streets of Milan with a large sack of apples. He began to throw apples to boys who were roaming the streets. With the apples he persuaded them to follow him to a church. There he and Father Castellino began to speak to the boys about salvation: they offered to teach them how to make the sign of the cross, promising an apple to the one who learned it first. When they had finished their instruction, they promised the boys more apples if they would return on the next holiday. They encountered opposition and ridicule, as some onlookers threw rotten apples and snowballs back at them.[13] But Castellino and his lay colleagues persevered until they had established holiday Schools of Christian Doctrine across the city.[14]

A lay confraternity called Compagnia della Reformatione Christiana in

---

[9]Tamborini, 1939, pp. 32–34, 36–38.

[10]Pellegrini, 1986, pp. 23–24; also see the sources listed in ch. 13 n. 112.

[11]Tamborini, 1939, pp. 40–42. For more on Merici and the Ursulines, see ch. 13 and the sources cited there.

[12]Cajani, 1978, summarizes what is known.

[13]"Andava per le strade predicando & esortando il popolo à frequentare la Dottrina Christiana; ma era burlato, perseguitato, e spreggiato con gettarli contro delle palle di neve, e pomi marci reputandolo pazzo. . . ." Porro, 1793, pp. 106–7. This was first published in 1640.

[14]Tamborini, 1939, pp. 50–52. Despite its uncritical viewpoint and occasional careless documentation, this account is fundamental and full of information.

Carità was founded in 1539 under Castellino to carry on the schools. The provocative name "Reformatione" and the use of laymen to teach laymen aroused the hostility of the Milanese hierarchy, which suspended the company in 1540. But in 1546 Castellino succeeded in winning approval for his catechetical efforts and the confraternity under the more modest name of Compagnia dei Servi di Puttini in Carità (Company of the Servants of Children in Charity).[15] The schools were universally called Scuole della Dottrina Christiana (Schools of Christian Doctrine).

Castellino probably looked forward from the beginning to the spread of the schools. The earliest surviving book of rules (Milan, 1555) directed the company to choose by ballot two members to found schools in the next town. In imitation of Christ's command to the apostles, they should take nothing with them, but might enter the houses of those prepared to receive them, eating and drinking according to their need (Matt. 9:5–15, Mark 6:7–13, Luke 9:1–6).[16] Indeed, the Schools of Christian Doctrine spread very rapidly, appearing in Pavia in 1538, Venice about 1540, Genoa, Verona, Vigevano, and Piacenza in 1541, Mantua and Parma in 1542, Lodi in 1545, Cremona in 1547, Varese in 1550, Novara in 1553, Bergamo and Brescia in 1554, Rome in 1560, Monza, Asti, and Ascoli in 1562, Desio, Belgioioso, Savona, Turin, and Ferrara in 1563, and Como in 1565. By the time Castellino died in 1566, he and his collaborators had achieved remarkable success in bringing the schools to the cities and towns, and to a limited extent, the countryside, of northern Italy.[17]

Lay confraternities under various names operated the schools. As always with Renaissance religious organizations, the confraternities combined an elaborate system of rotating elective offices with an intense concern for the spiritual welfare of the members. Castellino's movement fostered extensive adult lay participation. Twenty-five laymen assisted Castellino in leading the Milanese confraternity; additional laymen and laywomen taught, acted as ushers, maintained silence in the schools, and kept records, according to the Milanese rule of 1555.[18] Group religious exercises, such as reception of the Eucharist on specific days, promoted the spiritual welfare of the members. Confraternities in other cities followed the same pattern.[19]

---

[15]Porro, 1793, pp. 4–5; and Tamborini, 1939, pp. 86–92.

[16]*La regola della compagnia delli servi dei puttini in carita* (Milan, 1555) is reprinted in Marcora, 1960, pp. 470–81. The reference is to ch. 12 on p. 477. I have added the precise biblical citations.

[17]See Castiglione, 1800, passim; and Tamborini, 1939, passim. Cajani, 1978, p. 787, collects the towns and dates.

[18]Marcora, 1960, pp. 470–81, esp. pp. 479–80. *Regola*, 1566, esp. sigs. A7ᵛ–A8ʳ, shows that the Milanese confraternity had the same structure in 1566.

[19]In addition to the *regola* of Milan, 1555, in Marcora, 1960, pp. 470–81, see the fourteen other *regole*, 1566 through 1685, listed in Appendix 3.

Especially after the Council of Trent endorsed them and local bishops promoted them, the Schools of Christian Doctrine taught a large number of children. In Milan in 1564 about 200 adults taught more than 2,000 students in 28 catechism schools.[20] Bolognese schools enrolled close to 4,900 children in 1568. In 1577, the next year for which figures are available, average Sunday and holiday enrollment ranged from 3,000 to 4,000. Bolognese catechism attendance averaged about 3,300 for every Sunday through the first ten and a half months of 1579.[21] Bologna had between 7,000 and 10,000 boys and girls aged 5 through 14, so at least 40 percent of the children attended on any given average Sunday. More than 600 adults taught in the Bolognese catechism schools in 1583.[22] Milan had about 120 catechism schools in 1591.[23] Approximately 7,000 Milanese boys and 5,750 girls attended Schools of Christian Doctrine in 1599, when the city had about 200,000 people overall. At that time about 7,700 adults (3,730 men and 3,970 women) participated in the confraternity, a figure that may have included casual and inactive members.[24] Venice in the 1590s had 500 who taught 6,000 boys and girls in 30 or more schools, in a total population of about 150,000.[25] The Schools of Christian Doctrine flourished in Florence under the leadership of Ippolito Galantini (1565–1619).[26] The Roman confraternity had about 730 male members, including 270 active ones, plus 370 women, the majority active, in 1609. Its membership came from all ranks of society. A small sample included two ambassadors, a "gentleman," a lawyer, merchant, barber, carpenter, cloth dyer, stonecutter,

[20]Tamborini, 1939, p. 194.

[21]As Turrini, 1982, p. 458 n. 271, points out, it is not clear whether the figures of 1579 include boys and girls or boys only. If the latter is the case, then about two-thirds of the circa 5,000 Bolognese boys aged 5 through 14 attended catechism schools at this time.

[22]Prodi, 1959–67, vol. 1:182–87; Turrini, 1982, pp. 458, 461.

[23]Morigia, 1592, p. 407.

[24]Tamborini, 1939, pp. 323–26.

[25]The estimate of 6,000 pupils is the product of two sources. Venice in 1591 had thirty catechism schools, according to VC, Ms. Cicogna 3062, fasc. 4, a packet of materials on Venetian catechism schools, no pagination (Baldo, 1977, p. 8 n. 1, first noted this source.) In 1596 Lodovico Carbone reported that Venice had twenty-two schools for girls alone, that each school (boys or girls) had 200 pupils, and that about 500 adults labored in the Venetian catechism schools (Carbone, 1596, pp. 117, 130, 132). A minimum of thirty schools with 200 pupils each yields enrollment of at least 6,000 pupils. The figure may have been higher, because Patriarch Lorenzo Priuli actively encouraged the Venetian catechism schools. Carbone's figures deserve respect, because he was active in the Venetian catechism schools at the time. A layman born circa 1545 in Urbino, Carbone earned a doctorate in theology and philosophy, taught in Perugia (perhaps at the university), may have been a Jesuit at one time, wrote a treatise on sacred eloquence, and taught independently in Venice in October 1587. ACPV, "Professioni di fede," fols. 322^r–323^r. His *Dello ammaestramento de' figliuoli nella dottrina Christiana* of 1596 is a mine of information.

[26]See Sorgenti, 1825; D'Addario, 1972, pp. 45–47, 298–301; and *La comunità cristiana fiorentina*, 1980, pp. 120–29.

waller, and glass blower among the men, plus a duchess, weaver, carpenter, and vendor of olive oil among the women.[27]

The catechism schools met on Sundays and religious holidays, a total of eighty-five or more days a year.[28] They began at an unspecified time after the midday meal and continued until three hours before sunset in the summer (ending at about 5:00 P.M. in July) and until a half-hour before sunset in winter (about 4:30 P.M. in January).[29] The instruction probably averaged two hours or a little more per day.[30] Supporters felt that the schools should not last too long: "Many of them [i.e., children] spend the whole day in the shop or in school and, therefore, need some relaxation, a necessity for their age. The same can be said for many members of the confraternity, who also have other things to do."[31] Confraternities used various devices to encourage parents to send their children, including the device of "fishermen" (*pescatori*). Members walked the streets with two children, ringing a little bell and calling out, "Fathers and mothers, send your children to learn Christian doctrine. Otherwise you will have to render a strict accounting to God on Judgment Day!"[32]

Having been "fished" from homes and streets, the boys went to one church, girls to another to be taught. Men instructed boys, and women taught girls; the sexes did not mix. Pupils ranged in age from 5 or 6 to 14 or 15, with younger children probably dominating. The schools divided the pupils into three or more levels of difficulty and might add an additional class for pupils aged 15 and older.

READING AND WRITING

The catechism schools taught reading and writing as well as religion, according to sixteenth-century *regole*. An independent source confirms that Milanese catechism schools continued to teach reading and writing in

[27]Rivabene, 1982, p. 302, based on two documents.
[28]See, for example, the calendar in *Regole*, 1598, sigs. C3v–C4v.
[29]"Che li figliuoli si tengano occupati nell'essercitio della Scola solamente dal doppo disnare lo inverno fin' a le vintitre hore e meza in circa: E la estade, fin' alle vintiun'hora in circa, e poi subito siano licentiati." Montorfano, *Ordini*, 1568, p. 45, cited in Appendix 3. Sunset times are for central and northern Italy.
[30]Turrini, 1982, p. 413, suggests that the schools lasted an hour and a half in the two winter months and two hours in the summer.
[31]"Molti di loro stanno tutto il giorno nelle boteghe, o nelle schuole, è però hanno bisogno di qualche relassamento, cibo necessario alla loro età. Il medesimo diresti di molti operarij: i quali anco hanno qualche loro negotio da fare." Carbone, 1596, p. 192. Confraternities invariably referred to their members who taught as "operarii."
[32]"Padri e Madri, mandate i vostri figliuoli alla dottrina Christiana, altrimente n'haverete da render stretto conto a Dio nel giorno del Guidicio." *Regole*, 1598, pp. 26r–v. Exactly who initiated the practice is not clear, though Carlo Borromeo's early biographers credited him. All that can be said for certain is that "fishing" for students early on became standard.

1591 and probably beyond.[33] Venetian catechism schools may also have taught elementary Latin grammar in 1568.[34]

The catechism schools taught reading and writing as well as religion for two reasons. First, the early Catholic reformers did not envision religious training in isolation; rather, it was part of a broader charitable thrust. Miani and others developed comprehensive programs for needy children which combined spiritual and physical charity, that is, religious training, a place to live, and vocational instruction including that leading to literacy. Castellino and his followers shared this vision; indeed, the language of charity permeated the *regole* of the confraternities. The confraternities viewed spiritual ignorance and illiteracy as two aspects of a deprived condition. Second, Castellino and his disciples regarded elementary religious instruction and learning to read as synonymous. Children learned the fundamentals of religion by chanting and memorizing the Our Father, Hail Mary, and so on. Children also learned to read and write by chanting and memorizing prayers. The pedagogy employed and the elementary catechisms made this clear.

A typical school had at least three teachers: a chief teacher (called the prior) who taught the children the fundamentals of Catholicism, a second teacher who taught reading, and a third who taught writing.[35] Several *regole* stressed that a teacher should instruct only eight to ten pupils. The large number of adults involved in the confraternities and the ample space afforded by churches meant that the schools could easily heed this directive. Small group instruction obviously facilitated learning. Teachers arranged the children in a circle so that each could recite individually, slowly and distinctly. The teacher should spoon feed (*imboccandoli*) the material as the children held their books.[36] The confraternity provided books for

---

[33]". . . come in Milano oltre alle cento e venti scuole della dottrina Christiana, che mostrano leggere, & scrivere gratamente. . . ." Morigia, 1592, p. 407. Also see Turrini, 1982, pp. 428–31. Toscani, 1984, emphasizes the role of the Schools of Christian Doctrine in spreading literacy in the early modern period.

[34]"Prima, che se introduchino solamente nelle Scole per l'imparar i Putti questi libri, cioè, il libretto overo tavola, il Donato, a tempo, & l'ufficio della Madonna . . . & si metti a imparare, sopra ogni cosa, lo Interrogatorio. . . ." Montorfano, *Ordini*, 1568, p. 43. I have been unable to verify that Venetian catechism schools taught Latin, and I have my doubts.

[35]"In tutte le scuole, si di putti quanto di puttine, gli siano cinque operaii, vidilicet. Uno Priore che habbia il governo della scuola, et che insegni dire a mente li commandamenti d'Iddio, et le opere della misericordia, etc. Uno Sottopriore, che insegni leggere. Uno che insegni scrivere. Uno che mantenghi il silentio. Uno portinaro." The *regola* of 1555 in Marcora, 1960, p. 479. The identical words are found in *Regola*, 1566, sigs. A7v–A8r.

[36]"Gli faranno recitare separatamente ad uno ad uno, commandando però, che tutti stiano in piedi in modo di circulo a sentire gl' altri, saranno patienti nell'insegnar' ad agio distintamente, & a sillaba per sillaba bisognando massimamente a coloro c'hanno qualch' impedimento di lingua, perche in somma in questo consiste gran parte del guadagno spirituale dell'operare" (*Regole*, 1598, p. 24r). ". . . imboccandoli non solo le parole, ma anche le sillabe

those too poor to purchase their own. In other words, the catechism schools employed the same painfully slow but thorough teaching pedagogy of the primary school: the students spoke aloud and memorized letters, then syllables, then words, sentences, whole prayers, and the questions and answers of the *Interrogatorio,* the advanced catechism.

A few other members of the confraternity assisted in non-teaching roles. A *portinaro* (doorkeeper) opened the school, kept it clean, set the benches in order, kept out dogs and troublemakers, relieved the boys of sticks, and admonished those who entered to kneel and say an Our Father. When nature called, he made sure that only one boy went out at a time, leaving his book behind. Venetian catechism schools added a *scrivano* (scribe), who kept records, filled the inkwell, and gathered the textbooks.[37]

The schools divided the two hours or so into shorter periods for different kinds of instruction. The whole school might begin with fifteen minutes of prayers and hymns before splitting into smaller groups according to age or activity. The prior could spend an hour or more teaching from the *Interrogatorio* (see below) and then lead a question-and-answer session for thirty minutes to ensure that the pupils retained what they had learned. A group of younger children studied the basic prayers from the *Summario* (see below). Another group learned to read by reading and reciting the Pater Noster. The schools took advantage of the space afforded in a church and the numerous teachers available to send the children from place to place to learn different things. Sometimes a series of signs directed the children to where they could learn the alphabet, read and memorize the *Summario,* read the *Interrogatorio,* learn to write and count, or learn about Holy Communion.[38] The ringing of a bell signalled the end of one activity and the beginning of another. Two or more pupils might hold a disputation (*disputa*) in front of the entire school. However, here the traditional term for a formal academic disputation meant only a question-and-answer quiz on points memorized from the catechisms. The victor earned holy pictures and prayer books as prizes. Then a pupil might ascend the pulpit to deliver a little sermon (*sermoncino*). A litany led by a child or two and joined by all was a common closing exercise. The students then left "two by two in silence." Dismissal by pairs not only evoked Christ

ad una ad una, tenendo esse il libro in mano" (*Regole,* 1668, pp. 75–76). Also see *Regole,* 1678, pp. 38–39. ". . . avertendo li maestri di dover tutti insegnare ad litteram . . . essendo di mediocre capacità." Cabrini, *Ordini,* 1685, p. 19. Also see Turrini, 1982, pp. 423–25.

[37]Marcora, 1960, pp. 479–80; *Regola,* 1566, sig. A8r; Montorfano, *Ordini,* 1568, pp. 27–28, 34–35.

[38]Cabrini, *Ordini,* 1685, contains a number of fold-out diagrams showing where the teacher is to stand, where the pupils should sit, how to conduct a procession in church, etc. Also see Tamborini, 1939, pp. 76–77; and Turrini, 1982, p. 420.

sending his disciples out into the world, but also discouraged screams and scuffles on a Sunday afternoon.

Proponents of the Schools of Christian Doctrine endorsed a simple, commonplace psychology of education. The schools should "print Christ on the blank minds of children."[39] The minds of the young must be "stamped" with notions of good belief and behavior. Boys must be properly formed because they will become fathers and teach their sons.[40]

The confraternities tried to make the voluntary schools enjoyable. The *regole* repeatedly expressed such sentiments as "Children are happy with the promise of rewards and the admiration of their peers. They love to answer questions when publicly praised. Children enjoy singing, which banishes boredom." In hot weather the doorkeeper should bring in a bucket of "good water" for the pupils to drink.[41] Donations received by the confraternity went toward the purchase of prizes, books, benches, and "good water."[42]

The *regole* admonished teachers to avoid using corporal punishment: do not hit the children, lest you drive them away and anger their parents. Teachers should use charm rather than severity, words rather than deeds. The Milanese schools added a "silencer" (*silentiero*) who with a long rod might touch a noisy child on the shoulder.[43] The rules permitted teachers to impose a "mortification," such as ordering a miscreant to kiss the floor. They were forbidden to slap pupils except as a last resort, and then only with the permission of the prior.[44]

The Venetian catechism schools of the 1560s incorporated a limited amount of teacher training. A veteran teacher, called the "novice-master,"

[39]". . . imprimere Christo nelle nude menti de' fanciulli. . . ." Carbone, 1596, p. 93.

[40]". . . perche stampandosi nelle menti pure de' fanciulli quello, che devono credere, e quello che havro à fare. . . . formaranno la vita loro, e dovendo col tempo esser padri di famiglia, quello stesso insegnaranno à i loro figliuoli. . . ." Quoted from an undated letter of Venetian Patriarch Lorenzo Priuli, Patriarch of Venice, 1591–1600, in *Regole*, 1678, sigs. A2r–v.

[41]"Che la Estade per rispetto de i gran caldi si lascino alle volte bevere i figliuoli con ordine & ubbidientia: tenendo li Portinari, con licentia del Reverendo Prior, ò Sottopriore in loro custodia uno mastelletto di buon'acqua preparata per tempo, con delle scudelle da bevere, a spesa delli Fratelli." Montorfano, *Ordini*, 1568, p. 48.

[42]Carbone, 1596, p. 121.

[43]The *regola* of 1555 in Marcora, 1960, pp. 479, 480; *Regola*, 1566, sig. A8r.

[44]The emphasis on making the schools joyful and the prohibition of corporal punishment except in extreme circumstances appeared in the first *regola*, that of Milan, 1555, and continued throughout the literature. Here is a typical statement: "Quando bisognerà castigare i fanciulli per alcuno difetto, si facci con molta discretione, adoperando più tosto la piacevolezza, che il rigore, & le parole, che i fatti, ne mai si dia loro palmate, ne altre pene, se prima non haveranno provate alcune mortificationi, come di fargli baciare la terra. . . ." *Constitutioni*, 1611, p. 52. Also see Carbone, 1596, pp. 179–80, 188–90, 195, 232. The only exception was *Libretto*, 1593a, sigs. A2r, A3r, which permitted the teachers more latitude in administering physical punishment.

drew aside the newcomers (called "novices") who had volunteered to assist in the schools and taught them how to read, if they could not, and instructed them in the material of the *Interrogatorio,* if they could. The novices were not to be embarrassed by their ignorance in front of the children.[45] In addition, older pupils helped instruct younger ones. Such procedures demonstrate the popular base of the schools and the secondary result of adult education.

The Schools of Christian Doctrine probably taught both boys and girls from the beginning, for the earliest *regola* of 1555 endorsed the teaching of girls by female instructors.[46] Girls' schools were identical to those of boys. Both had the usual complement of three teachers, a doorkeeper, and a silencer, and the *regole* sometimes insisted that both must follow the same procedures and obey the same rules.[47] Catechisms often explicitly stated in their title pages or introductory material that they were intended for both sexes.[48]

Women teaching religion in church provoked some criticism, which Lodovico Carbone answered. Some say that women should not teach, because St. Paul wrote that a woman must be silent in church (1 Cor. 14:34–35; 1 Tim. 2:12–15), he began. But Paul meant only that she should not speak in the presence of men and must avoid usurping man's function. St. Paul wrote elsewhere that women can and should speak in church (1 Tim. 3:11–12). Moreover, deaconesses taught in the early church. The schools ignored objections to female teachers and similar opposition to laymen teaching in church for pragmatic reasons. Do you want to close down the catechism schools? Carbone asked rhetorically.[49] The laity furnished the personnel who enabled the catechism schools to function.

How much reading and writing did children who attended the catechism schools, but not formal schools, learn? The Schools of Christian Doctrine met eighty-five or more days a year for about two hours or a little

---

[45]"I Maestri de' Novitij, cioè delli Giovani & huomini, che vengono di nuovo con buon'animo di servir, & aiutare le Scole . . . perche poi questi tali hanno gran bisogno di essere particolarmente bene instrutti di tal'impresa, gli attenderanno con ogni destrezza & charità, retirandosi in qualche luogo separatamente dalli Putti, acciò non si vergognano di essi, e gli facciano imparare a lettere per una meza hora alla volta, se non saperanno leggere, e che siano atti a imparare, & che vogliano." Montorfano, *Ordini,* 1568, pp. 30 (quote), 31.

[46]"Però studiaranno tutti gli fratelli et sorelle della compagnia. . . ." *Regola* of 1555 in Marcora, 1960, p. 470.

[47]"In tutte le scuole, si di putti quanto di puttine, gli siano cinque operarii, vidilicet." *Regola* of 1555 in Marcora, 1960, p. 479; repeated in *Regola,* 1566, sig. A7v.

[48]See the title pages of *Modo,* 1566; *Dottrina Christiana,* 1579; Montorfano, *Interrogatorio,* 1560; plus editions of 1570, 1585, and 1595, as listed in Appendix 3. See also catechisms nos. 10, 16, 24, 65, 66, 67, 79, 109, and 110, listed by Turrini, 1982, pp. 474, 475, 479, 481, 483.

[49]Carbone, 1596, pp. 145–46. I have filled out and corrected some of Carbone's scriptural references. On the pedagogical role of deaconesses, see Thurston, 1913.

longer, with prayers and other activities occupying part of the time. This did not allow for a great deal of instruction. Hence, progress depended mostly on the aptitude of individual children. Some probably learned to read with little instruction; others could not learn thus. The regular phonetic structure and orthography of Tuscan Italian, which was becoming the norm in the Cinquecento, enabled beginners to move quickly. Reinforcement also played a key role. Encouragement and supplemental instruction by parent, sibling, or colleague in the shop obviously helped, a particularly relevant point for girls. Although generally confined to the home, girls did attend catechism schools. Regular attendance, plus support at home, may have enabled a number of girls to acquire rudimentary literacy. Some adults also probably acquired basic literacy through the Schools of Christian Doctrine, because confraternity members instructed illiterate volunteers.

A bound volume of four catechism booklets published in Milan and Brescia in 1567 and 1568 suggests that some individuals certainly did learn reading and writing in the catechism schools. On the inside of the front cover a crude hand wrote out the alphabet and Pater Noster, and added a name: "sia datta in mane del s^r. barba Szaba" ("written in the hand of Mr. Barba Szaba"). The back cover carries a laboriously written Ave Maria and the alphabet twice, in two equally unpracticed hands.[50] Although the writing cannot be dated, the location and contents of this crude writing suggest that it was the result of catechism school instruction.

THE *SUMMARIO*

The Schools of Christian Doctrine began with a combination primer and list of the fundamentals of Catholicism most often called *Summario* (Summary) or *Summario della vita Christiana*, a little booklet of sixteen pages in the textbook size of duodecimo (15 × 10 cm.).[51] The typography of the *Summario* was as conservative as that in other elementary textbooks: a first page in Gothic and antique Roman type, the rest in antique Roman type. Like copies of other elementary textbooks, copies of the *Summario* usually contained typographical errors.

The first page—which sometimes also doubled as the title page—began with IESUS in capital letters. Next came crosses signifying the sign of the cross, followed by the alphabet and words of the sign of the cross: "In nomine Patris, et Filij, et Spiritus Sancti."

---

[50]MA S.N.F.I.62. The bound volume includes Pius V's letter of 6 October 1567, a short collection of prayers to Mary of 1567, a *Summario* of 1567, and an *Interrogatorio* of 1568.

[51]The following remarks are based on six *Summarii*, 1566 through 1593, listed in Appendix 3. They are very consistent in format and content.

The Schools of Christian Doctrine gave the sign of the cross an iconographical prominence not found in earlier catechetical instruction. As mentioned before, Castellino started the movement by teaching the sign of the cross to Milanese street urchins. Later teachers also began by explaining the hand movements and the words of the sign of the cross, although they did not interpret it at length. The title pages of *Summarii* and *Interrogatorii* often displayed one cross, three crosses, or a crucifixion scene of Christ between the two thieves. An additional woodcut or engraving might appear within the text of the booklets.

After the alphabet and sign of the cross, the *Summario* proceeded to prayers in Latin: Pater Noster, Ave Maria, Credo, and Salve Regina (Queen of Heaven). The *Summario* then switched to Italian for the baptismal promises, the Ten Commandments, two precepts of the law of grace ("Love one God alone with all our heart, with all our spirit, with our whole mind, and with all our force, and our neighbor as ourselves"). Then followed two canons of the natural law: "Do not do to others what you do not wish them to do to you"; "Do unto others what you reasonably wish for yourself." Next came lists of the four cardinal virtues, seven gifts of the Holy Spirit, seven spiritual works of mercy, seven corporal works of mercy, seven capital sins, the opposite seven virtues, the three powers of the spirit ("memory, intellect, and will"), the five senses of the body (sight, hearing, smell, taste, and touch), seven sacraments of the Church, and ten commandments of the Church.

The *Summario* offered, without explanation, prayers, precepts, and lists to be memorized. Just as letters of the alphabet and syllables served as the building blocks of reading, so these rudiments were the bricks of Catholicism. The rest of the *Summario* presented more of the same with a minimum of instruction. It continued with a list of what the Christian had to do to keep holy the sabbath: abstain from sin and servile work, be contrite for your sins, adore God, give thanks for benefits received, and spend the day attending mass, including listening to the sermon. Do not pass the day playing, dancing, wandering about the piazza, or in debauchery and nonsense. Next followed the eight beatitudes, grace before meals (in Latin—the first use of Latin since the opening two pages), the four fruits of confession, the twelve fruits of Holy Communion, and hymns.

The contents of the *Summario* came from the Middle Ages. St. Augustine pioneered teaching through numerical multiples, especially multiples of seven, as a mnemonic device. He and various medieval authorities developed most of the rest of the standard elementary catechetical material found in the *Summario*. The pedagogical separation of basic principles from a biblical context or the life of Christ also came from the Middle Ages. Like their predecessors, Schools of Christian Doctrine catechists assumed that a student's verbal mastery of the truths of Catholicism under summary headings indicated an adequate conceptual grasp for this stage of instruction.[52]

But the *Summario* did not replicate previous manuals. Its organization—which matters as much as or more than content in elementary textbooks—showed the difference. Early Quattrocento vernacular manuscripts entitled "Trattato della Dottrina Christiana" presented the Credo, Ten Commandments, seven mortal sins, seven gifts of the Holy Spirit, four cardinal sins, and so on, with a minimum of explanation, but in a different order.[53] An anonymous *Libreto dela Doctrina Christiana,* printed at least nine times between 1473 and 1500, listed and explicated the Ten Commandments, Credo, seven sacraments, seven gifts of the Holy Spirit, seven works of corporal mercy, seven works of spiritual mercy, eight beatitudes, three theological virtues, four cardinal virtues, seven deadly sins, seven cardinal virtues, five senses of the body, and a praise of eternal life attributed to St. Bernard.[54] But it lacked the alphabet, sign of the cross, prayers, hymns, and occasional advice on behavior found in sixteenth-century *Summarii.* The fifteenth-century work offered different and theologically more complex explanations than the *Summario.* In short, the unknown compilers of the *Summario* rearranged traditional lists of religious information, and combined this material with the primer, in order to produce an elementary booklet suitable for the Schools of Christian Doctrine.

THE *INTERROGATORIO*

The *Interrogatorio,* a larger question-and-answer catechism of 120 to 220 pages, depending on printing format, served as the textbook for more advanced religious instruction.

Nothing is known about the authorship and publication of the first *Interrogatorio,* because the earliest printings have not survived.[55] For example, a seventeenth-century source credited Castellino da Castello with composing the first one in 1537, a claim that cannot be confirmed or denied.[56] The earliest surviving *Interrogatorio* appeared in Venice in 1551 or

[52]See the perceptive remarks of Sloyan, 1967.

[53]See FR Ms. 1716, fols. 1–12^v; and FR Ms. 1657, fols. 80^v–81^r. The latter manuscript carries the date 1410 and was copied by a Florentine.

[54]It was appended to St. Antoninus's *Confessionale.* See Goff A-845, 849, 851–55, 859–60. I have examined the editions of Venice: Antonius de Strata da Cremona, 13 July 1486 (A-854, GW 2165); and [Hermannus Liechtenstein for] Franciscus de Ragazonibus, 8 October 1491 (Goff A-859, GW 2167).

[55]Some of the vernacular catechisms for the laity which reforming clergymen wrote in the 1540s have not survived. Older sources mention editions of the *Interrogatorio* of 1542, 1547, and Brescia, 1551, which cannot be located today. See Turrini, 1982, items II, 2a, 3a, and 5, on pp. 471–73.

[56]Porro, 1793, p. 106.

1552: *Interrogatorio del maestro al discepolo per instruir li fanciulli & quelli che non sanno nella via di Dio.*[57]

The preface explained that the book intended to teach boys and girls everything that a faithful Christian needed to know. If parents lacked such information, they also should come to learn. All must honor God rather than dance, gamble, and sin on feast days.[58] The preface continued its argument for religious instruction by attacking secular learning based on the classics of antiquity, a target of some Catholic reformers.[59] In his effort to persuade readers to turn from secular to religious learning, the author held up "the Lutherans" as an example to emulate: they scorn worldly wisdom in their public and private schools. Their children attend only to the law of Christ, even though they interpret it according to the flesh and not the spirit of Christ.[60] No other catechetical work mentioned Protestants.

The text proper began by describing how to make the sign of the cross with the aid of a crucifixion woodcut and explaining the significance of the words (sigs. A4v–A6r). It then initiated the questions and answers: What is the sign of the good Christian? Answer: The sign of the holy cross. Like the *Summario,* the *Interrogatorio* went on to prayers such as the Apostles' Creed and the Pater Noster, adding explanation and elaborate details.

The 1551/52 *Interrogatorio* introduced early on two themes prominent in future catechisms. The fear of the Lord was the beginning of wisdom (sig. A2r), and the Christian must do good works. Will he who believes in God be saved? No. Why not? Because many false Christians who fail to do works will not be saved. A few lines later, the text posed the question anew: Will he who believes in God be saved? Yes, because he will strive to love Him with his whole heart, to do works, and to obey the commandments for love of Him (sigs. B7r–v). Despite awkward presentation, the text made the point very clearly: faith without works will not save, but active faith that moves man to do good works will. However, the 1551/52 *Interrogatorio* did not pursue the point.

The 1551/52 *Interrogatorio* highlighted many themes characteristic of late

---

[57]See *Interrogatorio,* 1551/52, in Appendix 3, for full title, description, and discussion of the publication date.

[58]Condemnation of holiday merrymaking marked the literature of the Schools of Christian Doctrine, because Castellino and his followers saw restoring holiness and sobriety to the Sabbath as part of their mission.

[59]See P. Grendler, 1977, pp. 67–70.

[60]"Excitivi in questo la cecita de Lutherani, li quali postergata ogni altra Sapientia in li loro studii publici & privati, & le loro figlioli solo attendano a la legge di Christo, benche la intendino, & interpretino a loro modo secondo la carne & non secondo lo Spirito de Christo. Ne vi scusate dire che non si trova Libri catholici di elegante & sottile Latinita, peroche, & Santo Augustino de Civitate Dei, & al Santo Hieronymo in le Epistole sue, & Lattantio Firmiano, & altri libri santi non manchariano. . . ." *Interrogatorio,* 1551/52, sigs. A3r–v.

medieval catechesis. It spent a good deal of time on a symbolic theology of praise by introducing descriptive names for Jesus Christ. Why do we call Him physician? Because by the virtue of His passion through the holy sacraments, He cures the infirmity of our souls. Why do we call Him saint of saints? Because all the saints are saints through His sanctity. Why do we call Him lion? Because through His bravery He has thrown to earth the devil and death. And much more (sigs. A7^v–A8^r). Other medieval motifs included renunciation of the world, a tendency to condemn many human acts as mortal sins and, above all, devoting much attention to making a good confession. The *Interrogatorio* did the last by cataloguing numerous possible sins. It even listed sins and sinners, such as inquisitors who misused their office, which only pope or bishop could absolve (sigs. D3^v–F8^r). On the other hand, the *Interrogatorio* avoided the medieval preoccupation with dying well. The *Interrogatorio* studied virtues mostly through their opposed vices; it emphasized obedience to superiors fairly strongly. Although clearly part of Catholic Reform catechesis, the text perpetuated much medieval content in a disorganized way. Above all, it did little or nothing to adapt doctrinal material to the intended audience, lay children and the adults who would teach them. The 1551/52 *Interrogatorio* did not chart a new catechetical direction; perhaps for this reason it failed to become the normative text.

The next *Interrogatorio* did become the standard text: *Modo breve et facile, utile, et necessario, in forma di dialogo, di amaestrare i figliuoli mascoli, & femine, & quelli che non sanno, nelle divotioni, & buoni costumi del viver Christiano* (A brief, easy, useful, and necessary method, in the form of a dialogue, to instruct boys and girls and those who do not know, in the devotions and good customs of Christian life), published in Venice, 1560.[61]

Contemporaries attributed this anonymous work to Giovanni Paolo Montorfano (or Giovanpaolo da Como), a Theatine priest from Como with much experience catechizing children in Venice and elsewhere.[62] He became a Theatine in 1553 and died in 1580; very little else is known.[63] Subsequent printings appeared under Montorfano's name; he also drafted and published in 1568 the rules of the Venetian confraternity of the Schools of Christian Doctrine.[64]

A question-and-answer text of 220 pages, the 1560 *Interrogatorio* was divided into three parts, each with its own title page displaying the three crosses. The clean typographical format set off the pupil's questions with appropriate spacing and large Roman type; the teacher's responses ap-

---

[61]See Montorfano, *Interrogatorio*, 1560, cited in Appendix 3.

[62]See the letter of Alessandro Sauli of 6 September 1564, as quoted in Premoli, 1913, p. 470.

[63]Vezzosi, 1780, vol. 2:78–79.

[64]Montorfano, *Ordini*, 1568.

peared in smaller Roman type. In his unsigned preface Montorfano stated that with the permission of his superiors he had "reformed and renewed" the text for the Schools of Christian Doctrine. Indeed, he completely rewrote the previous work. He further explained that the three parts of the book corresponded to rising levels of difficulty (pt. 1, pp. 2ʳ–3ʳ). Certainly the second level exhibited more complexity than the first, but little difference between second and third can be ascertained.

Part 1 took a statement from the 1551/52 text and elevated it to an important religious and organizational principle: the fear of God is the beginning of wisdom. Fear of God induces us to learn what is necessary for good spiritual health, to do good, to flee evil, and attain salvation (pt. 1, p. 5ᵛ). With the fear of God as his arm, the Christian conquers the world, the flesh, and the devil, and reaches eternal reward. The text calls on St. John Chrysostom, who says that the fear of God corrects the mind; only then does one flee sin, preserve the innocent, and do good.[65] The fear of God acts in us in seven ways: (1) it is the beginning of delight in God, (2) it is a fountain of life, (3) it is the discipline of wisdom which justifies our hearts, (4) it gladdens the heart, (5) it is the fruit and treasure of health, (6) it gives us long life in the world and eternity in the next, and (7) it chases sin away (pt. 2, pp. 4ᵛ–5ʳ). Indeed, the *Interrogatorio* promises that the goods of this world will enter the house of the man who fears God (pt. 2, p. 6ʳ). The fear of God was a key theme throughout the book, almost always used to exhort the Christian to live a good life.

The 1560 text vigorously emphasized works, as Montorfano again strengthened a theme from the 1551/52 *Interrogatorio*. Works give proof of the good Christian: one's good works demonstrate that one fears God. One must love God with one's whole heart, keep His commandments, and do good works for His love (pt. 2, pp. 10ʳ–ᵛ). In a discussion of the seven corporal works of mercy, the text posed the question: Are we all obligated to do these works? Answer: For those who lack the means, it is enough to do them in desire. But it is a grave sin for those who possess the means but fail to do them. Where does it say this? The Gospel proves this, because the Lord threatens with damnation the man who does not do the works of mercy for the poor (pt. 1, p. 18ʳ). Doing good works earned the Christian peace, success in this world, and salvation in the next.

The book might have emphasized the importance of sanctifying grace acquired through frequent reception of the sacraments. But it did not. Nor did it stress the mass as a channel of grace. It mentioned but did not

[65]Despite the focus on the fear of God and the reference to St. John Chrysostom, it does not appear that Benedictine spirituality as described by Collett, 1985, influenced the *Interrogatorii*. The Benedictines strongly emphasized grace and faith, the *Interrogatorii* stressed works.

underscore purgatory and devotion to Mary (pt. 1, pp. 18ʳ–19ʳ, 24ʳ–25ʳ).
By contrast, learning prayers mattered a great deal.

Montorfano deleted or reduced in importance parts of the 1551/52 text.
He dropped most of the discussion of the meaning of the names of Jesus.
He eliminated the exhaustive analysis of sins and the legalistic discussion
of the different kinds of absolution required by canon law in favor of
outlining briefly the procedure for making a confession (pt. 2, pp. 43ʳ⁻ᵛ;
pt. 3, pp. 13ᵛ–14ᵛ). Montorfano retained some of the puritanism and
renunciation of the world of the 1551/52 *Interrogatorio* by regarding dances,
extravagant dress, "dishonest songs," and games of chance as sinful (pt. 2,
pp. 10ᵛ, 41ᵛ–42ʳ). But he eased somewhat the notion that conjugal sex and
reception of the sacraments were incompatible. The 1551/52 *Interrogatorio*
(sigs. D3ʳ⁻ᵛ) had instructed married couples to abstain from conjugal
relations for three days before receiving Holy Communion, throughout
Lent, and at other times. Montorfano advised married couples to abstain
from conjugal relations before Holy Communion and a few vigils of holy
days (pt. 1, p. 16ᵛ). Overall, Montorfano softened the asceticism of the
earlier version and kept in mind an intended audience of lay persons.

The 1560 *Interrogatorio* seldom called on the Bible to support its positions. It did underscore the Apostolic origins of the Church and its
continuity since. Christian doctrine and practices appeared as a seamless
historical robe: Jesus to the Apostles to the faithful. But priests as inter-
mediaries and bishops as leaders of their flocks played small roles.

Overall, Montorfano's revision presented a better-organized text and a
more positive tone. In place of the commands not to sin characteristic of
the 1551/52 version, Montorfano frequently exhorted the Christian to do
good. For example, when discussing appropriate behavior for the Christian, he listed loving God, imitating the Saviour, keeping the commandments, holding oneself pure from the contamination of the world, remembering death, always doing good, and so on (pt. 3, pp. 16ᵛ–18ʳ). A
few pages later he only briefly mentioned the horrors of eternal damnation
(pt. 3, pp. 20ʳ–21ʳ). The 1560 *Interrogatorio* emphasized the positive far
more often than the negative; it exhorted the Christian to do good rather
than examine his conscience for sin. While repeating some material from
the 1551/52 *Interrogatorio*, Montorfano deleted, softened, reworked, and
reorganized the text to achieve balance and a more positive tone.

This catechism presented the basic elements of Catholicism in an un-
complicated way to the layman in order to urge him to do good, avoid
evil, and attain salvation. It presumed that he lacked interest in the intellectual origins and justifications of his faith. The 1560 *Interrogatorio* did not
teach him to defend his beliefs against others; it never mentioned Protestants and contained no polemical matter. Nor did it offer much to those
with a professional religious commitment, the boy or girl intending to

become a priest, monk, nun, or theologian. The Schools of Christian Doctrine set out to instruct the uneducated, or the minimally educated, layman in the rudiments of the faith. Like the *Summario,* the *Interrogatorio* seemed well designed to accomplish its purpose.

Montorfano's revision, reprinted without alteration several times, became the standard for the catechism schools. The slight variations that crept into regional editions confirmed its normative status. After approving the confraternity and Schools of the Christian Doctrine for the Archdiocese of Milan in 1566, Cardinal Carlo Borromeo appointed in 1567 a commission to revise the *Interrogatorio.*[66] The Milanese *Interrogatorio* (1568) reprinted part 1 of the 1560 version.[67] The few changes made it slightly more theological in tone. For example, while the 1560 text had ignored the Trinity, the Milanese *Interrogatorio* mentioned but did not explain the Trinity.[68] It also added grace as an aid to do good works: we must do good works with the aid of divine grace. Why do we need grace? Because we cannot act unless God helps us. How do we get this help from God? Through prayer.[69] The Milanese text also emphasized "churchly" things, such as hearing mass reverently, a little more. These minor changes did not alter the central conception of the striving Christian who did good works.

The Schools of Christian Doctrine sought to confirm and deepen in traditional ways the religious knowledge of laymen and to persuade them to live good lives. They provided religious instruction for the members of a long-established, highly structured church with definite ideas on doctrine, practices, and behavior. Catechetical instruction did not attempt to deepen theological knowledge; it certainly did not encourage the pupil to speculate about his faith. If a pupil seeks to learn more than what is suitable, if he asks about difficult and hidden things, the teacher should admonish him to be silent, wrote one teacher.[70]

The catechism schools offered clear, unambiguous doctrine. In particular the *Summario* and *Interrogatorio* probably succeeded in putting to rest the great insecurity of late medieval men, the uncertainty about salvation. The catechetical books admitted no doubts; if one did good works, kept the commandments, and prayed, one would be saved. The unrepentant sinner would be damned. The worry that man could not merit salvation by his own efforts, however many good works performed, and that he depended solely on God's gift of salvation, which might not be forthcoming, did not

[66]Tamborini, 1939, pp. 204–5. Also see the prefaces to the Milanese *Interrogatorio,* 1568; Milanese *Interrogatorio,* 1574; and Milanese *Interrogatorio,* 1593b.

[67]See Milanese *Interrogatorio,* 1568, cited in Appendix 3.

[68]Milanese *Interrogatorio,* 1574, sig. A3ᵛ.

[69]See ibid., sig. A7ʳ; Milanese *Interrogatorio,* 1593b, p. 13.

[70]Carbone, 1596, pp. 201–2.

13. Title page of *Interrogatorio della Dottrina Christiana*. In Milano, per Valerio & fratelli da Meda. Colophon: 1574. MB ZY.I.48.

exist. The Schools of Christian Doctrine offered reassurance of just rewards and punishments.

However, the *Summario* and *Interrogatorio* presented an impersonal Christianity. They omitted the life of Christ. The catechisms did not link the prayers, commandments, and sacraments to the birth, life, death, and resurrection of the founder of Christianity. The texts lacked warm stories and anecdotes demonstrating that Jesus loved the sinner and that Mary interceded for him. The child imbibed a series of disembodied prayers and precepts through the genre of the catechism, an impersonal package of religious principles to be memorized. Of course, teachers may have filled the lacunae with loving stories of Jesus and the saints.

Comparison with German Lutheran religious instruction underlines the character of the Schools of Christian Doctrine. German Lutherans and Italian Catholics shared the aim of implanting simple religious material through repetition and memorization. But subtle and real differences separated them. Luther began his catechism with the Ten Commandments;[71] the *Summario* began with the Our Father, the *Interrogatorio* with the fear of God quickly followed by prayers. Luther went from law to faith to prayer, the Schools of Christian Doctrine from prayer to works to law, with faith assumed. German Lutheran catechisms taught that man was a sinner while expressing optimism about salvation; works were neither stressed nor ignored. The Schools of Christian Doctrine taught that man should strive to do good works in order to win salvation. Protestant catechisms stressed Scripture a great deal more than did the Catholic texts. They also condemned Catholicism, because rebellion against Rome helped to define Protestantism. The *Interrogatorio,* which represented the traditional church, ignored the existence of Protestants.

Lutheran catechisms emphasized respect for authority and good social conduct more than the books of the Schools of Christian Doctrine. For example, Luther's *Small Catechism* helped the reader examine his conscience through self-accusatory statements: "I am unfaithful to my master. . . . I have made my master angry, caused him to curse, neglected to do my duty. . . . I have grumbled and sworn at my mistress." Similarly, master and mistress had to review their conduct toward those in their care: "I have not been faithful in training my children, servants, and wife to the glory of God."[72] The Schools of Christian Doctrine had none of this, and only briefly admonished children to respect authority. Catechisms made the differences between Italian Catholicism and German Lutheranism quite clear.

[71]See the English translation of Luther's *Kleine Cathechismus* (1529) in Janz, 1982, pp. 179–215; and Strauss, 1978, esp. ch. 8.
[72]As translated in Janz, 1982, p. 203. Also see Strauss, 1978, ch. 11, esp. pp. 239–40.

OTHER TEXTS

The Schools of Christian Doctrine and some formal schools also taught the *Officium Beatae Mariae Virginis* (usually called the *Little Office of Our Lady* in English). It imitated the Divine Office, the group of prayers that by custom, and later in obedience to canon law, priests, monks, and nuns recited at different hours of the day. Possibly compiled at the end of the eighth century and lacking canonical force, the *Little Office* grew in popularity until the regular clergy regarded it as obligatory in the fourteenth century.[73] Lacking a fixed form through most of its history, the *Little Office* included a variety of prayers, hymns, canticles, litanies, and especially psalms, many in praise of Mary. It usually borrowed the liturgical calendar from the Divine Office, and might include prayers from the mass, prayers for the dying, chapters from the gospels, and prayers to various saints. In 1571 Pope Pius V standardized the text and made it optional, an action that did not lessen its popularity.

Its position as a prayer book in nearly universal use brought it into catechism and formal schools. It appeared more often than any other title in the libraries of lay persons, including those who had only a book or two.[74] An enormous number of manuscripts and printed copies survive.[75] Indeed, publishers defied papal threats of excommunication in order to print it.[76] In 1572 the papal nuncio to Venice reported that not only members of religious orders but "every other sort of person, laymen, women, and children" commonly read the *Little Office*.[77] Self-appointed spiritual advisers recommended the book, especially to women and girls.[78] The catechism schools used the *Little Office* as a prayer manual. In

[73]For a brief history, see Toke, 1910.

[74]For its frequent appearance in Florentine private libraries, 1415–1605, see Bec, 1984, pp. 151–316 passim. It would take too much space to list all the private library and bookshop inventories that included either manuscript or printed copies. Suffice to say that it appears in practically every one examined.

[75]See, for example, Mss. 429, 432, 444, 456–58, 463–69, 472–74, 480, and 483, most of them fifteenth-century works, in the Riccardiana Library in Florence, and manuscripts from various *fondi* in the Laurenziana Library in Florence. The Fondazione Giorgio Cini, Venice, houses a superb collection of eighteen or more printed editions, many of them illustrated, dated 1493 through 1545. Printed versions almost always appeared in small formats (12 × 7, 15 × 10, or 20 × 15 cm.), in red and black ink, and in gothic or semi-gothic lettering. Many other Italian libraries and major non-Italian libraries hold additional manuscripts and printed works. Camerini, 1962–63, passim, lists most of the *Little Offices* published by the Giunti press of Venice. Bohatta, 1909, the standard bibliography, is far from complete.

[76]P. Grendler, 1977, pp. 169, 174–81.

[77]"Ma in particolare di questi offitiuoli della Madonna . . . sendo communi non solo a' religiosi, ma ad ogni altra sorte di persone, laici, donne, et putti." Letter of Nuncio Giovanni Antonio Facchinetti, 9 August 1572, as quoted in P. Grendler, 1977, p. 174 n. 35.

[78]See Sabba Castiglione, 1554, p. 94ᵛ; and Antoniano, 1852, bk. 3, ch. 46, p. 425.

addition, its hymns and psalms offered attractive material for singing and chanting.

The Schools of Christian Doctrine occasionally used other texts as well. Cardinal Carlo Borromeo authorized "capable" teachers to go beyond the required *Summario* to teach the *Parvus catechismus catholicorum* (or *Minor;* first Latin edition Vienna, 1558 or 1559, with subsequent Italian translation) of the Dutch Jesuit Peter Canisius (1521–97). The "best" teachers might instruct the *Catechismus ad parochos* (both Latin and Italian first editions appeared in 1566), the so-called Roman or Tridentine catechism intended for priests. But they should teach only the easier parts, such as the sections on the Ten Commandments, the Pater Noster, and those dealing with morals, Borromeo decreed.[79] In similar fashion, some seventeenth-century *regole* recommended the *Dottrina christiana breve* (1597) of Robert Bellarmine (1542–1621) for advanced classes of students 15 years of age and older.[80]

At the other extreme, some catechisms taught doctrine and morals with the aid of pictures. For example, *Dottrina Christiana nella quale si contengono li principali misteri della nostra fede rappresentati con figure per istruttione de gl'idioti, & di quelli che non sanno leggere* (Christian doctrine which contains the principal mysteries of our faith represented with pictures to instruct the simple and those who do not know how to read) of Rome, 1587.[81] It came from the fertile imagination of Giovanni Battista Eliano or Romano (1530–89), a converted Jew who became a Jesuit, taught Hebrew at the Collegio Romano, translated a catechism into Arabic, and went on missions to Egypt and Lebanon.[82] This small work (15.8 × 10.5 cm.) of seventy-nine pages used numerous woodcut illustrations prepared by an unknown artist to teach standard *Summario* content.

Before long, this work became a picture book teaching good morals and a little doctrine to the illiterate or barely literate. The edition of Rome, 1608, presented twenty-seven illustrations in the thirty-two pages of a very small booklet (10 × 7.5 cm.).[83] Each illustration occupied about 80 percent of a page; a few lines of text explained the concept further. For example, one picture had three scenes: (1) encouraged by demons, two men take the name of God in vain; (2) a blasphemer's tongue is pierced; and (3) a perjuror's hand is cut off. The text mostly repeated the pictoral message: "Do not take the name of God in vain. We must praise and thank God, not

[79]See Borromeo's letter of 20 December 1568, in an undated (but seventeenth-century) printed pamphlet, *Instruttione*. For the texts of Canisius's catechisms, see Canisius, 1933. Comparison shows the *Interrogatorio* in any version to be very different in organization, spirit, and content.

[80]*Regola*, 1649, p. 73.

[81]See Eliano, *Dottrina Christiana*, 1587, cited in Appendix 3.

[82]On Eliano, see Scaduto, 1974, pp. 97–98, 101, 105–8; and MP, vol. 3:293.

[83]See *Sommario*, 1608, cited in Appendix 3.

14. Illustrations from *Sommario delli misterii della Dottrina Christiana con le sue figure*. In Roma, appresso Guglielmo Facciotto, 1608. RV S. Borr. E.V.32.

only with the heart but with the tongue. But the tongue of the blasphemer is pierced and the hand of the perjuror cut off." An illiterate could comprehend the message without undue difficulty, while a reader might further explain it to him.

HIGH AND LOW IN THE CATECHISM SCHOOLS

The founders and teachers of the Schools of Christian Doctrine gave themselves to their volunteer labors in order to save the souls of the young and to earn eternal merit for themselves. They also wished to bring their young, poor charges into the mainstream of upright morality, a goal that had a social dimension. To some extent Castellino and his successors saw the schools as a mission from high to low, from the respectable upper classes to the degenerate lower classes. Such snobbery limited the involvement of the upper classes. The schools needed the participation of a great many people, and those from the middle and lower ranks of society probably played the major role. Their participation probably helped the Schools of Christian Doctrine to maintain their original purpose.

The drafters of catechism school guidelines often described the pupils in harsh terms. Montorfano in the 1568 Venetian *regola* urged instructors to teach with patience and pity, taking into account "the imbecility, ignorance, and great imperfections of the poor boys who lack intelligence and do not recognize their own good."[84] The *regole* also described those to be taught as *rozzi* and *rudes,* meaning uncultivated, coarse, or unskilled, and even *idiote*—illiterate and stupid. The terms convey the condescension of the educated toward the uneducated in a hierarchical society.

The leaders of the Schools of Christian Doctrine sometimes saw themselves as missionaries saving Italian "pagans." Lodovico Carbone, a teacher in and a fervent supporter of the catechism schools, made the point in 1596: just as the catechism has rescued the pagans of America and the New World from their ancient errors and brought them to the light of truth, so can it do the same in the Old World.[85] He expressed a fairly common view. The Jesuits also compared Italian *rudes* to the pagans of Peru and the Indies. In 1556 one Jesuit described Corsicans and inhabitants of the rural areas of the Kingdom of Naples as "a people . . . so ignorant through lack of instruction that they have only the name of Christians."[86] They do not know the sign of the cross, the Pater Noster, or the Ave Maria, cannot read or write, and believe that there are a hundred or more

[84]"Acciò tal'ufficio & impresa si faccia con riverentia e timor d'Iddio, con buona patientia & con pietà, considerando la imbecillità, ignorantia, & imperfettioni assaissime de' poveri figliuoli, che non hanno intelletto, e non conoscono il suo bene, per farglielo conoscere." Montorfano, *Ordini,* 1568, p. 19. Also see Eliano, 1587, pp. 5, 71; and Carbone, 1596, p. 2.
[85]Carbone, 1596, p. 36.
[86]As quoted in Prosperi, 1982, p. 221.

gods. They live in conditions of bestiality, carnality, superstition, and violence, he reported.

Proponents of the catechism schools knew that the *rudes* and *idiote* of northern and central Italy were not so ignorant of Christianity as New World Indians and Corsican peasants. But they did perceive a spiritual and moral ignorance. They hoped that the catechism schools would eradicate such popular beliefs as: fasting is required only of members of religious orders; one may work to earn a living on holy days; the devil is not so ugly nor hell so awful as pictured, because such descriptions are intended to frighten the crowd; it is not such a great calamity to go to hell because the majority of people including the great and noble are there; it is permitted to the young to have a good time so that they will not age so quickly; fornication is only the lightest of venial sins; one may take an oath and testify falsely in order to save a comrade or anyone else; to forgive an injury is the mark of a coward (*animo vile*); the first sign of madness is to give away one's goods for the love of God.[87] Such "abominable blasphemies" expressed the irreligious and hedonistic traditions of some members of the lower classes.[88] They demonstrated an earthy skepticism toward the church that bombarded them with commandments.

Supporters of the Schools of Christian Doctrine promised social and moral benefits to society through teaching good doctrine. Civil rulers should favor the Schools of Christian Doctrine in order to have a strong, devout, and well-ordered state. Religious instruction will give you "merciful lawyers, just judges, constant captains, prudent senators, pious princes, and good ministers," promised Carbone. A populace well instructed in Christian Doctrine is peaceable, obedient, just, constant, and a faithful defender of the *patria*.[89] Pastors who support the work of the Schools of Christian Doctrine will have an obedient, faithful, and devout flock who will fill the church, confess, and communicate.[90] But parents who do not send their offspring to the catechism schools will have restless, immodest, disobedient, and dissipated children who will become disturbers of the peace.[91]

Despite such promises, the instructional books and the *regole* of the Schools of Christian Doctrine did not stress respect for authority a great deal. Of course, they exhorted boys and girls to obey parents, elders, and

[87]Carbone, 1596, pp. 33–34.

[88]One might also call these beliefs "popular libertinism," an echo of the learned libertine view that saw religion as a fraud employed by princes to keep the populace in check. See Ginzburg, 1986, pp. 193–94.

[89]Carbone, 1596, pp. 114–16, 118; *Constitutioni*, 1611, p. 22. For additional praise of the catechism schools for leading the common people away from riotous behavior on *feste*, see the comments of Stefano Guazzo (1530–93) in Guazzo, 1586, pp. 188ʳ–189ᵛ.

[90]Carbone, 1596, p. 104.

[91]Ibid., p. 110.

teachers. But the catechisms did not uphold social distinctions until the early seventeenth century, by which time Italy had become an Old Regime society. Later versions of the *Interrogatorio* sometimes expanded advice on behavior in the light of social class. For example, a Sienese *Interrogatorio* of 1610 gave different advice to boys of different classes. A boy of noble blood, it counselled, should not shun the company of his inferiors so long as the latter behave well, pursue their studies diligently, or work attentively. But he must not become too familiar with servants and those of "low condition." He has an obligation to hear debates and preaching in church. But he should not attend when he has a cough; nor may he spit on the kneeler.[92]

Since supporters viewed catechism schools as a mission from high to low, they naturally held up for emulation members of the nobility who participated. Don Ferdinando of Toledo, an illustrious and rich cavalier, declined the cardinal's hat in order to devote himself to teaching Christian doctrine, according to Carbone. In Brescia, many gentlemen, including the "leading ones," teach Christian doctrine. Every feast day they visit schools in the countryside (*ville* and *terre*) throughout the diocese; gentlemen of Milan and Naples do the same. High-born ladies also contribute. Eleonora of Austria, the duchess of Mantua, founded a teacher-training institute to train ninety girls to teach in the Schools of Christian Doctrine. The duchess visits the schools of Mantua, exhorting the gentlewomen accompanying her to support this Christian exercise. Noblewomen of Brescia, Milan, Naples, Parma, Piacenza, and Venice act similarly, according to Carbone.[93]

Despite such examples, it is not likely that many members of the upper classes taught in the catechism schools. In 1609, Giovanni Pietro Giussani (1540–1615), a Milanese patrician priest, published an open letter urging nobles to teach Christian doctrine. He lamented that few nobles participate in this "glorious enterprise." He tried to respond to their objections: it was not appropriate for nobles to join in where only the "lower classes" (*gente bassa*) assembled, and the schools were "a low and plebeian thing" (*cosa vile & da plebeo*). Giussani presented the example of Christ, who taught the lowly. He even resurrected in these aristocratic times the fifteenth-century argument that true nobility was based on virtue, not rank or birth. One might demonstrate virtue by helping in the Schools of Christian Doctrine, he urged.[94]

The catechism schools probably recruited the bulk of the large number of adults needed to operate the schools from much the same middle- and working-class ranks that provided the pupils. Carbone suggested as much:

[92]*Dottrina Cristiana*, 1610, pp. 92–96.
[93]Carbone, 1596, pp. 129–32; also see Cabrini, 1685, sigs. A3ᵛ–A5ᵛ.
[94]Giussani, 1609, pp. 85, 90–91.

many times I have seen laymen and artisans who, after having worked all day in their shops, spend two or three hours on feast days teaching Christian doctrine in the churches without any priest or ecclesiastical person joining them. He went on to criticize priests who did less than artisans.[95] Indeed, having foreseen this problem, Castellino had organized the schools so that laymen, even the semiliterate, could help teach.

Upper-class parents did not normally send their children to the Schools of Christian Doctrine. Carbone lamented that some noble parents would not send their offspring because they did not want them to mix with boys of "inferior class" (*bassa conditione*). Why can't noble parents send their sons to common catechism classes? Are we not all equal in the eyes of God? he asked. Resignedly, he offered an alternative: he urged noble parents to send their sons to a separate catechism school reserved for those of "higher condition."[96]

Despite the perspective of a mission from high to low and the condescension involved, the Schools of Christian Doctrine remained reasonably faithful to their original charitable purpose, to impart religious instruction and rudimentary reading and writing to ignorant and poor children.

THE RELIGIOUS KNOWLEDGE OF THE LAITY

A single priest and a group of laymen founded the Schools of Christian Doctrine; later the hierarchy endorsed the movement. In 1542 Pope Paul III approved the catechism schools recently founded at Parma, and he may have approved schools elsewhere. The Council of Trent took a step toward recognition on 17 June 1546 by decreeing that parish priests (who might use helpers) should teach the laity "what was necessary for salvation" on all Sundays and feast days. Then, on 11 November 1563, the council commanded parish priests to teach the rudiments of the faith to children and charged parents to take responsibility to see that their offspring were taught.[97] These general exhortations acknowledged the utility of catechetical instruction for children but did not suggest means of implementation. Pope Pius V did in the papal bull "Ex debito pastoralis officii" of 6 October 1567. He noted that some children had been raised well, but others lacked good habits and had fallen into spiritual ruin because they lacked fathers, were poor, or their spiritual training had been overlooked. If they

---

[95]"Io in questa parte dirò quello, che sento havendo veduto molte volte secolari, & artegiani, i quali tutto il giorno stanno nelle loro botteghe a lavorare, stare due, & tre hore il dì della festa nelle chiese, & insegnare la dottrina Christiana, & ivi non essere alcun Sacerdote, o persona Ecclesiastica, & se pur vi erano non dare aiuto alcuno, mi sono stupito. . . ." Carbone, 1596, p. 231.

[96]Ibid., pp. 112–13.

[97]Tamborini, 1939, pp. 168–71.

had been "nourished and instructed" in Christian doctrine every Sunday and feast day as some children "and other miserable persons" have been, this would not have happened. Therefore, the pontiff commanded all bishops to make arrangements to have Christian doctrine taught on Sundays and holidays and to establish "companies or confraternities" to carry on the work. He granted indulgences to those engaged in catechism teaching.[98]

Some prelates threw their considerable weight behind the catechism schools. Cardinal Carlo Borromeo (1538–84), archbishop of Milan from 1565, vigorously supported the schools with his usual combination of effective organization and imperiousness. He drafted extensive rules for the catechism schools and ordered parish priests to compile a list of all boys aged 5 to 14 in their parishes with the view of making sure that they attended catechism schools.[99] Cardinal Gabriele Paleotti (1522–97), bishop of Bologna from 1567, and Lorenzo Priuli, Patriarch of Venice from 1591 until his death in 1600, also worked hard to establish more catechism schools and to increase attendance.[100] The Jesuits and other religious orders engaged in catechetical instruction.[101]

Some bishops also succeeded in introducing religious instruction into formal schools. Cardinal Paleotti of Bologna may have been the first. On 15 October 1575, he ordered all current and future teachers of the city and diocese of Bologna to teach their pupils Christian doctrine, with the content of the instruction to be determined by the archdiocese. He directed this decree to be printed in all Latin textbooks, Donatus and Guarino grammars, and primers.[102] He did not mention vernacular textbooks. Bishop Domenico Bollani did the same in Brescia in the late 1570s.[103] And in 1592 Patriarch Lorenzo Priuli directed all Venetian schoolmasters to

---

[98]*Bullarium,* 1882, pp. 945–46. It is appended, in Latin and Italian, to Montorfano, *Ordini,* 1568, no pagination; and to other books of the catechism schools. Pius V's bull in combination with other papal briefs granting indulgences for catechism teaching sometimes appeared as Italian leaflets. See *Breve,* 1593.

[99]Milanese *Interrogatorio,* 1568, p. 2. For Borromeo's detailed rules of 1569 for the Schools and Confraternities of Christian Doctrine, see *Acta Ecclesiae Mediolanensis,* 1846, pp. 1029–1131. Also see Tamborini, 1939, pp. 210–21. Borromeo's biographers exaggerate his contribution to the catechetical movement, in my view. See P. Grendler, 1988a.

[100]For Bologna, see Prodi, 1959–67, vol. 2:182–87; and Turrini, 1982, pp. 458–63. For Venice, see Priuli's decrees reprinted in *Regole,* 1678, sigs. A2r–A4v; and Carbone, 1596, p. 128. For Rimini, see Turchini, 1978, pp. 114–19.

[101]See the interesting account of how in 1576 a Jesuit initiated catechism schools for boys and girls in Forlì and its countryside, in MP, vol. 4:637–39. For further Jesuit activity, see Scaduto, 1974, pp. 614–20. See Turrini, 1982, pp. 452–54, for other religious orders.

[102]*Psalterio,* 1575, sig. B8v.

[103]Castiglione, 1800, pp. 202–3.

teach Christian doctrine at least once a week.[104] Thus, beginning at some point in the last quarter of the sixteenth century, schoolteachers in many Italian cities were obliged to teach the fundamentals of Catholicism as a regular part of their instruction.

Pedagogues did teach the catechism. Although not yet ordered to do so, in 1587, 56 of the 245 active Venetian teachers stated that they taught "Dottrina Christiana," or "Vita Christiana," or "il Cathechismo." Further statements demonstrated that they taught their pupils to memorize the contents of the *Summario*. For example, one teacher stated that he and his pupils made the sign of the cross and recited the Pater Noster, Ave Maria, Creed, Salve Regina, and Ten Commandments every morning.[105] Sometimes a teacher devoted one day a week to the catechism; the majority did not indicate the amount of time given over to religious instruction. The vast majority probably used the *Summario, Interrogatorio,* or the primer for catechetical purposes.

The teaching of the catechism schools, and the contents of the *Summario* in particular, defined the formal religious knowledge of the bulk of the laity. In addition to the foregoing evidence, a number of observers' comments confirmed the point. In his discussion of the religious training of youth, Silvio Antoniano in 1584 praised the Schools of Christian Doctrine and recommended that those fathers "who do not know what every Christian is obligated to know" should attend catechism schools. They could then teach their sons and especially their daughters.[106] Cardinal Agostino Valier (1531–1606) of Venice made a similar point for women and girls. He urged upper-class mothers to teach Christian doctrine, "especially that little book that contains Christian instruction." They should memorize it in order to teach their children and serving girls. He meant the Pater Noster, Credo, Ten Commandments, sacraments—the contents of the *Summario.*[107] He also urged "modest virgins," that is, unmarried adult laywomen, to teach the contents of the catechism to the children of the household and to assist in the Schools of Christian Doctrine.[108] Such remarks indicated that prelates and religious pedagogues did not expect members of the laity, especially women, to know more. At least they made no serious efforts to teach them more.

Thus, the Catholic reformers for charitable motives made two academic innovations in the second half of the Cinquecento. They provided

---

[104]*Regole,* 1678, sig. A4ᵛ.
[105]ACPV, "Professioni di fede," fol. 72ʳ.
[106]Antoniano, 1852, bk. 2, ch. 2., pp. 87–88.
[107]Valier, 1740, pt. 4, pp. 29, 31–32.
[108]Ibid., pt. 3, p. 36.

free rudimentary reading and writing instruction on Sundays and holidays to those who had no other opportunity to learn. And they gave the populace considerably more religious instruction than they had had before, through the Schools of Christian Doctrine and by insisting that formal schools teach the catechism.

CHAPTER THIRTEEN

The Schools of the Religious Orders

he new religious orders of the Catholic Reformation altered the educational landscape in the second half of the sixteenth century. In contrast to the medieval mendicant orders, several of the new orders devoted themselves to teaching lay children. Unlike the Companies of Christian Doctrine, they established formal schools that daily taught a Latin or vernacular curriculum. The Jesuits and the other religious orders who followed their pedagogical example founded new schools and sometimes took control of existing ones. Because they did not charge fees initially, the new schools of the Jesuits, Barnabites, Somaschi, and Piarists expanded educational opportunity. But from the beginning they began to alter the organization of Italian education by assuming control of communal schools, displacing independent masters, and adding an ecclesiastical presence to the academic landscape. Indeed, the Church through the new orders made itself felt in Italian preuniversity education for the first time in centuries. But the new orders did not change the curriculum. The Jesuits and their imitators continued to teach the *studia humanitatis,* the Piarists the vernacular curriculum.

JESUIT SCHOOLS

The Jesuits had not intended to become educators. Ignatius Loyola (c. 1495–1556) had in mind more dramatic service to God, beginning with a mission to the Holy Land. When that proved impossible, the small band vowed, upon receiving papal approval in 1540, to devote themselves to traditional religious activities such as preaching, doing charitable works, and especially teaching the catechism.[1] Events conspired to bring schooling to their attention. Francis Xavier in 1543 reported the excellent results that he had achieved with his school in Goa which trained Indian and

[1]Tacchi Venturi, 1950, pp. 270–71.

Portuguese youths in Christian doctrine and the humanities. Closer to home, Francis Borgia (1510–72), duke of Gandía (in Valencia) and a future Jesuit, offered to endow a university level school to educate members of the Society. Loyola accepted the offer, and the school opened in 1546. Its energetic rector invited laymen to attend the lectures, and in this way the Jesuits first began to teach external students, that is, those who were not members of the Society.[2] The Gandía school again turned Loyola's attention to education, but it could hardly have mattered as much to him at the time as oriental missions and serving the pope.

Then, in December 1547, the Commune of Messina, firmly nudged by the Spanish viceroy, petitioned Loyola to send ten Jesuits for a different mission.[3] The commune wanted five to teach, and the rest to undertake charitable activities. The commune, in turn, promised food, clothing, and a building for the Jesuits. Recognizing the invitation as an opportunity, and that one did not refuse a viceroy, Loyola managed to dispatch seven Jesuits from his already overextended band. Representing five nationalities, the group included some of the ablest Jesuit scholars, including the Dutchman Peter Canisius, who taught rhetoric the first year. The new school opened its doors on 24 April 1548, but soon closed them again, because the unfinished building afforded little protection against the Sicilian heat.

By the autumn the city council of Messina, the viceroy, and the Jesuits had entered into a formal agreement.[4] The Jesuits would not charge fees for their instruction. Instead, the people of Messina would support the Jesuits through freewill offerings, and the viceroy would supply food and clothing. And, of course, the city had erected the building. The Jesuit fathers would teach nine classes, beginning with the alphabet, reading, writing, and elementary Latin grammar in the first. Classes in rhetoric, oratory, Greek, Hebrew, Aristotelian logic, Aristotelian ethics, "scholastic theology," and casuistry would follow. The Jesuits also promised to give catechetical instruction to young and old. The school formally opened on 1 October 1548, in the presence of the viceroy and the local nobility.

The school achieved instant success. Enrollment in the elementary grammar class had already passed 180 in December 1548. Continuing expansion led the Jesuits to modify their original organization: by the end of 1549 the single reading, writing, and Latin grammar class had become three classes of ascending difficulty enrolling 78, 56, and 42 students respectively. A newly christened humanities class had 14 students, fol-

[2]Farrell, 1938, pp. 14–17.

[3]For the story of the Messina school, see MP, vol. 1:509–11; Farrell, 1938, pp. 25–29; and Tacchi Venturi, 1951, pp. 331–37, 358–61.

[4]See MP, vol. 1:383–86, for the undated proclamation embodying the terms of the agreement.

lowed by a rhetoric class of 15 or 16, making a total of 205 or 206 students in what was, in effect, the lower school. A preponderance of lower-school students would characterize almost all future Jesuit schools; three grammar, one humanities, and one rhetoric class became the pattern for Jesuit external colleges.[5] The higher-level classes had smaller numbers: dialectic 16, philosophy 13, scholastic theology 3, Greek 10, Hebrew 3 or 4, and a newly added mathematics class 10 or 12, for a total school enrollment of 260 to 264 students.[6] Enrollment in the Messina college reached a maximum of 370 students in September 1556, descended to a low of 240 students in May 1563, and averaged 295 students in its first two decades.[7] The Messina experiment yielded other fruits as well. In February 1550, the Jesuits opened a novitiate house, with the rent largely paid by the Messina Senate. Ten youths aged 15 to 20, including members of Messina's aristocratic families, enrolled.[8]

Gratuitous instruction largely explained the instant success of the Messina school. Free education on this scale was new to Italy. A handful of communal schools had offered free education to smaller numbers, and some masters were obligated to teach gratis the occasional poor boy. But the principle of free formal education, which went beyond the limited reading and writing instruction of the catechism schools, was new. The Jesuits inaugurated the first systematic effort to provide free education for one to three hundred students in a town. The opportunity must have seemed heaven-sent to boys—the Jesuits did not teach girls—and their parents.

Loyola repeatedly insisted that the Jesuit schools had to be free, believing the provision of free education consistent with the Society's vow of poverty.[9] The Jesuits clung to this principle despite the privations members suffered in the struggle to establish colleges.[10] They viewed teaching Latin, offering catechetical instruction, and leading schoolboys to receive

[5]I use the term *college* to mean a Jesuit day or boarding school on the pre-university level for lay boys, unless otherwise indicated. Sixteenth-century Jesuit sources used the term broadly to mean day schools, boarding schools, seminaries, and residences (sometimes with limited instruction) for their members. Indeed, the multiple meaning of *college* has persisted to this day in British or British-influenced education.

[6]The figures come from the annual report for 1549 in MP, vol. 1:515. See also Farrell, 1938, pp. 37–38.

[7]Scaduto, 1974, p. 358.

[8]Tacchi Venturi, 1951, pp. 362–63.

[9]Farrell, 1938, pp. 28, 137, 221, 253 n. 13, and 436–40. See also the portions of the Jesuit *Constitutions* which dealt with free schooling in MP, vol. 1:267, 269, and 307. A typical statement in the first rules for the rector of the Collegio Romano in 1551 is: "13° Anchora che non è serrata la porta alli benefactori, non si accetti, per conto del insegnar, cosa alcuna delli padri o parenti delli scholari che vengono; per il premio delle fatiche nostre in servitio de Dio, de lui solo l'habbiamo a aspettare." MP, vol. 1:88, with the Latin version on p. 89.

[10]Scaduto, 1974, pp. 441–44.

the sacraments as religious deeds akin to converting pagans. The decision to offer free education as a charitable act stemmed directly from the central theme of the Catholic Reformation, doing good in this world in order to ensure salvation in the next for doer and recipient. Only later did the Jesuits modify the principle of gratuitous education in order to accept payment from boarding-school students.

At the same time, the Jesuits at Messina accepted gifts from the wealthy and sought ties with the powerful. Indeed, the Messina experience anticipated most of the future development of Jesuit education. The Messina college taught a Latin humanities curriculum. The Messina Jesuits played a role in communal education and displaced independent masters. And the first school helped recruit new members of the Society.

Flushed with the success of the Messina experiment, Loyola began to see educating boys as one of the prime activities of the Society. He gave founding schools precedence over building residences. Italians responded enthusiastically by bombarding Loyola and his successors with five or six times as many requests to open schools as they could accept.[11] Although they did not always spurn petitions from provincial towns, the Jesuits preferred to establish colleges in larger cities. And when they lacked an invitation to open a school in a key political and intellectual center, they contrived to obtain one or founded a school without invitation.

For example, Loyola wished to establish a college in Florence, but Duke Cosimo I, always cool to any enterprise that he could not personally control, ignored him. Loyola then prompted Jaime Lainez (1512–65), his able associate and successor as general of the order, to write in the summer of 1551 a long memorandum to win over Cosimo I.

A Jesuit school would teach the boys of the city good learning, pious religion, and good moral habits, Lainez promised.[12] In the Jesuit schools of Messina and Palermo the pupils studied, heard mass daily, attended catechetical classes every Friday and feast day, and confessed monthly (all mandatory at Jesuit colleges). As a result, the boys had abandoned their "rude games, rowdiness, blasphemies, lies, and dishonesties," and had become "temperate and devout, obedient to their parents." A Jesuit school would produce loving and faithful subjects whose example would spread throughout the ducal state. Moreover, since a Jesuit college taught only Latin and Greek, it would not entice students away from the Medici-sponsored University of Pisa, but prepare them well for higher studies in law and medicine. Lainez then listed the crowned heads of Europe whom Cosimo I should emulate. Charles V had given an abbacy to the Jesuit college at Palermo. His Most Christian Majesty of France had authorized

---

[11]Ibid., pp. 227–31.

[12]Tacchi Venturi, 1951, pp. 420–33, for the story of the foundation of the Florentine college; pp. 422–24, for long quotations from the memorandum.

the Jesuits to found colleges in France. The King of the Romans (later Emperor Ferdinand I) had brought the Jesuits to Vienna. The king of Portugal had founded several Jesuit colleges including that at Coimbra. The duke of Bavaria had done the same in Ingolstadt. And the viceroy of Naples, Cosimo's father-in-law, had welcomed a Jesuit college in Naples.

Cosimo conceded under further pressure from his consort, Duchess Eleanora of Toledo. She promised a subsidy of 250 scudi annually plus enough grain and wine to feed twelve persons. The Jesuit school in Florence opened in January 1552 with the usual public oration delivered by one of the ablest Jesuit scholar-teachers. But the college did not prosper, partly because Eleanora's premature death in 1562 deprived it of court support. Her legacy permitted the college to continue in a modest way, but Cosimo I remained cool and the Florentines indifferent. According to the Jesuit rector, the Florentines lacked enthusiasm for study because they were merchants, the same complaint that the Jesuits levelled against the Venetians.[13] In the late 1550s and early 1560s, the Florentine college limped along with an enrollment that never climbed much above one hundred and sometimes fell well below.[14] The college eventually prospered, and it endured until dissolution of the Society in 1773.

As a new religious order, the Jesuits had to rely on benefactors for initial and continuing support. They needed a church in which to preach, hear confessions, and give catechetical instruction; a building in which to teach; and funds for food, shelter, and clothing for their members. But they lacked the churches, monasteries, properties, and benefices that the mendicant orders had accumulated over the centuries. Members of the ecclesiastical hierarchy seldom supported the Jesuits in the early years, because they viewed them as rivals in the competition for funds. The papacy supported the Collegio Romano in Rome itself, because it filled a unique role as the educator of clergymen and seminarians from many lands. But the papacy went little further in the early decades. Hence, the Jesuits tried to win over lay rulers by promising spiritual, intellectual, and civic benefits, plus the snob appeal of imitating the mighty. They had a great deal of success.

The Jesuits preferred the patronage of princes because it seemed more secure, but they would also accept communal support. Communal councils in smaller towns often invited the Jesuits to found a school and then asked them to assume direction of communal education. In Tivoli the Jesuits started a school in 1550[15] which nearly failed in 1553, when their rented house was put up for sale. At the last moment a priest rescued them

[13]Letter of 29 April 1564 as quoted in Scaduto, 1974, p. 370 n. 14. For the complaint against the Venetians, see Tacchi Venturi, 1951, p. 374.

[14]Scaduto, 1974, pp. 368–71.

[15]Some sources say 1549.

with a gift of 330 ducats to purchase the house. The Este governor of Tivoli then began to interest himself in the fortunes of the small band of five Jesuits and their school of 120 pupils. The school only became secure in 1563 when the commune assigned the Jesuits an annual subsidy of 60 scudi in exchange for teaching 160 students and carrying on charitable activities.[16] Their school at Frascati followed a similar development. The town invited the Jesuits in 1559 to take charge of a church and adjacent house. The Jesuits accepted because of the town's proximity to Rome and its salubrious climate. Then in 1563 the commune paid the Jesuits an annual subvention of 60 scudi with which to maintain two instructors and a building in which to teach. The Jesuits became the communal masters.[17] In similar fashion, in 1564 the Commune of Messina began to give the Society an annual payment for the maintenance of the school.[18] In this case the commune's money supplemented other support.

In time, princely support and communal subventions became the twin financial pillars of the Jesuit schools. Donations from lay and clerical benefactors plus some benefice income completed the balance sheet.[19] For example, the dukes of Savoy invited the Jesuits to establish schools in their state with support from four sources: private gifts, papal reassignment of some benefice income from abbacies and priories to the schools, ducal taxes on salt and wine, and communal support, the last under pressure from the ducal authority.[20]

The Jesuits won over public opinion by convincing parents that the Jesuits were better educators than their rivals. They did this through public academic exercises, such as inaugural orations delivered by the ablest resident Jesuit. If independent masters, fearing the loss of students and diminished income, challenged the Jesuits to a public disputation, so much the better. Almost always the Jesuit scholar vanquished rival masters and enrollment spurted, even if the brilliant Jesuit soon moved elsewhere (see below).[21] The Jesuits continued to woo public opinion throughout the year with prize days, disputations, and drama performances to which they invited parents, nobles, civic officials, and members of the ecclesiastical hierarchy.[22]

Jesuit schools failed when local support faltered. The Society founded a school in 1559 in Amelia, a small hill town about fifty-five miles north of

---

[16]Scaduto, 1974, pp. 336–37.

[17]Ibid., pp. 337–38.

[18]Batllori, 1983, p. 127.

[19]Ibid.; and Scaduto, 1974, passim.

[20]A. Erba, 1979, pp. 413–14.

[21]For the public disputations between the Jesuits and the *maestri dei rioni* in Rome in October 1552, see ch. 3 herein. For several academic competitions in Perugia, 1552–54, see Tacchi Venturi, 1951, pp. 451–55.

[22]Farrell, 1938, pp. 38–39; Scaduto, 1974, p. 429; Brizzi, 1976, p. 92.

Rome, and in 1562 accepted direction of the communal school. But townspeople and especially the local bishop opposed the Jesuits; the bishop restricted their preaching, in particular forbidding them to preach to nuns. In the face of this opposition, the Jesuits closed the doors of their school and withdrew completely in 1567.[23] The Jesuits had little success in Venice, where a juicy scandal concerning a confessor (not a Jesuit) who seduced the nuns in his charge heightened the republic's traditional hostility toward clergymen identified with Rome. When enrollment dwindled, the Jesuits closed the Venetian school in 1560.[24] The Jesuit school in Modena began with generous financial support and the approval of the bishop, but ran into local opposition that might have been the residue of Protestant sympathies.[25] When in the summer of 1555 the Modena school attracted only fourteen students, it closed. The Jesuits returned to Modena in the last decade of the sixteenth century to open a boarding school for nobles.[26]

Sometimes the Jesuits persevered in the face of daunting problems. The Jesuit school in Ferrara barely survived a series of conflicts perhaps endemic to small academic and religious communities. The school began in 1551 with support from the duke but not the townspeople. It declined to eighty-five pupils in two classes and barely kept its head above water financially. Then a noble widow rescued the school with a large gift; she also promised continuing support to the school's rector. In 1556, however, the new general Lainez ordered the rector transferred, replacing him with another man whom the widow disliked. She would have only the deposed rector as her confessor, he refused to leave, and tongues began to wag. With the Ferrara Jesuits now also divided by the dispute, the court withdrew support. Local clergymen, led by the Dominican inquisitor, harassed the Jesuits. In the middle of these troubles, illness carried off one teacher and laid the rest of the Ferrara Jesuit community low. Discipline and the quality of instruction deteriorated. Even General Lainez's appeal to Cardinal Ippolito Este, the Ferrarese cardinal, did not retrieve the situation, and the Jesuit college barely survived.[27]

Two broader if more mundane problems hampered the Jesuits more than headstrong benefactresses. Finding adequate quarters for teaching and living was a recurrent problem. The school building or residence was too expensive, too small, needed costly repairs, was unhealthy, or was about to be sold from under them. The Jesuits learned through experience that ownership of their own quarters for teaching and living was the only

[23]Scaduto, 1974, pp. 334–35.
[24]Ibid., pp. 418–22; Tacchi Venturi, 1951, pp. 372–78.
[25]For Protestant sympathies in Modena, see Rambaldi, 1979.
[26]Scaduto, 1974, pp. 415–18.
[27]Ibid., pp. 406–15; Tacchi Venturi, 1951, pp. 393–99.

sure solution. Before long they began to negotiate tenaciously for a building to be given them, or a new one constructed, before agreeing to establish a school.

The insufficiency of good teachers proved the more intractable problem in the early decades. The rapid expansion of schools in the 1550s and 1560s severely strained the Society's personnel. Sometimes the correspondence between the rector of a Jesuit college and the general in Rome was embarrassingly frank: enrollment had dropped because the rhetoric teacher was incompetent; could he be replaced? The general reluctantly replied that he did not have another teacher to send. In the early decades Loyola and his successors frantically shifted their better teachers around in order to deal with emergencies. One Jesuit taught in Rome, Forlì, Bologna, Milan, and Rome again between September 1562 and January 1565, five postings in twenty-eight months.[28] The rectors of Jesuit colleges repeatedly criticized transfers as counterproductive. For example, in 1571 the rector at Forlì complained to Rome that the nobles did not wish to send their sons to the Jesuit school because of the constant teacher changes. Today one teaches this, tomorrow another teaches something else; the students learn so little that they leave the school. One teacher of ordinary competence who stays will yield greater fruit than several brilliant ones who come and go, he concluded.[29] Probably no teacher in any century would dispute the wisdom of his statement. The problem reached such proportions that in 1565 one Jesuit addressed a long memorandum to the newly elected general urging a halt to the founding of new colleges until the teacher shortage had been solved.[30] The general did not heed him, and expansion continued.

Despite the difficulties, the Jesuits between 1548 and 1565 opened numerous colleges across Italy and the adjacent islands: Messina in 1548; Palermo in 1549; Tivoli in 1550; the Collegio Romano, Bologna, Ferrara, and Venice in 1551; Florence, Gubbio, Modena, Naples, Padua, and Perugia in 1552; Monreale (Sicily) in 1553; Argenta (near Bologna), Genoa, and Siracusa in 1554; Loreto in 1555; Bivona and Catania in Sicily, and Siena in 1556; Amelia (in Umbria) and Montepulciano (Tuscany) in 1557; Forlì and Nola (near Naples) in 1558; Caltabellotta (Sicily), Frascati, and Sassari (Sardinia) in 1559; Como, Macerata, Mondovì in 1561; Cagliari (Sardinia), Catanzaro, Milan, and Parma in 1564.[31] Not all the colleges succeeded;

[28]Scaduto, 1974, p. 450, and pp. 448–50 for fuller discussion.
[29]"Li gentil'homeni non vogliono mandar li suoi figlioli alle nostre scholle, per questa tanto spessa mutationi di mastri, che hoggi uno insegna una cosa, diman' un'altro insegna altro . . . che li scholari non fanno profitto, et cosi lasciano le schole." Letter of Filippo Trivisano, 15 April 1571, in Forlì, in ARSI, Epistolae Italiae, R. 141, pt. 1 (1571), fol. 144[r-v].
[30]Scaduto, 1974, pp. 803–4.
[31]The foundation dates and the number of schools are based on the best available information, but there are a few inconsistencies in the sources, especially for the dates. The

seven (Amelia, Argenta, Forlì, Gubbio, Modena, Montepulciano, and Venice) closed their doors within two to six years for lack of local support. Nevertheless, the number of functioning Italian Jesuit schools steadily increased from 18 in 1556 to 30 in 1565, 49 in 1600, about 80 in 1630, and 111 at the end of the seventeenth century.[32] The Italian Jesuits added only about a dozen more colleges in the eighteenth century before suppression of the Society in 1773.

Growth in membership of the Society roughly paralleled the increase in the number of colleges. The Italian provinces of the Society had 428 Jesuits of all ranks in 1556, 876 in 1565, 1,068 in 1574, and so on.[33] Numerous novices came directly from the colleges into the Society, which normally accepted them at the age of 15.[34]

All but one or two enjoyed local support and substantial enrollments. Italian Jesuit colleges usually reached enrollments of 100 or more within a year after opening. Most then reached and settled at a normal enrollment of 200 to 300, often closer to the higher figure, by the mid-1560s.[35] A popular college such as Messina went beyond 300 in some years, and the Brera in Milan had 500 students in 1580.[36] Colleges in small towns, such as Como, and the struggling schools remained at the lower end of the normal range. For example, the college in Bologna founded in 1551 reached a figure of 115 students in 1554, but still had only 108 and 112 students respectively in February and March 1560.[37] Although impressive by Italian scholastic standards, enrollment in Jesuit schools in the peninsula did not compare with that in Jesuit colleges in France, Germany, and Portugal, where figures of 500 to 1,500 students were common.[38] Only the Collegio Romano, the showpiece of Italian Jesuit education, boasted very large enrollments. By the end of its first year (1551), it had nearly 300 students.[39] By 1561–62, enrollment had grown to about 900 students, of whom approximately 530 studied grammar, humanities, and rhetoric, and the rest higher studies.[40] Another count at the end of 1571 showed a student body (excluding Jesuits) of more than 800, of whom approximately 570 studied grammar, humanities, and rhetoric, and the rest logic, philosophy,

---

map in Scaduto, 1974, following p. 800, is particularly useful. See also Farrell, 1938, pp. 431–35.

[32]Brizzi, 1982, p. 919, based on archival evidence found in ARSI for the last three figures.

[33]MP, vol. 2:10*.

[34]Scaduto, 1964, pp. 72, 254–55.

[35]Ibid., pp. 344–436 et passim for the figures.

[36]MP, vol. 4:345.

[37]For the 1554 enrollment, see Scaduto, 1974, p. 398; for the 1560 figures, see ARSI, Epistolae Italiae, R. 116 (1560), fols. 29ᵛ, 39ᵛ.

[38]Farrell, 1938, pp. 219–20.

[39]Ibid., p. 67.

[40]Scaduto, 1974, p. 281.

and theology.[41] The Collegio Romano continued to grow, reaching an overall total of about 1,500 in 1594, a figure that probably included Jesuit students plus philosophy and theology students.[42]

SCHOOLMASTERS TO THE ELITE

The Jesuits probably attracted their student body from a fairly broad spectrum of society at first. Indeed, a college of 160 students in a small town such as Tivoli had to draw the majority of its students from commoners, including artisans, because few of the wellborn and wealthy lived there. Scattered remarks confirm that some students came from the lower ranks of society in the early years of a college. The Florentine rector reported that the majority of the students came from the families of artisans and others of modest means.[43] At Monreale (Sicily), many students were so poor that they did not have enough to eat; they missed classes because they had to help their parents.[44] In Perugia the students deserted the school in the autumn of 1556 in order to help gather the harvest.[45] Such evidence demonstrates that early Jesuit schooling was a partial experiment in mass education.

Despite the lack of fees, a schoolboy from artisan ranks or modest economic background still had to overcome obstacles in order to attend Jesuit schools. The family had to have enough income or expectations to allow a son to follow the Latin curriculum, which yielded a financial return only if the boy could attend university or otherwise join professional ranks. The social gulf between the Latin and vernacular curricula must have discouraged most artisans from sending their sons to the Jesuit schools but beckoned to a few as a tantalizing opportunity. An artisan father now had the option of sending his son to learn Latin at the free Jesuit college in the hope that the boy might climb the social ladder. Upon graduation he might find a position with a noble needing a secretary fluent in Latin or with the commune as a civil servant. Finally, the free Latin schools probably made it easier than before for boys to enter the service of the church. The Jesuit schools did not lower social barriers, but they helped a few boys to climb over them.

Although the Jesuits taught all who came, they preferred sons of the upper classes. A rector rejoiced when the students in his college were "almost all nobles and from the most important (families) of this city."[46] The Jesuits gloated when sons of the principal nobles of a city abandoned

[41]Polanco, 1917, p. 124.
[42]Farrell, 1938, p. 220.
[43]Scaduto, 1974, p. 462.
[44]Letters of 10 October and 30 November 1557 in *Litterae quadrimestres*, 1921, pp. 406, 445.
[45]Letter of 7 September 1556, in *Litterae quadrimestres*, 1897, p. 489.
[46]". . . et i scholari quasi tutti nobili et di più principali di questa città. . . . Li gen-

other teachers in order to enroll in Jesuit schools.[47] The rector of the
struggling Bologna school believed that it turned the corner toward
success when the majority of the students were sons of nobles, of solid
citizens, and of the learned. Such pupils included nephews of a bishop and
the son of a well-known humanities professor at the University of Bologna.[48]

But they also made pedagogical decisions almost from the beginning
that transformed them into teachers of the upper and middle classes. The
earliest Jesuit schools, such as Messina, accepted very young illiterate boys
and taught them the alphabet, syllables, reading and writing, a little
arithmetic, and the first rules of Latin grammar.[49] But when the Collegio
Romano opened its doors on 22 February 1551, it admitted only students
who already knew how to read and write and, if possible, had begun the
study of Latin.[50] In November 1551 Loyola ordered the elimination of
alphabet, reading, and writing instruction in all Jesuit colleges, citing the
shortage of teachers.[51] Townspeople and benefactors, especially in the
smaller towns, strongly objected; they wanted the Jesuits to teach beginners.[52] When the Jesuits sought to eliminate the reading and writing class
at Tivoli, the commune argued that dropping the *ABC* class would
deprive the poor of all instruction.[53] Faced with such opposition, Loyola
implemented the new policy gradually. Existing colleges might continue
to teach the *ABC* class until conditions permitted its suppression, while
new schools would not teach reading and writing. Loyola also made a few

---

tilhuomini principali reputano a favore di poter mandar alle nostre schole i suoi figliuoli."
MP, vol. 4:589, letter of the rector of the school at Milan, 30 June 1575.

[47]Scaduto, 1974, p. 354, referring to Siracusa in the early 1560s.

[48]"La maggior parte però di loro sonno figliuoli di persone nobili, dotte, et da bene, et fra
gl'altri vi sonno tre nipoti del R.ᵐᵒ Mons. vescovo di Ragusi, et due altri della casa sua. Item il
figliuolo del s.re Francesco Robortello, il quale tiene il primo loco delli professori di lettere
latine et grece in questa città, et è persona dottissima. Oltre di questi vi sono molti cittadini et
figliuoli di gentil'huomini bolognesi." *Litterae quadrimestres,* 1932, p. 328, letter of 16 May
1561.

[49]MP, vol. 2:560; Farrell, 1938, p. 55. For other evidence from 1551 and 1552, see MP, vol.
1:95, 137.

[50]MP, vol. 1:89, 90 (n. 69), 91, and vol. 2:177; Farrell, 1938, p. 72.

[51]MP, vol. 1:526 (and n. 9), 530, 537–38, 558, 575; Farrell, 1938, pp. 73–74, 88 n. 21.

[52]For example, the rector of the school at Padua reported that the school was resisting
with difficulty the addition of a beginners' class, which, if opened, would attract "hundreds"
of students. "Hora gran difficultà a resistere di non accettare una classe di grammatica più
bassa, perché veniano le centenaie." MP, vol. 3:282, letter of 2 December 1558.

[53]Scaduto, 1974, p. 462. For other examples of the policy and the opposition engendered,
see Tacchi Venturi, 1951, p. 469; and Scaduto, 1964, p. 402. Also in France when the Jesuits
took control of municipal *collèges* (schools supported by town governments) in the late
sixteenth and early seventeenth centuries, they dropped the ABC class. Again townspeople
strongly protested. "When the Jesuits succeeded in eliminating beginners from the *collège,* the
first step had been taken toward eliminating children of low condition." Huppert, 1984, pp.
126 (quote), 127.

exceptions in heavily Protestant lands on the grounds that German boys, for example, needed to live in a totally Catholic educational environment from the earliest possible age.[54] But in Italy the Jesuit colleges eliminated the teaching of reading and writing. The Tivoli Jesuit school closed its elementary class, probably one of the last surviving ones in Italy, in 1574.[55]

Considerations other than a shortage of manpower also moved Loyola, because he ignored alternative solutions. For example, the Messina school had assigned a more advanced pupil to teach the alphabet, reading, and writing class.[56] The Jesuits decided to concentrate their energies on those likely to stay in school for many years and to become society's leaders. Was it worthwhile spending time and resources on poor students who only attended school until the age of 10 or 12 and would not join the elite? they wondered. The Jesuits might argue that they better served the lower classes through public preaching, charitable work, catechetical instruction, and missions to the backward regions of Italy, all pursued vigorously. The colleges, on the other hand, would teach Latin plus spiritual and moral values to members of the upper and middle classes who, in turn, would guide society in righteous ways as adults. Quattrocento humanistic pedagogues and communal councils had similar if more secular goals in mind and excluded the poor by charging fees.

With the suppression of the introductory reading and writing class, the Jesuit schools narrowed their educational mission chronologically and socially: they taught the *studia humanitatis* to upper- and middle-class boys aged 10 to 16. Having learned reading, writing, and a little Latin grammar elsewhere, the typical middle- and upper-class student entered the Jesuit college at the age of 10 or 11 in the lowest grammar class. He progressed through the next two grammar classes, went on to the humanities class (which normally required two years), and finished with the rhetoric class at about the age of 16.[57] Some students went on to more advanced studies.

As time passed, the Jesuits focussed more attention on training the aristocracy by operating boarding schools. They began with the Collegium Germanicum in Rome in 1552, a residence for German priesthood students aged 15 to 21 who returned to Germany after ordination.[58] These students lived in and received some tutoring at the Collegium Germanicum but attended classes at the Collegio Romano. Although admitting Germans of all classes, the Collegium Germanicum had by the seven-

---

[54]Farrell, 1938, pp. 196, 208, 302.

[55]Scaduto, 1974, p. 336.

[56]Farrell, 1938, p. 73.

[57]Ibid., p. 373.

[58]See the 1552 constitution of the Collegium Germanicum in MP, vol. 1:110–11; and Farrell, 1938, p. 433.

teenth century become the training ground for the sons of nobles destined for high ecclesiastical preferment in Germany.[59] The great deal of time and concern devoted to the establishment and operation of the Collegium Germanicum in its first decades may have awakened the Society to the potential of boarding schools for changing society.[60] In any case, the Jesuits founded their first boarding school for lay boys in Vienna in 1553 or 1554, and others quickly followed, especially in northern Europe.[61] The Jesuits founded or assumed direction of fifty boarding schools of various kinds (seminaries, schools for lay boys, or some combination of both) across Europe between 1552 and 1599.[62]

Boarding schools necessarily enrolled only the wealthy who could pay the fees. But some went further: princes and others founded boarding schools limited to boys of proven noble lineage. The Jesuits did not originate the concept of the academy for aristocrats, but they willingly accepted the role of schoolmasters to the nobility.

In Italy the Jesuits began to teach in boarding schools reserved for nobles in the mid-1570s. Carlo Borromeo, archbishop of Milan, probably founded the first ecclesiastically sponsored Italian boarding school limited to boys of verified noble blood. Borromeo brought to the Catholic Reformation the traditional pedagogical strategy of educating princelings elsewhere than in paternal courts in order to shield them from temptation. He feared that doting fathers would nourish their offspring in sensuality. By contrast, princelings should learn how to lead society in righteousness.[63] Hence, in 1574 he founded a Milanese boarding school for nobles from Lombardy and asked the Jesuits to assume direction. They declined, because they wished to maintain their independence from the imperious Borromeo. But they agreed to play a major role: they taught the nobles as day students in their existing Milanese school, they sent over one Jesuit to teach Latin grammar to the youngest boys within the walls of the boarding school, and they heard the boys' confessions.[64] In future decades the Jesuits alternated with another religious order in directing the Milanese school for nobles.

The Jesuits took full responsibility for subsequent schools for nobles. A new Jesuit boarding school for nobles in Turin enrolled "ninety to one hundred noble youths from all of Piedmont" in 1580.[65] Under pressure

[59]Schmidt, 1984.

[60]See MP, vol. 2:318–419, 799–1004; and MP, vol. 4:32–77.

[61]Farrell, 1938, p. 433, says 1553; Brizzi, 1976, pp. 21–22, argues for 1554.

[62]Brizzi, 1976, p. 22; and Barbera, 1946–47.

[63]Giussano, 1612, bk. 3, ch. 4, pp. 137–38.

[64]MP, vol. 4:345, 590.

[65]". . . del collegio M. Nicolino di convittori, del quale si dovria far gran conto, perché vi sono ordinariamente 90 o 100 giovani di tutto il Piamonte." MP, vol. 4:348, 18 January 1580.

from the local bishop, the Jesuits in 1582 opened a boarding school for nobles in Padua which enrolled seventy noble boys in 1589.[66] Other noble academies followed.

The famous school for nobles in Parma illustrates how successfully the Jesuits adapted to the role of educators to princes. Ranuccio I Farnese (ruled 1592–1622), duke of Parma and Piacenza, founded the school in 1601.[67] An accord of 1604 gave the Jesuits direction of the school and laid down the rules. The school accepted boys between the ages of 11 and 14 of verified noble lineage who might stay until the age of 20. In the beginning the boys boarded at the college and attended the existing Jesuit day school in Parma; before long, they received all their instruction at the boarding school. The school supplemented the standard Jesuit Latin curriculum with lessons in singing, dancing, designing fortifications, French, and, above all, riding. Indeed, the school's emphasis on horsemanship earned it a European-wide reputation. When the Jesuit general objected that riding practice caused the boys to miss the morning philosophy class, the father-provincial of the Lombard Province strongly defended riding as appropriate to the boys' "noble natures" and future station in life. Parents paid very high annual fees of 84 ducatoni ("big ducats" worth 7 lire 10 soldi instead of the normal 6 lire 4 soldi). Other fees for books, linens, clothes, and some special lessons added to the cost. For their money, the boys enjoyed the right to hunt in the duke's preserve and the privilege of occupying seats of honor at public ceremonies. Thirty-four Jesuit teachers, prefects, and servants taught and served 98 boarders in 1610. The majority of the boys came from Italy, a minority from the rest of Europe. Enrollment grew to 260 boys by the middle of the seventeenth century and a peak of 550 to 600 boys between 1670 and 1700 before the school began a slow decline. Other Italian Jesuit schools for nobles exhibited the same enrollment curve.[68]

By the first quarter of the seventeenth century, the Jesuits operated boarding and non-boarding schools for nobles, north to south, in Verona, Brescia, Milan, Turin, Genoa, Parma, Bologna, Ferrara, Ravenna, Prato, Siena, Rome, Naples, Palermo, and Cagliari.[69] As Italy became more aristocratic, princes and nobles increasingly did not wish their sons to associate with their inferiors in communal schools or even in other Jesuit colleges. Although other schools offered training for aristocrats, the Jesuit noble school dominated this part of the educational landscape.[70]

---

[66]Donnelly, 1982, p. 48.
[67]Capasso, 1901, pp. 1–38.
[68]Brizzi, 1976, p. 65 et passim.
[69]Ibid., p. 26.
[70]In addition to schools for nobles operated by other religious orders, the Venetian government in 1619 established a school for impoverished nobles which did not succeed. See Zenoni, 1916.

THE JESUIT CURRICULUM

The Jesuits taught the Latin curriculum exclusively. They explicated the same texts and led the students through the same kinds of exercises that humanistic masters had, but they organized the syllabus more rigidly than their predecessors had.[71]

Loyola and his early followers believed that they brought a new, more rigorous, syllabus of studies modeled on the *modus et ordo Parisiensis* to the undisciplined Italians, a claim echoed by modern Jesuit historians.[72] Loyola certainly remembered Paris. After his unhappy attempt at acquiring an essentially medieval education (including the study of Albertus Magnus and the *Sentences* of Peter Lombard) at Alcalá, he moved to the University of Paris in early 1528 and remained until 1535. Loyola and his first disciples arrived in Paris at the happy moment when the university had completed its transition from a medieval to a Renaissance curriculum of studies. Loyola never wavered in his admiration for Paris; he recalled with pleasure his studies at the Collège de Montaigu and the Collège de Sainte-Barbe. He and the early Jesuit schoolmasters frequently cited with approval "the method and order of Paris."[73] The term signified to them (1) a solid foundation in classical Latin grammar; (2) concentration on Cicero and Vergil more than any other authors; (3) emphasis on speaking Latin; (4) repetition, constant review, memorization, disputation, and composition exercises; and (5) an orderly, somewhat rigid progression of studies.

But the *modus Parisiensis* and the Jesuit *ratio studiorum* mostly imitated the humanistic curriculum developed by fifteenth-century Italians. Long before the Jesuits, Italian humanistic masters had begun with an intensive study of Latin grammar, had placed Vergil and Cicero at the center of the curriculum, and had employed a great deal of repetition, review, and drill. The close resemblance between the Italian *studia humanitatis*, the *modus Parisiensis*, and the Jesuit syllabus is obvious.

After the elimination of the reading and writing class and some experimentation with a Greek class, the Jesuit schools adopted a five-class system. They were (in ascending order), the first, second, and third grammar classes, humanities, and rhetoric. A class represented a unit of work to be mastered rather than a period of time. Hence, a student graduated to the next class when he mastered the material of his current class. The year-round calendar facilitated frequent promotions, although the Jesuits soon limited promotions to a few predetermined dates in the year. The Jesuits viewed each of the three grammar classes as requiring

[71]Scaglione, 1986, appeared too late to integrate into this section. It is in basic agreement with what is written here and adds interesting details on the Jesuit colleges in Savoy.
[72]Farrell, 1938, p. 29; Tacchi Venturi, 1951, pp. 338, 347, 354.
[73]Farrell, 1938, pp. 3–5.

about a year to complete, and the humanities class as needing about two years.[74] The rhetoric class also took about a year. Hence, an average student completed the course of study of a normal Italian Jesuit college in approximately six years, between the ages of 10 and 16. But the early syllabus and even the definitive *Ratio studiorum* of 1599 permitted flexibility. In a large college the three grammar classes might be further divided and streamed, so that some students moved ahead rapidly and others took additional months or years.

The Jesuits taught the standard classical curriculum authors with the same academic exercises used by Italian humanistic masters circa 1450 to 1600.[75] The lowest grammar class began with intensive memorization of the rudiments of Latin from an elementary manual. As noted in chapter 7, the Jesuits initially used the manuals of Despauter from northern Europe. But they quickly switched to *Ianua*, Guarino's *Regulae,* and other more local manuals in the face of protests from teachers and parents. Students were abandoning Jesuit schools because they used the wrong grammar! In the late sixteenth century Jesuit schools adopted the grammar of Manoel Alvarez, one of their own members. The lowest grammar class also read the *Disticha Catonis* and engaged in the usual intensive drill and agreement exercises. Teachers were permitted to explain grammatical points in the vernacular.

The second grammar class concentrated on analyzing several of the letters in Cicero's *Epistulae ad familiares* plus Vives' *Colloquia*. Sometimes the class read other books, such as Ovid's "chaste" *Tristia.* Intensive grammar drill with the same grammar manuals continued. The *Aeneid* or *Eclogues* of Vergil dominated the third grammar class and led the students through *ars metrica*. This class might also study Ovid's *Tristia* or *Epistulae ex Ponto* (elegaic letters) or Sallust's *Bellum Iugurthinum.* The study of Cicero's *Ad familiares* and grammar drill continued. And the students might be asked to write a short composition daily.

The two-year humanities class broadened the students' horizons. The

[74]Ibid., pp. 77, 161.

[75]For the following discussion of the Jesuit curriculum, I have relied heavily on early *catalogi lectionum* of various Italian Jesuit colleges. These brief catalogues listed the books actually taught class by class: Messina, 5 November 1558, in MP, vol. 3:534–36; the Collegio Romano, 1560, in MP, vol. 3:536–37; Palermo, 1561, in MP, vol. 3:537–38; Forlì, 1561–62, in MP, vol. 3:552; Naples, 1564, in MP, vol. 3:554–56; and Milan, 1565, in MP, vol. 3:564–65. Early *rationes studiorum* tended to be more general and optimistic, in effect academic wish lists, much like humanistic pedagogical treatises. Nevertheless, the following pair are particularly informative: the letter of Hannibal du Coudret of 14 July 1551, Messina, describing three to four years' experience in Messina, in MP, vol. 1:95–106; and the first attempt at a *ratio studiorum,* the "De studii generalis dispositione et ordine" of Hieronymus Nadal of 1552 in MP, vol. 1:136–42. The analysis of Farrell, 1938, pp. 47–64, 77–78, 95, 153–87, is also helpful.

class read one or more historical books, typically Sallust's *Bellum Iugurthi-num* but also Caesar's *Commentarii*. Students might also read Horace's *Ars poetica* and another work of Cicero, perhaps one of his moral treatises such as *De amicitia* or selections from the *Epistulae ad Atticum*. Jesuit schools usually avoided Terence for moral reasons (see ch. 9). The humanities class sometimes read the "chaste" parts of Martial. It often studied Erasmus's two great style compendia, *De conscribendis epistolis* and *De copia*, in the 1550s, but not after the mid-1560s, when Italian Catholics almost univer-sally condemned Erasmus as a heretic and Luther's precursor. And the humanities class began the study of Greek, invariably using the grammar of Cleynaerts. The class studied Isocrates' *To Nicocles;* it also sometimes read one or more of Aesop's fables in Greek and something from Pindar, Demosthenes, or another author. The study of Cicero's *Ad familiares* and Vergil continued, as well as limited grammar review, exercises, and prose composition.

In rhetoric, the fifth class, students concentrated on the theory and practice of oratory. They invariably read Cicero's *Partitiones oratoriae* and one or two of his orations, such as *Pro Milone* or *Pro lege Manilia*. They might also study Quintilian or the *Rhetorica ad Herennium* and occasionally a non-rhetorical Latin author. Students could be required to compose an oration or composition every week. The study of Greek continued with the same grammar and texts used in the humanities class.

The Jesuit curriculum differed significantly from the *studia humanitatis* only in that it elevated the study of Greek to a secure, important position in the syllabus. Although humanistic pedagogical treatises had praised the study of Greek, Italian masters had not taught much Greek. The Jesuits did much more. At first they taught Greek in the humanities class; after discussion and experimentation, they integrated Greek into the entire curriculum by introducing a little in the lowest grammar class and con-tinuing to teach it throughout the other classes. The trial *Ratio studiorum* of 1586 and the definitive version of 1599 confirmed this arrangement for Greek.[76]

Otherwise, the Jesuits simply added more structure to the humanistic curriculum. Italian pedagogical theorists and communes urged or ordered masters to teach grammar, poetry, rhetoric, and history, and they some-times named the texts. But they did not insist on a single pattern of studies. All of the Jesuits taught the same texts and authors in a methodical progression of classes. Grammar drill, composition exercises, and the paraphrase-commentary dominated the Jesuit classroom as they did other schoolrooms. Jesuit academic principles insisted that students and teachers speak only Latin in the classroom. But the Society sensibly modified the

[76]Farrell, 1938, pp. 96–97, 229–30, 237–39, 346–47, 349–52.

rule in practice in order to permit the use of the vernacular, especially in the grammar classes.[77] With much less fanfare, Italian humanistic masters and students had also tried to use Latin in the classroom and had not always succeeded.

In the first years the grammar class met six hours a day, evenly split between morning and afternoon, and the humanities and rhetoric classes met only four hours, two in the morning and two in the afternoon.[78] In 1567 the Jesuit colleges adopted for all classes a five-hour school day evenly divided between morning and afternoon.[79] Classes met six days a week. School was in session the year around except for a vacation of one or two weeks in the summer. The *Ratio studiorum* of 1599 permitted colleges to follow local vacation customs so long as the annual vacation did not exceed two weeks.[80] Classes met about 270 days in the calendar year. Like other schools, Jesuit colleges celebrated approximately thirty holy days, saints' feast days, and so on, by suspending classes, although they required their students to attend public assemblies marked by disputations and orations on some of these.[81]

The Jesuits handled large classes imaginatively. They developed an ingenious system of student assistants for large grammar classes of fifty or sixty. The master divided the class into groups of ten (*decuriae*), each headed by a leader (*decurio*) who heard the recitations and memory exercises of the other nine, collected their written work, took attendance, and kept track of those who recited well or poorly.[82] Students took turns serving as *decurio,* which also meant reciting before the master himself. A teacher streamed his students through *decuriae;* for example, a class of sixty might have six *decuriae* of varying levels of ability. When the entire *decuria* had mastered a body of material, it moved forward as a group.

Jesuit schools used competitions extensively and imaginatively. Whereas Renaissance pedagogy, with the endorsement of Quintilian and Erasmus, strongly approved of scholastic competition, the Jesuits wove it into the very fabric of the college. The *decuriae* might become the locus of various kinds of competitions. In monthly composition contests, the pupils turning in the best papers earned such titles as Imperator, Praetor, Tribune, and Senator, and held them until the next competition. Classroom contests led to schoolwide events and eventually to public appearances before parents and townspeople in which the best students read

[77]MP, vol. 1:377; vol. 2:538–39; vol. 4:8, 9.

[78]See Farrell, 1938, p. 49, for the Messina schedule.

[79]Ibid., p. 63 n. 17.

[80]Ibid., p. 97.

[81]See, for example, MP, vol. 2:550–51.

[82]For *decuriae* and the following paragraph on competition, see Farrell, 1938, pp. 119–21, 291–96.

their compositions, orated, or disputed. Competition for prizes seemed a natural development for an order founded by an ex-soldier and manifesting a robust esprit de corps. And like Renaissance teachers generally, Jesuit masters did not worry much about the adverse psychological effects on students who always lost.

The Jesuits also handled discipline and punishment adroitly. They relied mostly on the system of competition and rewards, cautioned their teachers to punish sparingly, and hired a non-Jesuit to administer corporal punishment when necessary.[83]

The consistently higher enrollment in the lower classes indicates that many students did not complete the approximately six-year-long program of grammar, humanities, and rhetoric. As in other schools, students might leave at any time. The boy who completed the five classes of the humanistic curriculum boasted facility in reading, writing, and speaking classical Latin, plus some competence in Greek. He then had several options. Since very few of the Jesuit colleges in Italy went beyond the rhetoric class, those who wished to continue studying under Jesuit auspices had to go to another school, such as the Collegio Romano, where they found classes in logic, philosophy, theology, and Hebrew. Many who followed this road may have entered the religious life. Others desiring further education enrolled in a university at the age of 16, 17, or 18. And still others entered the adult world prepared by the religious training imbibed at the college to be upright leaders of society—or so the Jesuits hoped.

THE SCUOLE PIE

The Jesuits offered free Latin schooling to boys of all classes at first, and to members of the upper and middle classes later. The Society added doctrinal instruction and obligatory religious practices to the humanistic curriculum of the Renaissance. Moreover, the schools for nobles adapted the Renaissance boarding school to the aristocratic world of the late sixteenth century and the seventeenth century. In these ways the Jesuits moved education from the Renaissance into a new era.

But the Jesuits ignored the vernacular curriculum. José Calasanz brought the charitable impulse and innovative energies of the Catholic Reformation to the vernacular schools enrolling middle- and working-class boys. Calasanz had the revolutionary idea of providing universal free education for boys. He offered free instruction in vernacular reading, writing, and abbaco, plus some Latin, six days a week throughout the year. His Scuole Pie aimed to educate poor and working-class boys so that they might attain salvation and earn a living; a few might move up the

[83]Ibid., pp. 74, 148, 244–45, 354–55.

social ladder. He and his schools remained basically faithful to this goal, although, in time, they taught more Latin and accepted some nobles and fee-paying boarders. Like the Jesuits, the Piarists, as Calasanz and his followers were called, reorganized a part of Italian pedagogy and helped Renaissance education become Old Regime schooling.

José Calasanz (Giuseppe Calasanzio in Italian), possibly the son of an impoverished *hidalgo* turned blacksmith, was born circa 1557 in a small village in Aragon.[84] University trained and ordained a diocesan priest, Calasanz rose in the administrative hierarchy of his diocese until 1592, when he went to Rome in search of a prebend. In the years that he waited for the Curia to act, he immersed himself in charitable activities, especially teaching in the catechism schools. He became president of the Roman company of the confraternity of the Schools of Christian Doctrine in 1593.

As he worked with the poor of Rome, Calasanz discovered that a large part of the population remained unschooled because parents could not afford even the modest fees of *maestri dei rioni* or independent masters. The unschooled had been there for centuries, but only Calasanz seemed to see them. He embarked on a fruitless quest to find teachers for the poor. He asked the *maestri dei rioni* to take into their classes all the poor boys in a *rione,* not just one or two. The *maestri* responded that they would need larger stipends from the city if additional nonpaying students replaced paying students.[85] Calasanz then urged the city either to increase the salaries of the *maestri dei rioni* or to open additional schools for the poor. The civil government declined, citing the lack of funds. He then turned to the religious orders. Calasanz asked the Jesuit father-general to establish a school for the illiterate poor. But the Jesuits reaffirmed their policy of accepting only boys who had already mastered the rudiments of Latin. Calasanz asked the Dominicans to establish such a school, but they responded that their work as preachers and missionaries made it impossible to take on such a heavy and different charge.

Calasanz took matters into his own hands. Sometime in the year 1597 he and two other priests began to teach poor boys without payment in two rooms supplied by the pastor of Santa Dorotea in Trastevere, a poor parish near the Ponte Sisto. Calasanz called his classes Scuole Pie (Pious Schools), a name derived from *pietà* (piety or mercy). Word spread very quickly; more than a hundred boys attended by the end of the first week, and the

---

[84]My account of Calasanz's life and the beginning of the Scuole Pie is based on Calasanzio, 1950–55; Tosetti, 1824; Timon-David, 1884; Caballero, 1945; Santoloci, 1948; Sántha, Aguilera, and Centelles, 1956; and Giordano, 1960. Despite a hagiographical tone, the older studies offer much detailed information that is consistent with modern studies. See Volpicelli, ed., 1960, pp. 561–85, for important Piarist documents.

[85]Although required by the city to teach all the poor in a *rione,* the *maestri dei rioni* constantly evaded their responsibility; see ch. 3. Of course, given the numbers of the poor in Rome (or any other Renaissance city), it was an unrealistic requirement.

school continued to grow. Calasanz coped with the spectacular enrollment growth by soliciting support and persuading others to come and teach. Popes Clement VIII and Paul V, Cardinals Cesare Baronio and Silvio Antoniano, and others provided the funds to rent additional rooms, to hire teachers when volunteers could not be found, and to buy the paper, pens, ink, and books furnished without charge to the students. The Scuole Pie moved across the Tiber to larger quarters in the district of Sant'Andrea della Valle in 1600. The school survived an inspection ordered by the pope in response to the complaints of the unhappy *maestri dei rioni* who saw their livelihood imperilled. Enrollment climbed to five hundred or more by 1602. Thanks to additional donations, the Scuole Pie purchased a building contiguous to the church of San Pantaleo just off what is now the Corso Vittorio Emanuele II, and the school moved there in 1612. This building in the heart of Rome remains the headquarters of the Piarist Fathers today. By 1612 the Scuole Pie enrolled eight hundred or more students.

Calasanz developed a school uniquely designed to teach poor boys. Indeed, the Scuole Pie differed substantially from the other religious order schools of the Catholic Reformation in the first twenty years, 1597 to 1617. Calasanz accepted only pupils presenting certificates of poverty issued by parish priests. The certificates guaranteed that those pupils most needing free schooling received it, even though Calasanz broke his own rule to accept a few wealthy pupils. The Piarists accepted barefoot students clad in rags. Once enrolled, the school furnished books, paper, pens, ink, and, on occasion, food to those needing nourishment. To maintain the integrity of the principle of free schooling, the Piarists discouraged gifts: they did not want pupils to bring firewood to school or mothers to wash the teachers' clothes.[86]

Like all the new educators of the Catholic Reformation, Calasanz made religious instruction and practices an integral part of the school, because he judged inculcating good morals and saving souls to be as important as learning.[87] The school day began with attendance at mass and recitation of the Litany of the Blessed Virgin Mary. Students confessed and received Holy Communion at least once a month. On Sundays and holidays students had to come to the school for a short session of prayers and catechetical instruction. Classes ended half an hour early on Tuesdays and Saturdays so that students might give ear to spiritual exhortation. Finally, the Scuole Pie practiced perpetual prayer during the day: a priest and nine students knelt and prayed in the church for fifteen to thirty minutes until relieved by the next group.

The most interesting part of the Piarist attempt to reach beyond the walls of the school was accompanying: at noon and again at the end of the

[86]Liebreich, 1985–86, pp. 73–74.
[87]In addition to the other sources, see ibid., pp. 256–59.

school day, teachers escorted groups of students to their homes across the city.[88] Calasanz probably initiated accompanying to keep the boys off the streets on the way home; clerical educators worried a great deal about street activities—games, gambling, and bad associates—in the Renaissance. The Piarists also did it to protect their students from stone and mud throwing. But teachers hated going out in all kinds of weather, and older boys did their best to slip away. Still, accompanying helped advertise the school.

The Piarists tried harder than other teaching orders to involve parents in their sons' schooling. They consulted parents on whether students should take the abbaco class or pursue the Latin curriculum. They hoped that boys would instruct their poorly educated parents in Catholic doctrine. The Piarists invited parents to attend musical, theatrical, and academic exercises and might heed parental criticism.[89]

The school met for two and one-half hours in the morning and another two and one-half hours in the afternoon except during the hottest days of the year.[90] School bells divided the day into quarter-hour segments, as teacher and students moved briskly from one exercise to another in the lower classes. The most elementary classes followed the vernacular curriculum; in the ninth or lowest class, boys learned "la Santa Croce"—the alphabet and how to read syllables. Because the teacher could not possibly hear individual recitations from the sixty or seventy boys in attendance, he wrote the letters of the alphabet on large sheets of paper attached to the wall, and touched the letters and syllables with a stick while the students spoke them in unison. Upon learning a few words, the boys graduated to the eighth class. Here another group of sixty or more boys read the entire primer in a similarly regimented fashion. They recited in unison the Latin prayers of the primer in six- or eight-line segments; then the boys recited individually. To make sure that the material was learned, the teachers quizzed the students, asking them to divide a word into syllables. At this stage, the students also recited in unison the opening sections of a catechism and various prayers. The teacher examined individual students throughout the day; a student who had mastered the primer moved up to the seventh class.

In the seventh and sixth classes (really one class of about 130 boys divided into a slower and an advanced section) boys learned to read vernacular religious books. Here and throughout the school, the teachers

[88]Ibid., pp. 60–62.

[89]Ibid., pp. 66–68.

[90]The following is based on "Breve relazione sul modo usato nelle Scuole Pie per insegnare agli alunni poveri," attributed to Calasanz between 1604 and 1610. It is printed in Volpicelli, ed., 1960, pp. 561–65; and Santoloci, 1948, pp. 89–96. Also see De Vivo, 1960, pp. 145–58; and Liebreich, 1985–86, pp. 225–42, for Piarist pedagogy.

encouraged better performance through contests and rewards. For example, teachers divided the classes into competing groups: Romans and Carthaginians, *pars pia* vs. *pars angelica, equites* vs. *pedites.* In the fifth class, two teachers instructed about 140 boys in various subjects. This class tried to meet both vocational and academic needs. In the morning one part of the class studied abbaco and the other memorized Latin nominatives. In the afternoon, all students learned to write. The better ones wrote well-formed letters in three or four months, Calasanz reported. This class marked a dividing point. Those who studied abbaco often left the school for an apprenticeship or employment upon finishing abbaco instruction at about the age of 12.[91] The school had accomplished its purpose of taking illiterate, poor boys and preparing them to earn a living, a goal that Calasanz kept always in sight.

Those boys who remained in school studied a standard Latin curriculum from this point. The fourth class declined and conjugated, did agreement exercise, and worked a little on verbal syntax. They also memorized the catechism. Teachers taught Latin in the vernacular; unlike the Jesuits, the Scuole Pie did not try to make Latin the language of instruction. The third class studied active and passive verbs and read the *Colloquia* of Vives. The second class continued to study verbal syntax and read a few letters from Cicero's *Epistulae ad familiares.* At the end of the year the students might also audit classes at the Collegio Romano. The first (highest) class studied gerunds and supines and read parts of Cicero's *De officiis* and Vergil. The Scuole Pie did not teach Greek; indeed, the Roman Piarist school ended at this point. Some boys would continue their studies at the Collegio Romano. Others would find employment or enter the religious life. Calasanz accomplished his purpose of giving several hundred boys from poor and modest family backgrounds academic and religious training. It was a major achievement.

Calasanz borrowed curricular content and pedagogical techniques from several sources but harnessed them to his own vision. The idea of a spiritual and intellectual mission to teach rudimentary education and religious instruction to the poor probably came from the Schools of Christian Doctrine. The highly structured system of classes came from the Jesuits, as, possibly, did some of the techniques for handling very large classes. But the notion that students might in one school learn vernacular reading, writing, and abbaco to prepare them for artisanal and merchant careers, or study Latin to rise socially, was his original insight.

Although conceived in a spirit and for a purpose very different from

[91]The Florentine Piarist school in the late seventeenth century seems to have followed the traditional Florentine practice of a separate, intensive abbaco class lasting about a year. The Florentine Piarists placed the abbaco class a little apart from the mainstream of the school. Liebreich, 1985–86, p. 237.

those of the Jesuits and other religious orders, the Piarists moved into the mainstream of Catholic Reform education after 1617. Calasanz organized his followers into a religious community sanctioned by the papacy as a congregation in 1617, and as an order called the Clerics Regular of the Mother of God of the Pious Schools in 1621. Contemporaries and historians usually called them Scolopi (a contraction of Scuole Pie), Padri Scolopi, Escolapios (in Spanish), and Piarists.

Calasanz eagerly expanded to other towns. The Piarists founded schools in Frascati in 1617; Narni (in Umbria) in 1618; Carcare (Liguria), Fanano (near Modena), and Norcia (southern Umbria) in 1621; Savona in 1623; Genoa in 1624; Messina in 1625; Naples in 1626; Florence in 1630; Ancona and Cosenza in 1631; and Palermo in 1634. Other schools followed. By 1646 the Piarists had five hundred members in thirty-seven houses in Italy and elsewhere in Europe.[92] Many were located in relatively isolated smaller cities and towns in northern and central Italy. In time the Piarists also became communal schoolmasters like the Jesuits, Barnabites, and Somaschi.

Calasanz relied on volunteers and gifts from prelates to finance the first school in Rome. After 1617 and expansion beyond Rome, the Piarists relied on much the same mix of benefactors as did the Jesuits: princes, prelates, nobles, some clergymen, numerous legacies, and the commune. The Florentine Piarists, for example, received support from the Medici court plus legacies of property, rents, and cash, for which they said numerous masses for the souls of the givers. Unlike the Jesuits, the Piarists went on begging expeditions, which they called "searches" (cerche). That is, they went door-to-door "in search of" grain, wine, and olive oil to feed the teachers, wood to heat the school, and so on.[93] The Piarists may not have enjoyed the success of the Jesuits in loosening the purse strings of the very wealthy, but they tried hard to obtain broad support from the giving public.

As they grew in number the Piarists succumbed to the intellectual temptation of more advanced teaching and study. They began to offer instruction in more Latin authors in the grammar classes, and they added a rhetoric class and some philosophy which included Galilean physics.[94] The Piarist syllabus began more closely to resemble the Jesuit curriculum, but it retained elementary reading and writing instruction and abbaco.

The Piarists moved farthest from their origins when they opened

[92]Timon-David, 1884, vol. 1, ch. 17, pp. 382–419, provides a list of the new schools. Also see Cordella and Severini, 1982; and Sindoni, 1971. Sometimes the sources differ with one another slightly on opening dates of schools.

[93]In addition to references to benefactors throughout the Piarist sources, see Liebreich, 1982, pp. 295–98.

[94]Ibid., pp. 278–81; Liebreich, 1985–86, pp. 248–55.

schools for nobles, though they did so on a limited basis. Cardinal Michelangelo Tonti (1566–1622) left the Piarists a legacy to establish a free boarding school for a limited number of poor boys between the ages of 12 and 18. However, a bitter legal battle with the cardinal's relatives, not finally resolved until 1679, seriously depleted the legacy. When the school, called the Collegio Nazareno, finally opened its doors in 1630, it could accept only eight pupils. A combination of heavy debts and nobles clamoring to get in persuaded Calasanz to accept fee-paying boarders in 1643. Before long the Collegio Nazareno, instead of a school for the poor, was a college of nobles pursuing a full Latin humanities curriculum.[95] The Piarists made a similar accommodation to the aristocratic times in Florence. One of the teachers there suggested adding a separate school for the sons of the nobility because "they do not wish to mix with the others or to go to the Jesuits."[96] Calasanz initially rejected the idea but later conceded, probably under pressure from Grand Duke Ferdinand II, the Piarists' chief Florentine benefactor. A school for nobles (really a separate class within the existing Scuole Pie) opened in Florence in 1638. It enrolled about twenty-five students, compared with the three hundred to five hundred in the main Florentine school. The Piarists did not go much further. They operated only one other Italian school full of nobles and did not teach courtly skills. Despite these compromises with the times, they remained primarily committed to educating the poor.

Consequently, after 1617 the Piarists turned contradictory faces to the world. On the one hand they taught the poor and helped the lower classes move up the social ladder through free Latin instruction. This face probably attracted the most attention, not all of it favorable. On the other hand they competed with the Jesuits and others as conventional pedagogues to the middle and upper ranks of society. Not surprisingly, some of the older orders of the Catholic Reformation resented the Piarists for this.

The Piarists endured considerably more criticism than the other teaching orders of the Catholic Reformation, much of it from defenders of the social status quo. Free schools for the poor undermined the right arrangement of society, in their view. Tommaso Campanella (1568–1639), in his defense of the Scuole Pie (written 1631–32 but not published), summarized the views of those who believed that educating the lower classes deprived the state of the useful services of those who worked.[97] These critics judged society to consist of different orders, each with its unique function, Campanella began. Patricians ruled, the clergy performed sacred duties,

[95]See Vannucci, 1930, for the story.

[96]As quoted in Liebreich, 1985–86, p. 85. For more on the Florentine school for nobles, see Picanyol, 1939; and Liebreich, 1985–86, pp. 82–86.

[97]For the Latin text and English translation, see Jensen and Liebreich, 1984; an Italian translation can be found in Volpicelli, ed., 1960, pp. 571–85.

and artisans, farmers, servants, and soldiers worked. If the working classes received a Latin education, they would try to become clergymen and university graduates, thus depriving the commonwealth of their useful labor. If artisans became learned and ceased to fill productive roles, patricians would be forced to work and would neglect the administration of the state. Similarly, schools would graduate too many clergymen; the natural balance and right functioning of society would be upset.[98] Thus Campanella outlined the rationale of the hierarchical state which schools for the poor threatened.

Campanella did not agree. He responded that education would enable artisans, peasants, and servants to discharge their duties better. In addition, more schooling would yield an improved and happier citizenry ready to oppose tyrants and able to avoid the snares of heretics. And he saw no ill effects for society if members of the lower classes rose through education.[99]

The Piarists' abandonment of the requirement of poverty and their move into the educational mainstream also provoked opposition. Upon receiving papal approval in 1617, the Piarists dropped the certificate of poverty, probably under papal pressure.[100] The Piarists continued to insist that the poor were their primary student constituency, but they now taught all who came. Discarding the certificate of poverty as a prerequisite for enrollment and teaching a full classical curriculum to those who wanted it transformed the Piarists into scholastic rivals to the Jesuits, Barnabites, and Somaschi. Naturally, these orders grumbled. Campanella tried to answer them, as well.

If the Jesuits teach their students piously and well, they need not fear defections to the Piarists, he began.[101] Moreover, the Scolopi do not teach singing, horsemanship, or fencing, but only learning and the fear of God.[102] Campanella argued that the two complemented each other—the Jesuits teach the wealthy in large cities, the Piarists the poor in small towns—a statement with some validity.[103] He could not resist jabbing the Jesuits for betraying their origins: if the Jesuits had devoted more time to helping the poor, the Piarists would not have arisen.[104] Overall, Campanella argued that the Piarists had as much right to teach Latin as the Jesuits did, and that the availability of more schooling benefited all.

[98]Jensen and Liebreich, 1984, pp. 41–42 (Latin), 58–59 (English).
[99]Ibid., pp. 43–46 (Latin), 60, 62–63 (English).
[100]Tosetti, 1824, p. 97.
[101]Jensen and Liebreich, 1984, pp. 52 (Latin), 69 (English).
[102]Ibid., pp. 57 (Latin), 75 (English).
[103]Ibid., pp. 46–47, 52 (Latin), pp. 64, 70 (English).
[104]Ibid., pp. 48 (Latin), 65 (English).

The Piarists also came under attack because Calasanz welcomed contro-
versial figures and new ideas.[105] Perhaps because they taught abbaco,
some Piarists went on to higher mathematical and scientific study. Moreover, Calasanz found mathematics interesting. These pursuits led to a
close association with Galileo in 1634, shortly after his condemnation and
sentence to perpetual house arrest in Arcetri on the outskirts of Florence.[106] Some Florentine Piarists assisted the blind scientist and followed
his teachings.

But not all. In 1640 one of the Florentine Piarists began to denounce his
colleagues to the Inquisition for alleged internal abuses and for holding
Galilean views. The latter charge was both serious and true. Urban VIII,
no friend of Galilean science, launched an investigation that essentially
culminated in the suppression of the entire order in 1646. Calasanz died
during these dark days, still expecting that his order would be vindicated.
He was right. The papacy restored the Piarists to the status of a congregation with simple vows in 1656 and to a full religious order with solemn
vows in 1669. A later pope canonized Calasanz in 1767. The order grew to
great size in Italy, Spain, and northern Europe in the eighteenth century
(218 houses in 1784), and numbered important scholars and scientists
among its members.

It has been said that the Jesuits educated the nobility and upper bour-
geoisie, the Barnabites the middle class, and the Piarists the humble.[107]
The limited, impressionistic available evidence cannot verify such a
sweeping statement but does suggest its accuracy. Records from the
Florentine Piarist school for the period 1680 to 1703 demonstrate that boys
from artisan, small shopkeeper, and merchant families composed 70 to 88
percent of the school's average enrollment of three hundred to four hundred; sons of professional men (notaries, physicians, etc.), important
merchants, and civic officialdom made up 6 to 24 percent; and sons of the
nobility 4 to 7.5 percent. Probably most of the last enrolled in the *classe dei
nobili* within the larger school. As might be expected, almost all the boys in
the upper-level rhetoric class were sons of *signori*, whereas nearly all the
boys in the abbaco class were the sons of artisans and tradesmen. Very
limited information on the immediate occupations of forty-nine boys who
left the school in the 1680s demonstrates that they followed three paths.
About one-third continued their studies at the University of Pisa, with the

---

[105]According to Sindoni, 1971, p. 376 n. 1, Calasanz's Roman school enrolled Jewish boys
as well as Christian ones.

[106]The story can be found in most of the Piarist sources cited in n. 84 and is conveniently
summarized in Liebreich, 1982, pp. 288–94. I have not seen Leodegario Picanyol, *Le Scuole
Pie e Galileo* (Rome, 1942).

[107]From a Piarist historian commenting on Florence, as cited by Liebreich, 1982, p. 272.

Jesuits, or in other schools. About one-fourth entered the religious life, and about two-fifths joined a merchant firm, worked in banks, or became artisans.[108]

Although some observers criticized free education for the poor, many more, including wealthy and powerful individuals, endorsed and supported free schooling for a broad spectrum of society. They did so basically from charitable motives. Hence, the number of Piarist schools grew, and the schools found imitators. For example, a group of priests and laymen supported by the archbishop founded a free school in Bologna in 1616 which they called Scuole Pie. The school's curriculum and internal organization imitated the Piarist model, although the Piarists had no role. The Bolognese group formed a local confraternity to operate the school, which began with 150 boys. A large gift from Pope Gregory XV in 1621, smaller gifts from individuals, and a subsidy from the Commune of Bologna enabled it to survive an early financial crisis and grow to 800 to 900 students in the late seventeenth century.[109]

Historians correctly honor Calasanz as one of the first, possibly the first, to offer free comprehensive and universal education to boys (but not girls). Even though he could not maintain the integrity of his early vision, his schools marked a significant innovative achievement.

THE SCHOOLS OF THE OLD REGIME

The Jesuits started it, other religious orders followed. Together they changed the face of Italian education. They moved from the Renaissance with its emphasis on independent and communal schools to the Old Regime of religious order and endowed schools. Thanks to the charitable impulses of the Catholic Reformation, these new schools probably offered more instruction to poor boys and all girls, who had been left out before.[110]

The Barnabites or Clerics Regular of St. Paul followed in the footsteps of the Jesuits. Antonio Maria Zaccaria (1502/3–39) and two companions founded the order in Milan in 1530 to carry on catechetical, devotional, pastoral, and preaching activities. The Barnabites declined invitations to teach until 1605, when they accepted a large legacy left them to open a school. The Barnabites amended their constitution to add the education of youth as an activity, and the Scuole Arcimboldi (named for the benefactor)

---

[108]The data indicated the immediate occupation, not necessarily permanent careers. Ibid., pp. 284–88, 302–4.

[109]Fantini, 1971, pp. 3–23.

[110]This section only outlines the transition. A full account of seventeenth-century education would require at least another volume.

opened in Milan in 1608. Other schools followed: Asti and Foligno in 1626, Florence in 1629, Pisa in 1632, Casalmaggiore in 1638, Vigevano in 1644, Livorno in 1650, and so on. Like the Jesuits, the Barnabites offered free instruction in the Latin curriculum to boys who had a grounding in the rudiments of Latin grammar. They operated a limited number of boarding schools, and probably drew the majority of their students from the middle and upper ranks of society.[111]

The Somaschi or Clerics Regular of Somascha followed a slightly different path. Girolamo Miani (or Emiliani, 1486–1537), a Venetian nobleman, founded the order in 1534.[112] He rescued orphan boys in Venice and other towns of the Venetian Dominion from a life of begging in the streets by housing them and teaching them Christian doctrine, reading, writing, arithmetic, and a trade. He also established orphanages for girls. The Somaschi saw instruction as only a small part of their mission to orphans at first; later they became pedagogues. In 1583 Cardinal Tolomeo Gallio, secretary of state to the reigning pope, gave the Somaschi a sum of money to found a school in his native town of Como. The Collegio Gallio admitted fifty boys at least 10 years old, giving preference to orphans but accepting fee-paying boys as well, to be trained according to their aptitudes. They might stay until they reached the age of 18. In 1595 the Somaschi opened the Collegio Clementino in Rome, a boarding school for noble boys endowed by Pope Clement VIII. By 1602 it enrolled ninety-four noble boarders who studied Latin letters and "arti cavalleresche," which meant riding, jumping, using the pike, fencing, fortifications, mathematics, painting, music, and vernacular languages. Numerous Italian future rulers and prelates, including one pope, studied there in the next three and a half centuries.[113]

In 1600 the Somaschi stood poised between their original role of preparing orphans for a trade and the new role of instructors to the elite. In the seventeenth century they increasingly followed the example of the Jesuits and Barnabites and became schoolmasters to the upper classes. They played a particularly important role in the Venetian state, partly because of their Venetian roots and because the government banished the Jesuits in 1606 during the Interdict fight and did not readmit them until 1657. In these years the Somaschi established a boarding school in Padua in 1606, a school for nobles in Brescia in 1628, another school for nobles with foreign boarders in Bergamo in 1632, and a third in Verona in 1639. Like all

[111]Premoli, 1913, pp. 387–91; Premoli, 1922, pp. 18–20 et passim; Le Scuole, 1933; De Vivo, 1959; and A. M. Erba, 1975.

[112]Zonta, 1932; De Vivo, 1958, pp. 263–82; Marcocchi, 1967–70, vol. 2:162–66; Bianchini, 1975; Bianchini and Pellegrini, 1977.

[113]Zambarelli, 1936, passim, but esp. pp. 13, 18.

religious orders, the Somaschi operated some seminaries. But they also continued to operate orphanages that prepared their charges to become tradesmen.[114]

A few religious order schools for girls also appeared in the sixteenth and seventeenth centuries. Angela Merici (1470/75–1540) showed the way. Although illiterate, Merici began to catechize girls and women in her native town of Desenzano on Lake Garda. In Brescia in 1535, she and twenty-eight female companions formed the Company of St. Ursula, a group of women who, much like men in a confraternity, did not profess vows but engaged in religious and charitable activities. Little by little they became more involved in educating girls through catechetical instruction and vernacular reading schools. In 1585 many of Merici's successors joined together in a formal order of professed nuns called the Order of St. Ursula. In the 1640s they operated two kinds of schools for girls. They taught a vernacular curriculum of reading, writing, arithmetic, domestic arts, music, painting, dance, and deportment to a limited number of daughters of the wealthy who were paying boarding students. This was a continuation of the traditional practice of the girls paying to live and study in the convent for a number of years. The Ursulines also taught without charge external students, girls who came daily to learn a limited amount of vernacular reading, writing, and domestic arts.[115] Eventually, other orders of nuns followed the same pattern of operating two kinds of schools for girls. The Maestre Pie Venerini founded by Rosa Venerini (1656–1728) opened in Viterbo in 1685; it was a free school modelled on the Scuole Pie to teach vernacular reading and writing to girls. By the time Venerini died, her order had opened forty schools across Italy, especially in towns and small cities in central Italy. Support came from communal governments and benefactors.[116]

Religious order schooling for girls grew very slowly because of papal restrictions on the movement of nuns. Pius V's constitution *Circa pastoralis* of 29 May 1566 ordered strict cloistering of all professed nuns.[117] They could not come and go freely to teach elsewhere in the town, because they had to remain in the convent except in dire emergencies. The female religious orders could instruct only those girls who lived in the convent as boarders or came as external students. Cloistering made it extremely difficult for nuns to teach, found schools, ask princes and lay benefactors for funds, or even to shift personnel from one convent to another. Cloistering also prevented nuns from improving their academic skills by study-

[114]Tramontin, 1983, pp. 46–47.

[115]Ledóchowska, 1974; "Orsoline," 1980, coll. 836, 841–42, 849–50; De Vivo, 1960, pp. 327–29.

[116]Rocca, 1978.

[117]"Clausura," 1975, col. 1174.

ing outside.[118] By contrast, professed male religious were not normally cloistered and could carry on teaching and other activities outside the monastery.

Establishing schools for girls without a religious order did not succeed, either. Countess Ludovica Torelli of Guastalla (1500–1569) tried this path. She founded in 1530 the Angeliche or Congregation of the Angelic Sisters of St. Paul, an uncloistered religious order of women closely associated with the Barnabites. They worked to reform female convents and to assist and educate girls. When the Council of Trent and Pius V ordered strict cloistering, Torelli left her order and founded in 1565 a secular boarding school for girls, possibly the only one in Italy at the time. Her Collegio della Guastalla in Milan accepted twenty-five poor noble girls at least 10 years of age. After studying reading, writing, and domestic arts, they left by the age of 21 with a marriage dowry provided by the college. But without the institutional strength of an order of professed nuns, Torelli could not recruit others to perpetuate and expand her initiative.[119]

The male religious orders became even more important when members became communal schoolmasters. Already in the sixteenth century the communal council or the prince sometimes subsidized the Jesuits to teach a certain number of boys of the town. It was a short step from a communal or princely donation to a contract in which a religious order took over communal schools. It began with the Jesuits in the sixteenth century and became common in the seventeenth century. Again and again communal councils, especially those of medium-sized towns, turned over their communal school to a religious order.

The schools of Novara, a medium-sized town and episcopal seat located about thirty miles west of Milan, illustrated what happened.[120] In the fifteenth century, the commune sponsored a Latin school to which it tried to appoint prestigious humanistic masters. In 1431 the commune appointed Guiniforte Barzizza, son of Gasparino, and in 1446 the commune tried to hire Francesco Filelfo, apparently without success. The communal school continued through the fifteenth century, but suffered in the six-

---

[118]Paradoxically, while the papacy hampered the spread of religious order schools for girls, it provided a good deal of education for Roman girls of all classes. Beginning in 1655 the papacy gave the funds to hire numerous female teachers for free neighborhood schools for girls across Rome. Each schoolmistress taught vernacular reading and writing to between a handful and more than seventy girls. As a result of this and other charitable initiatives, the majority of Roman girls could attend school at the end of the seventeenth century, a far cry from the situation in other cities and earlier centuries. Pelliccia, 1980; Pelliccia, 1985, pp. 393–417.

[119]A. M. Erba, 1974; Marcocchi, 1967–70, vol. 1:338–46; vol. 2:154–59; Premoli, 1913, passim.

[120]Lizier, 1908.

teenth century when armies marched back and forth across Lombardy. By 1575 the commune supported only one grammarian.

Then a bequest revitalized the communal school in 1603. Under the new name of Le Scuole Canobiane, it taught a standard Latin curriculum somewhat modelled on that of the Jesuits. The school did not charge fees, and enrollment rose. In 1612 the commune decreed an enrollment cap of 190 students of whom no more than 10 might come from outside Novarese territory. Five teachers and three *ripetitori* appointed by the commune taught them. Teachers might also accept up to 20 boarding students, so long as at least 10 came from Novara and its *contado* (countryside).

However, by 1624 the commune became dissatisfied with the operation of the school. Citing the lack of progress of the pupils, the administrative burden, and the difficulty of finding good teachers, the commune turned over direction of the Scuole Canobiane to the Jesuits, rejecting the bid of the Barnabites, who also wanted the Novara school. The Jesuits demanded an annual subsidy of 1,000 scudi, which the commune raised. The original bequest to the Scuole Canobiane provided 600 scudi, a legacy from a Roman Jesuit added 150, another 100 scudi came from the Novara seminary in exchange for the right of the seminarians to attend classes, and the final 150 scudi came from the *contado* of Novara. The Jesuits took over the school in 1624.

The Novarese citizens praised the Jesuits at first, but then found the school's discipline too restrictive. Indeed, the Jesuits kept the students on a tight leash. They expelled students who fought or threw rocks. They attempted to segregate the students from the life of the town: pupils were forbidden to associate with "bad women" and to loiter in the shops. Some financial difficulties also arose. Teaching came to a halt while the city and the Jesuits attempted to iron out their differences. Eventually an agreement was reached, and the school reopened. The Jesuits remained in control of the school until the Society's suppression in 1773.

The same thing happened repeatedly across Italy as communal councils called in the Jesuits, Barnabites, Piarists, or Somaschi to take direction of the communal schools.[121] The Barnabites were particularly active in Lom-

---

[121]In addition to the examples noted in the section on Jesuit schools, the Jesuits also became communal schoolmasters in other towns; Spoleto, see Fausti, 1943, pp. 44–51; Mantua, see Mainardi, 1871, p. 6; Pistoia, see Zanelli, 1900, pp. 112–13; Forlì, see Pasini, 1925, pp. 79–86, 179–92. The Barnabites became communal masters in Casalmaggiore, Vigevano, and Asti; see *Le Scuole*, 1933, pp. 120, 123, 148. The Somaschi replaced the Jesuits as communal masters in Brescia and took charge of the communal school in Udine; see Zanelli, 1896, pp. 22–23, 29–32; and Marchesi, 1890, pp. 15–20. The Piarists became the communal masters in Volterra; see Battistini, 1919, p. 54. This list is far from complete. Much the same happened in France. Many French towns had established municipal *collèges* for the *studia humanitatis* between 1530 and 1560. Then, in the seventeenth century, the monarchy encouraged and pressured the Jesuits and other religious orders to take over the municipal *collèges*. See Huppert, 1984.

bardy, the Somaschi dominated in the Venetian state, and the Jesuits and Piarists operated communal schools throughout Italy and Sicily.

Pedagogical, administrative, financial, and numerical reasons moved communal councils to bring in the fathers. First, the religious orders enjoyed excellent pedagogical reputations. Indeed, some members of the religious orders were excellent scholars and teachers in the humanities and the coming sciences. But, just as important, the other activities of the orders added luster to the schools. Surely the miracle-working Jesuits who converted oriental pagans and led obstinate heretics back to the true faith could stimulate the boys of the town to learn more. The orderly, somewhat regimented curriculum seemed to guarantee academic progress. The heavy dose of doctrinal instruction and enforced participation in religious exercises persuaded parents that their sons would become upright, devout citizens, always a concern to city fathers.

Other educational features also found favor. Jesuit theater, copied by the Piarists and others, seemed exciting and wonderful. Parents and townspeople flocked to these extravaganzas involving elaborate stagecraft, musical interludes, and dramatic thrills. The Piarists stressed music in their schools until circa 1641. It must have been more stimulating to attend a school of two hundred to three hundred pupils in a large building with many activities underway than an independent school of twenty-five pupils in a single room. Those who attended or supported religious order schools could feel with justification that they marched in the educational vanguard.

The commune lightened its own administrative burden when it called in a religious order. It did not have to recruit teachers, negotiate contracts, supervise the curriculum, and inspect the schools. A communal council no longer needed to pursue a famous teacher in order to bring renown to the city. The commune shifted responsibility for the school to other shoulders.

Above all, the religious order communal schools probably cost less. The lack of figures with which to compare the outlay for a communal school before and after a religious order assumed direction makes this judgment tentative. But the fact that towns and cities across Italy frequently made the change argues strongly that expenses dropped. Certainly local governments found it increasingly difficult to pay communal masters as economic depression and price inflation overtook Italy in the seventeenth century. The initial outlay for bringing in a religious order might be quite high, but the long-term disbursements may have been considerably lower. Erecting a building or providing a subsidy sometimes cost more immediately than paying salaries and housing allowances of communal masters. But often a rich benefactor paid all or part of the original outlay. Thereafter, the religious order schools taught by celibate clergymen vowing poverty probably cost less than the previous system of annual salaries, housing allowances, and renting schoolroom space.

Finally, the religious order communal school taught more students at lower direct expense to parents. Two or three salaried masters might teach 50 to 100 boys; a Jesuit college normally enrolled 150 to 300. Parents had to pay supplementary fees to earlier communal masters and larger amounts to independent teachers. The religious order schools were free to the pupils, because a prince, nobles, or the commune endowed the school. For these reasons, the communally sponsored religious order schools probably enlarged educational opportunity.

As the Novara example and others noted earlier in this chapter indicate, bequests and endowments played an increasingly prominent role in late-sixteenth- and seventeenth-century education. Endowed schools had been important elsewhere in Europe, especially England, from the late Middle Ages onward, but not in Italy.[122] Now for the first time wealthy Italians left substantial sums of money to endow elementary and secondary schools. Bequests were closely linked to the rise of the pedagogical orders and the emphasis on religious charity of the Catholic Reformation. A benefactor established a small school to tend to the intellectual and spiritual needs of a limited number of poor students. A donor typically left a legacy to found a free school to be run by a priest or two for ten or twenty "poor but nobly born" boys. Or a noble left money so that a religious order could establish a new school.

Endowed schools of limited enrollment dotted the academic landscape by 1600. They usually remained small, but often added fee-paying students to the original students taught gratis. Milan had several endowed schools in 1591.[123] The Scuola de' Calchi, founded by a nobleman named Girolamo de' Calchi who had left his palace and garden for a school, boarded and educated fifteen noble boys gratis. A supplementary bequest enabled the school to add twenty-five paying boarding students. One teacher and a *ripetitore* instructed the boys in the Latin curriculum. A Milanese count endowed the Collegio San Simone for the free education of twelve "poor but nobly born" boys, to whom were added another twenty-three upper-class boarding students. They studied the Latin curriculum plus theology on holidays, and did regular spiritual reading. A priest lived and slept in the dormitory with the boys in order to guide their spiritual development. The Collegio Dugnano educated ten aspirants to the priesthood chosen from a local orphanage. The Collegio della Guastalla, previously mentioned, trained twenty-five girls.

---

[122]Although the kind and quantity of endowed schools has been a matter of discussion, there is no doubt that they were an important part of English schooling much earlier than in Italy. See Moran, 1985, pp. 82–85 et passim.

[123]For the following and other Milanese endowed schools, see Morigia, 1592, pp. 407–8; and Bendiscioli, 1957, pp. 460–62.

Although most Milanese endowed schools taught the Latin curriculum to a small number of noble youths, some taught the vernacular curriculum to many commoners. The Scuola de' Taverni, endowed by a member of the Taverna family, paid the salaries of four reading teachers and one writing master who instructed about five hundred youths without charge. Like the Scuole Pie, it taught rudimentary vernacular literacy skills to a large number of children, presumably mostly or exclusively boys, by means of mass instructional techniques. More endowed schools followed in the seventeenth century in Milan and throughout Italy.

The combination of religious teaching orders, endowed schools, and targeting the "poor but nobly born" for special consideration while providing some free education for poor commoners substantially changed the pedagogical world of seventeenth-century Italy. Aristocrats took a leading role in endowing schools, just as they loomed larger in other areas of life. The poor noble claimed more free education than the poor commoner in this climate. Schools, as always, reflected the values of society, or at least of its leaders. The communal school, which expressed the will of the self-governing, wealthy, but not nobly born merchant class of the Renaissance city-state, gave way to the endowed school founded by an aristocrat and guided by the regular clergy. Italy had moved a long way from the Trecento organization of schooling.

But not completely. Tiny towns in particular continued to maintain communal masters. For example, numerous villages in the Pisan *contado* supported at communal expense a physician, a surgeon, and a teacher in the seventeenth century.[124] Communes paid these masters modestly, perhaps twelve to fifty scudi annually, to teach vernacular reading and writing, abbaco, and sometimes Latin. Priests and men in minor orders lacking benefices, as well as the occasional parish pastor, held the majority of these teaching posts; laymen occupied the rest. Students normally paid no fees. The villages in the Pisan *contado* managed to support teachers more or less continuously through most of the seventeenth century except for the plague years of 1630 to 1633. These villages were too small in population to support a religious order school. Not enough wealthy parents existed to support an independent master, and no parents could afford to send their sons elsewhere for instruction. Hence, the commune used part of its sparse revenues to provide for the training of its youth, just as it hired a physician and a surgeon to cure the sick. Other regions of Italy did the same.[125] Three centuries earlier cities and towns had inaugurated commu-

---

[124]Pesciatini, 1982. Pesciatini discovered that 34 of the 139 communes examined, some with only a handful of people, supported teachers through 1672, the concluding point of her research.

[125]For schools in the Sienese *contado*, see Imberciadori, 1959, pp. 432–37. For schools in

nal education because they had no alternative. Small villages continued to maintain communal schools in the seventeenth century for the same reason.

Probably the independent schools became the chief victims of the changing scholastic times. A Florentine noble diarist writing about 1665 noted their decline and the loss of prestige of the independent master. Every father with the means had a priest in the house to teach his sons and to accompany them throughout the city, he wrote. The many who could not afford a home tutor used to send their sons to a "public" (i.e., independent) school. But learning of the high reputation of the Jesuit schools, parents turned to them because they were free. Thus, the independent schools had gone into decline. And what was worse, few if any scholars wished to become teachers, because "the job is swinish." The majority of scholars learn just enough to pass the examination and become priests, he concluded.[126] The caustic opinion of one noble may not convey a wholly accurate picture. Nevertheless, his assessment of the declining ranks and prestige of independent masters seems reasonable.

THE ROLE OF THE CHURCH

The Catholic Reformation marked a decisive change in the organization of education. Starting from a deeply felt religious impulse to teach the word of God to children, priests and lay persons initiated a variety of educational thrusts. The Schools of Christian Doctrine, the starting point for so much Catholic Reform pedagogy, added informal holiday and Sunday reading, writing, and religious instruction. They reached out to those previously ignored, poor boys and most girls. The new religious orders added formal schooling and significantly altered the governance and financing of Italian education. The Jesuits, Piarists, Barnabites, and Somaschi founded new schools and often assumed direction of communal schools. Or perhaps it is more accurate to say that princes and communal

---

the Luccan *contado,* see Adorni-Braccesi, 1986, pp. 587–94. For clergymen who taught in the tiny villages and countryside of the diocese of Novara, see Deutscher, "Growth."

[126]Maestri di squola della Grammatica. Ciascun padri [*sic*] di famiglia, che haveva facultà di poterlo fare, teneva in casa un Preto, perche insegnasse à figlioli, e per accompagnarli fuori di casa, e ci essino suggetti di lettera, e di bontà riguardevoli. E per quelli che non potevano tenere il Maestro in casa ci erano parecchi, che tenevano sguola [*sic*] publica, e vi si mandavano i figlioli con un servitore, ò con altri. Havendo poi preso credito le sguole che tengono i Jiesuiti, ogn'uno è voltato à loro per non spenderi, e si sono dimesse le sguole publiche; e quel ch'è peggio nessuno studioso, ò pochi, per applicarsi à far mestiero del Maestro, perchè impiego è suanito; ma a i più basta imparar tanto, che basti loro per passar all'esame, e divenir Preti.

VM, MS. Italiani, Classe V, 39 (5859), "Memorie del Sig. Cavaliere Tommaso Rinuccini, gentilhuomo fiorentino, circa l'usanza mutate nel presente secolo 1600 notate e scritte da lui nell'età sua d'anni 69," fols. 166ᵛ–167ʳ. Rinuccini lived from 1596 to 1682.

councils abandoned independent masters and gave up direction of communal schools because the religious orders offered what they judged to be better education at lower cost.

The Italian Renaissance lacked a concept of free education for the benefit of the community and its members. At best, the commune or an individual teacher educated a handful of poor boys *ad amorem Dei*. Catholic reformers did not endorse free education as a secular value, but believed in it as a spiritual good, a means of saving the souls of the lower classes. The religious order schools all began by offering free schooling to boys drawn from all classes. But the desire to influence society's leaders in a very hierarchical age led the Jesuits and, to some extent, the other teaching orders to concentrate a significant part of their energies on the training of the upper class. When this happened the Piarists created new schools for the non-elite. The Catholic Reformation even managed to offer more education for girls than the Renaissance. Overall, Catholic reformers enlarged the pool of available elementary and secondary schooling.

But they did not change the curriculum, except to add much more religious instruction. They maintained the distinction between the Latin curriculum and the vernacular syllabus. The Jesuits, Barnabites, Somaschi, and later the Piarists taught the Latin *studia humanitatis* to the upper and middle classes. The Schools of Christian Doctrine, the Piarists, and the schools for girls taught vernacular reading, writing, and arithmetic for working boys and almost all girls.

One cannot quite say that the church took over Italian education circa 1600, because the line between ecclesiastical and lay society hardly existed in a modern sense in the several centuries covered in this study. But certainly the church was a stronger institution after 1550 than before. And some components of this vibrant church played the dominant role in Italian education in the seventeenth century. Together the Renaissance and the Catholic Reformation bequeathed to the future the curricula and structure of Italian pre-university schooling that lasted to the Risorgimento and beyond.

CONCLUSION

Italian Renaissance schooling met the needs of its own times well. Its mix of practical skills and moral values, intellectual creativity and tedium, mirrored the society from which it sprang. The Renaissance also strongly influenced European and North American schooling for the next four centuries. Hence, it is hardly surprising that Italian Renaissance education continues to attract attention and excite controversy. Its accomplishments and values are part of western civilization.

CHAPTER FOURTEEN

The Role of Education in the Italian Renaissance

arents and communal councils organized the schools of the Italian Renaissance. After the collapse of church schools, parents in the fourteenth century provided for society's needs by paying numerous laymen and clerics to teach their sons as independent masters, either in small neighborhood schools of ten to thirty pupils or as household tutors. Communal councils, especially in smaller urban centers, also contracted with a master to teach a limited number of boys. A small number of towns supported communal masters through the university; that is, some teachers listed on university rolls taught children in different parts of the city. The structure of Italian schooling was set in the fourteenth century. It did not change for three centuries.

A close look at Venice in 1587 indicates the distribution of schools and pupils in a major city. Venice had a large number of independent schools, a small number of communal Latin schools, and a few church schools to train future clerics. About 89 percent of the students attended independent schools, about 4 percent studied in communal Latin schools, and 7 percent church schools. About 47 percent of the students followed the Latin syllabus and 53 percent the vernacular curriculum. All but a handful of the pupils attending formal schools were boys, but some other boys and girls received a limited amount of informal schooling. Overall, probably 33 percent of the boys of school age and about 12 percent of the girls of school age acquired at least rudimentary literacy. Perhaps 23 percent of the inhabitants of Venice in 1587 were literate, a figure that may have been typical of an Italian Renaissance city.

The schools of Florence and Rome exhibited the same pattern as those in Venice, with minor variations. Giovanni Villani's famous statistics on Florentine schooling circa 1338 are probably wrong. But other data suggest that about one-third of Florentine boys aged 10 through 13 attended formal schools in 1480. No figures have been located for Rome, but the history of the *maestri dei rioni* illustrates some of the features of communal education. Although expected to teach the poor of the *rione* for free, the *maestri* consistently evaded their obligation. The city government failed to enforce the rule because it did not see free education promoting the public good.

Although Renaissance schools were intended for upper- and middle-class boys and were staffed by men, female teachers and pupils played a small role. Female teachers appeared in limited numbers but in many places from the fourteenth century onward. They usually taught vernacular reading and writing to girls. Theorists recognized and approved of education for girls in order to make them more attractive and useful wives and mothers. But educational opportunity for girls depended heavily on class: the higher a girl's social position the greater the possibility that she would attend school. Girls usually studied with household tutors or as long-term boarders in convents. They also learned rudimentary vernacular literacy from catechism schools and from relatives. Although subject to some of the same disabilities as girls, working-class boys enjoyed greater opportunity to learn.

The humanists of the fifteenth century changed the Latin curriculum, a major academic revolution. They discarded the late medieval Latin curriculum of verse grammars and glossaries, morality poems, a handful of ancient poetical texts, and *ars dictaminis*. In its place they substituted grammar, rhetoric, poetry, and history based on Latin classical authors and texts just discovered or newly appreciated. Above all, they inserted the letters of Cicero as the Latin prose model. The early humanistic pedagogues Gasparino Barzizza, Guarino Guarini, and Vittorino da Feltre implemented the new curriculum among the sons of the powerful in northern Italy. Communal councils and parents responded by hiring schoolmasters trained in the new Latin humanistic curriculum. By about 1450 schools in a majority of northern and north-central Italian towns taught the *studia humanitatis.*

Chapters 6, 7, 8, and 9 describe the Latin curriculum in detail. All children, whether in Latin or vernacular schools, began by learning the alphabet, syllables, and words from a hornbook or primer consisting of a few Latin prayers. Children continued to use such hornbooks and primers through the nineteenth century. Learning to read at this level followed a pedagogy originating in ancient Greece and Rome. Teaching consisted of breaking the language down into its smallest parts (letters) and then reassembling it (syllable, word, phrase, and sentence) in an almost mechanical way.

Led by Valla, the humanistic pedagogues proclaimed their allegiance to grammar based on ancient usage. They dropped the medieval verse grammars in favor of new grammars, such as Guarino's *Regulae grammaticales,* and the ancient *Ars minor* of Donatus. But *"Donatus"* turned out to be a late medieval Italian composition that circulated under Donatus's name. Similarly, Guarino and other Renaissance grammarians retained a certain amount of medieval grammatical principles in their manuals and teaching. In time a Renaissance grammatical tradition combining old and new emerged. Classroom instruction consisted of patient memorization of discrete bits of grammar plus agreement exercises. Elementary Latin reading began with the *Disticha Catonis;* sixteenth-century teachers added Vives' *Colloquia.* Overall, grammar had a lower position in the *studia humanitatis* than in the medieval liberal arts because the Renaissance saw grammar as a preparatory study.

Renaissance Latin schools focused on secondary rhetoric (letter writing) rather than primary rhetoric (oratory). All teachers agreed that a good Latin style depended on imitating classical authors. But should students learn an eclectic style based on several authors or a unified style following a single model? Italians overwhelmingly chose to imitate a single prose model, Cicero, especially his *Epistulae ad familiares.* They admired his periodicity, use of dramatic contrast, and the content, which showed a Roman patrician conducting the affairs of state, family, friends, and self. Like medieval teachers of *dictamen,* the humanists taught rhetoric through imitation. But they loosened the structure and put a higher value on concreteness and human expression. Teachers also expected students to learn from the content: *verba* (words) led to *res* (knowledge of life). Hence, they required students to copy and memorize *sententiae* from Cicero's works.

The humanists gave poetry an independent position in the *studia humanitatis* which the medieval liberal arts had denied it. Humanists saw poetry as a model of good style and eloquent description; they defended ancient poets from the charge of corrupting youth. Teachers used the paraphrase-commentary, a comprehensive analysis ranging from synonyms to extended rhetorical explanation, to teach Vergil above all, but also Terence, Horace, and Ovid. History was a new subject not found in the medieval curriculum. Since no commentary tradition existed for ancient historians, the humanists created their own which emphasized geographical and historical information. They preferred Caesar, Sallust, and Valerius Maximus. Schools did not teach moral philosophy as a separate subject, but extracted moral lessons from most curriculum texts. Finally, Renaissance schools in Italy taught a limited amount of Greek and logic, the latter by means of both medieval and Renaissance texts.

The vernacular schools, by contrast, did not undergo a curriculum revolution, but inherited various medieval texts and added some from the Renaissance. Lacking guidance from commune or pedagogical theorist, the vernacular schools brought books already popular with adult readers into the classroom. These included medieval religious works such as the

Fior di virtù, but also chivalric romances and a sixteenth-century pseudo-classical work, Guevara's *Vita di Marco Aurelio.* In addition to teaching reading, some of these texts tried to promote good morality and the worldly wisdom needed to survive. Others simply entertained. The vernacular schools ignored the classics of Italian literature but read Ariosto's *Orlando furioso* as a chivalric romance.

The vernacular schools also taught the mathematical, accounting, and writing skills needed for commerce. They taught abbaco, the business mathematics created by Leonardo Fibonacci in the early thirteenth century. Classical, humanistic, and medieval university Latin mathematics had little to offer future merchants and were ignored. The vernacular schools also taught the double-entry bookkeeping that medieval and Renaissance Italians invented.

The Catholic reformers of the second half of the sixteenth century and the early seventeenth century brought change to the organization but not the curriculum of Renaissance education. Moved by charitable and religious motives, Castellino da Castello and others reached out to the working class and the poor. Viewing spiritual ignorance and illiteracy as two aspects of deprivation, the Schools of Christian Doctrine taught elementary doctrine and rudimentary reading and writing to the uneducated. Unlike previous schools, the catechism schools taught large numbers of girls, but not alongside boys. Catechetical instruction also became a feature of formal schools at this time.

The new religious orders brought more educational change to Italy. The Jesuits and other orders established free Latin schools for boys which enrolled larger numbers of pupils than earlier schools. The Jesuits taught a Renaissance Latin and Greek humanities curriculum identical to or slightly richer than that taught earlier. Soon the Jesuits, followed by the Barnabites and the Somaschi, concentrated their educational energies on members of the middle class and the nobility. José Calasanz and the Piarists established universal schools for boys which taught both vernacular and Latin curricula to all, including the poor. The new religious orders proved so successful that city councils invited them to assume direction of communal schools. The religious orders also attracted legacies, which permitted the establishment of endowed schools. The religious order and endowed schools played major roles in seventeenth-century education, while independent and lay communal schools declined. These new schools probably taught a larger percentage of the school-age population than had Renaissance schools. They also perpetuated the humanities curriculum far into the future.

Renaissance Latin schooling has come under attack recently. One eminent scholar judges it to have been mentally rigid, full of tedium, and stifling to the imagination. It intended to "exalt authority, sanction imitation, and promote compliance."[1] A very recent book levels the broader charge that Renaissance humanistic training failed to inculcate moral values and eloquence, and degenerated into grammatical drill lacking originality. It taught future civil servants to write "a stylized setpiece in a stylized way."[2] Instead of producing the free, honorable, and eloquent citizen, Latin humanistic schools produced docile, obedient, upper-class servants of the state. The charges can be summarized under three headings: a concentration on tedium, the stifling of originality, and a failure to implant values.

The Latin humanistic curriculum lasted so far beyond the Renaissance that a twentieth-century perspective may underlie some of the criticism. But a curriculum and educational structure need satisfy only its own era. Viewing Renaissance schooling within the context of the Italian fourteenth, fifteenth, and sixteenth centuries makes it difficult to agree with the criticism.

Certainly Italian Renaissance Latin education required an enormous amount of grammatical drill and exercises. But whether students and teachers found it very tedious and oppressive is another matter. Learning to write and speak fluently a non-native language, especially one as complex as classical Latin, requires an enormous amount of drill and practice. Renaissance schoolboys put forth this effort because society valued these skills highly and rewarded those who mastered them. And many Renaissance men loved Latin and the civilization that its mastery unlocked.

High motivation mitigates what outsiders see as drudgery. This point can be better understood through a modern analogy. Today learning Latin rouses few. But mastering a musical instrument or developing an athletic skill sufficiently well to perform at a high level of proficiency excites many. Both skills require an enormous amount of drill and practice that non-participants may judge tedious. But youthful musicians and athletes rarely complain. Most are so fascinated by the skill itself that they eagerly practice hours a day for years, just as Renaissance students studied Latin. Of course, learning musical or athletic skills today is a voluntary activity, whereas learning Latin was obligatory in the Renaissance. But the main point remains: much depends on the involvement and motivation of the learner, which outsiders may not comprehend. Proficiency in classical Latin during the Renaissance had much the same high visibility as proficiency in music and sports today, and earned many of the same rewards.

The charge that a humanistic education stifled originality is difficult to sustain. By any standard of judgment the Italian Renaissance was a period

---

[1]Strauss, 1985, p. 366.

[2]Grafton and Jardine, 1986, p. 17 et passim. I hasten to add that this study and Strauss, 1978, deal with much more than the criticism noted here, and that I have learned much from them.

of great originality and genius. A Latin education did not throttle the
creativity of a Pico, Machiavelli, or Galileo, but provided linguistic skills
to serve it. What of the rest of Italian schoolboys, who may have had their
potential originality stifled by immersion in Vergil, Cicero, and the rest?
They met the standards of creativity decreed by their times. The Renaissance wanted them to exhibit their limited originality within the boundaries of classical expression, philosophy, science, and so on. The vast
majority did so reasonably well.

The third objection is that Italian Renaissance Latin education failed to
inculcate the values of the citizen-orator, partly because of a preoccupation
with the minutiae of learning Vergil, Cicero, and others. Obviously,
schools devoted a great deal of effort to the minutiae, particularly at the
primary and secondary levels. But there seems no reason to doubt that
teachers and theorists who asked students to compile notebooks of moral
and civic *sententiae* tried to teach these values. And the reading, from the
Disticha Catonis to Cicero's letters, was full of moral and social commonplaces. Vernacular school students read Guevara's *Vita di Marco Aurelio,* which offered more of the same. Renaissance education definitely
included a great deal of moral and civic exhortation. The second half of the
sixteenth century added catechetical instruction. Did all this moralizing
have any effect? In particular, did the schools produce men embodying the
ideal of the citizen-orator, or servile courtiers who only mouthed the ideal?

The fact that Italian intellectuals and others clung to and repeated the
values of the citizen-orator in the midst of the disasters of the Cinquecento
argues that they took these commonplaces seriously, and that the values
taught in humanistic schools had some impact. The historical circumstances had degenerated, to say the least. Several Italian states had lost their
political independence to ultramontane "barbarians." Italian merchants no
longer dominated European commerce. And the Italy of republican city-
states was turning into an Old Regime society of *bravi.* That Italian intellectuals continued to voice the values of Ciceronian *humanitas* in the face of
these circumstances testifies to their commitment.

But what of the intellectuals who lavished praise on the undeserving
and thereby seemed to indicate that the values learned in school were only
words? The answer is that Renaissance humanism had always had the
capacity to adapt to different political ambiances without betraying its
nucleus. Recent studies of Roman, Venetian, and Neapolitan humanism
demonstrate this, and offer a more complete portrait of the humanistic
movement than the earlier studies on Florence.[3] Renaissance humanism
remained faithful to its core, which was a combination of classically
derived moral values and a critical approach to scholarship and life, in quite

[3]D'Amico, 1983; King, 1986; Bentley, 1987.

diverse political and social circumstances. Indeed, the humanistic rhetoric of praise for human and civic values showered on a blackguard of a prince or a rapacious city council was not completely hypocritical or worthless. Epideictic oratory sought to promote at least a generalized ideal of the upright society even when it could not be realized. Orators in all centuries do the same; they remind their listeners of values to be upheld.

Education always reflects the society it serves. Italian Renaissance schooling suggests several characteristics of the age.

Some common traits appeared across the educational spectrum. Despite different subject matter and a large social gap, Latin and vernacular schools shared a pedagogical approach. The subject matter, whether beginning reading, Latin grammar, advanced rhetoric, or abbaco, had to be divided into very small individual bits of knowledge. Teachers and textbooks taught by breaking a skill down into its smallest components, drilling them intensively, and then assembling the bits to make the whole. It was pedagogy based on the belief that if the student learned the pieces thoroughly, he would grasp the whole. Teacher and pupil had to comprehend perfectly every step of the process; intuitive leaps of learning were distrusted. This same habit of mind can be found elsewhere in the Italian Renaissance, especially in legislation and procedural guides.

Renaissance schools sought to teach practical skills for different social roles. Latin schools taught the Latin that enabled students to go on to university studies and prepared them for careers in the civil service, the church, or the highest ranks of society, where a knowledge of Latin was expected. Vernacular schools taught the essential commercial skills of reading, writing, abbaco, and bookkeeping. The two streams prepared boys for different roles in a fairly rigid social order. Society's leaders learned Latin, those who would work at commerce or the trades learned vernacular skills. The two streams obviously reinforced existing social divisions. But they also facilitated a little upward mobility. Boys of modest circumstances fortunate enough to join the Latin stream almost automatically climbed a few rungs up the social ladder.

Both Latin and vernacular schools attempted to instill personal and social values based on classical and Christian sources and standards. They attempted to teach pupils how to behave honorably without losing any appreciable social or other benefit. One should do one's duty to family, *patria,* and God, without losing legitimate opportunity for personal advantage. If a choice had to be made, the texts exhorted the pupil to choose honor over gain. These values are found in both the Latin and vernacular texts, in Vergil's poetry and the *Fior di virtù.* Renaissance men mostly ignored contradictions between pagan classical and Christian moral and social values.

Renaissance education was secular. It inculcated civic morality for the ruling class and the professionals who served them. Humanistic and vernacular schools taught morality through classical examples. They did not stress Christian religious doctrine and practices until the advent of the Catholic Reformation. The church played no institutional role in Renaissance education until the late Renaissance. Indeed, most clergymen seem to have received the same education as laymen. This may help explain the nature of ecclesiastical life in the Renaissance, and why churchmen often behaved like laymen.

One cannot overestimate the importance of education in the Renaissance. The extraordinary political, social, economic, and even linguistic diversity—divisiveness would be the better term—threatened to pull the peninsula apart at any moment. But schooling united Italians and played a major role in creating the Renaissance. Humanistic pedagogues developed a new educational path very different from education in the rest of Europe in the early fifteenth century. Thereafter, Italy's elite of rulers, professionals, and humanists shared the language of classical Latin. They shared a common rhetoric. And they drew from the same storehouse of moral attitudes and life examples learned in school.

The humanistic curriculum unified the Renaissance, making it a cohesive cultural and historical epoch of great achievement. When humanistic education crossed the Alps, it created a similar cultural accord that endured beyond the shattering of religious unity. Jacob Burckhardt argued that individualism was the unifying force, the essence, of the Italian Renaissance and the modern world. He would have been better advised to look into the schoolroom for the spirit of the age.

Behind Renaissance education lay the optimistic presupposition that the world was susceptible to understanding and control. Through education the mind can be trained to understand, the will can be persuaded to choose good. With a few notable exceptions, Renaissance men believed that through learning people could improve themselves and their world. It may have been a utopian belief, but all education is based on belief in a civilized, rational universe.

APPENDIXES

Sixteenth- and Seventeenth-Century Italian Printings of Some Elementary Latin Grammars

This appendix gives an idea of the format and diffusion of sixteenth- and seventeenth-century Italian printings of *Ianua, Donato al senno*, the *Donatus melior* of Antonio Mancinelli, and Guarino's *Regulae grammaticales*. No incunabular printings are listed, because they can readily be found in the standard catalogues of incunables. The editions listed here undoubtedly represent only a small fraction of those issued. The fact that only a single copy of a printing has been located in almost every case suggests that many, perhaps most, entire printings of these universally used grammars have disappeared.

In addition to the library abbreviations listed at the front of this book, the following abbreviations of bibliographical works are used in Appendix 1.

Annali dei Giunti, Firenze	*I Giunti tipografi editori di Firenze. Annali 1497–1625.* Edited by Decio Decia, Renato Delfiol, and Luigi Silvestro Camerini. 2 vols. Florence, 1979.
Annali dei Giunti, Venezia.	*Annali dei Giunti.* Vol. 1: *Venezia* 2 parts. Edited by Paolo Camerini. Florence, 1962–63.
Cinquecentine della Trivulziana	*Le cinquecentine della Biblioteca Trivulziana.* Vol. 1: *Le edizioni milanesi.* Edited by Giulia Bologna. Milan, 1965.

IANUA

Aelij Donati grammatici pro impetrando ad rempublicam litterariam aditu novitijs adolescentibus grammatices rudimenta que aptissime dedicata. Colophon: Impressum Venetijs . . . impensis Lucantonij de giunta florentini, . . . 1510 Tertio idus Novembris.

21 × 14.7 cm. Gothic type. Title page in red and black ink. 40 pp. Includes *Disticha Catonis*. VCini. Also listed in *Annali dei Giunti, Venezia*, no. 142.

Aelij Donati grammatici pro impetrando ad rempublicam litterariam aditu novitijs adolescentibus grammatices rudimenta que aptissime dedicata. Colophon: Venetiis per Guilielmum de Fontaneto, 1525.

19.6 × 14.3 cm. Gothic type, red and black ink. Title page has figured border. 40 pp. Includes *Disticha Catonis*. IU.

Aelij Donati grammatici pro impetrando ad rempublicam litterariam aditu novitijs adolescentibus grammatices rudimenta que aptissime dedicata. Colophon: Venetiis . . . Luce Antonij Junta florentini impressa, . . . 1525 die xviii Maij.

Gothic type. 40 pp. Not seen, but identical with printing of Venice, 1510, according to *Annali dei Giunti, Venezia,* no. 296.

Aelij Donati grammatici pro impetrando ad rempublicam litterariam aditu novitijs adolescentibus grammatices rudimenta que aptissime dedicata. Colophon: Venetiis per Guilielmum de Fontaneto, 1530.

19.8 × 14.3 cm. Gothic type, red and black ink. Title page has figured border. 40 pp. Nearly identical, even to contents of individual pages, to 1510 printing above. NNC Catalogue gives date as 1503. However, the cropped date is 1530. Moreover, Guglielmo da Fontaneto was not active before c. 1512. NNC Clark Collection.

Aelii Donati grammatici brevissimae puerorum institutiones. Colophon: Brixiae per Ludovicum Britannicum, 1536.

21 × 15 cm. Title in roman type, red ink. Text in gothic type, black ink. Title page has figured border with school scenes. 40 pp. Includes *Disticha Catonis.* BQ 4ª.I.XI.30.

Aelii Donati grammatici brevissimae puerorum institutiones. Colophon: Brixiae per Ludovicum Britannicum, 1548.

20.2 × 14.3 cm. Title in roman type, red ink. Text in gothic type, red and black ink. Title page has figured border with school scenes. 40 pp. Includes *Disticha Catonis* and *De Constructione* review material partially attributed to Priscian. IU.

No title. Incipit: Ianua sum rudibus. . . . Colophon: Impressum Florentiae per Benedictum Iunta, 1548.

20.8 × 14.1 cm. Roman type. 48 pp. Includes *Disticha Catonis.* FN Palat. 19.6.109. Also listed in *Annali dei Giunti, Firenze,* no. 260.

Aelii Donati rudimenta grammatices. Studio & opera Barptolomaei Moirani. . . . Mediolani, ex officina Valerii & Hieronymi fratrum de Meda, 1568.

19.3 × 14.6 cm. Semi-gothic type. 48 pp. Includes *Disticha Catonis* and a small amount of additional material. MB ††.V.28.2.

Donati institutiones grammatices a Dionysio Malatesta de Civitate Ducali, summa diligenta recognitae, atque ad puerorum utilitatem nuper impressae. Addita, artis metrices, per brevi regula. Romae, 1575. Apud Victorium Elianum.

15.4 × 10.6 cm. Roman type. 84 pp. Includes *Disticha Catonis* and other material. RAng 11.1.69. This edition expands the declensions and conjugations slightly, presents a small amount of Italian translation, and presents very short examples. It resembles the *Donatus melior* as much as it does *Ianua.*

Donatus ad lectorem. Venetijs, apud Io. Gryphium, 1575.

14.3 × 9.6 cm. Title page in gothic and roman type, red and black ink. Text in gothic type. 72 pp. Includes *Disticha Catonis.* RCas Misc. 452.10.

Aelii Donati rudimenta grammatices incipiunt. Colophon: Florentiae apud Iuntas, 1578.

19.8 × 13.6 cm. Roman type. 48 pp. Includes *Disticha Catonis* and a small amount of additional material. RVE 6.2.D.50. Also listed in *Annali dei Giunti, Firenze,* vol. 2, no. 79.

Aelii Donati grammatices erudimenta. . . . Romae, apud Antoniam Facchettum, 1595(?).

13.7 × 9 cm. Roman type. Title page in red and black ink. 68 pp. Includes *Disticha Catonis.* An occasional word has been translated into Italian. RVE 34.5.A.10.4. The copy has been badly cropped, rendering the date illegible. Because it is bound with a 1595 *Regulae* of Guarino by the same printer, type, and format (see below), it is reasonable to assume that the date is 1595.

Aelii Donati grammaticale. . . . Colophon: Mediolani, apud Franciscum Paganellum, 1597.

21.1 × 14.8 cm. Roman type. Title page in red and black ink. 40 pp. Includes *Disticha Catonis.* MT H 1898/1. Listed in *Cinquecentine della Trivulziana,* no. 174.

Aelii Donati grammaticale. . . . Colophon: Mediolani, apud Gratiadeum Feriolum, 1597.

21.1 × 14.8 cm. Roman type. Title page in red and black ink. 40 pp. Includes *Disticha Catonis.* Contents identical with that of preceding edition. Berg Mai 3815.

Donatus ad lectorem. Patavij apud Laurentium Pasquatum, 1608.

14.4 × 9.2 cm. Title page in roman type, red and black ink. Text in gothic type. 72 pp. Includes *Disticha Catonis.* VM Misc. 642.12.

Aelii Donati grammaticale. . . . Colophon: Mediolani, apud Franciscum Paganellum, 1611.

20.1 × 14.5 cm. Roman type. Title page in red and black ink. 40 pp. Includes *Disticha Catonis.* MB AB.XI.73.

Aelii Donati grammatici de octo partibus orationis, libellus recens castigatus. Et ad grammatices Catholicae normam. per R. P. Hieronymum Agnesium . . . redactus. Accededit Cato. Genuae apud Iosephum Panonem, 1636.

14.1 × 9.6 cm. Roman and italic type. 96 pp. Includes *Disticha Catonis.* RAles O.e.66. This edition begins with syllables, includes some material possibly borrowed from Guarino's *Regulae,* and adds some Italian translation. Nevertheless, it is a modified *Ianua.* It was probably intended for use in Piarist schools; see Pseudo-Guarino, 1638, in the Bibliography, which was issued by the same publisher.

Aelii Donati grammatices erudimenta. Nunc demum post omnium editiones, quae ad hanc usque in lucem prodiere, novo, ac faciliori ordine digesta. Accuratius, ac diligentius emendata, & ab innumeris erroribus purgata. Romae, Typis Vitalis Mascardi, 1638. Ad instanza di Mauritio Bona all'insegna del Marion d'Oro.

416   Appendixes

15.2 × 9.8 cm. Title page in roman and italic type, red and black ink. Text in roman type. 68 pp. Includes *Disticha Catonis.* RAng II.1.72. *Ianua* text influenced by *Donatus Melior.* Printed with Guarino, *Regulae,* by the same printer, same year, using continuous signatures (see below).

Donatus ad lectorem. Maceratae, apud Curtium Gobbum, & Iosephum Pandarum, 1645.

14.3 × 9.8 cm. Roman type. Title page has school scene. 72 pp. Includes *Disticha Catonis.* RVE 34.5.A.10.2.

Aelii Donati rudimenta grammatices. Nuperrimè ad innumeris erroribus repurgata. . . . Florentiae Typis Massae, 1645.

15.1 × 10 cm. Roman type. 64 pp. Includes *Disticha Catonis.* FM 6.G.XI.22.1.

DONATO AL SENNO

No title. Incipit: Ianua sum rudibus. . . . Colophon: Venetiis per Manfredum de Monteferrato de Sustreno de Bonelli. A di xxii de Aprile del 1503.

19.9 × 14.6 cm. Roman type. Title page in red and black ink. 59 pp. Includes *Disticha Catonis.* VM Rari V.495.

No title. Incipit: Ianua sum rudibus. . . . Colophon: Venetiis per Melchiorem Sessa (*sic*) 1508 die xxix Aprilis.

19.7 × 14.5 cm. Roman type. 59 pp. Includes *Disticha Catonis* and a short review section. IU.

Donato al senno con il Cato volgarizato, novamente stampato, & con somma diligentia castigato, & corretto. Colophon: In Venetia, per Francesco de Leno, 1570.

14.6 × 9 cm. Roman type. Title page in red and black ink. 96 pp. FLaur 22.5.15.

Donato al senno con il Cato volgarizato, novamente e diligentemente corretto & stampato. In Milano, 1570. Si vendono al segno della Stella. Colophon: Mediolani per Iacobum Girardonium, ad instantiam D. Matthaei Besutij, ad signum Stellae, 1570.

19.3 × 14.6 cm. Semi-gothic type. 68 pp. MB††.5.28.

Il Donato al senno con li versi di Catone volgarizati. . . . In Trevigi, 1636. Per Girolamo Righettini.

14.8 × 9.4 cm. Roman type. 124 pp. RAng III.1.27.

Il Donato al senno et il Cato volgarizato. . . . In Verona, appresso Bortolamio Merlo.

13.8 × 9.5 cm. Roman and italic type. Title page in red and black ink. No date, but typography indicates 1600–1650. PU 102.b.220.

Donato al senno con il Cato volgarizato. . . . In Bergamo, per Marc' Antonio Rossi, 1653.

16 × 10.4 cm. Roman and italic type. 114 pp. Berg Mai.

Donato al senno, come si dice, co' versi di Catone, volgarizzato in lingua Toscana. Con diligenza riveduto, e corretto da A. M. Aggiuntovi un breve trattato de' primi principij della grammatica, e della costruzzione, non più stampato. In Bologna, per Domenico Barbieri, 1654. Ad instanza di Gio. Francesco Barbetti.

14.6 × 10.4 cm. Roman and italic type. Title page has school scene. 128 pp. FN 22.B.9.26.

Il Donato al senno, et il Catone volgarizato. . . . . In Trevigi, per Francesco Righettini, 1660.

15 × 10.3 cm. Roman type. 126 pp. Berg Mai Locatelli 1–954.

Donato al senno come si dice, co' versi di Catone. Volgarizato in lingua Toscana. Con diligenza riveduto, e corretto da A. M. . . . . Fiorenza & in Bologna, per Gioseffo Longhi, 1670.

14.3 × 10 cm. Roman and italic type. 112 pp. FM 6.D.XI.51.1.

Il metodo d'Elio Donato, e i versi di Dionisio Catone. . . . . In Firenze, nel Garbo, da Giuseppe Manni.

15.8 × 10.2 cm. Roman and italic type. 124 pp. No date, but 1650–1700. VM 64.D.185.

DONATUS MELIOR OF ANTONIO MANCINELLI

Donatus melior. Catonis carmen de moribus. De arte libellus. Colophon: Impressum Mediolani. Per magistrum Leonardum Pachel. Anno 1501 die xyiii Maii.

19.5 × 13.4 cm. Roman type. 80 pp. FN Palat. Misc. 3.E.2.12; BA 16.C.IV.55.3.

Donatus melior. Catonis carmen de moribus. De arte libellus. Colophon: Venetiis per Ioannem de Cereto de Tridino cognominatum Tacuinus. 1502 die xxviiii Octobris.

20.4 × 14.7 cm. Roman type. BA 16.C.V.43.

Donatus melior. Catonis carmen de moribus. De arte libellus. Colophon: Mediolani per Petrum Martyrem de Mantegatiis. 1503 die xxii Septembris.

19.5 × 13.6 cm. Roman type. 79 pp. Berg Mai Inc. 5/48/2.

Donatus melior. Catonis carmen de moribus. De arte libellus. Colophon: Impressum Mediolani. Per magistrum Petrum Martirem de Mantegatiis. 1506 die x Februarii.

Roman type. Printed as part of an *Opera omnia* edition. PU 107.b.140/2.

Donatus melior. De arte libellus. Catonis commentariolus. Colophon: Impressum Venetiis per Ioannem Tacuinum de Tridino. 1508 die v Augusti.

Roman type. Printed as part of an *Opera omnia* edition. FN Magl. 1.6.150.

Donatus melior. Catonis carmen de moribus a Mancinello & Ascensio explanatus. De arte libellus. Colophon: Impressam Venetiis per Georgium de Rusconibus, 1519 die xyiii Aprilis.

Roman type. Title page in red and black ink. Printed as part of *Opera omnia* edited by Josse Bade. These three works have title page, colophon, and pagination distinct from those in the other works. BA 16.K.V.4.

Donatus Antonii Mancinelli meliori quadam via nuper quam unquam antea castigatos a D. Ioanne Martello Verolano. . . . Romae apud Antonium Facchettum, 1594.

15.1 × 10.4 cm. Roman and italic type. Title page in red and black ink. 84 pp. Contains *Donatus melior, Catonis carmen de moribus,* and *De arte libellus.* RAng 11.1.71.

THE *REGULAE GRAMMATICALES* OF GUARINO GUARINI

Guarini Veronensis viri peritissimi grammaticales regulae incipiunt. Et noviter correctae fuerunt. Colophon: Impressum Venetiis per Pietrum de Quarengius Pergomensem, die xxvii Maii 1506.

20.8 × 15.1 cm. Roman type. 48 pp. Includes *Carmina differentialia* and a small amount of additional grammatical material. VM Misc. 2585.3.

Regulae Guarini nuperrime impressae & emendatur cum expositione versuum heteroclitorum & differentialium & cum suis diphthongis expositis: tam graecis que latinis additamentis foeliciter incipiunt. Colophon: Impressum Venetiis per Ioannem de Cereto de Tridino alias Tacuinum, 1507 die xxv mensis Augusti.

19.1 × 14.1 cm. Title page in gothic type with school scene. Text in roman type. 95 pp. Contains the additional grammatical material listed in title. PU 44.a.134/1.

Guarini Veronensis viri doctissimi institutiones grammaticales nuper emendatae: foeliciter incipiunt. Colophon: Impressum Venetiis per Magistrum Petrum Bergomensem die x Novemb. 1515.

19.2 × 14.4 cm. Roman type. 48 pp. Includes *Carmina differentialia,* etc. FN 1.D.17.12.

Guarini Veronensis viri peritissimi grammaticales regulae incipiunt. Colophon: Impressum Venetiis per Alexandrum de Bindonis. 1516 die 26 Iunii.

15.6 × 9.6 cm. Roman type. Title page has border with a few school figures. 64 pp. Incipit: Quid est grammatica? Includes *Carmina differentialia,* etc. FPed '500.61.

Guarini Veronensis viri peritissimi grammaticales regule incipiunt: & noviter correcte fuerunt. Venetiis. In Casis Guilielmi de Fontaneto Montisferrati, 1530 die primo Octobrii.

19.2 × 14.4 cm. First 18 leaves in gothic type, last 2 in roman type. Title page has figured border. 40 pp. Includes *De heteroclitus, Carmina differentialia,* etc. MH.

Grammatica Pyladis. Colophon: Venetiis in aedibus Francisci Bindoni ac Maphei Pasini sociis, 1534 mensis Iulii.

14.6 × 9.3 cm. Roman type. The first half is Guarino's *Regulae,* the rest new material prepared by Gianfrancesco Boccardo of Brescia called Buccardus Pylades, d. 1508. PU 105.b.216/2.

Guarini Veronensis viri peritissimi grammaticae institutiones. Colophon: Brixiae Ludovicus Britannicus . . . imprimi curabat. Mense Februarij 1535.

20.7 × 15.3 cm. Gothic type. Title page has border. 36 pp. Includes *De heteroclitus, Carmina differentialia.* BQ 4ᵃ.I.XI.29.

Guarini Veronensis viri peritissimi grammatice institutiones. Colophon: Brixiae Iacobus Philippus Turlinus . . . imprimi curabat. Mense Novemb. 1538.

20.9 × 15 cm. Gothic type. Title page has figured border. 36 pp. *De heteroclitus, Carmina differentialia.* ICU.

Grammaticae institutiones Guarini Veronensis, suis exemplis & aliis rebus auctae. Et noviter maxima cum diligentia correctiae. Colophon: Venetijs per Franciscum Bindonum & Mapheum Pasinum socios. 1546.

15 × 10.3 cm. Title page in roman type. Text in italic type. 127 pp. Morphological material in Latin and Italian precedes the *Regulae.* Verbal syntax in the *Regulae* has been expanded with additional examples, some with Italian translation. Includes *Carmina differentialia.* RAles O.c.16.

Grammaticae institutiones Guarini Veronensis suis exemplis et aliis rebus auctae. Colophon: Venetiis apud Petrum de Nicolinis de Sabio, ad instantia Melchioris Sessae, 1549.

14.6 × 9.3 cm. Title page in roman type. Text in italic type. 119 pp. Content is the same as in preceding volume. PU 105.b.216/1.

Guarini Veronensis viri peritissimi grammatice institutiones. Colophon: Brixiae apud Damianum Turlinum . . . mense Iunii 1550.

21.4 × 15.1 cm. Gothic type. Title page has figured border. 36 pp. CU.

Guarini Veronensis grammaticales regulae, noviter diligentiori cura recognitae. Brixiae apud Iacobum Britanicum, 1566.

20.8 × 15.6 cm. Title in roman type. Text in gothic type. Title page has border with portraits of Vergil, Horace, Ovid, Lucretius, Terence, Cicero, Sallust, Livy, Valerius Maximus, and Pliny. 48 pp. Includes *De heteroclitus, etc.* IU.

Io. Alberti Bossii institutiones grammaticae . . . a Bartolemaeo Moirano scholiaste recognitae. . . . Mediolani apud Valerium ac fratres Metios, 1566.

19.3 × 14.6 cm. Semi-gothic type. 48 pp. This is a slightly modified version of the *Regulae* with a small amount of borrowing from *Ianua.* MB ††.5.28.3.

Regule grammaticales Guarini Veronensi denuo correcte. Colophon: In Milano, appresso Francesco Magrega, 1567.

18.1 × 13.4 cm. Semi-gothic and italic type. MB XM★.V.11.

Ex Guarino Veronensi . . . regulae grammatices latinique sermonis institutiones pueris utilis . . . a Dionysio Malatesta . . . excerptae, & ab ipso nuper castigatae, & auctae. Romae, apud Victoriam Elianum, 1574. Colophon: 1575.

15 × 10.4 cm. Roman type. Incipit: Quid est grammatica? RAng 11.1.69. This is a slightly revised version of the *Regulae.* Although it has its own pagination, it is

bound with Malatesta's version of *Ianua,* also published in Rome, 1575, by Vittorio Eliano (see above).

Guarini Veronensis, viri peritissimi regulae grammatices. . . . Venetiis apud Io. Gryphium, 1575.

14.6 × 8.8 cm. Roman type. 48 pp. Incipit: Quid est grammatica? Includes *De heteroclitis,* etc. RVE 34.5.A.1.2.

Io. Alberti Bossii institutiones grammaticae multi iugis mendis, quibus scatebant, expurgatae, & demum à Bartholomaeo Moirano scholaste recognitae. . . . Mediolani apud Pacificum Pontium, 1579.

19.6 × 14.5 cm. Title page in roman and italic type. Text in semi-gothic type. 56 pp. RVE 6.2.D.50.2.

Guarini Veronensis viri peritissimi regulae grammatices. . . . Romae apud Antonium Facchettum, 1595.

13.4 × 8.9 cm. Roman type. 64 pp. Incipit: Quid est grammatica? This is a companion printing to the 1595(?) *Ianua* listed above. RVE 34.5.A.10.5.

Guarini Veronensis viri peritissimi regulae grammatices. . . . Veronae apud Petrum Diserolum, 1595.

14.2 × 9.5 cm. Title page in roman and italic type. Text in roman type. 64 pp. Incipit: Quid est grammatica? Includes *De heteroclitis,* etc. PU 2.b.239/b.

Io. Alberti Bossii institutiones grammaticae . . . *a Bartholomaeo Moirano recognitae.* . . . Mediolani apud Pandulfum Malatestam, 1597.

20.9 × 15 cm. Roman type. Title page in red and black ink. 56 pp. MT H 1898/2. Also listed in *Cinquecentine della Trivulziana,* no. 81.

Guarini Veronensis viri eruditissimi regulae grammatices. . . . Patavii, ex Typogr. Laurentij Pasquati, 1608.

14.4 × 9 cm. Roman and italic type. Includes *De heteroclitis,* etc. VM Misc. 642.13.

Io. Alberti Bossii institutiones grammaticae a Bartholomaeo Moirano . . . *recognitae.* . . . Mediolani, apud Marcum Tullium Malatestam, Typographum Regium Cameralem, 1611.

20.1 × 14.5 cm. Roman type. Title page in red and black ink. MB AB.XI.73.2.

Guarini Veronensis viri peritissimi rfgulae (sic). . . . Perusiae apud Ered (sic) Alexandri Perutij, 1616.

14.3 × 9.9 cm. Roman type. 48 pp. Incipit: Quid est grammatica? Includes *De heteroclitis,* etc. A printing full of typographical errors. FM 6.D.XI.51.3.

Donati erotemata grammatices rudibus pueris per necessaria recognita. A Cantalycio Epis. Pennensi nunc demum exacta cura & castigatione emendata. Romae, Apud Gulielmum Facciottum, 1627.

15.1 × 10.1 cm. Title page in roman type, red and black ink, with a school scene. Text in roman type. 188 pp. This is a combination *Ianua* and *Regulae*. The first half is a slightly expanded *Ianua*, the second half a slightly altered *Regulae*. RCas Misc. A.46.3.

Guarini Veronensis viri peritissimi regulae grammatices pristinae lectioni restitutae. Maceratae, apud Curtium Gobbum & Iosephum Pandarum, 1635.

14.4 × 9.6 cm. Roman type. 56 pp. Incipit: Quid est grammatica? Includes *De heteroclitis*, etc. Slightly expanded version. RVE 34.5.A.10.3.

Guarini Veronensis viri peritissimi regulae grammatices. Nunc denuo recognitae & summa ac diligenti cura ab innumeris erroribus emendatae. Romae, Typis Vitalis Mascardi, 1638. Ad instanza di Mauritio Bona all'insegna del Marion d'Oro.

15.2 × 9.8 cm. Roman and italic type. Title page has school scene. 64 pp. Incipit: Quid est grammatica? Includes *De heteroclitis*. RAng 11.1.72. This is a companion printing to an *Ianua* issued by the same publisher in the same year, with continuous pagination (see above).

Guarini Veronensis viri peritissimi grammaticales regulae. Bononiae, Typis Iacobi Montij.

14.7 × 9.5 cm. Roman type. 80 pp. Includes *De heteroclitis*, etc. Although lacking a date, it is clearly a seventeenth-century printing. BU Raro A.25.

Italian Translations and Printings
of the *Libro aureo de Marco Aurelio*
# of Antonio de Guevara

Guevara's *Libro aureo de Marco Aurelio* of 1528 first appeared in an Italian translation by Mambrino Roseo da Fabriano in 1542:

Vita di M. Aurelio Imperadore, con le alte, & profonde sue sentenze, notabili documenti, ammirabili essempi, & lodevole norma di vivere. Nuovamente tradotta di Spagnuolo in lingua Toscana per Mambrino Roseo da Fabriano. In Roma per Baldasare de Cartolari Perugino nel MDXLII.

Copy: FN Palat. 4.3.3.3. None of the bibliographies of Guevara's works lists it.

This volume of 256 pages in a small format (20 × 13 cm.) shortened and freely translated the original Spanish text. It was reprinted three times:

Roma: Baldasare de Cartolari Perugino, maggio 1543. FN Palat. 4.3.3.4.

Vinegia, no printer, 1543. VM 227.D.191.

Vinegia, Comin de Trino di Monferrato, 1544. ICN.

This translation by Roseo did not become the standard Italian text.

The second Italian translation appeared in 1544:

Vita, gesti, costumi, discorsi, lettere di M. Aurelio Imperatore, sapientissimo filosofo, & oratore eloquentissimo. Con la gionta di moltissime cose, che ne lo spagnuolo non erano, e de le cose spagnuole, che mancavano in la tradottione italiana. Il Petrarca di M. Aurelio ne'l trionfo d'amore. Vedi il buon Marco d'ogni laude degno pien di filosofia, la lingua, e 'l petto. In Vinegia, appresso Vicenzo (*sic*) Vaugris a'l segno d'Erasmo, MDXLIIII. ICU.

In the introductory letter, Fausto da Longiano related that a Spanish gentleman had complained about the inadequacy of the previous translation. It omitted entire chapters and letters, did not follow the order of the original, and transposed words and clauses, according to the Spaniard. This new translation was intended to set matters straight. Although Fausto da Longiano did not claim to be the translator, bibliographers, lacking other information, have assumed that he was.

This nearly complete translation restored the 48 chapters and 19 letters of the original. But it was not particularly faithful, and it interpolated a small amount of material from Guevara's expanded version. Nevertheless, it became the standard

Italian translation: at least twenty additional printings appeared before 1600, plus another five in the seventeenth century. Printings of this translation usually contained 300 to 350 pages in a small (about 15 × 10 cm.) format. Some editions subdivided Guevara's 48 chapters into between 61 and 68 chapters. Because the title corresponds to the information given by the teachers, and printers kept issuing it, the schools very likely used this version. The known printings are listed below.

*2. In Vinegia, 1546. Colophon: In casa de' figliuoli di Aldo.

*3. In Venetia per Francesco Bindoni, & Mapheo Pasini compagni, del mese di Ottobrio.

*4. In Vinegia. Alla Bottega d'Erasmo, appresso Vincenzo Valgrisi, 1548.

5. In Vinegia. Colophon: Per Pietro di Nicolini da Sabbio. 1548.

*6. In Vinegia per Giovambattista Buccida a San Luca al segno della Cognitione, 1549. Colophon: Per Comin de Trino di Monferrato.

*7. In Vinegia, appresso Gabriel Giolito de Ferrari, 1549. Colophon: 1550.

*8. In Vinegia, Agostino Bindoni, 1550.

*9. In Venetia, Francesco Bindoni & Mapheo Pasini compagni. Del mese di Luglio, 1551.

*10. In Vinegia, appresso Gabriel Giolito de Ferrari e fratelli, 1553.

11. In Vinegia, appresso Gabriel Giolito de' Ferrari, 1556.

*12. In Vinegia, appresso Gabriel Giolito de' Ferrari, 1557.

13. In Venetia, herededi (sic) di Gioanne Padovano, 1557.

14. In Venetia, appresso Francesco Bindoni, 1559.

15. 1561. Colophon: Stampata in Venetia per Alessandro de Viano.

*16. In Venetia, appresso Francesco Rampazetto. Colophon: 1564.

*17. In Venetia, appresso Domenico, & Gio. Battista Guerra, fratelli, 1572.

18. In Venetia, appresso gli Heredi del Bonelli, 1574.

19. In Venetia, appresso Alessandro Griffio, 1578.

*20. In Venetia, appresso Domenico Cavalcalupo, 1583. ICN; not in the bibliographies.

21. In Venetia, 1593. Presso Gio. Fiorina.

22. Venetia, no printer, 1609.

*23. In Vinegia, presso Giovanni Antonio Giuliani, 1615.

24. In Venetia, 1625. Appresso Ghirardo, & Iseppo Imberti.

25. In Venetia, appresso Gio. Battista Cester, 1646.

26. In Venetia, 1663. Appresso Gio. Battista Brigua.

Guevara's larger work, *Libro llamado relox de principes en el qual incorporado el muy famoso libro de Marco Aurelio*, also had two different Italian translations.

---

*The asterisked printings have been examined by me.

Aureo libro di Marco Aurelio con l'horologio de principi in tre volumi. Composto per il molto Reverendo Signor don Antonio di Guevara. . . . Nuovamente tradotto di lingua spagnuola in italiano dalla copia originale di esso auttore. . . . In Vinegia, Francesco Portonaris da Trino. MDLIII.

Translated by an unknown hand, this version of three books had about 560 pages. The same publisher reprinted it in 1555/56*, 1560, and 1562.

An expanded version appeared in 1562. It added as a fourth book a translation of another of Guevara's works, *Libro llamado aviso de privados y doctrina de cortesanos* (Valladolid, 1539).

Libro di Marco Aurelio con l'horologio de principi distinto in quatro volumi. . . . Nel quale sono comprese molte sententie notabili, & essempi singolari appertinenti non solamente a i Prencipi Christiani, ma a tutti coloro che desiderano di vivere civilmente, e da veri & honorati gentil'huomini. Con l'aggiunta del quarto libro novamente tradotto di lingua spagnola in italiano. . . . In Venetia, appresso Francesco Portonaris da Trino, MDLXII.

This fat volume of nearly eight hundred pages was reprinted in 1568*, 1571, 1575*, 1581*, 1584*, 1591, 1605, and 1606 (twice), always in Venice.

The standard bibliographies of Guevara's works are as follows.

Lino Gómez Canedo, "Las obras de fray Antonio de Guevara: Ensayo de un catálogo completo de sus ediciones," *Archivo Ibero-Americano* 6 (1946):441–601. This bibliography supersedes the previous ones. However, the older bibliographies are still useful for more complete descriptions of some editions and other information.

Raymond Foulché-Delbosc, "Bibliographie espagnole de fray Antonio de Guevara," *Revue Hispanique* 33 (1915):301–84.

Hugues Vaganay, "Antonio de Guevara et son oeuvre dans la littérature italienne: Essai de bibliographie," *La Bibliofilia* 17 (1916):335–58.

Eduart Toda y Güell, *Bibliografía Espanyola d'Italia dels origens de la imprempta fins a l'any 1900.* Vol. 2: D–L (Barcelona, 1928), pp. 233–48.

Books of the Schools of Christian Doctrine

REGOLE

I have located and examined the following *regole* in addition to that of Milan, 1555, which is found in Marcora, 1960, pp. 470–82. Titles have sometimes been shortened and capitalization and punctuation standardized.

Regola, 1566. *Regola della Compagnia delli servi de i puttini in carità.* Si vendano al segno della Stella. In Milano, 1566.

Copy: Flaur 22.5.16.

Libretto, 1567. *Libretto per conoscere il governo delle scuole de' putti & putte, & come si debba orare.* Colophon: In Cremona, Appresso Vincenzo Conti à nome delli fratelli della Dottrina Christiana nel 1567.

MA S.*N*.F.I.62.

Montorfano, *Ordini,* 1568. *Iesus Maria. Ordini et capitoli della Compagnia dell'Oratorio. Il quale è nell'hospitale de gli incurabili in Venetia, circa il governo delle schole de putti, che sono in detta città; nelle quali s'insegna la Dottrina Christiana a' figliuoli il giorno della festa doppo il disinare. Raccolti dal Rev. Padre Don Giovanpaolo da Como, preposito delli Reverendi Padri Clerici Regolari di San Nicola.* In Vinetia, Appresso Gabriel Giolito di Ferrarii, 1568.

V Stamp. Barb.D.II.149; MB ZCC.III.83.10.

Regola, 1568. *La regola della Compagnia delli servi dei puttini in carità.* Si vendono al segno della Stella. In Milano, 1568.

MA S.*N*.F.I.62.

Regola, 1583. *Regola della Compagnia delli servi delli puttini in carità.* In Brescia, Appresso Giacomo Brittanico, 1583. Colophon: A istantia de Gio. Martino Fanzano libraro in Cremona al segno della Balla d'Oro.

MA S.*C*.R.I.66; MA S.*N*.F.I.9.

Libretto, 1593a. *Libretto per conoscere il governo delle scuole de putti et putte, & come si debba orare.* In Brescia, Appresso Policreto Turlini, 1593.

V. Ferr. St. 8011 int. 5.

Libretto, 1593b. *Libretto per conoscere il governo delle scuole de putti et putte, & come si debba orare.* In Brescia, 1593. Colophon: In Brescia, per gli Heredi di Giacomo Brittanico.

MA S.N.F.I.9; MA S.C.R.I.66.

Ordeni, 1596. *Ordeni della Congregatione che governa la Compagnia della Dottrina Christiana.* In Padova, per il Pasquato. 1596.

MB ZCC.III.83.H.13.

Regole, 1598. *Regole della Compagnia della Dottrina Christiana di Roma. Fatte e stabilite d'ordine de suoi fratelli dal Rever. D. Angelo Baldi definitore di detta Compagnia l'anno 1598.* In Roma, Appresso li Stampatori Camerali, 1598.

RV S. Borr. D.V.118 (4).

Constitutioni, 1611. *Constitutioni della ven. Archiconfraternità della Dottrina Christiana di Roma.* In Roma, nella Stamperia della Cam. Apost., 1611. Ad istanza di detta Archiconfraternità.

V R.G. Storia IV.11054 (7).

Regole, 1649. *Regole della Congregatione, et scuole della Dottrina Christiana della città, diocesi, e provincia di Milano. Fatte da Santo Carlo Borromeo. . . . Con molti nuovi ordini aggionti dell'Eminentiss. . . . Cardinale Federico Borromeo. . . . Et di nuovo ristampato per ordine dell'Eminentiss. Cardinal Monti al presente Arcivescovo di Milano.* In Milano, nella Stampa Archiepiscopale, 1649.

MT L126; IU Cavagna 2379.

Regole, 1668. *Jesus Maria. Regole della Compagnia della Dottrina Christiana per le scuole de gl'huomini. Fatte di ordine di Monsign. . . . Bartolomeo Gradenico Vescovo di Trevigi.* In Trevigi, 1668, Appresso Francesco Righettini.

V R.G. Storia V.2148 int. 2.

Regole, 1678. *Regole della Compagnia della Dottrina Christiana per le scuole de gl'huomini stampate già per ordine dell'Eminentiss. . . . Cardinale Priuli. . . . Et nuovamente reviste & ristampate per ordine di Mons. . . . Gio. Francesco Morosini Patiarca (sic) di Venetia.* In Venetia, Per Antonio Bosio, 1678, Ad istanza del Scalvinoni.

VC Op. 439.29.

Cabrini, *Ordini*, 1685. [Agostino Cabrini], *Ordini con li quali devono essere regolate le scole della Santissima Dottrina Christiana et instituto de laici secolari con suoi Oratorij. . . .* In Venetia, 1685, Per Francesco Basetto.

V R.G. Storia V. 2148 int. 1.

SUMMARII

The following *Summarii* have been located and examined.

Modo, 1566. *Modo et ordine trovato novamente per tutte quelle persone che si voranno esercitare à imparare la Dotrina* (sic) *Christiana et è fatta à utilita de figlioli è figliole, et anco per persone grandi.* Ad instantia di M. Vittorio Rondo Mantuano Ebreo fatto Christiano. In Roma dell'Anno 1566.

14.5 × 9 cm. Roman type. 24 pp. V Racc. I.V.277(5).

Summario, 1567. *Summario della vita Christiana, qual s'insegna alli fanciulli di Cremona.* Colophon: In Milano, per Vincenzo Girardoni, ad istantia de Mattheo da Besozzo, 1567.

15 × 10 cm. Gothic and roman type. 16 pp. MA S.N.F.I.62.

Dottrina Christiana, 1579. *Dottrina Christiana con la dichiaratione divisa in tre parti, da insegnarsi à putti, e putte della Città, e Diocesi di Vicenza.* . . . In Vicenza, per Giorgio Angelieri, 1579.

15.3 × 7.2 cm. Roman type. 120 pp. MB ZY.1.50. This is a combination of *Summario* and *Interrogatorio*.

Sommario, 1585. *Sommario delle cose principali che si contengono nel libro dell'Institutione Christiana. Stampato per ordine di Monsignore* . . . *Hieronimo Della Rovere Ar-civescovo di Torino.* In Torino, Presso l'Herede del Bevilacqua, 1585.

14.6 × 9.6 cm. Roman type. 16 pp. MB ZY.1.52.

Eliano, *Dottrina Christiana*, 1587. *Dottrina Christiana nella quale si contengono li principali misteri della nostra fede rappresentati con figure per istruttione de gl'idioti, & di quelli che non sanno leggere.* . . . *Composta dal P. Gio. Battista Romano della Com-pagnia de Iesu.* In Roma, Nella Stamperia de Vincentio Accolti in Borgo, 1587.

15.8 × 10.5 cm. Roman type. 79 pp. V Barb. V.XIV.92. This is an expanded and illustrated *Summario*.

Summario, 1593. *Summario della Vita Christiana qual s'insegna alli fanciulli di Cremona. IESUS.* Colophon: In Brescia, per gli herede di Giacomo Britanico, a istantia de Gio. Martino Fanzano libraro in Cremona al segno della balla d'oro, 1593.

15.1 × 9.7 cm. Gothic type. 16 pp. MA S.N.F.I.9.

Sommario, 1608. *Sommario delli misterii della Dottrina Christiana con le sue figure: Il segno della Santa Croce, il Credo, il Pater Noster, l'Ave Maria.* . . . In Roma, Appresso Guglielmo Facciotto, 1608.

10 × 7.5 cm. Roman type. 32 pp. 27 illustrations. RV S. Borr. E.V.32. This is a fully illustrated *Summario*.

Summario, n.d. *Summario della Vita Christiana qual s'insegna alli fanciulli di Cremona.* Colophon: In Brescia, per Vincenzo Sabbio, ad instanza di Pietro Gennari, libraro in Cremona.

15 × 10 cm. Mostly gothic type, with a small amount of roman. 16 pp. Sabbio began to publish in 1566. V Ferr. St. V. 8011 int. 3.

INTERROGATORII

The following *Interrogatorii* have been located and examined.

Interrogatorio, 1551/52. *Interrogatorio del Maestro al Discepolo, per instruir li fanciulli: & quelli che non sanno nella via di Dio. Nel quale si contiene tutte le cose che debbe sapere ogni fidel Christiano: cavate dal Santo Evangelio, & dalli Santi, composto & stampato con alcune cose aggionte, a beneficio di quelli che desiderano vivere secondo Dio, & la Santa Madre Chiesa.* Colophon: In Venetia, Appresso di Agustino Bindoni nell'anno del Signore. M. D. II. (*sic*).

15 × 9.6 cm. Antique roman type in two columns, some chapter headings are in gothic type. 112 pp. FN Guic. 2.6.42. The date is obviously a misprint, because the text twice mentions "Lutherani," and because Agostini Bindoni published between 1524 and 1558. The printer probably substituted *I* for *L*; hence the date should be M. D. LI (1551). Possibly he omitted the *L*; hence, the date could be 1552.

Montorfano, *Interrogatorio,* 1560. *Modo breve et facile, utile, et necessario, in forma di dialogo, di amaestrare i figliuoli mascoli, & femine, & quelli che non sanno, nelle divotioni, & buoni costumi del viver Christiano.* In Vinegia, Appresso Gabriel Giolito de' Ferrari, 1560.

15 × 10 cm. Roman type. 220 pp. VM 71.C.178.

Milanese *Interrogatorio,* 1568. *Interrogatorio del maestro al discipulo per instruere li fanciulli & quelli che non sano nella via de Dio. Visto & corretto dal R. P. Inquisitore Generale nel Stato di Milano, il R. P. F. Angelo Avogadro de Verona . . . et di novo ristampato con certi agionti d'ordine dell'Illust. . . . Cardinal Borromeo Arcivescovo de Milano l'anno 1567 a di 24 marzo.* Si vendono al segno della Stella. Colophon: In Milano, per Vicenzo Girardoni, ad instanza de M. Mattheo da Besozzo, al segno della Stella, nell'anno 1568.

This is a slightly revised version of part 1 of Montorfano, *Interrogatorio,* 1560. 15 × 10 cm. Gothic type in two columns. 36 pp. MA S.N.F.I.62.

Montorfano, *Interrogatorio,* 1570. *Iesus Maria. Bellissimo, et devotissimo dialogo, overo interrogatorio diviso in tre parti. . . . per amaestrare i figliuoli mascoli e femine, secolari e religiosi, donne & huomini, che non sanno, la instruttione delle cose della fede. . . . Raccolto dal Reverendo P. Don Giovanpaolo da Como. . . .* In Vinegia, appresso Gabriel Giolito de' Ferrari, 1570.

The title page of part 3 carries the date 1571. 14.7 × 9.5 cm. Roman type. 216 pp. FN Guic. 12.4.21[1].

Milanese *Interrogatorio,* 1574. *Interrogatorio della Dottrina Christiana. Visto, et corretto, et di nuovo ristampato per ordine dell'Illust. & Reverendiss. Cardinal Borromeo Arcivescovo di Milano, in essecutione del Concilio Provinciale dell'anno 1569.* In Milano, per Valerio & fratelli da Meda. Colophon: Per Valerio & Hieronimo fratelli da Meda, 1574.

15.5 × 10 cm. Gothic type in two columns. 32 pp. MB ZY.I.48.

Montorfano, *Interrogatorio*, 1585. *Iesus Maria. Bellissimo, et devotissimo dialogo, overo interrogatorio diviso in tre parti . . . per amaestrare i figliuoli mascoli e femine . . . delle cose della fede. . . . Raccolto dal Reverendo P. Don Giovanpaolo da Como. . . .* In Venetia, presso Domenico Imberti, 1585.

 15 × 9.5 cm. Roman type. FN Magl. 15.7.165.

Milanese *Interrogatorio*, 1593a. *Interrogatorio della Dottrina Christiana. Visto, et corretto, di nuovo ristampato per ordine dell'Illustriss. & Reverendiss. Cardinal Borromeo Arcivescovo di Milano, in essecutione del Concilio Provinciale dell'Anno MDLXIX.* Stampato in Milano, & ristampato in Brescia, per gli Herede di Giacomo Britannico, 1593.

 15.1 × 9.7 cm. Title page in roman type. Text in gothic type. MA S.N.F.I.9.

Milanese *Interrogatorio*, 1593b. *Interrogatorio della Dottrina Christiana, visto, corretto et di novo ristampato per ordine dell'Illustrissimo, & Reverendiss. Cardinal Borromeo, Arcivescovo di Milano, & in essecutione del Concilio Provinciale, dell'Anno. 1583.* Stampato in Cremona, Per Barucino Zanni, 1593.

 15 × 10 cm. Title page in roman type. Text in gothic type in two columns. 36 pp. V Ferr. V.8011.4.

Montorfano, *Interrogatorio*, 1595. *Iesus Maria. Bellissimo et devotissimo dialogo, overo interrogatorio diviso in tre parti . . . per amaestrare i figliuoli mascoli e femine. . . . Raccolto dal R. P. Don Giovan Paolo da Como . . . & di nuovo con somma diligenza ricorretto.* In Cremona, Per Barucino Zanni, 1595.

 13.5 × 9.2 cm. Roman type. 182 pp. MA S.C.R.I.66.

Dottrina Cristiana, 1610. *Dottrina Cristiana stampata d'ordine dell'Illustrissimo & R.do Sig. Alessandro Petrucci, Arcivescovo IX di Siena. . . . Aggiuntovi le Letanie della Madonna: Alcuni utilissimi costumi morali, & civili. E quarantacinque laude spirituali, da cantarsi in tutto l'anno.* In Siena, Appresso 'l Bonetti, 1610.

 13.2 × 7.2 cm. Roman type. Title page in red and black ink. 144 pp. FN Magl. 15.7.220. An *Interrogatorio* with some variations for use by the Sienese Confraternità della Dottrina Cristiana.

Dottrina Christiana, 1617. *Dottrina Christiana e sua dichiaratione, divisa in tre parti, da insegnarsi à putti, e putte della città e diocese di Bologna, per ordine dell'Illustriss. e Reverendiss. Sig. Card. Lodovisi Arcivesc. In questa nova impressione da molti errori ricoretta.* In Bologna, presso Bartolomeo Cochi, 1617.

 13.2 × 7 cm. Roman type. Title page in red and black ink. 120 pp. BA 2.hh.IV.10.

BIBLIOGRAPHY

ARCHIVAL

Rome, Archivio Storico Capitolino
  Registro di Decreti di Consiglio e Magistrati e Cittadini
Rome, Archivio di Stato
  Archivio della Università di Roma
Rome, Archivum Romanum Societatis Iesu
  Epistolae Italiae
Vatican City, Archivio Segreto Vaticano
  Miscellanea Armadio XI
Venice, Archivio della Curia Patriarcale
  "Maestri de' sestieri de S. Polo et S. Croce"
  "Professioni di fede richiesta agli insegnanti, 1587"
  "Visite alle monasteri di monache"
Venice, Archivio di Stato
  Collegio, Notatorio
  Procuratori di San Marco de supra
  Riformatori dello Studio di Padova
  Senato Terra

MANUSCRIPTS

Florence, Biblioteca Nazionale Centrale
  Ms. Magliabechiano I 45, *Ianua* and *Disticha Catonis*.
  Ms. Nazionale II - 111, Italian to Latin translation exercises.
  Ms. Nazionale II - 156, Ioannes Angloriensis, Italian to Latin translation exercises dated 29 April through 30 May 1536.
  Ms. Nazionale II.II.89, *Fior di virtù* and other material.
  Ms. Nazionale II.VII.3, "Storie Narbonesi nella traduzione di Andrea da Barberino."
  Ms. Nazionale II.IX.69, "Libro di pistole vulgari rivoltate in latino et date da mz. Gio. Bat. Conti mio maestro cominciate a scrivere . . . a dì 19 di maggio 1590 in Fiorenza . . . ad usum Bernardi de Salvestris fu Inquilini, Florentiae apud Plateam Antinoream."

An uncatalogued manuscript of a Latin grammar with *Disticha Catonis* bound with a printed book, Landau-Finaly Inc. 49.

Florence, Biblioteca Riccardiana

Ms. 720, "Regole di Palla figliuolo di Bernardo Rucellai e degli ami."

Ms. 1657, miscellaneous vernacular religious material, including "Articoli della Dottrina Christiana" on fols. 80–81.

Ms. 1716, "Trattato della Dottrina Cristiana."

Ms. 4039, Gaspare da Verona, "Grammaticae Regulae."

Milan, Biblioteca Trivulziana

Ms. 2163, "Libretto dell'Iesus."

New York, Columbia University Library

Ms. Plimpton 138, *Ianua* and *Disticha Catonis*.

Venice, Biblioteca Marciana

Ms. Italiani, Classe V, 39 (5859), "Memorie del Sig. Cavaliere Tommaso Rinuccini, gentilhuomo fiorentino, circa l'usanza mutate nel presente secolo 1600 notate e scritte da lui nell'età sua d'anni 69," fols. 153^r–172^v.

Ms. Italiani, Classe VII, 1847 (9617), "Miscellanea veneta."

Ms. Latini, Classe XIII, 8 (3937), *Ianua* and *Disticha Catonis*.

Venice, Museo Civico Correr

Ms. Cicogna 3062, "Materie ecclesiastiche veneziane."

Ms. Cicogna 3160, miscellaneous documents on Venetian schools and the University of Padua.

Ms. P D C 2250/VIII, "Copia di parti del Senato relative al insegnamento pubblico in Venezia, 1443–1651."

PRINTED SOURCES

The bibliography includes works cited in the notes but not those listed in the appendixes. Nor does it include manuscripts, incunables, and sixteenth-century editions, such as multiple printings examined, which are mentioned only in passing in the notes.

Primary Sources

Acta Ecclesiae Mediolanensis, 1846. *Acta Ecclesiae Mediolanensis*. Edited by Carlo Cajetano. Vol. 2. Milan.

Alberti, Leon Battista, 1969. *I libri della famiglia*. Edited by Ruggiero Romano and Alberto Tenenti. Turin.

Alvares, Manoel, 1575. *De institutione grammatica libri tres*. Venetiis, apud Iacobum Vitalem.

Andrea da Barberino, 1947. *I Reali di Francia*. Edited by Giuseppe Vandelli and Giovanni Gambarin. Bari.

———, 1972. *L'Aspramonte*. Edited by Luigi Cavalli. Naples.

Antoniano, Silvio, 1852. *Dell'educazione cristiana e politica de' figliuoli libri tre*. Florence.

Baron, Hans, ed., 1969. *Leonardo Bruni Aretino Humanistisch-Philosophische Schriften mit einer Chronologie seiner Werke und Briefe*. Leipzig and Berlin, 1928; rpt. Wiesbaden.

Battelli, Guido, ed., 1928. *Le più belle leggende cristiane tratte da codici e da antiche stampe, commentate e illustrate.* 3d ed., rev. Milan.

Bertanza, Enrico, and Dalla Santa, Giuseppe, 1907. *Documenti per la storia della cultura in Venezia.* Vol. 1: *Maestri, scuole e scolari in Venezia fino al 1500.* Venice.

Boccardo, Gianfrancesco, 1508. *Carmen scholasticum. De nominum declinationibus, prima declinatio.* Colophon: Venetiis per Ioannem Rubeum Vercellensem X. Kal. Sept. FN Misc. 2585.4.

Bonamico, Lazzaro, and Paleario, Aonio, 1567. *Concetti per imparare insieme la grammatica, & la lingua di Cicerone. Di nuovo ristampato. . . . Et il dialogo intitolato il grammatico overo delle false essercitationi delle scuole.* In Venetia, per Francesco Franceschini. Although the work appears under Paleario's name, Bonamico wrote the *Concetti* and Paleario the *Dialogo.*

Bonciari, Marco Antonio, 1603. *Donatus et Guarinus emendati, aucti, illustrati. . . .* 4th ed. Perusiae, Apud Petrumiac Petrutiam. Copy: RVE 34.5.A.1 (4).

———, 1620a. *Donati, et Guarini grammatica institutio. . . .* Trevigi, Apud Angelum Reghetinum. RVE 34.5.A.1 (5) & (3).

———, 1620b. *Grammatica institutio, & in eam notae ampliores. . . .* Venetiis, Apud Petrum de Farris. FN Misc. Capretta 1711.12.

———, 1623. *Grammatica institutio, & in eam notae ampliores. . . .* Florentinae, Apud Stephanum Fantuccium. FN Magl. 3.4.2.

———, 1651. *Grammatica institutio, et in eam notae ampliores. . . .* Tarvisii, Apud Simonem à Ponte. BU A.V.Y.XII.48.

Borghi, Pietro, 1501. *Libro de abacho. . . .* Colophon: In Venetia, per Zuane Baptista Sessa. 1501 a di 10 Decembrio.

Bracciolini, Poggio, 1974. *Two Renaissance Book Hunters: The Letters of Poggius Bracciolini to Nicolaus de Niccolis.* Translated by Phyllis W. G. Gordan. New York and London.

Breve, 1593. *Breve col quale nostro S. Pio Papa V essorta gli ordinarij de' luoghi, che nelle loro città e diocesi deputino chiese, ò altri luoghi, nelli quali si debbano ammaestrare i fanciulli nella Dottrina Christiana. . . .* In Brescia, appresso Vincenzo Sabbio. Ad instanza di Pietro Gennaro. V. Stamp. Ferraioli V. 8011. int. 1.

Brown, R. Gene, and Johnston, Kenneth S., 1963. *Paciolo on Accounting.* New York, San Francisco, Toronto, and London.

Bruni, Leonardo, 1987. *The Humanism of Leonardo Bruni. Selected Texts.* Translations and Introductions by Gordon Griffiths, James Hankins, and David Thompson. Binghamton, N.Y.

Bullarium, 1882. *Bullarium diplomatum et privilegiorum summorum Romanorum Pontificum.* Vol. 7: *Pio IV ad Pium V.* Naples.

Caesar, Gaius Julius, 1482. *Commentariorum de bello Gallico* (and other works). Colophon: Venice, Octaviano Scoto, 21 August 1482. Hain-Copinger 4218*; GW 5829.

———, 1518. *Commentarii di Iulio Cesare tradocti* (sic) *di Latino in lingua fiorentina per Dante Popoleschi.* Colophon: Firenze, per Io. Stephano di Carlo da Pavia. 30 October.

———, 1569. *Commentariorum de bello Gallico, libri viii. De bello civili Pompeiano, lib. iii. Alexandrino, lib. i. Africano, lib. i. Hispaniensi, lib. i . . . cum scholiis Enrici Glareani.* Venetiis, Ex Bibliotheca Aldina.

———, 1571. *Commentariorum de bello Gallico, libri iix. Civili Pompeiano, libi iii.*

Alexandrino, lib. i. Africano, lib. i. Hispaniensi, lib. i. Eiusdem fragmenta A. Fulvio Ursino collecta . . . Scholia Aldi Manutii. Venetiis, In Aedib. Manutianis.

Cafaro, Girolamo, 1560. *Grammatices epitome.* Venetiis apud Paulum Erardum. FPed '500.22.

Calandri, Filippo, 1518. *Pictagoris arithmetrice introductor.* Colophon: Firenze per Bernardo Zucchecta, 1518 a di XX di Luglio.

Calasanzio, 1950–55. *Epistolario di San Giuseppe Calasanzio.* Edited by Leodegario Picanyol. 9 vols. Rome.

Canisius, Peter, 1933. *Catechismi Latini et Germanici.* Edited by Fridericus Streicher. Pt. 1: *Catechismi Latini.* Rome.

Carbone, Lodovico, 1596. *Dello ammaestramento de' figliuoli nella dottrina Christiana.* In Venetia, appresso Giovanni Guerigli.

Cato, 1922. *The Distichs of Cato, a Famous Medieval Textbook.* Translated and introduced by Wayland Johnson Chase. University of Wisconsin Studies in the Social Sciences and History, 7. Madison, Wis.

———, 1952. *Disticha Catonis recensuit et apparatu critico instruxit.* Edited by Marcus Boas and Henricus Johannes Botschuyver. Amsterdam.

Cavalca, Domenico, 1915. *Le vite dei Santi Padri.* 2 vols. Milan.

Cicero, M. Tullius, 1942. *Brutus. Orator.* Edited and translated by G. L. Hendrickson and H. M. Hubbell. Cambridge, Mass., and London.

———, 1948. *De oratore. De fato. Paradoxa stoicorum. De partitione oratoria.* Edited and translated by E. W. Sutton and H. Rackham. 2 vols. Cambridge, Mass., and London.

———, 1948–53. *The Verrine Orations.* Edited and translated by L. H. G. Greenwood. 2 vols. Cambridge, Mass., and London.

———, 1958–60. *The Letters to His Friends.* Edited and translated by W. Glynn Williams. 3 vols. Cambridge, Mass., and London.

———, 1978. *Cicero's Letters to His Friends.* Translated by D. R. Shackleton Bailey. 2 vols. Harmondsworth, Middlesex.

Clarenzio, Lorenzo, 1591. *Grammaticae institutiones.* Florentiae apud Philippum Iunctam. FM G.G.XI.22 (int. 7).

Clavius, Christophorus, 1586. *Aritmetica prattica . . . tradotta . . . in italiano dal Lorenzo Castellano.* Roma, per Domenico Basa.

Codice diplomatico, 1971. *Codice diplomatico dell' Università di Pavia.* 2 vols. in 3 pts. Pavia, 1905–15; rpt. Bologna.

Conciliorum, 1973. *Conciliorum oecumenicorum decreta.* Edited by Giuseppe Alberigo et al. 3d ed. Bologna.

Conversino da Ravenna, Giovanni, 1980. *Dragmologia de eligibili vite genere.* Edited and translated by Helen L. Eaker and Benjamin G. Kohl. Lewisburg and London.

Corradi, Giovanni Battista, 1653. *Schola humanitatis sub praeceptore Aelio Donato Romano.* Romae, Formis Francisci Monetae.

———, 1654. *Elio Donato Romano . . . overo di tutta la grammatica Latina e volgare.* Romae, ex officina Michaëlis Cortellini. RVE 42.1.F.2.

Dallari, Umberto, 1888–1924. *I rotuli dei lettori legisti e artisti dello Studio Bolognese dal 1384 al 1799.* 4 vols. Bologna.

De Luca, Giuseppe, ed., 1954. *Prosatori minori del Trecento. Scrittori di religione.* Milan and Naples.

Dolce, Ludovico, 1559. *Dialogo della institution delle donne.* In Vinegia, appresso Gabriel Giolito de' Ferrari.

Donatus, Aelius, 1926. *The Ars Minor of Donatus, for One Thousand Years the Leading Textbook of Grammar.* Translated by Wayland Johnson Chase. University of Wisconsin Studies in the Social Sciences and History, 11. Madison, Wis.

Donatus diligenter recognitus. No date. Mutinae. Colophon: Ex Officina Gadaldina. FPed '500.68.

Epistole et Evangeli, 1495. *Epistole et evangelii in vulgare storiate.* Florence [Bartolomeo de' Libri], 24 ottobre 1495. Hain 6643; IGI 3703.

Erasmus, Desiderius, 1965. *Ciceronianus.* Edited and translated by Angelo Gambaro. Brescia.

————, 1985. *Collected Works of Erasmus.* Vols. 25 and 26: *De conscribendis epistolis formula, De civilitate, De pueris instituendis, De recta pronuntiatione.* Edited by J. K. Sowards. Toronto, Buffalo, and London.

————, 1986. *Collected Works of Erasmus.* Vols. 27 and 28: *Panegyricus, Moria, Julius Exclusus, Institutio Principis Christiani, Querela Pacis, Ciceronianus.* Edited by A. H. T. Levi. Toronto, Buffalo, and London.

Feliciano, Francesco, 1536. *Libro di arithmetica & geometria speculativa & practicale: Composto per maestro Francesco Feliciano da Lazisio Veronese intitulato Scala Grimaldelli. Novamente stampato.* Colophon: Vinegia, per Francesco di Alessandro Bindoni & Mapheo Pasini compagni, 1536 del mese di Zenaro. VM 224.D.117.

Fieschi, Stefano, 1534. *De componendis epistolis opusculum* (i.e., *Synonyma sententiarum*). Colophon: Venetiis in aedibus Francisci Bindoni ac Maphei Pasini socii, mensis Iunii.

Fior di virtù, 1949. *Fior di virtù historiato.* Colophon: Florence, Compagnia del Drago, 1498; rpt. Florence.

————, 1953. *The Florentine Fior di Virtu of 1491. Translated into English by Nicholas Fersin with Facsimiles of all of the original wood cuts.* Introduction by L. J. Rosenwald. Washington, D.C.

Folengo, Teofilo ("Cocai, Merlin"), 1911. *Opere italiane.* Edited by Umberto Renda. Vol. 1. Bari.

————, 1958. *Il Baldo.* Edited and translated into Italian by Giuseppe Tonna. 2 vols. Milan.

Fonte, Moderata (Modesta da Pozzo), 1600. *Il merito delle donne in due giornate. Ove chiaramente si scuopre quanto siano elle degne, e più perfette de gli huomini.* In Venetia, presso Domenico Imberti.

Garin, Eugenio, ed., 1952. *Prosatori latini del Quattrocento.* Milan and Naples.

————, ed., 1958. *Il pensiero pedagogico dell'umanesimo.* Florence.

————, ed., 1959. *L'educazione umanistica in Italia.* Bari.

Garzoni, Tommaso, 1601. *La piazza universale di tutte le professioni del mondo.* In Venetia, appresso Roberto Meietti.

Geijsbeek-Molenaas, John B., ed., 1914. *Ancient Double-entry Bookkeeping: Lucas Pacioli's Treatise . . . and Abstracts from Manzoni, Pietra, Mainardi. . . .* Denver.

Ghaligai, Francesco, 1552. *Pratica d'arithmetica.* In Firenze, appresso i Giunti.

Gherardi, Alessandro, 1881. *Statuti della Università e Studio Fiorentino dall'anno 1387.* Edited by Alessandro Gherardi. Florence; rpt. Bologna, 1973.

Giussani, Giovanni Pietro, 1609. *Lettera . . . ad una persona nobile per animarla al perseverare nell'insegnar la Dottrina Christiana.* In Milano, appresso Gio. Battista Alzato. Colophon: Appresso Bernardino Lantoni.

———, 1612. *Vita di S. Carlo Borromeo.* Brescia, Per Bartolomeo Fontana.

Gorra, Egidio, ed., 1887. *Testi inediti di Storia Trojana preceduti da uno studio sulla leggenda Trojana in Italia.* Turin.

Grammatica latina in volgare, 1529. *Grammatica latina in volgare.* Verona. Colophon: Per Maestro Stephano Nicholini & Fratelli da Sabio. A di 23 decembrio 1529.

Grant, Edward, ed., 1974. *A Source Book in Medieval Science.* Cambridge, Mass.

Guarino, 1967. *Epistolario di Guarino Veronese.* Edited by Remigio Sabbadini. 3 vols. Venice, 1915–19; rpt. Turin.

Guazzo, Stefano, 1586. *Dialoghi piacevoli.* In Venetia, presso Gio. Antonio Bertano, ad instantia di Pietro Tini, Libraro in Milano.

Guevara, Antonio de, 1572. *Vita, gesti, costumi, discorsi, et lettere di Marco Aurelio Imperatore.* . . . In Venetia, appresso Domenico & Gio. Battista Guerra, fratelli.

Harvard, Stephen, 1981. *An Italic Copybook. The Cataneo Manuscript.* New York.

Horace (Horatius Flaccus), Q., 1566. *L'opere . . . commentate da Giovanni Fabrini da Fighine.* . . .In Venetia, appresso Gio. Battista, Marchiò Sessa, & fratelli.

Instruttione, n.d. *Instruttione per maestri e per scolari sottoscritta di mano di S. Carlo et autentica col suo sigillo.* n.p. MT E 730.

Isocrates, 1928–45. *Isocrates.* Edited and translated by George Norlin and Larau Van Hook. 3 vols. London and Cambridge, Mass.

Jacobus de Voragine, 1969. *The Golden Legend.* Translated from Latin by Granger Ryan and Helmut Ripperger. New York.

Janz, Dennis, 1982. *Three Reformation Catechisms: Catholic, Anabaptist, Lutheran.* New York.

Jensen, K., and Liebreich, A. K., 1984. "Liber apologeticus contra impugnantes institutum scholarum piarum," *Archivum Scholarum Piarum* 6, pp. 29–76.

King, Margaret L., and Rabil, Albert, Jr., eds., 1983. *Her Immaculate Hand: Selected Works by and about the Women Humanists of Quattrocento Italy.* Binghamton, N.Y.

Keil, Heinrich, ed., 1857. *Grammatici Latini ex recensione Henrici Keilii.* Vol. 1. Leipzig.

———, 1868. *Grammatici Latini ex recensione Henrici Keilii.* Vol. 5. Leipzig.

———, 1880. *Grammatici Latini ex recensione Henrici Keilii.* Vol. 7. Leipzig.

Leyva, Maria de, 1985. *Vita e processo di Suor Virginia de Leyva Monaca di Monza.* Milan.

Lily, William, and Erasmus, Desiderius, 1564. *De octo partium orationis constructione.* Venetiis apud Michaelem Tramezinum. FPed '500.67.

———, 1570. *De octo partium orationis constructione.* Parmae apud Seth Viottum. FM 6.G.XI.22 (2).

Litterae quadrimestres, 1897. *Litterae quadrimestres ex universis, praeter Indiam et Brasiliam, locis in quibus aliqui de Societate versabantur Roman missae.* Vol. 4 (1556). Madrid.

———, 1921. *Litterae quadrimestres ex universis, praeter Indiam et Brasiliam, locis in quibus aliqui de Societate versabantur Romam missae.* Vol. 5 (1557). Madrid.

———, 1932. *Litterae quadrimestres ex universis, praeter Indiam et Brasiliam, locis in quibus aliqui de Societate versabantur Romam missae.* Vol. 7 (1561–62). Rome.

Lombardelli, Orazio, 1594. *Il giovane studente.* In Venetia, presso la Minima Compagnia.

Mancinelli, Antonio, 1493. *Scribendi orandique modus.* Colophon: Venetiis per Bernardinum Benalium. No date, but introductory letter of 14 May 1493. Hain *10591.

Manuzio, Aldo, 1493. [No title but *Institutiones grammaticae*]. Colophon: Venetiis, [Andrea Torresano], septimo Idus Martias [9 March]. IGI 6139. VM Inc. V. 632.

———, 1501. *Aldi Manutii Romani rudimenta grammatices Latinae linguae.* Venetiis Mense Iunio.

———, 1508. *Aldi Manutii Romani institutionum grammaticarum libri quatuor.* Colophon: Venetiis apud Aldum Aprili Mense.

———, 1549. *Institutionum grammaticarum libri quatuor.* Venetiis. Colophon: In aedibus Francisci Bindonei, & Maphei Pasini. Mense Aprilis.

———, 1975. *Aldo Manuzio Editore. Dediche, prefazioni, note ai testi.* Introduction by Carlo Dionisotti. Edited and translated by Giovanni Orlandi. 2 vols. Milan.

Manuzio the Younger, Aldo, 1585. *Locutioni di Terentio overo, modi famigliari di dire. . . .* In Venetia.

Manzoni, Alessandro, 1977. *I promessi sposi.* Edited by Guido Bezzola. Milan.

Manzoni, Domenico, 1540. *Quaderno doppio col suo giornale. . . .* Venetia, per Comin da Tridino de Monferrato, del mese di Luio. FN and CU.

———, 1550. *La vera et principal ricchezza de giovani, che desiderano imparar ben legere, scrivere, & abaco. . . .* In Vinegia, per Comin de Trino di Monferato. PN Rés p.X.90 (105.621).

———, 1553. *Abachetto nuovo. . . .* [Venezia.]

———, 1564. *Libro mercantile ordinato cul suo giornale & alfabeto, per tener conti doppi al modo di Venetia. . . . Con alcune sorti di lettere cancellaresche, mercantesche, et bastarde. . . .* In Venetia [Comin da Trino di Monferrato] CU.

Marinella, Lucrezia, 1601. *La nobilta, et l'eccellenza delle donne, co' diffetti, et mancamenti de gli huomini. . . .* Accresciutto in questo seconda impressione. In Venetia, appresso Gio. Battista Ciotti Sanese, all'imsegna della Aurora.

Mattaini, Adelaide, ed., 1957. *Romanzi dei Reali di Francia.* Milan.

Monumenta paedagogica Societatis Iesu. Edited by Ladislaus Lukács. Vol. 1: *1540–1556;* vols. 2 and 3: *1557–1572;* vol. 4: *1573–1580.* Rome, 1965–81.

Morigia, Paolo, 1592. *Historia dell'antichità di Milano . . . dal principio della sua fondatione sino l'anno presente 1591.* In Venetia, appresso i Guerra.

Morrison, Stanley, 1929. *Eustachio Celebrino da Udene* (sic). *Calligrapher, Engraver and Writer for the Venetian Printing Press.* Paris.

Ognibene (Bonisoli) da Lonigo, 1506. *Grammatices erudimenta.* Colophon: Impressum Vicentiae per magistrum Henricum de Sancto Urso. Anno salutis MDVI die vii Iulii.

Ordinationi, 1566. *Ordinationi pertinenti alle monache della citta, e diocesi di Milano . . . sotto . . . Carlo Borromeo.* In Milano, appresso di Gio. Battista Ponte & fratelli, MB ZCC. III.83.2.

Ovid (Ovidius) Naso, Publius, 1555. *Epistole d'Ovidio di Remigio Fiorentino.* In Vinegia, appresso Gabriel Giolito de Ferrari, et Fratelli.

Pacioli, Luca, 1523. *Summa de arithmetica.* Colophon: [Paganino de Paganini], in Tusculano, xx Decembre 1523.

Perugia primer, 1578. No title. Perusiae, apud Petrumiacobum Petrutium. 1578. NYPL Spencer Collection Ital. 1578.

Petrarca, Francesco, 1982. *Letters on Familiar Matters. Rerum familiarium libri IX–XVI.* Translated by Aldo S. Bernardo. Baltimore and London.

Petrucci, Armando, ed., 1982. *Scrittura e popolo nella Roma barocca 1585–1721.* Rome.

Piccolomini, Alessandro, 1560. *Della institutione morale libri xii.* In Venetia, appresso Giordano Ziletti.

Platina, Bartolomeo, 1948. *Vita di Vittorino da Feltre.* Edited by Giuseppe Biasuz. Padua.

Plazon, Stefano, 1557. *Secunda editio Donati correcticum vera ortographia.* . . . Colophon: Venetiis per Haeredum Ioannis Patavini. FM 6.A.VIII.III.

———, 1565. *Secunda editio Donati, noviter correcti et emendati.* . . . Venetiis apud Hieronymum Cavalcalupum. DFo.

———, 1574. *Secunda editio Donati, noviter correcti, et emendati.* . . . Venetiis apud Iacobum Leoncinum. RAng 11.1.68.

———, 1578. *Secunda editio Donati . . . novissime correcta per Raphael Bovium Veronensem grammaticam.* Venetiis apud Alexandrum Gardanum. RAng 11.1.70.

Polanco, Juan, 1917. *Polanci Complementa. Epistolae et commentaria P. Ioannis Alphonsi de Polanco, e Societate Iesu, addenda caeteris eusdem scriptis dispersis in his monumentis.* Vol. 2. Madrid.

Porro, Ippolito, 1793. *Origine e successi della Dottrina Christiana in Milano, e suo augumento.* In Milano, nella Stampa di Carlo Federico Gagliardi.

Possevino, Antonio, 1604. *Il soldato christiano.* In Venetia, appresso Domenico Imberti. ICN.

Priscianese, Francesco, 1540. *Della lingua romana.* Colophon: In Vinegia, per Bartolomeo Zanetti da Brescia nel mese d'Agosto.

———, 1552. *De' primi principii della lingua latina, overo il priscianello.* Nuovamente con somma diligenza corretto, et ristampato. In Vinegia, per Giovan Maria Bonelli.

Psalterio, 1575. *Psalterio per putti principianti con la Dottrina Christiana aggionta.* In Bologna, per Alessandro Benaecio, Stampatore Episcopale, 1575. BA 16.Q.IV.29.

Pseudo-Guarino, 1638. *Guarini regulis grammaticis penitus suppressis . . . R. P. Hyeronimum Agnesium cum synonimorum additione. Ad Scholarum Piarum usum potissimum opus absolutissimum.* Genuae, Ex Typographia Io. Marie Farroni, Nicolai Pesagnij, & Petri Francisci Barberij soc. RAles O.e.66(2).

Quintilian, 1966–69. *Institutio oratoria.* Edited and translated by H. E. Butler. 4 vols. Cambridge, Mass., and London.

Ravizza, Giovita, 1544. *Iovitae Rapicii sermo de praestantia earum artium, quae ad recte loquendi, subtiliter disputandi, et bene dicendi rationem pertinent.* Colophon: Venetiis apud Hieronymum Scotum. IU.

Reichling, Dietrich, 1893. *Das Doctrinale des Alexander de Villa-Dei.* Berlin.

Rhetorica ad Herennium, 1954. *Ad C. Herennium de ratione dicendi (Rhetorica ad Herennium).* Edited and translated by Harry Caplan. London and Cambridge, Mass.

Ricci, Lodovico, ed., 1790. *Biblioteca Ecclesiastica e di varia letteratura antica e moderna.* Vol. 2. Pavia.

Sabba Castiglione, 1554. *Ricordi overo ammaestramenti*. In Vinegia, per Paulo Gherardo.

Sallust (Sallustius Crispus), Gaius, 1521. *Opus . . . cum . . . commentariis . . . Laurentii Vallae, Omniboni Leoniceni, & Jodoci Badij Ascensij in eiusdem bello Catilinario. In bello vero Jugurthino fratris Joannis Christostomi Soldi Brixiani, eiusdemque Ascensii . . .* (and minor works). Colophon: Venetiis, per Bernardinum de Vianis de Lexona Vercellensem. 15 Novembris.

———, 1564. *La historia di Gaio Sallustio Crispo, nuovamente tradotta dal signor Paulo Spinola*. In Venetia, per Gio. Andrea Valvassori, 1564. Colophon: 1563.

———, 1971. *Sallust*. Edited and translated by J. C. Rolfe. Cambridge, Mass., and London.

Saxo, Cristoforo, 1562. *Grammaticae institutiones . . . et cum arte metrica*. Venetiis, 1562. Colophon: Ioannis Griphyus excudebat. MB XM*.V.II (int. 7).

Scalzini, Marcello, 1599. *Il secretario. . . . Nel quale si vedono le varie, & diverse sorti, & vere forme di lettere cancellaresche corsive romane nuove. . . .* In Venetia, appresso gli Heredi di Francesco de' Franceschi.

Scoppa, Lucio Giovanni, 1616. *Epitome, cum adverbijs, praepositionibus . . . arte metrica . . . alphabeto Graece. . . .* Venetiis apud Lucium Spinedum. FM 6.G.XI.22 (int. 3).

Segre, Cesare, and Marti, Mario, eds., 1959. *La prosa del Duecento*. Milan and Naples.

Sole, Alessandro, 1623. *Grammatices rudimenta. . . . Ad usum alumnorum suorum in facilem hanc methodum digesta*. Ferrariae apud Franciscum Typographum Camer. RVE 34.5.A.1.

Tagliente, Giovanni Antonio, 1524. *Libro maistrevole*. Opera nuovamente stampata del M.D.xxiiii in Venetia la quale insegna maistrevolmente con nuovo modo & arte a legere a li grandi et piccoli & alle Donne. . . . ICN.

Tagliente, Girolamo, 1520. *Libro da abaco. . . . El qual libro se chiama Tesauro universale*. Colophon: Impresso in Venetia del Anno MDXX nel mese di Septembrio.

Terence (Terentius Afer), Publius, 1524. *Comoediae in sua metra restitutae*. Interpretantibus Aelio Donato . . . Guidone Juvenale . . . Jo. Calpburnio . . . Iodocoque Badio Accensio. . . . Venetiis, in aedibus Guillielmi de Fontaneto Montisferrati, die xxi Iulii.

———, 1542. *Comedie di Terentio nuovamente di latino in volgare tradotte*. Colophon: Venetia per Giovan' Battista da Borgofrancho pavese, del mese di maggio.

———, 1565. *Comoediae*. Ex vetustissimis libris & versuum rationea Gabriele Faerno emendatae. Florentiae, Apud Iuntas.

———, 1567. *Il Terentio Latino, comentato . . . da Giovanni Fabrini da Fighine Fiorentino. . . .* In Vinegia, Vincentio Valgrisi.

———, 1570. *Comoediae sex, infinitis fere locis emendatae:* Unà cum Vinc. Cordati Vesul. Burg. commentariis in Andriam. . . . Venetiis, ex Bibliotheca Aldina.

———, 1612. *Le comedie di Terentio*. Tradotte nuovamente in lingua toscana. Roma, appresso Bartolomeo Zannetti.

———, 1912. *Terence*. English translation by John Sargeaunt. 2 vols. London and New York.

Terracina, Laura, 1564. *Discorso sopra il principio di tutti i canti d'Orlando Furioso.* . . . In Venetia, appresso Francesco Rampazetto.

Thorndike, Lynn, 1971. *University Records and Life in the Middle Ages.* New York, 1944; rpt. New York.

Three Classics of Italian Calligraphy, 1953. *Three Classics of Italian Calligraphy. An Unabridged Reissue of the Writing Books of Arrighi, Tagliente and Palatino.* Introduction by Oscar Ogg. [New York.]

Toscanella, Orazio, 1559. *I modi piu communi con che ha scritto Cicerone le sue epistole secondo i generi di quelle, con altre cose.* In Vinegia, appresso Bolognino Zaltieri. Colophon: Per Francesco Marcolini.

————, 1562. *Precetti necessarii . . . sopra diverse cose pertinenti alla Grammatica, Poetica, Retorica, Historia, Topica, Loica.* . . . In Venetia, appresso Lodovico Avanzo.

————, 1566. *Modo di studiare le pistole famigliari di M. Tullio Cicerone.* In Vinegia, Gabriel Giolito de' Ferrari.

————, 1567a. *Quadrivio. Il quale contiene un trattato della strada che si ha da tenere in scrivere istoria. Un modo, che insegna à scrivere epistole latine, & volgari; con l'arte delle cose, & delle parole che c'entrano. Alcune avvertenze del tesser dialoghi. Et alcuni artificii delle ode di Oratio Flacco.* In Venetia, appresso Giovanni Bariletto.

————, 1567b. *Arte metrica facilissima.* In Venetia, appresso Giovanni Bariletto.

————, 1567c. *Osservationi sopra l'opere di Virgilio, per discoprire, e insegnare à porre in prattica gli artifici importantissimi dell'arte Poetica con gli essempi di Virgilio stesso.* In Vinegia, appresso Gabriel Giolito de' Ferrari.

————, 1568a. *Institutioni grammaticali volgari et latine.* In Vinegia, appresso Gabriel Giolito de' Ferrari.

————, 1568b. *Libro primo de gli artifici osservati . . . sopra l'orationi di Cicerone, sopra Virgilio, le ode d'Oratio, & le comedie di Terentio.* In Venetia, appresso gli Heredi di Marchio Sessa.

————, 1574. *Bellezze del Furioso di M. Lodovico Ariosto, con gli argomenti, et allegorie de i canti: con l'allegorie de i nomi proprii principali dell'opera: et co i luochi communi dell'autore, per ordine di alfabeto; del medisimo.* In Venetia, appresso Pietro de i Franceschi, & Nepoti.

————, 1575. *Discorsi cinque. I. Per studiare una epistola di Cic. II. Per tradurre. III. Per studiare diversi autori di humanità. IIII. Per studiare un poeta volgare, & latino. V. Per trovar materia da discorrere sopra ogni occorrente concetto.* In Venetia, appresso Pietro de' Franceschi, & Nepoti.

Urbani, Girolamo, 1615. *Discorso in difesa di Donato, et di Guarino.* In Camerino, appresso Francesco Gioiosi, RAng SS.11.34.

Valerius Maximus, 1482. (*Factorum ac dictorum memorabilium liber.* Edited by Raphael Regius. Com. Omnibonus Leonicenus.) Colophon: Venice: Johannes de Forlivio & socios, 28 June 1482. Hain–Copinger 15786.

————, 1487. (*Factorum ac dictorum memorabilium liber.* Com. Oliverius Arzignanensis.) Colophon: Joannes & Gregorius de Gregoriis de Forlivio, 8 March 1487. Copinger–Reichling 5928.

Valier, Agostino, 1740. *La istituzione d'ogni stato lodevole delle donne cristiane.* Edited by Gaetano Volpi. Padua.

Valla, Giorgio, 1514. *Grammatica.* Colophon: Venetiis arte Simonis de Luere, sumptibus vero Laurentii Orii de Portesio, mensis Martii.

Valla, Lorenzo, 1543. *Elegantiarum latinae linguae libri sex.* Venetiis, apud Ioan. Gryphium.

———, 1962. *Opera omnia.* Introduction by Eugenio Garin. Basel, 1540; rpt. Turin.

Varanini, Giorgio, ed., 1965. *Cantari religiosi senesi del Trecento.* Bari.

Varese, Claudio, ed., 1955. *Prosatori volgari del Quattrocento.* Milan and Naples.

Vegio, Maffeo, 1933–36. *De educatione liberorum et eorum claris moribus libri sex.* Edited by M. W. Fanning and A. S. Sullivan. Washington, D.C.

Verde, Armando F., 1973–77. *Lo studio fiorentino 1473–1503.* 3 vols. in 4 pts. Florence and Pistoia.

Vergerio, Pier Paolo, 1917. "De ingenuis moribus et liberalibus studiis adulescentiae." Edited by A. Gnesotto. In *Atti e memorie della R. Accademia di scienze lettere ed arti di Padova* 34 (1917): 95–154.

———, 1934. *Epistolario di Pier Paolo Vergerio.* Edited by Leonardo Smith. Rome.

Vergil (Vergilius Maro), Publius, 1573. *Opera . . . restituta.* His accessit XIII. Aeneid. liber, Maphaei Vegii poetae clarissimi lucubrationib. scite artificioseque conflatus. Brixie, Apud haeredes Damiani Turlini.

———, 1576. *P. Virgilii Maronis . . . notationibus illustrata opera. et. industria Io. A. Meyen Bergizonii Belgae.* Ven., Apud Aldum.

———, 1580. *P. Virgilii Maronis . . . notationibus illustrata opera. et. industria Io. A. Meyen Bergizonii Belgae.* Ven., Apud Aldum.

———, 1581. *L'Eneide di Virgilio Mantovano commentata volgare Toscana da Giovanni Fabrini da Fighine, & Filippo Venuti da Cortona. . . .* In Venetia, appresso Gio. Battista Sessa, & Fratelli.

Villani, Giovanni, 1844–45. *Cronica.* Edited by F. G. Dragomanni. 4 vols. Florence.

Vives, Juan Luis, 1753. *Ludovico Vives tradotto in lingua volgare dal Dottor D. Giacinto Garcea.* Napoli, per il Valiero.

———, 1908. *Tudor School-boy Life: The Dialogues of Juan Luis Vives.* Translated by Foster Watson. London.

———, 1964. *Opera omnia.* Edited by Gregorio Mayáns y Siscar. 8 vols. Valencia, 1782–90; rpt. London.

Volpicelli, Luigi, ed., 1960. *Il pensiero pedagogico della Controriforma.* Florence.

Watson, Foster, 1971. *Vives: On Education. A Translation of the De Tradentis Disciplinis.* London, 1913; rpt. Totawa, N.J.

Weinberg, Bernard, ed., 1970–74. *Trattati di poetica e retorica del Cinquecento.* 4 vols. Bari.

Woodward, William H., 1963. *Vittorino da Feltre and Other Humanist Educators.* Cambridge, 1897; rpt. New York.

Secondary Sources

Adorni-Braccesi, Simonetta, 1986. "Maestri e scuole nella Repubblica di Lucca tra Riforma e Controriforma," *Società e storia* 9:559–94.

Allen and Greenough, 1931. *Allen and Greenough's New Latin Grammar for Schools and Colleges.* Edited by J. B. Greenough, G. L. Kittredge, A. A. Howard, and B. L. D'Ooge. Boston.

Ariès, Philippe, 1962. *Centuries of Childhood: A Social History of Family Life.* Translated by Robert Baldick. New York.

Arnaldi, Girolamo, 1976. "Scuole nella Marca Trevigiana e a Venezia nel secolo

XIII." In *Dalle Origini al Trecento,* vol. 1 of *Storia della Cultura Veneta.* Vicenza, pp. 351–86.

———, 1978. "Discorso inaugurale." In *Le scuole degli ordini mendicanti (secoli XIII–XIV).* Todi, pp. 11–32.

Artese, Luciano, 1983a. "Orazio Toscanella: corrispondenza con il Granduca di Toscana e documenti inediti," *Atti e memorie dell' Accademia Toscana di scienze e lettere, La Colombaria* 48:27–68.

———, 1983b. "Orazio Toscanella, un maestro del XVI secolo," *Annali dell' Istituto di filosofia dell'Università di Firenze* 5:61–95.

Ashworth, E. J., 1974. *Language and Logic in the Post-Medieval Period.* Dordrecht.

———, 1982. "The Eclipse of Medieval Logic." In *The Cambridge History of Later Medieval Philosophy,* edited by N. Kretzmann, A. Kenny, J. Pinborg, and E. Stump. Cambridge, pp. 787–96.

Avesani, Rino, 1969. "Bonamico, Lazzaro," DBI, vol. 11, pp. 533–40.

———, 1970. "La professione dell'*umanista* nel Cinquecento," *Italia medioevale e umanistica* 13:212–24.

Bacci, Orazio, 1895. "Nota di tutti li maestri di grammatica che sono in Toscana nel '300," *Miscellanea storica della Valdelsa* 3:88–95.

Baebler, J. J., 1885. *Beiträge zu einer Geschichte der lateinischen Grammatik im Mittelalter.* Halle a. S.

Baldo, Vittorio, 1977. *Alunni, maestri e scuole in Venezia alla fine del xvi secolo.* Como.

Ballistreri, G., 1970. "Bonisoli, Ognibene," DBI, vol. 12, pp. 234–36.

Banker, James R., 1971. "Giovanni di Bonandrea's *Ars dictaminis* Treatise and the Doctrine of Invention in the Italian Rhetorical Tradition of the Thirteenth and Early Fourteenth Centuries." Ph.D. diss., University of Rochester.

———, 1974. "The *Ars dictaminis* and Rhetorical Textbooks at the Bolognese University in the Fourteenth Century," *Medievalia et Humanistica,* n.s., 5:153–68.

Barbera, M., 1946–47. "L'educazione nei convitti della Compagnia di Gesù nel secolo XVI," *La civiltà cattolica,* Anno 97, quaderno 2306 (20 July 1946), pp. 117–23; quaderno 2317 (4 January 1947), pp. 50–58; anno 98, quaderno 2323 (5 April 1947), pp. 57–64; quaderno 2324 (19 April 1947), pp. 144–51.

Baron, Hans, 1938a. "Franciscan Poverty and Civic Wealth as Factors in the Rise of Humanistic Thought," *Speculum* 13:1–37.

———, 1938b. "Cicero and the Roman Civic Spirit in the Middle Ages and the Early Renaissance," *Bulletin of the John Rylands Library* 22:72–97.

———, 1966. *The Crisis of the Early Italian Renaissance.* Rev. ed. Princeton, N.J.

———, 1968. *From Petrarch to Leonardo Bruni: Studies in Humanistic and Political Literature.* Chicago and London.

———, 1977. "The Year of Leonardo Bruni's Birth, and Methods for Determining the Ages of Humanists Born in the Trecento," *Speculum* 52:582–625.

Barone, Giulia, 1978. "La legislazione sugli 'studia' dei predicatori e dei minori." In *Le scuole.* Florence, pp. 205–47.

Barone, N., 1893. "Lucio Giovanni Scoppa, grammatico napoletano del secolo XVI," *Archivio storico per le provincie napoletane* 18:92–103.

Barsanti, Paolo, 1905. *Il pubblico insegnamento in Lucca dal secolo XIV alla fine del secolo XVIII.* Lucca; rpt. Bologna, 1980.

Bateman, John J., 1976. "Aldus Manutius' *Fragmenta Grammatica,*" *Illinois Classical Studies,* 1. Urbana, Chicago, and London, pp. 226–61.

Batllori, Miquel, 1983. "Economia e collegi." In Batllori, *Cultura e finanze: Studi sulla storia dei Gesuiti da S. Ignazio al Vaticano II.* Rome, pp. 121–38.

Battaglia, Salvatore, 1971. *La letteratura italiana.* Vol. 1: *Medioevo e umanesimo.* Florence and Milan.

Battistini, Mario, 1919. *Il pubblico insegnamento in Volterra dal secolo XIV al secolo XVIII.* Volterra.

Bec, Christian, 1967. *Les Marchands écrivains: affaires et humanisme à Florence, 1375–1434.* Paris.

———, 1984. *Les livres des florentins (1413–1608).* Florence.

Bellemo, Vincenzo, 1888. "L'insegnamento e la cultura in Chioggia fino al secolo XV," *Archivio veneto,* N. S. Anno 18, vol. 35, pp. 277–301; vol. 36, pp. 37–56.

Beloch, Karl Julius, 1961. *Bevölkerungsgeschichte Italiens.* Vol. 3: *Die Bevölkerung der Republik Venedig, Des Herzogtums Mailand, Piemonte, Genuas, Corsicas und Sardinens. Die Gesamtbevölkerung Italiens.* Berlin.

Beltrami, Daniele, 1964. *Storia della popolazione di Venezia della fine del secolo XVI alla caduta della Repubblica.* Padua.

Bendiscioli, Mario, 1957. "Vita sociale e culturale." In *L'età della Riforma Cattolica (1559–1630),* vol. 10 of *Storia di Milano.* Milan, pp. 353–495.

Bentley, Jerry H., 1987. *Politics and Culture in Renaissance Naples.* Princeton, N.J.

Bertoni, Giulio, 1964. *Il Duecento.* 6th printing of 3d ed. Milan.

Bertoni, Giulio, and Vicini, Emilio P., 1904–5. "Gli studi di grammatica e la rinascenza a Modena," *Atti e Memorie della R. Deputazione di Storia Patria per le Provincie Modenesi,* 5th ser., 4:145–258.

Bettazzi, Enrico, 1928. "Emanuele Filiberto: Riordinamento degli studi in Piemonte." In *Emanuele Filiberto.* Turin, pp. 305–58.

Biadego, Giuseppe, 1895. "Bernardino Donato a Vicenza e a Parma," *Nuovo archivio veneto* 10, pt. 2, pp. 365–69.

Bianchini, P., 1975. "Chierici Regolari Somaschi," DIP, vol. 2, cols. 975–78.

Bianchini, P., and Pellegrini, C., 1977. "Gerolamo Miani," DIP, vol. 4, cols. 1108–10.

Bietenholz, Peter G., 1985. "Nicolaus Clenardus." In *Contemporaries of Erasmus: A Biographical Register of the Renaissance and Reformation,* edited by Peter G. Bietenholz and Thomas B. Deutscher. Vol. 1. Toronto, Buffalo, London, pp. 312–13.

Billanovich, Giuseppe, 1965. "Auctorista, humanista, orator," *Rivista di cultura classica e medioevale: Studi in onore di Alfredo Schiaffini* 7, nos. 1–3, pp. 143–63.

Black, Robert, 1985. *Benedetto Accolti and the Florentine Renaissance.* Cambridge.

———, 1987. "Humanism and Education in Renaissance Arezzo," *I Tatti Studies. Essays in the Renaissance* 2:171–237.

Boas, Marcus, 1914. "De librorum Catonianorum historia atque compositione," *Mnemosyne* 42:17–46.

Bohatta, Hanns, 1909. *Bibliographie des livres d'heures (Horae B. M. V.) Officia, Hortuli Animae, Coronae B. M. V., Rosaria und Cursus B. M. V. des XV und XVI Jahrhunderts.* Vienna.

Boldrini, Luigi, 1904. *Della vita e degli scritti di Messer Giovita Rapicio.* Verona.

Bolgar, R. R., 1955. "Classical Reading in Renaissance Schools," *Durham Research Review* 6:18–26.

———, 1964. *The Classical Heritage and Its Beneficiaries.* New York.

444 Bibliography

Bolognini, Giorgio, 1896. *L'università di Verona e gli statuti del secolo XIII.* Verona.

Bolzoni, Lina, 1983. "Le 'parole dipinte' di Orazio Toscanella," *Rivista di letteratura italiana* 1:155–86.

Bonaventure, Brother (J. N. Miner), 1961. "The Teaching of Latin in Later Medieval England," *Mediaeval Studies* 23:1–20.

Bongi, Salvatore, 1890–97. *Annali di Gabriel Giolito de' Ferrari.* 2 vols. Rome; rpt. Rome, n.d.

Bonilla y San Martin, Adolfo, 1929. *Luis Vives y la Filosofia del Renacimiento.* 3 vols. Madrid.

Bonner, Stanley F., 1977. *Education in Ancient Rome: From the Elder Cato to the Younger Pliny.* Berkeley and Los Angeles.

Borracini Verducci, Rosa Marisa, 1975. "La scuola pubblica a Recanati nel sec. XV," *Università di Macerata. Annali della Facoltà di Lettere e Filosofia* 8:121–62.

Boswell, John E., 1984. "*Expositio* and *Oblatio:* The Abandonment of Children and the Ancient and Medieval Family," *American Historical Review* 89:10–33.

Bouwsma, William J., 1968. *Venice and the Defense of Republican Liberty.* Berkeley and Los Angeles.

Boyle, Leonard E., 1962. "The Constitution 'Cum ex eo' of Boniface VIII," *Mediaeval Studies* 24:263–302.

Branca, Daniela Delcorno, 1968. *I romanzi italiani di Tristano e La Tavola Ritondo.* Florence.

———, 1974. *Il romanzo cavalleresco medievale.* Florence.

Branca, Vittore, 1973. "Ermolao Barbaro and Late Quattrocento Venetian Humanism." In *Renaissance Venice,* edited by John R. Hale. London, pp. 218–43.

Brand, C. P., 1974. *Ludovico Ariosto: A Preface to the "Orlando Furioso."* Edinburgh.

Brinton, Anna Cox, 1930. *Maphaeus Vegius and His Thirteenth Book of the Aeneid: A Chapter on Virgil in the Renaissance.* Stanford, Calif.

Brizzi, Gian Paolo, 1976. *La formazione della classe dirigente nel Sei-Settecento. I seminaria nobilium nell'Italia centrosettentrionale.* Bologna.

———, 1982. "Strategie educative e istituzioni scolastiche della Controriforma." In *Letteratura italiana.* Vol. 1: *Il letterato e le istituzioni.* Turin.

Brown, Allison, 1979. *Bartolomeo Scala, 1430–1497: Chancellor of Florence.* Princeton, N.J.

Brown, Judith C., 1982. *In the Shadow of Florence: Provincial Society in Renaissance Pescia.* New York.

Brown, Richard, 1905. *A History of Accounting and Accountants.* Edinburgh and London.

Brown, Virginia, 1976. "Caesar, Gaius Julius." In *Catalogus Translationum et Commentariorum,* edited by F. Edward Cranz and Paul O. Kristeller. Vol. 3. Washington, D.C., pp. 87–139.

Brucker, Gene, 1969. "Florence and Its University, 1348–1434." In *Action and Conviction in Early Modern Europe,* edited by T. K. Rabb and J. E. Seigel. Princeton, N.J., pp. 220–36.

Bullough, Donald A., 1964. "Le scuole cattedrali e la cultura dell'Italia settentrionale prima dei Comuni." In *Vescovi e diocesi in Italia nel medioevo (sec. IX–XIII).* Padua, pp. 111–43.

Bursill-Hall, Geoffrey, L., 1971. *Speculative Grammars of the Middle Ages.* The Hague and Paris.

————, 1978. "A Check-List of Incipits of Medieval Latin Grammatical Treatises: A–G," *Traditio* 34:439–74.

Caballero, Valentin, 1945. *Orientaciones pedagogicas de San Jose de Calasanz, el gran pedagogo y su obra cooperadores de la verdad.* 2d ed. Madrid.

Cajani, L., 1978. "Castellino da Castello," DBI, vol. 21, pp. 786–87.

Callahan, William J., 1984. *Church, Politics, and Society in Spain, 1750–1874.* Cambridge, Mass.

Camerini, Paolo, 1962–63. *Annali dei Giunti.* Vol. 1: *Venezia.* 2 pts. Florence.

Cammelli, Giuseppe, 1941. *I dotti bizantini e le origini dell' umanesimo.* Vol. 1: *Manuele Crisolora.* Florence.

Capasso, Gaetano, 1901. "Il Collegio dei Nobili di Parma. Memorie storiche pubblicate nel terzo centenario dalla sua fondazione (28 ottobre 1901)," *Archivio storico per le provincie Parmensi,* n.s., 1:1–285.

Caponetto, Salvatore, 1979. *Aonio Paleario (1503–1570) e la riforma protestante in Toscana.* Turin.

Casalini, Mario, 1932. *Le scuole di Roma.* Rome.

Casamassima, Emanuele, 1966. *Trattati di scrittura del Cinquecento italiano.* Milan.

Casella, M. T., 1963. "Il Valerio Massimo in volgare: dal Lancia al Boccaccio," *Italia medioevale e umanistica* 6:49–136.

Casini, Tommaso, 1886. "Appunti sul Fiore di Virtù," *Rivista critica della letteratura italiana* 3:154–59.

Castiglione, Giambatista, 1800. *Istoria delle scuole della Dottrina Cristiana fondate in Milano e da Milano nell'Italia ed altrove propagate. Parte prima.* Milan.

Cavazza, Francesco, 1896. *Le scuole dell'antico Studio Bolognese.* Milan.

Cavedon, Annarosa, 1983. "Un umanista-rimatore del sec. XV: Gian Nicola Salerno." In *Umanesimo e rinascimento a Firenze e Venezia.* Miscellanea di studi in onore di Vittore Branca, vol. 3, pts. 1 and 2. Florence, pp. 205–19.

Cecchetti, Bartolomeo, 1886. "Libri, scuole, maestri, sussidii allo studio di Venezia nei secoli XIV e XV," *Archivio veneto* 32:325–63.

Cerasoli, F., 1891. "Censimento della popolazione dall'anno 1600 al 1739," *Studi e documenti di storia e diritto* 12:168–98.

Cessi, Camillo, 1896. *La scuola pubblica in Rovigo sino a tutto il secolo XVI.* Rovigo.

Cessi, Roberto, 1968. *Storia della Repubblica di Venezia.* 2 vols. Rev. ed. Milan and Messina.

Chambers, D. S., 1976. "Studium Urbis and *Gabella Studii:* The University of Rome in the Fifteenth Century," in *Cultural Aspects of the Italian Renaissance,* edited by Cecil H. Clough. Manchester, pp. 68–110.

Chiappa, Franco, 1964. *Una pubblica scuola di grammatica a Palazzolo nella seconda metà del 1400.* Brescia.

Chinea, Eleuterio, 1953. *L'istruzione pubblica e privata nello Stato di Milano dal Concilio Tridentino alla Riforma Teresiana (1563–1773).* Florence.

Chiuppani, Giovanni, 1915. "Storia di una scuola di grammatica dal medio evo fino al seicento (Bassano)," in *Nuovo archivio veneto,* n.s., 15, Tomo 29, pp. 73–138.

Cioni, Alfredo, 1962. *Bibliografia de "Le Vite dei Santi Padri" volgarizzate da Fra Domenico Cavalca.* Florence.

"Clausura," 1975. In DIP, vol. 2, cols. 1166–83.

Collett, Barry, 1985. *Italian Benedictine Scholars and the Reformation: The Congregation of Santa Giustina of Padua.* Padua.

Comparetti, Domenico, 1896. *Virgilio nel Medio Evo.* 2d ed., rev. 2 vols. Florence.

La comunità cristiana fiorentina, 1980. *La comunità cristiana fiorentina e toscana nella dialettica religiosa del Cinquecento.* Florence.

Cordella, Romano, and Severini, Eusebio, 1982. "I primi tempi delle Scuole Pie a Norcia," *Archivum Scholarum Piarum* 6, no. 12, pp. 205–56.

Corradi, Augusto, 1887. "Notizie sui professori di latinità nello Studii di Bologna. Parte prima," *Documenti e studii pubblicati per cura della R. Deputazione di Storia Patria per le provincie di Romagna* 2:355–514.

Cortesi, Mariarosa, 1981a. "Alla scuola di Gian Pietro d'Avenza in Lucca" *Quellen und Forschungen aus italienischen Archiven und Bibliotheken* 61:109–67.

———, 1981b. "Un allievo di Vittorino da Feltre: Gian Pietro da Lucca." In *Vittorino e la sua scuola,* 1981, pp. 263–76.

Corti, Maria, 1959. "Le fonti del 'Fiore di virtù' e la teoria della 'nobiltà' nel Duecento," *Giornale storico della letteratura italiana* 136:1–82.

Costes, René, 1925–26. *Antonio de Guevara: sa vie et son oeuvre.* Paris and Bordeaux.

Cressy, David, 1980. *Literacy and the Social Order.* Cambridge.

Curcio, Gaetano, 1913. *Q. Orazio Flacco studiato in Italia dal secolo XIII al XVIII.* Catania.

Curtius, Ernst Robert, 1963. *European Literature and the Latin Middle Ages.* Translated by Willard R. Trask. New York and Evanston.

Cutolo, Alessandro, 1944. *I romanzi cavallereschi in prosa e in rima del Fondo Castiglioni presso la Biblioteca Braidense di Milano.* Milan.

D'Addario, Arnaldo, 1972. *Aspetti della controriforma a Firenze.* Rome.

D'Amico, John F., 1983. *Renaissance Humanism in Papal Rome.* Baltimore and London.

———, 1984. "The Progress of Renaissance Latin Prose: The Case of Apuleianism," *Renaissance Quarterly* 37:351–92.

Da Mosto, Andrea, 1966. *I Dogi di Venezia nella vita pubblica e privata.* Milan.

Davidsohn, Robert, 1965. *Storia di Firenze.* Translated by E. Dupré-Theseider. Vol. 4, pt. 3: *Il mondo della chiesa. Spiritualità ed arte. Vita pubblica e privata.* Florence.

Debenedetti, Santorre, 1906–7. "Sui più antichi 'doctores puerorum' a Firenze," *Studi medievali* 2:327–51.

De Caprio, Vincenzo, 1984. "La rinascita della cultura di Roma: la tradizione latina nelle 'Eleganze' di Lorenzo Valla." In *Umanesimo a Roma nel Quattrocento,* edited by Paolo Brezzi and Maristella de Panizza Lorch. Rome and New York, pp. 163–80.

De la Mare, Albinia, 1972. "The Shop of a Florentine 'cartolaio' in 1426." In *Studi offerti a Roberto Ridolfi,* edited by B. M. Biagiarelli and D. E. Rhodes. Florence, pp. 237–48.

Delcorno, Carlo, 1977–78. "Per l'edizione delle 'Vite dei Santi Patri' del Cavalca. La tradizione manoscritta: I codici delle biblioteche fiorentine," *Lettere Italiane* 29 (1977):265–89; 30 (1978):47–84.

———, 1979. "Cavalca, Domenico," DBI, vol. 22, pp. 577–86.

Delhaye, Philippe, 1947. "L'organisation scolaire au XII siècle," *Traditio* 5:211–68.

Della Torre, Arnaldo, 1902. *Di Antonio Vinciguerra e delle sue satire.* Rocca S. Casciano.

De Maio, Romeo, 1965. *Bonsignore Cacciaguerra. Un mistico senese nella Napoli del Cinquecento.* Milan and Naples.

Denley, Peter, 1981. "Giovanni Dominici's Opposition to Humanism." In *Religion and Humanism,* edited by Keith Robbins. Studies in Church History, 17. Oxford, pp. 103–14.

Deutscher, Thomas, 1981. "Seminaries and the Education of Novarese Parish Priests, 1593–1627," *Journal of Ecclesiastical History* 32:303–19.

———, "Growth." "The Growth of the Secular Clergy and the Development of Educational Institutions in the Diocese of Novara, 1563–1772," *Journal of Ecclesiastical History,* in press.

De Vivo, Francesco, 1958, 1959, 1960. "Indirizzi pedagogici ed istituzioni educative di ordini e congregazioni religiose nei secoli XVI e XVII," *Rassegna di Pedagogia* 16:263–85; 17:22–57, 255–62; 18:145–58, 326–33.

Dionisotti, Carlo, 1959. "Entrée d'Espagne, Spagna, Rotta di Roncisvalle." In *Studi in onore di Angelo Monteverdi.* 2 vols. Modena, 1:207–41.

Dizionario degli istituti di perfezione. Rome, 1974– .

Donnelly, John Patrick, 1982. "The Jesuit College at Padua: Growth, Suppression, Attempts at Restoration: 1552–1606," *Archivum Historicum Societatis Iesu* 51:45–78.

Dorati da Empoli, Maria Cristina, 1980. "I lettori dello Studio e i maestri di grammatica a Roma da Sisto IV ad Alessandro VI," *Rassegna degli Archivi di Stato* 40:98–147.

Drury, Martin, 1982. "Metrical Appendix." In *The Cambridge History of Classical Literature.* Vol. 2: *Latin Literature,* edited by E. J. Kenney and W. V. Clausen. Cambridge, pp. 936–39.

Duff, J. Wight, 1970. *A Literary History of Rome.* Edited by A. M. Duff. Vol. 1, 3d ed.; vol. 2, 2d ed. London.

Edler, Florence, 1934. *Glossary of Mediaeval Terms of Business: Italian Series, 1200–1600.* Cambridge, Mass.

Erba, Achille, 1979. *La chiesa sabauda tra Cinque e Seicento. Ortodossia tridentina, gallicanesimo savoiardo, e assolutismo ducale (1580–1630).* Rome.

Erba, A. M., 1974. "Angeliche di S. Paolo," DIP, vol. 1, cols. 635–37.

———, 1975. "Chierici Regolari di San Paolo," DIP, vol. 2, cols. 945–74.

Ermini, Giuseppe, 1947. *Storia della Università di Perugia.* Bologna.

Falanga, Mario, 1979. *La scuola elementare nell'antica Roma.* Bari.

Fantini, Rodolfo, 1971. *L'istruzione popolare a Bologna fino al 1860.* Bologna.

Farrell, Allan, P., 1938. *The Jesuit Code of Liberal Education: Development and Scope of the Ratio Studiorum.* Milwaukee.

Faulhaber, Charles B., 1978. "The *Summa dictaminis* of Guido Faba." In *Medieval Eloquence: Studies in the Theory and Practice of Medieval Rhetoric,* edited by James J. Murphy. Berkeley, Los Angeles, and London, pp. 85–111.

Fausti, Luigi, 1943. *Le scuole e la cultura a Spoleto.* Spoleto.

Field, Arthur, 1978. "A Manuscript of Cristoforo Landino's First Lectures on Virgil, 1462–63 (Codex 1368, Biblioteca Casanatense, Rome)," *Renaissance Quarterly* 31:17–20.

Fiumi, Enrico, 1953. "Economia e vita privata dei fiorentini nelle rilevazioni statistiche di Giovanni Villani," *Archivio storico italiano* 111:207–41.

Foffano, Francesco, 1904. *Il poema cavalleresco.* Milan.

Fonseca, Cosimo Damiano, 1984. "Canoniche regolari, capitoli cattedrali e 'cura animarum.'" In *Pievi e parrocchie in Italia nel basso medioevo (sec. XIII–XV).* 2 vols. Rome, 1:257–78.

Fossati, Felice, 1902. "Le prime notizie di una scuola pubblica in Vigevano," *Archivio storico lombardo,* 3d ser., 29:156–67.

Foster, Kenelm, 1976. "Vernacular Scriptures in Italy." In *The Cambridge History of the Bible.* Vol. 2: *The West from the Fathers to the Reformation,* edited by G. W. H. Lampe. Cambridge, 1969; rpt. Cambridge, pp. 452–65.

Franci, Raffaella, and Rigatelli, Laura Toti, 1982. *Introduzione all'aritmetica mercantile del Medioevo e del Rinascimento.* Urbino.

Frati, Carlo, 1893. "Ricerche sul 'Fiore di virtù,'" *Studi di filologia romanza* 6:247–447.

Fryde, Edmund, 1980. "The Beginnings of Italian Humanist Historiography: The 'New Cicero' of Leonardo Bruni," *English Historical Review* 95:533–52.

Fumagalli, Giuseppina, 1912. *La fortuna dell'Orlando Furioso in Italia nel secolo XVI.* Ferrara.

Fusinato, Guido, 1883. "Un cantastorie Chioggiotto," *Giornale di filologia romanza,* 2d ser., 4:170–83.

Gabotto, Ferdinando, 1895. *Lo stato Sabaudo da Amedeo VIII al Emanuele Filiberto.* Vol. 3: *La coltura e la vita in Piemonte nel Rinascimento.* Turin and Rome.

Gardner, Edmund G., 1930. *The Arthurian Legend in Italian Literature.* London.

Garibotto, Celestino, 1921. *I Maestri di Grammatica a Verona (dal '200 a tutto il '500).* Verona.

Garibotto, Eloisa, 1923. "Le scuole d'abbaco a Verona," *Atti e Memorie dell'Accademia di Agricoltura, Scienze e Lettere di Verona,* 4th ser., 24:315–28.

Garin, Eugenio, 1954. *Medioevo e rinascimento, studi e ricerche.* Bari.

———, 1957. *L'educazione in Europa (1400–1600).* Bari.

———, 1961. *Medioevo e rinascimento, studi e ricerche.* 2d ed. Bari.

———, 1967. *Ritratti di umanisti.* Florence.

Gerini, G. B., 1897. *Gli scrittori pedagogici italiani del secolo decimosesto.* Turin.

Gibson, Eleanor J., and Levin, Harry, 1975. *The Psychology of Reading.* Cambridge, Mass., and London.

Ginzburg, Carlo, 1986. "The Dovecote Has Opened Its Eyes: Popular Conspiracy in Seventeenth-Century Italy." In *The Inquisition in Early Modern Europe: Studies on Sources and Methods,* edited by G. Henningsen, J. Tedeschi, and C. Amiel. DeKalb, Ill., pp. 190–98.

Giordano, Francesco, 1960. *Il Calasanzio e l'origine della scuola popolare.* Genoa.

Gnoli, Domenico, 1938. *La Roma di Leone X.* Milan.

Goldthwaite, Richard A., 1972. "Schools and Teachers of Commercial Arithmetic in Renaissance Florence," *Journal of European Economic History* 1:418–33.

———, 1980. *The Building of Renaissance Florence.* Baltimore and London.

Goodyear, F. R. D., 1982. "Sallust." In *The Cambridge History of Classical Literature.* Vol. 2: *Latin Literature,* edited by E. J. Kenney and W. V. Clausen. Cambridge, pp. 268–80.

Gorrini, Giacomo, 1931–32. "L'istruzione elementare in Genova durante il medio evo," *Giornale storico e letterario della Liguria,* n.s., 7:265–86; 8:86–96.

Gotoff, Harold C., 1979. *Cicero's Elegant Style: An Analysis of the Pro Archia.* Urbana, Ill., Chicago, and London.

Graff, Harvey J., 1983. "On Literacy in the Renaissance: Review and Reflections," *History of Education* 12:69–85.

Grafton, Anthony, 1977. "On the Scholarship of Politian and Its Context," *Journal of the Warburg and Courtauld Institutes* 40:150–88.

———, 1981. "Teacher, Text, and Pupil in the Renaissance Class-Room: A Case Study from a Parisian College," *History of Universities* 1:37–70.

Grafton, Anthony, and Jardine, Lisa, 1982. "Humanism and the School of Guarino: A Problem of Evaluation," *Past and Present*, no. 92 (August 1982), pp. 51–80.

———, 1986. *From Humanism to the Humanities: Education and the Liberal Arts in Fifteenth- and Sixteenth-Century Europe.* Cambridge, Mass.

Gratwick, A. S., 1982. "Drama." In *The Cambridge History of Classical Literature.* Vol. 2: *Latin Literature,* edited by E. J. Kenney and W. V. Clausen. Cambridge, pp. 77–137.

Grendler, Marcella T., 1973. *The "Trattato politico-morale" of Giovanni Cavalcanti (1381–c. 1451): A Critical Edition and Interpretation.* Geneva.

———, 1980. "A Greek Collection in Padua: The Library of Gian Vincenzo Pinelli (1535–1601)," *Renaissance Quarterly* 33:386–416.

Grendler, Marcella, and Grendler, Paul F., 1976. "The Survival of Erasmus in Italy," *Erasmus in English* 8:2–22.

———, 1984. "The Erasmus Holdings of Roman and Vatican Libraries," *Erasmus in English* 13:2–29.

Grendler, Paul F., 1969a. *Critics of the Italian World, 1530–1560: Anton Francesco Doni, Nicolò Franco, and Ortensio Lando.* Madison, Milwaukee, and London.

———, 1969b. "Francesco Sansovino and Italian Popular History, 1560–1600." *Studies in the Renaissance* 16:139–80.

———, 1971. "The Concept of Humanist in Cinquecento Italy." In *Renaissance Studies in Honor of Hans Baron,* edited by A. Molho and J. A. Tedeschi. Florence and De Kalb, Ill., pp. 447–63.

———, 1977. *The Roman Inquisition and the Venetian Press, 1540–1605.* Princeton, N.J.

———, 1978. "The Destruction of Hebrew Books in Venice, 1568," *Proceedings of the American Academy for Jewish Research* 45:103–30.

———, 1988a. "Borromeo and the Schools of Christian Doctrine." In *San Carlo Borromeo,* edited by J. M. Headley and J. B. Tomaro. Washington, London, and Toronto, pp. 158–71.

———, 1988b. "Chivalric Romances in the Italian Renaissance," *Studies in Medieval and Renaissance History,* 10:57–102.

———, 1988c. "Schools, Seminaries, and Catechetical Instruction." In *Catholicism in Early Modern History: A Guide to Research,* edited by J. W. O'Malley. St. Louis, pp. 315–30.

Grey, Ernest, 1973. *Guevara: A Forgotten Renaissance Author.* The Hague.

Gualdo Rosa, Lucia, 1984. *La fede nella "Paideia." Aspetti della fortuna europea di Isocrate nei secoli XV e XVI.* Rome.

Hankey, A. T., 1957. "Domenico di Bandino of Arezzo (?1335–1418)," *Italian Studies* 12:110–28.

Hardison, Jr., O. B., 1962. *The Enduring Moment: A Study of the Idea of Praise in Renaissance Literary Theory and Practice.* Chapel Hill, N.C.

Herlihy, David, 1972. "Some Psychological and Social Roots of Violence in the Tuscan Cities." In *Violence and Civil Disorder in Italian Cities, 1200–1500,* edited by Lauro Martines. Berkeley, Los Angeles, and London, pp. 129–54.

Herlihy, David, and Klapisch-Zuber, Christiane, 1978. *Les Toscans et leurs familles.* Paris.

⸺, 1985. *Tuscans and Their Families.* New Haven and London.

Hoffman, Philip T., 1984. *Church and Community in the Diocese of Lyon, 1500–1789.* New Haven.

Holtz, Louis, 1981. *Donat et la tradition de l'enseignement grammatical.* Paris.

Horkan, Vincent J., 1953. *Educational Theories and Principles of Maffeo Vegio.* Washington, D.C.

Houston, Rab, 1983. "Literacy and Society in the West, 1500–1850," *Social History* 8:269–93.

Huntsman, Jeffrey, 1983. "Grammar." In *The Seven Liberal Arts in the Middle Ages,* edited by David L. Wagner. Bloomington, Ind., pp. 58–95.

Huppert, George, 1977. *Les Bourgeois Gentilshommes: An Essay on the Definition of Elites in Renaissance France.* Chicago.

⸺, 1984. *Public Schools in Renaissance France.* Urbana and Chicago.

Imberciadori, Ildebrando, 1959. "Spedale, scuola e chiesa in popolazioni rurali dei secc. XVI–XVII," *Economia e storia* 6, no. 1, pp. 422–49.

Inama, V., 1896–97. "Una scuola di grammatica in Cles nel secolo XIV," *Archivio Trentino* 13:231–34.

Jardine, Lisa, 1982. "Humanism and the Teaching of Logic." In *The Cambridge History of Later Medieval Philosophy,* edited by N. Kretzmann, A. Kenny, J. Pinborg, and E. Stump. Cambridge, pp. 797–807.

⸺, 1983. "Isotta Nogarola: Women humanists—Education for What?" *History of Education* 12, no. 4, pp. 231–44.

Jayawardene, S. A., 1974. "Pacioli, Luca." In *Dictionary of Scientific Biography.* New York, 10:269–72.

Jones, Joseph R., 1975. *Antonio de Guevara.* Boston.

Kallendorf, Craig, 1983. "Cristoforo Landino's *Aeneid* and the Humanist Critical Tradition," *Renaissance Quarterly* 36:519–46.

Kennedy, George A., 1980. *Classical Rhetoric and Its Christian and Secular Tradition from Ancient to Modern Times.* Chapel Hill, N.C.

⸺, 1985. "Oratory." In *The Cambridge History of Classical Literature.* Vol. 1: *Greek Literature,* edited by P. E. Easterling and B. M. W. Knox. Cambridge, pp. 498–526.

Kenney, E. J., 1982. "Ovid." In *The Cambridge History of Classical Literature.* Vol. 2: *Latin Literature,* edited by E. J. Kenney and W. V. Clausen. Cambridge, pp. 420–57.

Kent, F. W., 1977. *Household and Lineage in Renaissance Florence: The Family Life of the Capponi, Ginori, and Rucellai.* Princeton, N.J.

King, Margaret L., 1986. *Venetian Humanism in an Age of Patrician Dominance.* Princeton, N.J.

Klapisch-Zuber, Christiane, 1984. "Le chiavi fiorentine di barbablù: l'apprendimento della lettura a Firenze nel XV secolo," *Quaderni storici,* no. 57 (dic. 1984), pp. 765–92.

————, 1985. *Women, Family, and Ritual in Renaissance Italy.* Translated by Lydia Cochrane. Chicago and London.

Kohl, Benjamin G., 1974. "Petrarch's Prefaces to *De viris illustribus,*" *History and Theory* 13:132–44.

Kristeller, Paul O., 1979. *Renaissance Thought and Its Sources.* Edited by Michael Mooney. New York.

————, 1981. "Niccolò Perotti ed i suoi contributi alla storia dell'Umanesimo," *Res Publica Litterarum* 4:7–25.

Labalme, Patricia H., 1969. *Bernardo Giustiniani: A Venetian of the Quattrocento.* Rome.

————, 1981. "Venetian Women on Women: Three Early Modern Feminists," *Archivio veneto,* 5th ser., 117:81–109.

————, ed., 1984. *Beyond Their Sex: Learned Women of the European Past.* New York and London.

Lane, Frederic C., 1944. *Andrea Barbarigo: Merchant of Venice, 1418–1449.* Baltimore; rpt. New York, 1967.

————, 1973. *Venice: A Maritime Republic.* Baltimore and London.

Le Coultre, Jules, 1926. *Maturin Cordier et les origines de la pédagogie protestante dans les pays de langue française (1530–1564).* Neuchatel.

Ledóchowska, T., 1974. "Angela Merici," DIP, vol. 1, cols. 631–34.

————, 1976. "Educazione della gioventù femminile nei conventi," DIP, vol. 3, cols. 1055–57.

Lee, Egmont, 1984. "Humanists and the *Studium Urbis,* 1473–1484." In *Umanesimo a Roma nel Quattrocento,* edited by Paolo Brezzi and Maristella de Panizza Lorch. Rome and New York, pp. 127–46.

Lenzi, Maria Ludovica, 1982. *Donne e madonne. L'educazione femminile nel primo Rinascimento italiano.* Turin.

Levi, Ezio, 1914. *I cantari leggendari del popolo italiano nei secoli XIV e XV.* Turin.

Liberali, Giuseppe, 1971. *Le origini del seminario diocesano.* Treviso.

Liebreich, A. K., 1982. "The Florentine Piarists," *Archivum Scholarum Piarum* 6, no. 12, pp. 273–304.

————, 1985–86. "Piarist Education in the Seventeenth Century," *Studi secenteschi* 26:225–77; 27:57–88.

Liruti, Gian-Giuseppe, 1780. *Notizie delle vite ed opere scritte da' letterati del Friuli.* Vol. 3. Udine.

Lizier, Augusto, 1908. *Le scuole di Novara ed il Liceo-Convitto.* Novara.

Lowry, Martin, 1979. *The World of Aldus Manutius: Business and Scholarship in Renaissance Venice.* Oxford.

Lucchi, Piero, 1978. "La Santacroce, il Salterio e il Babuino: libri per imparare a leggere nel primo secolo della stampa," *Quaderni storici,* no. 38 (maggio-agosto), pp. 593–630.

Lynch, Joseph H., 1976. *Simoniacal Entry into Religious Life from 1000 to 1260.* Columbus, Ohio.

Maccarrone, Michele, 1984. " 'Cura animarum' e 'parochialis sacerdos' nelle costituzioni del IV concilio lateranense (1215). Applicazioni in Italia nel sec. XIII," *Pievi e parrocchie in Italia nel basso medioevo (sec. XIII–XV).* 2 vols. Rome, 1:81–195.

McManamon, John M., 1982. "Innovation in Early Humanist Rhetoric: The Oratory of Pier Paolo Vergerio the Elder," *Rinascimento*, 2d ser., 22:3–31.

Mahoney, Michael S., 1972. "Mathematics." In *Science in the Middle Ages,* edited by David Lindberg. Chicago, pp. 145–78.

Maierù, Alfonso, 1978. "Tecniche di insegnamento." In *Le scuole degli ordini mendicanti,* pp. 305–52.

Mainardi, Antonio, 1871. *Dello studio pubblico di Mantova e de'professori che vi hanno insegnato a tutto l'anno 1848.* Mantua.

Mambelli, Giuliano, 1954. *Gli annali delle edizioni virgiliane.* Florence.

Manacorda, Giuseppe, 1914. *Storia della scuola in Italia: Il medio evo.* 2 vols. Milan, Palermo, and Naples; rpt. Bologna, 1978.

Mantese, Giovanni, 1964. *Memorie storiche della chiesa vicentina.* Vol. 3, pt. 2 (*Dal 1404 al 1563*). Vicenza.

Mantova. Le lettere, 1962. *Mantova. Le lettere.* Vol. 2. Edited by Emilio Faccioli. Mantua.

Mantovani, E., 1950. *Grammatichetta latina.* Milan.

Marchesi, Vincenzo, 1890. "Le scuole di Udine nei secoli XVI e XVII," *Annali del R. Istituto Tecnico di Udine,* 2d ser., anno 8:3–20.

Marchi, Gian Paolo, 1965–66. "Martino Rizzoni, allievo di Guarino Veronese," *Atti e Memorie dell'Accademia di Agricoltura, Scienze e Lettere di Verona,* 6th ser., 17:291–325.

———, 1981. "Discepoli di Vittorino da Feltre tra Mantova e Verona." In *Vittorino e la sua scuola.* Florence, pp. 285–98.

Marcocchi, Massimo, 1966. *La riforma dei monasteri femminili a Cremona.* Cremona.

———, 1967–70. *La Riforma Cattolica. Documenti e testimonianze.* 2 vols. Brescia.

———, 1974. *Le origini del Collegio della Beata Vergine di Cremona, istituzione della Riforma Cattolica (1610).* Cremona.

Marcora, Carlo, 1960. "La Chiesa Milanese nel decennio 1550–1560," *Memorie storiche della Diocesi di Milano* 7:254–501.

Marrou, H. I., 1964. *A History of Education in Antiquity.* Translated by George Lamb. New York.

Marsh, David, 1979. "Grammar, Method, and Polemic in Lorenzo Valla's *Elegantiae,*" *Rinascimento,* 2d ser., 19:91–116.

Martellotti, G., 1960. "Albanzani, Donato," DBI, vol. 1, pp. 611–13.

Martinelli, Lucia Cesarini, 1980. "Nota sulla polemica Poggio-Valla e sulla fortuna delle *Elegantiae,*" *Interpres* 3:29–79.

Martines, Lauro, 1968. *Lawyers and Statecraft in Renaissance Florence.* Princeton, N.J.

Martini, Giuseppe Sergio, 1956. *La bottega di un cartolaio fiorentino della seconda metà del quattrocento.* Florence.

Masetti Zannini, Gian Ludovico, 1982. *Motivi storici della educazione femminile. Scienza, lavoro, giuochi.* Naples.

Masi, Michael, 1983. "Arithmetic" in David L. Wagner ed., *The Seven Liberal Arts in the Middle Ages.* Bloomington, Ind., pp. 147–68.

Massa, Angelo, 1906. "Documenti e notizie per la storia dell'istruzione in Genova," *Giornale storico e letterario della Liguria* 7:169–205, 311–28.

Mathews, Mitford M., 1966. *Teaching to Read Historically Considered.* Chicago and London.

Mazzatinti, Giuseppe, and Pintor, Fortunato, 1901. *Inventari dei manoscritti delle biblioteche d'Italia.* Vol. 11: *Firenze (R. Biblioteca Nazionale Centrale).* Forlì.

Mazzuconi, Daniela, 1981. "Stefano Fieschi da Soncino: un allievo di Gasparino Barzizza," *Italia medioevale e umanistica* 14:257–85.

Mercati, Giovanni, 1925. *Per la cronologia della vita e degli scritti di Niccolò Perotti Arcivescovo di Siponto.* Rome.

Mercer, R. G. G., 1979. *The Teaching of Gasparino Barzizza.* London.

Mesini, Candido, 1981. "La catechesi a Bologna e la prima compagnia della dottrina cristiana fondata dal B. Nicolò Albergati (1375–1444)," *Apollinaris* 54:232–67.

Mols, Roger, 1974. "Population in Europe, 1500–1700," in *The Fontana Economic History of Europe: The Sixteenth and Seventeenth Centuries,* edited by Carlo M. Cipolla. Glasgow, pp. 15–82.

Monfasani, John, 1976. *George of Trebizond: A Biography and a Study of His Rhetoric and Logic.* Leiden.

———, 1988. "Humanism and Rhetoric." In *Renaissance Humanism: Foundations, Forms, and Legacy,* edited by Albert Rabil, Jr. Vol. 3: *Humanism and the Disciplines.* Philadelphia, pp. 171–235.

Moran, Jo Ann Hoeppner, 1985. *The Growth of English Schooling, 1340–1548: Learning, Literacy, and Laicization in Pre-Reformation York Diocese.* Princeton, N.J.

Morf, H., 1892–95. "Notes pour servir à l'histoire de la légende de Troie en Italie," *Romania* 21:18–39; 24:174–96.

Murphy, F. X., 1967. "Creed." In *New Catholic Encyclopedia,* 17 vols. Washington, D.C., 1967–79. Vol. 4, pp. 432–38.

Murphy, James J., 1981. *Rhetoric in the Middle Ages.* Berkeley, 1974; rpt. Berkeley.

Nardi, Bruno, 1971. *Saggi sulla cultura veneta del quattro e cinquecento.* Edited by Paolo Mazzantini. Padua.

Negri, F., 1969. "Bonciari, Marco Antonio," DBI, vol. 11, pp. 676–78.

Nesi, Emilia, 1903. *Il diario della Stamperia di Ripoli.* Florence.

Noakes, Susan, 1981. "The Development of the Book Market in Late Quattrocento Italy: Printers' Failures and the Role of the Middleman," *Journal of Medieval and Renaissance Studies* 11:23–55.

Novati, Francesco, 1890. "Donato degli Albanzani alla corte estense," *Archivio storico italiano,* 5th ser., 6:365–84.

Ogilvie, R. M., 1982. "Caesar." In *The Cambridge History of Classical Literature.* Vol. 2: *Latin Literature,* edited by E. J. Kenney and W. V. Clausen. Cambridge, pp. 281–86.

O'Malley, John W., 1979. *Praise and Blame in Renaissance Rome: Rhetoric, Doctrine, and Reform in the Sacred Orators of the Papal Court, c. 1450–1521.* Durham, N.C.

Origo, Iris, 1963. *The Merchant of Prato: Francesco di Marco Datini.* Harmondsworth, Middlesex.

Orme, Nicholas, 1973. *English Schools in the Middle Ages.* London.

"Orsoline," 1980. DIP, vol. 6, cols. 834–57.

Osley, A. S., 1972. *Luminario: An Introduction to the Italian Writing-Books of the Sixteenth and Seventeenth Centuries.* Nieuwkoop, Netherlands.

Parenti, G., 1973. "Cafaro, Girolamo," DBI, vol. 16, pp. 240–41.

Park, Katharine, 1980. "The Readers at the Florentine Studio According to Communal Fiscal Records (1357–1380, 1413–1446)," *Rinascimento,* 2d ser., 21:249–310.

———, 1985. *Doctors and Medicine in Early Renaissance Florence.* Princeton, N.J.

Pasini, Adamo, 1925. *Cronache Scolastiche Forlivesi.* Forlì.

Paternoster, Paolo, 1883. *Le scuole pubbliche a Venezia ai tempi della Repubblica. Nozze Levi-Rava.* Venice.

Pavanello, Giuseppe, 1905. *Un maestro del quattrocento (Giovanni Aurelio Auguerello).* Venice.

Pecchiai, Pio, 1948. *Roma nel Cinquecento.* Bologna.

Pellegrini, Carlo, 1986. "San Girolamo Miani, i Somaschi e la cura degli orfani nel sec. XVI." In *San Girolamo Miani e Venezia nel Vº centenario della nascita.* Venice, pp. 9–38.

Pelliccia, Guerrino, 1980. "Scuole di catechismo e scuole rionali per fanciulle nella Roma del Seicento," *Ricerche per la storia religiosa di Roma* 4:237–68.

———, 1985. *La scuola primaria a Roma dal secolo XVI al XIX.* Rome.

Percival, W. Keith, 1972. "The Historical Sources of Guarino's *Regulae Grammaticales:* A Reconsideration of Sabbadini's Evidence." In *Civiltà dell'Umanesimo,* edited by Giovannangiola Tarugi. Florence, pp. 263–84.

———, 1975a. "The Grammatical Tradition and the Rise of the Vernaculars." In *Current Trends in Linguistics,* edited by T. A. Sebeok. Vol. 13: *Historiography of Linguistics.* The Hague, pp. 231–75.

———, 1975b. Review article in *Language* 51:440–56.

———, 1976. "Renaissance Grammar: Rebellion or Evolution?" In *Interrogativi dell'umanesimo,* edited by Giovannangiola Tarugi. 3 vols. Florence, 2:73–90.

———, 1978. "Textual Problems in the Latin Grammar of Guarino Veronese," *Res Publica Litterarum* 1:241–54.

———, 1981. "The Place of the Rudimenta Grammatices in the History of Latin Grammar," *Res Publica Litterarum* 4:233–64.

———, 1982. "Changes in the Approach to Language." In *The Cambridge History of Later Medieval Philosophy,* edited by N. Kretzmann, A. Kenny, J. Pinborg, and E. Stump. Cambridge, pp. 808–17.

———, 1986. "Early Editions of Niccolò Perotti's *Rudimentes Grammatices,*" *Res Publica Litterarum* 9:219–29.

Pesce, Luigi, 1969. *Ludovico Barbo vescovo di Treviso (1437–1443).* 2 vols. Padua.

———, 1983. *Vita socio-culturale in diocesi di Treviso nel primo Quattrocento.* Venice.

Pesciatini, Daniela, 1982. "Maestri, medici, cerusici nelle comunità rurali pisane nel XVII secolo." In *Scienze, credenze occulte, livelli di cultura.* Florence, pp. 121–45.

Petrocchi, Massimo, 1978. *Storia della spiritualità italiana.* Vol. 1: *Il Duecento, il Trecento, e il Quattrocento.* Rome.

Petrucci, Armando, 1978. "Scrittura, alfabetismo ed educazione grafica nella Roma del primo Cinquecento. Da un libretto di conti di Maddalena pizzicarola in Trastevere," *Scrittura e Civiltà* 2:163–207.

Petrucci, F., 1979. "Sabba (da) Castiglione," DBI, vol. 22, pp. 100–106.

Petti Balbi, Giovanna, 1975. "Salvo di Pontremoli maestro di scuola a Genova tra secolo XIII e XIV," *Studi medievali,* 3d ser., 16, no. 2, pp. 787–94.

———, 1979. *L'insegnamento nella Liguria medievale. Scuole, maestri, libri.* Genoa.

Pfeiffer, Rudolf, 1976. *History of Classical Scholarship from 1300 to 1850.* Oxford.

Picanyol, Leodegario, 1939. "La Scuola dei Nobili nelle Scuole Pie Fiorentine e il suo fondatore P. Giovan Francesco Apa," *Rassegna di Storia e Bibliografia Scolopica* 5:1–28.

Pigman, G. W., III, 1981. "Barzizza's Studies of Cicero," *Rinascimento* 21: 123–63.

Pinborg, Jan, 1982. "Speculative Grammar." In *The Cambridge History of Later Medieval Philosophy,* edited by N. Kretzmann, A. Kenny, J. Pinborg, and E. Stump. Cambridge, pp. 254–69.

Post, R. R., 1968. *The Modern Devotion: Confrontation with Reformation and Humanism.* Leiden.

Premoli, Orazio M., 1913. *Storia dei Barnabiti nel Cinquecento.* Rome.

———, 1922. *Storia dei Barnabiti nel Seicento.* Rome.

Prodi, Paolo, 1959–67. *Il Cardinale Gabriele Paleotti (1522–1597).* 2 vols. Rome.

———, 1961. "Antoniano Silvio," DBI, vol. 3, pp. 511–15.

Prosperi, Adriano, 1965. "Note in margine a un opuscolo di Gian Matteo Giberti," *Critica storica* 4:367–402.

———, 1969. *Tra evangelismo e controriforma: G. M. Giberti (1495–1543).* Rome.

———, 1982. "*Otras Indias:* Missionari della Controriforma tra contadini e selvaggi." In *Scienze, credenze occulte, livelli di cultura.* Florence, pp. 205–34.

Pullan, Brian, 1971. *Rich and Poor in Renaissance Venice: The Social Institutions of a Catholic State, to 1620.* Cambridge, Mass.

Rabil, Albert, Jr., 1981. *Laura Cereta: Quattrocento Humanist.* Binghamton, N.Y.

Ragni, Eugenio, 1974. "I cantari." In *Dizionario critico della letteratura italiana.* 3 vols. Turin, 1:480–88.

Rajna, Pio, 1872. *I Reali di Francia. Ricerche intorno ai Reali di Francia seguite dal libro delle storie di Fioravante e del cantare di Bovo d'Antona.* Vol. 1. Bologna.

———, 1900. *Le fonti dell'Orlando Furioso. Ricerche e studi.* 2d ed., enlarged. Florence.

Ramat, Raffaello, 1954. *La critica ariostesca dal secolo XVI ad oggi.* Florence.

Rambaldi, Susanna Peyronel, 1979. *Speranze e crisi nel Cinquecento modenese. Tensioni religiose e vita cittadina ai tempi di Giovanni Morone.* Milan.

Rashdall, Hastings, 1936. *The Universities of Europe in the Middle Ages.* Edited by F. M. Powicke and A. B. Emden. Vol. 2: *Italy-Spain-France-Germany-Scotland, etc.* Oxford.

Reames, Sherry L., 1985. *The Legenda Aurea: A Reexamination of Its Paradoxical History.* Madison, Wis.

Redondo, Augustin, 1976. *Antonio de Guevara (1480?–1545) et l'Espagne de son temps. De la carrière aux oeuvres politico-morales.* Geneva.

Renaissance Eloquence, 1983. *Renaissance Eloquence: Studies in the Theory and Practice of Renaissance Rhetoric.* Edited by James J. Murphy. Berkeley, Calif.

Renazzi, Filippo Maria, 1803–6. *Storia dell'Università degli Studi di Roma.* 4 vols. Rome.

Renouard, Ant. Aug., 1953. *Annali delle edizioni aldine.* Bologna (rpt. of 3d ed. of 1834).

Resta, Gianvito, 1964. *Giorgio Valagussa, umanista del Quattrocento.* Padua.

Reynolds, L. D., 1965. *The Medieval Tradition of Seneca's Letters.* Oxford.

Reynolds, L. D., and Wilson, N. G., 1974. *Scribes and Scholars*. 2d ed., enlarged. Oxford.

Reynolds, Robert L., 1937. "Two Documents concerning Elementary Education in Thirteenth-Century Genoa," *Speculum* 12:255–56.

Riché, Pierre, 1976. *Education and Culture in the Barbarian West, Sixth Through Eighth Centuries*. Translated by J. J. Contreni. Columbia, S.C.

———, 1979. *Les Ecoles et l'enseignment dans l'Occident chrétien de la fin du Vᵉ siècle au milieu du XIᵉ siècle*. Paris.

Rigon, Antonio, 1984. "Organizzazione ecclesiastica e cura d'anime nelle Venezia. Ricerche in corso e problemi da risolvere," *Pievi e parrocchie in Italia nel basso medioevo (sec. XIII–XV)*. 2 vols. Rome, 2:705–24.

Risse, Wilhelm, 1964. *Die Logik der Neuzeit*. Vol. 1: *1500–1640*. Stuttgart and Bad Cannstatt.

Rivabene, Sergio, 1982. "L'insegnamento catechistico dell'Arciconfraternita della Dottrina Cristiana a Roma nei secc. XVI–XVIII," *Archivio della Società Romana di Storia Patria* 105:295–314.

Robey, David, 1980. "Humanism and Education in the Early Quattrocento: The *De ingenuis moribus* of P. P. Vergerio," *Bibliothèque d'Humanisme et Renaissance* 42:27–58.

———, 1984. "Humanist Views on the Study of Poetry in the Early Italian Renaissance," *History of Education* 13:7–25.

Robins, R. H., 1951. *Ancient and Medieval Grammatical Theory in Europe with Particular Reference to Modern Linguistic Doctrine*. Port Washington, N.Y., and London.

Rocca, G., 1978. "Maestre Pie Venerini," DIP, vol. 5, cols. 835–40.

Ronconi, Giorgio, 1979. "Il grammatico Antonio Beccaria difensore della poesia e la sua *Oratio in Terentium*." In *Medioevo e rinascimento veneto con altri studi in onore di Lino Lazzarini*. 2 vols. Padua, 1:397–426.

Roover, Raymond de, 1942. "The Commercial Revolution of the Thirteenth Century," *Bulletin of the Business Historical Society* 16:34–39.

———, 1966. *The Rise and Decline of the Medici Bank, 1397–1494*. New York.

———, 1967. *San Bernardino of Siena and Sant'Antonino of Florence: The Two Great Economic Thinkers of the Middle Ages*. Boston.

———, 1974. "The Development of Accounting prior to Luca Pacioli according to the Account Books of Medieval Merchants," in de Roover, *Business, Banking, and Economic Thought in Late Medieval and Early Modern Europe*. Edited by Julius Kirshner. Chicago and London, pp. 119–80.

Rose, Paul Lawrence, 1975. *The Italian Renaissance of Mathematics: Studies on Humanists and Mathematicians from Petrarch to Galileo*. Geneva.

Ross, James Bruce, 1974. "The Middle-Class Child in Urban Italy, Fourteenth to Early Sixteenth Century. In *The History of Childhood*, edited by Lloyd deMause. New York, pp. 183–228.

———, 1976. "Venetian Schools and Teachers Fourteenth to Early Sixteenth Century: A Survey and a Study of Giovanni Battista Egnazio," *Renaissance Quarterly* 39:521–66.

Rossi, Vittorio, 1901. "Un grammatico cremonese a Pavia nella prima età del Rinascimento," *Bollettino della Societa Pavese di Storia Patria* 1:16–46.

———, 1907. "Maestri e scuole a Venezia verso la fine del medioevo," *Rendiconti del*

Reale Istituto Lombardo di scienze e lettere, 2d ser., 40:765–81, 843–55.

———, 1949. *Il Quattrocento.* 3d ed., rev. Milan

Rudd, Niall, 1982. "Horace." In *The Cambridge History of Classical Literature.* Vol. 2: *Latin Literature,* edited by E. J. Kenney and W. V. Clausen. Cambridge, pp. 370–404.

Ruggiero, Guido, 1980. *Violence in Early Renaissance Venice.* New Brunswick, N.J.

Russo, Luigi, 1951. "La letteratura cavalleresca dal 'Tristano' ai 'Reali di Francia,'" *Belfagor* 6:40–59.

Sabbadini, Remigio, 1878. "Antonio Mancinelli, saggio storico-letterrario." In *Cronaca del R. Ginnasio di Velletri.* Velletri, pp. 7–40.

———, 1885. *Storia del ciceronianismo e di altre questioni letterarie nell'età della rinascenza.* Turin.

———, 1897. "Biografi e commentatori di Terenzio," *Studi italiani di filologia classica* 5:289–327.

———, 1914. *Storia e critica di testi latini.* Catania.

———, 1922. *Il metodo degli umanisti.* Florence.

———, 1924. *Giovanni da Ravenna, insigne figura d'umanista (1343–1408).* Como.

———, 1964a. *Guariniana. Vita di Guarino Veronese.* Edited by Mario Sancipriano. Turin. First published in 1891.

———, 1964b. *Guariniana. La scuola e gli studi di Guarino Veronese.* Edited by Mario Sancipriano. Turin. First published in 1896.

———, 1967. *Le scoperte dei codici latini e greci ne' secoli XIV e XV.* Edited by Eugenio Garin. 2 vols. Florence.

Salvioli, Giuseppe, 1912. *L'istruzione in Italia prima del Mille.* Florence.

Sanford, Eva M., 1960. "Juvenalis, Decimus Junius." In *Catalogus Translationum et Commentariorum,* edited by Paul O. Kristeller. Vol. 1. Washington, D.C., pp. 175–238.

Sansonetti, Vincenza, 1952. "Le pubbliche scuole in Vicenza durante il medio evo e l'umanesimo," *Aevum* 26:156–79.

Sántha, G.; Aguilera, C.; and Centelles, J., 1956. *San José de Calasanz. Su obra. Escritos.* Madrid.

Santoloci, Quirino, 1948. *Giuseppe Calasanzio, educatore e santo, 1648–1948.* Rome.

Sapegno, Natalino, 1952. *Il Trecento.* 6th ed., rev. Milan.

Sarri, Francesco, 1939–41. "Giovanni Fabbrini da Figline (1516–1580?)," *La rinascita* 2 (1939):617–40; 3 (1940):233–70; 4 (1941):361–408.

Sassi, Daniele, 1880. *L'istruzione pubblica in Torino dal 1300 al 1800.* Turin.

Scaduto, Mario, 1964. *L'epoca di Giacomo Lainez, 1556–1565. Il governo.* Rome.

———, 1974. *L'epoca di Giacomo Lainez, 1556–1565. L'azione.* Rome.

Scaglione, Aldo D., 1970. *Ars Grammatica. A Bibliographic Survey, Two Essays on the Grammar of the Latin and Italian Subjunctive, and a Note on the Ablative Absolute.* The Hague and Paris.

———, 1986. *The Liberal Arts and the Jesuit College System.* Amsterdam and Philadelphia.

Scarafoni, Camillo Scaccia, 1947. "La più antica edizione della grammatica latina di Aldo Manuzio finora sconosciuta ai bibliografi." In *Miscellanea bibliografica in memoria di Don Tommaso Accurti,* edited by Lamberto Donati. Rome, pp. 193–203.

Scarpati, Claudio, 1982. *Studi sul Cinquecento italiano.* Milan.

Scheyen, Renate, 1973. *Guarino Veronese. Philosophie und Humanistische Pädagogik.* Munich.

Schmidt, Peter, 1984. *Das Collegium Germanicum in Rom und die Germaniker: Zur Funktion eines römischen Ausländerseminars, 1552–1914.* Tübingen.

Schmitt, Charles B., 1983. *Aristotle and the Renaissance.* Cambridge, Mass., and London.

———, 1985. *La tradizione aristotelica: fra Italia e Inghilterra.* Translated by Antonio Gargano. Naples.

Schmitt, Wolfgang O., 1969. "Die Janua (Donatus)—ein Beitrag zur lateinischen Schulgrammatik des Mittelalters und der Renaissance," *Beiträge zur Inkunabelkunde,* Dritte Folge, vol. 4, pp. 43–80.

Schullian, Dorothy M., 1984. "Valerius Maximus." In *Catalogus Translationum et Commentariorum,* edited by F. Edward Cranz and Paul O. Kristeller. Vol. 5. Washington, D.C., pp. 287–403.

Schutte, Anne Jacobson, 1986. "Teaching Adults to Read in Sixteenth Century Venice: Giovanni Antonio Tagliente's *Libro Maistrevole,*" *Sixteenth Century Journal* 17, no. 1, pp. 3–16.

Scott, Izora, 1910. *Controversies over the Imitation of Cicero as a Model for Style and Some Phases of Their Influence on the Schools of the Renaissance.* New York.

Le Scuole, 1933. *Le scuole dei Barnabiti nel IV° centenario dell'approvazione dell'ordine, 1533–1933.* Florence.

Le scuole degli ordini mendicanti, 1978. *Le scuole degli ordini mendicanti (secoli XIII–XIV).* Todi.

Secco, Luigi, 1973. *La pedagogia della Controriforma.* Brescia.

Segarizzi, Arnaldo, 1913. *Bibliografia delle stampe popolari italiane della R. Biblioteca Nazionale di S. Marco di Venezia.* Vol. 1. Bergamo.

———, 1915–16a. "Cenni sulle scuole pubbliche a Venezia nel XV e sul primo maestro d'esse," *Atti del Reale Istituto Veneto di scienze, lettere ed arti* 75:637–67.

———, 1915–16b. "Una grammatica latina del secolo XV," *Atti del Reale Istituto Veneto di scienze, lettere ed arti* 75, pt. 2, pp. 89–96.

Seigel, Jerrold E., 1968. *Rhetoric and Philosophy in Renaissance Humanism.* Princeton, N.J.

Serena, Augusto, 1912. *La cultura umanistica a Treviso nel secolo decimoquinto.* Venice.

Serio, Bernardo, [1845]. *Discorso sulla Istruzione Pubblica ne' secolo XVI° e XVII° in Sicilia.* N.p.

Setton, Kenneth M., 1956. "The Byzantine Background to the Italian Renaissance," *Proceedings of the American Philosophical Society* 100:1–76.

Sforza, Giovanni, 1870. "Della vita e delle opere di Gio. Pietro d'Avenza, grammatico del secolo XV," *Atti e memorie delle RR. Deputazioni di Storia Patria per le provincie Modenesi e Parmensi* 5:393–411.

Shelby, Lon R., 1983. "Geometry." In *The Seven Liberal Arts in the Middle Ages,* edited by David L. Wagner. Bloomington, Ind., pp. 196–217.

Simeoni, Luigi, 1940. *Storia della Università di Bologna.* Vol. 2: *L'età moderna (1500–1888).* Bologna.

Sindoni, Angelo, 1971. "Le Scuole Pie in Sicilia. Note sulla storia dell'ordine scolopico dalle origini al secolo XIX," *Rivista di Storia della Chiesa in Italia,* 25:375–421.

Sloyan, G. S., 1967. "Catechism." In *New Catholic Encyclopedia*, 17 vols. Washington, D.C., 1967–79. Vol. 3, pp. 225–31.

Sorbelli, Albano, 1942. "La libreria di uno stampatore bibliofilo del Quattrocento." In *Studi e Ricerche sulla Storia della Stampa del Quattrocento*. Milan, pp. 259–336.

Sorgenti, Fabio, 1825. *Vita del Beato Ippolito Galantini fiorentino, fondatore della Congregazione della Dottrina Cristiana*. Rome.

Sowards, J. K., 1982. "Erasmus and the Education of Women," *Sixteenth Century Journal* 13, no. 4, pp. 77–89.

Spadolini, Ernesto, 1900. *Briciole d'Archivio*. Ancona.

Spagnolo, Antonio, 1904. "Le scuole accolitali di grammatica e di musica in Verona," *Atti e Memorie dell'Accademia d'Agricoltura, Scienze, Lettere, Arti e Commercio di Verona*, 4th ser., 5 (vol. 80 of the entire journal):97–330.

Strauss, Gerald, 1978. *Luther's House of Learning: Indoctrination of the Young in the German Reformation*. Baltimore and London.

———, 1985. "Liberal or Illiberal Arts?" *Journal of Social History* 19:361–67.

Tacchi Venturi, Pietro, 1950. *Storia della Compagnia di Gesù in Italia*. Vol. 2, pt. 1: *Dalla nascita del fondatore alla solenne approvazione dell'Ordine (1491–1540)*. 2d ed. Rome.

———, 1951. *Storia della Compagnia di Gesù in Italia*. Vol. 2, pt. 2: *Dalla solenne approvazione dell'Ordine alla morte del fondatore (1540–1556)*. Rome.

Tagliaferri, Amelio, 1966. *L'economia veronese secondo gli estimi dal 1409 al 1635*. Milan.

Tamborini, Alessandro, 1939. *La compagnia e le scuole della dottrina cristiana*. Milan.

Tartaro, Achille, 1972. *La letteratura civile e religiosa del Trecento*. Bari. Rpt. of part of *Letteratura Italiana Laterza*.

Texts and Transmission, 1983. *Texts and Transmission: A Survey of the Latin Classics*. Edited by L. D. Reynolds. Oxford.

Thomson, David, 1983. "The Oxford Grammar Masters Revisited," *Mediaeval Studies* 45:298–310.

Thurston, Herbert, 1913. "Deaconesses." In *The Catholic Encyclopedia*, vol. 4. New York, pp. 651–53.

Timon-David, Joseph, 1884. *Vie de Saint Joseph Calasanct, fondateur des Écoles Pies*. 2 vols. Marseille.

Toke, Leslie A. St. L., 1910. "Little Office of Our Lady." In *The Catholic Encyclopedia*, vol. 9. New York, pp. 294–95.

Toscani, Xenio, 1984. "Le 'Scuole della Dottrina Cristiana' come fattore di alfabetizzazione," *Società e storia* 7, no. 26, pp. 757–81.

Tosetti, Urbano, 1824. *Compendio storico della vita di S. Giuseppe Calasanzio, fondatore delle Scuole Pie*. Florence.

Tramontin, Silvio, 1965. "Gli inizi dei due seminari di Venezia," *Studi veneziani* 7:363–77.

———, 1983. "Ordini e congregazioni religiose." In *Storia della Cultura Veneta*. Vol. 4, pt. 1: *Il Seicento*. Vicenza, pp. 23–60.

Tuer, Andrew W., 1979. *History of the Horn Book*. London, 1897; rpt. New York.

Turchini, Angelo, 1978. *Clero e fedeli a Rimini in età posttridentina*. Rome.

Turrini, Miriam, 1982. " 'Riformare il mondo a vera vita christiana': le scuole di catechismo nell'Italia del Cinquecento," *Annali dell'Istituto storico italo-germanico in Trento* 8:407–89.

Ullman, B. L., 1960. *The Origin and Development of Humanistic Script.* Rome.

Vaccari, Alberto, 1952–58. *Scritti di erudizione e di filologia.* Vol. 1: *Filologia biblica e patristica.* Vol. 2: *Per la storia del testo e dell'esegesi biblica.* Rome.

van der Haeghen, F., 1961. *Bibliotheca Erasmiana.* Ghent, 1893; rpt. Nieuwkoop.

Van Egmond, Warren, 1976. "The Commercial Revolution and the Beginnings of Western Mathematics in Renaissance Florence, 1300–1500," Ph. D. dissertation, University of Indiana.

––––––, 1981. *Practical Mathematics in the Italian Renaissance: A Catalog of Italian Abbacus Manuscripts and Printed Books to 1600.* Florence.

Vannucci, Pasquale, 1930. *Il Collegio Nazareno, MDCXXX–MCMXXX.* Rome.

Varanini, Giorgio, 1974. "Andrea da Barberino." In *Dizionario critico della letteratura italiana.* 3 vols. Turin, 1:65–67.

Vasoli, Cesare, 1968. *La dialettica e la retorica dell'Umanesimo. "Inventione" e "Metodo" nella cultura del XV e XVI secolo.* Milan.

Venezia ebraica, 1982. *Venezia ebraica.* Edited by Umberto Fortis. Rome.

Verde, Armando, 1973. "Niccolò Machiavelli studente," *Memorie Domenicane*, n.s., 4:404–8.

Verger, Jacques, 1978. "*Studia* et universités." In *Le scuole degli ordini mendicanti.* Todi, pp. 173–203.

Vezzosi, Antonio Francesco, 1780. *I scrittori de' Cherici regolari detti Teatini.* 2 vols. Rome.

Vicini, Emilio P., 1935. "Le 'Letture Pubbliche' in Modena nei secoli XV–XVII," in *Rassegna per la Storia della Università di Modena e della cultura superiore modenese.* Fascicolo 5 (Modena):47–170.

Villoslada, Riccardo G., 1954. *Storia del Collegio Romano dal suo inizio (1551) alla soppressione della Compagnia di Gesù (1773).* Rome.

Vittorino e la sua scuola, 1981. *Vittorino da Feltre e la sua scuola: umanesimo, pedagogia, arti.* Edited by Nella Giannetto. Florence.

Vogel, Kurt, 1971. "Fibonacci, Leonardo." In *Dictionary of Scientific Biography.* New York, 4:604–13.

Ward, John O., 1978. "From Antiquity to the Renaissance: Glosses and Commentaries on Cicero's *Rhetorica.*" In *Medieval Eloquence: Studies in the Theory and Practice of Medieval Rhetoric*, edited by James J. Murphy. Berkeley, Los Angeles, and London, pp. 25–67.

––––––, 1983. "Renaissance Commentators on Ciceronian Rhetoric." In *Renaissance Eloquence: Studies in the Theory and Practice of Renaissance Rhetoric*, edited by James J. Murphy. Berkeley, Los Angeles, and London, pp. 126–73.

Weiss, Roberto, 1977. *Medieval and Humanist Greek: Collected Essays.* Padua.

Wieruszowski, Helene, 1971. *Politics and Culture in Medieval Spain and Italy.* Rome.

Wilkinson, L. P., 1955. *Ovid Recalled.* Cambridge.

––––––, 1982. "Cicero and the Relationship of Oratory to Literature." In *The Cambridge History of Classical Literature.* Vol. 2: *Latin Literature*, edited by E. J. Kenney and W. V. Clausen. Cambridge, pp. 230–67.

Witt, Ronald, 1982. "Medieval 'Ars Dictaminis' and the Beginnings of Humanism: A New Construction of the Problem," *Renaissance Quarterly* 35:1–35.

———, 1983a. "Brunetto Latini and the Italian Tradition of *Ars dictaminis*," *Stanford Italian Review* 3:5–24.

———, 1983b. *Hercules at the Crossroads: The Life, Works, and Thought of Coluccio Salutati.* Durham, N.C.

———, 1986. "Boncompagno and the Defense of Rhetoric," *Journal of Medieval and Renaissance Studies* 16, no. 1, pp. 1–31.

Woodward, William H., 1968. *Studies in Education during the Age of the Renaissance, 1400–1600.* Cambridge, 1906; rpt. New York.

Zabughin, Vladimiro, 1921–23. *Vergilio nel Rinascimento italiano da Dante a Torquato Tasso.* 2 vols. Bologna.

Zaccagnini, Guido, 1924. "L'insegnamento privato a Bologna e altrove nei secoli XIII° e XVI°," *Atti e Memorie della R. Deputazione di storia patria per le provincie di Romagna,* 4th ser., 14:254–301.

———, 1926. *La vita dei maestri e degli scolari nello Studio di Bologna nei secoli XIII e XIV.* Geneva.

Zafarana, Zelina, 1984. "Cura pastorale, predicazione, aspetti devozionali nella parrocchia del basso medioevo," *Pievi e parrocchie in Italia nel basso medioevo (sec. XIII–XV).* 2 vols. Rome, 1:493–539.

Zama, Piero, 1920. *Le istituzioni scolastiche faentine nel medio evo (sec. XI–XVI).* Milan.

———, 1938. *Il monastero e l'educandato di Santa Umiltà di Faenza dalle origini ai nostri giorni (1266–1938).* Faenza.

Zambarelli, Luigi, 1936. *Il Nobile Pontificio Collegio Clementino di Roma.* Rome.

Zanelli, Agostino, 1896. *Del pubblico insegnamento in Brescia nei secoli XVI e XVII.* Brescia.

———, 1899. "Maestri di grammatica in Foligno durante il secolo XV," *L'Umbria, Rivista d'arte e letteratura* 2, nos. 13–14 (15 luglio 1899), pp. 102–3.

———, 1900. *Del pubblico insegnamento in Pistoia dal XIV al XVI secolo.* Rome.

Zanette, Emilio, 1960. *Suor Arcangela monaca del Seicento veneziano.* Venice and Rome.

Zenoni, L., 1916. *Per la storia della cultura in Venezia dal 1500 al 1797. L'Accademia nei Nobili alla Giudecca (1619–1797).* Venice.

Ziliotto, B., 1963. "Baratella, Antonio," DBI, vol. 5, pp. 778–80.

Zonta, Giovanni, 1932. *Storia del Collegio Gallio di Como.* Foligno.

INDEX

Abbaco: classroom instruction in, 311–19; compared with Latin schooling, 319; compared with twentieth-century mathematics, 317–18; definition and history of, 306–9; and interest-bearing loans, 318–19; not taught in Latin schools, 309–11; taught by Scuole Pie, 385

Abbaco schools: in Florence, 72–73; in Lucca, 22–23; in Pistoia, 22; in Rome, 84; in Venice, 50; in Verona, 22; in Volterra, 23

Abbaco teachers: additional duties of, 22–23; communes prefer foreigners as, 23; incomes of, 23; not household tutors, 51; in Verona, 5

Abbecedario. See Primer

Accursius, Bonus, wrote grammar, 192

Adriani, Antonius (teacher), 54

Aesop (*Liber Aesopi*), 17, 69, 197; identified, 112; in medieval schooling, 114–17; taught in Jesuit schools, 379

Agricola, Rudolph, works of, taught, 268–70

Aimeric of Angoulême, 170

Alain de Lille (author), 114

Alani parabolae, 197

Albanzani da Casentino, Donato degli, teaching career of, 39

Albergati, Nicolò (bishop), religious instruction by, 333

Alberic of Monte Cassino (supposed author), 115

Alberti, Carlo, 131

Alberti, Leon Battista: recommends

abbaco, 310–11; studies with Barzizza, 131

Albertus grammaticus of Noàntola, 4

Albertus Magnus, 377

Aldine Press: editions of classics, 249; publishes Vergil, 240

Alexander de Villedieu, 126
—and Barzizza, 166
—*De algorismo,* 307
—*Doctrinale,* 136, 164, 201; available, 174; contents, 112; criticized, 139; and Guarino, 168; not read, 182; on poetry, 139, 235–36; taught, 33, 140; word order, 208

Alfonso I (king of Naples), 324

Alfonso of Portugal, 131

Al-Khwarizmi (mathematician), 318

Alvares, Manoel, 191, 378; writes grammar, 192

Ambrose, St., adapts Cicero's work, 216

Amelia, Jesuit school in, 370–71

Ancona, Piarist school in, 386

Andrea da Barberino, works of, 289–90, 292, 294–97

Andreucci, Antonio (teacher), 24

Angeliche (female religious order), 393

Anianus de Salvis (teacher), 54

Anthonius (teacher), 56

Anthony, St. (founder of monasticism), 283–84

Antoniano, Silvio: on educating lower-class boys, 102, 106–7; on female education, 89; praises Schools of Christian Doctrine, 361; supports Scuole Pie, 383

Schooling in Renaissance Italy

Designed by Ann Walston

Composed by Village Typographers, Inc.,
in Bembo text and display type